ERASING THE BINARY DISTINCTION OF DEVELOPED AND UNDERDEVELOPED

ERASING THE BINARY DISTINCTION OF DEVELOPED AND UNDERDEVELOPED

A Comparative Study of the Emergence of the Large-Scale Steel Industry in Imperial Russia, Imperial Britain, Imperial America, and Colonial India, 1880-1914

VINAY BAHL

AAKAR

Erasing the Binary Distinction of Developed and Underdeveloped
Vinay Bahl

First Published in India 2022

ISBN 978-93-5002-766-0

Readers should be aware that all online references listed in this book were working at the time of publication

Published by
AAKAR BOOKS
28 E Pocket IV, Mayur Vihar Phase I
Delhi 110 091, India
www.aakarbooks.com

Printed at
Sapra Brothers, Noida

Dedication

To the late Professor Ramkrishna Mukherjee,
Professor Rifa'at Abou-El-Haj Sultan,
late Professor Eric J. Hobsbawm, &
Professor Immanuel Wallerstein.

CONTENTS

Preface and Acknowledgments

Preface and Acknowledgments

I wrote this book from the margin, as a migrant woman of 'color' from the lower-middle class, born in a third world (tricontinental) country now living and working in the US. I neither claim (nor apologize) to have any expertise in Western or Eastern philosophies or theories, and I do not believe in disciplinary boundaries. My intent here is to present a line of thinking that might enable us to discard the use of the binary distinction of "developed/underdeveloped" to categorize all countries because it has a negative affect on most of the people around the world. It is this existential issue (negative experiences) that compelled me to take up this project, which has evolved over time as I was trying to make sense of my own life experiences in India and in the US.

My study does not defend any particular existing theoretical perspective, as I wish to benefit from some of the vast human knowledge available, which was created by our common human ancestors. Moreover, it is my understanding that theories are merely tools (and not a faith to be defended or rejected) to help comprehend and analyze our social reality to some extent, and also to challenge different theories in order to create new, more useful tools that can help explain the social reality of our own time. With that in mind I gainfully employed ideas from various disciplines of social sciences as well as from other sciences, including technology, for this project. Since I was not following a set formula based on any particular theoretical framework, nor writing an exhaustive chronological history for each of the four countries selected for comparison, this book evolved somewhat haphazardly. It was during the process of simultaneously writing various chapters—as and when any idea would occur, or as and when I read about these countries and the related debates, as well as gleaning other information from different fields of studies—that I began to see the possible methodology and concepts that might be useful for this work.

This project began with a question that I have been wrestling with for some time: why are we so strongly stuck with the binary distinction of "developed/underdeveloped" to categorize all societies, and why until now have no alternatives emerged that would eliminate the need for this binary? Over time I realized that it is difficult for scholars to break out of this dichotomy because all schools of thought dealing with this binary distinction remained grounded within the "transition" debate. This realization led me to the idea of using a yardstick of parity to evaluate any society so that this binary distinction will become redundant. However, I was somewhat concerned that this approach involving parity might be criticized as promoting "universalism." Therefore, the challenge became how to explain my ideas in a way that retains both universal and specific characteristics in every society and does not promote the "universalism" of European thought, and does not defend imperialism, neo-liberalism, fundamentalism (Hindu, Islamic, Judaic, Christian, Buddhist), or indigenism. The concept of "human creativity," which was articulated initially in my last published volume in 2005, continues to seem appropriate for achieving this goal. However, reacting to this volume, one scholar reminded me that the issue of "human nature" is very problematic. This comment did not make any sense to me because my use of the concept of "human creativity" is not the same as that of the concept of "human nature." I believe that human creativity is an innate capability (not genetic) that humans have inherited from nature itself, as humans are part of nature itself and one of the infinite expressions of nature's creativity. Every person is born with this creativity and it is not something that is formed by external forces. Whereas, the concept of human nature is a social construct because (1) humans are born with all possible traits and every society makes choices to promote certain traits among its members—violence or peacefulness, for instance—based on various existential needs and their perception of reality. As Karl Polyani pointed out, the idea of human nature itself is the product of market society *(bourgeois ideology,* my emphasis) and not the other way around. Earlier exchanges existed to satisfy the needs of people and not to create markets and make profits, and there is nothing automatic about the growth of a market society.

Later, I became aware that the concept of human creativity (as explained in this volume) has also been promoted by various scholars in certain disciplines. However, after I completed the initial drafts of Chapters One and Two, I found myself reviewing Professor Immanuel Wallerstein's books, *Geopolitics and Geoculture* and *The End of the World as We Know It: Social Science for the Twenty-First Century.* I found that in addition to his well-known theory of World-System, Professor Wallerstein has also noted and explained the importance of the concepts of "creativity," "complexity," and "arrow of time," while quoting Nobel Laureate scientist Ilya Prigogine. This line of thought intrigued me so much that I went on to explore more about complexity studies, learned many things about the cosmos, science, and synergy—while also becoming more confident about what I was trying to unravel in my work. I discovered the work of other physicists who have written about "morphic resonance" and interconnection of various elements—web of life matters—that are similar to what sociologists also investigate. I came to realize that physicists and sociologists are likely examining similar processes that exist in nature and the cosmos as well as within society through the process of human interaction. This perception called to mind the ideas of Eastern philosophies (not as promoted by Hindutva forces) and the yoga that I was exposed to while growing up in India. I recognized that what I had read in the works of these Western physicists and sociologists sounded familiar, even though it was presented in a Western language within a Western context and within Western theoretical framework. This realization diminished the alienation in my mind that I had experienced during the process of reading Western works. I also discovered that similar ideas existed before the Enlightenment, and that most of these ideas had been suppressed over time and removed from common knowledge. Reading the history of the Freemasons clarified my understanding of the development of various historical processes in the West that contributed to the creation of an international bourgeois class. It was this bourgeoisie class that promoted capitalistic ideas and created a myriad of social and financial institutions to promote them. Books such as Clifford D. Conner's *People's History of Science,* and Lewis Mumford's *The Myth of the Machine* provide further affirmation of my own thinking. The all-embracing ideas about a holistic history, holistic medical system, and cosmic and nature's connections with human life have always made sense to me, and I had been using the holistic approach for many years as a teacher of sociology. In fact, it is difficult to ignore the interconnectivity of all elements and all living beings with the cosmic world because this is something all of us witness every day (an observable reality), whether we consciously agree with it or not (2). Interestingly, eco-sociologists are also now emphasizing this holistic understanding of our social reality and the planet.

Thus, it was natural for me to also look for an holistic approach for this endeavor. Consequently, I decided to use a yardstick of parity to understand the making and industrialization of each of the four chosen societies for this volume without categorizing any one of them as either developed or underdeveloped. I have also provided a sample of comparative study of these chosen four countries to show how the yardstick of parity can be used while considering the issue of the emergence of the large-scale steel industry between 1880 and 1914. Hopefully, the ideas suggested in this volume might help in breaking the trap of fatalism (the stage theory and inevitability of transition), and open up a space for thinking of alternative paths that would lead to the improvement of living conditions everywhere; friendly to all people and the planet.

This project evolved with the encouragement, support, and comments of many scholars whom I wish to thank and express my gratitude. I am thankful to Professor Rifa'at Abou-El-Haj Sultan for introducing me to the concept of "human creativity" and also for long discussions on various topics and subjects over the years. I am grateful to him for his continuous encouragement of my academic pursuits and his comments on all of my academic works. I am thankful to the late Professor Ramkrishana Mukherjee for his continuous encouragement and his comments. I thank Professor Amiya Kumar Bagchi for his encouragement and his comments on my initial ideas of this project. I thank late Professor Terence K. Hopkins for commenting on my initial preliminary ideas on this project. I wish to thank the late Professor Eric J. Hobsbawm for his continuous encouragement, his comments on my work, and academic support during the most crucial time in my academic life. I am thankful to Professor Immanuel Wallerstein for his continuous support and encouragement. I wish to thank Doctor (MD) Arno Vosk for his continuous encouragement and comments on the initial drafts of several chapters. I also benefited from his deep, personal knowledge of Russian history, politics, culture, and society. I am thankful to my colleague Professor Carl Milofsky for reading and commenting on this manuscript. I have greatly benefited from the scholarly website Abhinavagupta@yahoogroups.com and I am grateful to Dr. Sunthar Visuvalingam for introducing it to me. I am thankful to Dr. Nandini Assar for her moral support and being a soundboard for my initial ideas for this project. My thanks to Denise Ramp for her continuous support. My thanks also goes to Barbara Andreassen for helping in the creation of the final form of this manuscript. However, I am responsible for any errors.

ENDNOTES

1. Graham-Leigh has pointed out that the idea of human nature as a stand-to-reason view has its roots in the foundations of bourgeois ideology. Descartes' description of the human body as machine-like and separated from human consciousness was an expression of the "emerging capitalist view of workers as reducible to interchangeable moving parts." (Elaine Graham-Leigh, "Marxism and Human Nature," June 23, 2018. (https://www.counterfire.org/articles/opinion/19716-marxism-and-human-nature). Posted on MR online July 13, 2018).

   More recently it was pointed out in an article, "Is the Answer Really in Genes?" that the concept of 'human nature' has no scientific evidence. According to Karl Marx, "human essence" was not a fixed entity located physically in every individual, but rather "the ensemble of the social relations" which also keep changing over time. (Full Marx, from Marx Memorial Library, MR online, November 6, 2018).
2. It was interesting to note in the editorial of *SPANDA Journal* the use of the concepts of "unified field of consciousness" and "spirituality" in making connections with the changing social reality of our time. This particular issue of *SPANDA* focused on the theme of "Anarchy and Non-Profit." (Sahlan Momo, "Mesoeconomy and the Clean Code." Editorial in *SPANDA Journal*, IV, 1. January–June, 2013.) This particular issue of the journal was brought to my attention by Professor Carl Milofsky.

INTRODUCTION

"Let us not forget what it is we are studying and how little we know of man, of history, of biography, and of the societies of which we are at once creators and creatures. Realizing this, perhaps we should be at once more careful and less pretentious about the methods we would employ when we get down to our work" (Mills, 2009).

"Every speech, act and more generally, every action, is a conjuncture and encounter between independent causal series" (Bourdieu, 1991).

"There's nothing fundamentally wrong with the people. Given a story to enact that puts them in accord with the world, they will live in accord with the world. But given a story to enact that puts them at odds with the world, as yours does, they will live at odds with the world. Given a story to enact in which they are the lords of the world, they will ACT like lords of the world. And, given a story to enact in which the world is a foe to be conquered, they will conquer it like a foe, and one day, inevitably, their foe will lie bleeding to death at their feet, as the world is now" (Quinn, 1995).

"How have we been led to believe that the English Civil War, which led to the execution of Charles I in 1649, and the 'Glorious' Revolution of 1688, which dethroned Charles I's son James II, were advances in the history of limited government, whereas the regicide of the Ottoman Sultan Ibrahim in 1648, and the deposition of Ibrahim's son Mehmed IV in 1687, for instance, were simply signs of decline" (Tezcan, 2010)?

"World-system has reified a whole series of binary distinctions, and given them political importance to a degree unknown before: bourgeois middle class/proletariat-working class; man/woman, White/Black (or person of color); breadwinner/housewife; productive worker/unproductive person; sexually mainstream/sexually aberrant; the educated/the masses; honest citizen/criminal; normal/mentally abnormal; of legal age/a minor; civilized/uncivilized. ... these binary distinctions, all elaborated theoretically in great detail in the nineteen century, is that they build on ancient distinctions, but give to them a salience, an interconnectedness, and a rigidity that they seldom had before. ... consequence ... restriction of effective citizenship ... being distinctive reduced this 'everyone' to a relatively small minority of the population" (Wallerstein, 2003).

"Historical knowledge and understanding advance incrementally ... and even the most original interpretations shifts the emphasis rather than rewrite the script ... professional scholars can hope, at best, to reshuffle the pack" (Cains and Hopkins, 1993:52).

By opening up an old debate about the conceptual binary distinction of "developed/underdeveloped" I am hoping to reshuffle the historical pack. However, this revisiting of the old debate is not due to any newly discovered sources or data, as all the information for this volume is derived from existing published secondary sources in the English language only. Instead, this volume argues for the erasure of the binary distinction of developed/underdeveloped in classifying societies in order to spare people—those living in so-called "underdeveloped," ex-colonial societies—from having to re-prove their abilities, creativity, and achievements every time a comparative history is attempted. Moreover, this erasure would open a space to find an alternative perspective to not only understand different societies by using a yardstick of parity, but also to improve their poor conditions without resorting to the Western formula of growth and development. It should be taken into account that independence from colonialism did not liberate these societies and countries from the clutches of neocolonialism and the status of backwardness. The ideology of "development" has claimed millions of lives around the world in the name of progress and prosperity in the twentieth century. It has become a nightmare for billions of people who experience the impact of so called development.

Erasing this binary distinction will also erase the labels of "backward," "lacking," and "not yet" attached to these poor societies and ex-colonies, thus making redundant the "civilizing mission" of Western neocolonialism. The liberation from these labels will empower these societies to reject Western projects of development, which continue to bleed the world through exploitation and genocide—including the millions who perished in China and Soviet Russia in the name of the ideology of scientific history and socialist development. The erasure of this binary distinction will allow these societies to imagine and find humane and ecologically friendly alternative forms of a good life that creates conditions for the flourishing of human creativity, while allowing for a plurality of practices and beliefs based on new forms of reasoning. I believe that it is possible to erase this binary distinction through a refined perspective that allows the study of all societies with a yardstick of parity on equal terms. This suggestion was initially articulated in my last volume (Bahl, 2005a) and it is further extended in the present volume along with an example showing how it can be done through a comparative historical study. For this comparative study (offered only as an example, and not as an in-depth study of each chosen country) I have focused on four countries—Imperial Britain, Imperial Russia, Postcolonial Imperial USA, and Colonized India—to understand the question surrounding the emergence of the large-scale steel industry from 1880–1914.

I used the term 'country' here so that the reader will be able to relate to these boundaries, as scholars have dealt with the issue of industrialization and development within the context of country boundaries that were established between 1880 and 1914. However, I wish to point out that the term country, as well as the concept of nation-state, are problematic as they are continuously being constructed and reconstructed through various historical processes (including imperialism, colonialism, and neoliberalism) created by human interactions. Similarly, society is not a given entity and it is not a fixed unit of analysis because it exists only when people interact regularly over time and create social structures (cultural and social institutions) to meet their human needs. This process itself is continuously changing and evolving all the time and changing social formation, as all societies are also interacting with other societies. My ideas are based on this understanding of the formation of society and not on the concept of nation-states or country.

WHY THIS PARTICULAR COMPARATIVE STUDY?

The idea for this volume initially emerged when I was working on my doctoral thesis involving a case study of the Tata Iron and Steel Company, 1880–1946 (Bahl, 1995). I was intrigued by the fact that Russia had a large-scale steel industry in the 1880s, yet Russia was considered "backward" in comparison to the US and to many European countries at that time. I was also puzzled by the fact that the US and Germany's advances in industrialization during that time period were attributed to their having large-scale steel industries, while Russia was not considered in the same light even though it, too, had a large-scale steel industry. Furthermore, Imperial Britain did not have a large-scale steel industry at that time yet it was considered "developed." Moreover, during my research, I found that the information regarding the question of industrialization and development was always presented within the binary frameworks of "progressive/backward" and "developed/underdeveloped" connected to the role of colonialism and dependency, core, and periphery [(1)]. It was obvious to me that no society can escape this categorization as there was no other framework available which would treat all societies on par with one another.

In addition, the labeling of India as "backward" has long puzzled me because I was born and grew up in India with the knowledge that Bengal was considered a "Golden Bird" well before the advent of British colonialism. I also knew of Naoroji's "Drain Theory" that explains how India was made poor by British colonization. During my life I have visited many magnificent forts, temples, monuments, cave paintings, and schools of painting in both the north and the south of India that were built over the span of 5000 years. I have seen various forms of arts and artifacts, building materials, and unique products retrieved from the excavations of the Indus Valley civilization. I was exposed to knowledge gleaned from Ayurvedic medicines and herbs; matters my own uncle and brother were deeply involved with and were part of our daily life. This knowledge exposed me to various medical systems—Yunnani, Homeopathic, Ayurvedic, Nature cure and Herbal cure—and Yoga, both as a philosophy and practice. I was exposed to a variety of practices and expressions within the Hindu religion that included Sikhism, Buddhism, Sanatan Dharma, and Arya Samaj—as well as Sufism and festivals celebrated by Muslim people. I spent my childhood in Calcutta (now called Kolkata), and was exposed to the Bengali version of Hindu religious practices and rituals, including those revering local gods and goddesses. From a very early age, I heard my father regularly recite passages from Persian and Urdu poetry; a practice that made me aware of the beauty of Urdu *ghazals*. I was exposed to different traditions (including Bengali songs that we were taught in elementary school in Kolkata) and types of Indian classical music such as the Dhrupad form of singing, reputed to have emerged from ancient temple chants during the Aryan period (circa 1500–1000 BC). Growing up, I heard stories about the great city of Baghdad, about the interaction of Chinese, Persian, and Indian people and traders, about Egypt and its great pyramids, about the inventions of the Chinese, and about the spread of Buddhism and Hinduism in the Eastern countries and the great temples and monasteries built in those countries. I have seen King Ashoka's Edicts of ancient times, as well as the steel column at Kutub Minar that was built before the coming of the Mughals. I have seen the legendary Taj Mahal, the great temples of Southern India, and the ancient cave paintings at

Ajanta and Ellora. I heard about Dhaka muslin and all the great textile and weaving, about wood craft, about magnificent designs and about much more that Indian craftsmen created in the past and continue to create in the present time. Today, one can find examples of the many varieties of these crafts at cottage emporiums in many big cities throughout different provincial states. India's knowledge of and contribution to mathematics is well known. I could go on and on.

All this information and knowledge made it clear to me that precolonial India was not originally a "backward" country and that it had contributed to all fields of knowledge—architecture, science, astronomy, technology, mathematics, arts, music, performing arts, and medicine—along with the creation of environmental, political, social, religious, and literary works. However, I also heard while growing up that independent India was "backward," lacking all the facilities and infrastructure found in the Western world. I observed that one would get more respect if one could communicate using the English language, and more so if one was fortunate enough to be born into a wealthy family able to afford for its children to study at an English medium school. It was the same with higher education; one would be respected and taken seriously and considered scholarly if one could speak English with a British accent, preferably acquired from Oxford or Cambridge.

It is no different in present-day India even though there has been a big push towards "Indian-ness." Middle-class Indians are proud that they are able to consume the same things Americans do, that so many imported goods are available in big malls, and that they can go there to participate in this "progress," even if only for a day. To middle-class Indians it feels as though India has arrived. They measure their "progress" by standards set in the West. They continue to work towards "catching up" through "development" projects, yet these projects themselves are displacing large numbers of poor people who are migrating to urban areas that make their lives more miserable, while despondent farmers are committing suicide in large numbers. One can go on adding information about the negative and disastrous impacts of these ongoing "development" projects. It seems as if there is no alternative to this idea of development, and there is no solution to the misery of millions of people who are victims of these projects, except for protesting against them.

The issue of the binary distinction of developed/underdeveloped is not simply an academic exercise, but an existential issue for me and for those countries that are forced to accept these development projects, or for those who opt for them believing in its promise. For me, this has been an existential issue both in India and now in the US (as it is for many others like me from various so-called third world countries). In India, I confronted the challenges of patriarchy in society and academia, academic snobbery and discrimination, including casteism, sexism, colorism and classism; and in the US, I am continuously facing sexism, classism, racism, ageism, colorism, and patriarchy in and outside of academia, as well as academic snobbery and discrimination [(2)]. These issues, encountered earlier in India and now in the US, affect me every day throughout all of my interactions: market, public, official, academic, cultural, personal, and professional. Academically, as one Subaltern Studies scholar pointed out previously, in order for Indian (or any other non-Euro-American) scholars to remain up to date they must be acquainted with the writings of leading European historians and/or social scientists. However, Euro-American scholars can seemingly ignore the writings of their colleagues in India, China, Brazil, Iran, and Kenya without feeling inadequate or that they are missing anything important. Moreover, they do not appear to feel either "provincial" or "backward" (3). Notwithstanding, this scholar did not mention that Indian scholars within India and abroad have also internalized the same Euro-American attitude and display it in their interaction with other Indian scholars. Most likely the same must be the case with other non-European scholars.

Thus, this intellectual exercise became an imperative for me. Since academically, politically, and internationally every country is considered to possess the binary distinction of being either developed or underdeveloped based on Western concepts of modern technology and industrialization, I decided to generate a comparison of two countries that have been labeled developed, and two that have been labeled underdeveloped. The common feature among three of the selected countries is this: the existence of a large-scale steel industry during 1880–1914. Normatively, however, I could not ignore Britain, the major superpower of the time and labeled as developed, even though it did not have a large-scale steel industry until the 1930s. I chose the large-scale steel industry because it was considered the basis for the development of both Germany and the US during this time.

I have found that this binary approach of developed/underdeveloped has continued into the present time and that every underdeveloped country is now running at full-speed to achieve the impossible task of "catching up", which is creating more problems in those countries than solving them. These countries, labeled as underdeveloped (or "backward"), have no alternative narrative or framework to define and improve their economic and social conditions except for the metric guiding the projects of development that are defined and imposed by the IMF and the World Bank. As McCaffray and Malancon have pointed out, "it may be a time to abandon the great interpretative tool of 'backwardness' … if Russia adopted (as it did) a program of universal accident insurance in 1912, but the United States failed to do so until the Depression, should we consider the United States to have borrowed this idea from backward Russia" (McCaffray and Melancon, 2005:9)? I believe that an alternative perspective will help former colonized countries find their own narrative and unique strategies to improve their present conditions without the projects of Western development. Instead, they would benefit from the accumulated human knowledge available within their society and country as well as around the world. This goal can be achieved not by refining or redefining the concept of development/underdevelopment, but by erasing it.

It was a long time before this project could take off. Following the completion of my dissertation, I published my first book on the case study of the Tata Iron and Steel Company, 1880–1946 (Bahl, 1995). But, even before it was released, I became a casualty of the globalization that was pushing for the restructuring of the US educational system to create more business and technical colleges that would produce more technocrats, mid-level managers, paramedics, nurses, and other skilled technical workers, in both high-tech and low-tech areas, that the new global economy demanded. During a two-year span spent at the University of Pennsylvania in Philadelphia as an independent scholar in the South Asia Studies department, I acquired stronger exposure to the ideas and questions raised by the Subaltern Studies collective as well as postcolonialism that were then in vogue. In addition, I had negative experiences that were sometimes patronizing, patriarchal, sexist, racist, and classist with many South Asian and other third world scholars as well as with whites and Afro-American scholars, both men and women, and with white feminists. It was in that context that I decided to analyze my experiences with these feminists, whites, Afro-American, South Asian, and other third world scholars in general, as well as to investigate various issues that the Subaltern Studies collective and postcolonial theory were raising.

This effort took the form of an article on the critique of Subaltern Studies and another article dealing with globalization and women's movements [(4)]. However, I also realized that the issue of "specificity and differences," that both Subaltern Studies and postcolonial scholarship have raised to challenge the prevailing meta-narrative and modernity, can be dealt with by providing an alternative question. To me that alternative question was this: If specificity is so important to the understanding of each society, then why are historians in all countries today raising similar historiographical questions and not specific concerns of their own society? This similarity of historiographical questions compels us to evaluate the larger historical forces of our time that interact with the specificity of each society. Specificity is equally important, but in and of itself it is not sufficient. It is the complex interaction process between both specificity and the larger historical processes and forces emerging within a society along with inter-societal and intra-societal interactions that are created through the choices and actions of people in each society based on how they perceive their situations. This alternative question was worked out in the publication (2000) of a co-edited volume, *History after the Three Worlds: Post-Eurocentric Historiographies* [(5)]. While working on that volume, the issues of modernity, subjectivity, differences, and specificity raised many more questions pertaining to my own project on the erasure of the binary distinction of development/underdevelopment. It became clearer to me that there is a need for an alternative narrative because the existing perspective of this distinction is self-serving to the interests of the Western world, as is the concept of "modernity." Lamentably, the alternatives put forth by Subaltern Studies and the postcolonialists only led us up a blind alley.

The ideas constituting post-development theory are not much different than those of Subaltern Studies or postcolonial theory, as they propose alternatives using local solutions (something people are already trying, but are unable to change, such as the development projects). I realized that we cannot find an alternative perspective and an alternative narrative by redefining, refining, or tweaking the existing ones. It was becoming clear that the existing perspective and narrative of the binary distinction of developed/underdeveloped must be erased, even though it may be useful in highlighting matters such as the adverse effects of development projects. I say this because we need to not only expose the ruinous impact of imperialism, but also to eliminate imperialism in all its forms that are creating such disastrous conditions for people and for the planet. In addition to intellectual exercise, this realization was validated by the earlier mentioned matter of my day-to-day existential experiences, not only with European and American whites, feminists, Afro-Americans, South Asian, and other third world—tricontinental—scholars, both male and female, but also with my own college students (white and Afro-American from various socio-economic backgrounds), my Afro-American and white colleagues, my Afro-American and white college administrators, and communities in both the northern and southern US.

Moreover, the events of 9/11 affected me in a fundamental way. From that day forward my regional Punjabi dress, a *shalwarkamiz*, which is similar to Muslim women's attire (Bahl, 2007), was judged negatively by my students and the public at large. One particular incident even before 9/11 was most shocking and revealing. The head of my department in a Southern college asked me to attend, on her behalf, a meeting of sociologists from various colleges. That day I was wearing my regional Punjabi dress along with a Kashmiri *phiran*. When I entered the room, there was a pin-drop silence and I saw terrified faces. I did not understand this reaction. I then introduced myself, and heard sighs of relief. The chairperson, a sociologist who should know better, later explained to me that they thought I might have been a terrorist because I was wearing Muslim (Punjabi) attire. Today, as I have discussed elsewhere, my regional Punjabi dress has become a national dress for working women all over India, and that women's attire from other regions have become obsolete (Bahl, 2005b). According to the logic of these American sociologists, all Indian women who wear Punjabi dress could be considered terrorists! No wonder many women from Pakistani or Indian backgrounds living in the US switched to western attire after 9/11, as I also had to do for existential reasons.

The point I want to make is that the binary distinction of developed/underdeveloped has affected me every day in very profound ways, both in the US to which I migrated, as well as in India where I grew up. However, as it so often happens, I am now treated like an outsider in India while I remain an "other" and a foreigner in the US. I am constantly judged, as many people are, as either "modern" or "traditional" by peers, teachers, students, and others based on Western binary ideas of "modern/traditional" and "progressive/backward" [(6)]. This judgment process renders me either "capable or incapable" in the eyes of the person judging me, which has not only affected me psychologically, undermining my self-confidence (a hazard that few women and most minority group members can escape), but it has also affected my chances for better opportunities throughout my life, both in India and in the US. (I have addressed some of these issues in *What Went Wrong with "History From Below": Reinstating Human Agency as Human Creativity*. Bahl, 2005a). Moreover, the negative experiences of people like me are typically explained away as problems involving "cultural deficiencies," similar to the rationale in the modernization theory for the third world as being "culturally deficient." Wallerstein has summed up this rationalization of modernization theory as follows:

> First of all, here is the universalist theme. All states can develop; all states shall develop. Then comes the racist theme. If some states have developed earlier and faster than others, it is because they have done something, behaved in some way that is different. They have been more individualist, or more entrepreneurial, or more rational, or in some way more 'modern.' If other states have developed more slowly, it is because there is something in their culture … which prevents them or has thus far prevented them from becoming as 'modern' as other states (Wallerstein, 1989:18).

The idea of cultural deficiency is further reinforced with the concept of the 'melting pot', which sends the message that people like me must assimilate and if not then any "failure" is my own fault. There is no place for multiculturalism even though there are so many programs in US universities, colleges, and businesses to incorporate diversity and multiculturalism, which is a multimillion-dollar industry. In the US, the words diversity and multiculturalism actually mean only the diversity of appearances (which does not mean you will not suffer for being non-white), and not the diversity of cultural, moral, spiritual, and intellectual norms. The future of diversity and multiculturalism does not look good in the US in light of the racist, anti-immigrant, and Islamophobic statements that US President Donald Trump made during the 2016 election campaign, which gave a big boost to extreme white supremacist forces. Recent events between 2017 and 2019 have confirmed this earlier assessment.

Thus, my ideas for this volume crystallized over the years through personal life experiences as a migrant in the US and as a visiting NRI in India, and through the close observation of larger global processes and their disastrous impact on people, the ecology, and the planet. Specific recent examples include the disturbing news about five hundred thousand farmers in India committing suicide during the years of liberalization and structural adjustment since 1995 following the introduction of genetically modified cotton and cash crops (Shiva and Jalees, 2009); news about various development projects, such as the Sardar Sarovar Dam project, that have uprooted, disrupted, and ruined millions of lives. Time and again I have asked myself, why do we not have an alternative to these development projects? Why do the people of the so-called third world have to prove themselves continuously with no end to their subordinate status? Why does the Western news media report on deaths in so-called terrorist attacks in Europe or in the US with such urgency and sympathy, while similar deaths in Iraq, Syria, Afghanistan, Palestine, Somalia, Yemen and other non-European countries are treated as non-news or are generalized with little or no focus on the lives of individuals or their relatives? If at all, pictures of suffering children from affected areas in the third world are shown in the Western media for obtaining Western support to justify further bombing in those regions. In 2016, the US dropped 26,171 bombs on seven Muslim-majority countries, while Muslims in general have been labeled as "terrorists." A recent report from Brown University's Watson Institute for International and Public Affairs noted that since 9/11 the War on Terror has killed over a half million people in Iraq, Afghanistan, and Pakistan. However, this number does not include those who died due to the impact of war (such as disease and devastated infrastructure), and those 110,000 who died after August 2016 (Crawford, 2018). When civilians die in these bombings they are dismissively labeled as collateral damage. At the same time, the continuous War on Terror is fed by the unending vicious cycles involved in the development of a neo-liberal financial imperialism.

Under neo-liberalism the global financial system has become a means of controlling and pillaging poor countries. For example, third world countries are forced to take loans for development projects even when the lending parties know that those countries will not be able to pay them back. Thus, the lending countries, mostly Western and specifically the US through the IMF and World Bank, are able to control these poor third world countries by dictating terms of repayment that often involves selling their resources to the lending countries below market price. A recent estimate of Global Financial Integrity (GFI) and the Center for Applied Research at the Norwegian School of Economics (2015) shows that the net drain from the global South since 1980 adds up to $16.3 trillion. During 2012 alone, net resource transfers from developing and emerging economies to rich countries were estimated $2 trillion (quoted in Suwandi, Jonna, and Foster, 2019:5). Moreover, developing countries have transferred $4.2 trillion to developed countries by way of interest payment on debt (quoted in Gurukkal, 2018). This is the direct result of a debt service trap. The World Bank and IMF force these countries to introduce structural adjustment programs that impose austerity measures eliminating welfare programs and funding for education. These projects push more people into poverty, and these countries then lose their standing with foreign lenders. In order to control this volcanic situation of discontent and poverty, the governments of these poor countries use repression techniques that often involve buying more weapons from countries such as the US and the UK. Thus, a vicious cycle is established. These poor countries become mired in continuous conflict—civil war amongst different factions—and corruption, which then requires more weapons, more debt, more control by outside forces, and the continuation of the Global War on Terrorism. Outside forces are not neutral in these situations, and they tend to exploit different factions to their own advantage to gain and retain access to resources and control over these governments.

However, as Banerjee et al. (2016) pointed out, the operation of neo-liberalism and its consequences have not changed the terms of theoretical understanding, as their origin remains the same—Europe. In the long historical process of imperialism and colonialism, Banerjee et al. explained, Europe was able to monopolize and define the theory that created a binary of theory/practice and later created additional binaries: mind vs matter, subject vs object, and idealism vs materialism. Over time, the binary of ideal/real was created, while the Christian ideal of divine perfection was replaced by a rational subject as a new perfection. Banerjee et al. suggest that through the idea of a rational subject (existed outside of society) it became possible for Europeans to separate theory from people's thought and everyday-ness. However, most scholars who use European theories often do not question their European origin. For example, as Banerjee et al. (2016:43) pointed out, Indian Marxist scholars in the 1970s and 1980s were concerned with finding out whether or not the Indian economy was capitalist. By raising this question, Indian Marxist scholars remained entangled in the European "transition debate." In the late 1980s and 1990s, postcolonialism and the Subaltern Studies collective challenged these Marxist ideas with an historical counter-evidence of differences. However, their challenge did not bring any theoretical breakthroughs either, as Subaltern Studies scholars admit that it is not possible to avoid using Western criteria while showing differences or similarities from the West because that criteria is already explained within the Western theoretical framework. Consequently, as Banerjee et al. pointed out, scholars have only three choices: show limits of universal categories, use Western theoretical concepts to our favor, or invoke an authentic indigenous mode (7) or, I will add, the availability of a fourth option—keep critiquing Eurocentrism.

My suggestion is that in order to avoid these four choices above, and to break out of the European theoretical framework and the binary of developed/underdeveloped, we need an alternative theory that does not defend imperialism, neo-liberalism, fundamentalism (Hindu, Islamic, Judaic, Christian, Buddhist), indigenism, or any other type of binary distinction. The alternative perspective should be constructed in such a way that it can be used for all societies and for all historical times and places, and that perspective should not treat the existing perception of any society (superior/inferior, progressive/backward) as that society's original autochthonous condition. In this way, we shall be able to move from critiques of Western theoretical frameworks and start creating an alternative theoretical framework that will erase binary distinctions. It seems to me that Banerjee et al. are also pointing in the same direction.

THE MAJOR QUESTION IN THIS STUDY

Attempts to write comparative history on equal terms has been an issue for many scholars for a long time, and this is also my main concern in the present volume. Initially, I fleshed out my ideas about this question in my last volume (Bahl, 2005a). I suggested the erasure of the binary concepts of developed/underdeveloped and modern/traditional by using the alternative yardstick of human creativity, which would allow us to treat all countries and societies with parity[(8)]. In the present volume, I have further expanded on these alternative ideas, and have included the metaphor of Indra's Net (discussed in Chapter 2), which helps in understanding and imagining how all societies can be envisioned as equal, unique and interconnected, while influencing one another at the same time. This metaphor is also useful in understanding the integral unity of the parts and whole of society. Indra's Net is similar to the idea about networks that emerged later in the Western physics that influenced cybernetics (Capra, 1984).

Besides elaborating on the aforementioned ideas, I have provided a sample in the present volume to show that it is possible to do a comparative historical study without categorizing any society as developed or underdeveloped. To demonstrate the application of this idea, I have focused on a comparative study of the emergence of the large-scale steel industry between 1880 and 1914 in four countries: Imperial Russia, Imperial Britain, postcolonial Imperial US, and colonial India. As noted earlier, Britain, while labeled a developed country, did not have a large-scale steel industry until the 1930s. I have not treated these countries as nation-states because state formation and re-formation or dissolution (as is happening increasingly in the twenty-first century under continuous regime changes and US foreign policies involving the perpetual War on Terror) is an ongoing process, so is never complete. With new technological developments there is the possibility of redefining what it means for a state to have geographical borders. For example, Estonia is experimenting with the idea of digital residency, which means that stateless people anywhere in the world can register with Estonia as e-residents (Haley, 2016). The concept of nation-state (a Western racist project, see Abou El-Haj, 2005) is a relatively recent phenomenon, and none of the four countries examined herein started as a nation-state [(9)]. Moreover, each of these four chosen countries was at a different stage of state formation during the years 1880–1914. Two of them, Imperial Britain and Imperial Russia, were not just states but large empires (although the nature of these empires were different; Britain expanded its power around the world by violently colonizing distant lands to exploit their resources and markets for its own benefit, while Russia expanded within the continent eastward following a very different agenda). The postcolonial US, based on an imperialist project from the start, was an emerging nation-state at the time and was not truly one nation as one state. Moreover, in the 1890s the US was already expanding its own empire overseas in the Philippines, Cuba, Guam, and

Puerto Rico after having first taken over the land of the Native Americans, and part of Mexico; the south and west portions of the continent itself. Colonial India was not an independent state during this time as it was part of the British Empire.

In the following, we begin with the basics of the theory of development/underdevelopment and challenges posed to it. After that our discussion focuses on highlighting the problems in this binary distinction, as well as problems in other alternative perspectives: Post-development thinking, the Subaltern Studies alternative, and Marxist alternative. A question is then raised as to why and how we can explore another perspective, which hopefully would help us break out of this binary distinction of developed/underdeveloped.

THE THEORY OF "DEVELOPMENT AND UNDERDEVELOPMENT" AND CHALLENGES TO IT

Rostow's theory of modernization (1960) was a development paradigm that came into being in the mid-twentieth century and dominated the thinking of both academicians and policy makers. According to his development paradigm, development happens in five stages. Based on these stages he classified economies of different societies as traditional, underdeveloped, developing, developed, or post-industrial. His ideas were based on the model of Euro-American economic evolution, and he advocated that the development in poor countries would (and should) take a similar unilinear path (Rikodi, 2015). Thus, he put forward an historical and normative model of development for poor countries. According to Rostow, traditional societies are underdeveloped because of their ignorance of modern technology, their having fatalistic ethos, and their strong family and kin ties, which, according to Rostow, were hindrances in their development. These characteristics, as Rostow opined, limited the investment and rational decision making that are necessary for economic prosperity. Therefore, he proposed a theory on stages of economic growth for the development of these societies which would enable them to "take off" and become prosperous like other countries. One of the strategies for facilitating these stages of economic growth was to change the values, habits, and attitudes of traditional societies to modern ones so that these people would think more rationally about making investment decisions that would make them prosperous. Countries in the Global South and the Global North, as well as aid agencies, accepted these ideas and started implementing them without recognizing that mainstream theories of development are based on a fundamental paradox: It promises on one hand an improvement in the conditions of the world's poor, and on the other hand, in practice, it increasingly facilitates the exploitation of the world's poor pushing them further to the brink (Ibid.).

However, the theory of modernization (development/underdevelopment) that blames the culture of the so-called underdeveloped society for its woes has been challenged. The initial challenge came from neo-Marxist theories of dependency (Frank, 1967) and world-system (Wallerstein, 1974a), both popularized in the 1970s. Dependency theory is based on a "center/periphery" binary distinction that parallels the dichotomy of "modernity/tradition." According to this theory, development and underdevelopment are two inseparable parts of the global economy which do not allow the periphery—third world countries—to develop along the same path as the countries in the center (Frank, 1967). Frank also argues that underdevelopment must be seen not as set of initial conditions that capitalist development is meant to transform, but as an outcome of the very process of capitalist development itself. However, this theory does not challenge the basic assumptions of modernization theory: "the idea of growth," and the final aim to modernize, industrialize, and capture foreign markets. Some critics of Dependency theory have pointed out that it attributes underdevelopment solely to external factors, and does not take into account the fact that external forces also interact with local conditions bringing a different outcome based on different specific context of each society (Rikodi, 2015). However, this theory lost its appeal as it did not provide any viable alternative strategy for change, and the collapse of the Soviet Union further added to scholars' skepticism.

Renowned sociologist, Immanuel Wallerstein, structured and systematized the idea of a world-economy in *The Modern World System* (1974). Wallerstein's approach is different yet complementary to the dependency theory. His focus is also on core and periphery as two integral elements of a structure that he calls the world-economy, but he explores the core and periphery relations from a different perspective. While dependency theorists question how the integrated world-economy hinders development prospects at the periphery, Wallerstein explains how the same world-system also helps in sustaining capital accumulation that promotes development at the center. Thus, the dependency and world-system theories together were able to break out of orthodoxy (Rikodi, 2015). However, while welcoming this departure from orthodoxy the Marxist camp also criticized them for defining their theory entirely in terms of the sphere of circulation (exchange).

For example, Brenner criticized Wallerstein and the dependency theory for not focusing on production, class relations, and class struggle. Brenner stated that the sphere of circulation does not determine class relations; instead, it is the class struggle that determines the trajectory of capitalist development and underdevelopment (Brenner, 1977). With his critique, Brenner introduced the questions of agency, power, and subjectivity that were missing from the discussion of the process of capitalist transformation. However, as the Indian economist Kalyan Sanyal has pointed out, both Marxists and liberals have problematized the economic formation of the third world within a framework of a European transition debate—from tradition to modernity, from unreason to reason, from pre-capitalism to capitalism—which keeps third world countries within the same binary distinction of developed/underdeveloped (Sanyal, 2007).

The binary distinction of developed/underdeveloped raises questions: Who is benefiting from this binary, and how is it a challenge to Western modernity? Moreover, this claim that there is something peculiar to Western culture that generates a desire for basic liberties, is problematic, because there is nothing Western about these values—standing up against oppression or looking for a better life—as these values are universal and necessary to advance solutions to peoples' basic needs. Examples of such mobilizations can be found everywhere in the former colonies. As Chibber has pointed out, "Modernity on both sides of the world was brought into being by agents still immersed in pre-modern culture" (Chibber, 2013:206). Chibber further suggested that one does not first become modern and then demand these liberties. It is through a process of struggle that people attain the liberties, and thus make a society "modern."

Another critique of modernization theory came from Indian historians who also accepted the binary distinction of developed/underdeveloped, but blamed underdevelopment on the colonizing countries (Morris et al., 1969). As mentioned earlier, in the late 1980s and 1990s these Indian historians were challenged by the emerging ideas of the Subaltern Studies (hereon as SS) collective and postcolonialist theories which served as a severe critique of Western colonial projects, and were put forth as an alternative to the metanarrative of capitalism, colonialism, and imperialism. These theories were focused on individual actions, choices, their agency, and differences, which, in turn, promoted the notion of identity politics and fragments. With this new focus on the individual, agency and differences, the larger metanarrative—capitalism, colonialism, imperialism, globalization—within which every individual life unfolds as each individual makes choices and differences are invented and promoted—simply disappeared from academic discourse.

However, the Indian scholars of the SS collective did not rule out the issues of modernity and empiricism and proposed the idea of "*Provincializing Europe*" (Chakrabarty, 2000, 2007). Chakrabarty, the most influential spokesperson of the SS collective, has discussed in detail the issue of empiricism that is connected to the questions of development and his term of phrase, "not yet." Chakrabarty is rightly worried, as Brennan points out, about a historiography that sees India only from the perspective of "developmental" schemes that portray the country always as "lacking." However, Chakrabarty's charge is not a new one and is common-place in postcolonial studies (Brennan, 2006:314). He also writes that while he wishes to challenge the concept of modernity, he finds it indispensable because it is only through modernity that we can ask for democracy, equality, justice, and so on (Dietz, 2008:72). He believes that it is possible to challenge the hegemony of the nation-state and the modernity of our time by celebrating indigenous religious "fragments." Therefore, the alternative to the basic assumption in understanding the history of the West, according to Chakrabarty, is to emphasize culture, identity, and subjectivity, and to promote the "communitarian" mode of history writing (Chakrabarty, 2007).

Influenced by postmodernism and postcolonialism, a similar critique by post-developmentalists (most of whom are anthropologists) emerged within development studies. They rejected, as Rikodi noted, the structuralist, materialist, and reductionist approaches of the social sciences and instead advocated constructive, multidimensional, and holistic views. Based on these alternative views, they criticized modernization theory and development models for creating a simple dichotomy between traditional and modern societies. They stressed that traditional societies have a complex relationship with modernity and that the diversity of cultures, religions, ethnicities, and indigenous social institutions within these societies are important actors that should not be ignored in policy making. According to these alternative views, a model of development should be local, self-reliant, and egalitarian in which it will be the people of a society that define their lives as they want, in accordance with their own values and cultures (Rist, 2008; Rikodi, 2015). The advocates of post-development theory demonstrated that these concepts, such as poverty, needs, resources, and the environment, that serve as the basis of development practices are products of the development discourse itself. This dominant discourse of development does not allow for many other alternative ways of interpreting and relating to the world around us. Moreover, development has failed hopelessly to deliver to the poor of the third world, and therefore, according to post-developmentalists, the entire paradigm of development must be abandoned, and based on ideas produced at the grass root level people should look for new imaginaries of human possibilities—in other words, an alternative to development (Rikodi, 2015; see also Sylvester, 1999).

Lieten, a Dutch historian, noted that both Wallerstein and Frank seem to have made the transition toward post-developmentalism. While they advocate "new social movements" as a possibility of stimulating an "ecocentric, humanocentrist, and decentralized development," they do not offer any specific details about how that would happen. However, Wallerstein advocates for a new concept that he invented, *utopistics*, whereas Franks merely suggests that the struggle continue, "A Luta Continua!" Both of these ideas, as Lieten observed, are calling for collective engagement to invent a future system and implement it through new types of social institutions [(10)].

Another alternative model that came into being was based on faith traditions such as liberation theology within the Catholic Church in Latin America, engaged Buddhism, and Islamic economics. These religious institutions were engaged in charitable welfare and development work along with providing guidance about values, behavior, and right social ordering. However, as Rikodi noted, this alternative model, which privileges religious authority and solidarity, clashed with modern values of individual reason and experience because it promotes the idea of equality and dignity (Rikodi, 2015).

A more recently emerged alternative idea is the concept of "degrowth" (Jackson, 2009; Schor, 2011; Victor, 2012). However, the concept of "degrowth" has a different meaning in the Global South and the Global North. In the North, it refers to dematerialization, de-commodification, and decentralization followed by rationality, and a planned, sustainable state economy that distributes aid internationally based on need. The gist of the idea is by following this path it would be possible to diminish Global North and Global South inequality, and that would lead to a lower demand on natural resources and "sustainable development" in the Global South. However, Global South countries like to "follow their own trajectories to what they conceive as a good life ... while claiming global environmental justice, indigenous rights, and rights for nature" (Veciana, 2016).

It is evident that each side is defining its strategy based on its own assumptions and values. The Global North defines the meaning of *wellbeing* as overcoming growth pattern while fostering deeper democracy through autonomy and self-determination. Whereas, the Global South focuses on building moral economy and "traditional social and environmental ties based on giving, receiving, sharing, and reciprocity" (Ibid). Despite these differences in assumptions and values, all the proponents of degrowth believe that growth is uneconomic, unjust, and ecologically unsustainable. However, as Robert Pollin pointed out, this perspective ignores the reality of neoliberalism and maximization of profit in the contemporary world. He noted that even when growth rates decline, as happened under neoliberalism, there was no slowing down of the concentration of wealth and income (Pollin, 2018). Moreover, the aims of degrowth is the "decolonization of imaginaries" (similar to the earlier mentioned SS, postcolonial, and post development projects) (see Escobar, 1995; Sachs [Ed.], 1992) that seems to Schmelzer as naively idealistic perspectives. He suggests "in order to dismantle the hegemony of growth, degrowth has to develop a profound and critical understanding of the real societal contradictions, hierarchies, and power dynamics shaping capitalism and transform them in new ways" (Schmelzer, 2016). These ideas do not seem to be the goal of the proponents of degrowth.

PROBLEMS WITH THE BINARY DISTINCTION OF DEVELOPMENT/UNDERDEVELOPMENT

Those who advocate the binary distinction of developed/underdeveloped ignore the fact that all societies change through inventions within the society as well as through ideas borrowed from outside during the process of society-to-society interactions in various forms. Reciprocal diffusion of ideas and technology remains the most prominent form of change in most societies because human beings also imitate others in the process of their interaction. If we examine the history of various societies in the world, it would be possible to show that the ideals of the Enlightenment are neither unique to Europe, nor was Europe the first region to come up with these ideals. European societies, like all other societies, were (and still are) constantly going through the historical process of cultural diffusion as they interacted (and currently interact) with other societies (see Anievas and Nişancioğlu, 2015, see also Mishra and Argullol, 2008).

For example, Voltaire viewed India as an enlightened civilization with its inventions of numbers and chess. Europe, during the nineteenth and twentieth centuries, also discovered that Indian linguistic science has a high degree of sophistication (Pujol, N.d.). There are ample examples of Europeans interacting with Asian and South Asian societies well before the Industrial Revolution came into being [(11)]. For example, Alexander of Macedon's invasion of India in 327 BC is well known to have brought Greeks in contact with Indians, although the mingling of Greeks with Indians came later in the second century BC (Thaper, 1966). It is also well established that before the Christian era, the continents of Europe, Asia, and North Africa were connected by trade routes, which allowed the exchange of goods from the Mediterranean to China via Central Asia and Southeast Asia. Being uniquely placed, India became an important facilitator of trade between Rome and the Orient. Later on, as Sanskrit scholar Oscar Pujol noted, the Toledo School of Translators made Latin versions of the fundamental works of Greek and Indian sciences accessible to Christian Europe (Ibid.). Another research scholar recently came across a large number of religious icons of Orthodox Christian art which show Jesus, Mary, and the saints using the exact hand-gestures as performed in specific yoga *mudras* (bibhudevmisra.com/2017/11/yoga-mudras-in-orthodox-christian-art-html). Jana L. Igunma (2019) informs that Christian Europe used to celebrate the story of Buddha without even knowing it. However, Europeans tend to deny any connection with Afro-Asian interaction, and trace their ideas only from the Greeks and the European Enlightenment. This denial, according to Clifford Conner, puts them in the category of nativists, not the universalists they claim to be.

Conner also refutes the thesis that the classical Greeks suddenly burst onto the scene out of nowhere in the sixth century BCE, and asks this question: How is it possible that the existence of high civilization in Egypt and Mesopotamia for thousands of years had no impact on Greek culture? Referring to Martin Bernal's *Black Athena*,

Conner shows the Afroasiatic roots of Greek culture (Conner, 2005:118). Conner explains that European scholars in the nineteenth century wanted to avoid acknowledging that the roots of civilization are Afroasiatic, and therefore, minimizing the importance of Egyptian, Sumerian, and Semitic contributions was necessary. These European scholars kept the focus almost entirely on the Greeks, who they considered to be of Aryan stock as their language is part of the Indo-European family (Ibid.). These European scholars then claimed that the Greeks developed their culture all on their own. From Germany, the idea of this "Greek Miracle" spread to England, France, and the US—creating a body of ideas, known as the "scientific laws of race" that were considered to be science, which has negatively impacted the lives of people of 'color' in profound ways. However, ancient Greek authors recognized that their culture was rooted in the wisdom and accomplishments of earlier civilizations and especially that of Egypt (Ibid., 122).

Europeans also conveniently forget that the three most important inventions that helped them become a colonial power were the printing press, gun powder, and the compass, which were all invented in China and not in Europe (Hobson, 2004; van Zanden, 2008). Moreover, China's industrial revolution, which spanned a period of 1500 years,

> culminated in the Sung revolution in some 600 years before Britain entered its industrialization phase. China's iron and steel industry began between the fifth and second centuries BCE and reached its peak between 800 and 1100 AD. By the end of the eleventh century, China was already producing as much steel as all of Europe put together would as late as 1700. By the twelfth century, the Chinese had a relatively advanced market economy, with paper money and a taxation system based on cash (Nigam, 2011:66; see also Wagner, 1993).

Is it possible to say that the Europeans, who used China's inventions of the printing press, gunpowder, and the compass to their advantage, ignored learning about iron and steel or the market economy and paper money?

In fact, according to Conner (2005), many important technical innovations that took place in China were transmitted over time to Europe, which in turn sparked the Scientific Revolution. Besides printing, gun powder, and the magnetic compass, China produced hundreds of technical inventions that influenced European society—sometimes in stunning ways. Conner listed such technical inventions: mechanical clockwork, the casting of iron, stirrups and efficient horse harnesses, the Cardan suspension and the Pascal triangle, segmental-arch bridges and pound-locks on canals, the stern-post rudder, fore-and-aft sailing, and quantitative cartography. Needham also came to a similar conclusion as he wrote that basic inventions and discoveries that the modern world was built upon came from China (quoted in Conner, 2005:173). We can observe this fact by locating the breadth of Chinese artisans' knowledge and its antiquity in all areas including biology, mechanics, geology, metallurgy, chemistry, agriculture, and navigation, to mention a few. Moreover, Enlightenment thinkers in eighteenth century Europe held the Ming and the early Qing societies in high esteem (Dirlik, 2013).

Needham has challenged the notion that Chinese achievements were *merely technical,* as if they were not worthy of being deemed scientific. Expanding on this issue, he informs that in ancient and medieval China one can find not only a large body of naturalistic theory but also records of systematic experimentations, as well as an accurate measurement system (cited in Connor, 2005:167). Moreover, people from all walks of life in China were honored for their creative deeds. For example, a minor military officer and sword maker, Chhiwu Huai-Wen, was honored for "the co-fusion process of steelmaking" (Ibid., 169). Chinese knowledge was transmitted to other societies by itinerant merchants. For example, the principles of Chinese alchemy were transmitted by Hu merchants during the T'ang dynasty to the Islamic world during the seventh through ninth centuries CE. The Hu merchants were Persian and Arabic traders who traveled the famous Silk Road connecting their native lands with China. They did not include the lands of Europe in their trade route at that time. However, several centuries later, Hu merchants carried alchemical knowledge to the West by using similar methods. It appears that Chinese knowledge also spread through exported slaves, as Needham further explains referring to the near-simultaneous appearance of numerous Chinese innovations in Europe that he called "transmission clusters." Needham suggested that in medieval times slave trade brought thousands of Tartar (Mongolian) domestic servants who embodied all kinds of know-how to Italy. This slave trade peaked in the middle of the fifteenth century (quoted in Ibid., 171). Europe was introduced to Chinese plows with moldboards by Dutch sailors in the seventeenth century, which revolutionized European agriculture. Later, the Dutch brought their Chinese plows with them when they were hired by the English to drain the East Anglian Fens and Somerset Moors. This agricultural knowledge spread from England to Scotland, and from Holland to America and France (Ibid., 179). The Chinese method of making steel from cast iron dates to the second century BCE. The eventual invention of the Bessemer steel process in the West in 1856 was, in fact, anticipated in 1852 by William Kelly, who had brought four Chinese steel experts to Kentucky in 1845 from whom he learned the principles of steel production used in China for over two thousand years previous (Ibid., 177).

Connor has pointed out that European explorers, looking for resources and domination, acquired and seized the knowledge of various technologies for navigation, maps, and other important information by using brute force and by the kidnapping of people from Africa, Arab regions, and India, as they possessed that knowledge which they had accumulated over generations through years of hard work and observation (Conner, 2005). Later, when European elite scientific thinkers appropriated this artisan knowledge and systematized it, they did not credit it to these artisans, who were reduced to wage laborers. These scientists also appropriated scientific and technical knowledge from other countries while denying the role of any artisans and resultantly, their debts to other countries. Thus, a myth of European superiority was created, along with the myth that everything began from the Renaissance with famous scientists such as Galileo, Newton, and Gilbert. In reality, it was ordinary people working in different fields for their daily existence who generated the scientific knowledge and various instruments, technology, and mathematics. But their knowledge was not considered worthy of respect. Today, the average person has no knowledge about those artisans, sailors, and others who cultivated scientific and artisanal knowledge later "invented" by Europeans, instead we keep repeating, and teaching about famous names as the pioneers of science (Ibid.).

In light of the aforementioned, the questions, "why was Britain industrialized first, and why did China not industrialize first," are self-serving, as they promote the binary distinction that automatically bestow a superior status to Britain. For example, the question as to why England was successful in becoming the center of capital is generally explained with regard to its initial advantage in defeating its primary challengers. But this is a circular argument, as it does not first explain the historical contingency of various forces within which the initial advantage of England was largely grounded (van der Pijl, 1998:89). For example, how do we explain why "Germany bypassed Britain in 1910 in qualitative terms ... specifically in steel production Germany had already bypassed Britain in 1900 and enjoyed a 4.3 percent advantage over Britain and French combined in 1910 [?] Similarly, the so-called 'backward' Russia's energy consumption was roughly equal to Austria-Hungary's, and in steel, to France's on the eve of the war" (Ibid., 93–94). Moreover, Russia had become the world's largest iron producer and an important exporter way back in 1716, and by 1913 it possessed a substantial industrial sector ranking fifth in the world after the US, Germany, Britain, and France. It had a well-developed, heavy industrial sector, and in coal and pig iron Russian production was in fifth place and fourth in steel [above France] (Falkun, 1970:20).

If the problem of not having industrialization was due to cultural "backwardness" then how do we explain why the Indian capitalist Tata acquired local capital in 1912 for investment in a large-scale steel industry that could produce the cheapest pig iron by the late 1920s (Bahl, 1995)? How do we explain that India, after being bled white—Britain drained 45 trillion dollars from India between 1765–1938 (Banerjee and Chandrashekar, 2018, quoted in Hickelby and Hickel, 2018; Polya, 2018; Patnaik, 2017b in Chakrabarti and Patnaik)—for 200 years for anything from 3 to 10 percent of its GDP annually, saw its per capita income after independence grow annually at 1.4 percent for several decades (three times faster than its best phase 1870–1913 under colonialism) and much faster (3.01 percent) for the nearly next 30-year span, 1973–2001? During the years 2003–2004 and 2006–2007, India's GDP grew at 7 percent—comparable to the rates achieved by Japan between 1950 and 1973 (Mukherjee, 2010). India developed as much in 30 years as Britain did in 150 years.

However, if our goals are to understand social reality and to eliminate binary distinction, then the question of why England was industrialized first has no relevance. Critics who promote Enlightenment ideals for the advancement of European values have ignored the fact that in the sixteenth century the Indian emperor Akbar, based on his Islamic faith, already supported the ideas of reason, tolerance, and the rights of women, while trying to promote a universal religion, *sulh-i kul.* Meanwhile, his contemporary, Prince Philip II of Spain, was engaged with the Spanish Inquisition. Enlightenment ideas were nowhere in sight in Europe at that time (Ibid.). Many scholars have already made this point. Going back further in Indian history, it should be noted that King Ashoka (third century BC), based on his Buddhist faith, promoted the ideas of human rights, animal rights, secular religion, and tolerance way before the Enlightenment or any UN human rights manifesto. His edicts are recorded on *stupas,* carved into pillars, all over India as documented proof of his humanitarian ethos.

Curiously, there was no immediate cause of the English Industrial Revolution, as it took three centuries to manifest (Hobsbawm, 1968). Actually, as Heller has pointed out, it is possible to describe all historical processes in the West without

European periodization and "without adopting the nineteenth century notion of the emergence of capitalism as a specific stage in the development of world society, and we can dispense with the supposed sequence of periods of production leading to it that are confined to Europe" (Heller, 2011:225).

The problem with Eurocentrism is that "Western civilization has been constructed on a perverse and mistaken idea of human nature ... that we are condemned by an irresistible human nature to look to our own advantage at the cost of whomever it may concern and thus menace our own social existence ... it is probably true, however, that this perverse idea of human nature endangers our existence" (Sahlins, 2008:112). Therefore, the question is this: If Western civilization is constructed on a perverse idea of human nature that is endangering the existence of human species, then how can this be a sign of progress or development? Moreover, why should societies that did not follow the Western path to "progress" (that is, endangering human existence) be labeled as backward unless one thinks that endangering the human existence is a sign of progress?

Noam Chomsky recently remarked that it is ironic that "the so-called 'least advanced' people are the ones taking the lead in trying to protect all of us, while the richest and most powerful among us are the ones who are trying to drive this society to destruction" (quoted in Mukherji, 2016:32). Indigenous communities in Bolivia, Ecuador, and in India are the leading forces in trying to prevent a race to disaster (Alexandra, 2016). Similarly, writing about indigenous knowledge, Mukherji points out that, "Liberal education, with its species-terminating edifice of knowledge, is often ascribed absolute value, since any alternative form of education is viewed as either inconceivable or politically incorrect" (12). The reality is that an entire range of indigenous "adult" knowledge systems have existed simultaneously, though in isolation, for thousands of years (Mukherji, 2016), whereas modern liberal knowledge systems are a more recent phenomenon. It is the indigenous people with their accumulated knowledge of thousands of years that can help save the planet and not the "development" projects of the West.

Agreeing with these ideas, I will point out that while establishing the validity of indigenous knowledge is important, we also need to claim all human knowledge as a common human heritage that has been created by our collective human ancestors on the planet over thousands of years. We should learn from all collective human knowledge (East, West, North, South) and improve human conditions, the planet, and all living beings, and not privilege one human group or one particular form of knowledge over another (13). This is possible when we stop thinking in binary terms. Or else, we will remain trapped into choosing from indigenism, or fundamentalism, or Enlightenment rationality. For example, as Almond points out, some Muslims fear that a complete rejection of modernity will allow more fundamentalist versions of Islam to take its place—therefore, they do not wish to challenge modernity. However, postmodernists who challenge modernity by calling it "a cluster of cultural contingencies" remain trapped in indigenism and local solutions (Almond, 2010:4). Both of these approaches are problematic as they both promote binary distinction. We need to break out of these binaries and false choices and find an alternative perspective.

THE PROBLEM WITH POST-DEVELOPMENT ALTERNATIVE

The post-development theory (Ferguson, 1990; Sachs, 1992; Escobar, 1995; Rahnema, 1997) that came into being in the 1980s and 1990s promotes more pluralism in ideas about development. These theorists were influenced by wider intellectual trends, including the constructivist turn in the social sciences, postmodernism, post-colonial, and populism (Rikodi, 2015:24). The central premise in all these strands is that "the idea of development is founded upon the European tradition of knowing; a tradition which creates its own grounds for ... domination, and thereby forcible eliminating non-European forms of knowledge. It is the culture of the West, and the movement of this culture 'Westernisation,' which is ... taken to mean development" (Sanyal, 2014:80–81). Development was perceived as a discourse, and Escobar, an anthropologist, provided a detailed discourse analysis of development as a regime of representation and power. His project was inspired by Edward Sa'id's *Orientalism* (1978) in which Sa'id deconstructed the concept of the Orient produced by European thought. Following Sa'id, Escobar deconstructed this "colonization of imagination" to show how development became an elaborate mechanism of control through the interplay of knowledge and power (Rikodi, 2015). Post-development theory also focuses on local culture, knowledge, and grassroots movements (Sardar, 2007).

Post-development scholars' ideas of the celebration of a plurality of voices, and multiplicity of local practices of resistance are surely welcoming because they challenge the mainstream development model. They also reject the entire paradigm of development based on its failure to deliver to the poor of the third world. However, their counter-model of development, which rejects development, turns out to be another grand narrative that replaces one dogmatism with another (Lieten, 2002:78). Their approach perpetuates cultural relativism, which, in turn, promotes neoliberal ideals. They are criticized for portraying modernity and development as "monolithic, depoliticizing processes, everywhere the same and always tainted beyond redemption by their progressive European provenance" (Rikodi, 2015:27). However, by equating modernity with being Western, post-developmentalists seem to be suggesting that non-Western societies do not value reason, science, and rationality (Rist, 2008:259). Their ideas privilege local, community, culture, and indigenous knowledge, and they do not take into account how all local cultures are not only continuously changing by migration, trade missions, technology, and colonialism, but also maintaining existing local power relationships, hierarchies, and inequalities (Rikodi, 2015; see also Sylvester, 1999). Moreover, in recent times, the role of NGOs has increased at the local level, and religious organizations are also equally important actors in influencing local thinking on the matter of development. However, post-developmentalists do not clarify which "people" are being identified with "local", as there are many social groups in every locality. Do they mean marginalized people, or sub-caste or a regional sub-caste within the group, or a localized village population with an adult male culture of domination, or culture and interests of the poorest and lowest-caste females (Lieten, 2002)? The post-developmentalists reject modernity and development without realizing that most contemporary national development plans (e.g. Uganda Vision 2040, Vietnam's Sustainable Development Strategy for 2011–2020) express a widespread desire to achieve both modernity and development (Rikodi, 2015, see also Dirlik, 2013).

Recently, Kalyan Sanyal made an interesting critique of Escobar's ideas about post-development while also appreciating his efforts to create new possibilities. According to Sanyal, Escobar conflated development and capitalism while depoliticizing development. This strategy "leaves no space where the relationship between the dynamics of the postcolonial capital and the dominant imaginaries of development can be addressed" (Sanyal, 2014:86). Moreover, Escobar's assumption that there exists some original and authentic tradition which is pristine and indigenous and can be located by displacing the modernization project of development, as Sanyal points out, is problematic. This approach ignores that indigenousness has its own oppressive system, and moreover, that development programs are popular with the marginalized people (Ibid., 93). One can also observe in everyday interactions how structures of tradition negotiate with modernity and help to achieve development goals. However, in the process of negotiation, tradition and modernity constitute one another, which then eliminates any "pure authentic tradition." Similarly, David Lehmann noted that grassroots movements—which are projecting an image of being authentic and untouched—are in fact part of a larger dialogue within a global social movement, and they could not function without a global NGO network available to them (Lehmann, 1997:577).

Notwithstanding these criticisms, post-development ideas have undoubtedly generated new insights. As Lieten has pointed out, "If post-development theories had an explicit political, social and economic program, and a way of galvanizing social forces to reach that aim, dialogue, discussion and dispute could follow, but as it stands, post-modern/post-development is a hollow and yet seductive position" (Lieten:79).

In the following, we shall review similar problems with the alternatives provided by the SS collective, which embraced Western postcolonial theory and postmodernism—as was also done by the followers of post-development theory.

THE PROBLEM WITH SUBALTERN STUDIES ALTERNATIVE

Subaltern Studies challenge the categories and assumptions of the European project of development, but has failed to provide a viable alternative. For example, they raised the issue of historiography that sees India only through "developmental" schemes that always portray the country as "lacking" and "not yet." However, instead of offering an alternative to the existing developmental narrative, the SS collective simply rejects metanarrative (Marxism, globalization, imperialism). By rejecting metanarrative, Harriss pointed out, the SS collective unwittingly reinforces the neo-liberal agenda to change the discourse from the binary of capitalism/socialism to one of democracy/totalitarianism, and then uses anti-totalitarian concepts to any effort to understand the society as a whole, or the world at large. Thus, by denying the existence of larger historical forces, it closes any possibility for the people to resist against these forces (Harriss, 2001) and makes it difficult to find alternatives to the narrative of developed/underdeveloped.

This is not surprising, because the SS collective had been shifting its focus as they rose in prominence in the Western academic world. They shifted their focus "from inquiry into Subaltern 'autonomy' at moments of rebellions through representations of the subaltern in the colonial archives and in mainstream histories, to a whole range of subjects connected to colonial governance, education, movements of religious and social reforms, the state and public institutions, modern ideas of rationality, science, regimes of power" and differences based on identities [14]. This shift in focus is due to the SS collective's entry into the milieu of postcolonial theory, which was already focusing on similar issues and questions. Thus, the SS collective acquired their theoretical credentials in the US, and they rose to international prominence while becoming a "conduit for postcolonial notions in the social sciences" along with their general reach (Brennan, 2014:71). (To understand how the SS became acceptable in the US, and how the members of the SS collective became internationally known, Kaiwar's book is very enlightening)[15]. No wonder that both Subaltern Studies and postcolonial theory are unable to provide a useful alternative narrative as they are more concerned with deconstructing history and finding multiple modernities (Brennan, 2014).

Their idea of multiple modernities could not be the basis for an alternative narrative because it suggests that modernity is a superior form of living, and we (non-Europeans), too, are modern as we are keeping up with Europe (Dietze, 2006; see also Dirlik, 2013). Similarly, their rejection of metanarrative does not allow a focus on the process of globalization, which keeps people diverted from focusing on the larger system that produces and reproduces the differences of race, ethnicity, gender, and other local identities. Consequently, the SS and the postcolonial theory's focus on these differences has marginalized the need for an understanding about the growing underdevelopment of large regions throughout the world.

Furthermore, the SS and postcolonial theory's focus on identities and differences unwittingly legitimized the promotion of "multicultural neoliberalism," which was able to promote all types of differences while keeping class structure intact. However, with "multicultural neoliberalism" identity became a question of choice including "Choice Feminism," like choices of consumer products, while giving the illusion of empowerment without any change in status quo. In fact, as Kymlicka explains, gender identity politics became a substitute for feminism and by broadening its definition feminism was depoliticized (the LGBT acronym has grown to LGBTQQ1P2SAA and a greater number of possible permutation of identities can be created by adding race to this mix). Thus, "multicultural neoliberalism" was able to reshape the construction of diversity in a way that radically atomized society, in which an autonomous individual is emancipated from social bonds and solidarity (Kymlicka, 2012). Consequently,

> Neoliberal multiculturalism enacted a structure of public recognition, acknowledgment and acceptance of multicultural subjects, based on an ethos of self-reliance, individualism and competition, while simultaneously (and conveniently) undermining discourses and social practices that call for collective social action and fundamental structural change (Darder, 2012:417, see also Pierscionek, 2018).

As a result, any interpretation was dismissed as an "alternative point of view" or an "opinion" because it is "all relative" and "everyone has their own truth," as we see it actually existing in the world of the Internet (Pomerantsev, 2016).

Unfortunately, even though the SS collective and the practitioners of philosophical postmodernism were generally from the political left, their focus on identity has unwittingly facilitated the rise of "several religious revivalists, chauvinist, xenophobic, autarkic, reactionary trends, which, in the name of fighting the evils of capitalism [a leftist agenda now used by reactionary forces], want to turn back the clock of history by counterpoising 'Internationalism' with 'localism" (James, 2017; see also Mirkovic, 2015:190). Even in the context of progressive and democratic demands, the same reactionary trends are on display. For example, when certain people of different ethnicities residing in Europe try to keep their lifestyle intact and not "ape" the West, they are criticized for rejecting Western values: progress, openness, and democracy. The recent banning of the hijab, burqa, and burkini, in the name of security and openness, is a case in point. Muslim women are asked to show their bodies in the name of openness and democratic values, while denying them their democratic right to choose their own attire, their comfort level, and the manner of showing or not showing their bodies. Instead, in the name of security and democracy, Islamophobia is being promoted.

To "provincialize Europe" is the more recent concern of the SS collective even though Huntington said years ago that Europe is not universal but unique (Kaiwar, 2015). So, how do we provincialize Europe when it is already provincialized? Anievas and Nişancioğlu clarify that the SS idea of the provincialization of Europe is not about a region of the world called Europe, but rather the generalization of its (European) forms and categories. However, the SS collective has never provided an "alternative substantive historical sociology of the European experience" from which these categories and forms were derived (Anievas and Nişancioğlu, 2015:40). Instead, they "uncritically presuppose a discrete and hermetically sealed European history in which modernity was created before being subsequently expanded globally" (Ibid.). Obviously, the project of *Provincializing Europe* (Chakrabarty, 2000, 2007) has not been able to decenter Europe and thus has not made former colonies free from "the taint of inadequacy in relation to the West" (Kaiwar, 2015:xiii–xv). Consequently, the SS collective is not able to provide any alternative perspective to modernity or to the European project of development.

AFTER SUBALTERN STUDIES

Interestingly, when I was halfway into my current volume, the Subaltern Studies disbanded in 2012 and one of the founders admitted there were problems in their theoretical understanding (Chatterjee, 2012). In 2013, a scathing attack on the SS collective came from a young Marxist scholar of Indian origin residing in the US (Chibber, 2013). In 2014, another Marxist scholar of Indian origin (Kaiwar, 2015) also published a book with a thorough and detailed critique of SS, specifically focusing on their ideas of "provincializing Europe" and "dominance without hegemony." Coincidently, this attack came at a time when Marxism as metanarrative—which has been rejected by SS and postcolonial theory—was once again becoming fashionable amongst US historians and other scholars, while younger students were becoming more curious about it. Chibber also noted this fact and wrote,

> The global economic crisis has brought into relief the basic fact that the entire world is now part of the same universal history, subject to the same underlying forces … For the first time since the 1980s, *everyone* is talking about capitalism—not alterity, or hybridity, or the fragments, but the ubiquitous, grinding, crushing force of capital. This certainly makes for

a friendlier environment for the arguments I have been developing in this book [(16)].

No wonder Chibber's book was so widely discussed and received with great warmth. In addition to renewed interest in Marxist ideas in the US, efforts to make young people interested in Marxist ideas are increasing in China. For example, the Chinese government has released a rap song about Karl Marx in an effort to make young people interested in reading his works and to support the Chinese Communist Party (teleSUR, 2016), while Chinese universities are asked to teach Marxist Theory (scmp.com, January 20, 2015). In the US, Bernie Sander's presidential campaign of 2016 helped make socialism a popular topic among the younger generation, many of whom are now interested in understanding this alternative social system and are not shy in talking about it.

Although these changes are welcome, the people from former colonies and their societies are still perceived through the lens of the developed/underdeveloped binary distinction, and are assessed according to the tenets of Eurocentrism. During the 2016 presidential campaign, Donald Trump openly supported Islamophobia and hatred towards immigrants. Black lives are erased with impunity and a disproportionately large number of black men are incarcerated. A self-proclaimed socialist, Sanders clearly supported the droning of third world people and the imperial goals of America. He also addressed Hugo Chavez, who, like himself, was a social democrat, as "a dead communist dictator." He supported the return of Special Forces (death squads) to Iraq. He also backed Bill Clinton's illegal bombing of Serbia (Pilger, 2016). He is also not against the military industrial complex, as it generates jobs for his constituency and keeps him in the Senate. He is also in favor of regime change in Syria by force.

Moreover, people from non-European countries are treated with the same binary distinction under which they are always considered "less" and "deficient" in comparison to the European West. Within the US, there is a systematic attack on programs and academic courses that challenge Eurocentrism, and in many American universities programs in Afro-American Studies, Women's Studies, and Hispanic Studies are being eliminated (Azikiwe, 2016; see also Democracynow.org, July 17, 2017 to learn about the court case in Arizona on the banning of books and Hispanic Studies). Attacks on gender studies are also becoming more common in Europe. The World Bank and the IMF always offer the same elusive solution of "development" to improve poor conditions in poor countries. The consequences of these solutions are so devastating that recently twenty-four groups in India working on environmental, labor, and human rights wrote to the executive directors of the World Bank petitioning them not to dilute the environment or defray social safeguards [(17)].

In addition, the US continues to invade and drone other societies (mostly third world) compelling them to accept US hegemony, values, and way of life—while forcing them to live in poverty. At the same time, the US is forcing these societies to provide cheap labor and open access to their resources for exploitation by multinational corporations. Islamophobia is at an all-time high in Europe as well as in the US and other rich countries. People and societies of poor countries and ex-colonies are still being defined as backward, tribal, and underdeveloped. This is reflected clearly in the reporting bias among Western media that treats the killing of people by American drones or by a "terrorist" group in non-European countries as non-news while regarding the terrorist attacks and killing of people in France, Germany, and Britain with an astounding level of sympathy, concern, and urgency. A recent survey made by Fairness and Accuracy in Reporting (FAIR) observed that the US media considers ISIS attacks and subsequent deaths in Europe as 1800 percent more newsworthy than ISIS attacks and deaths in the Middle East (Johnson, 2016). This sends a clear message that European lives are more valuable and therefore more worthy of sympathy, concern, and news than others. Flags are flying at half-mast for European deaths but not for the Iraqi people who are being killed by the same forces. Hurricane Harvey's flood disaster in Houston and the subsequent death toll of 65 people was reported continuously for days all over the world. However, the South Asia floods (India, Bangladesh, and Nepal), which occurred at the same time, where 45 million people were affected and 1200 people died, did not receive much coverage in Western media. On September 2, 2016, an estimated 180 million workers throughout India went on strike for one whole day, the largest workers strike in human history, yet it was ignored by Western media.

Thus, in the twenty-first century, the perspective about and treatment of third world people remain contemptuous and racist in the Euro-American world. In this current historical context, even though Marxism seems to be making a comeback, it is doubtful if it can help change the conditions and treatment of third world people with the formula of "development of productive forces for transition to socialism."

THE PROBLEM WITH THE MARXIST ALTERNATIVE

Kenneth E. Boulding wrote, "Anyone who believes in indefinite growth in anything physical on a physically finite planet, is either mad or an economist" (Goodread. com). In May 2016, the IMF released a report admitting that its formula of neoliberalism and perpetual growth is unsustainable and that it was a mistake [(18)].

However, both capitalists and Marxists believe in the same ideology of growth and development. The policies of global institutions such as the UN, IMF, and the World Bank to improve the conditions in third world countries are based on the ideas of growth and development. Even those countries in Latin America that claim to be pursuing an alternative to neo-liberalism are following these same ideas of growth and development. The recent reemergence of Marxism does not challenge the destructive growth model of the capitalist system as many Marxists, blindly following scripture, also promote the further development of capitalism (productive forces), believing this to be a logical transition to their goal of socialism. This strategy has done a great deal of harm to people, to societies and countries, to the environment, and to the planet. Moreover, as Lummis (2005) pointed out, according to Marxists, history has a determined course and political actors are the agents of history. However, many of these political actors do not take responsibility for the consequences of their actions (atrocities against people) as they believe they are merely the tools of history. Marxists are only interested in creating conditions to reach their goal of socialism, even if it has to be on the dead bodies of those in whose names socialism would be (if at all) attained. With this approach political actors, while believing in their innocence, are able to commit horrendous atrocities and cruelties as are also being done in the name of modernization and development (Lummis, 2005:178–9). It reminds me of the US government's invasion and destruction of Iraq in the name of "saving it."

The Marxist model also perpetuates the binary distinction of developed/underdeveloped by promoting only the capitalist forces of production. Question: How many more people (mostly poor and marginalized) have to be sacrificed at the altar of socialism? How many more people have to suffer the consequences of development projects, and how much more environment has to be destroyed before we reach the heavenly socialism? It is insane to talk of socialism in the same breath while promoting destruction of people's lives (dispossessed from their lands and homes) and destruction of environment in the name of development of productive forces. This brand of Marxists do not realize that people want to live a better life in the present, and cannot wait for elusive socialism to arrive (if at all) someday. However, it seems that few Indian Marxist thinkers have begun to address these issues (Patnaik, 2011).

It should also be noted that Marxists do not see any problem with technology, nuclear power, or machines under a socialist system, as if machines will treat workers differently, and growth and development would not create environmental destruction, or nuclear plants would not be hazardous (Lummis, 2005). This denial on the part of Marxists is not surprising because, "Marxism has no metaphysics" as Camille Paglia pointed out, "it cannot even detect, much less comprehend, the enormity of the universe and the operation of nature ... Marxism is only a fragment of the totality of life" (quoted in Lehmann, 2018). Many Marxists, who are ready to quote Marx about everything, are not capable of finding an alternative, as they stay very close to the scripture. They have forgotten Marx's advice to "let the 'dead generations' rest in peace. Awake from 'nightmarish' mimicry. Make your own case. Use your own words, use your own examples. Stop 'borrowing.' Create" (Albert, 2016).

FAILING TO IMAGINE ALTERNATIVE PERSPECTIVES

There seems to be a failure of imagination in finding alternative perspectives. The elite intelligentsia from former colonies are generally trained in Western universities where they learn from the same Eurocentric models, and they easily accept the IMF and World Bank's suggested solutions [(19)]. We cannot expect this intelligentsia to come up with an alternative narrative or solutions for our present plight.

Even leftist intelligentsia have not done any better. For example, the socialist magazine *Monthly Review* published an article in its May 2017 issue on the Legacy of A. G. Frank's "Development of Underdevelopment" which offers no alternative theory, but instead invites us "to further expose the fallacies of mainstream development strategies" (de Oliveira, 2017:58). Similarly, Tina Renier (2018) finds that the Dependency theory has a prevailing relevance in understanding persistent poverty and underdevelopment of the Caribbean. It may be so, but it does not provide any alternative framework (that does not include "development" ideology) to find an alternative path to improve the poor conditions of these countries.

The incapability of Marxists to imagine an alternative perspective can be discerned from the following example from India. In 2006–2007, the left-front government of West Bengal dispossessed peasants in Singur, Kalinganagr, and Nandigram from their lands and handed them to the Tata Company to manufacture cheaper cars for the lower middle class in India (Nigam, 2009). (These processes have not stopped, in fact, they have picked up speed under the new Indian government.) (Basu and Biswas, 2017). This process involving the state confiscation of peasant land to benefit the growth of the manufacturing industry led the peasants to revolt, which was violently suppressed by the state police who killed many people. It is worth noting that this brand of Marxists in the West Bengal leftist party defended their actions on the basis of the desirability of "historical necessity" of industrialization and development [20]. This defense is based on their ideological belief that capitalism is a progressive force as it would lead to socialism. (It is forgotten in this belief that capitalism will not convert to socialism on its own. It would be, if at all, resistance movements based on class consciousness against capitalism which might, or might not, have the potential—not guaranteed—for creating such possibilities. However, the outcome may not necessarily be the one that Marxists hope for. Moreover, the consciousness of the working class itself is now in danger of being controlled and manipulated remotely with new pulse microwave technologies.)

Moreover, Marxists also believe that the move from agriculture to industry is inevitable and necessary because this is how it had happened everywhere else in the world (Nigam, 2011:26). Even when so many economic historians have concluded in their studies that there is no standard experience of industrialization, it has not occurred to this brand of Marxists of the West Bengal leftist party that the same process which happened in England 200 years ago does not, and cannot, necessarily repeat itself everywhere in the same way. For example, as Nigam pointed out, capitalism did not destroy feudalism and the old property form. Instead, it led to the destruction of small peasants only (Ibid., 59). Moreover, the same process did not take place in other areas of Europe. "Till well into the twentieth century, the peasantry actually remained an important segment of west Europe's population" (Ibid., 61). Recently, the renowned Indian Marxist economist Prabhat Patnaik also pointed out that "the discourse propagated by capitalism on 'development' is neither theoretically nor historically valid" (Patnaik, 2018).

The other myth about the standard experience of industrialization—that the history of industry, science, and technological development begins with the West around the fifteenth and sixteenth centuries—has also been refuted by historians such as Janet Abu-Lughod and John Hobson. For example, the idea that Vasco de Gama "discovered India" is not correct. "Sassanid Persians had been sailing across to India and China from the early centuries of the first millennium as did the Black Ethiopians and, later on the Muslims (after about 650 AD)" (Nigam, 2011:63; Abu-Lughod, 1989; Chaudhuri, 1990). According to Hobson,

> 'Islamic navigator Ahmad bin-Majid had already, decades before Vasco de Gama, circled around the Cape of Good Hope and entered the Mediterranean via the Strait of Gibraltar ... virtually all of the nautical and navigational technologies and techniques that made De Gama's journey possible were invented in either China or the Islamic Middle East' and that he apparently managed to navigate across because he was guided by an 'unnamed Gujarati (Indian) Muslim pilot' (Hobson, 2004 quoted in Nigam, 2011:64).

Recently, Conner has provided information that Hippalus was the first Greek to comprehend the weather patterns of the Indian Ocean. His knowledge came from anonymous Arab and Indian navigators, who themselves had learned from the two-thousand-years-old tradition of using monsoon winds to understand weather patterns (Conner, 2005:207). However, this knowledge of monsoon winds was lost to the Europeans for centuries with the disappearance of the Western Roman Empire. In 1497, when Vasco de Gama entered the Indian Ocean, he found that people were not willing to share the secrets and sophisticated traditions of navigation. Therefore, he used the methods of seizing and kidnapping people who possessed that knowledge (Ibid., 203).

Conner informs that at the end of the fourteenth century, Chinese sailors were the most advanced in the world and their ships were more than four hundred feet long. One Chinese ship could accommodate Columbus' ships—the Nina, Pinta, and Santa Maria—on its deck with room left over. However, the Chinese decided to scrap their fleets in 1433 as they found that they had nothing to gain from trading with "barbarians" (Ibid., 217), instead, they should protect their territory from continuous nomadic threats on its inner land frontiers (Anievas and Nişancioğlu, 2015:72). Philippe Beaujard (2009) also pointed out that the Ming dynasty pulled back because Mongols were seriously menacing them as they captured the Emperor in 1449 and held him for ransom. Another problem, due to deforestation, accessible timber for building huge ships was running out and it was expensive to source from remote forests (cited in Anderson, 2018).

Many more scholars have challenged prevailing Marxist assumptions that the world before 1500 was a stagnant one "mired in tradition with insulated societies." These scholars have produced an alternative narrative showing that:

> Right from the seventh century onwards, there has been a flourishing global economy with considerable trade and other forms of interaction. This was a global economy that was powered by the major achievements of the Arabs and the Chinese. Between 650 and 1000 AD ... the leading edge of global power lay in the Islamic Middle East and north Africa. Islamic/Arabic breakthroughs in astronomy, mathematics, paper manufacturing are well known—apart from a range of textile and silk manufacturers. Right down to the eighteenth century, Muslims of the Arab world led over the Europeans in iron and steel production; they also made impressive strides in sugar refinement, construction, furniture manufacture, glass, leather tanning, pottery and stone cutting. Apart from these, they created a whole range of economic institutions relating to partnership, banking, contract law, credit and such other matters—some of these pre-dating the advent of Islam (Nigam, 2011:64–65).

Recently, one scholar claimed that Adam Smith learned about the division of labor from Sharia Law even though he did not acknowledge it. However, Smith did praise Ibn Khaldun in his work (Barsocchini, 2016; Oweiss, faculty/Georgetown.edu).

Based on the research of various scholars, Aditya Nigam has noted that 600 years before Britain entered its phase of industrialization, China's industrial revolution, which spanned a period of 1500 years, had already culminated in the Sung period. The Chinese iron and steel industry probably began between the fifth and second century BC, and it reached its high point between 800 and 1100 AD. Nigam pointed out that China was able to produce a large quantity of steel by the end of the eleventh century comparable to what Europe combined would produce in the late 1700s. Moreover, the Chinese had developed a relatively advanced market economy with paper money and a taxation system based on cash by the twelfth century (Nigam, 2011:65). We also learn from Conner that from the second century BCE the Chinese had developed methods for making steel from cast iron, which over time eventually reached Europe through traders, merchants, slaves, and other travelers.

Besides providing steel making methods to the West, China also invented printing, gun powder, and the compass, which later made it possible for the West to colonize the whole world (Nigam, 2011). Based on these studies and resultant information, one can refute the assumption that until the beginning of England's Industrial Revolution in the eighteenth century, the world was simply an unchanging and traditional world, caught up in stagnation and backwardness. It seems a strange logic, as Nigam pointed out, to believe that while markets, trade, and industry emerged and developed over a long period in pre-industrial societies, but somehow these developments did not eliminate existing modes of living (Nigam, 2011:66; Nigam, 2007).

The historian Raj Chandavarkar raised similar questions in connection with the debate about India's industrialization. He pointed out that both Marxists and functionalists derived models of industrialization and social change largely from the historical experience of Western Europe, especially of Britain (Chadavarkar, 1985). However, the critics of these theories have not rejected these models as a whole. They remain pervasive in the analysis of economic development both in the West and in the third world.

> Industrialization is taken to constitute an autonomous force, determined by a neutral technology, whose 'imperatives' and 'inherent tendencies' appear to lie beyond the realm of social choice or political control, and which acts to shape society inevitably in a single direction .... Consequently, they have generated endless false analogies between fundamentally different societies and inspired scores of meaningless computations of industrial achievement (Ibid., 627–628).

According to Chandavarkar, various forms of Marxist analysis seem to resemble functionalist sociology. Moreover, the factors they identify as the "preconditions" of economic development have more often turned out to be the consequences rather than the causes of growth (Ibid.).

Renowned Indian Marxist historian Sumit Sarkar highlighted the complex circulatory processes in various economic and environmental interactions within colonial India in his recent volume about India that was based on numerous historical studies (Sarkar, 2014). He writes, "'Development' and 'underdevelopment' thus fed each other, not just globally, but also with regard to relationships within the colonized country" (Ibid., 127). He elaborates that "Relations between traditional and modern, indigenous and European business life in late-colonial India were marked by both interconnections and varying degrees of mutually beneficial adjustments, as well as by a basic and growing subordination of the traditional indigenous. The latter produced conflicts, but did not rule out collaboration" (Ibid., 191–192).

Earlier in 1995, in the case study of the Tata Iron and Steel Company, I showed that the anomaly of the emergence of the large-scale steel industry in India with native capital under British colonial rule can be explained by focusing on the interaction and conjunction of various historical forces internationally and nationally—within England, within the US and within India—that allowed the indigenous entrepreneur J. N. Tata to develop the enterprise (Bahl, 1995). The Tata steel factory was successful, whereas earlier attempts by British entrepreneurs to produce steel in India did not succeed. The success of one and failure of the others cannot be explained simply by focusing on individual entrepreneurship, the availability of capital, any so-called cultural or technological "superiority," or deficiency, or colonial government support or lack of support. It is more complex, and I have further expanded on this point with a revised version of my research efforts in Chapter 7 of the present volume.

It is now well documented that there was no standard experience of industrialization worldwide, and that there is no inevitability that agriculture must be replaced by industry, nor any inevitability of capitalism to move towards socialism. Similarly, there are no pre-conditions for the emergence of industrialization and it does not occur the same way everywhere, and it does not have to. (For more detail, see Chapter 1, section on "Preconditions.") With this understanding it may be possible to find a much-needed alternative perspective, which will enable us to write a comparative history on equal terms with a yardstick of parity without categorizing societies as either developed or underdeveloped.

THE NEED FOR AN ALTERNATIVE PERSPECTIVE

Alternative perspectives and alternative narratives can only provide alternative strategies to improve human lives as well as save the planet. Otherwise, as Nigam observed, during various revolutionary takeovers of state power most often the revolutionaries did not build a socialist system but instead opted to build a capitalist one, which only destroys autonomous life forms and reduces everyone to wage laborers (Nigam, 2009).

However, we also need to worry about the problem of other vested interests taking over the leadership of social movements and directing them toward different outcomes in the name of 'democracy' and 'revolution' (Bisnoff, 2019). For example, the CIA, USAID, George Soros, and others are either creating or using genuine popular uprisings (as in Egypt and Tunisia) to their own ends by directing and training their energy towards a different outcome. (Interestingly, Pakistan has recently asked groups affiliated with George Soros to leave the country). For example, the Soros funded Open Society and the CIA were deeply involved in training and organizing the Orange Revolution in the Ukraine, Rose Revolution in Georgia, and the Tulip Revolution in Kyrgyzstan. The Serbian OTPOR symbol of a black-and-white-fist as a sign of resistance has been used in different colors during subsequent revolutions. An open hand symbol was used to symbolize an uprising in Venezuela. Many young students and young Venezuelans from the opposition party were involved in this uprising and trained by OTPOR members on how to build the movement to overthrow the country's president. These movements are funded by quasi-private "foundations" and NGOs such as the Albert Einstein Institute (AEI) and the National Endowment for Democracy (NED), and both are connected to USAID through which money is channeled [(21)]. The organization Moveon.org, which has coordinated many demonstrations and social movements in the US, is also funded by George Soros (Maclean, 2017). Other organizations funded by the US for regime change in other countries include the Agency for International Development (AID), United States Information Services (USIS), International Republican Institute (IRI), and The Atlas Network. The goal of the Atlas Economic Research Foundation, called Atlas Network, is to defeat socialism at all levels from university campuses to whole countries and remove constitutional governments from power as was recently done in Brazil (Aharonian and Rangel, 2018). Atlas Network has adopted the operative strategy spelled out by

Nobel Laureate economist James McGrill Buchanan from the University of Chicago—that "it is necessary to put chains on democracy" and subordinate government models in defense of the sanctity of private property rights (quoted in Ibid). Even the World Social Forum, which is supposed to be challenging neo-liberalism and capitalism globally, is funded by neo-liberal and capitalist forces such as Rockefeller and others (Chossudovsky, 2018; Welch, Feldman and Morningstar, 2018).

It would seem that revolutions and social movements have been used as effective tools by imperialist forces for regime change, and not so much for the social change that discontented people are clamoring for. Tragically, the genuine discontentment of people towards appalling conditions is channeled to fulfill an imperial agenda. In this context, people need to be vigilant that the movements they are supporting (for socialism or for any other system) are not hijacked by such elements. Similarly, Marxists should be careful not to blindly support the development of productive forces while believing in the myth of transition to socialism because it is the Western transnational companies that are promoting development in poor countries in order to plunder their resources while controlling their land and agriculture; in other words, the re-colonization of poor countries.

As we approach the end of the second decade of the twenty-first century, there is no new alternative perspective on the horizon. All scholars, both pro-and anti-modernization theorists, are using the same binary distinction of development/underdevelopment to explain their argument. Their questions and answers remain Eurocentric, which eliminates the possibility of an alternative perspective, even though these scholars are claiming to do the opposite. The problem is that the assumptions behind these ideas do not allow us to think about societies in any other way. Consequently, it becomes very difficult to find a solution to the prevailing problems in poor societies, except with the fixed formula of development. We continue looking at each society through a lens of its being developed or undeveloped, as if every society is static with no prior history and as if every society began with a given condition (developed or underdeveloped) that never changed. This approach denies the historical processes that make any society what it is in the present time and it ignores the fact that changes in any society are not based only on the actions of individual societies. As Immanuel Wallerstein has pointed out, "the fundamental error of ahistorical social science (including ahistorical versions of Marxism) is to reify parts of the totality into such units and then to compare these reified structures" (Wallerstein, 1974b:388). As scholars and as historians, we should be aware of our responsibility in the production of related knowledge and history writing because both play an important political role in shaping ideas and government policies.

How do we write comparative history without the binary distinction of developed/underdeveloped and give equal weight to every society, while not undermining their specificities nor the roles of imperialism and capitalism and their ramifications on the entire world? It would be difficult to do so if one keeps on reiterating the old ideas of "superior west and inferior rest." However, even when one tries to conduct research in these areas, one's findings may not be considered serious "unless the conclusions are guaranteed by the concepts and models of 'normal science' which is defined by European assumptions" (Rist, 1997:246). In other words, it would not be possible to discover anything new. The question is this: How can "'normal science' [based on

European assumptions] which has significant numerous anomalies be a model for normal science?" (Rist, 1997:246). If we are to fulfill the demands of European criteria regarding "ideal normal science," then surely we shall never move out of it. For example, a recent study of German Indology has shown German Indology's claim to be based on an historical-critical method and on the ideal of objective, scientific investigation of Indian texts is not correct because of its theological and Neo-Protestant inheritance (Adulari and Bagchee, 2014).

I am well aware that country-to-country relationships today are based on global power structures. The renowned Indian scholar A. K. Bagchi recently examined and explained how Western projects of development have negatively affected various countries (Bagchi, 2005; see also Rodney, 1983). In addition to grasping this important knowledge about the negative effects of development projects, we also need to find a methodology that does not trap us into choosing those same negative solutions for our economic and social problems. To achieve this goal, we need to cultivate a different perspective.

TOWARDS A POSSIBLE ALTERNATIVE APPROACH

We have yet a long way to go in determining a non-binary, non-centric holistic approach towards writing and analyzing history. Most of the time, we do not realize how various binaries creep into our analyses and writing of history. It is important that scholars keep striving to erase these binaries from their writing and to not reinforce the violence of these distinctions. It is generally forgotten that all binary distinctions are a human construct, that they are not inevitable, naturally given conditions, and that they can be erased. An alternative argument is possible only if we are prepared to ask an alternative question. A recent work by Parthasarathi, *Why Europe Grew Rich and Asia Did Not: 1600–1850* (2011), is an attempt to rectify this tendency. However, the title of the book and the questions raised in it remain within the same binary and defensive framework. We have yet to find a way that does not require us to defend our capabilities (as ex-colonies and ex-colonized people) every time we make a comparative study.

Possibilities and alternatives have always existed, in the past as well as in the present time. However, if our assumptions are based on a "context-free" approach that promotes only one criterion of truth and right action (universalism) at all times and places, then it will always lead to binaries such as, "development/underdevelopment," "traditional/modern," "backward/progressive," as if they are a naturally given condition of a society and that no other alternative was or is possible. In the absence of "a context-sensitive" approach, unsurprisingly, the question as to why, by 1850, "Western Europe was the undisputed center of a new global manufacturing order" (Parthasarathi, 2011:1) remains the only valid one for those scholars who wish to understand the increasing inequalities among different societies.

These questions—Why was England industrialized first? or Why did China not industrialize first?—do not allow us to consider an approach that provides for multiple possibilities and historical processes that are complementary and interactive. We need to break out of Eurocentrism, but also to avoid any centrism while treating all societies on equal terms with mutual respect in understanding their social reality. We need an approach that will include a complex historical understanding of life that is always becoming, with multidimensional realities that have both micro and macro elements existing simultaneously in a deeply connected and interdependent relationship—not as binary distinctions. Such an alternative approach is possible only by asking an alternative question, while also reevaluating both the assumptions and the yardsticks that are used in understanding and interpreting both Western and non-Western societies.

Thus far, the binary distinction of developed/underdeveloped is defined only in relation to modern large-scale industrialization, subsequent mass production, and consumerism. In order to refute and erase this binary, we need to demonstrate how a country moves from point A to point B with the combined action and creativity of various players. With this approach, industrialization would be explained *only* in terms of the choices and actions people made in these societies in a particular historical time and context while also interacting with other societies. In this way, no country would be judged based on its industry, culture, or technology but rather by the context of its history, the choices made by different groups of people (based on geography, along with traditional thinking processes, philosophies, and practices) its conflicts, creativity, and social structure along with the conjunction of world political, economic and other forces in relation to each society that has contributed to its evolution in one direction or other. In other words, we need to reflect upon the dynamic relationships among nature, self, culture, market, and society as well as their interactions with larger historical forces both outside and inside of a society.

With this understanding, an alternative question might be the following: How do people in any given society, while making everyday choices to meet their human needs, come to acquire specific economic, political, religious, social, technological, and cultural conditions? This question would direct our focus on the continuously changing specificities of a society—a product of human creativity (which is dynamic), choices, and actions in the process of human interactions within a society—as well as its relations and interactions with larger historical forces (including nature) and its interactions with other societies in different historical times that also shaped the historical trajectory of that society. Moreover, this would compel us to make a comparative study without a prior assumption about these societies as being developed or underdeveloped. It would also free us from the Western conceptualization of society and individual imprisoned in "Enlightenment black boxes" that have no connection with nature and transcendence (Giri, 2015:212). It would eliminate the need to continuously prove the capitalist or modernist credentials of a so-called underdeveloped society. In other words, we do not have to worry about proving why Asia or any other region of the world did not industrialize first. By eliminating the need to answer this question we can stop being complicit in the promotion of Western binaries and Western myths about the baseless and irrelevant "lacking" and "not yet" labeling. This alternative question will also help create a space wherein we can find an alternative theoretical framework that is sorely needed to break out of this so-called development model in which the world is mired, along with the sense of fatalism and hopelessness that accompanies it.

The assumption of the alternative question is that all humans are part of a larger ecological system and part of nature/cosmos (as suggested in Big History, see Christian, 2011) itself—it is a self-regulating system. (The food we eat and air we breathe come from nature and sustain our bodies, while those bodies provide home to trillions of bacteria and microbes.) Thus, humans are one of the infinite expressions of Nature's creativity. Without this innate attribute of creativity Nature could neither exist nor create anything. Humans, being one of the infinite expressions of Nature, have thus inherited Nature's innate capability of creativity, which made it possible for humans to create the human world as we know it. Human beings created societies in the process of interaction among people within and outside of each society to fulfill their daily human needs for existence (Bahl, 2005; Conner, 2005). Moreover, all humans and their societies try to attain four primary valuations: "(a) ever expanding span of survival of the species, (b) better and better security of life, (c) even more material prosperity for ensuring the above two valuations while enjoying further wholesome life, and (d) deeper and deeper mental peregrination for systemising the above three valuations as well as for continually unfolding the potentialities of the species" (Mukherjee, 2009:1). However, these can never be fully realized because life is an ongoing process (Ibid.) and human life is also part of the continuously changing larger ecological system of nature. Moreover, human beings (with their inner creativity) in an attempt to realize reality, seek access to the spiritual, idealist view of life, irrespective of place-time-people variations (Ibid., 5). It is this eclectic energy of humans that has kept the field of scientific inquiry open.

Geographic location also plays an important role in shaping the possibilities for interactions among a particular group of people within a given geographical region, thus creating a particular cultural outlook and philosophy of life. It also contributes to the possibility of self-sufficiency in food or increased dependence and a need for acquiring more land. If we look into all these forces and human choices in these contexts, we can understand why Russia (or any other country) did not follow the same so-called "stages" (there are no fixed stages) of development as the Western world, and why Russian society (or any other) evolved in its own specific way considering it had a different historical trajectory. No society can be a replica of another (and need not be). However, all societies are similar in the sense that they all deal with the needs of their members. All members of each society create its social institutions, languages, and cultures in the process of social interaction using their innate capacity for creativity. They all develop their particular point of view and notion of self. However, differing notions of self do not make any society either superior or inferior. Based on this understanding, I believe that it is possible to erase the binary distinctions developed/underdeveloped, modern/traditional, and progressive/backward from our perception of societies and instead, look for commonalities that are universal in all societies without denying any society its unique specificity and differences.

The most important commonality among all societies is the human interaction involved in creating events that makes all societies possible, which includes the cultures, the social institutions (e.g. family, polity, economy, religion, education, and technology) and the social structures that fulfill the human needs of every society's members. In this process of the making of a society, the important common factor is human creativity (more on this later)—an innate human capacity to imagine, think, create language—naming, reifying, communicating, and taking action. But this human creativity manifests itself only in the process of interaction with other human beings, as well as with "inner conversation," in their struggle for everyday survival—not only within their social, political, and cultural environment, but also biologically and ecologically, as both are part of a larger nature. However, "social becoming" (Sztompka, 1994) does not take place separately from nature (which includes non-human entities) because it is through nature that human existence is possible. For example, the human body contains nature within itself in the form of trillions of microbes through which humans are able to do anything. Similarly, the human body is sustained through food, which is produced outside of the human body in nature (Capra, 1996).

Human creativity, an innate capacity within all human beings, is a universal trait, as pointed out earlier, because humans are one of the infinite expressions of Nature's creativity. In my understanding, human creativity manifests itself through human actions and interaction processes. There is no conflict, as body-mind-self-nature emerge out of one another and remain an integrated whole all the time, as it is a unified whole (non-duality which is different from unity. See Rambachan, 2015), and not a separate process [(22)]. One can observe this process in the making of any social event. It is human action and interaction with other humans and their choices at any given geographical and historical time and place that create all social institutions, and that determine the nature of various social, economic, technological, cultural, historical, and political forces. In turn, these various forces and social structures create conditions within which people make their choices and take actions at a particular time and place. In this process of interactive and interdependent relationships (humans created social institutions, social structure and culture) everyday life is played out creating small and big events [(23)]. A similar process occurs in society-to-society interactions because all human beings (and their societies) are interdependent, they are not autonomous beings living in a vacuum. Similarly, microcosm is connected to macrocosm, as part and whole are held together in integral unity as is also suggested in "Indra's Net" (discussed below). Thus, human agents can be understood as bio-psycho-spiritual-social structures that have the power of interactivity and innate creativity (Gorski, 2013). Creativity does not unfold as a fixed plan because it is an impetus of life, and a current of life itself (Sheldrake, 2012), and I should add, it is unceasing, always present everywhere in all living beings, as it is the basis of both existence and reproduction of the cosmic whole (see also Koch, 2016).

In addition to human creativity, I am also using the concept of "humaneness," (for details see Chapter 2) which signifies that human beings in every society are able to set their own life agenda by creating and recreating a society at the bottom, even when the social (and outer) structures of the society (government, rulers, constitution) are repeatedly destroyed. One can find examples of this in all societies [(24)].

Another commonality among societies is "unified field of consciousness." Physicists, psychologists, and ancient mystical philosophies are increasingly converging in their views about cosmic reality. All of them seem to point to a reality of a "unified field of consciousness" [(25)]. According to this understanding, all pervasive awareness of consciousness gives us self-awareness of our cosmic selves. However, it is through the process of interaction, communication, and language that all human beings not only realize their innate creative genius, are aware of their cosmic self and consciousness, but also become social humans in the sense that we understand today. Human interaction inevitably creates events leading to group formation and social relationships—household, tribe, locality, trade, guild, and so on—for their survival and to fulfill their human needs. Historians should explore how an evolving human goes about everyday life to meet daily needs, and how that human must have adjusted, compromised, challenged, and reconfigured the environment to make sense of that daily life, as well as how that human created new circumstances in the existing environment. Human beings should be considered as both an integrated being with a separate body structure having an innate creative capability and potentialities, as well as a social being who realizes her/his innate potential creativity through social interaction only, while forming social relationships and simultaneously using "inner conversation" (Archer, 2000; Collins, 1998) to interpret those social relationships. In this way, it will be possible to eliminate the conceptual divide between evolving human beings and their creation of a society.

I have also used the metaphor of "Indra's Net" as it captures my idea about all societies—that while remaining interconnected, they are also unique and equal at the same time. In the metaphorical Indra's Net there is no hierarchy; each jewel (in our case society), though unique, resembles the others and connects with the others to construct the whole and infinite net. In this infinite net each node has a jewel and each one reflects all other jewels. Thus, there is no separate self-existence of any jewel, however, each one is unique in its reflection of the others. The net symbolizes a universe of infinite dependencies and relations interwoven among all its members (individual human as well as individual society) as all exist in the context of a collective reality. The metaphor of Indra' s Net allows us to perceive the existence of a creative intelligence (not to be confused with "intelligent design," as promoted by Christian Evangelicals), cosmovision and spirituality (not religion) that permeates all life and the whole cosmos. It also illuminates the reason why all appearances of separateness (dualism; See Rambachan, 2015) are in fact *maya* (illusionary). However, this does not mean that we do not have separate physical identities or that the physical world is not real. Both situations are real and each one of these realities needs to be respected on its own terms while also understanding their connectedness as a part of larger whole, which is non-dual. "The non-duality does not require a denial of the reality of the world" (Rambachan, 2016:66). These ideas are further elaborated in Chapter 2.

Based on alternative questions and assumptions, concepts of human creativity and the metaphor of Indra's Net, I have attempted to show (as a sample only) how it is possible to write comparative history with a yardstick of parity and without categorizing societies as developed/underdeveloped and thus, making this binary distinction redundant. My hope is that by making this binary distinction redundant, it will open up a space where we can imagine alternative ideas and visions, which will make it possible for former colonized societies to visualize a different path to improve their living condition. This alternative possibility will give them confidence to step out of the Western "catch up" game of "development and progress," and they will be able to liberate themselves from the clutches of neo-liberalism; the present avatar of capitalism.

LASTLY, AN IMPORTANT CLARIFICATION

I decided to add this clarification because it became clear to me during my presentation of the preliminary ideas for this volume in an Indian university that under the changing political conditions my ideas can be easily mislabeled. For example, I have raised the issues and concepts of human creativity, universal consciousness, (cosmos, spiritual ideas, mindfulness and inner-self—see Chapter 2 for details), and together they can easily be mistaken as some sort of New Age spiritual fusion, and irrelevant for academic exercise. Therefore, I will explain how I perceive these issues including the controversy over religion and science.

First of all, to those readers who might incline towards mislabeling my ideas, I have the following to say: When we want to learn about social reality and about human beings, we need to include all possible aspects of life—the usual economic, social, cultural, historical, and political factors—and importantly, include human creativity, human consciousness, inner-self, inner conversation, spiritual life, and the cosmos (nature) at large. This is necessary because human beings do live and deal with all of these aspects of their everyday life by using innate creative capabilities. Those who label any discussion about Hindus or collective ancient Indian traditions and religion as "Hindu Fundamentalism" should remember that labeling is not a counter-argument, and that the holistic approach and heritage of vast Indian knowledge are not the monopoly of any one religious group. We should not abdicate our right to benefit from our collective human knowledge to Hindutva forces. Moreover, we need to be clear that Hindutva is not equal to Hinduism or Hindu, and all Hindus are not followers of Hindutva (Pandey, 2018).

As Kasbekar wrote recently in a letter to the editor in *Economic and Political Weekly* (a center-left weekly), "Hindu-bashing has become a symbol of intellectual progressivism … is it not strange that Indian intellectuals have no qualm in being called Marxists, Leninists, Trotskyists, or Maoists—all progressive labels—but being called a Hindu, is regressive or troglodyte" (Kasbekar, 2017:4)? He also pointed out that the recent (2014) victory of Bhartiya Janta Party (BJP-right-wing party) became possible with the votes of non-Hindus as well as Hindus who are far from hard-core Hindu sympathizers. He questions, Why are the genuine sentiments of millions of Hindus labeled contemptuously as "Hindu nationalism?" (It is similar to the rise of the far right in the EU and in the US as reflected in the elections of 2016 and 2017 where everyone who voted for right wing parties is labeled nationalist). These are valid concerns and rightly challenge the blind labeling of people's actions in the name of progressivism as if there is no other possibility beyond the binary of Hindutva versus progressive. How can progressives claim to be rational and scientific if they cannot see beyond the binary distinction of a social reality?

However, I understand that if we keep denying ourselves all the tools we need to imagine and develop an alternative view point in the fear of being labeled this or that, we shall not be able to find an alternative to Eurocentrism and its binaries that can open the possibilities for a new approach to understanding our social reality in such a way that will free us from the taint of "inadequacy" as well as from a colonial mind set. We need to reclaim our power to imagine an alternative perspective to achieve our goal and we should not lose sight of our objective while exposing and condemning the growth of fascist forces.

To me, being scientific means (not simply a method of static rationality and systematic study of a phenomenon, because there exist other ways of knowing reality as well) that we keep examining critically our constantly changing social reality to understand why things are the way they are, while also continuing to explore other mysteries of the universe and to understand how humans are part of and connected with this vast nature and cosmos. As Hancock writes, "We will never know unless we try to find out. And, so far we haven't tried because our rational, scientific culture regards myths and traditions as 'unhistorical'" (Hancock, 1998). Exploring the unknown world is what scientists do. For example, some scientists are exploring the world as being four dimensional and theorizing that there are no fixed rules in the cosmos. (These scientists may be working based on faith rather than science, but faith and fantasy are essential to exploring the unknown.) Scientists are also exploring invisible matters such as the "God Particle" (aka Higgs boson), life in the universe, and a myriad of unknown phenomena. The US military has experimented (secretly) with many ideas such as remote viewing and other "occult" activities to determine whether or not they might be useful to the US militaristic agenda (Targ, 2012; Salazar, 2017). Until recently, the idea of "human aura" was not considered to be scientific, however, now there are cameras that can take pictures of anyone's aura. More research is being done in the West on these various "irrational" and "unscientific" ideas, including yoga, meditation, mindfulness and the use of herbs from India and Africa than in the places of their origin (Hathaway, 2015; Zaitchik, 2017). Erin Connelly (2019) recently reported that research is now being conducted to look into medieval books to find recipes for new antibiotics. Through scientific research, the stigma of "irrational and unscientific" has been removed from some of these ideas and practices, and they have become normalized and appropriated in the West without any identity crisis, as the Western users generally do not see the need to recognize their source. For example, a few years ago, several Western corporations were trying to patent two Indian herbs—namely, turmeric and neem. Fortunately, that effort was defeated by a huge social movement in India against it.

In the US, we have witnessed the emergence of integrated medicine that includes acupuncture, spirituality, yoga, and other so-called "alternative" medical systems that previously were treated as "irrational" or "unscientific." Feminists in the field of medicine as well as in medical sociology have been challenging mind-body dualism and focusing on the unity of medicine and holistic health while explaining how medicine has been masculinized, and how all aspects of human life and culture are medicalized under the capitalist-patriarchal system (Hubbard, N.d. ; Lowenberg and Davis, 1994; Kheel, 1989; Pieri, 2008; Scott, 1998). Within the field of science there are those involved in complexity studies who are also challenging dualism and the epistemological status of sciences as discoverer, guardian, purveyors of authoritative knowledge and truth (Lee, 2001a). The Nobel Laureate scientist Ilya Prigogine has argued that the "sciences are not the reflection of a static rationality to be resisted or submitted to; they are furthering understanding in the same way as are human activities taken as a whole" (Prigogine cited in Lee, 2004a:202). Furthermore, Prigogine and Driebe maintain that,

> [T]he laws of nature now express possibilities instead of certainties … entropy expresses a fundamental property of the physical world, the existence of a broken time symmetry leading to a distinction between past and future that is both a universal property of the nature we observe and a prerequisite for the existence of life and consciousness (quoted in Lee, 2004b:115).

Thus, by emphasizing "contingency, context dependency, and multiple, overlapping temporal and spatial frameworks," complexity studies have shifted the direction of science towards historical social science (Ibid., 117).

In the light of these developments we should not simply dismiss people's religious practices and beliefs in "alternative" medicines as "superstitions" without, at the very least, conducting scientific research and testing these so-called alternative practices. The problem is that the labels of superstition, unscientific, and irrational are also applied on those people who are struggling to save their agricultural land, or a river or a hill from governments' development projects. A most recent example is the Bhangar movement in the state of West Bengal (Basu and Biswas, 2017). This type of labeling raises the question about the genuineness of those seemingly promoting rationality and science. They seem to forget that there is no one truth, and science, which is also an interpretative subject, is similar to all other forms of interpretation that utilize the cultural framework of its time. As Esha Shah pointed out, "all interpretations and knowledge of risk, including empirically-driven scientific knowledge, are inherently a matter of perception and hence subjective and political ... There is no one truth, there are no facts outside the interpretations of values based on context, position, perspectives, interest, and power" (Shah, 2011:36; Glieiser, 2014).

The Western version of the history of science excludes, according to Conner, the role of anonymous masses of humble people—the common people—in creating science. For example, the knowledge of nature, which is the basis of science, was first generated by people who were closest to nature, as their survival required a daily encounter with nature, such as hunter-gatherers, peasant farmers, sailors, miners, blacksmiths, folk healers, and others (Conner, 2005:2). In the same way, it was prehistoric people who gathered the knowledge of the therapeutic properties of plants, from which the modern science of medicine continues to draw from for information. Their knowledge was stored in songs, stories, rituals, and folklores that are considered unscientific or superstitious today. It was astrology that fostered astronomy (an exact science) and alchemy that fostered chemistry (another exact science). In fact, the practice of early modern astronomy depended on the observational data compiled by the ancients, which means that modern astronomers cannot claim to be better than their predecessors (Shapin, 1996). Both Copernicus and Kepler used to cast horoscopes, and both closely observed planetary movements and made tedious mathematical calculations (Mumford, 1970:31). As Lachmann has noted, the intellectual environment favorable to experiment and induction emerged "when some Europeans expressed their skepticism toward church institutions by seeking to harness natural and supernatural forces themselves. Magic, astrology, and alchemy all flourished during the Renaissance, and especially in the post-Reformation era" (Lachmann, 2000:2).

Moreover, it is a mistake to think that the Enlightenment was a movement of rationalism against passion, of science against superstition, of progressive politics against conservative tribalism (Smith, 2019; Storm, 2017). On the contrary, it placed a high value on the role of sensibility, feelings, and desire. Especially in France, *the philosophes* were enthusiastic about the passions, emphasized sensation, imagination and embodiment, and they were deeply suspicious of abstractions. According to them, it was the speculative system-builder who was the enemy of scientific progress, who saw the body as a mere machine (Lloyd, 2018). It should be noted that even at NASA the cosmonauts perform some bizarre rituals (superstitions) to ward off ill omen (e.g. fear of number 13) before space travel. Even the Enlightenment is deeply shaped by the values of Christian traditions and moreover, "Enlightened liberals served as the legitimating ideology of a capitalist culture more steeped in blood than any other episode in human history" (Eagleton, 2009:68–69; see also Oak, 2019). An Indian philosopher, Manesh Firaq Bhattacharjee, stated:

> [T]he age of reason gave us colonialism, the Holocaust, Stalinist gulags, the death of collective conscious, and did not prevent us from being unethical intermediaries of power. Reason does not make us ethical. Reason can not be our master. We must believe in miracles, too. Miracles of life that enhances life and imagination, not of fake gurus that hoodwink people (Oak, 2019).

The question is: Why should we promote such an ideology which is "steeped in blood" rather than seek an alternative?

Why it is so difficult for scholars to recognize a reality that humans, using their creativity, have produced all types of knowledge while fulfilling their daily human needs? This includes the creation of myths, legends, and mysticism that often reflect opposition to the dominant narrative of the time (Chakraborty, 2018c). However, their knowledge was appropriated by elite thinkers, called "science," and in this way was separated from people's daily lives. Interestingly, physicists now talk about a holistic view of science, which includes the whole cosmos and all living beings (Capra, 1996). They admit that life cannot be understood in fragments as the whole cosmos and all living beings on the earth are connected to and interdependent with one another in the web of life. This approach breaks away from the Cartesian binary distinction of mind and body. If we look deeper into this shift toward holism in physics, we will find that much of what these physicists are suggesting already existed in common parlance for years including in the Hindu religion (not of the Hindutva type). Moreover, both Western and Indian religious ideas were shaped through a complex intertwined process of the exchange of ideas between them as Goldberg pointed out,

> Western philosophists influenced by Indian philosophy groomed an Indian lad [Jaddu Krishnamurti], who became an independent thinker whose Vedantic principles, converted into philosophical English, passed through quantum theory, context organization theory and landed, unrecognizable in corporate team-building sessions (Goldberg, 2010:55).

In light of these ideas, it is not easy to label anything as science (rational) or religion (irrational) (see also Rosa Silva, 2017).

Even though some scientists are moving towards a more holistic approach, some other scientists are choosing to serve the agenda of global capitalism. For example, 100 Nobel Laureate scientists have put their names to a letter urging Greenpeace to end its opposition to genetically modified organisms (GMOs produced by Monsanto) (Todhunter, 2016). Similarly, the IMF and World Bank are using science for destructive development projects. In the nineteenth century, science was used to reinforce gender roles.

> Medical scientific theory stated first that women were ill because they were women, and second that they became ill if they tried to do anything beyond their conventional female roles, a Catch 22 situation. The 'illness' almost always related to the woman's reproduc-

tive system which, it was thought … was by its very nature pathological (Conner:472).

Moreover, scientists who conduct research to produce medical knowledge have a conflict of interest, as their knowledge becomes the private property of corporations that are funding the universities, along with public dollars (Ibid., 473–475; see also Stuber and Rampton, 2001). Almost one hundred years ago, Bertrand Russell pointed out that, "Science is used for three purposes: to increase the total production of commodities; to make war more destructive; and to substitute trivial amusements for those who had some artistic or hygienic values" (Russell, 1923:187).

It is no surprise that in the late-twentieth century a widespread distrust of modern science emerged and people began to perceive scientists as paid apologists for the interests of giant corporations or government bureaucracies (Conner, 2005). For example, in 1973, a campaign challenging the "myth" of "medicine as science" exposed the workings of the medical establishment in suppressing alternative medical practices such as home births and nurse midwives. Moreover, while challenging the "myth' that "medicine is a science" the authors of *Our Bodies, Ourselves* declared, "Much of the theory on which modern medical practice is based actually derives from the untested assumptions and prejudices of earlier generations of medical leaders" and pseudo-scientific statements that have been used to deprive 'inferior' groups, like women and blacks, of social control and political power (quoted in Ibid: 471; see also Saini, 2019). These ideas continue to guide doctors and interns' behavior towards Afro-American patients, as a study shows that they assume that black people do not feel pain due to their thick black skin, and therefore are not given pain medicine (Noonan, 2012; Fernandez, 2018). This is also confirmed in recently published articles (2019) with titles like, "The Disturbing Return of Scientific Racism," and "The Return of Scientific Racism."

Besides using science for controlling different minority groups, Western modern science also refuses to recognize many discoveries of old civilizations. For example, Hancock has long explored information about lost civilizations that has led to a greater understanding of the technological, astronomical, mathematical, and other achievements of many civilizations that existed perhaps more than 10,000 years ago. His observations are corroborated by geological and genetical evidence (Hancock, 2019), which shows that the Western world does not have a monopoly over creativity in science, astronomy, and mathematics. It also indicates that a long time ago our ancestors had achieved a vast quantity of knowledge about mathematics, astronomy, and other "sciences," and by using this knowledge were able to build humungous structures without the help of machines. Hancock noted that by not recognizing these discoveries, Western modern science wishes to maintain their version of history of human evolution according to which it is only now, in our time, that humans (read Western) could achieve such heights of technology and science (Hancock, 2015:425–440; Hancock, 1995).

A similar problem is found in connection with traditional indigenous knowledge and practices. Traditional indigenous knowledge is not recognized by Western scientists except when it either supplements or supports their own findings (Nicholas, 2018). Western scientists generally dismiss traditional indigenous knowledge as a myth whenever it challenges scientific "truths." However, they could not do so with recent evidence of archeological findings in coastal British Columbia about the existence of marine culture, maintaining "clam gardens," that predate European settlement. This finding shows that indigenous groups of people were practicing resource management strategies and had an ecological understanding that predates modern management systems by a millennia (Ibid.). Clearly these systems are not the modern inventions Western scientists claim them to be. Currently, Zapatistas are struggling to decolonize science (Meek, 2018) because they see that the crisis of climate change and epidemics of disease are perpetuated by links between science and capitalism. At the same time, they think that science can be used as a tool of resistance by reimagining it from the grassroots. Terri Hansen provided examples of how traditional practices of indigenous people, informed by a millennium of traditional ecological knowledge, have contributed to modern science knowledge (Hansen, 2018).

While some Western scientists refuse to recognize the scientific contributions of other cultures, the American Left and progressive thinking people refuse to accept the findings (challenging official story of 9/11) of professional architects, engineers, physicists, nano-chemists, firemen and first responders, airline and military pilots based on scientific data and the analysis of the 9/11 tragedy. Is it not puzzling that the American Left defends the US government's account of 9/11, even when they are well aware that "the Tonkin Gulf was an orchestration for war, that Saddam Hussein had no 'Weapons of Mass Destruction,' that Iran had no nukes"? A recent book titled *Conspiracy Theory in America* published CIA dispatch #1035-960 that explains the idea of the "conspiracy theory" as a campaign to discredit those who were suspicious of the Warren Commission's conclusion about John F. Kennedy's assassination by a lone gunman in 1964. Since then, the label "conspiracy theory" has been applied to humiliate and delegitimize any challenge to an official version of war or any major event in which state involvement is suspected [(26)]. In 2016, the label of "fake news/ alternate facts" began to be used for similar purposes (Parry, 2018).

It seems the American Left is more concerned about not being labeled "conspiracy theorists" than about being scientific, which has effectively destroyed the anti-war movement in the US. These leftists should note that many lawyers and others did not worry about being labeled as conspiracy theorists, and went on doing the hard work of finding evidence to challenge official narratives. Through their hard work and commitment to scientific thinking they have been successful in getting the attention of the US Attorney General who agreed on November 7, 2018 to establish a grand jury to investigate the attack of 9/11 based on the evidence submitted by the Lawyers Committee for 9/11. Similarly, Kennedy and King family members have asked the US Congress to reopen the assassination cases of John F. Kennedy, Robert Kennedy, Martin Luther King, and Malcolm X (Roberts, 2019). My question is this: What is so good about beating the drums of science and rationality while using it selectively in a way that is killing those very forces and ideas that could promote human welfare? Ironically, in India, there is a huge social movement promoting science and rationality while condemning 'superstitions' (Quack, 2012). Meanwhile in the West, where rationality and science have long been practiced, people are looking for a return to enchantment, magic, meditation, and Eastern religions without suffering from an identity crisis or being labeled as irrational or superstitious. It is no wonder that Harry Potter books and movies, and superhero films and TV shows are popular among all sections of society and in high demand in the West. Tapping into this need for experiencing magic (not rational), entrepreneurs are offering consumer technology in a form that provides that experience and it's no wonder that it sells so well.

While Western people are trying to return to magic and enchantment, social scientists in independent India remain dependent on Western "scientific thinking" (disseminated by colonial knowledge), methodology, and concepts to create knowledge, even though they wish to break away from colonial knowledge. For example, sociologist M. N. Srinivasan, who focused on indigenous traditions, did not realize that his so-called "'traditional' features of Indian society were mere attributes constructed by modernity to make Indian society's modern and colonial character" (Patel, 2006:391). Indian sociologist Sujata Patel explains that this indigenization created an Indian ethnosociology that essentializes Hindu traditions while demanding that these values become the basis for creating new epistemologies (Ibid., 394). Moreover, the indigenous knowledge perspective, as Patel clarifies, not only essentializes indigeneity and reproduces binaries by focusing on nativism, it also leads to the essentialization of the "nation" and the "nation state" that denies global inequalities. The consequences of this indigenous knowledge perspective are not very pleasant as the Hindu right and other related identity movements are, by identifying with this ethnosociology, able to redefine nation and nationhood in religious and chauvinist terms. These developments have contributed to an increase in violent conflicts within India, as well as causing a backlash from the anti-superstition movement (Ibid.).

With the coming (2014) of the new government of the Bhartiya Janta Party in 2014, the ongoing debates in India about rationality, science, superstitions, and local knowledge has once again come to the forefront (Quack, 2012). What is strange is that social scientists and historians tend to simply dismiss any alternative claim as "irrational," or "ideological" just because it does not fit into their preconceived idea of so called "rationality and science." One possible reason for this is that academic professionals become like an interest group that protects itself from new and uncomfortable competitive ideas. At the same time, they do not consider the difficulty in strictly applying the same science and experimental methods, hard data, and quantitative analysis to soft disciplines such as social sciences in order to supposedly yield accurate predictions. As Heredia pointed out, new and deeper insights and understanding can come only through interpretative disciplines and with reflexive sociology (Heredia, 2016). However, Varma challenges defenders of science for not being scientific themselves:

> The defenders of science talk about the principles of scientific investigation, yet do not apply the same principle [and] ... dismiss ... [critics of science] with caricature, condescension, and parody ... they do not provide a 'scientific proof' why scientific epistemologies are necessarily better than alternative ones; instead, they keep reiterating their ideological convictions (Varma, 2001:4799–4800).

This dilemma is reminiscent of Gödel's proof and "incompleteness of theorems." Gödel's ideas show that science is based on philosophical assumptions that you cannot prove scientifically. The scientific method can only infer and not prove (Cubitt, Perez-Garcia and Wolf, 2018). Similarly, economics touted as science is actually based on faith[27]. Terry Eagleton has also raised similar question as he writes, "Is it equally reasonable for science to place its faith in the consistency of mathematics, even when Gödel's second theorem demonstrates that it cannot be proved" (Eagleton, 2009:12)? Highlighting the role of mathematicians (in the seventeenth century) in creating abstract form in scientific thought, Robert Young pointed out that it was from these abstract forms that mathematicians derived clear cut demonstrative trains of reasoning which was then accepted as concrete rendering of fact (Young, 1990:3).

We do not have to perpetuate the binary distinction of Western "scientific rationalism" and Indian religions as "superstitions," a concept that was introduced in India during the nineteenth century under colonial rule. Today, this binary has created a huge social movement in India and has led two provincial Indian states to adopt a law banning "superstitions" (*Indian Express,* 2013). Some scholars (Nanda, 2005; Nanda, 2008) have criticized theories of post-colonialism and alternate science for legitimizing Hindutva arguments for "Vedic science," because these theories are promoting cultural relativism, constructionism, focusing on local and indigenous while abandoning Enlightenment thinking. These defenders of modern science believe in secularism and Enlightenment ideas of science, and consider any effort to challenge this Western legacy (which is rooted in Christian theology) as dangerous to humanity. Ranjit Sau's (2006) critique of Meera Nanda's article, "How Modern Are We?" (Nanda, 2006) is very instructive in this regard. He explains how Nanda's formulation of the term "counter-Enlightenment" is false. He also writes, quoting Kant, "reason itself does not operate on instinct, but requires trial, practice, and instruction in order to gradually progress." Sau questions, "How can such a faculty, which is inherently tentative so as to 'require trial, practice and instruction,' deliver moral judgment and guide science to comprehend the world?" (Ibid.). Regarding Nanda's concern about misinterpretation of modern science, especially quantum mechanics, by neo-Hinduism, I find it very interesting that Sau's explanation is similar to what I have already discussed in connection with Sheldrake's "morphic resonance" and Nobel Laureate Ilya Prigogine's ideas of uncertainty, complexity and auto-organization (discussed in Chapter 2).

Summarizing quantum mechanics in three theorems Sau writes that it consists of,

> (a) 'non-locality', which shows interconnectedness between all matter in the universe, and universal equality of all points of the universe in respect of possessing information; (b) 'a tendency to exist' rather than existence as such, of matter which points to the illusory (maya) nature of the physical world and (c) 'reassembly' or 'self-organisation' that hints at the presence of a sort of consciousness in the apparently non-living system as well (Sau, 2006).

Moreover, the idea of consciousness as being all pervasive in the universe, and matter transforming into energy and waves (Quantum mechanics), are also found in old Hindu scriptures. Thus, as Sau pointed out, modern science does not seem different from mysticism to those who wish to humanize mysticism or use it for some other vested interest (Ibid.). Therefore, if we wish to refute the claims of neo-Hindus, we need to understand how they are misinterpreting old Hindu scriptures and using them for their own agenda. In this way, we should be able to benefit from the old Hindu scriptures—which is, in fact, a collective human knowledge created by our collective ancestors including the knowledge generated by everyday folks (see A. K. Ramanujan's famous essay, "Three Hundred Ramayanas," in Dharwadker, 1999)—while not letting Hindutva forces to have monopoly over them and not let them define the Hindu religion (which is different from Hindutva) based on their own agenda.

The idea that Vedanta was the dominant tradition of Hinduism was constructed by colonialists and they created a homogenized Hinduism. Nationalist leaders upheld this Hinduism as the anchor of an Indian identity (Chandhoke, 2018). Neera Chandoke pointed out that this textualized Hinduism ignored the strong strain of atheism, naturalism and heretical materialist school of Carvaka philosophy, which promoted anti-Vedic materialism. It also ignores materialistic visions of various indigenous mystical trends such as Siddhacharyas from the ninth century AD. The rebellious groups such as Bauls like Lalan Fakir, modern day songs of Bauls in Bengal, fishers of the eleventh century, and farmers in the nineteenth century had materialistic vision similar to Siddhaas. They rejected ritual ceremonies, religion, customs and rituals of empowered elite (Chakraborty, 2018c). Thus, by ignoring these traditions of rational, atheist, materialist thinking, which also existed along with other philosophical traditions in India, it became possible to label India as spiritual, and thus creating the binary of West as rational/scientific, and India as irrational/spiritual. It also ignored the fact that Hinduism, as we know today, has been assimilating and appropriating many other regional and local traditions and concepts for centuries as Atindriyo Chakraborty explains (Chakraborty, 2018a; see also Jain, 2015). At the same time, people went on resisting this cooptation by connecting with different stream of faith such as *Vaishnavism, Shaivism, Shakto Islam,* and creating new forms (Charkaborty, 2018b). For example, Dhamma worship is the mix of Buddhism and certain indigenous cults of the Dom; the *Vaishnava-Sahajiya* stream of faith is a mix of Buddhism and *Vaishnavism* (Ibid.). Sunthar Visuvalingam, a renowned scholar of Abhinavagupta, informs, "there would have been no Hinduism without Buddhism" (Visuvalingam 2017, Abhinavagupta@yahoogroups.com). This statement is well corroborated by Atindriyo Chakraborty as he explains how the concept of *Shunya* (or emptiness, as related to the negation of duality between being and non-being) was assimilated in Hinduism. This concept of *Shunya* was introduced by Buddhist philosopher Nagarjuna long ago. Later on, *Shunya* was mentioned in Sanskrit literature as *Advaita Shunya* (non-dual void). However, in the hands of a Brahmin named Gaudapada, *Shunya* was replaced with *Vedanta,* thus converting the whole concept into *Advaita Vedanta.* From this time on *Advaita Vedanta* philosophy was preached by Gaudapada's followers and later by Shankaracharya. However, the concept of *Shunya* was not lost among many Indian faiths including Kabir panth and Sikhism, which arose across the Middle Ages as a counter-reaction to Brahmanical oppression. For these faiths, the concept of *Shunya* (non-dual void) was important as it challenged the very foundation of caste-division (Chakraborty, 2017). Andrea Jain has traced a similar story (discussed later) about the appropriation of yoga, which was heterogeneous in origin, by Hinduism (Jain, 2015).

Three noted rationalists who dedicated their lives to countering superstition and who championed scientific thought, were murdered recently in India and the Modi government has created a climate of religious intolerance and political interference in the academic affairs of many important universities and institutions. This has led to a signed statement by 100 prominent scientists and heads of institutions protesting "the ways in which science and reason are being eroded in the country" (Mandavilli, 2016). A recent documentary, "Reason," by Anand Patwardhan (shown on September 8th at the Toronto International Film Festival 2018) has well documented the terroristic activities of Hindutva forces in India. These are extremely important efforts to expose Hindutva's fascistic intentions. However, what I find problematic is that critics do not try to understand why there is such a reaction in India to Western secularism, Enlightenment traditions, and universalism, and why there is a huge move towards "critical traditionalism" (Juluri 2016)? Why are masses flocking to RSS programs of spirituality and yoga? People take refuge in religion out of desperation and hopelessness, as religion provides an alternative reality filled with solace and hope. Rather than condemn those people—who really are suffering—as "superstitious," we need to understand their suffering and work towards improving their lives, which, in turn, will eliminate the need for superstitions (Moore, 2018). At the same time, it is necessary to condemn and expose those forces that are abusing religion and rituals, as well as science and medicine, to harm people. However, in order to change people's attitudes and behavior we need to do more than pass legislation or condemn people for their beliefs. The job of the social scientist is to understand all dimensions of a social reality and then suggest useful, probable solutions—and not simply condemn people as being "irrational or superstitious." For example, the Karnataka government has passed laws to criminalize black magic and discriminatory rituals that target lower caste people and women. Such actions will help in changing people's attitude and behavior over time. This is an important step, as we need to scrutinize our beliefs, and not justify them, by looking into likely consequences of a specific change whether it would benefit the society at large (Sau, 2006). However, both the Hindutva group and anti-Hindus, being unhappy with this Karnataka law, do not seem to be thinking about the social advantages of this law (Bhatia 2017, Scroll.in November 28).

We should also keep in mind that by following the Western ideology of progress and Enlightenment, we have repressed and erased our historical legacies that could serve as precious resources for finding a better future (Eagleton, 2005:90). That repressed past is now returning as various forms of fundamentalism, including Hindutva forces, which are considered by Enlightenment rationalists as superstition and childish irrationality. Eagleton advises that rather than arrogantly condemning religion as opium, we need to patiently decipher it because, "no polemic against religion pitched simply at the level of rational argument can hope to succeed" (Ibid., 90–91). He explains how the relations between knowledge and belief are notably complex. A belief can be rational but not true. For example, the early belief that the sun circled the earth was based on what they were physically seeing. Similarly, claims about the world can be true but not, in a sense, rational, such as nuclear particles that can pass through two different apertures at the same time (Ibid:112–113). Another example is that we have never seen the unconscious (and consciousness) but a large number of people believe in its existence (including psychologists; for instance, Freud focused on the depth of the unconscious) as it makes sense to them based on their experience in the world. These days, neurobiologists are deeply involved in studying the human brain to find consciousness, and many universities in the US now offer consciousness programs. We should also not forget that the idea of working-class consciousness has been the main focus of Marxists in order to achieve their goal of socialism. Richard Rorty once noted that "the implication of the theory of unconscious is that there is something in us like another person that has just as good a claim to be 'us' as our conscious minds" (quoted in Sam Dresser, 2019). The question for me is that if the concepts of unconscious and working-class consciousness have been accepted as legitimate for academic debate, then why are the concepts of universal consciousness, or unified field of consciousness, not given the same status but instead treated as a religious or metaphysical concern? After all, working class consciousness can happen only if everyone has a consciousness, or in other words, consciousness itself is universal.

There is no denying that there is a genuine crisis of history and people everywhere are looking for alternatives to the modernity (Dirlik, 2013) that has oppressed them with development projects, imperialism, and globalization. Postcolonialism, Subaltern Studies, and post-development all emerged as a reaction to these very historical processes. The dilemma is this: How do we find an alternative that does not trap us in indigenism, localism, fundamentalism, or Eurocentrism? I pointed out this problem in my last volume as follows: "It is very easy to lose the sight of specific differences among individual scholars: (a) those supporting Subaltern Studies which mainly derived from leftist ideology, (b) culturalist scholars who are reacting to the adverse impact of modernization on the Indian people and ecological imbalances, and (c) the Hindu fundamentalists who have totally different agendas from the previous two groups of scholars. The problem is that all three groups seem to be raising similar issues and similar arguments and ultimately suggesting similar solutions. This similarity does not mean they are all alike with similar agendas, but it does mean that there is a real historical crisis and that the major social and historical issues cannot be ignored any longer. It is puzzling to note that both the Right and the Left are suggesting a turn back to a 'pure' past which can never be found. This puzzle raises the following question: Why have progressive scholars given up on the futurist agenda and exploration of any other alternative path, and instead are echoing ideas that are similar to the rightist agenda" (Bahl, 2005:6–7)?

The issue is not that Hindutva forces are successful, but why are they successful today more than ever? Why are people attracted to their ideas now (Moore, 2018)? Why are Dalits joining Hindutva forces? That is what we need to understand so that we do not become unwitting apologists of the West or of Hindutva forces. At the same time, we need not throw away all that is useful in Western ideas, in traditional ideas, or in traditional resources for the well-being of humankind and the planet. This is what I feel is not being discussed, as scholars move between the vague binary of "science and superstitions." Critics fail to consider the fact that no group has a monopoly over collective human knowledge, and we should not allow Hindutva forces to appropriate collective Indian knowledge and heritage as their personal property. We all should be able to benefit from that knowledge by using it critically and advisedly. (Interestingly, in 2017, the Marxist party—CPI(M)—in Kerala made an effort to spread awareness through a series of seminars about the various versions of the Ramayana in order to prevent the Hindutva forces from appropriating the ancient epic for political gain. They also plan to do the same for the Mahabharata, Vedas, and Upanishads) (Amerudheen, 2018). It is through such efforts that we shall be able to find alternative ideas to deal with the crisis of epistemology in the historiography of our time, and not simply by accusing one another for either supporting a "scientific" and therefore Eurocentric approach, or for challenging the "scientific" (Eurocentric) approach and therefore supporting Hindutva forces. Moreover, simply erasing Eurocentrism will not solve the crisis of our time because Eurocentrism is not only a cultural expression of the capitalist imperial system but is also used as an ideological tool to maintain this system.

We also need to remember that the term Hinduism is incompatible with any adequate understanding of the religious outlook of Hindus. Classical Hindu scholars discussed religious questions critically and profusely, but did not name it Hinduism [(28)]. Besides the critical analysis of classical Hindu scholars, there have also existed, side by side, diverse beliefs and practices in different regions of India. When colonial "Orientalist" scholars, missionaries, and administrators gave the name "Hinduism" to this totality of diverse practices, they defined it according to the beliefs and practices associated with the priestly Brahman caste and the elite Sanskrit traditions, and not on the colloquial, village, or popular religion that most people were engaged in. This colonial definition reflected the Christian idea of what a religion should look like. According to Christian ideas, people are not permitted to belong to more than one religion (Black, Hyman and Smith, 2014). That is why we should be careful when we use the term "Hinduism" and give Hindutva forces a monopoly over Hindu religion (as faith), while denying the rest of the diverse Hindu population a chance to define what they think it is based on their own specific beliefs and practices. The problem today is worse; with the emergence of Hindutva ethnic plurality itself is being eliminated. As Ashis Nandy explains, this elimination is done by not only removing folk elements from Hinduism and turning it into a classical Vedantic faith, but also by eliminating ethnic plurality within India itself (Nandy, 1990).

In eliminating ethnic plurality, the state ideology of secularism has also played a decisive role. Nandy explained that modern nation-states, which have internalized the colonial concept of state, are carrying on the civilizing mission of the colonial state in the garb of secularism. According to him, nation-state secularism treats religion-as-ideology and considers it to be in opposition to the state ideology of secularism and therefore, it is important for state to contain diverse ethnic religions. Since secularism has nothing to say about culture, it does not treat religion as a way of life, thus denying its diversity and notion of tolerance among religions (Nandy, 1990:69), while at the same time, ideologies of secularism, development, and nationalism have become faiths which are intolerant of other faiths (Ibid., 71). These ideologies are used to justify the use of violence against those groups of people who follow their religion as a way of life (Ibid., 90), and thus destroy ethnic plurality in India.

However, as Nandy noted in recent years, those who understand "religion-as-faith" are rejecting the state's claim of being the sole authority and arbitrator among different religions and communities. In any case, in practice it is not possible to make a distinction between religion and secularism in India, as religion remains in the public sphere in spite of the urbanization of India. Moreover, cultural nationalists and cultural movements are also challenging the universal modern Western science (part of the package of ideology of secularism) by promoting alternative science. For example, the Nazis' "Aryan science" versus "Jewish science," and Hindu fundamentalists' "Hindu science," and Islamic fundamentalists' "Islamic science." Even though these alternative "sciences" are not about gaining knowledge of nature but are used only to exercise ideological authority and justify ancient superstitions to keep people in bondage (Conner, 2005:462), they have become a threat to the authority of Western science.

By now the theory of secularization as well as the desirability or inevitability of the spread of the secular has been debunked (Tomalin, 2007; see, Stark and Finke, 2000). Nandy also suggested that the ideology and politics of secularism have exhausted all of their possibilities and we have reached a point of time "when old-style secularism can no longer pretend to guide moral and political action" (Nandy 1990:81). Banerjee et al. have also pointed out the limitations of the idea of secularism in India, where the mass mobilization for the Babri Masjid demolition made this limitation apparent. Moreover, it is not possible to escape the implicit Christian concept of the secular (Banerjee et al., 2016). In addition to these problems in the idea of secularism, there is another important related issue that needs attention as Camille Paglia stated in a recent interview, "Secular humanism has failed ... if religion is erased, something must be put in its place. Belief systems are intrinsic to human intelligence and survival. They 'frame' the flux of primary experiences which would otherwise flood the mind. Politics cannot fill this gap" (quoted in Lehmann, 2018). Her suggestion to fill this gap with art, is something worth consideration.

While challenging alternate sciences such as "Islamic Science," "Hindu Science," "Aryan Science," and "Jewish Science" is necessary, we also need to be careful not to dismiss useful traditional ideas and practices such as yoga and pranayama exercises and various other practices. These ideas are of universal value as recognized by the UNO and it officially adopted June 21st as the International Day of Yoga [according to Resolution 69/131. December 11, 2014] (Nitesh, 2015) by 193 members and 177 co-sponsor countries of the UN General Assembly. Similarly, we should be careful to not conflate yoga as equal to Hindutva thereby abandoning our right to benefit from the useful knowledge of our collective ancestors. We need to also remember that yoga is not part of one particular religion as it has been "heterogeneous in practice and characteristics of the doctrinally diverse pre-modern culture of South Asia" (Jain, 2015:18). It is relevant to point out that after the waning of Buddhism, Brahmins gave lower caste identities to those who followed naturalism driven hatha-yoga involving body disciplines (Chakraborty, 2018b). Similar to any other cultural phenomenon, yoga has also been continuously constructed and reconstructed by individuals and institutions in different social, cultural, and historical contexts in different countries/societies. Andrea Jain pointed out that modern yoga is a product of colonial context as Europeans and Americans began to visit India. Some of them became interested in various subjects including metaphysics and fitness. At the same time, wishing to promote yoga, Indian nationalists and reformers began to endorse yoga as a universal system compatible with modern thought and science (Jain, 2015:42). Thus, Europeans and Americans learned this new version of yoga and carried it to their countries while adapting it to their own context and needs.

It should be noted that yoga's popularity in the US today is not a new phenomenon, as it was quite popular across the country during the 1920s. While facing unemployment and denaturalization due to a US Supreme Court ruling in 1923, which made South Asians ineligible for citizenship, some of them reinvented themselves as yoga teachers and metaphysical lecturers. They interpreted yoga in a variety of ways to attract followers across the country, except in the South. However, they were also influenced in the US by everything from the positive thinking New Thought movement to Spiritualism and occultism, while also influencing them in return. After WWII, people in the US began viewing yoga as something postural and physical, rather than mental and magical. Nevertheless, these Yoga teachers served as an important bridge between the Hippie movement of the 1960s and those who would come after them and develop American yoga into a billion-dollar industry (Deslippe, 2018).

As we should not conflate yoga with Hindutva, similarly we should not conflate Hindutva with Hindus either, because all Hindus are not supporters of Hindutva. Unfortunately, this fact is completely overlooked in the controversy in California over text books. For example, Indian American Hindus (all are not supporters of Hindutva) are objecting to the way in which Hinduism is presented in California school text books (Juluri, 2016; de Roover, 2006). The Hindu protagonists perceive that other major religions, which are in no way perfect even by their own standards, get a much kinder treatment in these text books while Hinduism is presented with complete negativity. These Hindus in the US want scholars of religion to work from a position of respect for the faith of their religion [(29)]. Thus, the issue is about equity in the depiction of Hinduism in comparison to the depiction of Islam, Christianity, and Judaism in the curriculum. This concern of Indian-Americans is condemned by Jangam and other activists as the "replication of the Hindu right-wing government's attempt in India both at provincial and national levels to rewrite the historical narrative of India from the nostalgic Hindu Brahminical hegemonic perspective" (Jangam, 2016:20). Jangam's claim about the Hindu right-wing government's attempt to rewrite Indian history is correct, and it is also the case that there are religious advocacy groups in the US that have a different mandate than those who want equity. However, lumping all Indian American Hindus into the same Hindutva category is not fair either. We should be aware that the California textbook problem is also part of a specific American minority issue. For example, Native Americans have been fighting for a long time over the issue that their religious practices and sacred symbols (head feathers, sacred paints and dances) are being used for sports entertainment and profit making. The matter is similar to the objections of Muslim people in the US over labeling Islam as a terrorist religion because ISIS promotes its own version of Islam. The issue of including caste and Dalit oppression in the California school text books is definitely valid and should not be sidelined. However, maintaining a focus only on equity, or only on caste, has turned the controversy into a binary: you are either with Hindutva forces or with Dalits. In this binary division the existing plurality of faiths in India receive no attention. I wonder who is benefiting from this binary distinction. In this regard it is instructive to read David Washbrook's remarks written in 1997:

> The image of 'holistic' ideology mainly [was achieved] by marginalising in India's historical culture all those elements which might conceivable correspond to some kind of 'individualism'—such as Brahmanic ethic and *bhakt*-ism, ... just as it achieves its image of Modern West as 'individualistic' by overlooking Europe's own holistic ideologies—Catholicism, monarchism, Fascism. Similarly, it denies Traditional India ideologies of equality by focusing exclusively on caste at the expense of systems of kinship, temple sect and 'community,' where hierarchy was never easy to establish. Just as its inference that Modern Western society is no longer dominated by ideologies of hierarchy disposes, at a stroke, of the entire subject matters of the sociologies of gender, generation and race (Washbrook, 1997:415).

Leaders from the left and progressive forces in India excluded from their analysis religion, caste, and gender—politics of recognition (Babar, 2018). Conversely, Hindutva forces have been able to monopolize the discourse on religion and caste. Consequently, a genuine debate on these issues has become difficult for fear that one will be labeled as promoting Hindutva or as being against science. Recently, the Dalit people have begun emerging as a challenging force demanding both recognition (identity) and redistribution (equity). However, it has not made any difference in the left's analysis of social reality, and there is no inclusion of Dalits in their top leadership, as they remain committed to class analysis only[(30)] even though there are a few young left activists and Dalit activists who are beginning to combine politics of recognition and politics of redistribution in their speeches and slogans (Kundu, 2018).

Defending either Marxism or anti-Marxism (as do the Subaltern Studies) should not be the basis or goal of our analysis if we are trying to understand and change social reality for the better. We need to recognize the difficulty of comprehending how freedom, tradition, and imagination are always connected in so many ways. Instead of denouncing tradition, we can learn from the example of the Zapatistas of Chiapas who are able to root themselves in a deep traditional past and draw from a mixed and complicated narrative to build their society in the twenty-first century (Graeber and Wengrow, 2018). We can also find perspectives and narratives to help improve our collective human condition and the planet, without becoming pawns in the hands of either neo-imperialism or Hindutva type forces, or some variant of them, or indigenism. In this effort we all can draw from the reservoir of collective human knowledge (including science not just from the West but from every region of the world) developed over the centuries by our collective ancestors on the planet, and find alternatives to the existing capitalist modernity, which promotes the binary of development/underdevelopment. This common human legacy of past treasure of knowledge is for all humans on the planet to use, as it is not a monopoly of one nation, one group, or one religion.

Based on this understanding I used the metaphor of Indra's Net and other concepts in making my argument and raised various issues, while hoping to liberate ex-colonies from the humiliating label of "not yet" by erasing the Western conceptual binary distinction of developed/underdeveloped.

ORGANIZATION OF THE STUDY

This study focuses on the erasure of the conceptual binary distinction of developed and underdeveloped so that all societies can be examined with the same yardstick of parity. This idea is based on the following assumptions: All societies are equal in human creativity; in universal consciousness and humaneness; all societies have the same human needs of security, prosperity, reproduction and progress; all societies are connected and unique at the same time as in Indra's Net; and no country or society came into being with the original condition of "developed or undeveloped." I have tried to apply these ideas in a sample of comparative studies of four countries, specifically focusing on the question of the emergence of the large-scale steel industry between 1880 and 1914. The four countries chosen for this study are not treated as "nation-states" (a racist project of the Western world), because Imperial Britain and

Imperial Russia were empires that included many nationalities and cultures. Britain developed its national identity in the process of ruling its empire. Postcolonial Imperialist US was struggling to become a nation-state, however, it was also building an empire after expanding to the western end of the continent and then moving overseas. In colonial India, the impulses of nationalism started vibrating during the 1880s through 1914 and it was a huge subcontinent comprised of an enormous number of diverse societies and cultures.

In order to show how all societies can be treated as equals with a yardstick of parity (and not with the binary distinction of developed/underdeveloped), I have focused on the historical process of the making of each of these four countries in which the role of people's choices, interactions and actions in each society and their interaction within and outside considered primary. I have used the concept of human creativity as a yardstick of parity to understand four chosen societies, because human creativity is the same chemical composition for a person born in England or a person born in India, and it cannot be compared. I have used the metaphor of Indra's Net to explain how all societies are connected, equal, and unique at the same time. These assumptions, concepts, and metaphor enabled me to show that each of these countries/societies had both universal and specific characteristics, and they all can be compared using the same yardstick.

My study, thus, refutes the claim of the uniqueness of any society because, as Berreman has pointed out, "Everything in the world is ultimately unique." The only way we can find out "what is specific to one culture, society or situation, and what is common to types or categories of social organization, or is common to recurrent processes and historical circumstances" is by extracting "aspects, elements, principles or relationships which are (or thought to be) common, for the purpose of comparison." This can be done "without denying the uniqueness of every culture, every institution, every object and every event" (Berreman, 1971:21).

(It should be noted that certain ideas and examples are repeated in different chapters in order to reinforce the connections of these ideas and examples with various situations and historical contexts. This reinforcement was necessary due to the unconventional question raised and explanation offered in this volume.)

Chapter 1 focuses on the issue of the spurious binary distinction of "developed/underdeveloped." Before explaining how it is a spurious construct, I traced the origin of this dichotomy as well as the recent trichotomies in sociological theories followed by a discussion on the falseness of this binary. In this discussion, I consider the following questions: How has the idea of European "superiority" evolved? How did the binary of "development/underdevelopment" emerge and evolve, and how has it been reproduced over time? How has the West explained the phenomenon of underdevelopment using a misleading Western yardstick of "prerequisites for industrialization"? After examining the Western yardstick along with various challenges to modernity, an alternative question is suggested that might point to a different direction which could help in erasing this misleading binary.

In Chapter 2, the following question is raised: Why and how can this binary distinction be erased? In this chapter, I suggest a possible alternative approach and an alternative yardstick that is based on the concept of "human creativity" as I understand it. The chapter elaborates on the concept of "human creativity" and the assumptions behind it because this concept is not used simply as an add on to other factors. My yardstick is "human creativity" because every human being (one of the infinite expressions of Nature's creativity) in every society is born with this innate capability which they inherited from nature's creativity itself. It implies that one cannot compare the "human creativity" of a person born in England with that of one born in India because "human creativity," an innate human quality, remains the same within each human being. This concept does not simply reduce humanity into "labor" (Seabrook, 2012) as Western thinkers have done while explaining industrial or other revolutions. (However, Marx's concept of alienation includes alienation from human creativity.) This narrow version of "what it means to be human" denies the creativity, mind, spirit, diversity, richness and splendor of humanity, and instead reshapes humanity into a commodity (labor) like an object for sale and to profit from (Ibid.). This narrow version of human is supported by Western religious scriptures as follows: "In the sweat of your face shall you eat bread, till you return to the ground; for out of the ground you were taken; for dust you are and to dust shall you return" (Ibid., 55). Scriptural authority in the West has also, in addition to controlling the nature, sanctioned the ideological construct of modern time where the industrial model (buy and sell and exchange of money) is extended to other areas of life, to all that is precious and vital to survival including healthcare, education, leisure, entertainment, music, water, funeral, retail, and sex (Ibid., 54).

I then discuss the metaphor of Indra's Net while explaining how it can be useful in imagining and treating all societies as equal as well as connected. The focus is on the commonalities among societies and not the differences (but not denying them). One of the commonalities is "unified field of consciousness or universal consciousness," which is deeply connected to "human creativity" and the idea of equality. These connections have been corroborated with the findings of various physicists who have written about the universal consciousness and the oneness of humanity and planet, and the fact that more and more scientists are breaking away from the binary distinction of mind and body. The "complexity studies" (Waldrop, 1992) in the sciences has further contributed to this forward motion. All this knowledge from various scientists and physicists as well as from other sources [(31)] affirms my understanding of "human creativity" and my conviction that no society began as "inferior or backward." We should study each society with the premise that all societies are equal, although their present conditions are the products of a long historical process in which the role of capitalism, imperialism, colonialism, and neo-liberalism, along with brute military force, and globalization were/are predominant.

In Chapter 3, the focus is on the international context of the historical conditions of the 1880s to describe what types of historical, political, financial, technological, social, and religious developments had taken place, and setting the international scene within which the large-scale steel industry that emerged in four selected countries. What was the nature of the power structure in the world arena? This discussion allows us to understand European societies in the larger context of that time to see how they influenced the decisions and choices of people in different societies, and how these in turn interacted with each society in a specific way, creating specific historical condition for each society. The emphasis is on the dialectical (though not always opposite) process between countries, and not merely a one-way process in which only outside forces were affecting domestic conditions or only internal forces were creating their own dynamics. It was a complex process in which the formation and role of a transnational class—the Freemasons—were very important, as were the coercive powers and structures of the state system. For the sake of clarity and comprehension, I have elaborated separately on various broader historical processes and shifts that contributed to the creation of powerful historical forces at that time as follows: shifts in the ideas of science and religion, improvements in transportation and communication systems, demographic shifts, science-based industries, the new economic forces of colonialism and imperialism, the changing structure of the international political economy, international trade and tariffs, international monetary and financial systems, alliances and international treaties, the struggle in the international balance of power, the socialist challenge, labor movements, social movements, the emergence of new forms of art and aesthetics, social reforms and social changes. These myriad developments in Europe affected the Indian subcontinent, as Britain, France, the Netherlands and Portugal then all actively participating in the power struggles in India, and would do so later, in its successful colonization.

In Chapters 4–7, I have organized the information about each of the four countries in a similar fashion because the uniqueness of each country is also a universal situation. In other words, the uniqueness is nothing more than how the historical processes manifested themselves in each country during the process of the interaction of historical forces within and outside—web of interactions, like Indra's Net. No one disagrees that every country has distinct physical and geographical conditions that contribute to the specificity of its history. In that sense, India is no more unique than Russia, Britain, or the US. Therefore, the discussion in these four chapters revolves around the same two questions: How to erase binary distinction in comparative history? How can the suggested yardstick of parity be used to understand the emergence of the large-scale steel industry in these four societies during 1880–1914? For answers I dug into the history of each of these chosen countries and organized historical material of each chosen country according to these questions. Therefore, readers will not find a conventional in-depth chronological history of these four countries. Instead, they will find only the broad synoptic industrial history (1880–1914) of each country related to my argument.

The first question is dealt with by challenging the binary distinction of "universality/specificity" along with the binary distinction of developed/underdeveloped. It is maintained that every country has universal characteristics as well as a specific history unique to itself. Therefore, we do not have to accept European universalism to do a comparative history, or simply focus on the differences and specificities of every society (even when we recognize these differences and specificities). Instead, we can erase this existing binary distinction by explaining how each country is a product of similar universal (not universalism) processes as well as a product of its own specificity unique to that country. Dealing with the second issue—using the yardstick of parity—I tried to show how each society is a product of people's interactions within a society and also with international historical forces, which are products of society-to-society interactions. It is within this larger context of conjunction of historical forces within a society and internationally that I have tried to locate the emergence (or non-emergence) of a large-scale steel industry in each country.

This organizational method of historical information is necessary because I believe that the history of every present-day country is the history of its interdependence and interaction with other societies/countries, and these mutually influence one another in reciprocal or asymmetric perceptions and relationships. Through these entangled processes, countries co-constitute one another. That is why, the history of different societies/countries should not be dealt as separate units of nation-states (it is a modern construct and a racist project) for comparison, and not referred to as "core/periphery" or "developed/undeveloped." This approach is relevant for earlier historical periods as well. Our methodology does not deny that some countries do become powerful by controlling and colonizing other countries and societies, compelling them to become periphery and underdeveloped. Those events have also recently occurred through the services and power of the IMF, World Bank, and now Troika—IMF, World Bank and European Central Bank—by forcing structural adjustment programs on the ex-colonies, which then led to increased poverty in those countries. What is being suggested here is that no country or society should be considered developed or underdeveloped as an original, natural and inevitable given condition.

This methodology helped in erasing the Western conceptual binary distinction of developed/underdeveloped, and to move away from the simplistic narrative that underdevelopment is either due to capitalism, imperialism, and dependency, or it is simply a cultural "backwardness and resistance to progress" by those countries and societies. With the erasure of this conceptual binary distinction, poor countries (and their people) would not have to re-prove their capabilities and creativity anymore (referred as "not yet"), as they will be free to imagine different alternative approaches to understand their present conditions and find better solutions.

In the concluding remarks, some observations are made based on this comparative study to reiterate that it is possible to make a comparative historical study without categorizing any society as "developed or underdeveloped." Thus, removing the need for using this binary distinction will allow poor countries and their people to reclaim the space to define their lives, create new concepts to understand their present, and find alternative narratives of their histories using resources from the vast combined collective human knowledge, which is produced by our common human ancestors throughout human history. Through this process these countries would be able to recover their dignity and independence while improving the lives of their people.

ENDNOTES

1. See: Bahl (2005), "Introduction." I have heavily borrowed from the introductory chapter of my previous book wherein the main ideas for the present volume were initially articulated.
2. Academic snobbery and party politics (many Indian political parties have their student and teacher wings in the colleges and universities to promote their political agenda) is a staple in Indian higher education as they are able to influence the admission policies and teacher's appointments. Besides party politics, discrimination based on caste, gender, class, color, English speaking or not, modern or not, also goes on at every level (see recent articles in *Economic and Political Weekly*, April 1, 2017, about the Institute of Management at Kolkata. Joshi and Malghan, "Faculty Diversity at the Indian Institute of Management: A Preliminary Snapshot," and Thakur and Babu, "IIMs and Reservations"). If one does

not have a mentor, or higher-up connections, or a teacher who cares for you for various reasons mentioned above, who could help one navigate the academic territory, or if one happens to be the first generation in one's family going to college or university with no orientation about all these problems in university life, it is very easy to either become a drop-out or a pariah.

It was this impossible situation that compelled me to move to the US to complete my doctorate degree where somewhat similar processes (with an American flavor) was repeated in a different way.

I found that in 2011 Professor Sukhadeo Thorat had recommended various provisions to the Indian government to enable SC/ST (disadvantaged groups) students so that they would not be at a disadvantage to more privileged students. One of the recommendations was the development of the English and communication skills of these students and the establishment of NET of an equal opportunity cell coaching classes. (*Hindustan Times* 3/16/17. "JNU Dalit Scholar Muthukrishnan's body brought home, slipper hurled at the Union Minister"). These recommendations have not been implemented and some Dalit scholars have committed suicide, feeling the extreme bias against them in India's higher educational institutions, including the progressive Jawaharlal Nehru University (JNU). As I mentioned above (previous paragraph was written before the other information became available) I faced similar problems (even though I am not from the Dalit community) when I was in JNU. However, there was no help available on campus to improve communication skills or English language skills. At that time, the students' struggle at JNU was to change the admission policy to include people coming from Hindi speaking areas, and other disadvantaged groups in order to make JNU less elitist. However, I had to pay a very high price for joining this struggle and ultimately I was left with no choice but to leave the country to complete my doctorate degree in the US. It is sad to see that in the twenty-first century, Dalit scholars are treated with such contempt and bias at a place of higher learning (B. Prabhakarn, "Indian Academia and Institutional Injustice." countercurrents.org. March 18, 2017).

This universal need to learn the English language and to be fluent and articulate with a British or Boston accent in order to compete with privileged students, is a problem in itself. It is not possible for most of Indians to have access to such schools and environments because it requires a lot of money to study in English speaking schools and go abroad for education in order to acquire desirable accent. It seems Indians have not been liberated from the cultural imperialism of the English language as it is tied up with being considered smart, commanding respect, getting a higher education and better prospects for social mobility. This problem is well depicted in a parody *Jai Englis Mata* (Tr. Hail Mother English) recently made by few comedians in India (Scroll.in, July 26, 2018). In another recent (2018) experiment by Daily Hunt #HarBhashaEqual (Tr. every language is equal) campaign also confirmed that people consider a person smart, more capable of accomplishing something, if that person shows fluency in the English language (as opposed to regional language). What is the chance of those born in the "wrong place, wrong class, wrong caste, wrong gender" to study in English medium schools, and to speak fluently English language in order to be recognized as smart, to receive a higher education and attain social mobility?

3. Chakrabarty, D. (2000). *Provincializing Europe: Postcolonial Thought and Historical Difference.* Princeton, NJ: Princeton University Press. p. 28.

Most likely, similar concerns and confusions may have given rise to old Indian traditions and cultural practices so that people can feel proud of their culture. Unfortunately, in India, RSS (*Rashtirya Sevak Sangh*) and *Hindutva* forces are using these concerns to their political advantage and even trying to prove that all modern scientific developments were already achieved, or the basic scientific concepts and principles were already developed in Ancient India. Interestingly, this claim only establishes the importance of scientific thinking even though a large number of people follow rituals and beliefs that are considered superstitious. A recent book (*Homegrown Gurus: From Hinduism in America to American Hinduism,* Ann Gleig and Lola Williamson, (Eds.). SUNY Press. 2013), is instructive to understand how Hinduism was made palatable to a Western audience by incorporating Western values of rationality, and how Swami Vivekananda framed Hinduism as universal and scientific, and thus, a viable choice for modern Western people. Other gurus who came after him also adapted Hinduism in creative ways to make it more suitable for an American audience and thus thrust Hinduism into the global market place of ideas. The growth of Hindu nationalism in the last three decades is connected to globalization. With globalization, there is an increase in complexity—socially, conceptually, ideologically, economically—which created condition for defensive and nostalgic reactions from the more conservative religious groups (Christian, Islam and Hindu). ("Hinduism and Globalization," in Stanley D. Brunn (Ed.), 2015. *Changing World Religion Map: Sacred Places, Identities, Practices and Politics,* New York: Springer Science + Business Media. Vol. III. 1917–1932. See also Jain, A. R. (2015), *Selling Yoga,* Oxford University Press).

However, as I have discussed in the section titled "An Important Clarification," we need not throw away all that is useful in our collective human knowledge for the welfare of humanity just because fundamentalist forces are trying to monopolize this knowledge and interpreting it to suit their own fundamentalist agenda. We should claim our own human heritage of vast accumulated knowledge and put it to use for the welfare of humanity and the planet. We can learn from the Zapatistas at Oaxaca (Mexico) where they are building up an alternative society using ancient and modern knowledge and tools to reclaim community power and define how they want a society to work and to live with dignity (Gustav Esteva, "The Oaxaca Commune and the Zapatistas: Hope from the Margins," CounterCurrents.org. August 30, 2016).

4. Bahl, V. (1997). "Relevance (or Irrelevance) of Subaltern Studies." *Economic and Political Weekly,* 32(23):1333–44. June 7, 1997. A revised version of this article was also reproduced as "What Went Wrong with Subaltern Studies." In Bahl, 2005.

   Bahl, V. (1997). "Thinking Globally: Cultural Imperialism and Women's Movement." In *Gender and History,* April, 9(1):1–14.

5. Dirlik, A., Bahl, V. and Gran, P. (Eds.). (2000). *History After the Three Worlds: Post Eurocentric Historiographies.* Baltimore: Rowman and Littlefield.

   In the same year, another edited volume on Subaltern Studies was published that was a collection of selected essays written by both the Subaltern Studies collective and some of their critics, Vinayak Chaturvedi (Ed.), *Mapping Subaltern Studies and the Postcolonial.* London: Verso (2000). In 2003, an additional edited volume was published that contained essays critical of Subaltern Studies mainly written by Indian scholars, David Ludden, (Ed.), *Reading Subaltern Studies: Perspectives on History, Society, and Culture in South Asia.* Delhi: Oxford University Press.

   It is interesting to note that Ajay Gudavarthy recently suggested that "Indian subaltern is, ironically, local and very global at the same time." To substantiate this statement, he highlights the shifts in Subaltern Studies approaches that are in alignment with the shifts in global theoretical frames: from Althusserian structuralists to Gramsci, moved to Heidegger, then to Laclau and Mouffe and to Foucault, post structuralism and autonomist philosophers ("Brahmanism, Liberalism and the Postcolonial Theory," *Economic and Political Weekly,* July 11, 2016, 51(24):15–17, p. 16).

6. Throughout my life, in India as well as in the US, I have observed and personally suffered the consequences of how people judge others based on dress and color choice of attire, hair style, color of your skin, accent both in Hindi and in the English language. Sociological studies have confirmed that the social structure of any society is reproduced through every day interactions and in turn it limits the life chances of many people. A very important book (Gabriella Gutiérrez y Muhs, Yolanda Flores Niemann, Carmen G. González and Angela P. Harris (Eds.), *Presumed Incompetent: The Intersections of Race and Class for Women in Academia.* Utah State University Press. 2012) has documented all these experiences of various women of color specifically in the academic world in the US. More recently, in the wake of the #MeToo movement, *The Chronicle of Higher Education* has collected information about women's experiences in Academia, which corroborates similar experiences.

   Within India, only those who can speak English with an Oxford or Cambridge accent are respected as smart and true scholars. In the US, (see video: "American Tongues") in every state in the US, people make fun of any accent other than their own. In India, if you are lucky to be born into a wealthy family, can afford to study in English medium schools, as well as develop habits associated with Western lifestyles, you will be considered modern. If one does not fit into these criteria, one is relegated to being ancient, backward or traditional, and consequently, one's life chances shrink and life struggles become more tough and hopeless. It is not surprising that younger people in India are desperately trying to fit into this definition of 'modern' as young people did in my time.

At the same time, many people are disturbed by the effects of modernity, and want to stop this change by joining hands with fundamentalist forces. Thus, this struggle is about resisting cultural, social, political and financial imperialism. Of course, fundamentalist forces are using this situation to their advantage. Rather than understanding these conditions, scholars are getting bogged down in a dichotomy of modern/rational versus superstition/fundamentalism, which only creates more confusion. It forces people to take one side or the other as if reality of life, social traditions, and modernity are clear cut black and white. Those supporting rationality and science also ignore the grey area that exists in reality. Unsurprisingly, we look at the other side as the enemy and stop listening to what the other side might have to offer.

7. Discussion and information based on Banerjee, P., Nigam, A. and Pandey, R., "The Work of Theory: Thinking Across Traditions." *Economic and Political Weekly,* September 10, 2016. 51(37):42–50. p. 43.

Banerjee et al., write that Enlightenment thought was based on the rise of universal history, which in turn was based on the rise of universal history of philosophy. In this way it became possible for the West to imagine the whole world as potentially a boundless Christian imperium. Over time, universal history changed from being evangelical to being colonial with the emergence of modernity. Under modernity, the world was perceived to be ruled by reason and capital was perceived to be personified as the global agent of history. With this perception it became possible to automatically subsume histories of all people in the world under universal history.

With this mechanism, consequently, history of theory was subsumed within theory itself and in the process made "theory immune to historicisation and therefore to the challenge of counter-histories" (p. 46). That is how, as Banerjee et al. pointed out, it became possible for the West to treat European thinkers from diverse time and context in "seamless contemporaneity" while, non-West pre-colonial thinkers are so deeply historicized and contextualized. This treatment of non-West pre-colonial thinkers has made it "impossible to approach them from our modern locations, even though we find it perfectly legitimate to read archaic European thinkers such as Plato and Aristotle (Ibid.)."

Moreover, European thinkers' incorporation of the history of philosophy within philosophy itself is hegemonic, as it allows the "unmediated slippage between history and philosophy, fact and concept that we often encounter when we read European theory (Ibid.)." For example, the French Revolution is considered not a local occurrence but "the moment the philosophical concepts of liberty, equality and democracy were enunciated." Whereas, Chinese or Russian revolutions, and Asian and African liberation struggles are simply treated as purely empirical historical events (Ibid.).

8. Jason Moore has also recently rejected Cartesian binary in *Capitalism in the Web of Life: Ecology and the Accumulation of Capital.* London ; New York: Verso (2015). In the field of science, as Capra has noted, a shift away from Cartesian binary has been taking place for some time (Capra, F. (1996). *Web of Life: A New Scientific Understanding of Living Systems.* New York: Anchor Books).

9. Brennan, T. (2006). *Wars of Position: The Cultural Politics of Left and Right.* NY: Columbia University Press.

Regarding the formation of the nation-state Brennan writes, "The transition from the tributary state to the modern nation state in the Romantic period might be seen as the result of a management crisis created by foreign conquest and the wealth that it generated … Fences had to be set up at home in order to clarify jurisdiction over the spoils abroad.

The massive cultural confrontation of global settlement and business organization dictated a reactive fear of difference … In part, the nation was the result of a desire, again for reasons of jurisdiction, to codify the differences between home and territory, receiver and giver, owner and owned" (p. 230).

10. Lieten, 2002, p. 67–79.

    Wallerstein explains, "Utopistics is the analysis of possible utopias, their limitations and the constraints on achieving them … it is the analytical study of real historical alternatives in the present. It is the reconciliation of the search for truth and the search for goodness … if we are to be serious about utopistics, we must stop fighting about nonissues and the foremost of these nonissues is determinism versus freewill, or structure verses agency, or global verses local, or macro verses micro." (I. Wallerstein (1997) "Social Sciences and the Quest for a Just Society." *American Journal of Sociology*, 102(5). March 1997:1241–1257:1255)

11. Parthasarathi, P. (2011). *Why Europe Grew Rich and Asia Did Not: Global Economic Divergence 1600–1850.* Cambridge University Press. Mishra, V. N. and Argullol, R. (2008) *From the Ganges to the Mediterranean: A Dialogue between the Cultures of India and Europe.* Shubi Publishers.

    See also Martin Bernal (1987). *Black Athena: The Afroasiatic Roots of Classical Civilization,* New Brunswick: Rutgers University Press. See also Kapil Raj (2006). *Relocating Modern Science Circulation and the Construction of Knowledge in South Asia and Europe.* Delhi; Steven Shapin, (1996). *The Scientific Revolution*. Chicago; Harley. B and David Woodward (Eds.). (1992). *The History of Cartography* Vol. II. Book 1, *Cartography in the Traditional Islamic and South Asian Societies.* Chicago. pp. 388–493; Nathan Sivin, "Why the Scientific Revolution Did Not Take Place in China—Or Didn't It?" *Chinese Science,* 5 (1982):45–66.

    Banerjee et al. (op. cit) have provided the example of a Deleuze scholar Laura U. Marks (to be published, *Enfoldment and Infinity: An Islamic Genealogy of the New Media Art.* Cambridge, MA: MIT Press.), which traces the influences of other thinkers (Muslim) on Deleuze.

12. Nirmalangshu Mukherji makes a similar point by using the example of the decision of tribal indigenous people who rejected the corporation Vedanta's efforts to take over their hills and forest to mine Bauxite for aluminum. They used their accumulated knowledge, which was developed over thousands of years, to decide what is good for their region. Their knowledge is used for saving the planet and not for saving "development" projects. (Nirmalangshu Mukherji, "Education for the Species." *Economic and Political Weekly,* 6 August (2015), 51(32):30–35).

13. Clifford Conner has explained how the knowledge of technology and science was a collective effort that included ordinary artisans and other different types of professionals including women. Moore (2015) has also suggested the idea of "Web of Life" that shows the unified world in which society and nature are not seen as two separate entities but "humanity in nature and nature in humanity" as an organic whole co-produced. Earlier Capra (op. cit.) also wrote about the *Web of Life* (1996).

14. Kaiwar. p. 7.

    For more detailed and in-depth critique with arguments and rebuttal of Subaltern Studies, its ideology, its strategies, and its international reputation, read Vasant Kaiwar (2015), *The Postcolonial Orient: The Politics of Difference and the Project of Provincialising Europe.* Chicago: Haymarket Books; see also Vivek Chibber (2013). *Postcolonial Theory and the Spectre of Capital.* London: Verso.

15. Kaiwar, V. (2015). *The Postcolonial Orient: The Politics of Difference and the Project of Provincializing Europe.* Chicago: Haymarket Books.

    Kaiwar wrote, "The shift in the terminology reflects the moment and its use of the cardinal point is itself interesting, that is, North and South in place of West and East; North and South are essential to a postcolonial geography as West and East were to colonial geography, but the valances of the latter have often been quietly smuggled into the former" (pp. 64 fn. 120).

16. Chibber, p. 294.

A recent article by Lois Menand, "Karl Marx, Yesterday and Today," in *New Yorker* (October 10, 2016), further confirms this observation.

Timothy Shenk has pointed out that in the US, some young New York City journalists, who were also connected with the Occupy Wall Street movement at Zuccotti Park, started their career as Marxist intellectuals even when Marxists were skeptical of the Occupy movement. Most of these American journalists had no background in Marxism since Marxism had been out of public debate for a long time. In this situation, Marxism seem very daring to these journalists and they used their access to social media to disseminate Marxist ideas through web. Thus, according to Shenk, Marxism was reborn and became a minor genre in the US since that time. (Timothy Shenk: "What was Socialism?" Book Review. *The Nation,* May 5, 2013. pp. 27–37).

17. Countercurrents.org/2016/06/30/twenty-four-groups-write-to-the-world-bank-no-more-destructive-development

The letter is as follows:

June 25, 2016: Dear Executive Directors,

We are representatives of people's movements, civil society organisations, and other concerned citizens from India, who have been engaged with, or monitoring World Bank financed projects for the past many years.

In April 2013, around 60 of us jointly issued a statement titled 'Sham Consultations: No More' during the first phase of the Safeguard consultations. We have detailed our opposition to the consultations, citing examples of different projects to establish that "the so-called environmental and social safeguards of the Bank are nothing more than a veneer of protection to mask the real impacts of this dangerous financial institution which works only to increase profitability of its shareholders and furthering the cause of the extractive-accumulative large capital—at any cost."

While we stand by that, and despite many voices of opposition and concern from different parts of the globe, the Bank continued [the] process of consultations, without addressing the issues we collectively raised, and brought out two drafts of it. The drafts clearly demonstrated all that we said in our letter—the intentions are wrong, the process flawed and the purpose of this is to fool people, giving them a false sense of participation. The end result remains the same—to push investments in all possible sectors, with scant regard for social and environmental impacts and without any democratic and participatory processes. The World Bank projects are not only a contributor to climate change situation, the projects are also destroying the capacity of the people to adapt to changing climate.

To add insult to injury, our government has advocated for weakening of the policies claiming that these Safeguard policies are too costly and time-consuming to implement; inefficient when national systems could more quickly and easily be applied; and undermine national authority and sovereignty by putting harsh conditions on Bank lending.

We do not share this view with our government. Our opposition was on different grounds and it was not to weaken the policies.

We believe that unless there are genuine efforts to learn from past experiences, the consultations are more inclusive and participatory, and keeping people and environment in the core of any planning, these policies will only disempower the people, rob them off their natural resources and push them to destitution. — Signed by 24 groups.

18. IMF Report (2016), www.imf.org; See also Benjamin Dangl, "Lives Destroyed: Elite Admission that Neoliberalism has Failed." Alternet.org. June 2, 2016; Pritam Singh, "IMF's Autocritique of Neo-Liberalism." *Economic and Political Weekly,* August 6, 2016. 51(32):17–18.

Singh writes, "It seems that this new confession by IMF economists, over the kind of growth promoted by neoliberalism promotes inequality, is a step forward in recognising the dialectic of modern capitalism where massive increases in the income of the richest strata of society coexist with some modest improvements in the living conditions of the very poor. That the state needs to intervene through welfare measures to reduce poverty and inequality is also conceded in the IMF paper ... A glaring weakness of this otherwise praiseworthy IMF paper on many points remains the absence of recognition of the ecological implication of capitalist economic growth" (p. 18).

See also the information in the UNO's *Global Sustainable Development Report,* 2019. Saul Foster, "UN Scientific paper suggests Capitalism has to Die in Order for the Planet to be Saved." Posted September 3, 2018, MR Online.

19. Western educated intellectuals of Asian and other non-Western countries accept IMF ideas automatically because business schools in the West are teaching only about capital gains and profits and not much about the ethical and social consequences of these policies. (Recently, students in various countries are demanding to reform the economic discipline to include alternative economic ideas.) Patel has also noted a similar point in the context of sociological language that was diffused through universities and other academic institutions from the US to the rest of the world. S. Patel, "Beyond Binaries: A case for self-reflexive sociologies." *Current Sociology,* May 2006, 54(3):381–395.

Joseph Thomas explains how Asian leaders are groomed in the US and through them US interests are taken care of in those countries. "These cadre, with 'seed funding' provided through the US State Department and the YSEALI itself, will be building networks that serve US special interests, locked directly into the very institutions and networks YSEALI alumni met and worked with during their various fellowships." Thomas, Joseph: 2016: "US 'Cultural Colonisation' in Asia Pacific." (New Eastern Outlook). Viewed on August 30, GlobalResearch.ca.

The 2016 demonetization in India is a good example of how US interests are served in India through US trained Indian economists. In this regard, Colin Todhunter provides the following information: Raghuram Rajan who was the Governor of the Reserve Bank in India, was also chief economist at the IMF 2003–2007 and was a Distinguished Service Professor of Finance at the University of Chicago Booth School of Business from 1991 to 2013. He is back at the University of Chicago.

"Economist Norbert Häring implicates Rajan in the demonetisation policy. He indicates that the policy was carried out on behalf of USAID, Master Card, Visa and the people behind eBay and Citi, among others, with support from Gates Foundation and the Ford Foundation. Häring calls Rajan the Reserve Bank of India's 'IMF-Chicago boy' and based on his employment record, memberships, ... which includes heads of central, investment and commercial banks and links, place him squarely at the centre of Washington's financial cabal. Häring says that Raghuram Rajan has good reason to expect to climb further to the highest rungs in international finance and thus play bow to Washington's game plan." (Colin Todhunter, 2017a), "India, From the Destabilization of Agriculture to Demonetization, 'Made in America'." GlobalResearch.ca January 06.)

See also Norbert Häring (2017a), "A Well-Kept Open Secret: Washington is Behind India's Brutal Demonetization." January 3, GlobalResearch.ca. Norbert Häring (2017b), "How India Became Bill Gates 'Guinea Pig: A Conspiracy As Recounted by the Main Actors." Countercurrents.org. July 27, 2017. See also "Tata Corus Deal—Uncovering the Mystery of the White Knight." http://greatgameindia.com/tata-corus-deal-rothschild-mossad-white-knight 4/26/2017. See also Shelley Kasli Global #WaronCash, an impact study on India's demonetization drive. April–June 2017 Demonetization Issue of GreatGameIndia. Colin Todhunter (2017b), "Indian Independence: Forged in Washington?" GlobalResearch.ca, July 30.

Moreover, US think tanks (Carnegie, Rockefeller, Ford) are also opening shop in India to influence Indian government policies. For details see Urvashi Sarkar, "Carnegie Endowment in India: Promoting US Leadership with Indian Corporate Wealth." *The Wire,* August 31, 2017; See also Inderjeet Parmar (2012). *Foundation of the American Century: The Ford, Carnegie and Rockefeller Foundations in the Rise of American Power.* New York: Columbia University Press.

Parmar informs that these American corporates created these foundations in the early

1900s to develop American leadership to replace British and French rule as well as to challenge Communism and Socialism in the world. They hired people who were connected with the US State Department or other government agencies. Now they are exporting similar institutions to other countries (earlier to China and now to India) to influence and socialize the Indian elite (university academia, higher rungs of government services, business leaders, and the media) into the international order promoted by the US. These actions are based on their belief that US dominance in the world can be managed better with deep engagement in other countries.

20. Nigam, A. (2011).

    See also G. Kuppuram and K. Kumudamani, *History of Science and Technology in India*. Delhi: Sundeep Prakashan. (1990) in 12 volumes; S. H. Nasr, *Islamic Science. World of Islam Festival* (1976); George Saliba, "Arab Influences on the Renaissance." Paper at the 5th Annual Conference of the World Historical Association. Pomona, CA. June 21. Quoted in A. G. Frank, "Speaking Truth to Power about the Scientific Emperor's Clothes." *Economic and Political Weekly,* October 17–24, (1998); Jack Goody, *The East in the West.* Cambridge University Press. (1996); J. M. Blaut, *The Coloniser's Model of the World: Geographical Diffusionism and Eurocentric History.* New York ; London: Guilford Press. (1993); Jonathan Grant, "Rethinking the Ottoman Decline: Military Technology Diffusion in the Ottoman Empire, 15th–18th Centuries." Paper at the World History Association meetings in Pomona, CA. June 21–22, (1996).

21. Engdahl, W. F. (2017), "US Empire, CIA, NGOs," Countercurrents.org, July 17, 2017. See also Valerly Kulilov (2017), "Soros, Go Away." In https://journal-neo.org, October 22, 2017.

    Gerry Docherty and Jim Macgregor, (2013), *Hidden History: The Secret Origins of the First World War and Prolonging the Agony.* Edinburgh ; London: Mainstream Publishing. Brennan, C. L. (2015), *Fall of* the *Arab Spring: From Revolution to Destruction.* San Diego, CA: Progress Press. See also Eva Golinger, "Coloured Revolutions: A New Form of Regime Change, Made in USA." In Global Research.org. March 5 (2014).

    The documentary, "Weight of Chains," is informative in understanding how neo-liberalists aided by politicians, CIA, economists, banks, military and other institutions, tried to control social movements and bring about regime changes in various countries.

    See also Efe Can Gürcan, "The Non-Profit Corporate Complex: An Integral Component and Driving Force of Imperialism in the Phase of Monopoly Finance Capitalism." *Monthly Review,* April 2015, 66(11): 37–53.

    Gürcan writes, "Wikileaks documents and many other credible sources have unveiled how USAID as a 'civilian foreign-aid agency' transferred millions of dollars to Cuban and Venezuelan NGOs for pro-US regime change … non-profit corporate complex … under it the absorption of radical movements is ensured through the establishment of patronage relationships between the state and /or private capital and social movements …. The crucial involvement of monopoly capital (Mellon, Ford, Soros foundations) in the non-profit sectors helps transform political resistance projects into quasi-entrepreneurial, corporate style ventures … 200 non-profits controlled over 1.59 trillion in financial assets and had expenditure of over $822 billion … and … co-optation of radical movements in the name of promoting the interests of 'civil society' " (p. 42–44).

    More recently, the "Black Lives Matter" movement gained the support of the Ford Foundation, as reported by Gabriel Black on the GlobalResearch website October 12, 2016. Moveon.org which organizes demonstrations and such activities in the US, is supported by George Soros, who also funded the DNC. NGOs are part of one more industrial complex used as a front for multinational corporations and other vested interests.

    Welch et al. noted that most of the social movements confronting government or corporate actions are organized and directed by non-governmental organizations (NGOs), which are funded by philanthropic foundations established by various companies. For example, the Keystone XL pipeline protest of 2014, and the climate march was funded by the Rockefeller and Clinton Foundations among others. NGOs help in changing the issues of the protest movements and keep them fragmented by focusing on different issues and not let a united front to emerge. Thus, the foundations behind NGOs remain invisible while NGOs do their bidding. ("The Non-Profit Industrial Complex and the 'Parallel Left'." In GlobalResearch.ca, May 12, 2018).

22. Professor Rifaat Abou-El-Haj made me aware of the idea of human creativity and it appealed to me as it related to the personal questions that I had been contemplating for a very long time resulting from my own life experiences in India as well as in the US.

    To understand the meaning of non-duality, see Rambachan, 2015.

    Nobel Laureate physicist Ilya Prigogine has championed the idea of self-organizing systems. Waldrop noted, "Darwin did not know about self-organization—matter's incessant attempts to organize itself into ever more complex systems just as surely as they do to the formation of snowflakes or the appearance of convection cells in a simmering pot of soup. So, the story of life is, indeed the story of accident and happenstance, declared Stuart Kauffman, scientist from University of Pennsylvania. But it is also the story of order, a kind of deep inner creativity that is woven into the very fabric of nature (p. 102) … the view point of complexity does not accept duality between human and nature ... so once you drop duality … then the question changes … These ideas were not new to Eastern philosophy .... But it more recently becoming important in the West … both in science and culture at large (p. 333)." Mitchell, M. Waldrop, *Complexity: The Emerging Science at the Edge of Order and Chaos.* NY: Simon and Schuster, (1992).

    See also Sayers, Sean. (2003), "Creative Activity and Alienation in Hegel and Marx." *Historical Materialism,* 11(1): 107–128. A recent article focusing on mental health and capitalism shows how people under capitalist systems become mentally sick as they cannot express their creativity (Matthews, 2019). While I agree this analysis, I do not agree with Erich Fromm's ideas as author explained that creativity was a later development in the process of evolution of human beings. I believe that since we are the expression of Nature's creativity, and Nature is creativity itself, we all inherit it. Without this we could not have evolved into human beings who were then able to control nature itself.

    The ideas of "creative activity" were also used by Marx in the following ways: "Marx describes work as man's vital activity, his species activity, man's spiritual essence his human essence …. Man is a thinking consciousness … man duplicates himself in that (i) he is a thing in nature, but (ii) he is just as much for himself, he sees himself, represents himself to himself, thinks. Marx also maintains that since Aristotle and the Stoics, it has been common knowledge that human beings have 'intellect, emotion, and will.'" (CW, 5, p. 511: MEW, 3, p. 500. Quoted in Isidor Wellimann, *Estrangement: Marx's Concept of Human Nature and the Division of Labor.* Syracuse University. (2015). http.//surface.syr.edu/books/22).

    The following was also written by Marx, "Conscious life activity distinguishes man immediately from animal life." (CW, 3, p. 276): MEW, EB 1, T, p. 516). "Man also forms objects in accordance with the laws of beauty." (CW, 3, pp. 276–277; MEW EB1 T, p. 517). "Language, like consciousness, only arises from the need, the necessity, of intercourse with other men." (CW, 5, p. 44; MEW, 3, p. 30). "At this point [i.e. At the beginning of conscious social life] man is distinguished from sheep only by the fact that with him consciousness takes the place of instinct or that his instinct is a conscious one" (CW, 5, p. 44; MEW, 3, 31). Marx writes "free, conscious activity is man's species character."

    A recently published (2017) book title *The Runaway Species: How Human Creativity Remakes the World,* by D. Eagleman and A. Brandt seems to also emphasizing human creativity in the re-making of the world.

    One scholar has also tried to show how Marxism and Buddhism complement each other: Adrian Kreutz, "How Marxism and Buddhism Complement Each Other." (https://aeon.co/essays/how-marxism-and-buddhism-complement-each-other).

23. Bahl (2005).

    I should also clarify that my suggestion about Human creativity is not the same as one recent book suggests *The Rise of the Creative Class* by Richard Florida, 2004. He talks about the structural changes that have taken place in the US economy where the role of information, engineering, scientists, artists, theatre, biotech, architecture, education, and small businesses etc. has increased, and this workforce creates new ideas in these fields for a living; around 40 million people in America who form this group of "creative class." Whereas, I am suggesting that every human is born with innate creativity (which is inherited from nature, as humans are one of the infinite expressions of nature's creativity) and it is through human interaction and interaction with nature that inner creativity manifests in the making of social institutions and various products, ideas, and so on.

Earlier, Noam Chomsky pointed out the universality in language formation. Discussed in Agnihotri. R. K. (Postscript), "Gender Agenda." *Economic and Political Weekly,* September 10. 2016, 51(37).

24. Bahl, V. (2005). "Introduction."

Historical archaeologist Dan Sayers of American University of Washington D.C. wrote about Native Indians, Black slaves, and indentured white people who ran away from slavery and built their free lives on equal basis in the swamps of south east Virginia and north west North Carolina from 1680 to the Civil War. These people preferred to live a hard and difficult life as they were completely dependent on the place that was very difficult to navigate, and risked everything to live more just and equitable ways for more than ten generations. *The Desolate Place for Defiant People* (2012). Reported in Smithsonian Magazine. 1. September 2016 by Richard Grant. Smithsonian.com

25. Maheshvarananda, D. (2004). *After Capitalism: PROUT's Vision for a New World.* Proutist Universal Publication. Washington D.C. ; New Delhi: Belo Horizonte.

It is important to point out that this book was reviewed in *Monthly Review-An Independent Socialist* journal, by Hans G. Despain: "It's the System Stupid." *Monthly Review.* Vol. 65. November (2013) with a foreword written by Noam Chomsky.

It should be noted that Austrian theoretical physicist and Nobel Laureate Erwin Shrodinger wrote in his book, *My View of the World*, that "the plurality that we perceive is only an appearance, it is not real. Vedanta philosophy—has sought to clarify it by a number of analogies, one of the most attractive being the many-faceted crystal which, while showing hundreds of little pictures of what is in reality a single existent object, does not really multiply that object." Wikiquote.org

German theoretical physicist and Nobel Laureate Wemer Karl Heisenberg also noted that one cannot always distinguish between statements made by eastern metaphysics based on mystical insight, and the pronouncements of modern physics based on observations, experiments and mathematical calculation (Goldberg, 2010:285).

Recently Jeremy Sherman pointed out that science still cannot explain the biological mystery, that is, organisms: what they are and how they emerge from chemistry. Scientist simply assume them without explaining them. Whereas, the religious faithful people raise that question and try to answer them in a way that is really no answer. But they are honest at least in raising this question. Jeremy Sherman (2018), "Science Still Can't Explain This Biological Mystery, But Scientists Like to Pretend Otherwise." Alternet.org. March 18. See also Koch (2016), and Complexity Studies.

26. Norgaard, R. (2015). "The Church of Economism and its Discontents." Countercurrents.org. December 30.

Norgaard quotes Frank Knight to explain that economists themselves have acknowledged the ultimately religious nature of their discipline. Knight (1932) founders of the influential market-oriented Chicago school of economics, literally argues that economics, at a fundamental level, had to be a religion, the basic tenets of which must be hidden from all but the few: "there must be ultimates, and they must be religious, in economics as anywhere else, if one has anything to say touching conduct or social policy in a practical way. Man is a believing animal and too few, if any, criticize the foundations of belief 'intelligently.' To inquire into the ultimate behind accepted group values is obscene and sacrilegious; objective inquiry is an attempt to uncover the nakedness of man, his soul as well as his body, his deeds, his culture, and his very gods. Certainly, the large general [economics] courses should be prevented from raising any question about objectivity, but should assume that objectivity of the slogans they inculcate, as a sacred feature of the system." Frank Knight, "The Newer Economics and the Control of Economic Activity."

Journal of Political Economy, 1932, 40(4):448–9, 455.

See also a recent book by John Rapley (2017). *Twilight of the Money Gods: Economics as a Religion and How it All Went Wrong.* New York: Simon and Schuster.

27. Smith, C. W. 1991 [1962]. *The Origin and End of Religion.* Minneapolis, MN: Fortress Press. p. 6. Quoted in Emma Tomalin, "Introduction," in *The Routledge Handbook of Religions and Global Development.* London, Routledge. 2015. p. 8. See also Johannes Quack, *Disenchanting India: Organized Rationalism and Criticism of Religion in India.* Oxford: Oxford University Press. 2012.

Criticizing the Anti-Superstition Movement for attacking local, "small" godmen and healers instead of "big" godmen and gurus, Shubha Ranganathan suggests that it is important to acknowledge the efforts of the rationalist mission. However, we should also closely examine how the Anti-Superstition Movement (ANS) is implementing its agenda. She informs that ANS is targeting those godmen who are of a diverse group including local healers, herbalists, wandering monks, religious authorities, miracle men, tantriks, and mantriks. Each one of them uses different methods, substances, rites, and perform different rituals to appease the gods in healing people. However, rationalists treat all these small godmen as the same. Rationalists claim that they are opposed to both the "small babas" and "big babas" and prominent gurus. In practice they only target small, local, and unorganized healers and do not touch famous gurus.

She further points out that it is not possible to determine which healing practice can be considered as "superstition" (or not) in a pluralist and diverse society like India. Moreover, the ANS movement has led to greater opposition between science and religion. This situation leaves no space for the non-rational in a scientific discourse. Johannes Quack's (2012) detailed description and analysis of the ANS activities reveal that "their larger objective is to bring about a complete shift in world view, where rationality and science are presumed to be universal and ultimate ideals. In this rationalist world view, there is little space for the mystical, spiritual or even the cultural/symbolic" (quoted in Ranganathan).

Ranganathan worries that since fascist Hindu elements also oppose the rationalist movement, it has become difficult to raise questions against the extreme and all-encompassing nature of the ANS' activities, as one would be branded as right-wing and fascist. She writes, "No doubt there are local healers and black magicians who exploit the poor for personal gain. Yet, it is also important to critically examine the rationalist claims that the only path to progress is through modern science, and that the agenda of social reform justifies an aggressive crusade against non-rational beliefs and practices."

(Shubha Ranganathan, "The Rationalist Movement Against Quack Healing." *Economic and Political Weekly,* January 4, 2014. 49(1):13–15.)

See also B. M. Hegde (2017). "Science Needs To Be Set Free For The Good of Mankind." April 10. (http://www.countercurrents.org/201704/10/science-needs-to-be-free-for-the-good-of-mankind).

Ellen Weinstein (2018). *Recipes for Good Luck: The Superstitions, Rituals and Practices of Extraordinary People.* San Francisco: Chronicle Books.

28. Roberts, C. P. (2016), "What Became of the Left." Information Clearing House. Viewed on Aug, 21, 2016. See also Lance DeHaven-Smith; *Conspiracy Theory in America.* Texas Press; Jay Syrmopoulos, "Fifteen years later, Physics Journal Conceded, All Three WTC Towers Collapsed on 9/11 due to Controlled Demolition." GlobalResearch.ca 9/13/16; Jack Mullen, "September 11, 2001: 9/11, The Day the Laws of Physics were Suspended." Global Research.ca 9/13/16. A recent article on GlobalResearch.ca, 3/15/17, by Graeme McQueen is thought provoking; "The 'Inside Job' Hypotheses of the 9/11 attack: JFK, 9/11 and the American Left." Kevin Ryan, "Evidence for 'Informal Trading' on the Attacks of September 11, 2001, GlobalResearch.ca, September 4, 2018. Gary G. Kohls "Facts that Disprove official 9/11 White House "Conspiracy Theory": Why Are Good Americans Silent?" GlobalResearch.ca, September 7, 2018. Lawyers Committee for 9/11 Inquiry April 10, 2018 (www.lcfor911.org).

More recently, a left leaning magazine, *The Nation,* criticized even the art work displayed in the New York Metropolitan Museum of Art showcasing a critical perspective on the official narrative of major events including 9/11, as promoting and normalizing conspiracy theory (Zachary Small, "Conspiracy Theories Are Not Entertainment: New York's art world explores the paranoia of American politics." *The Nation*, October 31, 2018). See Max Parry's article, "In Defense of 'Conspiracy Theory': From 'Fake News' to the Art World." In GlobalResearch.ca, December 2, 2018.

29. Kumar, P. J. D. (2016), "Intellectual Analysis of Religion." Letter to Editor. *Economic and Political Weekly*, August 13, 51(33). Another scholar, Sudarsan Padmanabhan, explained this phenomenon as follows: "Most Indians who migrated to America belonged to upper middle classes ... The cultural distance between the Indians and the Indian Americans seems to have contributed immensely to the current textbook controversy ... Indian Americans retain their reified ideas about India...they do not want to lose their Indian cultural identity ... their yearning for Indian culture is exploited not only by the Hindu nationalist groups but also by Indian cinema, music, drama and dance artists ... The California textbook controversy is the latest attempt by the Hindu nationalist groups to create a wedge and polarize the Indian American population ... it is understandable on the part of those who espouse the cause of fair treatment of Hinduism to feel aggrieved at insensitive references that have to be interpreted in a specific context." ("Debate on Indian History: Revising Textbooks in California." *Economic and Political Weekly,* May 6, 2006: 1761–1763).

30. Dalit Camera: (2016) "Inquiring into the Role of CPI(M) In the Annihilation of Caste." Countercurrents.org 9/21/2016. This "open letter" to the Marxist Party of India brings out details not only about recent alliances between the Dalit movement and Marxist party, but also questions their sincerity and commitment based on their treatment of Dalits, poor peasants, land reforms, and Muslims in those states where the Marxist party was the ruling party. It also highlights the opportunism of the Marxist party in various political situations in general and in specific cases where Dalits were organizing and protesting more recently.

    See also Gopal Guru (2016), "Shifting Categories in the Discourse on Caste and Class." *Economic and Political Weekly,* 51(47):21–25. November 19.

31. Mann, Charles C. (2005). *1491: New Revelations of the Americas Before Columbus.* New York: Vintage Books; Bollier, D. (2016). "Beyond Development: The Commons as a New/Old Paradigm of Human Flourishing." In countercurrents.org, 6/30/2016. See also books by Graham Hancock on the lost civilizations where he demonstrates how different ancient civilizations in Mexico, Egypt, and Cambodia, that came into being before or at 10,000 BC, are similar in many ways. Hancock, G. (1998). *Fingerprints of the Gods.* NY: Crown Publishing; Hancock, G. (2015). *The Magicians of the Gods*. NY: St. Martin's Press; Hancock, G. (2019). *America Before: The Key to Earth's Lost Civilizations.* London: Hodder & Stoughton.

    Rodrigues et al. (2015). *From Big Bang to Galactic Civilizations: A Big History Anthology.* Vol. I. Delhi: Primus Books.

SECTION I

Defining and Explaining the Problem

CHAPTER 1

Spurious and Misleading Binary Distinction

"I do not see how the movement required can emerge as long as leftists and many others here are plagued by the false dichotomies and false dilemmas ... The reality in most cases is that there are many in-between or other alternative options, not just two mutually exclusive one ... There are two ways in which one can commit a false dilemma. First, one can assume that there are only two (or three ... that case is strictly speaking be a false 'trilemma') options when there really are many more. Second, one can take the options to be mutually exclusive when they really are not" (Paul Street, 2015).

"The last taboo is the myth of civilization. It is built upon the stories we have constructed about our genius, our indestructibility, our manifest destiny as a chosen species. It is where our vision and our self-belief intertwine with our reckless refusal to face the reality of our position on this Earth. It has led the human race to achieve what it has achieved; and has led the planet into the age of ecocide. The two are intimately linked" (Paul Kingsnorth, http://dark-mountain.net/about/manifesto).

"The civilized have created the wretched, quite coldly and deliberately, and do not intend to change the status quo; are responsible for their slaughter and enslavement; rain down bombs on defenseless children whenever and wherever they decide that their 'vital interests' are menaced; and think nothing of torturing a man to death; these people are not to be taken seriously when they speak of the 'sanctity' of human life, or the 'conscience' of the civilized world" (Baldwin, 1998).

"I shall not accept an inferior position in the art world. Nor have my art called African because I have not correctly and properly given expression to my reality. I have consistently fought against that kind of philosophy because it is bogus. European artists like Picasso, Braque and Vlaminck were influenced by African art everybody sees that and are not opposed to it. But when they see African artists, who are influenced by their European training and techniques, they expect that African to stick to traditional forms even if he bends down to copying them. I do not copy traditional art, I like what I see in the works of people like Giacometti but I do not copy them. I knew Giacometti personally in England, you know, I knew he was influenced by African sculptures. But I would not be influenced by Giacometti, because he was influenced by my ancestors .... Whites who are critical of the kind of things I do, do so because they do not want to see African life portrayed with dignity at all. They don't want to see that we have sophistication and dignity too. The kind of art I do annoys and frightens them because it proves to them that their theories of being better and more advanced than Blacks are false. ... they prefer to see weak distorted figures and forms, a childish kind of expression called primitivism—or child art—that remains perpetually in a child-art-state. Such an art of course, makes them feel superior." Nikiru Nzegwu's interview with Ben Enwonwu in 1989 ("Contemporizing NKA: Spirit, Mind and Medium in the Creation Process." Type script).

"Europeans have made great cultural contribution to our common human enterprise. But it is simply not true ... The active replacement of the current Eurocentric bias by a more sober and balanced sense of history and of its cultural evaluation will require acute and constant political and cultural struggle. It calls not for new fanaticisms but for hard intellectual work, collectively and individually … The North's wealth has in very large part been the result of a transfer of surplus-value from the South. It is this very fact which, over several hundred years, has led us to the crisis of the system. It is not a question of remedial charity, … Finally, the struggle will be an intellectual one, in the reconceptualization of our scientific canons, in the search for more holistic and sophisticated methodologies, in the attempt to rid ourselves of the pious and fallacious cant about the value-neutrality of scientific thought. Rationality is itself a value judgment … and nothing is or can be rational except in the widest, most inclusive context of human social organization" (Wallerstein, 1995).

"The mantra of liberals is rationality. Liberals are the most loyal scions of the Enlightenment … believe in the *potential* rationality of all persons … share the metaphor of Newtonian science: that complexity is best handled by reducing it to smaller parts, by differentiation and specialization … in order to perform their role … individuals have need of expert counsel to guide them, to delimit the alternatives, and to suggest criteria by which to judge political alternatives. If rationality, to be exercised, it also then requires the civic culture of giving the specialists pride of place. The modern educational system, whether in its humanistic or scientific form, has been intended to socialize citizens into accepting the edicts of experts … What we are seeing is the 'social scientization' of all knowledge … The idea that there are two cultures, a fortiori that these two cultures are in contradiction to each other, is a gigantic mystification. The tripartite division of organized knowledge is an obstacle to our fuller understanding of the world" (Wallerstein, 1999).

"Britain came to acquire the status of a universal model … Like the functionalist models, Marxist theory [also] built upon the English experience of industrialization …. Industrialization is taken to constitute an autonomous force, determined by a neutral technology, whose 'imperatives' and 'inherent tendencies' appear to lie beyond the realm of social choice or political control, and which acts to shape society inevitably in a single direction … These assumptions…have influenced the study of industrialization … Consequently, they have generated endless false analogies between fundamentally different societies and inspired scores of meaningless computations of industrial achievement" (Chandavarkar, 1985).

"Britain drained 45 trillion dollars from India between 1765–1938" (Patnaik, 2017).

"Development now has become an amoeba-like shapeless but ineradicable concept. It's contours are so blurred that it means nothing, but spreads everywhere because it connotes the best intentions. Though development has no content, it does possess one function, it allows any intervention to be sanctified in the name of the higher goal" (Basu and Biswas, 2017).

INTRODUCTION

Many modern historians are tirelessly looking for the origin of capitalism that seemed to one historian of comparative history, "not much better than the alchemists search for the philosopher's stone that transforms base metal into gold" (Chaudhuri, 1990a:87; Rist, 2008). While some historians are searching for the "origins of capitalism," others simply believe in the so-called "benefits" of capitalism as it supposedly leads to the "development" (progress) of poor societies. Interestingly, the investments in poor countries in the name of development is currently referred to as "philanthrocapitalism," "social entrepreneurship," and "social impact bonds." However, these investments and their stated benefits never worked as supposedly intended for development (Hobbs, 2014), but do contribute in perpetuating the Western binary of "(superior) West and (inferior) rest" as now does the perpetual War on Terror, which is justified in the name of protecting the "civilized and developed Western world" from the "barbarians" (underdeveloped) who "hate" Western values. Within this Western narrative it is suggested that "underdeveloped" societies can only be developed by adopting Western values, lifestyle, and technologies. In order to "develop" a country, if we accept Western ideas, narratives, and assumptions, then we also have to accept the Eurocentric idea of "superior West and inferior rest" as a naturally given original condition. Ashis Nandy has spelled out this dilemma as follows:

> We see all over the place, a kind of encroachment of concepts or ideas which didn't hegemonize a particular domain ... and ultimately get identified with the entire domain, and you cannot enter that domain without invoking that concept. For example ... from the social sciences to newspaper editorials, you do not hear the phrase 'social change' any more, it is 'development.' ... I don't see any effort to get out of the stranglehold and the result is this, that today, even in the southern hemisphere, ... there is no concept of thinking outside development ... how do we recover ... that space ... how do we get back to the simple concepts of everyday lives which have been hegemonized and have shrunk, shrunk to almost obscurity? (Nandy, quoted in Lal and Rajan, 2016:100–101).

It is not only "underdeveloped" countries which are treated as backward, as even the case of Russian imperialism is not treated on par with Western imperialism, as Western scholars often neglect in their general theories, history, and fiction, the entire matter of Russian imperialism. The reason for this neglect is an assumption that Russia was "too backward to have sustained a genuine imperialism" (Palat, 1988:160). However, the interesting thing is that the same idea of Russia's "backwardness" was also forcefully used by the Russian intelligentsia and imperial bureaucracy to measure the country's distance from their goal of an industrial society. According to Madhvan Palat, "The concept of her [Russia's] backwardness was as much a strategy as the fact of it might have been obviously true by the usual comparative indices of growth" (Ibid., 161). However, the fact is ignored that Russia was the "only colonial empire from which political unity and economic development ... emerged as congruent rather than divergent processes" (Ibid.). It seems that the concept of backwardness (and it is also not currently out of fashion), was useful for the agenda of both Russian bureaucrats and European elites. Given these complex realities, if we wish to understand any social reality and also replace the narrative of developed/underdeveloped, we need to be aware of the narrative, politics and assumptions behind these concepts and not simply accept them as a given natural condition of a society.

Let me clarify at the outset that I do not deny that today large numbers of countries in the world are poor, and that many people in these countries live in miserable conditions. However, it is no accident that most of these poor countries are also ex-colonies of the Western "civilized" world, and they now are incorporated into the world economy. My question is this: In order to improve the condition of people in poor countries, is the "development" model the answer as has been promoted for so long, even when scholars (including development promoters who have admitted its failure) have expounded the negative and tragic effects of these development models

(Bagchi, 2013)? For the last 60 years or so, we have not seen any alternative to the development model except for some efforts towards developing local production—producing community and production in community—as "commons" (Boiler, 2016) which are increasing in Latin American countries. By now, it has become clear that the prevailing conceptual binary distinctions—modern/traditional, developed/underdeveloped, progressive/backward, core/periphery—blur our vision in finding an alternative perspective that would free us from the development model and "corporate feudalism" (1). This situation raises an obvious question: How do we cultivate an alternative vision and create an alternative strategy for improving the human condition?

This question is not new. As Washbrook pointed out, the European sociological theories of development/underdevelopment are being challenged by historians of non-European countries and is based on a vast amount of evidence from indigenous sources. Using this new evidence, some historians have been able to show parallels in Indian history to modern European history, while others have been able to challenge the concepts of capitalism, development, and even modernization (Washbrook, 1988). Washbrook also thinks that generalizing about industrialization and capitalism based on the single case of England does not hold because connection between the social order of capitalism and the logic of technological development and modernizing social change has not been established by Western European historians (Ibid., 77). Moreover, it is strange that scholars expect non-European societies to repeat precisely the same history as Europe or England and not ask the question: How was capitalist development ever able to produce industrialization in the first place (Ibid., 83)? Furthermore, why do scholars not ask: What was the role of conjuncture in seventeenth and eighteenth century Europe which may have created conditions for the consolidation of social classes and right to private property; Why did South Asians not resist Europe's efforts in creating capitalist social relations in South Asia; and why were South Asians participating in their own colonization (Ibid., 84)?

With these questions in mind, the problems with the concept of developed/underdeveloped and possible alternatives are addressed in this chapter. One major problem with this conceptual binary distinction is that it is spurious and misleading as it is based on the false Western claim of its "superiority." This claim of "superior" West does not hold, as Washbrook clarifies that many features of Western Modernity were also present in 'post-Bronze Age civilization' across most of 'Eurasia.' For example, rise of a commerce and money-economy, which is considered to be the roots of modern capitalism, already existed in China, India, and the Islamic world. Similarly, a body of evidence shows conclusively that relations of property and class, which were considered the root of modern capitalism, were also prevalent in Asian societies as much as in the West. Furthermore, Washbrook explains, if the philosophical origins of 'science' were thought to lie in the emergence of formal rationality, then Greek logic was part of the Sanskrit and Arabic cultural universe long before it was part of an Anglo Saxon one. If modern society were forged in 'the city,' the quintessentially urban (and urbane) civilizations of Islam and of post-Sung China nurture it substantially ahead of that of the medieval West. In the light of these findings, most of the 'deep' historical and cultural foundations, thought to have underlain the West's distinctive road to Modernity, have come to look very insecure. This, in turn, has begun to make the perspectives of comparative sociology look no less dubious (Washbrook,

1997:414–415; see also Trojanow and Hoskote, 2012).

Recently, a short documentary video[2] has brought to light the existence of many pre-colonial African cities that were built featuring circular and linear design, representing various architectures and including large forts, long solid walls, huge palaces, and more. The documentary also noted that 1500 years ago Ethiopia minted coins using gold and East Africans were making steel. An astronomical observatory constructed in 300 BCE for mapping the stars has been found in Kenya. Of keen interest, the words "primitive" and "backward" do not come to mind while watching this video. In fact, the video includes footage of contemporary visitors from European countries commenting positively on these African architectures. More recently, Clifford Conner investigated the history of the West African city of Kumbi Saleh and illuminated the existence of various other ancient African cities such as Gao, Jenne, and Timbuktu. Most intriguingly, Kumbi Saleh was a thriving city 1000 years ago in the kingdom of Ghana, with a population of 15,000 to 20,000 inhabitants. Neither London nor Paris was anywhere near that size until hundreds of years later (Conner, 2015:131). Moreover, it was the Moors from Africa who ruled over South France, Spain, and Portugal for 700 years from 711 AD. They brought mathematics, art, astrology, and philosophy to Europe when Europe was barbarian. According to Garikai Chengu, Africans experimented with flying before Leonardo da Vinci came up with his flying hanger. In the 1920s, the historian Leo Weiner wrote about Africa's influence in the Americas before the "discovery" of Americas by Europeans (quoted in Chengu, 2017; Chengu, 2015b). Chengu wrote that while Europe was experiencing its Dark Age, which was a long period of intellectual, economic, and cultural backwardness, Africans were experiencing an almost continent-wide renaissance. The leading civilizations of this African rebirth were the Benin Empire, Kingdom of Ghana, and the Mali Empires (Chengu, 2016). The Mali Empire was larger than the Holy Roman Empire (Chengu, 2015b). These examples indicate that the claims of binary distinction related to a "civilized world" do not make any rational sense (Mumford, 1967).

While recognizing the spuriousness of the binary distinction of developed/underdeveloped, we also need to understand the philosophical origin of these dichotomies as well as the recent trichotomies in sociological theories. Therefore, in this chapter, after the discussion on the origin of dichotomies, the issue of spuriousness will be discussed with the following questions in mind: How has the idea of European superiority evolved? How has the binary of developed/underdeveloped emerged, and evolved, and how has it been reproduced over time? How is the phenomenon of underdevelopment explained with a Western yardstick of "prerequisites for industrialization?" After examining this Western yardstick along with various challenges to modernity, an alternative question is suggested that might open a different direction and space which could help erase this misleading binary.

DICHOTOMIES AND TRICHOTOMIES IN SOCIOLOGICAL THEORIES

Classical Western theories consider societies, existing before and after 1800, to be a series of dichotomies with each having a unitary and systematic character. For example, Saint Simon suggested that societies moved from a feudal to industrial form.

According to Comte, societies moved from a metaphysical to scientific stage. Spencer explained the movement from militant to industrialized societies. For Smith and Marx, the passage was from feudalism to capitalism. Durkheim suggested that societies moved from mechanical to organic forms of division of labor. Weber did not dichotomize, as he saw history as a singular rationalization process (Mann, 1993). Parson's (1950) fourfold dichotomy focused on interpersonal relations, and it was suggested that in pre-industrial societies interpersonal relationships were dominated by the following characteristics: particularistic, ascriptive, affective (emotion laden), and specific to a particular relationship. In industrial societies, these relations shifted to become universalistic, achievement oriented, instrumental, affectively neutral, and diffused across most relations (Ibid.).

Foucault reintroduced the distinction between the classical age and that of the bourgeoisie with the suggestion that each had its own "episteme," or "discursive formation" of knowledge and power. Giddens developed, based on Foucault's ideas, a distinction between the pre-modern and modern nation-state. In the late twentieth century, these binary distinctions shifted into trichotomies with the addition of a "post" classification. However, all of these distinctions suggest two transitions—from feudal to industrial to post-industrial; from feudal to capitalist to monopoly to disorganized post capitalist; and from pre-modern to modern to post-modern (Ibid., 12).

The assumption of these dichotomies and trichotomies is that there was a qualitative transformation of society as a whole, and it was in economic revolution. The key difference among them is in the essence of the new economy as either industrialist or capitalist. In general, these dichotomies and trichotomies seem to overlook the fact that capitalism and industrialization were two different processes that occurred at different times in so-called advanced countries (Ibid.). For example, Britain was capitalist before its Industrial Revolution. Interestingly, many current historians treat the First Industrial Revolution (circa 1760–1830) and Second Industrial Revolution (1880–1914) as two separate processes by downplaying the impact of the First Industrial Revolution while emphasizing the impact of the Second Industrial Revolution (Ibid.). Dichotomous theories came into being around 1880 when a single civilization (European) began to dominate the world through violence with the use of a massive military. Europeans considered this domination to be "progressive" and "modernizing" (Ibid., 14). However, as Mann has pointed out, this progress and modernization did not revolutionize the distributive power of the people. For example, in Great Britain the distributive power that came into existence in 1700 remained the same in 1914, even as it does today (Ibid., 15).

In the nineteenth century, the introduction of the idea of "equality of citizens" in the industrial world did not increase the power of the common man either, as it was limited by the creation of legal categories of distinction and new theoretical ideas. Of course, there existed in pre-industrial societies various types of distinctions based on class, race, and gender however, with the creation of the concept of citizen, who has "equal" rights, the anxiety of knowing, who is included in this "all" who have equal rights, increased (Wallerstein, 2011). Thus, on one hand equality was proclaimed as a moral principal, and on the other hand more obstacles were instituted to prevent their realization through juridical, political, economic, and cultural institutions (Ibid.) while creating various binary distinctions. Thus, the concept of citizen helped in the "crystallization and rigidification" of the long list of binary distinctions–bourgeoisie and proletarian, man and woman, adult and minor, breadwinner and housewife, majority and minority, white and black, European and non-European, educated and ignorant, skilled and unskilled, scientist and layman, specialist and amateur, high culture and low culture, heterosexual and homosexual, normal and abnormal, able bodied and disabled—both legally and intellectually. All these categories imply the former as civilized, and later as barbarian. These distinctions then came to form the cultural basis of the capitalist world economy in the nineteenth and twentieth centuries (Ibid., 147).

(It should be noted that a similar process followed in the formation of the concept of race within the US. The idea of race was fleshed out only when Blacks in the US were emancipated after the American Civil War, and suddenly it became important to understand what race meant. At the same time, various laws—Black codes, Jim Crow laws, and scientific racism—were created so that Blacks could not exercise their freedom.)

EVOLUTION OF THE IDEA OF EUROPEAN SUPERIORITY

Eurocentric beliefs such as "the West is the maker of history," "everything diffused from Europe," and "non-European societies are only recipients and not makers of history," were used to justify the looting and colonization of the Americas. Later, the same ideas were extended to justify the colonization of Asia, Africa, South Asia, and the Middle East. Even though these beliefs emerged from earlier conceptions of Christendom and the Roman imperial legacy, their present full form was developed in the nineteenth century (Blaut, 1993:18). In the formation of these beliefs, as Samir Amin pointed out, two simultaneous historical processes—the crystallization of the concept of Europe and Europe's conquest of the world—gave rise to the Eurocentric episteme which emphasized only the crystallization of European society, while ignoring Europe's conquest of the world (Amin, 2009). English and European empire builders deliberately used Eurocentric episteme to develop contradictory and convoluted arguments because they could not otherwise justify their unilateral, uninvited, and unprovoked invasions of cultures thousands of miles away in the name of self-defense. They needed to convince themselves that they were superior using the following narrative:

> Europeans … come through an extremely difficult and perilous time of troubles … they been challenged by Islamic and other non-believers … They had also been tested in horrendous trials by disease and other disasters. But they had survived … The faithful had survived and were moving toward the assertion of their superiority … and [thus] justified the imposition of imperial power on that basis (Williams, 1980:28–29).

The English elite also realized that in order to maintain their power to rule, they needed to adopt policies of freedom, prosperity, and social peace at home, while adopting expansionist policies abroad. In order to justify expansionist policies, the argument of "superior West and inferior rest" became a useful tool (Ibid.). However, to realize their imperial dream, British and European elites had to also convince the conservative segment of their societies to accept a new outlook; that "progress is inevitable, natural, and desirable." Therefore, these ideas were formulated in religious terms as follows: "European history was guided by God, and progressive innovation was a product of European mind and spirit, and thus ultimately products of Christian soul" (Blaut, 19). With this formulation, the concepts of inside/outside, and progress were created, which also prepared the common people to accept the upcoming, painful changes later imposed on them.

During the seventeenth century, in the debate about the humanity of Native Americans (Indians), which ensued with the Spanish invasion of the New World, the concept of "outsider as inferior" became useful to justify the invasion and taking over the land, labor, and products of the American Indians and African slaves without "guilt." By the eighteenth century, the reference of God and scriptures was eliminated from the justification for imperialist action. However, elites could not apply the concept of "outsider" to the Ottoman Empire at that time, as it was a formidable force and was expanding its territories in Southeast Europe while the Iberians were conquering the New World. Instead, the rest of the world was seen as lacking in rationality (Christianity) and therefore not "progressing," which was meant as lacking in freedom (Ibid.). However, after India, Southeast Asia, interior Africa, and China were colonized during the nineteenth century, the inhabitants were all considered "outsiders" and thus inferior.

Indian sociologist Sujata Patel pointed out that the binary distinction of insider/outsider was incorporated into the theory of Eurocentrism and was based on two narratives: One, the superiority of Western civilization (progress and reason) and two, a belief in the continuous growth of capitalism through modernization, development, and the creation of new markets. According to this ethnocentric theory the growth of Europe was assessed in terms of itself, while the rest of the world was considered an object to control, even though, as Patel pointed out, Europe itself had and did become modern through the control of its colonies. It must be noted that the assumptions of this ethnocentric theory also framed the ideas of many Western philosophers and thinkers, including Hegel, Kant, Durkheim, Weber, and Marx (Patel, 2016).

In the late nineteenth century, colonial agriculture was developing considerably, however, more efforts were increasingly being made worldwide in the mining of non-precious metal (Blaut, 1993). In this new context of increased wealth for colonialists, it became necessary to present a revised theory of progress which became known as the "diffusionism" model. According to this version, as Blaut explained, it was God's plan that Europe became a core society as it generates internally continuous progress, and that culture was a product of evolution from the very primitive beginning of the Stone Age. Believing in this new claim, Christian missionaries increased their efforts to gather information about the ethnography and geography of the colonized people with great zeal. Based on the information provided by missionaries, which is distorted by colonial interests, new theories were constructed in the nineteenth century that helped to strengthen the doctrine that European colonization was "scientifically natural, a matter of inevitable working out of social laws of human progress" (Ibid., 24). These ideas and doctrines were legitimized by lawyers, administrators, intellectuals, European colonial capitalists, and colonial officials. Their collective actions contributed to the creation of a legal basis for expropriating the land from colonized people by using the fictional notion that the colonized had no concept of land property rights. With this doctrine, legitimized by legal fiction, it became possible to gain the support of the European population for colonizing other countries. Blaut pointed out that Marx also accepted these ideas as Marx's theories about the evolution of "private property and the origin of capitalism" are based on the assumption that they were peculiar to European phenomena (Ibid., 25).

By the early twentieth century, spatial expansion was complete as the entire non-European world was divided among European colonialists who justified their colonization of other countries with so-called "scientific" proof of genetic and anthropological racism. However, the colonialists faced a new problem as the active resistance of the colonized people made it difficult for them to maintain exploitative control of certain territories. After World War II, when many of these colonies became independent, the old doctrines and ideas were given new identities under the labels of "modernization" and "development" (Ibid., 28). However, this definition of the new terminology conveniently overlooked the intense interaction between European and non-European societies after 1492, as if colonialism had not been important for Europe's modernization (Ibid.).

EMERGENCE OF THE BINARY CONCEPT OF DEVELOPED AND UNDERDEVELOPED

Following World War II, North America took over the torch of imperialism and the idea of "progress" while viewing itself as an agent of God's will and purpose. Godliness in America was equated with individual or collective success on earth. Their belief was that North Americans had discovered the ultimate solution for the proper way to organize society. Based on these assumptions, as Williams pointed out, they judged other people as "agents of the devil" if they refused to "open their minds to the idea of improvement [as defined by America]" (Williams, 1980:52). Using this false logic, Americans began to believe that it was their duty to deal with such people by force. Another justification for using force against people who did not agree with their ideas was that:

> Americans considered themselves perpetually beleaguered, an attitude that led on to the conviction that military security was initially to be found in controlling the entire continent—and ultimately prompted them to deny any distinction between domestic and foreign policy (Ibid., 53).

As Benjamin Franklin warned in 1760, "It [attitude] is leaving no medium between Safety and Conquest" (quoted in Ibid., 54). (It should be noted that this attitude continues even today as America keeps intervening—regime changing, bombing and droning—in other countries in the name of threat to America's security.)

The "development age" was inaugurated when the US took over the leadership role believing in its mission to spread its version of progress in the world (Rist, 1997:71). Consequently, international relations and modernization were conceived in a new way. Modernization meant the development of a modern economy, a modern public administration, and a modern technical infrastructure. All these developments generated wealth for the colonizers, and it is no wonder that modernization became their mission (Rist, 1997). However, this mission was presented as an act of benevolence and fairness as President Truman offered in his Point Four program:

> We must embark on a bold new program for making the benefits of our scientific advances and industrial progress available for the improvement and growth of underdeveloped areas ... in cooperation with other nations, we should foster capital investment in areas needing development ... The old imperialism—exploitation for foreign profit—has no place in our plans. What we envisage is a program of development based on the concepts of democratic fair-dealing (Ibid., 71).

Truman's Point Four program conceptualized almost all areas outside of the Atlantic Alliance as "backward" including Japan, and they were declared as in need of technological and psychiatric assistance to bring them into modern world. Rist observed that this Point Four program created both a new world view and a new adjective —"underdeveloped"—that was synonymous with economically backward. The "development" that was earlier presented as something intransitive that simply happened, now took on a transitive meaning (an action performed by an agent upon another) while "underdevelopment" became a "naturally occurring" (causeless) state of things (Ibid., 73). It should be pointed out that Indian nationalist leaders had developed the Drain Theory during the 1890s to explain how the British colonial government drained India's resources and made it poor. Such ideas had no place in Truman's concept of "underdeveloped."

Instead, the earlier connection of colonizer and colonized opposition was now replaced with a "developed/underdeveloped" dichotomy with a supposed (not real) *de jure* equality. This contradictory situation was presented in terms of a single family consisting of all societies in which some members were lagging behind. However, it was also assumed that these "lagging" societies would "catch up" as long as they played by the rules of the game. According to this assumption, underdevelopment was just an incomplete development and not an opposite of development, therefore, it will only go in the direction of development because it was, what Rist called, an "internal self-generated self-dynamizing phenomenon" (Ibid., 74). By treating each country as formally "equal"(3) and as an autonomous individual nation (as if there was no prior history of interaction among various countries/societies contributing to the making of the present state of affairs), the Western ideologies of "equal opportunities" and the "self-made man" were now transferred to underdeveloped countries. According to this ideology, through hard work and perseverance, any one (or any country) could move ahead: for example, a worker could become boss (or a poor "undeveloped" society could become a rich "developed" society). It implies that if a country remains poor, it must be that country's own fault for not pursuing these development goals and techniques. This is similar to the idea that individual success depends on hard work and perseverance, and that failure is the individual's fault.

However, the Indian economist, Kalyan Sanyal, has pointed out that this discourse of development emerged at a particular historical conjunction during the 1950s when Western powers were seriously concerned about the spread of communism. He substantiated his statement based on a 1949 Report by a committee headed by H. Rowan Gaither, which was given the task to assess what the Ford Foundation could do in the interest of the underdeveloped regions of the world. Sanyal observed that this committee had a deep concern about the possibility of another world war due to widespread poverty and deprivation in underdeveloped regions. Based on that concern, the committee suggested that the US must work to eradicate this poverty(4).

Sanyal noted that this element in the report was an "overt admission that development of the third world was due to the urgency to launch a battle against communism and establish political control over the newly decolonized countries" (Sanyal, 2014:129). Interestingly, while "development" was a political project, its aim was to totally depoliticize the process by making it purely the job of technology, experts, and professionals. This depoliticization, according to Sanyal, was useful in distinguishing the historicist term "transition from the capitalist industrialization" and thus changed the narrative away from "transition to communism" (Ibid., 131).

However, suggestions to check the spreading of communism were made even before the Gaither Report of 1949. Rosenstein-Rodan's seminal article in 1943 proposed the idea of industrialization as a check on the spreading of communism. According to the article, industrialization would be fundamentally different from the Soviet model of self-sufficient, heavy-industry oriented growth, because it would integrate the Eastern European economy into the global capitalist order dominated by the US (Ibid., 133).

Moreover, the idea of dismantling the earlier colonial empire fit nicely into the interests of North America, as it was eager to gain access to new markets through development programs and to stop the spread of communism. The binary distinction of developed/underdeveloped became useful as it maintained the gap between different parts of the world. It also justified the necessity of intervention in these countries on the grounds that "one cannot remain passive when one is confronted with extreme need" for resources (Rist, 2008:76). Making resources available would enable these societies to help themselves, and thus, everyone would emerge richer and more prosperous. According to this model, the prosperity and happiness of a society was possible only by increased production (development), and not through endless debates about the organization of society, or the ownership of means of production or the role of the state. In this way, development was presented as a set of technical measures outside the realm of political debate, while underdevelopment was defined as a "lack" that could only be improved with development policies of aid and growth (Ibid., 79). With this new standard set by the US, as it stood on the top at that time, Rist explains, it became impossible to question the concept and project of development.

This new distinction of developed/underdeveloped changed the course of world history in the mid-twentieth century as the US began to establish its hegemony worldwide. At the same time, as Rist pointed out, more than two billion inhabitants of the planet suddenly found, from 1948 onward, that their societies were now officially "underdeveloped," and that they were expected to disown their own values and further increase the Westernization of their lives and society at large. According to Rist, many former colonies, who were never treated respectfully with equality and denied a chance to prosper, found the new status of "underdeveloped" useful, as it gave them a legal status of "equality" with the colonizer along with the respectability, and a chance of attaining possible prosperity. However, they had to pay the price for this legal equality by sacrificing their identity and their economic autonomy, as they had to travel the "development path" that others had worked out for them (Ibid., 79).

UNO played an important part in establishing US hegemony by launching programs in underdeveloped countries. In addition, the US used bilateral agreements as well as "economic hit men" (Perkins, 2004) to bring more regions of the world under its hegemony. Moreover, the modernization project was intensified in order to prevent newly independent societies from joining the Soviet Union or communist China. Similarly, the US increased its investment in Latin America when Cuba underwent a successful revolution (Rist, 1997). Over time, when certain countries tried to break away from US dominance they faced dire consequences. For example, in the second decade of the twenty first century, Gadhafi in Libya attempted to build up the African Union and break away from US dollar hegemony. He was overthrown and killed with the help of NATO and other Western allies, and Libya was left in shambles. More recently, Venezuela, Iran, China and Russia are also attempting to break out of the dollar exchange system and the US has already targeted Venezuela for regime change, imposed more sanctions against Russia and Iran (while also pulling out of the nuclear agreement), and China is facing a tariff war. In the twenty first century, the US has been trying hard to maintain its hegemony and dominance in the world through various free trade agreements, numerous wars and increased military bases worldwide, and also by promoting so called development projects[(5)].

SHIFTING TERMINOLOGY AND IMPACT ON ACADEMIA

Around 1960, W. W. Rostow began promoting the binary distinction of development/underdevelopment in his theory of "modernization"—creating hope for every country to share in the promise of abundance [(6)]. This reassuring promise encouraged the Western world to continue to generate aid, not in the name of "civilization" but in the more ancient belief in "growth." Rulers of both the North and South acted as if growth meant compound interest, and as if it was true, desirable, possible and achievable goal (Rist, 1997). In the North, development was seen as gradual unfolding of a flower from a bud, or as a mental and physical development of a child. A similar image with substituted local words was promoted in the South (Rehnema, 2005:71).

However, in the 1970s a challenge emerged from the Dependency school of thought that blamed the industrialized nations for creating poverty in the South through dependent relations. To scuttle this claim, a proclamation from the New International Economic Order (NIEO) renewed the hope of reducing inequalities between nations by providing "basic needs" to those countries that had the least resources. This proclamation, as Rist explained, made development seem more durable and humane. However, with increased debt problems and environmental crises, the facade of durability and humaneness did not last long.

In the face of each new crisis, relevant terminology and meaning shifted once again so that the illusionary promise of material prosperity remained intact. Eventually the concept of underdevelopment was transformed into "underdeveloped countries" and again into "developing countries" (Ibid.). Like all magic words, no one knows exactly what "development" means (Ibid., 242). These terminological shifts and subsequent illusions of prosperity, Rist observed, were no different than,

> Those who think that illness is due to a sin against God or one's ancestors—and so considers forgiveness the first step to a cure—and the economists who identifies unemployment with weak demand and looks to renewed growth (and consumption) as the solution. In both cases, there is a premise which grounds the initial belief and determines the answer to the question posed. The believability structure necessarily confirms the

> belief as that which cannot be refuted, no one could prove that God does not exist (Rist, 1977:239).

This whole exercise of shifts in terminology was meant to keep a belief system intact by providing a few miracles (as happens in every religion) such as with the cases of the development of the Four Asian Tigers. Even the report of failures in many cases of development did not change the belief system, as these failures were presented as a triumph for "cultural diversity." Rist pointed out that this belief system in development is no different than an experiment involving religious devotees, who rationalize and convince themselves when faced by reality contradicting the faith, that they probably miscalculated (Ibid., 240).

The influence of the "development age" has also impacted the academic area studies that further reinforced this binary distinction. For example, in the 1970s the field of International Studies was renamed Global Studies which helped reinforce the concept of North/South and Right/Left division. Thus, the Western binary distinction has remained intact in one form or another despite ever-changing situations. The noun "underdevelopment" was introduced and altered the meaning of "development" in a new way. In the 1980s, the term "backward" transitioned from "underdeveloped" to "developing" and later, morphed into "newly industrializing" before becoming "emerging markets." In spite of changes in terminology, the assumptions of developmental trajectory (technological and cultural changes) remained based on Western experiences (Abu-Lughod, 2004). Terminology changes have been reflected in North American academia where Non-Western became "Non-Aligned nations" and then to "third world" area studies. Area studies came into being during the Cold War period when certain countries were trying to chart a different economic path through the formation of the Non-Aligned movement (NAM) (Ibid.). With the formation of NAM, the idea that development is necessary and that it should take place within the perspective of integration into the world economy, gained strength within the Western world (Rist, 1997:85). It also hastened the advent of international institutions like the World Bank and the International Monetary Fund to promote the development model of the industrialized (mainly US) countries. Thus, the "third world" became the ideological battleground of the major powers, and many new states benefited from the support of their powerful protectors. No wonder, as Rist pointed out, that the most important issue in the UNO during this period was development (Ibid.).

In the case of South Asia, the Massachusetts Institute of Technology (MIT) in the US played an important role through its Center for International Studies established in 1951 (Sanyal, 2014:157). Economists at MIT focused on South Asia, specifically on India and Pakistan, to find prospects for development in this region. MIT sought funding from the Ford Foundation for development projects after receiving initial funding from the US government. MIT's association with the Ford Foundation spurred its involvement in the Indian Planning Commission. The Ford Foundation also funded new research institutions in India: The Institute of Economic Growth in Delhi, Delhi School of Economics, Gokhale Institute of Politics and Economics in Pune, and interacted closely with the Indian Statistical Institute in Calcutta (Ibid.). These Indian institutions were then integrated into the network of Western institutions with the help of the Ford Foundation. This network of institutions started producing experts who became advisors on the question of development. These "development professionals" then guided Indian planning. To achieve the goal of integrating Indian institutions with the network of Western institutions, it was necessary to persuade Indian universities to adopt "a new vision of economics grounded in mathematical techniques, statistical calculations, and econometric tests" (Ibid., 158). This integration process ensured that development projects would proceed as intended according to Western conceptions. A similar process was followed in other newly independent colonies. In light of this, it is no surprise that Indian experts within the Indian government and other Indian academic institutions accept without questioning Western ideas of development projects.

In the area of social sciences, according to Patel, Indian academia ended up with a methodological binary that was institutionalized within the Eurocentric position, even though Indian social scientists wanted to break away from colonial or neocolonial tutelage. This problem arose, as Patel points out, due to the close functional relationship of Indian social scientists with the higher education policies of the Indian government. This relationship intertwined the project of knowledge creation and nationhood and thus, Indian social scientists remained tied up with policy orientation that was based on the Eurocentric Orientalist perspective [(7)].

In recent years, the Eurocentric perspective has come under attack by various Indian scholars and religious groups. This challenge came with a new perspective of indigenization, known as Indian ethnosociology, which, as Patel explained, essentializes Hindu traditions, while demanding that these values become the basis for creating new epistemologies. Moreover, ethnosociology has become "identified with the Hindu right and other related identity movements that are redefining nation and nationhood in religious and chauvinist terms" (Patel, 2016:38). (As I discussed in the introductory chapter, it is within this context that we need to understand the recent conflicts in India between the promoters of science—rationalist movement—who are waging a war against "superstitions," and the right-wing Hindutva forces and other identity movements.) However, the leaders of Hindutva forces (extreme right-wing fundamentalists), who came to power in 2014 and retained it in 2019, in addition to promoting indigenization, are also promoting development projects with full force—as did the Congress party (secular) when it was in power. It seems that the challenge of the academic and religious group to Eurocentric perspectives also did not make any difference in halting the project of development in India.

EVOLUTION OF THE CONCEPT OF DEVELOPMENT AND UNDERDEVELOPMENT

It is interesting to note that the US preferred to use the term "development" (as in achieving human welfare) to improve the conditions of former colonies instead of the term "civilization" (which was used until the end of World War II) or "Westernization," or "modernization," or even the military term "liberation." The term "development" was useful because "it already enjoyed a certain respectability within scientific discourse and it linked up with a tradition of thought which underwrote its legitimacy" (Rist, 1997:26). For example, one can grasp the concept of development as it relates to a child or a plant. That development entails, as Rist explains, directionality, continuity, moving from a lower to higher stage, and irreversibility. Therefore, taking this metaphor from a natural world and applying it to the social world can make social phenomena look natural, which in turn makes the idea of naturalized history possible (Ibid.).

Rist also observed that the concept of development (which can be traced back to early Roman times and to the ideas of Christianity) connotes both a belief (gradually constructed) and a series of practices forming a single whole, even though there are contradictions between them (Ibid.). In spite of contradictions, the concept of development gained ground when it was connected with the earlier doctrine of social evolution which was firmly rooted in popular imagination by the nineteenth century. Even though scholars had different ideas about the stages of social evolution, they generally agreed on three essential points: "Progress has the same substance (or nature) as history; that all nations travel the same road; and that all do not advance at the same speed as Western society, which therefore has an indisputable 'lead' because of the greater size of its production, the dominant role that reason plays within it, and the scale of its scientific and technological discoveries" (Ibid., 40). In other words, the "superiority of the West" lies above other societies.

This theory of "social evolutionism" also provided a philosophy of history in which "events follow one another according to a predetermined finality" (Ibid., 42). The concept of social evolutionism, which was closer to Darwinism, gained scientific acceptance. However, politically social evolutionism helped legitimize the new wave of colonization of Africa, Madagascar, and Indochina, and destruction of their culture, under the pretext of a "generous" undertaking to help "backward" societies to the road to "civilization" (Ibid., 43). At the same time, the destruction of colonized people's cultures was justified with the rationale as having predetermined fate (US idea of manifest destiny), and as "inevitable development" in the larger Western epic story.

Thus, a new linear reading of world history was created with new episteme and new values. In this new history of humankind, every nation (including ex colonies) was to have progressive access to the benefits of development. Development would be extended to the whole planet through endless growth (Ibid.). The promoters of Western development assumed that everyone would accept these goals, and, as Rist has pointed out, they ignored the fact that development discourse was built into the relationship of power that left no one any choice to do otherwise. They also ignored the fact that other cultures imagined the idea of "the good life" (development) differently. For these cultures, it is often the distribution of wealth and not the accumulation of wealth—as in the Western world—that helps define a good life.

In modern times, the shared belief in the concept of development—technological progress will solve problems—was promoted by the pronouncements of the economic experts using data and progress indicators, and opinion polls. This belief in technological progress is further strengthened through signs (new school opening, new dam constructed) and rituals (similar to religious practices), and through fairs and exhibitions of every kinds. However, any contradiction that inevitably emerges in this process is ignored, attributed to faulty interpretations, or to human failings or lack of information, while the belief in development is kept intact, as it is considered irrefutable (Ibid.).

Similar theories are employed to reinforce the myth of Europe's historical and cultural "superiority" (Ibid., 45). All scholarships are rooted in the belief of the "European miracle," and these statements about empirical reality are accepted as truths. The basic idea inherent in different models of core/periphery, that the "world has center and outside," is gradually changing into one in which the world is divided into zones, each representing a different level of "modernity, civilization, or development" (Blaut: 26). In the second decade of the twenty-first century, these terminologies remain in vogue in government policy decisions, and among many historians, sociologists, and other intellectuals dealing with global inequalities.

REASONS FOR THE PERSISTENCE OF THIS BINARY DISTINCTION

This conceptual binary distinction persists in our time because the issue of global inequality has been focused on only one question: Why was England industrialized first? This question is embedded in the Western dichotomy of "progress vs backwardness." It is not surprising that the question has been answered primarily in two ways: First, some scholars from former colonies have taken a defensive approach, and tried to prove that their societies were already on the way to industrialization before their colonization. Others have claimed that India's backwardness was due to colonial rule that drained her resources (Ranade, 1899). Additionally, challengers to the theory of modernization (Wallerstein, 1974; Frank, 1967; Harris, 1998; Amin, 1990, Rodney, 1983) have shown—based on the premises of developed/underdeveloped, and core/periphery—how backwardness is perpetuated through dependent relationship, and through the incorporation of these societies into the world economic system. Second, some scholars have defended colonialism and the "superiority" of westernization (Rostow, 1960; Landes, 1969; Landes, 1998), blaming the "cultural backwardness" of societies like India and China for not being the first in industrialization. They have ignored and undermined the technological accomplishments and industrial growth in China, India, and the Islamic world that were achieved long before European advancements and how Europeans actually learned from these earlier technological accomplishments (Conner, 2005; Hobson, 2004; Needham, 1996; Goody, 1996).

However, all scholars, whether for or against modernization theory, use the same binary distinction of developed/underdeveloped to explain their arguments. Their questions and answers remain Eurocentric, which circumvents the possibility of an alternative perspective, even when some scholars claim to be doing precisely that—generating an alternative vision. The recent work of Hobson (Hobson, 2004) is persuasive, however, even when he claims that he is not creating new binary with a China-centered world history, he does not escape it completely.

By accepting these binary distinctions as a predetermined fate, scholars have not only abandoned the search for an alternative future, but have also become unwittingly complicit in the promotion of these myths. They have ignored the fact that Western modernity is also based on tradition, ideology, and the myths of Christianity, and like all myths, those of Christianity are also based on trust and shared beliefs (Rist, 1997). Western binaries are based on Christian myths drawn from the story of Genesis. According to this story, in all polarities and opposites (good/evil; modernity/traditional) the second option is always considered absolutely dangerous, and therefore, it must be completely eradicated to restore order and uniformity (Malhotra, 2011:188). Western science and classical Western philosophy emerged from this premise, and scholars studying the West do not question them. It is then no surprise that Western binary distinctions have remained saddled in place and that the question of why, by 1850, Western Europe was the undisputed center of a new global manufacturing order, (Parthasarathi, 2011:1) remains a distinctly valid one for those scholars who wish to understand the increasing inequalities between different societies.

It has been ignored that the concept of development, (and later, that of underdevelopment) was constructed in a particular historical and cultural time—US President Truman introduced it in 1949 with his Point Four program (Rist:70–71). However, as Eric Helleiner has pointed out, the term "underdeveloped" was first used during the July 1944 Bretton Woods Conference in a proposal by the Indian delegation for a very different reason than that attributed to Truman. The Indian delegation employed it "as part of its demand for greater international support for [India's state-led] development goals" (Helleiner, 2015). However, the US at that time chose to oppose the inclusion of this phrase in the IMF's charter. As mentioned earlier, the idea of industrializing poor countries as a way to check the spread of communism was introduced in 1943 in the writings of Rosenstein-Rodan.

One reason among others to ignore historical context could be that the definition of development allows to depict the ideal conditions of social existence in different ways. For some, it may be a subjective feeling of fulfillment and for others it may be a series of operations. This binary also accommodates any new vocabulary that might emerge to challenge it without changing this binary distinction (Rist, 1997:123).

The effort to keep the Western narrative intact is so strong that when another society appropriates the Western binary distinction for its own advantage, these distinctions are immediately reformulated and reproduced in a new garb. For example, the Chinese Cultural Revolution and other movements within the "third world" demanded and built their own discourse based on the principle that it was necessary to act upon the causes of underdevelopment and not just minimize its effects (Ibid., 140). To achieve their goal, they created the Non-Aligned Movement (NAM) of "third world" countries. Unsurprisingly, this new group was not acceptable to the West (as the twenty-first century the BRICS organization is also not acceptable to the US), and not long after, a Western ecological movement emerged in the US that was headed initially by elite individuals who belonged to country clubs and who wanted to preserve land for fishing, hunting, and bird watching [(8)]. This ecological movement to "save the planet" was created at a time when Western corporations were moving their production into the low-wage regions of the world, which led to the deindustrialization of developed countries, (Rist, 1997) and increased pollution in the newly industrialized countries. Furthermore, during the world-wide oil crisis in the early 1970s, UNO joined in by declaring a second development strategy called Collective Self-Reliance [CSR] (Ibid., 143), intended to achieve peace and security in the world, which, according to the UNO's claim, would help poor countries "catch up" with the rich. The third world countries trying to "catch up" or identify the causes of their "underdevelopment" were soon divided into three groups: the ultra-rich countries with oil and rent money, the Least Developed Countries (LDC) that were sunk deeper in poverty, and the newly industrialized countries (NIC). This fragmentation, according to Rist, not only destroyed NAM, but also provided an opportunity to the industrial countries searching for new areas of investment with petrodollars to negotiate separately with each one of them, and to keep promoting the "development" agenda while reinforcing Western binary distinctions (Ibid., 153).

Western banks offered loans to poor countries on a large-scale (poor countries had no hold over any non-commodity money), which later led to a financial crisis and an economic restructuring of the Global South (Rist, 1997). In this context, the role of the World Bank increased as it became eager to intervene at a grass-roots level without ceasing to fund large-scale projects. To implement this new agenda, Rist informs, the idea of "solidarity with the poor" was introduced to justify Northern intervention in the countries of the Global South, and if necessary, sidestep the concerns of local government in these matters. It was further promoted using a slogan addressing "basic human needs" that was supported by the World Bank, ILO, third world Forum, and even by NGOS. All of them united against the third world nationalist bourgeoisies, accusing them of either "making off with the fruits of development or as refusing to comply with the funder's injunctions" (Ibid., 165).

In the 1980s, policies of structural adjustments were imposed on the countries of the Global South when they could not repay the loans. These structural adjustment policies were based on the assumption that the government, companies, and individuals of the third world were living beyond their means. Implementation first required adjustment (drastic cuts in social programs and social welfare) and then development. NGOs [(9)], supported by corporate money, played an important role in making people accept these drastic cuts and their catastrophic effects (Rist, 1997). Under the structural adjustment program development issues had been reduced to humanitarian initiatives of UNICEF and NGOs. With the fall of the Berlin Wall and the breakup of the Soviet Union, the ultimate blow was made to "third world-ism." However, the project of development was revived with the formation of the World Commission of Environment and Development (1983), which was concerned with sustainable development to resolve the dilemmas of justice and respect for nature. Since everyone was supposed to be responsible for "sustainable development," that actually meant that no one was (Ibid., 180; see also Edelman and Haugerud, 2005).

From then on, the diplomatic term "sustainable development" became part of the language of every developer as it brought together two opposites—structural development with a human face and humanitarian intervention (Ibid.). With the aid of this new terminology, an international division of the environment was created by allowing certain polluting industries to transfer their toxic waste more easily to regions that were relatively free of environment nuisance. To implement this new agenda, an international bureaucratic structure was built that tightly controlled the policies of dominated countries while imposing a program of structural adjustments on them (Ibid.). Before long, the United National Development Program [UNDP] came up with updated terminology, including, "human development," "human liberty," and the "global village," creating an illusion that something new was happening (Ibid., 205). People gave different meaning to these terms and used them at cross purposes, which, explained Rist, allowed everyone a good reason for continuing with their activities as usual, while maintaining the illusion of "change."

For example, "development" has now become a sector of economic activity such as tourism, computing, or consultancy. Many organizations—like UNICEF, FAO,

WHO, UNESCO, and ILO—are managing "development programs." NGOs are doing their part through "humanitarian aid" which allow them to redefine and reorganize the concepts of spaces and values, thus, preparing the ground for the globalizing forces of neoliberalism. These forces are stripping states in the Global South of their control of power by intervening and destabilizing the state. Thus, as Petras pointed out, the global implementation of neo-liberalism has diminished the power of the state with regard to its effective redistributing function and the power to maintain public order, which has resulted in increased pauperization and subsequent violence (Petras, 2017). NGOs have begun to take on the role played by the state as a part of the neoliberalism movement, and it is not a coincidence that NGOs numbers have increased with the expansion of neoliberalism worldwide. NGOs help soften the negative effects of neoliberalism by stepping up so-called "humanitarian" efforts (Gurcan 2015; Welch, Feldman and Morningstar, 2018). The case of Bangladesh is a good example with decades of NGO involvement and "pro-poor" microcredit operations. Today in rural Bangladesh, 56 percent of households are landless, and those who can be categorized as 'resource poor' consist of 82 percent of the rural population (Ibid.). NGOs, while doing the bidding of multinational corporations (MNC)s, have sabotaged peoples' movements that might have emerged in their absence. Godrej quoting from Arundhati Roy writes, "Armed with their billions, these NGOs have waded into the world, turning potential revolutionaries into salaried activists, funding artists, intellectuals and filmmakers, gently luring them away from radical confrontation" (Roy, 2014 quoted in Godrej, 2012:13). No wonder feminist movements in Africa are also now NGO-ized making them ineffective (Bah and Anumo, 2017).

Thus, by changing terminology and reformulating the concept of development, the conceptual binary distinction is kept intact. In this effort the role of scholars and policy makers is no less important, as they keep using the Western yardstick of prerequisites for industrialization to analyze "progress" in poor countries. These scholars and policy makers also ignore that this standard yardstick of prerequisites has been refuted many times. This deliberate ignoring requires showing a bright light on this ignoring with a fresh refutation of this yardstick of prerequisites.

MYTHS OF "PREREQUISITES" FOR INDUSTRIALIZATION

Many historians now recognize that industrialization was "a complex amalgamation of foreign and indigenous knowledge, techniques, and institutions ... essential for the exercise and consolidation of state power" (Parthasarathi, 2011:223–224). In spite of this consensus, the industrialization debate remains focused on its prerequisites and its related binaries (development/underdevelopment, modern/traditional, and progressive/backward). The debate about prerequisites revolves around concepts of "proto-industrialization," the "spirit of entrepreneurship," rationality, science, innovations, and technological advancements.

As it is pointed out in the following discussion, these concepts are not very useful for explaining many of the complex social conditions that prevailed under Imperial Russia, colonial India, in Belgium, or in Germany. Some of these societies were industrialized in the absence of all the classical "prerequisites." This contradiction between historical realities and the industrialization debate requires some rethinking and re-explaining.

a. "Proto-industrialization": An Inadequate Concept

Proto-industrialization refers to the following conditions of a region as being on its way to industrialization: if it is integrated with distant markets; if it has developed small-scale production (within rural households) commodities; and if it has wage labor available (Ågren, 1998). However, as Ågren pointed out, this definition excludes many types of production, including commodity production by urban craftsmen, agricultural production by rural households, and large-scale commodity production in factories. Additionally, the definition excludes production based on non-domestic organizations, such as the mines, mills, forges, and furnaces that existed within the agrarian economy. Moreover, based on this definition, she pointed out that London, the single largest industrial district in Britain, would not be considered a case of proto-industrialization (Ibid.).

A study of the iron industry in Russia and Sweden shows there is no evidence that proto-industrial regions were most successfully industrialized, or that such activities appeared solely in regions where pastoral farming and inheritance predominated (Ibid.). Similarly, there is no clear and simple connection between proto-industry on one hand, and demographic expansion and social stratification on the other. In the case of the iron industry in Russia, according to Ågren, there were no actual borders between domestic commodity production, larger production units, and urban commodity production (Ibid.).

The discourse on proto-industrialization does not explain the role and structure of the market in understanding the process of industrialization. For example, in the late eighteenth century, Swedish and Russian iron masters had to reconsider their choice of products because of changes in the British iron industry, which had started producing coke-based iron. Russian iron masters chose to produce for the growing domestic market, as local peasants bought scythes, spades, padlocks, smith tools, horseshoes, nails, frying pans, roof iron, saws, wire, oven doors and pots. During this process, Russian market became compartmentalized due to higher diversification in which there was no direct competition between different productions. Different items came from different production units, each of which specialized in a certain type of iron commodity (Ibid.).

Moreover, there was "no such thing as a single mode of production for the social organization of proto-industrial iron production, but a number of alternative ways" (Florén, 1994:83). Florén suggested that the dominance of one or another mode of production was dependent on its societal context, and not on the social relations of the rural world. Each mode of organization has its own peculiarities and generates its own contradictions and conflicts. For example, Sweden, Belgium and Russia played an important role in European production of iron in different periods between the sixteenth century to the nineteenth century. Economically and politically they all embodied different types of society. Feudal and Tsarist Russia was characterized by its reinforcement of serfdom parallel to its attempts to westernize, whereas, Sweden had small and weak towns with a traditionally free peasant class. The politically weak and scattered Walloon lands (Belgium) were divided principally between the House of Habsburg and the independent bishopric of Liège. This region was constituted of considerable economic as well as social differences between the urban culture of the north and the more traditional estate economy of the principalities of Namur and Luxembourg (Ibid., 83.).

Florén found that the technical process of large-scale iron production (except for forging) was similar in all parts of early modern Europe, and before the nineteenth century there was rarely any establishment that had a concentration of different stages of production, and integrated systems. The typical proto-industrial iron industry was a spatially disintegrated system due to the need for charcoal and water power. For example, in Sweden and Wallonia, mines furnaces dominated in some regions, while forges dominated in others. However, the units in the Russian Urals were the exception as they were centralized, including furnaces, forges and sometimes manufacturing workshops, as well (Ibid., 84–85). Some of them were of an impressive scale with 30 hammers and 8 furnaces at work. The technical and special aspects of iron production also shaped the organization of the labor process in these three regions. Apparently organization of labor process was similar in these three regions as skilled and professional workers were employed in the furnace and forges, while most of the unskilled labor was employed in the peripheral parts of production, i.e. mining, charcoal burning, and transportation (Ibid., 85). However, Florén pointed out that when viewed in greater detail the differences in the organization of labor process among these three regions were more striking than similarities.

The claim that proto-industrialization contributed to the dissolution of feudalism is also not correct. According to Ågren, large-scale centralized metal production in Russia was not hindered by either feudal or absolutist regimes because it was the state and the landlords who created and actively promoted industries. Many peasants, both serfs and well-to-do entrepreneurs, were running a *kustar* (cottage) industry—a practice widespread and flourishing. It was the same in the metalwork industry, which was large and based on centralized production (Ågren, 1998:18–19). It seems that Ågren's concept of "network of production" is more useful in understanding Russia's diversified economy and the wider regional context of social institutions within which these networks of productions were located.

For example, it was through established rules and practices that people organized their economic, social, demographic, political, and cultural activities, as well as their property rights, community systems, inheritance practices, and the new institutions of the early modern state (Ibid., 17). Similarly, as Ågren has pointed out, regions are both socially and politically constructed because people create these constructs by using certain resources that are to be found within a geographical space. For example, the region of iron production in early modern Sweden was the result of the way work was organized socially. But the demands of the state also affected the social organization of work. In the case of the iron industry, it led to a scattered form of production and several units had to interact by networking. State involvement also influenced the form of social tensions and conflicts that beset early iron production in Russia and Sweden (Ågren, 1998; see also Shaban, 2017).

In the case of the Netherlands, the concept of proto-industrialization seems irrelevant. The Netherlands had all the classical prerequisites: "A large and wealthy bourgeoisie, a singularly high rate of urbanization, a prosperous and relatively efficient agrarian sector, a commercial and financial superstructure that was without peer in Europe, and above all an abundance of capital that dwarfed any other country in Europe including England" (Mokyer, 1976:24). But it was Belgium that did not have any of these advantages, yet it became the most industrialized nation on the European continent—not the Netherlands. The Netherlands became an industrialized economy when, as Bagchi wrote, England made the East Indies and Indonesia available to both the Dutch government and Dutch businessmen for plunder (Bagchi, 2012).

b. The Spirit of Entrepreneurship: An Irrelevant Concept

Another prerequisite for industrialization, the "spirit of entrepreneurship," is based on the assumption that only one group of people is capable of having it. However, an historical account of different societies shows that "no class should be, on a priori grounds defined as incapable of entrepreneurial activity" (Rosovsky, 1954:207). Russian entrepreneurship came from all sections of society—merchants, nobility and serfs—and they were divided in order of rank. In Russia, the form of serfdom varied based on regional geographical conditions. These regional geographical considerations also created different incentives for serfs. For example, the black soil region of Russia, and the Volga region on the eastern steppe did not industrialize where serfs fulfilled their obligations through *barshchina* (labor services). The North Russian region became the main industrial area where serfs practiced *obrok* (quit rent) (Ibid.). In the promotion of serf bourgeoisie, the Russian nobility played a big role as they needed more cash to buy European luxury goods and lifestyle amenities at the beginning of the eighteenth century. Since these nobles were not much interested in entrepreneurship and serfs hated to work in estate factories, a solution was found in the *obrok* system: in exchange for a large obrok payment, the nobility helped the entrepreneurial serfs (Rosovsky, 1954).

These serf entrepreneurs contributed in the promotion of Russia's industrialization and some of them joined the nobility after buying their freedom. For example, Rosovsky informs that in the fourteenth century the Stroganovs (who would become the most prominent salt mine owners), were peasants who by the eighteenth century had achieved titles of nobility. The peasant "putting-out" system for the production of calico and linen was promulgated by those smaller enterprisers still nearer to *Kustar* status. The bigger businessmen did not join in until the early nineteenth century. Russian serfs were also very active in large manufacturing. For example, in the 1830s, the largest manufacturer of hats was a serf resident of Moscow. He was able to buy his freedom from serf status by paying 800,000 rubles to his master (Ibid). One can trace serf-entrepreneurship over the 150 years period and find that many of them were able to circumvent the disadvantage of their birth with imagination and ingenuity. For example, in the 1850s one serf entrepreneur named Ushkov produced and exported chemicals to Europe (requiring a considerable amount of technical know-how, capital, and a large plant) and became what was then the largest enterprise in the country (Ibid., 218). Throughout Russia, Rosovsky informs, many serfs were also involved in money lending and smuggling activities, while many peasants carried on with small trading businesses.

Between 1726–62, more and more items produced by serfs in their homes reached the larger markets of Russia controlled by the merchants. These items included, wool, leather, hemp, lard, iron, and linen, as well as the particularly coarse peasant canvas produced in such centers as Yaroslavl, Vologda, and Kastroma (Rosovky, 1954). These peasant serfs were skillful workers and their production began to influence the larger economy controlled by the merchants. In Moscow, so the account goes, three factory owners were crown peasants and it seems they were paying *obrok* to the crown. Threatened by peasant production, the merchants pressed on the government to issue a series of decree circa 1730–1750s in order to curb economic activities among the peasants. But the laws were not effective, and soon the prohibitions were lifted. In the end, the state decreed that all who desired could open manufacturing establishments, except in two cities: Moscow and St. Petersburg. By the 1770s, most manufacturing establishments enjoyed a situation of comparative freedom (Ibid.).

In addition, a general communal entrepreneurial system prevailed in the *mir* (self-ruled peasant community) however, the inhabitants organized their production differently. They formed a cooperative enterprise under the direction of the *mir*, thereby guaranteeing a more equitable distribution of income. Thus, no richer peasants could exploit others, and at the same time *obrok* payments could be made in an easy and secure way (Ibid.). Moreover, since the ancient times in North Russia, peasants had been engaged in the household industry fulfilling domestic needs. They produced a variety of textiles: yarned cloth, woolens socks, utensils, soap, spirits, sail cloth, and more. In spite of its connection with the market economy, Rosovsky explained, the household industry remained intact until well into the middle of the eighteenth century. The household industry in Russia was connected with agriculture and was organized on a part-time basis under the *barshchina* system (a portion of the products of the industry was frequently given to the landowner as payment in kind).

Similar to Russian society, the "spirit of entrepreneurship" has long been alive and well in India. For example, until the early nineteenth century, there were a large number of merchant entrepreneurs who were well respected by British officials (Raj, 2006; Parthasarathi, 2011). The great King Akbar and other local royalties promoted various industries and manufacturing, the results of which can be witnessed in the country's impressive record of art, architecture, literature, technology, manufacturing and textile. India had a large army of skilled workers in most of its regions and it had been booming early modern (1800–1850) textile-exporting regions: Gujarat, Bengal and South India (Parthasarathi, 2011): Steam engines, rolling mills, and spinning machines were introduced into South India, Bengal, and Bombay in the early years of nineteenth century. Indian workers quickly learned to operate, maintain and even build machines. Indian entrepreneurial ability, knowledge and skill were evident in the Indian Ocean trading system, as Pedro Machado wrote, "Guajarati cloth merchants out compete Portuguese and British traders because of their superior information and better connection to the sources of cloth" (quoted in Ibid., 240). These merchants were able to dominate these markets against European rivals during the early nineteenth century because they had highly efficient and superior networks that enabled them to connect efficiently with both consumer demand and producer centers. An official of the East India Company in Calcutta observed the following in this regard:

> The formerly timid Hindoo now lends money at respondentia on distant voyages, engages in speculations to various parts of the world, and as an underwriter, in the different insurance offices,—erects indigo works in various parts of Bengal, and is just as well acquainted with the principles and British laws respecting commerce as the generality of European merchants, and enjoys moreover two very great advantages over the latter, the first in trading on his own, instead of a borrowed capital, and secondly of living and conducting his business at probably $1/10^{th}$ of the expense of the Europeans (quoted in Ibid.; see also *Parliamentary Debates* 1813).

Asiya Siddiqi concluded from a study of the complex business world of Jamsetjee Jejeebhoy that during the early nineteenth century in western India there was no dearth of financial resources for business enterprise, or for entrepreneurial initiative and skill (cited in Parthasarathi:240). The problem was, as Parthasarathi pointed out, not the lack of capital but the raising of it, a task British firms also confronted. He explains further that the colonial government in India borrowed as much as it needed at 4 percent, a rate increased to 5 percent in 1825 with the onset of the Burmese War and greater government demands for funds (Ibid., 241). Similarly, the high levels of skill and technical abilities of Indian workers in the eighteenth century continued into the early British period. All this information points to the conviction that the idea of India's "underdevelopment" deriving from a "lack of entrepreneurship and shortage of skilled labor and capital" before 1850 is a myth (Ibid., 244).

The above discussion on proto-industrialization and the spirit of entrepreneurship suggests that every society is always in the making; never becoming a finished product. Many ongoing complex social realities of any historical time are created in the same way, and they cannot be reduced into a short list of prerequisites. Moreover, the spirit of entrepreneurship was not confined only to the Western world or to the eighteenth and nineteenth centuries, as is often believed. In our time, the entrepreneurship of poor people in so-called "underdeveloped" regions and immigrant stories of success in every country are very good examples in this regard. In every country, poor people have found a variety of ways to survive using their creativity during good times as well as during times of transition. Since the world-wide recession of 2008, many people have been able to survive by using their creative ideas. Similarly, refugees in Middle-Eastern countries, who have been created by the war games of the super powers of the Western world, are using their inventive minds to find solutions to everyday existential problems. They cannot depend on institutional support, they remain constantly creative and innovative to keep their spirit of entrepreneurship alive. In the late 1990s, when development practitioners realized that the informal sector was going to be present for a long time, they began to paint the informal sector in a positive light as one with "inherent creativity and ingeniousness" (Sanyal, 2014:204). Even the World Bank began to acknowledge that poor Indian women could be good entrepreneurs and that they should be eligible for micro-credit loans to improve their condition. Since then, a large number of poor women have been brought into the global market through the informal sector.

c. Technology and Science Are Not Autonomous Forces in Industrialization

Tools do not invent themselves or reproduce themselves; they can be created only by human beings. We need to explain why certain tools were invented, and we need to recognize by whom they were made, and not simply focus on the invention itself[(10)]. No one society typically creates a new technology all on its own; it is through a complex process of human interaction, diffusion, and expatiation that people are able to create new technology. For example, the claim that "Europeans were more inventive, innovative, rational and they were able to move society forward by inventing new technology"[(11)] is incorrect. Because, one of the most important skills for the Industrial Revolution was iron and steel making, which Europeans learned from the Middle-East and China (Blaut, 1993:111). Conner has further noted that China had developed a method for making steel from cast iron in the second century BCE. This method in due time led to the invention of the Bessemer steel process in England in 1856. For example, William Kelly (who also met Henry Bessemer) of Kentucky brought four Chinese steel experts to Kentucky in 1845 to learn from them the principles of steel production that were used in China for over two thousand years previously (Temple, 1999:49, cited in Conner, 2005:177) [(12)].

Moreover, plows pulled by teams of twenty-four oxen were used in northern India before the time of Christ. As noted earlier, it was Dutch sailors who introduced Chinese plows with moldboards into Holland in the seventeenth century. From Holland it spread to America and France and when English hired Dutch to drain the East Anglian fens and Somerset moors, they brought their Chinese plows with them, later named the 'Rotherham plough.' Thus, these Chinese ploughs spread from England to Scotland (Conner, 2005).

It is through this process of society-to-society interaction that people learn and share ideas as well as technology. All civilizations were inventing new technologies and sharing them around through various types of human interactions over centuries. For example, agricultural techniques passed from farmer to farmer, while other techniques moved through the mainly urban network of trade and transportation, and sometimes moved around with conquests (Blaut, 1993:115). China was an important source for many technical innovations that found their way into Europe and eventually stimulated the Scientific Revolution (Conner, 2005:165). Conner also pointed out, that it was during the T'ang dynasty—seventh century through ninth century CE— that Chinese knowledge was transmitted to the Islamic world through *hu* merchants, who were Persian and Arabic traders traversing the Silk Road between their native lands and China. Similarly, the export of slaves may have played a significant role in the transmission of Chinese knowledge to the Western world (Ibid., 171).

Joseph Needham's work has shown the development of Chinese technology and science in ancient times, which belies the claim of European uniqueness to their inceptions (Needham, 1996; Blaut, 1993:116). European technology acquired an edge over others only after 1492, which had revolutionary consequences. However, we need to explain why and how this happened rather than assume that Europeans gained this edge because they were "superior." As shall be discussed in Chapter 2, all human beings are born with the same innate capacity for creativity and no one is superior or inferior in that sense.

Critics who argue that China stopped advancement because it was not rational, and did not engender private property rights, typically fail to ask an important question: Why and how did Chinese advances happen? — not how and why they stopped happening (if, indeed, they stopped) (Blaut, 1993)? They do not explain how China came to be such a technologically innovative society that it outstripped other civilizations in many spheres of technology for many centuries, long before Europe started to industrialize. It is overlooked that after 1350 Europe stagnated both economically and technically because the Renaissance was not a technological revolution. After 1492, important European advances began only in certain technical spheres such as shipbuilding (Ibid.). Moreover, there were no prerequisites to the development of technology and science leading to the Industrial Revolution. It was the artisans, sailors, surveyors, lens grinders, blacksmith foundry men, mechanics, glass blowers, clock makers, shipwrights and manual workers who had been accumulating knowledge and information for centuries that made advances in science possible. Conner informs readers that Galileo, Bacon, and Gilbert admitted that their inspiration and information came from these earlier artisans and workers (Conner, 2005:276).

Similarly, Anievas and Nişacncioğlu (2015) have highlighted the role of the Mongol invasion and Ottoman Empire in facilitating the rise of the West, including its technology. Skilled workers in eighteenth-century England learned the trade by observation only and not through written documents. "Useful knowledge" (science and technology) was embodied in the artisans and skilled workers. These persons then carried this knowledge to different regions via migration in response to the demands of the commercial world (Mokyer, 2005). The transmission of this knowledge thus came from the migrant skilled workers and artisans, not from education, patents, or copyrights. However, in Germany, it was also the proliferation of books that played an important role in nineteenth-century industrialization (Thadeusz, 2010). Scientists in Germany were motivated to publish the results of their research so that they could reach a larger audience. "Scholars in Germany churned out tracts and handbooks on … chemistry, mechanics, engineering, optics and the production of steel, dike construction" and more (Ibid.).

The narrative of the Industrial Revolution claims that internal processes within European societies created the technical development leading to industrialization. This narrative ignores the long-time continuous interactions of European societies with many other societies in the East (Mongols, Ottoman Empire), in Africa and in the Americas (Blaut, 1993). If we examine the long-time histories of these different societies, we will find that these traits of entrepreneurship, innovation, invention and technological development are not unique to the modern Western world (Landes and Mokyer, 2010). India and China were highly developed civilizations way before the Western world could claim to be one. Centuries before England began to produce iron and steel, China was producing various forms of iron—using cast iron for shovels and ploughshares (as well as cannon), while simultaneously producing wrought iron for blades (swords and knives). China invented new smelting techniques (1400 years ago) to produce cast iron using blast furnaces and piston bellows. In the fifth century CE, Chinese steel was produced using a "co-fusion" process in which wrought iron and cast iron were melded together. To diminish the threat of deforestation, China innovated substitution of coke for charcoal in the eleventh century. Water-powered machines for hemp and silk were widespread after China began its silk industry in the fourteenth century BCE (Hobson, 2004).

The production of all of these goods imply the existence of a major infrastructural support network in China. For example, Temple (1999) informs that as early as 31 CE, Chinese water mills were developed to propel the bellows in blast furnaces using a piston-rod and driving belt that resembled the (not yet invented) steam engine. In 984, China developed the earliest known pound lock on a canal. China also tapped petroleum and natural gas for fuel, cooking, and lighting purposes around the fourth century BCE. It was also mass producing permanent asbestos lamps for homes around the tenth century CE (cited in Hobson, 2004). In the fifteenth century, the Chinese constructed the most accurate maps of that time when the difference between magnetic north and true north was discovered. They also built large numbers of high quality, physically and technologically sophisticated, large and small ships, which led to a navigational revolution. Temple noted that as late as 1800, "European ships were drastically inferior to Chinese ships in every respect imaginable" (Temple, 1999:186, quoted in Hobson:58).

China was also the first society that produced revolutionary military weapons between 850 and 1290. The Chinese invented rocket launchers that could dispatch 320 rockets instantaneously. The scale of Chinese arms manufacturing had no parallel at that time in history (Ibid.). During the following seven hundred years, Europeans assimilated many of China's technological inventions.

While Indian textiles were world famous until the mid-nineteenth century, India also had innovative skilled iron smelters. Parthasarathi informs that James Franklin, who toured the iron works of central India in the early nineteenth century as the Superintendent of Iron Mines, noted with surprise that Indian smelters built the interior proportions of smelting furnaces with precision (Parthasarathi, 2011:217). Observers have also noted that during the seventeenth and eighteenth centuries, India had medical practitioners, shipbuilder, surveyors, architects and many people who worked with manuals/texts. This tradition continued in the eighteenth and nineteenth centuries (Cook, 2007; Raj, 2007; Grove, 1991). Parthasarathi pointed out that various reports suggest that until the nineteenth century, Europeans were acquiring various types of knowledge from Indian workers and scholars (Parthasarathi, 2011).

Russia had to its credit a long list of achievements in the field of science and technology. For example, prior to the advent of steam-powered machinery, the Urals (in Russia) was the site of one of the world's great industrial centers. In the last half of the eighteenth century the Urals became one of the major iron-producing areas of the world; a top competitor in the international market, and one of the principal sources for England's supply of iron ore on the eve of the Industrial Revolution. By 1775, the Urals had the most integrated, complex and sophisticated iron industry in the whole world (Blackwell, 1968:20). The number of blast furnaces in the region increased from 15 in 1734 to 74 in 1807. Urals iron masters were able to reduce the cost of production and increase sales through innovations in charcoal-making technology and by creating integrated "factories" powered by hydraulic water wheel complexes. Without using any western technology, these iron masters were also able to increase sales twelve-fold by 1914 (Blanchard, 2005). According to Ian Blanchard,

> The Urals ferrous metal industry on the eve of the twentieth century secured its competitive position not by the availability of cheap timber and labor, rather its low input supply costs were a result of high productivity levels achieved by organizational and technological innovation within a water powered, charcoal fueled iron industrial structure very

> different from that 'western' coke fueled iron industrial structure contemporaneously employed in South Russia (Ibid., 136).

Russia also produced many scientists. In 1727, a Russian scientist worked on ballistics (Blackwell, 1968:33). In 1750, Mikhail Lomonosov was interested in mining, chemistry, electricity and more. He invented his own version of the light rod, compasses, thermometer, and other instrument of measurement (Ibid., 34). Ivan I. Polzunov invented a 32-horse-power steam engine designed to pump water from the Attaic mine, an engine that preceded James Watt by a few years. Ivan. P. Kulibin invented his own telescope, a searchlight, reflector lamps, and an electrostatic machine. He designed a single arch, wooden bridge to span the Neva River (Ibid., 36). By 1800, Russia had started using steam power in its industry, whereas water power continued to dominate in England until the second quarter of the nineteenth century, and in the US until mid-century (Ibid., 32). In 1858, the four largest factories in St. Petersburg had a quantity of spindles equal to the total of all spindles in the Philadelphia area (Ibid., 33). By the mid nineteenth century, Russian born machinists were building and producing machinery in quantities that at least equaled and sometimes surpassed the volume of machines imported. In 1829, Aleksandr Zasiadko manufactured gunpowder rockets (Ibid., 385–86). K. A. Shilder built the first Russian submarine in 1835 (Ibid., 397). Ignatii Safonov invented one of the world's earliest water turbines that was used in the Urals (Ibid., 398). In 1832, Paul Schilling invented the electromagnetic telegraph and made the first public demonstration of a telegraph, a decade before Samuel Morse (Ibid., 400). In 1838, Moritz von Jacobi demonstrated an electric-powered boat that was propelled using 320 galvanic batteries (Ibid.).

In addition to the fact that many other societies were highly inventive in the area of technology even before the Western Industrial Revolution, it also needs to be pointed out that no new technology emerges in a vacuum but through expatiation (Johnson, 2010). Expatiation occurs when a new invention is built using elements of preexisting inventions in different fields. For example, the printing press would not have been possible without the existence of all the different elements that went into the making of it. Each element—the mobile type, ink, paper, press—had been developed separately well before Gutenberg printed his first Bible (Ibid.). Moveable type was created by a Chinese blacksmith four centuries before the western printing press. The Chinese did not adopt it for mass printing of texts because they imprinted the letter forms in the page by hand rubbing—more efficient than using a medieval scribe. We should call Gutenberg's press a product of expatiation because he made modifications to the existing moveable type system. For the press, he borrowed an idea from a different field and put it to work in another area. He turned a wine-making press into an engine of mass communication[(13)]. However, we should keep in mind that each separate invention was as much the product of creativity of the inventor, as it was for the person who put together various inventions to make a new product out of that combination. In spite of this reality, we tend to glorify the creativity of the one who combined various separate inventions while dismissing all other inventions, without which no combination of inventions would be possible.

In the production of any new technology, other processes such as mutation, error, and serendipity, along with expatiation also play a part. For example, in 1800,

French weaver Joseph M. Jacquard developed the first punch card to weave a complex silk pattern. Several decades later Charles Babbage borrowed that punch card idea and created his analytical engine. Punch cards were crucial to programmable computers until the 1970s. The vacuum tube was originally adopted to make signals louder, but it was eventually used to turn these signals into data (zero and one) that could be manipulated in astonishing ways. In the 1950s, the vacuum tube helped further the creation of the World Wide Web (Berkun, 2007).

Besides expatiation and serendipity, each innovation is based on innovations in other areas over a long period of time (Ibid.). For example, the Bessemer system would not be usefully employed to produce mass scale steel without first having available the many other small innovations made by many other workers. Similarly, although Babbage formulated the concept of the computer in 1821, his conception could not be used at that time as many other inventions and innovations had to be in place first.

Moreover, technology is not just *there* as a disembodied historical force affecting people's lives—it is *people* who create technology. It works both ways, people create technology, which in turn creates new conditions in which people then change their habits, social relationships, and institutions, followed by the creation of a new technology to meet new needs that are generated by using the earlier technology. This is an unending process. Both processes, while reinforcing the existing social order, also undermine it[(14)]. When a particular technology is created in a society it does not mean that another range of possibilities did not exist. It means that a particular section of people in that society, who are then in control of the power structure, seized upon one particular concept rather than the other(s) for their own particular purpose at that time. The changes in technology and the technological revolution, in itself, cannot be the cause of industrialization as is generally believed (Noble, 1979). Technical parts, labor efficiency, and mass production (a major prerequisite) became important very late (1890s) in the process of industrialization and not at the beginning of it.

It is surprising to note that scholars often do not clarify what they mean by technology. This is important because technology can mean many things. For example, it could refer to technological procedures and know-how, to different ways of organizing the labor force, or to different institutional arrangements and management processes. Moreover, innovation occurs in the distribution process as well as in production, which leads to a competitive advantage in marketing and in manufacturing. Technology is also a social process because it is created and adapted by a human agency (i.e. an individual organization) as well as created and regulated with the support of the state. In other words, we cannot discuss the issue of technology without connecting it to the larger processes of state formation as well as human creativity in everyday life. For example, there was not one particular group of people called *scientists* (or one individual genius) who carried out scientific activities in Europe. Science evolved through the observations of various merchants, soldiers, surveyors of land, carpenters, traders and healers, not all of whom considered themselves scientific men and women. For example, the role of merchants in the development of the long-distance seaborne trade and transoceanic ventures gave rise to a European "Age of Discovery" that in turn paved the way for the Scientific Revolution (Conner:182).

Besides the observation of merchants in their transoceanic ventures, they also used, Connor noted, the methods of seizing knowledge by coercion and kidnapping knowledgeable local people—as Vasco De Gama did many times (Ibid., 203). However, well before the advent of European science, traders, sailors, and soldiers were interacting and exchanging ideas with others around the globe through vast networks, as the world under Oriental globalization was "polycentric" with China, India, the Middle East, Northern Africa, South East Asia and Japan, all being significant players (Hobson, 2004; Parthasarathi, 2011; Conner, 2005). These interactions and exchanges of ideas were crucial in the making of the "future European scientific enterprise."

Based on all of this information, the claim that scientific revolution was an "independent" European phenomenon does not make sense. However, the modernization theory continues promoting the idea of European advancement, prosperity and its technological development as a "model," which "underdeveloped" countries should follow to gain prosperity.

CHALLENGES TO MODERNIZATION THEORY

Since the 1970s, challenges have been made to the theory of modernization ("development/underdevelopment") that blames the culture of the so-called underdeveloped society for its woes. The initial challenge came from the neo-Marxist theory of Gunder Frank's Dependency theory and Immanuel Wallerstein's World System theory (Wallerstein, 1974) that became popular in the 1970s. Many Marxist scholars in North America as well as neo-Marxists and others from the third world (Amin, 1990; Rodney, 1983) have also challenged the theory of modernization. The Dependency theory is based on the center/periphery binary that parallels the dichotomy of traditional and modernity. This premise does not allow the Dependency theory to challenge the basic presupposition of the "idea of growth" which implies the need for modernization, industrialization, and capturing of foreign markets (Frank, 1967). This theory ignores the fact that the world is constantly evolving and all countries are not in the same position *vis a vis* to center. Moreover, the center itself continuously adapts to new conditions (Rikodi, 2015; see also Cowen and Shenton, 1996).

During the 1980s, Subaltern Studies, postmodernism and postcolonialism emerged, all rejecting the Marxist "grand narrative." The SS collective challenged the categories and assumptions of the European project of development, and raised the issue of historiography that sees India only from "developmental" schemes that portray the country always as "lacking" and "not yet." They made a severe critique of Western approaches and put forth an alternative, which focused on individual actions and their agency. However, by treating individuals as autonomous, they also fed into the Western conceptual binary distinction and thus, could not provide an alternative to the issue of "not yet." One prominent founder member of the SS collective recently admitted the limitations of this approach (Chatterjee, 2012). Similarly, the historians of colonized societies have accepted these conceptual binary distinctions, blaming the colonizing countries for the "underdevelopment" of ex-colonies.

It seems the violence of binary distinction—always about the absence of something—somehow also did not register in Gandhi's perception (Fox, 1990:249), as he accepted the Western-imposed binary distinction that India was radically different from the West. According to Gandhi, since India is spiritually superior to the West, there is a better possibility for a more humane and organic Indian society. However, Gandhi's acceptance of this particular binary is not surprising, because he supported similar ideas when he was in South Africa. According to Arundhati Roy in 1884, when Gandhi became the secretary of the Natal Indian Congress in South Africa, he petitioned the authorities for a third entrance to the Post Office be open for Indians so that they did not "need to use the same entrance as the 'Kaffirs'" (means Blacks) (Roy, 2017:51). In an open letter (December 19, 1884) Gandhi says that both the English and the Indians "spring from common stock, called the Indo-Aryan," and complained that the "Indian is being dragged down to the position of raw Kaffir" (Ibid). In another instance when Gandhi staged his visit to the Balmiki (converted untouchables) colony on Mandir Marg [in Delhi] in 1946, he refused to eat with the community" (Prashad, 2001 quoted in Roy, 2017:86). It seems Mahatma Gandhi's binary vision about Indians being "infinitely superior to black Africans" is now being challenged in South Africa and Ghana. In 2013, people in Johannesburg protested against Gandhi for his racist remarks about black people. In 2016 professors and students at the University of Ghana began a "Gandhi Must Fall" movement demanding to remove Gandhi's statue from the university, and it was ultimately removed in 2018 (Scroll Staff, 2018).

More recently, a critique within development studies emerged that was influenced by the ideas of postmodernism and postcolonialism (Nederveen, 2010). As a group, its adherents are called post-development theorists (mostly anthropologists). They rejected structuralist, materialist, and reductionist approaches to social science and instead advocated for constructive, multidimensional, and holistic views (Rikodi, 2015). They have criticized modernization theory and development models for creating a simple dichotomy between traditional and modern societies. Post-developmentalists have stressed that traditional societies have complex relationships with modernity, and that a diversity of cultural, religious, ethnic, and indigenous social institutions within these societies are also important actors in the making of this modernity (Rist, 2008). According to these alternative views, a model of development should be local, self-reliant and egalitarian, one in which the people of a society define their lives as they want in accordance with their own values and cultures (Rikodi, 2015; see also Sylvester, 1999; Ellerman, 2005).

The post-development challenge to the mainstream development model is welcoming (Ibid.; see also Gidwani and Sivaramakrishnan, 2003), as it celebrates a plurality of voices while also recognizing a multiplicity of local practices of resistance. Post-developmental theorists also reject the entire paradigm of development as it has failed hopelessly to deliver to the poor of the third world. However, their approach perpetuates a cultural relativism that in turn promotes neoliberal ideals (Leiten, 2002). Their counter-model of development, which rejects development, simply replaces one grand narrative with another (Rikodi, 2015). By equating modernity with the West they suggest that non-Western societies do not value reason, science, or rationality. These ideas privilege the local, communities, cultures and indigenous knowledge, while neglecting the fact that local culture keeps on changing through migration, trade missions, technology, colonialism and neocolonialism (Rikodi, 2015:27–28). The idea of local empowerment does not take into account local power relationships and inequalities. However, it is not clear in the post-development approach just whose interests are being identified: Is it a group of marginalized people, or a specific sub-caste or regional sub-caste within the group, or the localized village population which also has a culture of male dominance, or is it the culture and interest of the poorest and low caste females (Leiten, 2002)? Moreover, the widespread desire of people for development and modernity (for example, the national development plans of Uganda Vision 2040 and Vietnam's Socio-Economic Development Strategy for the period of 2011–2020), are ignored and devalued by the post-development approach (Rikodi:28).

In 2007, Kalyan Sanyal made an interesting critique of Escobar's ideas on post-development while appreciating his efforts to create new possibilities. According to Sanyal, Escobar conflated "development" and capitalism while depoliticizing "development." This strategy, according to Sanyal, "leaves no space where the relationship between the dynamics of the post-colonial capital and the dominant imaginaries of development can be addressed" (Sanyal, 2014:86). He is also critical of Escobar's assumption that there exists an original and authentic "tradition" which is pristine and "indigenous," and that this original tradition would replace the modernization project of development. Escobar's approach does not take into account the fact that indigenousness has its own oppressive system, and that marginalized people do want to be part of development (Ibid.). Moreover, traditions are not static as they change in the process of negotiating with modernity and ultimately both constitute one another. However, as Sanyal pointed out, in this process of constituting one another, modern is inserted in the structure of traditions, which makes it possible for the promoters of development to use these structures of traditions as an instrument to achieve their developmental goals (Ibid., 92).

Agreeing with Sanyal's critique, I also wish to point out that the idea of returning to the concept of "indigenous" in order to challenge Eurocentric binary distinction is problematic because these distinctions cannot be substantiated historically (Deshpande, 2011). Instead, we should learn from the multiple voices within European history, as well as from Asian, African, and Latin American voices, who have been challenging Eurocentric historiography and cultural imperialism. All are historically diverse in thought and practices. If "modern and contemporary Europeans and Americans have found Islam, Buddhism and Yoga interesting for a variety of reasons, we too could find the several European intellectual traditions rewarding for peculiar reasons" (Ibid., 88). As discussed earlier, all societies learn from others in the process of interaction. Why not deliberately learn in order to solve urgent human and societal problems of our time not only from within one's own society but also from others, including the West, as such a vast collective human knowledge (a common human heritage created by common human ancestors) has been accumulating for centuries in all countries and societies?

PROBLEMS WITH THE BINARY DISTINCTION OF DEVELOPED/UNDERDEVELOPED

"If 'development' is only a useful word for the sum of virtuous human aspirations, we can conclude at once that it exists nowhere and probably never will" (Rist:10). All these ideas and values, and presuppositions of "social evolutionism (catching up with the industrialized countries), individualism, (developing the personality of human beings), economism (achieving growth and access to greater income)," are simply tools to attain broad consensus at little cost (Ibid., 9).

The problem is that the assumptions behind these ideas do not allow us to think about societies in any other way. Consequently, it becomes very difficult to find a solution to prevailing problems in poor societies, except with the fixed formula of development. We keep looking at every society through the lens of "developed and underdeveloped" as if every society is static with no prior history and it began from a given condition of developed or underdeveloped that never changed. This binary approach denies the historical processes that make any society what it is in the present time.

The concept of development is actually a social construct, but, as Rist pointed out, development now has the appearance of a natural phenomenon with laws of its own that govern all societies. Marxists and liberals believe in the importance of the development of productive forces even when this process is extremely harmful to nature, increases inequalities, and leads to the universal commodification of everything (including human beings). According to this idea, industrialization, burgeoning trade, new agricultural technology, profitability requirements, and reinvestment of profits are all supposed to make it possible to create wealth by stimulating development. In reality, as Rist noted, development is a pretext to convert natural and social relations into commodities which is widening the gulf between rich and poor (Ibid., 216).

The developed/underdeveloped binary distinction ignores the fact that all societies change through inventions within a society as well as through ideas borrowed from outside in the process of diffusion. Reciprocal diffusion of ideas and technology remains the most prominent form of change in most societies because human beings tend to imitate others in the process of their interaction. The questions, Why was Britain industrialized first? or Why was China not industrialized first? are self-serving, as they promote a binary that automatically bestows a superior status to Britain. For example, the question of why England was successful in becoming the center of capital is generally explained based on England's initial advantage in defeating its primary challenger. But this is a circular argument, because, as van der Pijl pointed out, the initial advantage of England itself needed to be explained first as it was largely grounded on historical contingency of various forces (van der Pijl, 1998). For example, how do we explain:

> In terms of quantitative development, Germany in 1910 bypassed Britain ... in steel production Germany had already bypassed Britain in 1900 and enjoyed a 4.3 advantage over Britain and France combined in 1910 ... Russia['s] ... energy consumption was roughly equal to Austria-Hungary's, and in steel, to France's on the eve of the war (Ibid., 93).

Moreover, in 1716, Russia had already become the world's largest iron producer and an important exporter, and by 1913 it possessed a substantial industrial sector ranking fifth in the world after the US, Germany, Britain, and France. At that time, Russia had a well-developed heavy industrial sector, its coal and pig iron production ranked fifth place worldwide and its steel production ranked fourth (above France) (Falkus, 1972:13, 22–24, 27).

If cultural "backwardness" was the problem, then how do we explain the fact that the Indian capitalist Tata raised enough local capital in 1912 for investment in a large-scale steel industry that would produce the cheapest pig iron by the late 1920s (Bahl, 1995)? How do we explain that India, after being bled white—Britain drained 45 trillion dollars from India between 1765–1938 (Patnaik, U. 2017a and 2017b; Polya, 2018)—of 3 to 10 percent of the country's GDP annually, India's per capita income after independence in 1947 grew annually at 1.4 percent in the first couple of decades (three times faster than its best phase [1870–1913] under colonialism) and as quickly as 3.01 percent between 1973–2001? In the spans 2003–2004 to 2006–2007, India's per capita income reached at 7 percent, comparable to the rates achieved by Japan's between 1950–1973 (Mukherjee, 2010).

However, if our goal is to understand social reality and eliminate binary distinction then the question, Why was England industrialized first? has no relevance. Critics who promote Enlightenment values as the ideal for European advancement have ignored the fact that in the sixteenth century the Indian emperor Akbar, based on his faith in Islam, was already supporting ideas of reason, tolerance, and women's rights, while trying to promote a universal religion—*sulh-i kul*. Unfortunately, Akbar's contemporary, Prince Philip II of Spain, was engaged in the Spanish inquests, and Enlightenment ideas were nowhere in sight in Europe at that time (Mukherjee, 2010). Many scholars have made this point. Going back further in Indian history it should be noted that King Ashoka (third century BC), based on his faith in Buddhism promoted the ideas of human rights, animal rights, secular religion, and tolerance way before the Enlightenment or UN human rights manifesto. Ashoka's edicts are written in *stupas* (pillars) and rock edicts spreading all over India are documented proof of this fact. Based on this information, the argument that European advancement was due to the ideals of the Enlightenment does not hold. Moreover, the Industrial Revolution took three centuries to manifest in England as there were no immediate causes of it (Hobsbawm, 1968). However, the British plunder of the Americas, India, and enslaving of Africans for sugar, tobacco, and cotton plantations did provide the necessary capital for it.

If we look into the history of various societies in the world, it would be possible to show that the ideas of the Enlightenment were neither unique to Europe nor was Europe the first region that came up with these ideas. European societies, like all other societies, were (and are) constantly going through the historical process of cultural diffusion as they interacted with other societies. There are ample examples of Europeans interacting with Asian and South Asian societies before the Industrial Revolution came into being (Ridley, 2010; Parthasarathi, 2011; Hobson, 2004; Conner, 2005). The three most important discoveries that helped Europe to become a colonial power were the printing press, gun powder, and the compass, which were all invented in China (Nigam, 2011:65–66). Moreover, China's Industrial Revolution, which spanned a period of 1500 years, peaked during the Sung revolution 600 years before Britain entered its industrialization phase. China's iron and steel industries began between 400 and 100 BC and peaked between 800 and 1100 AD. By the end of the eleventh century, China was producing as much steel as all of Europe would as late as 1700. By the twelfth century, the Chinese had a sophisticated market economy with paper money and a taxation system (Ibid., 65). Is it possible to say that Europeans, who used China's invention of the printing press, gun power, and the compass to their advantage, overlooked learning about iron and steel or the market economy or paper money?

Jack Goody suggests that it is possible to describe all historical processes in the West without European periodization and "without adopting the nineteenth century notion of the emergence of capitalism as a specific stage in the development of world society, and we can dispense with the supposed sequence of periods of production leading to it that are confined to Europe. Such an account avoids European periodization and its assumption of long-term superiority" (Cited in Heller, 2011:225). Using Goody's suggestion we can explain the so-called "rise of England" by looking into the conjunction and contingencies of various social, economic, historical, political, and geographic forces of the time. England, like other European countries, borrowed various skills and ideas from others. Malleable iron, considered to be the major source of industrialization, was introduced to the British Isles in the late fifteenth century by migrant iron workers from Normandy within a particular historical context. As Evans and Ryden have pointed out, there was no indication that native English iron workers anticipated the idea of indirect reduction method of producing iron (Evans and Ryden, 2005:16).

Historically, technical development has always been a slow process because many preparatory things must come into being before a complete technical thing is created. Moreover, as discussed earlier, no technology develops in a vacuum and it is always a combination of small inventions in technology that over time lead to a major turnaround at the macro level. This macro level change in technology gets more attention and other historical processes that contributed in laying the groundwork for this technology are generally forgotten (Mokyr, 1990:116). To go back in time, as discussed earlier, European information about iron and steel actually traveled from China through migrants, *hu* merchants, traders, and visitors, because China had developed iron and steel of good quality centuries before England or Europe could produce it (Conner, 2005).

The binary distinction of developed/underdeveloped is not the natural, organic condition of any society. However, societies labeled as underdeveloped are under constant pressure to relate their history in a way that parallels the Western model, or to prove if they were on the verge of being a capitalist society, or to show if their working class is capable of developing class consciousness, or to prove that they were not primitive or undeveloped. These societies, vulnerable to continuous economic crisis generated in the Western world, can find an alternative to the current development model only when they understand their own history without reference to the Western model, while also emphasizing their interaction with the world *including* the West. This goal can be achieved by carefully avoiding and erasing the paradigms of development and underdevelopment and by questioning the assumptions and the yardsticks used in understanding and interpreting non-Western societies. This questioning can be followed up with the formation of a yardstick that should be applied equally to the understanding of *all* societies.

NEED FOR AN ALTERNATIVE PERSPECTIVE

Aside from changing the center of history from Europe to China (which also does not eliminate binary distinction. See Frank, 1998; Hobson, 2004), no new perspective is on the horizon in the second decade of the twenty-first century. Instead, the old colonial approach (Roy, 2012; Roy, 2006; Mukherjee, 2008) and Rostow's theory of modernization blaming backward culture on colonized countries, remain dominant. Joel Mokyer's (2016) most recent book, *A Culture of Growth,* reinforces the idea of a superior European culture that helped make Europe the first to undergo an Industrial Revolution (Mokyer, 2016; Landes and Mokyer, 2010). All scholars, whether for or against modernization theory, use the same binary distinction of developed/underdeveloped in explaining their argument. Their questions and answers remain Eurocentric, which eliminates the possibility of an alternative perspective. Scholars seem to be forgetting that Eurocentrism ideology is necessary in maintaining the hegemony of Western civilization. However, Western civilization is constructed on a perverse and mistaken idea of human nature that "we are condemned by an irresistible human nature to look to our own advantage at the cost of whomever it may concern and thus menace our own social existence ... It is probably true, however, that this perverse idea of human nature endangers our existence" (Sahlins, 2008:112). The question is: If Western civilization is constructed on a perverse idea of human nature that is endangering the existence of the human species, then how can any relationship to that idea be a sign of true progress or development? Moreover, why should those societies, which did not follow the Western version of "progress" (which would thus endanger human existence), be labeled as backward unless one thinks that endangering the human existence is a sign of progress? Should we not look for alternative perspectives that are not based on such a perverse understanding of human nature?

If we do not question "the tendency to hypostatize 'the West' as possessed of an original and authentic culture and history" (Washbrook, 1997:410), then we shall keep producing a history that validates this assumption. We shall keep believing that "the unique qualities of the West created a pathway to modernity that became universally available to the rest of the world" (Ibid.). As scholars and historians, we need to remember and shoulder this burden responsibly because the production of knowledge and the writing of history play an important political role in shaping ideas and government policies. The question is: Why don't scholars treat Western societies as traditional and as exotic as any other? Why do historians keep writing the history of non-European societies as a history of "absences" or "not yet?" Why is labor history always directed toward the issue of the absence of "revolutionary class consciousness" in comparison to Western society[(15)]? How do we write comparative history without binary distinction and give equal weight to every society while not undermining the role and ramifications of imperialism and capitalism on the whole world and planet? It will continue to be difficult to do so if scholars keep on reproducing old ideas of "superior West and inferior rest."

Joel Mokyr, in his book *Enlightenment and Industrialization* (Mokyr, 2012), also reinforces the idea of "superior Europe/England" even when his own argument and information contradicts it. All of the information in his book indicates the importance of the conjunction of the historical forces that created the conditions for the Industrial Revolution. However, Mokyr concludes (Ibid.) that it was Enlightenment ideas that created the conditions for England's Industrial Revolution. For example, he writes that the Industrial Revolution did not happen overnight as it was based on various innovations that were made over the course of centuries that together slowly changed the material conditions of Europe and Britain. He also states that the steam engine could have been developed earlier, but was not, as the time was not right and the necessary innovations were not in place. Similarly, he remarks that the Industrial Revolution would have happened in Europe, if not in Britain, but it so happened that things came together in the right way in Britain first. He treats Russia, which was also moving towards industrialization at the same time, as an outsider. Why does Mokyr reinforce the "special" characteristics of England while ignoring his own data to the contrary? Why does he not apply the same argument to understand non-European societies?

One can point out that the issue of binary distinction is nothing new. Historically, the dominant group in every society has always used binary distinction to control the subordinated group and retain its own power. This point is well taken, but leads us to this question: Should we keep repeating violence and injustice in our time just because violence and injustice has been going on through much of recorded history? In other words, according to such a view, there is no point in challenging the binary distinction because that is the way things are. This statement does not allow us to ask a concomitant question: Why are things the way they are? It reminds me of a workshop on South Asia I attended at the University of Iowa in 1994, where one scholar from India said there was no need to criticize American imperialism (or any imperialism) because India (and others) had also been imperialist in earlier times. It is a fallacy that one wrong committed by one country can right the wrong repeated later by another country. This argument also ignores the historical context that India as a nation-state came into being only in 1947, while also ignoring the fact that American and Western imperialism has brought the whole planet to the brink of disaster, which is not at all similar to simply spreading Indian culture and civilization throughout Eastern countries.

However, "Even if one tries to organize research in these areas, the problem is that it will not be considered serious unless the conclusions are guaranteed by the concepts and models of 'normal science" (Rist, 2008:246). This means it will not be possible to discover anything new unless we question the "normal science" itself, as it has many anomalies and it cannot claim to be a perfect model. However, there are signs that give some hope that this hegemony of "normal science" might change because many students at respected institutions around the world have begun demanding a change in the way economics (considered a science) is taught so that they can learn an alternative perspective to understand about real economics in present times. To pursue this agenda, certain British students have founded an organization called "Rethinking Economics," which will demand a complete overhaul of economic departments. In December 2017, a group of academics and media commentators affixed "33 Theses for an economic reformation" to the doors of the London School of Economics challenging the discipline's fundamental teaching[16]. Similarly, students in the US, Canada, Israel, Brazil, Argentina, Chile, Germany, France, and New Zealand are demanding alternative perspectives. For example, students in Chile founded Estudios Nueva Economia (ENE) with the aim of achieving pluralism in economic thought, and they demanded that economics should be taught by locating it in the larger context of both the history of the discipline as well as other social sciences—history, politics, sociology, and anthropology. They believe that this approach would provide a greater range of tools for students to analyze real world scenarios while looking critically at their own discipline (Russell, 2014). In the world-famous Cambridge University in England students have launched a movement in October 2017 for the "decolonization" of courses. A letter signed by 100 students sent to the English faculty demanding to broaden the English Curriculum to be more inclusive of literature from the Global South. This movement is now spread to other departments of Sociology, Philosophy, and Art History, as well (Savva, 2017). Hopefully, with changes in the discipline of economics and other disciplines future scholars would be able to break out of the binary distinction of developed/underdeveloped.

However, we have yet a long way to go to find a non-binary, non-Eurocentric approach to the writing of history. Most of the time we do not realize how various binaries creep into our analyses and history writings. Interestingly, even when the idea of grand unified theories (the quantum theory and chaos theory) have taken root in the disciplines of Western science, they have gained no acceptance in the social sciences or in the writing of history. It is important for scholars to keep striving to erase these binaries in their writing and not reinforce the violence of binary. It is generally forgotten that all binary distinctions are human constructs that are not inevitable or naturally-given conditions of any society, and that they can be erased. An alternative argument is possible only if we are prepared to ask an alternative question that precludes binary distinctions as a naturally-given condition of any society. Parthasarathi's recent work, *Why Europe Grew Rich and Asia Did Not: Global Economic Divergence, 1600–1850* (Parthasarathi, 2011), is an attempt to rectify this tendency. However, the title of the book and the question raised in this work remain within the same binary framework and defensive mode. We have yet to discover a way that does not require us to defend our capabilities (as ex-colonies and ex-colonized people) every time we make a comparative study.

It may be possible to find an alternative perspective by using a yardstick of parity to understand every society and focus on the conjunction of various historical forces; a product of human choices and actions in the process of interaction, that contribute to the making of any society. It means understanding each society's industrialization, culture, social structure and social institutions in its own context as well as in international historical context. For example, in the case of Russia, it is familiarly stated in history books that "Nicholas II decided to industrialize Russia." However,

> [T]his statement creates a false picture, not because the Tsar and his court were irrelevant, but because in a phase of generalized development capital was attracted to new countries [*conjuncture of historical force, my emphasis*] and this gave an incentive to the industrialization of Russia well before Nicholas II. It is, then, worthwhile not only in economics but also in 'general' history to inquire into the overall, spontaneous economic tendencies which bring complex factors into play: while the decisions of individuals and legislative initiative have their part to play, their significance and especially their effectiveness, depend on the 'conjuncture' in which they are located (Vilar, 1969:40).

Therefore, the question, Why was England industrialized first? does not make sense, and it does not allow us to consider an approach that provides for multiple possibilities and conjunction of historical processes that are complementary and interactive. We need not only to break out of Eurocentrism, but to avoid any centrism while treating all societies on equal terms (but not as ahistorical static individual autonomous entities) with mutual respect in understanding their social reality. For that we need a complex, multi-dimensional approach that includes both micro and macro elements in an interdependent relationship existing simultaneously. Such an alternative approach is possible only by asking an alternative question while also questioning both the assumptions and the yardsticks that are used in understanding and interpreting non-Western societies.

ALTERNATIVE QUESTION

If we wish to create a better world, we need to understand our present social reality not in terms of inevitability but as a product of a combination of contingencies and conjunctions of events that came into being through human creativity, actions, and human choices. There always existed in the past, as well as in the present time, many possibilities and many alternatives. However, if our assumptions are based on a "context free" approach, that promotes only one criterion of truth and right action (Western idea of universalism) at all times and places, then that will always lead to binaries such as developed/underdeveloped, modern/traditional, and progressive/backward as if no other alternative was/is possible. In the absence of a context sensitive approach, the question, "Why by 1850, Western Europe was the undisputed center of a new global manufacturing order" (Parthasarathi, 2011:1), remains the only valid one for those scholars who wish to understand the increasing inequalities between different societies. The need to eliminate binary distinction is urgent for two main reasons: it does not allow for an alternative approach, and it has negatively and tragically affected the lives of millions of people on this planet leading to a sense of hopelessness. Moreover, Parthasarathi's question above does not allow us to consider an approach that provides for multiple possibilities (not multi-modernities) and multiple historical processes that are simultaneous, complementary, holistic, and interactive.

Therefore, to eliminate the binary distinction of developed/underdeveloped from our understanding of any society, we can raise the following alternative question: How do people in any given society, while making everyday choices to meet their human needs, come to acquire specific economic, political, religious, social, technological, and cultural conditions? This question directs our focus to the constantly changing specificities of a society—a product of human creativity, human choices, and actions in the process of human interactions within a society—as well as its relations and interaction with larger historical forces (including geography and nature at large) and interaction with other societies in different historical times that shaped the historical trajectory of that society. Moreover, it compels us to make a comparative study without prior assumptions about other societies as developed or underdeveloped. It would spare ex-colonial societies from having to continuously prove their capitalist/modernist credentials. In other words, there will be no need to address questions of why Asia, or any other region of the world, did or did not industrialize first. By disregarding these questions, we can stop being complicit in the promotion of Western binary distinction and Western myths. Moreover, the alternative question will help in creating space where we can find an alternative theoretical framework, one that is sorely needed to break out of the "development model" mindset in which the whole world is mired and sustaining a self-defeating sense of fatalism and hopelessness.

The assumption of the alternative question is that all societies are created in the process of interaction of people within and outside of each society to fulfill their daily human needs for existence (Bahl, 2005). Moreover, all humans and their societies try to attain four primary valuations: "(1) an ever-expanding span of survival of the species, (2) better and better security of life, (3) even more material prosperity for ensuring the above two valuations while enjoying further wholesome life, and (4) deeper and deeper mental peregrination for systemizing the above three valuations, as well as for continually unfolding the potentialities of the species" (Mukherjee, 2009:1). However, as Mukherjee suggested, these valuations can never be realized fully and finally because life processes are immanent.

Moreover, human beings (with innate creativity) in an attempt to realize reality, seek access to the spiritual (not institutionalized religions), to an idealized view of life, irrespective of place, time, and people variations (Ibid., 5). Quoting from the Sankhya school, Mukherjee writes, "Germinating, decaying and again germinating denotes the course of scientific knowledge of what is reality—only which is true and everlasting" (Ibid., 6). But to keep this spirit of scientific inquiry alive and open we should know that we do not know everything, as mentioned (translated by physicist-statistician P. C. Mahalanobis, 1972) in the Article 10 of Kenopanishad: "I do not think I Know very well, nor that I do not Know, He Knows who knows this that I do not Know and I Know" (Ibid., 7).

Geographical location also plays an important role in creating the possibilities for interaction among particular groups of people within a given geographical region, thus creating a particular cultural outlook and philosophy of life. It contributes in the possibility of self-sufficiency with respect to food or an increased dependence and need for acquiring more land. If we consider all these forces and people's choices in these contexts, we can understand why Russia (or any other society) did not follow the same "stages" of development as the Western world (since there are no fixed stages), and why Russia (or any other society) evolved in its own specific way considering its unique historical trajectory. No society can be, nor is needed to be, a replica of another, although all societies are similar in the sense that they all are dealing with the needs of their members through an interdependent process of human creativity. It is possible to erase binary distinction (discussed in the following chapter) by looking for commonalities among all societies without denying any society its specificity.

All societies, their cultures, social structures, and social institutions are emergent processes. These social forces continuously keep changing in conjunction to various historical forces that are guided by human creativity, human choices, and human actions in their everyday struggle for survival and in the making of their society, both as individual beings and as parts of a larger social structure. Modern industrialization is one of many such phenomena that emerged in the same way. That is why, there is no need to look for the "prerequisites" or "fixed stages" that every society must go through during the process of industrialization or during any alternative form of existence and prosperity. With this approach, it becomes possible to eliminate both the Western binary distinction and the stage theory that many of Marx's followers promote by dispossessing peasants from their lands blindly believing (literally following the book) that the development of capitalism (in the name of development of productive forces) will lead to socialism. It is puzzling as to why these Marxist followers are unable to explore an alternative path that is more humane and non-violent. The poor are suffering the same fate (dispossessed from the land and becoming precariat and gigariat) under the capitalist system as well as under those claiming to be governing, as under Indian Marxists were doing in the name of socialism. Indian Marxists have not noticed, as Sanyal pointed out, that the narrative of "transition" has lost its validity as it is extricated from the concept of "development" which is depoliticized (Sanyal, 2014:206). Moreover, people need a better life right now, in the present, and cannot wait for elusive socialism to come someday (if at all). That is why it is easy to sell ideas of "development" even though the agenda is shaped by Western multi-nationals and transnational agribusinesses and has led to 500,000 farmer suicides since 1997 while many more are facing economic distress or leaving for the cities to join the informal labor market.

For example, Indian politicians continue using this magical word "development" in their speeches to get votes by creating a sense of drama while merging science and history with myth and folklore through catchphrases, such as 'good governance,' 'make in India,' 'development,' 'smart cities' (Antony, 2015). Whereas, in reality, the process of development has increased gender, caste, ethnic and class tensions in India because of its accompanied ideology of competition, individual success, and consumption. Thus, the legacy of development in India has created new crisis of identity and changed the ideas of freedom and citizenship to individual advancement and goods and services. The following quote sums up this change in present-day India,

> The pressures of a competitive society have generated a new crisis of self-esteem that take people back to the comforts of identity narratives. The murderous politics over Lingayat identity, or Shivaji and the Marathas, or Patels or Jats are not just contests over orthodoxy and dissent, they are also responses to the anxiety of mobility. And the crisis of masculinity is apparent in the kinds of mobilization we see in places like Mangalore and Mumbai. The language of development in India speaks a transactional language of goods and services, of individual advancement. It does not speak the language of freedom and citizenship, the restraints of reciprocity. It has no means of conceptualizing the tensions inherent to development (*Indian Express,* 9/1/2015; see also Hall, 2016).

The alternative to such a situation cannot be found within the binary distinction of developed/underdeveloped, but through the process of erasing it. The issue of erasure of binary distinction of developed/underdeveloped, along with a possible alternative suggestion, is deliberated in the following chapter.

ENDNOTES

1. Personal conversation (2014) with renowned Indian scholar Amiya K. Bagchi regarding his recent focus on the emerging "Corporate feudalism."
2. "Forgotten Ruins of Ancient Cities of Africa." http//www.facebook.com/mayada.amannan/videos/10153379937461209. I am grateful to Arno Vosk for this information.
3. This idea of "equality" is different from what I am suggesting in this volume as yardstick of parity to understand each society without any presumption of their being either "progressive or backward." Under the Western idea of "equal" means autonomous person without any connection with its society or nation-states and without any history.
4. Sanyal, K. 2014:129. Sanyal quoted from George Rosen's *Western Economists and Eastern Societies,* that deals with the role of the Ford Foundation in inaugurating development planning in South Asia in the period spanning 1950–1970s.

5. These "free trade" agreements may now be difficult to get through US Congress and other countries under the new climate of anti-establishment and anti-corporations. Obama suspended the TPP agreement immediately after the election of Donald Trump as President in 2016.
6. Rist calls it a kind of Marxism without Marx. p. 101.
7. Sujata Patel points out that after World War II, the discipline of sociology became a separate subject to be studied and learned both in Europe and America. However, it was the Parsonian school of sociology—taught in the US—that came to dominate the world of sociology. This school emphasized social integration and consensus while ignoring the issue of social change because it represented the aspirations of the American state, which wanted to ensure a stable world order and sought to establish its hegemony over the new world. To achieve the American goal of global hegemony, the Parsonian school created a new sociological language and body of knowledge, which were exported to rest of the world (including newly emerging nation-states) through universities and other academic institutions. In this diffusion process within all academic fields, the role of foreign students was important because it was through them that the US achieved its hegemony as these students returned home they established and legitimized those practices that they learned in the US through syllabus and curriculum, textbooks, and reference books (Patel, 2006:387).
8. Naomi Klein (2015), "This Changes Everything." Video. Western corporations are successful in creating doubt about climate change, which enables them to manipulate the debate on climate change to their advantage in order to gain more carbon taxes.
9. See *The New Internationalist,* December 2014. Whole issue is devoted to the workings and impact of NGOs in different countries.

   Gürcan's article (*Monthly Review*) is useful to understand the role and power of NGOs. He explains that after the end of the welfare state under the neoliberal development paradigm, the nonprofit sector became important for social engineering and the financialization of the wider social sphere. This nonprofit corporate complex was part of the international non-governmental organizations as in 1980s it became the third pillar of the contemporary imperialist structure. It was a response to the spread of revolutionary movement in 1968 as well as the rise of radical social movements in the 1970s. As Gürcan noted, Mellon, Ford, and Soros foundations got involved in the nonprofit sector and thus helped in transforming political resistance projects into quasi-entrepreneurial, corporate-style ventures. Gürcan provides details that the nonprofit sector controls over 1.59 trillion in financial assets and had expenditures of over $822 billion.

   Thus, "the growth of the nonprofit sector ended up with the professionalization of non-profit organizations acting as a 'shadow state' which coincided with a flurry of sectorial experts and the opening up of business schools, the entire curricula of which had been devoted to training high profile managers … Social services provide 'social service workers' with jobs and make them feel good about the work they do … NGOs creating a new privileged class of professionals, who serve the status quo, rather than working for social change … The process of NGO expansion is rooted in a problematic 'humanitarian view of development' … poverty as a quantitative problem … As a result, development is considered purely a technical matter that should be isolated from ideology and politics … The massive boom of NGOs in the 1980s … was supported by international institutions … IMF and World Bank and dominated by the US treasury and the department of finance of wealthy countries … NGOs are bureaucratic, hierarchical and professionally staffed organizations, serving imperialist interests … they are more accountable to the donors and less responsive to their constituencies … nearly 80 percent of Haiti's basic services (healthcare, education and sanitation) [run by NGOS] … NGOs also do the counterinsurgency and intelligence work for the donors" (Gürcan, 2015:41–49).
10. Blaut, 1993:108.

    Nobel Laureate scientist Ilya Prigogine writes,

    > The world lines, the trajectories followed by the atoms and particles that makes up our universe, can be traced toward the future or toward the past …. This static view of the

world is rooted in the origin of Western science. ... physicists and chemists know that a description in which past and future play the same role does not apply to all phenomena. Every day observes that two liquids put into the same vessel generally diffuse toward some homogenous mixture ... we observe progressive homogenization and the one sidedness of time become evident in the fact that we do not observe spontaneous phase separation of the two mixed liquids ... the concept evolution seems to be central to our understanding of the physical universe. It emerged with full force in the nineteenth century. It is remarkable that it appeared almost simultaneously in physics, biology and sociology although with quite different specific meanings. In physics it was introduced through second law of thermodynamics ... the law of increase of entropy ... However, in biology and sociology, the basic meaning of evolution was just the opposite, describing instead transformation of higher levels of complexity (Prigogine, 1980:xi).

11. Blaut, 1993:109. Blaut makes an important point about psychic unity of mankind when he writes, "If we accept the quite fundamental assumption that all human groups are truly human in their thinking apparatuses and therefore, broadly similar in their ability to invent and innovate—this assumption is known as 'the psychic unity of mankind' ... we would expect inventions to occur everywhere across the human landscape" (p. 16).

    See also Trojanow and Hoskote, 2012; Conner, 2015. Conner has emphasized the creativity of common people in creating technology and science, however that later became the monopoly of institutional science.

12. Conner, 2005:177. He quoted from Temple, 1999:49.

    Joel Mokyr also informs, "Bessemer invention occurred simultaneously with that of an American William Kelly, who patented an identical process in June 1857, a year after Bessemer read his famous paper to the British Association for the Advancement of Science. Eventually, Bessemer and Kelly came to an agreement to coordinate their patents" (Mokyr, 1990:117).

13. Conner:156.

    Matt Ridley also has suggested that technology and inventions were a collective phenomenon. For example, "No single person [or any one society] knows how to make a computer mouse [(4)]" because to create a new technology many ideas have to meet and mate. However, "there is no inevitable end to this process" (p. 7). All inventions are a product of accumulative knowledge (culture). Moreover, "knowledge does not exist in concentrated or integrated form but solely as the dispersed bits of incomplete and frequently contradictory knowledge which all the separate individuals possess"[(38)]. For example, "the bread you eat was first cross bread by a Neolithic Mesopotamia and baked in a way that was first invented by Mesolithic hunter gatherer" (Ibid.). Today we benefit from that knowledge as we have incorporated it into our machines and recipes. It is the same with all discoveries and labor of thousands of people (dead or alive) that we are able to produce and sell whatever we do today. Ridley also points out that accumulated knowledge was possible with exchange of ideas. However, exchange did not happen naturally, but evolved from the basic glue of society called, reciprocity. At the same time exchange is different from reciprocity because exchange is about giving each other different things at the same time (barter or trade). Reciprocity is about giving each other the same things in different times, for example, helping someone in need and later that person helps you when you need it (Ridley, 2010).

    See also a recent article (Sengupta, 2018) on the story of antibiotics explaining how the creation of scientific knowledge is a process and it is based on collective activity.

14. Noble, 1979:xvi.

    Ridley has also pointed out that "the European scientific revolution in the seventeenth century unleashed the rational curiosity of educated classes, whose theories were then applied in the form of new technologies, which in turn allowed standards of living to rise. China, on this theory, somehow lacked this leap to scientific curiosity and philosophical discipline, so it failed to build on its technological lead (p. 255)" is not valid, because "few of the inventions that made the industrial revolution owed anything to scientific theory" (Ibid.). His argument is that slaves in Rome knew how to make better watermills and wool looms, and many plutocrats knew how to save, invest, and consume. But they did not come together to create industrial revolution. Moreover, Ridley pointed out that Newton did not influence the creation of James Hargreaves's Spinning Jenny. All those technologies, like Jennies, gins, frames, mules, looms, and steam engines that revolutionized the working of cotton, were invented by tinkering businessmen. Ignorant of scientific theories, these businessmen made possible the theories of vacuum and the laws of thermodynamics that helped create the steam engine. Ridley thinks that scientists were the beneficiaries of technology and actual technical changes came from attempts to improve existing technology at the workplace on shop floors among apprentices and mechanics (Ridley, 2010).

Conner (2005) has also written on similar lines in his book, *A People's History of Science*. Information on the global diffusion process of technological knowledge is also dealt in many other books such as Steven Shapin (1996), *The Scientific Revolution*. Chicago, University of Chicago Press; Kapil Raj (2007). *Relocating Modern Science: Circulation and the Construction of knowledge in South Asia and Europe, 1650–1900*. New York: Palgrave.

Raj has provided example of the hybrid work of French text (fourteen volumes) on the plant life of eastern India. It was compiled in the early eighteenth century by Nicholas L. Empereur who drew upon Indian writings on medicine as well as the knowledge of Indian healers, botanists, gardeners and merchants (p. 44–45). Similar process of interaction took place in the making of modern mapping between British and Indian surveyors. Raj wrote, "The British depended crucially on their indigenous intermediaries" and local technical culture. "Only later did it come to be seen as a European or colonial enterprise and the Indian dimensions lost or excised" (p. 63).

Parthasarathi (2011) has also provided many examples of collaboration between Asians and Europeans that created over time the so called "European scientific Knowledge." (p. 192)

15. van der Linden, M. (2008). *Workers of the World: Essays toward a Global Labor History*. Brill. Highlighting the false dilemmas of leftist scholars and others, Paul Street wrote,

> I do not see how the movement required can emerge as long as leftists and many others here are plagued by the false dichotomies and false dilemmas … here is a useful definition and discussion of a false dichotomy, found online, 'a false dilemma, or false dichotomy is a logical fallacy which involves presenting two opposing views, options or outcomes in such a way that they seem to be the only possibilities: that is, if one is true the other must be false, or, more typically, if you do not accept one then the other must be accepted.' The reality in most cases is that there are many in–between or other alternative options, not just two mutually exclusive one … There are two ways in which one can commit a false dilemma. First one can assume that there are only two (or three … ; that case is strictly speaking be a false 'trilemma') options when there really are many more. Second, one can take the options to be mutually exclusive when they really are not." (*Z Magazine,* April 2015. Paul Street, "Beyond False Dichotomies" (16–22) p. 16).

16. Noted in a review article, "Want a Reformation? : Rethinking the Discipline of Economics." Rebecca L. Spang in *Times Literary Supplement*, February 9, 2018. pp 12–13. The following books are reviewed: Lilian Fischer et al. (Eds.), *Rethinking Economics,* Routledge; Giacomo Corneo, *Is Capitalism Obsolete: A Journey through Alternative Economic Systems*. Harvard University Press; Samuel Bowles, *The Moral Economy: Why Good Incentives Are No Substitute for Good Citizens*. Yale University Press; John Rapley; *Twilight of the Money Gods: Economics As a Religion and How It All Went Wrong*. Simon & Schuster.

Kate Raworth, *Doughnut Economics: Seven Ways to Think Like a 21st Century Economist*. Cornerstone, US: Chelsea Green.

SECTION II

A Possible Alternative Perspective

CHAPTER 2

Erasing the Binary Distinction

"Man is directly a natural being. As a natural being ... he is on the one hand equipped with natural powers, with vital powers, he is an active natural being; these powers exist in him as dispositions and capacities, as drives. On the other hand, as a natural, corporeal, sensuous, objective being he is a suffering, conditioned and limited being. Like animals and plants, that is to say, the objects of his drives exist outside him as objects independent of him, but these objects are objects of his need, essential objects, indispensable to the exercise and confirmation of his essential powers. To say that man is a corporeal, living, real, sensuous, objective being with natural powers means that he has real, sensuous object as the object of his being .... A being which does not have its nature outside itself is not a natural being and plays no part in the system of nature" (Marx, 1974).

"It is not our human nature that is universal, but our capacity to create cultural realities, and then to act in terms of them" (Mintz 1988, quoted in Wallerstein, 1989).

"The tripartite division of organized knowledge is an obstacle to our fuller understanding of the world" (Wallerstein, 1999).

"Nature and society are not two distinct poles, but one and the same production of successive status of societies-natures, of 'collectives.' It is by recognizing this and making it the center of our analyses of the world that we can go forward" (Ibid.).

"The ways of nature cannot be foreseen with certainty. The elements of accident therein cannot be eliminated ... Bifurcating nature is that in which small differences and insignificant fluctuation can, provided they occur in opportune circumstances, spread out through the whole system and bring into being a new mode of functioning" (Prigogine and Stenger, 1979).

"We live in an uncertain cosmos, whose single greatest merit is the permanence of the uncertainty, because it is this uncertainty that makes possible creativity—cosmic creativity and with that of cosmic human creativity" (Wallerstein, 1999).

"If everything is uncertain, then the future is open to creativity, not merely human creativity but the creativity of all nature" (Wallerstein, 1999).

"... complexity studies is emphasizing the arrow of time, a theme that has always been central to social sciences. It emphasizes complexity and admits that human social systems are the most complex of all systems. And it emphasizes creativity in nature, thus extending to all nature what was previously thought to be a unique feature of Homo Sapiens ... social science ... emphasizes the non-uniformity of social reality and the necessity of appreciating rationality of the other" (Wallerstein, 1999).

"Quantum as being individual and collective at the same time" (Sahlan Momo, 2013).

INTRODUCTION

Have-nots today are given only the following choices: "between the binaries of material destitution or acceptance of the market rules, traditional hardships or modern comfort, 'progress' or 'regress', 'development' or 'underdevelopment', advanced technology or primitive tools, high-tech medicine or second-rate shaman, school system or illiteracy" (Rahenema, 2005b:246). These binary choices have only increased the miseries of poor people and poor societies while benefitting imperialist countries in the form of higher profits and increased control of their ex-colonies. In order to find an alternative to these binary choices it is necessary to erase the existing conceptual binary distinction of developed/underdeveloped, which includes the other binaries mentioned above. The erasure of prevailing Eurocentric binaries will open up a space which will allow for the possibility of alternative perspectives to emerge along with a new set of concepts and narratives to explain our social reality. This will help us to find alternative strategies to improve our social conditions.

Therefore, in the following we discuss not only how to erase the binary distinction, but also alternative questions and related issues: the issue of binaries and evolution of the concept of human agency, a possible alternative approach along with related concepts of human creativity, humaneness, inner-self, and the metaphor of "Indra's Net." The last section of this chapter highlights how the corporate world is increasingly using modern technology to control human creativity and our inner-selves. The chapter ends with a summation and conclusion.

PROBLEMATIC ISSUE OF BINARY DISTINCTION

The issues surrounding binary distinction are not new, and have been critiqued by third-wave feminism, postcolonialism, postanarchism, and critical race theory. Proponents of these theories argue that the ideas of "civilized white man" and Western power structures are legitimized and perpetuated with the perceived binaries of man/woman, civilized/uncivilized, and white/black. Most of these theories focus on deconstructing the purported binaries but do not provide meaningful alternatives. The speed in which the contemporary historical process is moving and affecting the lives of billions of people in such a negative way has increased the urgency to find an alternative perspective to prevailing binaries, including that of developed/underdeveloped—the main focus of this study.

In order to find an alternative perspective, we need to understand the historical processes of social formation within both Western and non-Western societies as well as their interactions. Within these intersocietal and society-to-society interactions, the adaptation and exchange of cultures and cultural artifacts was and is inevitable as they co-constitute and co-produce each other. This exchange and adaptation of ideas and artifacts among societies can take place under different social relationships, although historically the predominant one has been the use of force. It cannot be claimed, as economist William Baumol suggests while rewriting the story of Western capitalism that, "Medieval China, for example, invented gunpowder, paper, the printing press and probably the compass and the waterwheel. But these inventions failed to raise living standards until adapted into consumer products by societies that were less hostile to commerce" (quoted in Weinstein, 1999). According to Baumol, "the genius of Western capitalism was to translate invention into the goods and services that enrich everyday life" (quoted in Ibid.). While making these suggestions, Baumol is only recognizing the genius of Western capitalism but not the genius of those who invented the new technology. The real irony is that today when China is able to adopt and adapt nuclear technology from the United States of America it is not considered a work of genius, but of espionage. How do we reconcile this double standard? Why is the marketing of products (advertising, promotional campaigns) and mass production processes (that have dehumanized the whole labor process) seen as the work of genius, while invention and the process of invention are not? One can see this happening in every field of human endeavor including music, art, fashion, education, technology, medicine, food, and so on. Every field is categorized in a way which erases the specificity and context of non-western countries. For example, music is categorized as Western (considered specific) and World Music (all the rest lumped together) (de Paor-Evans, 2018).

The process of mass production did not occur with a stroke of genius but in the undertaking of bitterly fought class struggles to control the hours of work, wages, and labor processes. At the heart of these developments are human labor and the human capability for creativity. Ignoring these historical processes of social production and reproduction is like saying that capitalism's exploitation of labor and the management of labor are the work of geniuses, but that the workers' initial knowledge of the production process, their knowledge of creating products in innovative ways, and their perfecting these processes with long time experience (all later appropriated by capitalists under the theory of scientific management) are not. Baumol's suggestions are based upon the assumption that the East is inferior to the West, a staple of Western thinking for a very long time, even when people in the East created these technologies that helped Western societies to achieve high standards of living for their middle classes. Thus, by ignoring the historical process of social formations within societies *and* their interactions (by force or mutual interests) in modern times, scholars such as Baumol can perpetuate the myth of the "genius" of Western capitalism and a "backward inferior" East, while keeping alive the binaries of tradition/progress and developed/underdeveloped. Such explanations call to mind the way in which philosopher and economist John Stuart Mill, while serving as an officer in the British East India Company for 35 years, studied the *Dharmashastras* in order to instruct the British on how to "manage" Indians socio-politically. His study of the *Dharmashastras* also influenced the "European liberalism" that Mill pioneered in Britain. Strangely, Mill did not consider India, the source of the *Dharmashastras,* ready for liberalism (Mehta, 1999).

This process of both appropriation and demonization of the source is ongoing and has been expanded to other cultures, as well. For example, North America is now appropriating Indic traditions (without having an identity crisis) such as yoga, and a knowledge of Ayurvedic medicines, while India is presented as other-worldly, pre-rational, and culturally backward. North America has exhibited similar behavior many times in the past when dealing with Native American and African cultures (Ibid.). This artificial binary of East (inferior) and West (superior) must be eliminated so that the continued expansion of this binary based on extreme nationalism or localism can be avoided. This does not mean that these regions are not different from one another historically, geographically, politically, economically and culturally. With a possible alternative approach suggested in this chapter, it will also be possible to eschew the artificial binary of developed/underdeveloped. England "developed" through the interaction process of plundering Latin America, North America, and later Asia and Africa, in order to advance materially. These were acts of robbery (as mentioned earlier, Britain drained 45 trillion dollars from India between 1765–1938), and aggression—not works of genius—against other societies that had neither provoked nor attacked England.

Hierarchical relationship between societies occurs when their interactions involve certain social elements of certain societies forcibly occupying (colonizing) other societies. By occupying another society and appropriating its resources (physical, material and human), the occupying society gains control over the institutions of knowledge production as well as the producers of knowledge in the colonized society. Through the control of this knowledge production, the occupying society is able to justify the exploitation of the colony to the members of the occupying society. In this way the colonizing society, while retaining the same social structure and inequalities within its own society, tries to solve the problems of its lower classes by stealing from others. For example, the foreign policies of different societies are mostly based on finding solutions to their own domestic economic and social problems, but only those societies with strong military force are able to rob others successfully (Chossudovsky, 1997; Chomsky, 1994; Eichengreen, 1997). In this process of stealing from others, the colonizing power also imposes its own ideas and cultural habits on the subordinated societies in order to guarantee a flow of human labor with colonial cultural ideas, tastes and habits, as well as natural resources.

At the same time, it is not to be assumed that the people of subordinated societies suddenly abandoned all their rituals of daily life. In fact, the subordinated people make sense (through "inner conversation"—that is, a process of comprehending one's everyday social reality through personal creativity and genius, also called "the consciousness of life") of their newly imposed social reality by creating and configuring a new, evolved culture. This new culture always accommodates parts of the imposed culture while continuing elements of the previous ones (Bahl, 2005). In all of these processes, it is the innate "humaneness (part of human creativity)" of human beings that creates a new agenda for life from an arbitrary life which looks like a seamless process to scholars who dwell only on colonial culture, Western science, or colonial imagination. It is ignored that human agency (as creativity) is not passive or simply receptive to an imposed agenda. Human beings are constantly creating and recreating their lives (and their culture) in the process of interacting with historical forces, as well as meeting their daily human needs, including their humaneness. No society can survive or progress without each individual member's capacity for humaneness. In other words, each human being's humaneness is what creates and sustains a society in the first place. At the same time, humaneness cannot be realized in a vacuum. It is realized while human beings (who are part of nature itself, as one of the species) interact with nature in all aspects, which includes non-humans, other human beings, and one's inner-self through "inner conversation," (Collin, 2004; Archer, 2000) while making sense of all these interactions through the use of some prevailing contemporary world view, or by creating one if none is available. Some scientists are also trying to understand this concept of inner conversation as observed by Nobel Laureate scientist Ilya Prigogine and author Isabelle Stengers:

> Scientists would be wrong to ignore the fact that theoretical construction is not the only approach to the phenomena of life: another way, that of understanding from within (interpretation), is open to us ... Of myself, of my own acts of perception, thought volition, feeling and doing, I have a direct knowledge entirely different from the theoretical knowledge that represents the 'parallel' cerebral processes in symbols. This inner awareness of myself is the basis for the understanding of my fellow-men whom I meet and acknowledge as beings of my own kind, with whom I communicate sometime so intimately as to share joy and sorrow with them (Prigogine and Stengers, 1984:311).

To fully comprehend the construction of social reality even under colonial rule and a hierarchical relationship, we need to understand the dynamics of human agency under various social conditions. In the following section, the concept of human agency is further expanded and deepened as "human creativity," which includes "humaneness" (discussed later). But first we need to understand how the concept of human agency evolved in the Western world.

EVOLUTION OF THE CONCEPT OF HUMAN AGENCY

Initially, the human social world was not given agency in Western history and sociology. However, agency was considered something located amidst the natural forces that were outside of society and history. Later, sociology was humanized by attaching the idea of human agency to "great" men (prophets, heroes, genius, and leaders) who supposedly "genetically" inherited the charismatic capacity, which they developed individually. Over time, the concept of human agency was extended to other people as producers, consumers, buyers, and sellers who were making collective, multiple, and dispersed decisions in everyday life (Sztompka, 1994:27). It was implicit in Merton's (1976:145–155) concept of "unintended consequences" which addressed the latent effect of human action. This idea further implied that the actions of each member of society contribute in bringing about the social change, therefore each member of society is an agent as well as an actor in the collective. Thus, it became possible to understand social change as "the aggregated and historically accumulated result of what each society member does for his/her own private reasons and egoistic purposes" (Sztompka, 1994:28). However, Marxian Conflict Theory emphasized dissension, strain, and tension within society. In the 1960s, with the emergence of new humanism and new subjectivity, the hermeneutic concern with individual people and actions became important. Based on these ideas, various theories of the new subjectivity school developed in the 1980s: the theory of postmodernism—which also influenced the Subaltern Studies Group in India—and post-modernist sociology. In these theories, as Piotr Sztompka quoting from Mongardini (1990) writes,

> [T]he urge for change became the glorification of change. Change was seen as a value in itself .... In all cultural forms, change, far from being the tool of modernity for achieving the goal of progress, has become an end in itself .... There begins a period of no progress and no history, a period of 'post culture' (Ibid., 32).

The social movements of the sixties and seventies also influenced a change in the subject matter of the social sciences, as social theorists acknowledged that individuals and their actions do count, sometimes, even under repressive structures. In addition, with the worldwide spreading of the ideas of pluralism and participation, representation made people aware that they had the power to improve their lives by changing the social structure. This realization of their own power to change their own living conditions allowed many people to respond strongly to economic recession, international conflict, as well as to the eruption of ethnic, racial, inter-generational, and class antagonism (Sztompka, 1994). Sztompka pointed out that the theoretical synthesis that emerged from these new realities was based on a binary approach that treated human agency as the opposite of structure/action, and historical sociology as the opposite of continuity/change. This new synthesis was in opposition to the earlier theorization of human agency, which was based on the concept of "morphogenesis" (Ibid., 35).

According to the concept of morphogenesis (Buckley, 1967), the structure is constantly being built and transformed. Similarly, Michel Crozier and Erhard Friedberg (1977) promoted the interdependence of actor and system as, according to them, "All change is the result of human inventiveness, creation, and search .... Collective learning is one of the fundamental mechanisms of social self-transformation" (Quoted in Sztompka, 1994:38). Even the rules and resources that actors use were seen as reshaped by social actors who use them (Giddens, 1985 cited in Sztompka, 1994) because people use the reflectiveness, and knowledgeability that are core properties of all human beings (Sztompka, 1994), including, I will add, human creativity. According to this thinking, while history making was contingent upon human agency, it did not match with human intentions. More recently, sociologist Margaret Archer added another layer to the concept of human agency. According to Archer, a social agent itself changes when it brings about social transformation because an agent has the "traits of reflectiveness, purposiveness, promotiveness, and innovativeness." Social agency shapes and reshapes structure while reshaping itself in the process of a "double morphogenesis" (quoted in Ibid., 42).

The notion of agency is also integrated in Historical Sociology, however, it did not make much of a dent in America, as America had poor historical traditions due to its adoption of the industrial capitalist economic system from its inception. Sociology in America has been more concerned with solving social problems and the functioning of the system such as eradicating crime and social disorganization, integrating local communities, improving the effectiveness of institutions, and raising the productivity of labor and efficiency of management. These concerns then guided American sociologists to rely on the empirical method along with psychology, which in turn helped in creating the theories of social behaviorism, symbolic interactions, and the exchange theory. In 1948, the theory of structural functionalism was formed in America under the influence of British functional anthropology. Since then, structural functionalist theory not only dominated American sociology, but was also transported and spread around the world. Sztompka pointed out that this theory has created an ahistorical bias and promotes the idea of presentism, as it is based on the assumption that society is an internally harmonious system which is self-regulating and equilibratory (Ibid., 46–47).

However, ahistoricism of the structural functionalist theory was challenged in the 1960s and 1970s by the conflict theory, which focused on the concept of "dialectics" of human agency and structure. The relation between human agency and structure was explained as a process of collective actions of individuals who can reproduce it and also transform it into a different structure through individual actions. Thus, Sztompka explained, it became possible to overcome the old dilemma of the binary distinctions of agency and structure, individual and holism. However, the dilemma was not completely resolved because, as Sztompka pointed out, the category of concepts such as representation, collectives, class consciousness, hegemony, praxis, agency, habitus, historicity, figurations, mobilization, anomie and duality of structure do not denote people or systems (Ibid., 270).

Sztompka offers a third theory saying that one cannot think of a human individual outside of some social context because the very definition of what it means to be an individual must contain reference to some social whole apart from the individuals who make it up (Ibid., 271). He further explains that in society, what exists is the unified socio-individual field where the ultimate atom in social reality is the living socio-individual field that is constructed in the process of being and events. In the making of an event, a fusion of the following takes place: individuality and totality, persistence and change, potentiality and actuality (Ibid., 273). Thus, praxis (events) and agency are connected because agency actualizes in praxis, and praxis reshapes agency, which actualizes itself in the changed praxis (Ibid., 275). Events (praxis) affect all aspects of life that together make up historical traditions: the material residue, memory traces, structural arrangements, and institutional forms. These events (praxis) could be intended, unintended, recognized, and unrecognized, but together they make up real circumstances, conditions and situations for further events (praxis). Thus, according to Sztompka, "history is simultaneously the continuous chain of praxis and conditions for praxis" (Ibid., 276).

In the 1970s, the sociological field became split between macro-theories emphasizing organizational, institutional, and structural aspects of society (conflict theory, structural Marxism, and neo-Weberian theory), and micro-theories emphasizing individual actions, meanings, symbols, awareness, and the subjective construction of reality (exchange and rational choice, symbolic interactionism, dramaturgical theory, ethnomethodology and phenomenology) (Ibid., 1994:xii). But there were also efforts to synthesize these theories (Bourdieu, Alexander, Giddens, Archer, Sztompka) that led to a debate over agency and structure (Ibid., xiii).

Recently, historian Lynn Hunt expressed a desire for a "theory of the mutual relationship between the individual self and the larger society" (quoted in Moyn, 2015:12). She seems unaware that it has already been developed by sociologists such as C. Wright Mills. Mills's notion of "sociological imagination" allows us to understand the relationship between history and biography at any given point in time. Samuel Moyn pointed out that relation of self and society has been the constant concern of social theory since its origin from Vico to Marx. Moreover, Marx did not treat human being and nature as two separate entities as he wrote, "To say that man's physical and mental life is linked to nature simply means that nature is linked to itself, for man is a part of nature" (Marx, [1844] 2007:107). Recently, sociologist Jason Moore reinforced Marx's idea noting, "Human agency is always within, and dialectically bound to nature as a whole … human agency is not purely human at all. It is bundled with the rest of nature" (Moore, 2015:37). Moore's ideas seem to reflect my understanding of human agency as human creativity (discussed later).

In my last book (Bahl, 2005), I suggested the idea of explaining "human agency as human creativity" in the sense that every human is born with an innate capacity for creativity that enables humans to create society, language, and everything else that humans need to survive and protect themselves from harmful forces and objects. It is a collective and collaborative act that makes human survival possible. My ideas on human agency as human creativity are further elaborated in the current chapter with the assumption that humans themselves are part of nature, because nature exists within the human body and helps the human body to function. Humans are one of the infinite expressions of nature's creativity. Thus, human beings have inherited this innate creativity of nature (some people refer it as intelligence or consciousness), which allows them to function using their bodies and minds, while interacting with other humans. Through these interactions human beings create, sustain, and reproduce society while fulfilling their needs.

NEED FOR AN ALTERNATIVE APPROACH

The question of finding an alternative perspective to this binary distinction has also been raised by many scholars for some time. For example, Terry Eagleton pointed out in his book, *Reason, Faith and Revolution,* that science, reason, liberalism, and capitalism do not deliver what is ultimately needed (Eagleton, 2009). He raises theological questions: Why is there anything in the first place? Why is what we do actually intelligible to us? And where do our notions of explanation, regularity, and intelligibility come from? Eagleton thinks that these questions cannot be answered by liberal rationalism and economic calculations, as people inhabiting in these fields believe in the superstition of "untrammeled human progress," as well as trusting in the efficiency of social engineering and liberal enlightenment. He writes, "If ever there was a pious myth and piece of credulous superstition, it is the liberal-rationalist belief that, a few hiccups apart, we are steadily en route to a finer world" (Ibid., 70). He points out that "all reasoning is conducted within the ambit of some sort of faith, attraction, inclination, orientation, predisposition or prior commitment" (Ibid., 120). Eagleton believes that there is no simple bare account of facts, and that we are still facing the problem of choosing between religious faith (with flaws) and hubristic faith in the power of reason and progress that has no content. According to Eagleton, a transformed future could come into being if these "liberal dogmatist, doctrinaire flag-wavers for Progress and Islamophobic intellectuals did not continue to stand in its way" (Ibid., 169). Another scholar made the following remarks:

> The fields of emergence, holism, and complexity are revealing entirely new dimensions of our existence, and work in the cognitive sciences is revealing what many of us have already known: that we are not discrete, autonomous machines, genetically driven in the mindless pursuit of self-interest … We are now learning things about ourselves that are in complete contrast to what we have been taught to be true for hundreds of years. The model of human agency and the assumptions that underlie it frame our entire political, legal and economic system. That model is now being shown to be false … This singular conception [rational] of mankind has served as justification for four hundred years of capitalism's systematic destruction of human community and eco system. The ecological and social catastrophic devastating the planet clearly shows that capitalism's hero 'the selfish

> individual' has no idea what he is doing, and now we know why: the hero's life is based on a lie ... The material conditions of daily life are changing rapidly, and the old narratives are no longer believable (Dardozzi, 2010, monthlyreview.org).

World renowned sociologist Immanuel Wallerstein also raised this question earlier:

> Physical scientists and mathematicians are now telling us that truth in their arenas is complex, indeterminate, and dependent on an 'arrow of time.' What does that mean for social scientists? For, it is clear that, of all systems in the universe, human social systems are the most complex structures that exist, the ones with the briefest stable equilibria, the ones with the greatest number of outside variables to take into account, the ones that are most difficult to study (Wallerstein, 2000:197).

Wallerstein also points out that "within the inner sanctum of physics, this world view [universalism] is being challenged ... with a sober insistence on the range of human possibility," and on scientific grounds (Wallerstein, 1991:219). He laments that "at this moment when physical scientists are experiencing a 'profound change in the scientific concept of nature,' many social scientists are still clinging to their version of universalism and linearly derived from the older view of physical science." He thinks that, "the implications for social decision making are obviously even more immediate and more threatening of established interests than the implications for engineering and technology" (Ibid.).

Complexity theory emphasizes complexity, focusing on the fact that "human social systems are the most complex of all systems. And [this theory] emphasizes creativity in nature, thus extending to all nature what was previously thought to be a unique feature of Homo sapiens" (Wallerstein, 1999:250). The Nobel Laureate scientist Ilya Prigogine explains that the complex nature of the world of dynamics was "a 'divine' world on which time has no impact, from which the birth and death of things are forever excluded" (quoted in Ibid: 250). This is indeed a more complex understanding of the nature of all living systems. Prigogine came to his conclusion about the deeper level of order in the universe based on his experiment of mixing together some chemicals where he saw how a new complex ordered system appeared spontaneously (Talbot, 1991).

Synthesizing the outline of emerging theories of living systems, physicist Fritjof Capra presented a unified view of mind, matter, and life. He purported that since our perception of reality is based on Cartesian duality, our crisis is really the crisis of perception (Capra, 1994). He suggested that by using a holistic perspective of "deep ecology" we shall be able to appreciate the intrinsic value of all living beings and view humans as just one particular strand in the whole web of life. Once we become aware that we are part of the whole web of life, it will be natural for us to care for all of living nature (Ibid., 12).

Capra observed that two concepts derived from the new science of ecology, community and network, are helpful in imagining the eco-system as a network with a few nodes. However, when these nodes are magnified, each one appears itself as a network. Moreover, each node in the new network may represent an organ which in turn will appear as a network magnified, and so on (Ibid., 35). According to this perspective, there is no above or below in nature, and there are no hierarchies—there are only networks nesting with other networks. Capra noted that the network concept has been central to recent advances in scientific understanding of not only ecosystem, but also the very nature of life (Capra, 1994:41; Avery, 2003). Imagining connections between societies on similar lines I have suggested the metaphor of Indra's Net (discussed later).

Furthermore, the concept of "bio-regulation" was developed in the sciences to show how a system regulates itself (Capra, 1996:45). This concept came into being in the context of the change that was taking place during the 1970s when a systematic concept of life, mind, and consciousness began to emerge, which helped in unifying various disciplines that were formally separated. Similarly, cybernetics represents a unified approach to problems of connection and control, involving a whole complex of novel ideas. However, the idea of self-regulation is not new, as it was already in common parlance for hundreds of years in the phrases like "self-fulfilling prophecy, vicious cycles, and bandwagon effect" (Ibid., 63).

A POSSIBLE ALTERNATIVE PERSPECTIVE

Obviously, the search for an alternative view has been a concern of many physicists and social scientists for a long time. My search is no different in that regard. However, my specific concern and focus is on the binary distinction of "development/underdevelopment" because it represents a false dichotomy, as does the distinction of "human agency" and "structure," in explaining any social reality. If we wish to create a better world (as most of the scholars writing on "human agency" seem to believe they do) then it is imperative that we find ways to erase these binary distinctions and to develop an alternative approach to understanding all societies. The matters of metanarrative (structure) and human agency (subjectivity) are connected and intertwined as already pointed out by various scholars such as Prigogine and Wallerstein. However, we need to cultivate a different and deeper understanding of "human agency" (not in terms of an "individual hero" within the capitalist system) as human creativity and humaneness (deepening the human agency), that will eliminate the need for this specific problematic metanarrative of development/underdevelopment. For that purpose, it will be helpful to look at the commonalities (universal elements) among all societies without undermining their differences (specificities). This can be done by using the same yardstick of parity to evaluate each society, while keeping in mind that all societies are equal and unique at the same time, as they are part of a larger web, or network, resembling Indra's Net (discussed later). With this approach it will be possible to eliminate the need for categorizing societies as developed or underdeveloped.

ASSUMPTIONS OF THE ALTERNATIVE PERSPECTIVE

The assumption of the alternative perspective is that all societies are created in the process of interaction of people within and outside of each society to fulfill their daily human needs for existence (Bahl, 2005). Geographical location has also an important role in creating the possibilities of interaction between particular group of people within a given geographical region, thus creating a particular cultural outlook and philosophy of life. It also contributes to the possibility of self-sufficiency in supplying food, or increased dependence and the need for acquiring more land. If we look at these forces and at people's choices in these contexts, we can understand why Russia (or any other society) did not follow the same so-called "stages" (there are no fixed stages) of "development" as the Western world did. Russian society (and others) evolved in their own specific ways as they had different historical trajectories. No society can be a replica of another society, and it does not need to be. However, all societies are similar in the sense that they all are trying to meet the needs of their members through an interdependent process in which all members use their human creativity/consciousness to not only create society, but also to reproduce it while solving the various problems of everyday life.

The suggested possible alternative perspective postulates that evolving humans are equal in the sense that they all are endowed with similar biological and genetical make-up as well as similar qualities of intelligence, humaneness, creativity, and a capability for self-learning including the capacity to make and enjoy music. All humans have the same goal—to achieve inner peace and happiness—and all humans are part of what physicist Capra called the "supreme consciousness" (Capra, 1996), or, in other words, unified field of consciousness. This idea is based on the understanding that every human being is able to learn and communicate with one or more languages (verbal or non-verbal) made up of abstract symbols. Every human being who is able to create, learn and use abstract symbols has an innate creative genius in her/him. Humans have inherited this innate creativity from nature, as humans are one of the infinite expressions of nature. With this capability for creativity, humans are able to create things or any social structures, which is different than saying that only artists or musicians are creative or that a computer whiz is creative—yes, they are all creative but only in the way all of us are creative in everyday life. As mentioned earlier, Connor observed that it was ordinary humble people and artisans who gathered knowledge about nature and who created tools and techniques which made it possible for modern science to emerge (Conner, 2005).

All societies and their cultures, social structures and social institutions are emergent processes and none of them is a finished product. However, when new structures come into being they eliminate earlier structures (Ibid.; Sztompka, 1994). Social forces also keep changing continuously with the conjunction of various historical forces that are guided by human creativity, human choices, and human actions in their everyday struggle for survival, both as individual and as a part of a larger social structure. One can observe the manifestation of human creativity in every aspect of human life including the creation of society through the process of human interaction. Therefore, continuously evolving (and becoming) human beings should be considered the real players in the formation of the history, social institutions, power relations and culture(s) of any society. However, "social structures have agency that transcends and influences the intentions of the individual agents that co-constitute them" (Gorski, 2013:668) and thus influences the actions of its members in a dialectical process. In this perspective, "culture" is continuously emerging from the historical process of interaction among human beings to meet their daily human needs in specific places and times (Bahl, 2005). There cannot be one culture in a society but many cultures based on various social relationships that emerge from the dynamic historical process of social formations that includes the geography of the region and intrasocietal interactions. In all these processes, human beings also use their "inner conversation" (a process of comprehending one's everyday social reality through her/his creativity and genius that is also called consciousness of life) to give meaning to their existence in everyday life [(1)].

The history of any society is constructed by each person in that society as each follows one's own consciously desired end which takes many different directions. However, as Indian sociologist Ramkrishna Mukherjee pointed out, people's choices and actions do not necessarily produce the intended results. This is because the outcome of the disparate actions of each person creates a series of manifold effects upon the outer world. Thus, each society develops a particular historical trajectory based on various random acts by various groups of people. However, this does not mean that every person in a society has a uniquely different idea about existence and a better quality of life. People in every society have a common goal to achieve four cardinal human values: survival, security, prosperity, and progress (Mukherjee, 1991:29). Another scholar reached a similar conclusion about the randomness of human action. "All long term changes were inadvertent" as "individual and groups affected change to solve their own problems that they defined within the actual existing contexts of their medieval and early modern societies" (Lachmann, 2000:8). Sociologist Randall Collins has analyzed how we create society (its components: social stratification, culture and social institutions) every day through symbols, and through interactive rituals that involves emotional energy. He wrote, "Instead of focusing on the individual, we can look at the structuring of an entire social arena or institution as a linkage of interaction ritual chains … The mechanism is the same whether these chains are focused on material economic activities or on purely sociable relationships" (Collins, 2004: xiv–xv).

During the last 500 years, with the advent of colonialism and imperialism, society-to-society interaction in the world has increased to an unprecedented degree, and this has injected an added dimension to the on-going process of social and cultural formation within these interacting societies. This understanding assumes that culture formation in societies consists of a complex, multi-dimensional process. Unlike hunting and gathering societies, which tended to develop more internally with person-to-person interaction (and interaction with neighboring societies), most societies are exposed more and more to external forces (including technology) and to increased society-to-society interaction since the advent of the agriculture age, and the age of imperial conquest (Bahl, 2005).

Based on the assumptions of these alternative ideas, and with the metaphor of Indra's Net in mind, we can understand all societies with the yardstick of parity while recognizing their specificities. This understanding does not make any society unequal, superior, or inferior. Societies do not move from primitive to modern or from underdeveloped to developed status. There is no single path of social evolution that all societies must pass through because the history of each society is a product of human actions creating a contingency of various events that come together in a particular way at a particular time. All living societies are constantly changing through human actions and interactions (intersocietal and intrasocietal), and they must adapt to change. However, a new situation does not necessarily engender superiority over an earlier condition. Moreover, change comes from within a society including its interaction with natural forces, as well as from its interaction with larger international historical forces. All of these forces, those within a society and those in the larger world (including nature and geography), create a specific history of each society that is distinct from every other society. At the same time, all societies also share many commonalities as the process of the making of every society is similar. Therefore, by looking into those commonalities it will be possible to conceive how we can erase the binary divide of development/underdevelopment in our analysis.

In the following we discuss the main commonalities among societies: Human Creativity and Human Interaction, Humaneness, Connectedness of all Societies, Universal Consciousness/Unified Field of Consciousness, and Collective Human Knowledge.

UNDERSTANDING COMMONALITIES AMONG SOCIETIES

1. Human Creativity and Human Interaction

The main commonality among societies is "human creativity" as "it is not our human nature that is universal, but our capacity to create cultural realities, and then to act in terms of them" (Mintz quoted in Wallerstein, 1989:5). Members of the human species (not a fixed entity but an evolving human—physically, spiritually, and socially) are born with an innate capability of creativity (Bahl, 2005). For example, a human child, only a few months old, is able to process various sounds possessing social meaning—language—and making connections between the sounds and their meaning is nothing short of an act of genius. What that child will do with her/his innate creativity when she/he grows up in a particular society and in a particular time is a different matter (Angier, 2012). According to developmental psychologist Rebecca Treiman, "Children at this very early age [3 years old] really know a lot more than we had previously thought," while a literacy development specialist Kathy Hirsh Pasek said, "those [tots'] squiggles, that ability to use lines to represent something bigger, to represent something deeper than what is on that page, is the great open door into the world of symbolic thought" (quoted in Neergard, 2016).

It is important to point out that all human beings are capable of symbolic thinking, such as languages (verbal and non-verbal). This implies that human beings everywhere in the past and in the present time are capable of developing consciousness that extends beyond their time and place, and also of developing perception of the world within and beyond one individual (Foer, 2011). The capacity for creating abstract symbols has helped people face numerous challenges in their day-to-day survival by tapping into their inner resources (Stix, 2011). Children, according to psychologist Michael Tomesello, are born equipped with a special set of abilities—cultural intelligence—that prepares them for learning from parents, teachers, and playmates (Ibid.). His research shows that at about nine months of age, children can engage in a figurative form of mind reading with their parents. Each has what psychologist call "a theory of mind." This capacity to engage with another person to play a game or achieve a common goal is what Tomasello calls "shared intentionality" (Ibid.). He describes this as an evolutionary adaptation that is unique to humans because humans have an inherited predisposition for a degree of cooperative social interactions that make culture based on cooperation possible. Based on this understanding, Tomasello thinks that toddlers have an intuitive understanding of iconic gestures for many familiar activities. Thus, the capability for cooperative social interaction has made other communication possible which has helped in creating institutions, culture and society at large (Ibid.).

In society, humans are not autonomous beings living in a vacuum. Human beings and their societies are interdependent similar to the way whole and part are held together in integral unity as in Indra's Net (discussed later). Roy Bhaskar's idea of dialectics is useful for understanding this mechanism (Gorski, 2013), and Archer's (1985) idea of "inner conversation" is useful for understanding human reflexivity in everyday life and how it works. Sociologist Margaret Archer explained that social systems undergo radical restructuring due to human agency, at the same time human agency is also transformed in the process. She proposed the concept of double morphogenesis in which "structure is the conditioning medium and elaborated outcome of interaction: agency is shaped and reshaped structure whilst reshaping itself in the process" (quoted in Sztompka, 1994:42). While summarizing the legacy of the theories of agency Sztompka also noted on similar lines that,

> Action occurs in the context of encountered structures, which it shapes in turn, resulting in the dual quality of structures (as both shaping and shaped), and dual quality of actors (as both producers and product); ... that the interchange of action and structure occurs in time, by means of alternating phases of agential creativeness and structural determination (Ibid., 43).

There is no binary distinction between human agency and structure, as society and individual life are not separate processes. Each makes the other simultaneously in what Sztompka calls, "social becoming" (Szrompka, 1994). (It is also like quantum physics; the individual in two places at the same time/being an individual and being part of collective both at the same time.) However, social becoming does not take place separately from nature (which is non-human) because nature not only provides the sustenance and all resources that are needed for humans to exist and flourish, but also lives within the human body itself where trillions of bacteria reside. Human creativity (inherited from nature itself) manifests itself only through human action (inner-conversation) and interaction processes. There is no conflict as body-mind-self emerge out of one another and remain an integrated whole all the time as it is a unified whole (non-duality is different from unity) and not a separate process. One can observe this process in the making of any social event. It is human interactions creating events that make all societies possible, which includes their cultures (values, beliefs, traditions, arts, and total way of life), and social institutions (family, polity, economy, religion, education, technology), and social structures (class, race, gender and other stratifications) to fulfill the human needs of their members. In this process of making of any society the important common factor is human creativity—an innate capacity to imagine, think, create language, naming, reifying, communicating, and taking action. Thinking is actually an inner-conversation we all do in our head, and it is quasi-verbal. Randall Collins explains that it is this internal ritual that makes our inner-selves different from our outer-selves (Collins, 2004:xvi).

In fact, everyday creativity is a routine thing that happens all the time. It includes commonplace ideas we have about how to do things, the things we create and produce, acts of management, or self-presentation or insightful speech and so on (Gauntlett, 2011). For example, the term *jugaad* in India refers to a traditional, frugal, innovative system that is followed in solving everyday challenges, such as, Indian villagers designing a rural vehicle by connecting an old chassis to the engine of an irrigation pump (Bahl, 2005). It is possible to find thousands of such examples not only in India but everywhere in the world. A recent book has provided numerous accounts of such examples (Banerjee and Duflo, 2011). These things do not require expert verifications. It is interesting to note that scholars are increasingly seeing potentials in the concept of *jugaad* for articulating ways of being, as human beings are an open system capable of creativity and resistance (Banerjee et al., 2016).

Human agents are bio-psycho-spiritual-social structures (Gorski, 2013) with the power of interactivity and innate creativity. Life does not happen inside a human alone, as life is achieved through larger dynamics of human interactions with social structures, with one another, as well as with nature, as humans are part of nature and thus nature itself. New ideas and collective consciousness are created through the meeting and mating of brains and with a cross-fertilization of ideas (Johnson, 2010). Recombining ideas happens with creativity, and social structures are the elaborated outcome of the interaction of human creativity that shapes and reshapes structure while reshaping itself in the process. It is up to us as to how we use our inner creativity to make a better society and better world by realizing how we are all connected, not only to other human beings, but to all inanimate and animate beings on, the planet and in the cosmos—as we are not only part of nature itself but also in it. Nature and humans are not two separate entities because every human is made out of same ingredients that are found in the stars (Jayawardhana, 2015; Lenton, 2016), and with the same process. "Billions of years of co-evolution have produced innumerable species and life webs that are metabolically connected at every level, from the smallest cell to the entire planet" (Angus, 2018 in countercurrents.org, April 23). With this knowledge, it is reasonable to assume that people in one society are as creative as any other society (as humans everywhere are part of nature, and creativity is inherent in nature) and no one is "superior/inferior; developed/underdeveloped" except when one society colonizes others and imposes these labels and conditions on them. This understanding is important in challenging the Western binary distinction of "developed/underdeveloped" and creating an alternative perspective.

All types of every day acts of creativity, including the making of art and creating technology and science, require a similar process involving an intuitive appreciation of the relationship among objects, ideas, and symbolic representation. In other words, symbolic cultural form comes into being because of the preexisting human potential to create or imagine music, or any other art form (Newberg, 2001; Tattersall, 2001). For example, according to psychologist Carl Rogers, everything we create is through a creative process. It could be anything from creating an instrument of murder to making music, poetry, and scientific theory (Rogers, 1954). On the same lines, de Certeau has suggested, this ability of human beings, i.e. to create a new set of everyday practices on the basis of a preexisting harmony and to maintain a formal relationship between them, in spite of the variation of the elements, should be treated on par with a similar process that takes place in both artistic production and serious thinking. In other words, "[I]t could be considered the ceaseless creativity of a kind of taste in practical experience" (de Certeau, 1988:73). Similarly, archeologists have also pointed out that "thinking and communicating through abstract symbols is the foundation of all creativity," in art, music, mathematics, science, and language (Wilford, 2002). More recently, David Gauntlett, while analyzing the development of the Web system in relation to everyday small acts of creation, wrote that it is something at the level of feeling (Gauntlett, 2011). In fact, creativity is something that happens quite routinely whenever any of us does something in an unexpected but striking and inventive way. For example, every day we have ideas about how to do things, how to create and produce things, how to manage a place or people, perform self-presentation, or come up with an insightful speech (Ibid.; see also Ashton, 2015). In everyday life, the role of memory is important as it is about "developing the capacity to quickly create images that link disparate ideas, while creativity is the ability to form similar connections between disparate images and to create something new and hurl it into the future so it becomes poem, a building, a dance, a novel" (Reitz, 2008).

The world of technology and business is more attuned to this understanding of "creativity" and corporate leaders are able to successfully tap into the collective genius of many people to develop new products. John Morse, president and publisher of Merriam-Webster, pointed out that people with their collective genius are developing vocabulary that is immediately accessible to all of us and, "It's sometimes absolutely poetic" (Reitz, 2008). Similarly, in the business world, the idea of using open source technology in Linux is promoted because it is powered by the brilliance of thousands of programmers who created it (Taylor, 2006.). Business executives are increasingly recognizing that it is more useful to tap into the collective mind of many people (needs an open system), as each one of them has a different set of life experiences that can help create amazingly new ideas and products. With this realization, the co-founder of the collective system, engineering and software company Rite-Solutions said, "At most companies, especially technology companies, the most brilliant insights tend to come from people other than senior management. So, we created a marketplace to harvest collective genius" (Ibid.). It is similar to what Rider (2010) suggested that many innovations take place with collective accumulated knowledge and not by the genius of a single person.

The same creative capabilities have also helped humans to develop cultural attributes, maintaining a common identity and communicating ideas that helped organize societies into stable, enduring regional groups. But the need to develop new symbolism and new identities arises when diverse cultures interact on a continuous basis. Such cross-cultural interaction, according to Rahman, becomes possible when people within a society try to fulfill their needs—food, labor force, trade, raw material, marriage—by venturing outside of their own territory. Many times, this cross-cultural interaction can be on unequal terms due to the colonial context; nevertheless, the contact itself creates possibilities for influencing one another's culture (Rahman, 1999).

But people forget these social realities and treat these environments as independent powerful forces. By understanding this process in each society (it is not a fixed, bound entity and it is not the same as a political nation-state that came into being in the nineteenth century), it will be possible to demonstrate that all societies are equal in their social formation process and in people's struggle to fulfill everyday human needs, even when they all vary in their actual material and physical manifestations. It will also help us to find out why and how people of some societies could invade and control other societies. How did the colonized people find ways to make life meaningful with their new living conditions? How did people re-define their roles and opportunities and adjust to their new circumstances? For example, P. B. Mukharji's study of Ayurvedic modernity is pertinent to understand the braiding process of religious ideas, Western science and medicine along with caste and *jati* beliefs in the small community of regional medical practitioners, called Kobirajes. They were trained in Western medicine and they used small modern Western technologies/instruments and adapted to various pressures (*jati,* religion, Western knowledge, foreign rule, local medical knowledge and needs and perceptions of local customers) in practicing Ayurvedic medicines while residing around Kolkata (earlier Calcutta) under the British colonial rule (Mukharji, 2016). Invariably, while making adjustments and compromises under their new circumstances, people create a new vocabulary (or sometimes modified existing terminology, as in the context of 'caste') to explain changes in their everyday lives, in their redefined goals, and in limitations of everyday life that tend to merge with the existing local cultures over time. For example, colonialism was also an interactive process. Indian nationalists and natives used interaction with the colonizers for their own purpose and created "a new synthesis" that in turn contributed in the process of decolonization (Iyer, 2011).

My idea of human creativity assumes (as discussed earlier) that all humans are born with similar creative capacities and thinking apparatuses. My ideas, like Sheldrake's "morphic resonance," is in tune with the idea of a "psychic unity of mankind" which is reflected in the similarities of ideas, images, patterns, concepts of space and time, concept of trinity and the Cross in vastly different cultures that are located on different continents worldwide (Koepping, 1983; d'Huy, 2016). However, these similarities are likely also due to human migration, as travelers carried their myths with them along with their knowledge of various technologies, art and other concepts that are refined and redefined across generations. According to Sheldrake, creativity does not unfold as a fixed plan because it is an impetus of life, and current of life itself (Sheldrake, 2012). Even when human beings are endowed with an inherent creative capacity, their actions (through the creative capacity) are produced as Sheldrake suggests, without the need for divine guidance or intervention (Ibid.). The merit of this approach is that individual agency gets a holistic treatment as being a part of larger cosmic world (that includes non-human entities also) that, according to Sheldrake, has an inherent quality of "morphic resonance." The idea of "field" was also used by sociologist Sztompka, to create a non-binary concept (mentioned earlier) called, "living socio-individual field in the process of becoming" (in short it is called "social becoming") to explain social reality (Sztompka, 1994:274).

Thus, each human being should be considered both an integrated being with a separate body structure having an innate creative capability and potentialities, and a social being who realizes all innate potential creatively through social interaction only, while forming social relationships and simultaneously using "inner conversations" (Archer, 2000) to interpret those social relationships. Having this understanding, it is suggested here that scholars should explore how these evolving humans went/go about in everyday life to meet their daily needs, and how humans must be adjusting, compromising, challenging, and reconfiguring their environment to make sense of their daily lives, as well as how they created new circumstances in their given environment. In this way, it will be possible to eliminate the conceptual divide between evolving human beings and their creation of a society, and instead imagine relationships of part (individual) and whole (society) as in Indra's Net (discussed later). Based on this understanding it can be further suggested that "consciousness/

creativity" as a non-dualistic concept is also the basis of all living beings in nature at large, and in all societies.

In light of all these ideas and understanding, it is not too farfetched to say that the *process* of learning and creating things is always the same everywhere. It is through the innate capacity of human creativity that human beings are able to form social institutions and various fine arts and artifacts, while interacting with other human beings (and through inner conversation) to fulfill their everyday needs for survival. Therefore, it is important to treat "human creativity" as a basic unit of analyses to understand how people in each society build their environments—social, political, economic, cultural, religious, and relations with outside forces—in which humans have as much to contribute as the environment they create and vice versa (Bahl, 2005).

Human Capacity for Reification

The innate creativity of humans also includes the capacity for reification (through inner conversation); treating an abstract concept or inanimate thing as if it were a person, has consciousness as if it had a reality of its own. Reification takes place at two levels: first, imagining a possible concrete form; and second, after converting the imagined form into a concrete form through words, sounds, or any other modality, providing meaning to these forms and then treating them as if they are real and true. This evokes what is known in India as *Maya*. According to the Hindu belief system, *Maya* means that everything in the world is an illusion, including one's wealth (for example, our belief in paper money and its exchange value in turn provides real value to that paper, which otherwise on its own has no value, and which is also called *Maya*, and therefore slippery), and the human body itself which is made of five elements and after death returns to those same five elements. Thus, according to this belief, we are all trapped in an earthly illusionary world of "*Maya Jal*" (network of illusion) while believing it to be the real world. When a person dies one leaves behind all accumulated wealth, as well as a body that disintegrates into the five basic elements it was originally made of. (Even science has now concluded that the apparent solidity of particles in an atom's nucleus is an illusion) (See Capra, 1984.). Our concrete "reality" of social structure and culture which emerges through the process of interaction and reification, gives people the impression that they have no control over social, political, economic, and cultural realities while forgetting that it is the creativity of people, not a god or nature, who created these social realities (including society and its social structures) in the first place. This explanation does not deny the role of natural forces such as physical geography and climate in the social formation processes within a given society (Bahl, 2005).

These reified social realities also change through the process of constant social interaction among people to fulfill their daily human needs and through their "inner conversation" to make sense of these realities. This whole process of fulfilling daily human needs, which I shall refer to as "humaneness" (discussed below), requires human communication and interaction through symbols (created through the innate capacity of creativity in human beings).

2. Humaneness

A human being becomes human in the process of realizing one's "humaneness." It includes all the physical, material, intellectual, emotional, and spiritual needs of human beings, as well as the sense of self-identity, creativity, personal fulfillment, cooperation, and compassion for others. But humaneness can only be realized in a social context where human beings interact with one another while using their creativity in everyday life.

All human beings are born with both capacities—creativity and humaneness—but we have relegated the power to define and interpret these capacities to the domain of institutionalized religion, which blinds us from using our own capacities to find an alternative historical perspective. However, neoliberals have been able to use religious institutions, religious vocabulary, and the concept of humanitarianism to promote their own agenda. Therefore, if we wish to find an alternative perspective, we need to first take back the power of defining our capacity for creativity and humanness. We need to reinforce the idea that an evolving generic human being learns to be human while interacting with other human beings, either "real" or, now-a-days "virtual." Human interaction is necessary for the reproduction of human beings, biologically (sometimes indirectly in the age of test tube babies and sperm banks), which includes everyday human reproduction, and socially. It is undisputable that every human baby needs other human beings for physical, emotional, and mental nourishment for a long time, and that these needs require some form of compassion on the part of adult human beings. Moreover, in this process of biological and social reproduction, human beings have to be constantly inventive to find new ways to meet their daily human needs in different social, historical and natural geographical environmental contexts. In this process of finding new ways of using their creative capabilities to adjust and to live in different natural and social conditions, human beings also create new social and historical conditions (including technology) in their societies (Bahl, 2005).

My use of the term "humaneness" implies both the capacity for innate human creativity enabling people to find ways to survive and fulfill their daily human needs, and people's capacity to care for others while transcending their selfishness (a recent report shows that humans are wired to care for one another), but not in the way neoliberals are using this concept to justify their goals. My understanding is that human creativity and its manifestation in humaneness are more easily discernible and displayed when humans find themselves under extremely oppressive social and political conditions in which they do not abandon their ingenuity while adapting or struggling to change their conditions. To illustrate, we draw on examples from the histories of the Americas, Africa, East Asia, and India.

Slaves in the US kept their creativity alive under the most adverse conditions by creating new music, thousands of quilt patterns, and various artifacts while also trying to keep their social bonds intact. There were many slaves who ran away to the marshlands to live under the most hazardous conditions in order to live a free life.

The form of oppression differed under a free labor market. In that economy, working masses were put under new oppressive working and living conditions, often alienating them from the work process, the finished products, their coworkers, and each other. In spite of these hurdles, the working masses were able to find ways to cooperate with one another (trade unions) to change their living and working conditions, while also expressing their creative ideas in poems, songs, art and other forms. They were also able to transcend many ethnic differences (but not gender differences, especially in North America) and to come together in their struggle against capitalist forces, often winning major victories (Bahl, 1995). A relatively recent example of such a victory is in South Africa where poor people are once again standing up together, in spite of ethnic differences (in some cases joining former enemies from the era of apartheid), against the ANC government to improve their living conditions (Desai, 2002). Similarly, in Mexico, where 40 percent of the population currently lives in extreme poverty, people are not passively waiting to be pulled out of the increasing immiseration (Bahl, 2005). Instead, they are searching for ways to exercise a modicum of self-governance to strengthen their organization and their ability to survive at the margins of a globalized society. They continued to produce their basic needs locally and are involved in projects and initiatives that attempt to identify ways of inserting innovations into existing community structures to produce new commodities and services (Barkin, 2003). More recently black working-class communities in Jackson, Mississippi have seriously begun to take control of their everyday needs by creating community cooperatives including banks, food production, pooling of skills, education, and so on (Akuno and Nangwaya, 2017). We can add similar examples from Brazil and Argentina as well. According to the IMF the *piqueters* (largely unemployed persons who are trying to survive by creating neighborhood unions) in Argentina are "the 'collateral damage' of neoliberalism—a fluke explosion that happened when rapid-fire privatization was mixed with 'shock' austerity in the mid-1990s" (Klein, 2003). These *piqueters* refused to disappear quietly into the scavenged shanty towns and slowly die. Instead, they organized picketing events to block highways and bridges until the government agreed to provide unemployment benefits (Ibid.). Nonetheless, as one observer noted, the Argentine government and capitalist forces treat the desperate quest of millions of Argentinians to stay alive as a threat to the economy's recovery, and they believe that people's efforts to stay alive must be halted, with brute force, in order to get more IMF loans (Ibid.).

Another illustration of human ingenuity can be seen in the ability of tribal workers in India to acquire new skills in record time as they adjusted and adapted to new factory life environments modeled on Western values that were completely alien to them until the 1920s. This example also refutes the prevailing myths—among both Western and Eastern scholars—about the "cultural backwardness" of the working masses in India (Bahl, 1995), a characteristic theoretically responsible for India's poverty. The Tata steel workers' struggle in colonial India demonstrates that between 1920 and 1940, tribal people who joined the modern Indian steel industry were able to run an entire rail mill on their own within a few years. Any lack of advanced knowledge about the machines or the discipline of factory life, did not stop them from becoming wholly skilled workers whose abilities matched those of the imported European workers who worked along them. These Indian workers also found ways to improve their living and working conditions when pushed to the extreme by company policies. Moreover, they used their existing cultural ideas of justice and fair play to resolve problems that arose from the emerging social relationships created by the modern steel industrial set-up (Ibid.). In all of these adaptations and maneuverings in new social conditions, it was their "humaneness" that guided the actions of the tribal workers. Therefore, while examining any historical process of social change, a scholar should also consider the role of people's daily life strategies that are guided by their very humaneness.

From the contemporary world, the East Asian countries referred to as the Four Tigers (Hong Kong, Singapore, South Korea and Taiwan), and China provide illustrative cases with regard to the concept of humaneness. Until relatively recently, these countries were considered by Westerners as culturally backward and were historically guided by Confucianism. In spite of this so-called backwardness, these countries have become able to compete with the Western world in the areas of productivity, living standards and export capacity within a short time span. The case of China is particularly stunning as it is now emerging as the second largest economy in the world over a short period of time with a high GDP growth rate. On similar lines, Russia was plundered for a decade in the 1990s by the Western world. However, within the last fourteen years it has gained international status while also challenging the hegemony of the United States.

The speed with which these East Asian societies have been able to adapt, change, and produce things comparable to the most industrially developed societies can be explained by looking at the common element in their society, the innate creativity and "humaneness" of people, and not their culture. People create culture in the process of interacting with people in their societies in order to fulfill their daily needs, including achieving their humaneness. That is why the so-called "cultural backwardness" did not hinder the Asian countries seeking equality with the West. Similarly, tribal workers in India had no problem acquiring high technical skills in such a short time, in spite of never having been exposed to any modern industry (Tata Steel was the first large-scale modern industry in that region of India under the colonial rule).

"Humaneness" in Everyday Life

"Humaneness" also means that human beings in every society are able to set their own life agenda by creating and recreating a society at the bottom, even when the upper (and outer) structures of the society (government, rulers, constitution) are repeatedly destroyed. One can provide numerous examples in this regard from every living society. For example, when Soviet Russia ceased to exist and its economy was in shambles, its people were able to maintain their way of life by falling back on a barter system. Similarly, poor people in the US keep on bartering their expertise and sharing their resources to cope with their situations in everyday life such as is also happening in contemporary times in the war-torn regions of Palestine and Afghanistan. Historically, India experienced numerous invasions along its western borders; people in these areas went on doing their daily chores within their existing social relationships, while submitting to the new forces temporarily when forced to pay more for rent or other services. The case of the Andaman Islands is a good example in which people from diverse cultures (all regions of India as well as from Burma, Thailand, Sri Lanka, Malaya, and China) have been able to live together for a long time while sharing their creativity and humaneness. In Middle-Eastern countries during medieval times followers of Islam, Christianity and Judaism lived side by side without much conflict

(Menocal, 2002). Many Christians and Muslims during the time of the Crusades, also tolerated each other and went on living together peacefully. This complex aspect of the Crusades is left out of the modern narrative, which was created by Europeans in the eighteenth and nineteenth centuries (Mourad, 2018). A recent publication (Rosenfeld and Tardieu, 2000; Bystydzienski and Schacht, 2001) based on selected European experiences illustrates how poor people are succeeding in creating alliances and overcoming social exclusion, while radically changing their inhuman living conditions. These people are, in fact, using their humaneness to make a difference in their lives by finding new ways to solve everyday existence problems with dignity and pride. This experience is directly opposite to the concept of engaging in private charity to elevate the conditions of poor people. In recent years, peoples' struggles in Mexico, Brazil, South Africa, and Argentina for their basic human rights have been revealing in this regard and confirms to the point made here. Maxwell Cele, one of the community activists in South Africa who fought the installation of water meters in Mpumalanga, said:

> No one is in charge of the protests, except the anger and hunger in every person ... What connects the militant community mobilizations springing up across South Africa is not ideology but need: for water, medicine, electricity, and land. It is the gut instinct that human needs should take precedence over the demands of the market and, more to the point, that any direct action taken by ordinary people to meet those needs is not only justified but heroic (Klein, 2002).

In 2008, with the economic meltdown in the US, people immediately created a network of barter systems and took control of their lives. Now an elaborate barter system has emerged all over the world through an internet system to deal with global meltdown (Castells et al., 2017). It should be noted that similar actions were taken in the Depression era of the early 1930s (Rowe, 2018). Anarchists have been also writing about the hidden history of people addressing their own needs and solving problems through collective actions voluntarily. Some recent books have reiterated the same point; that the majority of social relations are made up of alternatives to state power, as most people survive through mutual aid (Shantz, 2014). Unfortunately, conventional sociology ignores these hidden histories of people. Using an example of design and buildings, Colin Ward explained that non-experts have done most of the world's building construction and still do. The rise of professional creative and design experts is a recent development. Ward emphasized the creativity of ordinary people in their day-to-day lives (Ward, 2011). In Ward's view, people are capable of organizing their own affairs in cooperative and humane ways and will find creative and resourceful ways to do so when given a chance. James Scott provides similar ideas (Scott, 2013). In the face of years of austerity policies and a refugee crisis, many Greek anarchist groups are self-organizing (separately) to help people with food, medicine, and housing refugees in empty buildings. They fund their activities through private donations, and proceeds from street exhibitions, on-site books, and theater (Kitsantonis, 2017).

One can also add examples of human creativity and humaneness under other stressful circumstances, such as war conditions. For example, many Syrian refugees running away from Syrian conflicts used their creativity and humaneness to create meaningful life in the camps, as there was no help from any state system (Kimmelman, 2014).

Humaneness Through Cooperation

However, human social interaction is not a non-conflictual linear process, because one can find in various societies throughout history numerous examples of power relationships and power conflicts based on religion, gender, race, class, age, and other factors. Without denying the existence of these conflicts, we have chosen to emphasize human cooperation and compassion (the origin of *humane* likely having developed from the recognition of these human qualities), because those are the guiding forces for the sustenance of any living society, as human beings cannot live without other human beings. That may be why the worst punishment in the criminal justice system is solitary confinement. The examples of cooperation amongst people against extremely adversarial circumstances can be found in the case of working people's struggle for workers' rights, women's struggle for equality and justice, and people's struggle in general for universal human rights and human dignity, including circumstances related to natural disasters. (It does not mean that these cooperating processes are devoid of power struggles or hierarchical relationships within these social movements; rather, these hierarchical relationships are part of the larger social problem against which social movements emerge) [(2)].

Biologist Martin Nowak (2012) explained that cooperation is the architect of creativity throughout evolution; from cell to multicellular to anthills to village to cities and that our survival depends on cooperation. A more recent book of Berry Brown (2017) focuses on the issue of humanity and points out that cooperation, reciprocation, and kindness towards strangers were the rules for 99.9% of human existence. It seems to me that by focusing on the question of cooperation, and not dwelling on differences and conflicts—while not denying their existence in our daily lives—it becomes possible to explore an alternative theoretical framework.

This idea is not too far-fetched, because the neo-liberal state of the US is already employing such ideas to reduce social tension while the state withdraws from its welfare function. For example, under the Clinton administration, the US government advocated the idea of "people caring for people"—that is, volunteer work—to ameliorate the social tension created by the mass unemployment and underemployment of people resulting from the advent of the information age. The US government under the George W. Bush administration called on religious institutions to use their compassion to help the government achieve its goal of reducing social tension. Churches were asked to take care of ex-welfare recipients in exchange for government subsidies (Bahl, 2005). Britain has also moved in that direction by trying to abolish its social welfare system. This appropriation of volunteer work as a political and economic strategy of the state (used also by the World Bank and the IMF to promote the role of NGOs for the development of poor societies in the name of local empowerment) minimizes the spirit of volunteerism and humaneness. Moreover, it promotes the neo-liberal agenda of reducing the role of the state and making large cuts in public expenditure while simultaneously promoting the idea of people pulling themselves together [as self-help and non-dependence, taking responsibility of their lives] from below without much help from government or their privileged fellow citizens (Ibid.).

It should be noted how these neo-liberal forces appropriate progressive vocabulary and the concepts of self-help, and transcending selfishness, appealing to the subliminal instincts by using "religious" vocabulary to serve their own agendas without seeming to do so. Thus, they are able to create the illusion of people's empowerment, while cutting the welfare resources for many, and providing more resources to the already rich. This type of peoples' 'empowerment' should be treated with skepticism and rejection, and efforts should be made to find ways to empower people in the real sense and not promote a neo-liberal agenda.

3. Unified Field of Consciousness

The innate capacity of creativity in humans is not separate from human consciousness, and it is through this consciousness humans become aware of their surroundings and use their creativity to build their societies while interacting with other human beings. Humans have inherited these (creativity/consciousness) capabilities from Nature itself as humans are one of infinite manifestation of Nature. This is also confirmed by both physicists and ancient mystical philosophies(3) and psychologists (Hunt, 2018). Progressive Utilization Theory (PROUT) (Maheshvarananda, 2004) suggests that there is a fundamental Oneness in the universe as all minds and matters are composed of the same universal elements (earth, fire, air, water, light—where we all eventually end up). According to this understanding, all-pervasive awareness of consciousness gives us self-awareness of our cosmic self. However, as discussed earlier, it is through the process of interaction, communication, and language that all human beings not only realize their innate creative genius (cosmic-self and consciousness), but also become social humans in the sense that we understand today.

The existence of a unified field of consciousness can be further verified from recent developments in science. Until recently, as Capra pointed out, scientists were challenged to explain the connection between the physical universe to the living world; the living world to the world of society, and the world of society to the domains of mind and culture. More recently, physicists have been able to create an integrated and more unitary world picture by using a logical scheme enabling them to explain that fundamental fields and forces of nature have common origin (Capra, 1996). Four astrophysicists developed the idea in 1957 that "almost all the elements in the periodic table were cooked up over time through nuclear reactions inside stars—rather than in the first instant of the Big Bang, as previously thought ... science continues to show just how intimately connected life on Earth is to the extra-terrestrial processes" (Jayawardhana, 2015).

In recent years some Western scientists, breaking away from Newtonian ideas, began to interpret complex systems to show that we are the part of an "ever-changing, interlocking, nonlinear, kaleidoscopic world" (Capra, 1997:133). In other words, resembling Indra's Net. This change in outlook began to take place in the 1930s, as the simple and predictable understanding of the universe and the human world was challenged when mathematician Kurt Gödel explained how even some very simple mathematical systems (arithmetic) are inherently incomplete (Waldrop, 1992:328). Similarly, physicists in the 1960s and 1970s proved that one can produce surprising and unpredictable results from very simple equations.

A paradigm shift was identified in science in which the expansion of the self all the way to identification with nature was seen as the basis for deep ecology thus, overcame the Cartesian dualism and shifted emphasis on the whole (Capra, 1992). It should be noted that the idea of a unified cosmos is not new as Eastern philosophies (considered as spiritual) have been advocating this concept for a longtime, but were not considered scientific. Capra admitted that "the emerging new vision of reality based on deep ecological awareness is consistent with the so-called perennial philosophy of spiritual traditions, whether we talk about the spirituality of Christian mystics, that of Buddhists or the philosophy and cosmology underlying the Native American traditions" (Ibid.).

Moreover, various branches of sciences have shown the divergent creative potential of the universe which is random and unforeseeable (Capra, 1996). Physicists have discovered that life, mind, and culture are all part of this larger world's reality because, according to them, information extends far beyond the mind of an individual person or even all people put together (Capra, 1993; Sheldrake, 2012; Avery, 2003). The universe is constituted, according to physicist Sheldrake (2012), of continuous fields and forces (includes all non-human living beings, the entire web of life, and human consciousness) that carry and convey information as well as energy. This is a non-dualistic approach to understanding the universe as well as the social cosmos (Ibid.; see also Momo, 2013; Koch, 2016). Sheldrake's idea of morphic information implies that there is "some inherent creative intelligence in mind and nature" (Goswami, 2003). More recently, psychology professors, Tam Hunt, and Jonathan Schooler at the University of California Santa Barbara, have developed a "resonance theory of consciousness" suggesting that resonance (synchronized vibrations) is not only at the heart of human consciousness, but also animal consciousness and of physical reality more generally (Hunt, 2018). With their resonance theory of consciousness, they think they are providing a unified framework that includes neuroscience as well as more fundamental questions of neurobiology, biophysics, and philosophy of mind. Tam Hunt informs that mathematician Steven Strongatz provides various examples from physics, biology, chemistry and neuroscience that illustrates 'sync', his term for resonance, in his 2003 book, *Sync: How Order Emerges from Chaos in the Universe, Nature and Daily Life.* A similar idea was earlier promoted by the Nobel Laureate scientist Ilya Prigogine with his experiment of mixing together some chemicals where he saw how a new complex ordered system appear spontaneously (Talbot, 1991). One recent experiment by neurobiologist shows that thoughts can be directly sent to another person's brain (arxiv.org/abs/1809.08632). Scientists are also discovering that plants and water also have memories (See William Brown, Oct. 5, 2018, resonancescience.org/scientists-show-that-water-has-memory; See also Sara Abbott, "Plants Can Make Memories," untamedscience.com/biology/plants/plant-memory).

According to Goswami, a theoretical scientist, creative intelligence is consciousness itself, which is the basis of all being. "Consciousness acts on matter in conjunction with a vital body that contains the blueprints of biological forms. That is the source of morphic information" (Ibid.). Goswami explains how Sheldrake's idea of "morphic resonance" can be explained by using Quantum principles applied within the context of a new science—science within consciousness, a science based on primacy of consciousness. According to Goswami, consciousness is undivided and there is no subject/object split. It is a self-referential system, and consciousness is the same as *prana* in India and *Chi* in China and *Ki* in Japan. Both physical and vital worlds are "quantum superposition of possibilities," but it is consciousness that gives them substantiality (Ibid.). Sahlan Momo, the editor of journal SPANDA, also wrote that "Consciousness does not differ from the energy that constitutes it, it is itself that energy" (Momo, 2013, viii). We think that we cannot understand quantum mechanics as it is so far removed from our common experiences, however, we do not realize that an individual being both an individual and collective at the same time is a quantum phenomenon. We also forget that various modern communication systems we use every day—telephone, transistors, internet—are based on quantum mechanics.

With these scientific "discoveries," prevailing Enlightenment ideas seem to have come full circle, as they evolved by ignoring or rejecting these roots in earlier holistic approaches, and by promoting a separation of mind and body, while creating modern science based on logic and rationality (4). However, this view ignored the rich texture of Enlightenment itself, which placed a remarkably high value on the role of sensibility, feeling and desire (Lloyd, 2018). The same modern science, a product of prevailing Enlightenment ideas of reason and rationality, is now rediscovering the unity of the cosmos and human-kind that various religious traditions (for example, Hinduism which consists of heterogeneous practices, traditions, customs and ideas—not of RSS variety) including the holistic medicines of ancient India (such as Ayurveda and yoga—both products of heterogeneous and diverse local, regional and folk knowledge) and China have been promoting since antiquity (Capra, 1993). Physicists now suggest that all of our impressions of ultimate solid substance are deceptive (Goldberg, 1999).

This holistic approach is well developed in the Indian tradition of *Tat twam asi, Neti* and *Yoga*. The Nobel Laureate poet Rabindranath Tagore explained it as follows,

> The technique of *Tat twam asi* ('That is what you are'), like the *Neti* technique ('I am not that, it does not belong to me'), and the methods of *Yoga* for obtaining control over the automatic vital processes, thereby leading to awareness of all the bodily organs and the sensations, are simply three related procedures directed towards *the common aim of full community in suffering with the Universe.* The technique of *Yoga* dispenses the essentially living element in man from its individual status and makes it universal, in that it leads to an apprehension of the body as a mere object of consciousness alien to the self, a mere setting for the universal flow of life throughout all existence. The *Neti* technique puts an end to the parochialism of identifying oneself with some particular good or person or thing, in favour of identification with the universe in its undivided wholeness. But the technique of *Tat twam asi*, which presupposes the other two, is the most immediate preparation for the act of identification itself (emphasis in the original) (5).

Unfortunately, many people believing in modern Western science consider the concept of *Tat twam asi* as esoteric and therefore reject it. I find it strange that the academic community finds Freud's concept of unconscious and Marx's concept of working class consciousness as legitimate for academic consideration, but treat a holistic concept of *Tat twam asi*, which is also about consciousness, as esoteric. They ignore that the concepts of "unconscious" and "working class consciousness" are based on the assumption of their being universal.

4. Indra's Net

By dropping Cartesian dualism, it has become possible to focus on a non-dualistic approach. The metaphor of Indra's Net seems useful in this regard[6] because it enables us to visualize the interconnectedness and uniqueness of all societies (including their members), while treating all societies with a yardstick of parity.

What is Indra's Net? I first came across this metaphor in a quote from the dedication page of *The Sociology of Philosophies* book by renowned American sociologist Randal Collins[7]. It was referred by Fa-tsang during T'ang dynasty in the following couplet:

> In every hair there are an infinite number of lions, and in addition in all the single hairs, together with the infinite number of lions, in turn enter into a single hair. In this way the progression is infinite, like the jewels in Celestial Lord Indra's net (Fa-tsang, T'ang Dynasty).

The metaphorical Indra's Net is a conceptual matrix of integral unity. It refers to an infinite net that has a jewel in each node and each one reflects all other jewels. Thus, there is no separate self-existence of any jewel, however, each one is unique in its reflection of the others. This net symbolizes a universe and shows how there are infinite dependencies and relations interwoven among all its members (and societies) as all exist in the context of a collective reality. Later Buddhist texts mentioned that Indra's Net has no beginning or end and that every member of the universe is mutually related to every other member[8].

The metaphor of Indra's Net allows us to perceive the existence of a creative intelligence (not to be confused with "intelligent design" as promoted by Christian Evangelicals) that permeates all life and whole cosmos. It also illuminates the concept that all appearances of separateness (dualism) are in fact *maya* (illusory). However, this does not mean we do not have separate physical identities or that the physical world is not real. Both situations are real and each one of these needs to be respected on its own terms (Malhotra, 2011; Hathaway, 2015). Similarly, all societies are both unique as well as connected with other societies at the same time. Therefore, to understand any society we need to understand the complex interconnectedness and uniqueness of all societies.

Randall Collins's tome on *Sociology of Philosophies* (1998) is a good example of how the metaphor of Indra's Net can be applied in understanding the development of different philosophies in different societies. He explains how science and the occult originated from the same source, how the ideas of thinkers from different generations were built upon earlier ideas, and that every society follows a similar sequence of epistemology-metaphysics that is also a version of an abstraction-reflexivity sequence. He also explains that all thinkers develop ideas within a network system and that none of them develop ideas in isolation even when they work alone as individuals (Collins, 1998).

Complexity studies have also pointed out that the universe works in the same way as a network system (Kaufman, 1996). Unlike the Enlightenment viewpoint, the viewpoint of complexity study does not accept duality between human and nature.

> We are part of nature ourselves. We are in the middle of it. There is no division between doers and done-to because we are all part of this interlocking network. If we, as humans, try to take action in our favor without knowing how the overall system will adapt—like chopping down the rain forest—we set in motion a train of events that will likely come back and form a different pattern for us to adjust to, like global climate change (Waldrop, 1992:333).

Earlier, Albert Einstein also wrote in a similar vein,

> A Human being is part of a whole, called by us the universe, a part limited in time and space. He experiences himself, his thoughts and feelings, as something separated from the rest—a kind of optical delusion of his consciousness. The delusion is a kind of prison for us, restricting us to our personal desires and to affection for a few persons nearest us. Our task must be to free ourselves from this prison by widening our circles of compassion to embrace all living creatures and the whole of nature in its beauty (goodreads.com).

The metaphor of Indra's Net has already influenced and inspired other scientific models and computers. For example, the hologram, in which every area of a hologram contains the essential information of the whole, was inspired by this non-dualistic concept of Indra'a Net (Malhotra, 2011; Talbot, 1991). This concept has also influenced models of human brain interconnectedness and models of the way in which the internet functions. It also offers an ancient correlation to Bell's theorem in theoretical physics, according to which, there are no local events or local causes, because everything in the cosmos is inherently interconnected (Talbot, 1991). For example, the current netocratic system is based on an Eternalist world view, according to which,

> All existences, genes as well as memes, and the Deleuzian clusters, have a starting point, a singularity. From this singularity the phenomenon expand into eternity, that gives rise, time after time, to new singularities, new complex pattern ... universe itself ... has been transformed into a single, vast eternalistic phenomena ... When a series of such forces work together as a Deleuzian historical cluster, a body without organs, then ... a resonance-phenomenon or a feedback loop occurs (Bard and Soderqvist, 2012:95–96).

In the Eternalist world view, "These temporarily blossoming clusters and resonances make up the nodes of civilization, ... every single individual, the subject, is therefore a resonance-phenomenon rather than a fixed ego" (Ibid., 96). This working of resonance phenomenon is similar to an earlier concept of "morphogenesis" to which new principles—non-locality and downward causation—have been added by physicist, Rupert Sheldrake. These new principles are not in material form, and downward causation works through a new principle called "morphic resonance" (Goswami, 2003). Sheldrake, using the concept of "morphic resonance," explained that our habits draw upon cumulative collective memory and through that humans are able to create forms. Since "everything is enfolding into everything," these forms are transferred to other areas as they become part of the cumulative collective memory. It is through creativity (within nature and within human) that new patterns of organization arise; however, only those patterns survive that are repeated and thus become increasingly habitual. In fact, the possibilities of new patterns of organization that never existed before are latent in creativity. Under the appropriate circumstances, the latent pattern become actual (Ibid.). For example, we create technology, pictures, art and many other things that are latent in our consciousness, and we bring them to life through human creativity and actions. Furthermore, humans are part of nature and their innate creativity is part of nature's ongoing creativity as all creativity is part of a vast creative process that has been unfolding throughout the whole cosmic evolution (Sheldrake, 2012, Capra, 1996). Talbot's recent theory of the holographic nature of the physical universe, like Indra's Net, is a useful example in this regard because it helps reconceive "the unified *chita* (consciousness)" as the "unified field that ties all things in the universe together"(9). However, as Sheldrake points out, those who are more used to a narrative where there is a beginning, middle, and end will find it difficult to comprehend the idea of ever-expanding universe or expanding energy, and relate them to human creativity as part of this vast all-pervasive process (Sheldrake, 2012; see also Avery, 2003).

Based on the understanding of physicists and netocrats about universal oneness and connectedness of all, an understanding that is also well-established in Hindu traditions (but not the one promoted by RSS group in India) and probably in others as well, it is possible to imagine how all societies are both unique and connected as in Indra's Net. With this approach we can eliminate hierarchical relationship of societies and their knowledge, which will help in removing from our mind the binary distinction of East/West, North/South, traditional/modern, developed/underdeveloped, and so on. It will then be possible to use a yardstick of parity to understand all societies.

5. Collective Human Knowledge

All societies are also connected through collective human knowledge as culture and knowledge diffusion have been occurring since the time human societies came into existence. Collective human knowledge developed through the amalgamation of knowledge derived from various indigenous religions and other systems such as yoga, religious scriptures (from all over the world), and through all types of everyday workers who created techniques, technology and collected data, which was later used in scientific discoveries that have enhanced our human life experiences. However, under the influence of Enlightenment ideas, Cartesian duality separated mind and body, which contributed to the creation of other distinctions between rationality/irrationality, progressive/backward, and so on. The recent shifts in scientific thinking, which is now in agreement with ancient Indian philosophies about the existence of universal consciousness, has made it possible to break out of Cartesian duality. It is now possible to usefully apply and extend the metaphor of Indra's Net to understand social reality and observe how human creativity manifested in different places in the form of various inventions, and production of goods as well as institutions, innumerable ideas and how human collective knowledge was diffused everywhere over the course of thousands of years.

It is abundantly clear that creativity is not the monopoly of a single human group or of a particular historical time period. The existence across the world of myriad enormous and intricate monuments, vast hydraulic systems from ancient times, and sites showing the signs of large-scale mining as well as the production of copper and iron are some of the obvious examples of human creativity. Graham Hancock (2015) has explored ancient monuments that indicate the sophisticated knowledge of astronomy, architecture, and engineering among ancient builders that dates back well beyond 10,000 years. Similarly, traditional collective indigenous knowledge was developed over innumerable generations relating to ecology, biology, botany, medicinal plants, climate and other areas of nature and human life. The creation of these knowledge systems was a long process in which many individuals over many generations were involved. All of them learned collectively through their experiences the explanations of the world, which was also verified by their elders. Such knowledge systems were conveyed to other generations through oral traditions which guided their experiential learning. Thus, the record keeping of traditional indigenous knowledge can be found in the oral tradition and other experiential ways. It is interesting that many scholars in recent years have become aware of this vast traditional indigenous knowledge. For example, as Nicholas noted, recently archeologists and environmental scientists found evidence of mariculture (developed by Kwakwaka'wakw and other indigenous groups) that pre-dates European settlement in coastal British Columbia. This discovery shows that indigenous groups had already developed the skills—hundreds of years before the modern management systems—of a resource management strategy with a sophisticated body of practices and ecological understandings. However, many Western scientists only value the local knowledge that supports or supplements archaeological or other scientific evidence, while rejecting those that challenges science's "truth" as "myths" (Nicholas, 2018).

We learned from Clifford Conner that it was anonymous masses of people who gathered the knowledge of nature, because those closest to it were the hunter gatherers, peasant farmers, sailors, miners, blacksmiths, and folk healer, who encounter nature on a daily basis. Chemistry, metallurgy, and the material sciences in general originated in the knowledge produced by ancient miners, smiths, and potters. Mathematics owes its existence to surveyors, merchants, clerk accountants, and mechanics over many millennia. Drawing from these sources and artisans in the workshops, the Scientific Revolution could emerge (Conner, 2005:3). The birth of modern science occurred when gentlemen began to appropriate and systematize collective artisans' knowledge (Ibid., 19). However, we remember the names of those gentlemen who appropriated this knowledge (considered geniuses), and not those people's creativity who gathered the knowledge of nature over many millennia (our collective human ancestors), which allowed the emergence of modern science.

It is from this collective human knowledge that all of us are benefiting today. However, most of the time people do not recognize this reality and start claiming ownership over particular human knowledge, thus creating binary distinctions and boundaries. In the following, we shall try to understand how these binary distinctions are depriving people access to collective human knowledge as is happening in India recently.

CONTROVERSY OVER COLLECTIVE HUMAN KNOWLEDGE

In recent years, few vested interests in India and some fanatics (such as the RSS) are trying to monopolize collective Indian traditional knowledge while promoting their own version of Hinduism. One major problem is that once collective human knowledge is monopolized by fanatic groups, people wrongly tend to associate that particular collective human knowledge itself as fanatic (or worse, as undesirable), thus, depriving the rest of the population from accessing and applying that collective human heritage of knowledge to improve their lives. Instead, people start creating binary distinctions: science (as promoted by Enlightenment ideas and rationality) versus superstition (anything that concerns astrology, yoga, quantum physics, rituals and other religious traditions), as if there are no other explanations to our existence aside from these two. This binary distinction between science and superstition (let me make it clear that I am not supporting superstitions) being forcefully promoted in India today, actually reinforces the cultural hegemony of the West, and thus limits us from accessing the rest of the vast collection of human knowledge. It has also created an environment in India (especially with the election results in 2014 and, more recently, in 2019, in favor of Hindutva (literally means Hinduness) forces, who are bent upon transforming India according to their version of Hinduism) that it is impossible to raise this issue without being labeled as a "Hindu fundamentalist" (see Introduction chapter, section on "An Important Clarification").

Consequently, in this fight against Hindutva forces the collective traditional Indian knowledge (accumulated over thousands of years) is being thrown out the window in the name of Western science, while allowing Hindutva forces to claim a monopoly over yoga, Ayurvedic medicine, and other aspects of the collective heritage of Indian knowledge, as well as allowing them to define this knowledge according to their own political agenda. Both, those promoting Western science and rationality and those promoting Hindutva, seem to have forgotten that this heritage of common human knowledge is for everyone[(10)]. On a side note, it is interesting that people in the US who practice yoga of various types, and promote organic food and alternative medicine (including Indian herbs and Ayurvedic medicines), are seen as progressive and liberal, while in India the same is associated with Hindu nationalism. It is puzzling—how can the same practices and rituals be both "progressive (scientific) and nationalist (Hindutva)" at the same time in different locales [(11)]?

Hindutva crusaders are not only monopolizing collective traditional Indian knowledge but also establishing modern scientific credentials of Vedas and Upanishads with the claim that these old scriptures had already provided the science of quantum mechanics. These crusaders of Hindutva are in fact looking for validation from modern science even though it is for regressive reasons. They do not care to acknowledge that while Vedas do postulate the uncertain nature of reality, and old scriptures confirm the existence of all-pervasive consciousness and the idea of matter transforming into energy and waves, they did not provide any mathematical interpretation of quantum phenomenon (Betageri, 2015; Sau, 2006). Neo-Hindus are able to make such claims because the science of quantum mechanics (QM) is itself on the verge of mysticism as the following QM theorems indicate: its focus is on "(a) 'non-locality', which shows interconnectedness between all matter in the universe, and universal equality of all points of the universe in respect of possessing information; (b) 'a tendency to exist' rather than existence as such, of matter which points to the illusory *(maya)* nature of the physical world and (c) 'reassembly' or 'self-organisation' that hints at the presence of consciousness in the apparently non-living system as well" (Sau, 2006. http://www.epw.org.in).

Before blindly rejecting or accepting the validity of Hindutva crusaders' claims, they should be critically examined. No one group should be allowed to monopolize collective human knowledge (including QM) that is produced by our collective ancestors in all societies over the centuries. One cannot claim something as either a Hindu science or a Christian science. The knowledge of Vedas and Upanishads (they were a synthesis and products of accumulated various local, regional, and folk knowledge) and all other ancient knowledge available anywhere should be studied and, if possible, used to enhance human conditions. No one group should be allowed to own it as its "religion." Labeling a person who may try to use this knowledge to enhance our understanding of human life as a Hindutva promoter allows Hindutva forces to monopolize, misinterpret, and misuse this knowledge. While we should not simply throw away ancient knowledge as redundant, we should also not blindly accept all scientific ideas as "truths" either. Since scientific "truths" are also constantly changing, we can never be sure if one scientific truth is valid for all time. It should be pointed out that similar to the abuse of religions and cults for power and control over people, science has also been abused by vested interests like pharmaceutical companies, tobacco companies, and oil companies for nefarious ends. For example, scientific racism was used to justify keeping black people in menial jobs, and science was also used for controlling women's reproductive organs by claiming that women have smaller brains and that education would affect their reproductive organs. As mentioned earlier, scientific racism is, unfortunately, making a comeback.

The present binary debate in India between science and superstition is not very useful as it echoes the same binary distinction of the East (traditional/backward) and West (science/superior), and does not allow us to break out of it and find an alternative without getting entangled in Hindutva politics. It should be pointed out that faith in superstition and religion is not much different than having faith in science, markets, development, or economics. Interestingly, Richard Norgaard (2015) noted that economists themselves have acknowledged the ultimately religious nature of their discipline. More recently, John Rapley has discussed economics as religion (Rapley, 2017a; Rapley, 2017b). In 1932, Frank Knight, the most scholarly and broad thinking of the founders of the influential market-oriented Chicago school of economics, literally argued that economics, at a fundamental level, had to be a religion, the basic tenets of which must be hidden from all but a few" (Norgaard, 2015). The following is a direct quote from Frank Knight:

> The point is that the principles by which a society or a group lives in tolerable harmony are essentially religious. The essential nature of a religious principle is that not merely is it immoral to oppose it, but to ask what it is, is morally identical with denial and attack. There must be ultimates, and they must be religious, in economics as anywhere else, if one has anything to say touching conduct or social policy in a practical way. Man is a believing animal and too few, if any, is it given to criticize the foundations of belief 'intelligently.' To inquire into the ultimate behind accepted group values is obscene and sacrilegious: objective inquiry is an attempt to uncover the nakedness of man, his soul as well as his body, his deeds, his culture, and his very gods. Certainly the large general [economics] course should be prevented from raising any question about objectivity, but should assume the objectivity of the slogans they inculcate as a sacred feature of the system (Ibid.).

However, by mathematizing economics and other subjects (Davis, 2015; Conner, 2005), these disciplines are treated as "science." Other disciplines in social sciences and humanities are also struggling to achieve the status of science by following a similar strategy of mathematization. It seems strange that mathematization can turn any subject into a science when mathematics itself is not a natural science. Mathematics does not study any empirical reality, and it does not use the same methods as used in science to understand reality.

In view of these realities, the faith in science is as problematic as faith in economics, or faith in religion or its superstitions. Instead of fighting over the claims of any knowledge as being either science or superstition, or claiming ownership over a particular form of knowledge, we need to explore how we can benefit from collective human knowledge that might be useful to improve our present human and planetary conditions.

One of the many ways we can accomplish this goal is to treat all societies with the same yardstick of parity and make the binary distinction of developed/under-developed redundant. The yardstick of parity would be based on the commonalities among all societies as discussed above: human creativity, reification, humaneness, universal consciousness, interconnectedness (as in Indra's Net) of societies and collective human knowledge. Based on this yardstick, we can understand any event in any society including the Industrial Revolution by focusing on the conjunction of historical forces within and without a society, and not on some "superior" culture or "genius" of a social group.

BREWING PROBLEM

However, it should be noted that some of these commonalities—human creativity, which includes humaneness and inner self—are now under threat as the corporate world has been trying to control them for a long time. Scholars believe that this is the last area (inner life and reproduction of everyday life) where workers still have some control (not completely conquered by capital) as their innate creativity and inner-self allow them to re-appropriate their lives even though their labor is commodified (Anievas and Nişacncioğlu, 2015:37). As I discuss below, the corporate control and commodification of human creativity, inner-self, and human social reproduction has been increasing steadily. Many countries have already acquired the capability to control the human nervous system remotely with pulsed microwaves (Babacek, 2019). The corporate world understood a long time ago the importance of human creativity and inner-self to increase their profits. However, scholars are still clinging to the binary approach of rational/irrational, development/underdevelopment, progressive/backward and so on. It is time we start paying attention to these developments so that we can protect our inner-selves, creativity, and humaneness from the onslaught of corporations and their new technologies. It is only by protecting our inner-selves and our creativity that we would be able to find solutions to improve human and planetary conditions.

a. Corporate Threat to Human Creativity, Humaneness, Inner-self and Reproduction of Everyday Life

The actions of the working masses in connection with their social reproduction should not be considered simply as "resistance" to modernization, or as passive reactions to their circumstances as some scholars maintain. The creation of human bonds and human relations, and the subsequent actions of people to preserve these new bonds, are a part of their being human (humaneness). It may not be far-fetched to suggest that there exists a whole system in this social process of reproduction that is similar to the systems propounded in other fields such as physics and economics. In most instances, we witness only the attempts by powerful elements within a society who are able to destroy or subvert those systems of social reproduction through processes of control (Bahl, 2005).

For example, during the last two hundred years in the Anglo-American world, managerial ideologies to control workers have transitioned from:

(a) the theory of "dependence" (treating the worker as a child and dependent on the employer) to
(b) the theory of "laissez-faire" (responsibility of the employer for the worker was rejected) to
(c) the theory of "social Darwinism" (riches and poverty merely reflect differences of ability and efforts) to
(d) the theory of "human relation" (worker seen as an 'individual' whose skills could be improved by appropriate attention to her/his psychological makeup) to
(e) the theory of "team work" (workers controlling one another to increase productivity) to
(f) the theory of "happiness and wellbeing" that involves using yoga, meditation, and other reflective methods to deal with the enthusiasm gap among workers and stress in the workplace to
(h) the robotization of workplace (workers become obsolete) to
(i) the final corporate takeover of humanity and people's inner-selves with the emergence of trans-human machines incorporated in human bodies to enhance physical and cognitive capabilities.

In the contemporary era, the use of technological devices to watch, compute efficiently, and control working people's actions and thoughts is increasing every day. But this practice has a long history as William Davies observes in *Happiness Industry* that it started in the middle of the nineteenth century. He explains how the power of mathematics and measurement during the Industrial Revolution eliminated the basis for the Enlightenment idea that an "individual draws on his own judgment" (Davies, 2015) [(12)]. These techniques have been applied to understanding the inner-self of human beings by measuring sensations. Thus, the mystical was brought down to earth with psychophysics, which also refuted Kant's claim that the "science of psyche is impossible." By the end of the nineteenth century many new fields of study emerged that used measurement and scales to help understand the human mind—influencing psychologists, economists, and management consultants, as well as quantitative and economic psychology. All of them believed that individual behavior could be changed with the help of experts, and thus began the intimate micromanagement of the individual. These experts were technocrats who were not concerned with the intrinsic meaning of life or collective purpose. They were more concerned about industrial productivity. It is in this context that various solutions were found to increase workers' productivity at different historical times since the mid-nineteenth century. These technicians focused on the workers' inner-selves by using measurement, scale, and mathematics to understand worker fatigue because it was diminishing human resources. Taylor's scientific management was a product of similar industrial needs. These very same ideas and methods were extended later to workplace problems involving workers' enthusiasm levels, stress, and happiness. Scientific Management was also applied to consumers in terms of the "science of desire" as corporations promoted the idea of the perpetual growth of profit. Since the coming of social media and the internet, corporations now use the concept of "social" and social network analysis to reach consumers. Corporations have become "altruistic" and they want to be friends with consumers by giving away "free" things. In all these shifting methods, the basic idea involves using measurement to understand the minds of the consumers and the workers (who are also consumers) so that corporations can increase profits while also controlling their workers(13).

In the 1990s, an ingenious concept of "teamwork" was introduced that advanced the theory of scientific management and control of the labor process. This "teamwork" has created a system in the work place that increases productivity and creates a false sense of participation by having workers monitor one another. Furthermore, it is based on a temporary relationship with one set of workers completing a short project at one time, and then moving on to a new project with a different set of co-workers. In this new system, workers eliminate the "slackers" automatically and help reduce direct conflict with management. The whole set-up thus minimizes the chances of workers ever developing the bond needed for a united struggle. A further separation of workers in one factory is achieved by encouraging each department to treat other departments as clients for their products.

Along with the "teamwork" that actually prevents bonding, management promotes the idea of excellence by introducing such concepts as "everyday heroes" and "champions" in the work place. As Paul du Guy pointed out,

> "[C]ultural Excellence is a struggle for identities, an attempt to enable all sorts of people, from highest executive to lowliest shop-floor employee, to see themselves reflected in the emerging conception of the enterprising organization and thus to come increasingly to identify with it" (du Guy, 1991:53–54).

This is a clear case of manipulating people's "humaneness" in order to increase productivity and gain their loyalty with minimal conflict. Willmot explained that the 'new' corporate culturalism is about employees adopting and cherishing corporate values of 'quality,' 'flexibility,' and 'value added' as their own. This internalization of corporate values (culture) will direct employees to use their powers of judgment and discretion unequivocally toward working methods that will increase corporate profits (Willmot, 1993). This example shows that the idea of humaneness is not an abstract idea because it can be observed in a concrete and representative social situation. As suggested earlier, one form of humaneness is the bonding among workers which empowers them (individual power to use their civil, political, and economic rights) against capitalist exploitation. Conversely, another form of bonding called teamwork encourages corporate culture, which weakens the earlier forms of bonding among workers who could gain power to subvert the capitalist agenda.

The capitalist control of markets, workers, and consumers is now reaching a new high, thanks in part to the use of mathematical algorithms to identify and locate complex patterns in a matter of seconds. They played an important role in the 2008 economic meltdown and are now used for chasing stocks. Their use extends to many crucial decisions regarding public life. At MIT, there has been an effort to create an algorithm that would mimic the intuitions of human beings (Kole, 2016). Psychologist Robert Epstein noted that Google used a tool called "the autocomplete algorithm" to manipulate voters—without their knowledge(14). Franklin Foer (2017) informs about the danger that GAFA—the four technology giants Google, Apple, Facebook and Amazon—poses to our cultures and careers as they have become the new arbiters of media, economy, politics, and arts (see also Harari, 2017). Even the idea of subliminal messaging (theoretically banned in the 1960s) is coming back to influence consumers and working people. There is talk amongst American Navy research personnel of inserting chips in humans for complete control of their lives and minds (Hamill, 2016). Scientists are making chips to be inserted in our brains to read our thoughts. Recently, BrainCo, an education technology company based in Boston, has come up with a headband to measure brainwaves to gather data about student engagement in class. According to the CEO of the company, Bichen Han, "This will enable us to use artificial intelligence on what will be the world's largest database to improve our algorithms for think like attention and emotion detection" (Horowitz, 2017, Alternet.org, December 1). Already, brain-reading technology has been developed, which is an invasion of the basic human right to cognitive liberty (Ienca, 2017). Now the ability to send thoughts directly to another person's brain has become a real possibility with new tools as recently reported by Emerging Technology (arxiv.org/abs/1809.08632).

Neuroscientists are now venturing into studying inner speech (people talking/arguing to themselves in their head); something that was once considered impenetrable to science. They believe that by studying this intimate aspect of consciousness they can illuminate some important questions about the human mind—specifically, clues about the origin of human creativity (Fernyhough, 2017). *National Geographic* of May 2018 (pp. 110–111) noted that neuroscientists are measuring art's impact on the brain at the University of Houston in Texas by recording the brain waves of a painter, a dancer, and a musician in order to unlock the biology of creativity. In April 2017, one Swedish company offered its employees microchip implants (AP news April 16, 2017). The idea of mixing human and machine is picking up steam (NeuraLink Company) in the name of enhancing human life experience. The Pentagon wants to use this technology to allow soldiers to fire their weapon with their minds. Moreover, chips planted in soldiers' brains will allow them to control robotics by thought alone, and will also allow them to communicate with the squad via telepathy (Hedge, 2018). This technology will reduce time and cost in commanding the body to pull the trigger (Sputnik International, July 20, 2017). USSOCOM (US Special Operations Command) and DARPA (Defense Advanced Research Project Agency) documents clearly noted that they are planning to create an elite fighting force which will have invincible, extraordinary capabilities. One of the projects is to create software that can be uploaded directly to the brain to give soldiers heightened senses while also attempting to cure serious ailments (Hedge, 2018). NESD (Neural Engineering System Designing) is developing an implantable neural interface which will be able to provide advance signal resolution and brain computer interface (BCI) for data transfer between brain and electrons (Ibid.; see also Babacek, 2013). Shuja Haider highlights the challenge of Google's Deep Dream program, in which a neural network scans an image for recognizable patterns attempting to identify its contents the way a human would. The problem is that builders of technology are transmitting their values into machinery which will have widespread consequences, because as he notes, it is a synthesis of apparent opposites, "The New Left utopianism and Ayn Randian individualism" (Haider, 2017). Similarly, Jon Kofas has focused on the socio-economic, political, and ethical problems of artificial intelligence and biosynthetic engineering (Kofas, 2017). Harari also believes that the main product of the twenty-first century would be bodies, brains, and minds—and authority would shift from individual humans to networked algorithms. Humans won't fight machines, they will merge with them (Harari, 2017 quoted in Nour, 2018). Interestingly, this idea is now being picked up in the fashion world in the name of self-expression with bioreactive necklaces that sync with one's heart; bioluminescent filaments that serve as a Medusa-esque back ornament; pink, living eyelashes that responds to music, light, and mood; and a growth pattern that can be adjusted at will (Italie, 2018). Apple and Samsung expect that the direct connection with brains will gradually replace computer keyboards, touch screen, and mouse. With this new technology it will be possible to implant thoughts and emotions in people's minds and hearts when they connect to the internet and cell phone system (Babacek, 2019). There is already a warning about the rise of digital dictatorships because devices will know more about the person holding it than that person will. In 2016 and 2017, ten European organizations tried to convince the European Parliament and the European Commission to enact legislation that would ban the remote control of the human nervous system.

The concerns of these organizations are valid because all of these technologies and robotization of the work place will further yield more power to corporations and governments to more efficiently control the inner lives of soldiers, workers, and consumers who are also citizens. However, these efforts are not new. After World War II, as hundreds of recently released CIA documents reveal, a series of covert projects were conducted by the CIA and other US agencies. One program called MK-ULTRA involved psychological-warfare and was run by the CIA in the 1950s and 1960s. The goal of this program was to develop mind control techniques through the use of LSD and other drugs. Most interestingly, the CIA also tried to develop psychic and supernatural abilities (they must believe that such things are possible after all, and they are not some other worldly new age spirituality stuff) of selected people for military purposes, including psycho-kinesis and remote viewing (Salazar, 2017:10). All of the above information makes it clear that it is human creativity/consciousness (of workers' and consumers' inner-selves) that is being targeted for control and for profit making. What Marx wrote about workers' alienation from creativity (in the workplace) is now extending into all aspects of human life (Saner, 2018). As we pointed out earlier, with new technology even the inner-self and consciousness can be manipulated with remote control systems. However, in the meantime, the corporate world is also using the techniques of mindfulness and meditation, developed by ancient religions—Buddhism and Hinduism—to influence the inner-selves of workers so that they blame themselves for their poor wages, living and working conditions.

b. "Mindfulness" and "Inner-self" at the Service of Corporations

Corporate America is systematically using yoga and meditative practices as a tool to maintain the status quo of the workplace (Holloway, 2015). In 2002, several of the topmost neurobiologists and psychologists in America started a project with the help of the Dalai Lama, exiled Tibetan Buddhist religious leader, to learn how to manipulate the human inner creative mind to remain perpetually happy despite the presence of social, economic, and physical problems (Bahl, 2005). In San Francisco, an experimental project involving school teachers and medical patients has been conducted with this focus. Various projects (using yoga, Zen meditation, Transcendental Meditation, and other methods of poverty management, pain management, and stress management) focus on changing individual behavior through the manipulation of one's inner capacity for creativity so that one learns to accept one's social situation with contentment while blaming one's own self for personal failure. This method also eliminates the possibility of people connecting with others who are in similar situations and using collective action to demand broader structural changes (Ibid.). These methods of using the inner-self to achieve perpetual happiness calls to mind the idea of "contentment in one's destiny or status" that was earlier promoted for maintaining stability within the Indian social stratification system. Later, this ideology was considered a hindrance in the "development" (modernization) of people's mentality of "contentment"—ironically creating a myth that Indian people are supposedly more "spiritual" in their attitude towards life. In turn, such myths promoted the artificial and false binary of "spiritual East" and "modern technologically advanced West." It is not clear how promoting the very same ideologies once condemned as "anti- development" would help promote "modernization" (or so-called "development") (Ibid.). Obviously, the corporate world uses these methods and ideologies to its own advantage while promoting the illusion of empowerment and self-help for workers.

Recently, the concept of "mindfulness" has been redefined as a technique, giving it a secular makeover described as "the awareness [that arises] through paying attention on purpose in the present moment, and non-judgmentally" (Zahan, 2016). It has become a religion in the corporate boardroom as mindfulness is now commodified by eliminating all reference to the transcendent. Detaching the concept of mindfulness from dogma has created endless opportunities for its uses (Ibid.). Steve Jobs was an avid practitioner of meditation—one of the first tech industry icons to weave mindfulness with business practice. His heir apparent, Chade-Meng Tan, headed up the company's first "Search Inside Yourself" course, a two-day mindfulness-focused program. The program was adopted by Procter & Gamble, General Mills, and Aetna along with banking companies, law and advertising firms, and the US military. All this acceptance of meditation has to do with increasing productivity; it is a useful tool to squeeze even more work out of an already overworked workforce. According to one author of "McMindfulness," it is a commodified, secularized, corporatized version of the meditative practice. "Mindfulness training has wide appeal because it has become a trendy method for subduing employee unrest, promoting a tacit acceptance of the status quo, and as an instrumental tool for keeping attention focused on institutional goals" (Ibid.). Apple has developed a mindfulness tool for its newest Apple Watch to remind us to "breathe" (Ibid.). Mindfulness is now extracted from its communal context and has become "a catch all and cure all. Want to relieve stress, get more sleep, perform better at work … just meditate" (Ibid.). Mindfulness-Based Stress Reduction (MBSR) is a technique now spreading from hospitals to offices to the halls of Capitol Hill (Ibid.). The purpose of MBSR is to improve individual awareness and, in turn, business. In this way, mindfulness enables an ensuing preoccupation with social climbing and career advancement. Thus, MBSR is a form of "McMindfulness," which is a banal, therapeutic, self-help technique to improve employees' productivity for business gains. A new leadership description has recently come into being,

Zentrepreneur, or one who use "Zenergy" in the workplace to achieve their goal of "balance, sustainability, positivity, and consciousness." Thus, capitalism is seen as a spiritual practice and employees as templates for enlightenment. Lynn Stuart calls it, "Ayn Rand disguised in a saffron yellow meditation robe," something like a "spiritual materialism" (Paramore, 2016; Purser and Edwin, 2015). Curiously, there is scarce acknowledgement of the source of their practices, which is the usual habit of some in the Western world.

Being in a power position, the Western world is not interested in the exchange of culture, but rather an appropriation of culture with the freedom to participate in different cultures freely, which has usually led to the annihilation of many cultures as well as the colonization of other cultures (Mehta, 1999). In this ongoing process of appropriation, the idea of "mindfulness" is one of the more recently acquired. It should be noted that minority groups have started to object to the appropriation of their cultural items and traditions as they feel that this appropriation deprives them of their group identity and dignity (Jain, 2015). However, it is forgotten in these claims that no "pure" culture or tradition exists (no culture is a fixed entity as all cultures are constantly changing), and that the diffusion of culture has been an ongoing process; earlier, by human interaction through trade, travels, migration, cultural exchanges, and more recently through colonization and globalization. Our specific identities, which we believe we have today, are historically constructed and defined by the needs of Western imperialism for colonization and appropriation of resources. The fact is ignored that when the Western world appropriates other cultures it does not care to recognize the source, or if at all recognized, it is labeled as exotic and ethnic. Moreover, the West's appropriation of other cultures is not denigrated as aping others, but when people of other cultures try to adopt Western culture and lifestyle they are denigrated as aping the West or whites. This problem needs to be addressed and challenged.

A blogger in the *Economist* noted that, "Western capitalism seems to be doing rather more to change Eastern religion than Eastern religion is doing to change Western capitalism" (Schumpeter, 2013). It listed the names of companies like Google and eBay, and persons such as Rupert Murdock, who are adopting the practice of "mindfulness" at the workplace. Bill George, a former CEO of Medtrone (a medical technology development company) and a board member of Goldman Sachs, is introducing mindfulness at the Harvard Business School in an attempt to develop leaders who are "self-aware and self-compassionate." Similar attempts are being made at the Drucker School of Management at Claremont University, the International Institute for Management Development in Switzerland, and at the University of Nebraska-Lincoln College of Business. However, the Indian government under Prime Minister Narendra Modi, a member of the right-wing Hindutva party guided by RSS, has made yoga compulsory for soldiers in seven paramilitary forces, including the Central Reserve Police Force, the Central Industrial Security Force, and the Border Security Force, through a May 26, 2015 circular (Singh, 2015).

> Yoga is thus being used to serve the twin goals of (1) conditioning a soldier's psyche to submit to his superiors in the cantonments and (2) orienting his aggression in the battlefield in the direction ordered by his superiors—whether against Pakistani soldiers, or Indians in Chattisgarh, Jharkhand, or Kashmir (Bannerjee, 2015).

Military veterans' hospitals in the US are using meditation and yoga to cure PTSD among suffering soldiers. Even the World Economic Forum at Davos in 2016 invited a Buddhist monk to guide the attendees to learn mindfulness. No wonder, the "Happiness Industry" has become a corporate priority for the time being (Davies, 2015).

However, mindfulness is not only being used by corporations for their bottom line. Some young people in the US are trying to use mindfulness as a spiritual awakening in an effort to work towards a political change by combining mindfulness with political activism and anarchism through a website (the consciousresistance.com). Arielle Levites has also challenged the "Spiritual Left" to turn from "being a change" into "agitate for change" (Levites, 2017). Terry Patten is promoting the idea that Radical Activism is spiritual as well as political, something he learned from his own experiences during the 1960s. He noted that Martin Luther King Jr. and Daniel Berrigan set a powerful example of how to integrate personal spirituality with political commitment (Patten, 2018). It will be interesting to watch how this call will be heeded.

However, the highest humane ideals of altruism, volunteerism, philanthropy, and friendship, which are very important for human well-being, are also now targeted for commodification by corporations (Sen, 2015). When these higher ideals are used consciously as a resource for personal happiness and personal gains, they lose their true value and meaning. With this approach, it is the personal happiness that is sought after—not altruism or friendship for its own sake as a high value of life. Moreover, when corporations try to promote these behaviors, it cannot be out of altruism as their primary goal is profit making. There are currently two industries that use "altruism" specifically as a market strategy. One of them is philanthropy, where welfare is a part of the market activities (Ibid., 23). This has also created jobs for "philanthropic consultants" who give advice to rich people about where their money will be most efficiently utilized. This outcome-based giving has commoditized the idea of "doing good."

In addition to the commodification of "doing good," philanthropy is proving to be damaging for women, as Kathryn Moeller pointed out in her study of a Fortune 500 company's charitable program they launched in order to "give back" (quoted in Posner, 2018). She explained that this charity work, which is modeled around the 'girl effect,' actually shifts the burden of bringing social and economic change unfairly onto girls and women. With this shift two goals are accomplished: one, problems of women in the Global South are depoliticized, two, responsibility for bringing change is shifted from governments, corporations, and global governance institutions to women. Moreover, these institutions are able to disown their responsibility for creating conditions for "unequal distribution of resources, food insecurity, abusive labor conditions, unfair trade policies and environmental degradation that disproportionately affect girls, women and the poor around the world" (Ibid.). Furthermore, Moeller pointed out that by using terms like "empowerment," and not a political term such as "women's right," these companies are able to avoid working in those areas where sexist regimes explicitly suppress women for political gains. These strategies of companies also reflect in the type of education they encourage for women, which only focus on their becoming an economic actor, while not addressing the issues of racism, sexism, or other barriers these women will inevitably encounter in the job market (Ibid.).

Similarly, the industry of volunteering, or giving up your time for the purpose of social or communal good, is also now commoditized. As Jahanvi Sen has pointed out, most forms of volunteerism seem to suggest that it is not a resistance to capitalism but another way of legitimizing it, of minimizing community resistance, and of reinforcing certain hierarchies. The example of volunteer tourism or "voluntourism" is appropriate in this regard (Ibid., 24). These volunteers, mostly from the Global North, who get a chance to travel to exotic locations in the Global South and feel good about their contributions toward social causes, tend not to question the issues of inequality and redistribution in those regions. Their main concern is enhancing their CVs for better jobs by having cultural knowledge of exotic places in order to give them an edge over other applicants. Intermediaries, who make profit on people's time, promote "voluntourism" in the name of "giving back" to poor countries. Sen, quoting from Vrasti, wrote that it is the new formulation of a neo-liberal subject that,

> [I]nstead of the rational, calculating and cold-blooded American Psycho, the good neo-liberal subject of the twenty-first century is the rather schizophrenic figure of the compassionate entrepreneur, the happy workaholic, the charitable CEO, the creative worker, the frugal consumer and last but not the least, the volunteer tourist (Vrasti, 2013:21).

Besides making profit from voluntourism, companies and organizations are using voluntary free labor mostly through unpaid interns making it appear to be an obligation under the pretext of reciprocity. According to this idea, the unpaid labor of the intern is actually paid (gifted) by the organization in the form of giving them "experience" and "training" during internship, which adds to their CV points. All these different cases of philanthropy, volunteer tourism and free labor, remain a one way 'gift,' which provides a status of superiority and spiritual deference for the "gift giver." Thus, two goals are achieved with this new way of 'gifting': reduce the chance of uprising against oppression (as people feel inclusive), and keep the status quo intact by appearing more humane and less oppressive (Ibid). It is amazing how corporate creativity finds ways to appear humane and caring without meeting the real material needs of people. It reminds me of another instance of corporate creativity, which is to make workers feel good about themselves by defining their job status in glorious ways, but not increasing their wages or benefits. Corporations were successful for some time in keeping workers' discontentment at bay.

SUMMATION

Even when corporations are promoting philanthropy and voluntourism simply to gain profits and customers, hopefully, as William Davies points out, it can have a very positive effect in truly bringing people together and they might genuinely start caring for others (out of real altruism) and challenge these profit-making corporations. This is possible when people consciously use their inner creativity to change the course of history. We need to be aware that it is our human capacity for creativity that is universal, not human nature, and that it is we humans who create social and cultural realities using our capabilities and then act in terms of them. In order to understand our present social reality, we need a more complex interdisciplinary approach, including newly emerging social neuroscience (Harari, 2014, 2017) rather than simple binary distinctions of religion/science, developed/underdeveloped, or progressive/backward.

We also need to further explore the very system of social reproduction that these powerful elements in society control and subvert, instead of focusing on "superior" cultures, or "superior" industries of a society while creating artificial binaries. My suggestion is that if we really wish to treat every society with the same yardstick on an equal level, then we must focus not on their differences (while not denying their existence) but on their commonalities, which means we learn to look to the histories of societies in and of themselves, with all the contradiction and conflict therein, as well as their interactions with other societies, and with all the myriad aspects of power play involved. With this approach we will learn how, in fact, all societies are co-produced and co-constituted and interconnected as in Indra's Net, and that no society is superior or inferior except when some countries forcibly colonize other countries and force them into an inferior condition.

For example, all societies are based on some form of production, distribution, and exchange while fulfilling the basic human needs of their members. It is this basic need for survival that leads to group formation, small or large, which makes all human beings equal, not their physical or cultural differences. If we agree with this statement, then it means we do not have to start writing history by making Europe, Africa, or the Orient (Frank, 1998) or the East as the world's center. We must start by looking at world history as a simultaneous process of many societies interacting, as well as developing within their own permeable boundaries—hence modernity is not bound by boundaries—to deal with their survival questions by organizing societies according to specific forms of production, distribution, consumption, trade, and culture as way of life, and so on (Bahl, 2005). Using this approach, it will be possible to normalize Europe while critically studying the West (which also consists of a vast number of different complex societies) and its role along with other societies in the making of the global past. Moreover, with this approach it will be possible to write comparative histories of all societies without giving hegemonic status (this approach does not deny that some societies acquired hegemonic power through alliances with local elite groups, through force as well as through fraudulent means, and thus able to propagate its supposed superiority) to any one society based on either cultural (or spiritual) superiority, or industrial superiority. In other words, erasing the binary distinction of developed/underdeveloped is necessary in order to write a comparative historical study with a yardstick of parity.

CONCLUSION

The possible alternative perspective suggested in this volume was developed in the process of understanding various contemporary social issues that are fiercely debated by scholars in both Western and non-Western countries. These scholars use either economic or cultural arguments to explain social issues. In earlier days, grand theories of modernization, dependency, and the world system (all focused on economic arguments) were more popular. In recent years, the emphasis on culture, subjectivity, and identity to focus on the role of "human agency" has gained ground to the extent that it has closed all possibilities for the creation of new approaches, leading to a blind alley while promoting cultural determinism—a factor which hides various complexities, including material conditions, the class status, and economic conditions of people, which also interact with larger historical forces. These perspectives are not useful in removing the binary distinction of developed/underdeveloped that seems to define the status of every country. My understanding is that unless we move out of this binary distinction in our analysis it is not possible to develop an alternative perspective to the above two approaches. For that we need to raise alternative questions.

An alternative question might be the following: How do people in any given society, while making everyday choices to meet their human needs, come to acquire specific economic, political, religious, social, technological and cultural conditions? This question would direct our focus on the continuously changing specificities of a society—a product of human creativity (which is dynamic), choices and actions in the process of human interactions within a society—as well as its relations and interactions with larger historical forces (including nature) and its interactions with other societies in different historical times that also shaped the historical trajectory of that society. Moreover, this would compel us to make a comparative study without a prior assumption about these societies as being developed or underdeveloped. It would also free us from the Western conceptualization of society and individual imprisonment in the "Enlightenment black box" that has no connection with nature and transcendence (Giri, 2015:212). It would eliminate the need to continuously prove the capitalist or modernist credentials of a so-called underdeveloped society. In other words, we do not have to worry about proving why Asia (China) or any other region of the world did not industrialize first. By eliminating the need to answer this question, we can stop being complicit in the promotion of Western binaries and Western myths about the baseless and irrelevant labelling of "lacking" and "not yet". Thus, it will be possible to make redundant the binary approach of developed/underdeveloped. The alternative question will also create a space wherein we can find an alternative theoretical framework that is sorely needed to break out of this so-called development model in which the world is mired, with its sense of fatalism and hopelessness.

In the alternative hypothesized perspective offered in this volume, the focus is on two processes: one, the role of human agency (including structural agency), defined more broadly here as human creativity, that includes inner-self and humaneness (as well as subjective reactions to living and working conditions); two, uniqueness and inter-connectedness of all societies as in Indra's Net. With this approach, it should be possible to explain the issue of industrial development and underdevelopment as part of a larger process resulting from people interacting with others within a society while resolving their daily human needs through their humaneness and creativity, as well as people interacting with the larger historical forces developing outside of their society. The following example from India can be helpful to understand this point.

With the introduction of so-called development projects, people in India were compelled to leave their villages in massive numbers in search of a livelihood. But the fate of one Rajasthan village changed when Dhanoya, a poor man in that village, called on an old idea of saving rainwater naturally and made up his mind to implement this practice and saved the village from drought and extinction. He mobilized the village people, and in response, people from all castes and religions in the village came together. They were successful in saving their village from present and future extinction, and they soon became prosperous through their projects related to watershed development. This approach is now replicated in other regions as a weapon against poverty in India, and is preferred to the failed projects of "development" (industrial projects) imposed and suggested by the IMF and Western scholars, which is then, of course, implemented by the Indian government (Mahurkar and Parihar, 1999; Goodman, 2015). This has given the people of the village a sense of empowerment and ownership. As villager Kanhya Lal said, "We used to feel we could not change our fate, but now we have the confidence to look after ourselves" (Mahurkar and Parihar, 1999).

From the perspective of this volume, it is important to note that people from all castes and religions were able to come together to save this village, rather than reinforce their distinctive caste identities, thus refuting the widely propagated notion of rigid caste consciousness among Indian villagers and its hindrance of people's solidarity. However, this is not to say that the caste problem does not exist anymore. In fact, with the development projects caste identities are increasingly being used for political votes and economic gain, as well as for the politics of recognition. At the same time, it is also the case that the Dalits are still facing severe repression, even though many young Dalits are able to attain social mobility and higher education.

In another instance, when imported parts were not available for repairing existing tractors, some villagers used their ingenuity, called *juggad,* a Hindi term used colloquially, to create new ways for improving those tractors that did not depend on imported parts. In Bangladesh, the poorest country in the world, people have created many new schemes (such as the famous Grameen Bank) to take control of their lives. It is a different matter that such schemes have been hijacked many times by patriarchal power structures (and by NGOs) to their own advantage while marginalizing women, ironically in the name of improving women's lives. Nevertheless, the role of human creativity cannot be denied in the development of new ways to change society and living conditions. The example of the Workers' Party's success in Brazil is noteworthy in this regard (despite the fact that imperialist forces are once again successful in forcibly reversing these conditions), as are the actions of the poor people in South Africa who are once again standing up to the ANC administration and their draconian rules. Similarly, in India, people are successfully fighting against the projects of modernization (such as the Narmada Valley Dam), which are supported by the World Bank and other multinational companies in alliance with the government of India. In the Amazon forest, a tiny tribe has been able to stop oil companies from taking over its land. Recently, twenty-four organizations in India have written a letter to the World Bank about the tragic consequences of "development" projects.

It is important that scholars give credit where it is due and recognize the genius (creativity) of all those who are able to survive and manage their daily lives with ingenuity. It is the capitalist forces that learn from people's ingenuity and innovations and then appropriate these innovations and survival strategies for its own commercial ends through scientific management (Bahl, 2005). Thus, a so-called primitive culture is suddenly transformed—by the magic wand of a time and motion study—into a modernity and therefore, seemingly progressive Western, of course, "brand new", culture. For example, generations of women in Africa have been carrying enormous pots filled with water on their heads and loads of fire wood for long distances (as well as carrying their children) without straining their necks. US Pentagon authorities, after making a time and motion study of the African women's ability to function under such a load, found that this transport method could be adopted by the US army to train its soldiers to carry more weight while on the battle field and remain efficient and agile (Ibid.). Similarly, the creative fashion styles of inner-city Afro-American youths are profitably used by the high fashion industry to set new trends in teenage clothing, while these inner-city youths are treated as deviants of society. One can go on adding any number of similar cases from the world of music, art, scientific inventions, weapons, innovation in food, cooking, herbal plants, indigenous knowledge, yoga and other intellectual fields that are appropriated by corporations for profit. We applaud corporations for making a profit, but we do not appreciate the genius and creativity of the average person who is the real creator of ideas utilized by the corporations for profit making. Similarly, we tend to recognize the bravery of soldiers (those who kill people on behalf of their countries) and rich people who go for adventure tours, while ignoring the bravery of people who are able to survive their seemingly impossible everyday struggles against the onslaught of capitalist forces, while also keeping their creativity intact. Perhaps it is not all that surprising that a soldier's bravery and the glamorous life of rich people seem more interesting than the struggle for survival among poor people. Perversely, in 2000 the television industry found a way to market and profit from the common people's capacity to creatively survive extreme situations, as demonstrated by the record-breaking rating for the artificially created "real survivor" programs. More recently, poverty tourism (also called slum tourism) is gaining steam as some well-off people from the West are looking for the new adventure of experiencing poverty themselves by living with a poor family or homeless person for few days. The new trend in California is the gentrification of poverty where people drink raw water, and live in tiny houses with all the modern amenities and luxuries that only the rich can afford.

It cannot be denied that it is the creativity, genius, and average individual's capacity to provide labor power, as well as the reproduction of social and biological labor, that has created profits for the capitalist class in the form of inventions, innovations, and manual labor. Since capitalists are using all their resources to control the genius of the average person to maintain these profits and power, concerned scholars should try to understand this precious potential source of capitalistic profits and expose the hypocrisy of the theories of "development" and the politics of "identity and subjectivity." Using the metaphor of Indra's Net we can visualize all societies non-hierarchically as being part of a larger network interacting as unique and equals at the same time.

In the end, it may be pointed out that the suggestions hypothesized here might help in writing histories everywhere—of women, the working class, oppressed people, and colonized oppressed societies—from the vantage point of their own societies without the binaries of "traditional or modern," "core/periphery," "progressive or backward"—not as national or local history, but as a dynamic process of social interaction among people through their capacity for creativity, that in turn creates social institution and historical forces within a society as well as internationally. These social structures and historical forces, in turn, influence and affect people's choices and actions. The metaphor of Indra's Net is useful in explaining the interactive processes among societies. Questions automatically arise: Why have we not used our creative ideas to write and promote such histories rather than feel stuck in a blind alley?

In subsequent chapters, I shall provide a sample of how these ideas can be applied in a historical comparative study of four countries, and it will not cover an in-depth chronological history of each country. Instead, I shall explain by using the yardstick of parity (not the binary distinction of developed/underdeveloped), and focusing on the conjunction of historical forces, which are created through the interactions of societies, how the large-scale steel industry emerged in four countries—Imperial Russia, colonial India, Imperial UK and postcolonial Imperial US at the turn of the nineteenth century—each having a different historical trajectory with different characteristics. I chose the case of the large-scale steel industry because it was considered to be the basis of "development." However, England did not develop theirs until 1932, and that did not stop historians from treating England as a "developed" country. Colonial India and Imperialist Russia also had large-scale steel industries before World War I, but historians have referred to these societies as "underdeveloped/backward." These characterizations of different societies, besides being racist and inaccurate, have not helped in understanding these societies in all of their complexity. Each society contains universally common elements as well as very specific historical conditions, and they are all connected as in Indra's Net, thus they are all co-produced and co-constituted. The binary distinction that has been used so far does not allow us to see this complex relationship among societies.

However, before concentrating on each chosen society for this volume, it is necessary to locate all of them in the larger international historical context of that time period. Because each society, while created and guided by the needs, choices, and actions of its members (using their creativity), was simultaneously interacting with other societies and creating a specific international environment, which in turn influenced the choices and actions of each of these four societies, including the choices of whether or not to build a large-scale steel industry.

NOTE: In this chapter, I have developed and expanded on ideas that were initially articulated in the "Introduction" section of my last book (2005) and thus a heavy borrowing from it became necessary.

ENDNOTES

1. Conner, C. (2005).

It is important to point out that Marxist scholars use the concept "class consciousness" to explain how workers become conscious of being part of the larger working-class vis a vis capitalist class. This process of becoming *class conscious* also involves *inner conversation* that, in turn, is connected to the everyday interaction with others in the process of class struggles. Moreover, the inner conversation of workers and their sense of belongingness with the larger whole are similar to the experiences of human beings when they feel connected to the larger cosmos, and have a sense of belongingness with it. However, this experience is generally labeled as spiritual or religious, and then it is relegated to the realm of institutionalized religions for interpretation, thus unavailable to others for serious evaluation. If any academic person attempts to take it seriously, she/he is labeled as un-academic.

The following quote from Jiddu Krishnamurti is useful to understand the process of creative thinking: "Creative thinking is the infinite movement of thought, emotion and action ... thought, which is emotion, which is action itself, is unimpeded in its movement, is not compelled or influenced or bound by an idea, and does not proceed from the background of tradition or habit, then that movement is creative. Creative thinking is free of division, which creates conflict between thought, emotion, and action ... thinking is action, which is the relationship between individual and society" (Krishnamurti, 2009, IndiaTimes.com, May 26).

2. Marean, C. W. (2015). "The Most Invasive Species of All." *Scientific American,* August 2015. pp. 33–39. Marean explains that Homo sapiens managed to colonize the whole globe because of two major reasons: one genetically determined propensity for cooperation with unrelated individuals, and, two, advanced projectile weapons. Using the study of Sam Bowls, the author then explains how Homo sapiens came to have this cooperative trait. Bowls' work shows that an optimal condition under which genetically encoded hypersociality can propagate is, paradoxically, when groups are in conflict. Groups that have higher number of pro-social people will work together more effectively and thus outcompete others and pass their genes for this behavior to the next generation resulting in the spread of hypersociality.

3. Capra, F. (1984). *The Tao of Physics.* Toronto: Bantam Books.
Austrian theoretical physicist and Nobel Laureate Erwin Schrödinger wrote in his book, *My View of the World,* "The plurality that we perceive is only an appearance, it is not real. Vedanta philosophy—has sought to clarify it by a number of analogies, one of the most attractive being the many-faceted crystal which, while showing hundreds of little pictures of what is in reality a single existent object, does not really multiply that object." Wikiquote.org.

Schrödinger also wrote, "In all the world there is no kind of framework within which we can find consciousness in the plural; this is something we construct because of the temporal plurality of individuals, but it is a false construction ... The only solution to this conflict insofar as any is available to use at all lies in the ancient wisdom of the Upanishad."

German theoretical physicist and Nobel Laureate Wemer Karl Heisenberg also noted that one cannot always distinguish between statements made by eastern metaphysics based on mystical insight, and the pronouncements of modern physics based on observations, experiments and mathematical calculation (Goldberg, 2010:285).

See also *Engels on Feuerbach* (MECW Volume 5, p. 11 in http://www.marxists.org/archive/marx/works/1845/thesis/feuerbach.htm).

Frederick Engels quotes Feuerbach: "Isolated man by *himself* has not the essence of man in *himself,* 'the essence of man is contained only in the community, in the unity of man and man, a unity however, which depends only on the *reality* of the *difference* between I and you—Man by himself is man (in the ordinary sense), man *and* man, the unity of *I and you* is God' (i.e., man in the supra-ordinary sense)."

Another quote from Feuerbach: "the truth that no being on its own is a true, perfect, absolute being, that truth and perfection is only the association, the unity of two beings that are essentially alike."

4. Henry Martyn Lloyd pointed out that Enlightenment's contribution was to add science to this picture of reason, and religious superstition to the notion of passionate enslavement. Similarly, within the ancient Stoic philosophy, passion was a threat to liberty because it makes a weak person a slave. The strong remain free by asserting their reason and will. However, Lloyd thinks that it is a mistake to believe that the "Enlightenment was a movement of rationalism against passion, of science against superstition, of progressive policies against conservative tribalism" because the Enlightenment had a rich texture. According to him, the Enlightenment was a diverse phenomenon, as most of its philosophy stood far apart from Kantianism or Hegel's version of Kant. He thinks that Romanticism was a continuation of Enlightenment themes.

Elaborating on the diversity of Enlightenment ideas, Lloyd further pointed out that the French Enlightenment emphasized sensation and "many Enlightenment thinkers advocated a polyvocal and playful version of rationality" and were against the inwardness of speculative philosophy. The philosopher Etienne Bonnot de Condillac said, according to Lloyd, that "all aspects of human thought grew from our senses, specifically, the ability to be drawn toward pleasant sensations and driven away from painful ones. These urges gave rise to passions and desires, then to the development of languages, and on to the full flourishing of the mind." Referring to David Hume, Lloyd writes, "A person without the ability to be affected, either because of the absence of passions or the absence of senses, would be morally monstrous." However, as Lloyd pointed out, these ideas of Enlightenment were not a "rejection of science rationality per se, it was only a rejection of reason in *isolation* from the senses, and alienated from the impassioned body." (Henry Martyn Lloyd, "The Enlightenment was not the Age of Reason—Here's Why." Alternet.org, Nov. 17, 2018).

5. Scheler, op. cit. p. 80.

"'Tat Vam Assi' is an anti-individualistic concept contrary to what has been propagated. 'Tat Vam Assi' does not mean I am in you and you are in me. But in fact, similar to 'do to others as you wish to be done by.' Seeing others as yourself means treating others as human as you think you are. It is connecting with others on an equal level and not less or more than you. … No one is an island. More one realizes this more humane behavior is possible." *The New York Times,* "What Would Krishna Do?" August 3, 2014. (https://opinionator.blogs.nytimes.com/2014/08/03/what-would-krishna-do-or-shiva-or-vishnu).

Erwin Shrodinger provided another interpretation of this concept: "This life of yours and being is not merely a piece of this entire existence, but in a certain sense the *whole,* only this whole is not so constituted that it can be surveyed in one single glance. This, as we know, is what the Brahmins express in that sacred formula which is so simple, and so clear, tat vam assi, that is you" Wikiquotes.org.

It should also be pointed out that within science, which is treated as a symbol of modernity, objectivity, and progress, any new discovery that is "in conflict with the conventional wisdom, those are not easily accepted. This resistance to new discoveries does not seem to be a scientific way of dealing with them." As Igor Juricevic pointed out, "numerous reports indicate that scientists rate research more favourably if the findings agree with their prior belief … these prior beliefs often have nothing to do with science but are simply the scientists' personal views" (Igor Juricevic (2016), "Person's Beliefs versus Scientific Innovation: Getting Past a Flat Earth Mentality," Alternet.org. Viewed June 13, 2016).

See also Terry Eagleton (2009). He points out that science also has its high priests, sacred cows, revered scriptures, ideological exclusion and rituals to suppress dissent. This suggests that science is not opposite to religion (*Reason, Faith and Revolution: Reflections on the God Debate.* New Haven, CT: Yale University Press. p. 133).

6. It is only now that the idea of holography is succeeding and scientists are able to think of other possible dimensions of the cosmos. As noted in *Scientific American* (2014), scientists have started questioning that, "Perhaps the rules of the cosmos are written in another set of dimensions and translated into the three we perceive. Perhaps, like Plato's prisoners, our personal circumstances have tricked us into believing the world as three dimensional when in fact a deeper understanding of what we perceive will come only when we look for explanations in the fourth dimension … Our model of holographic big bang resolves not only the main puzzles of uniformity and near flatness of standard cosmology without resorting to inflation, but also nullifies the damaging effects of the initial singularity" ("The Black Hole at the Beginning of Time," Niayesh Afshordi, Robert B. Mann and Razieh Pourhasan. *Scientific American,* August 2014, pp. 38–43. p. 43).

The use of metaphor to understand social reality is not unique to social sciences. Even in science, which is supposed to be objective, also works mainly by metaphor because metaphors are the source of all thinking and speaking that includes sciences (Waldrop 1992). For example, the Western view of the world before the advent of Sir Isaac Newton was organic. However, that changed when in the 1660s Newton's laws and differential calculus showed that planets move in simple predictable orbits. With a predictable world, there was no need for either a God to hold things in place, or angels to push things around (Ibid.). According to this new understanding, the planets ran themselves in a simple regular and predictable Newtonian machine—like clockwork. That is how clockwork became the metaphor for the age of the Enlightenment.

7. Randall Collins (1998), *The Sociology of Philosophies: A Global Theory of Intellectual Change* 1998. Cambridge, Harvard University Press. He was quoting the saying of Fa-tsang writ-

ten during the Tang Dynasty.

When I gave a talk using the metaphor of Indra's Net in a university in Kolkata, a scholar present in the audience simply labeled it as an effort to promote Hindu fundamentalism. His reaction probably had something to do with a recent huge victory of Hindutva forces in the 2014 election, or perhaps this scholar was not aware that this metaphor has been used by a renowned sociologist (Randall, 1998), as well as by a physicist (Capra, 1993), and is certainly not connected with Hindutva forces. As I have discussed in this chapter, the whole web network system is based on the same principle as Indra's Net. Most of all, this metaphor is part of the accumulated knowledge of Indian heritage, which is (and should be) accessible to everyone, as it is not a monopoly of Hindutva forces.

Interestingly, on the issue of the Indian heritage of accumulated knowledge, Amritanshu Pandey (2015) has explained that various words, that seem synonymous today, had very different meaning and there were many different Vedic clans who followed different rituals and dialects. We cannot claim that Rig Veda was written by one tribe, as there was no united citizenry. He explains the diversity in ancient India as follows:

> We must note the fact that tribes such as the Bharatas never used the title of Manava or Purusha—indicating that they were each completely separate people. This gives us an ancient canvas where India was not populated by a united citizenry, but divided into dozens of clans that drew vital distinctions between each other. The Suryavamshi prayed primarily to their patron deity, Surya, and the Rig Veda (which Bharata tribe's compositions) contains only eight prayers to Surya. Eight among the 900+ prayers! It can thus be said that Surya worship was not an important ritual among those of Bharat blood, though it was vital to the Manavas and Aikashvakus that claimed descent from Surya himself. Is Suryanamaskara really a part of Indian culture then, when India's most prominent ancient tribe (Bharata) never indulged in it? With so many different tribes occupying different parts of ancient India's geography and cultural legacy how can we to say anything about our ancestors that may hold true for all of them? Can I even consider the Rig Veda representative of ancient Indian times when it was composed almost exclusively by a single tribe?

Regarding the un-scientific attitude of Indian Marxists towards religion, a Marxist journalist Vidyadhar Date (2008) pointed out in a left of center journal, *Economic and Political Weekly,* that this attitude of Indian Marxists has allowed Hindutva forces to monopolize the common Indian heritage of accumulated knowledge in the name of religion. For example, he wrote, "That Communist Party of India (Marxist) leaders in West Bengal show the same fascination for the expensive, time consuming, scandal ridden game of cricket and seek to control the Cricket Association of Bengal," while ignoring "yoga and pranayama that are excellent exercises which can play a great role in creating a healthy society at no cost what so ever." Date writes that yoga is becoming more popular and respectful in the West, and the best research in yoga is taking place in the West as they see it as a useful exercise to improve the mind and body. He suggests, that "the left should have championed these exercises long ago but has ignored them and has allowed the religious right to monopolize them" and capture the initiative of mass fitness with yoga. This initiative, he pointed out, made people flock to the organizations closer to *Rashtriya Sevak Sangh*, such as Brahmavidya Sadhak Sangh in Maharashtra. These organizations, while promoting yoga, are also able to instill their Hindutva ideology and politics into a large number of people using Sanskrit prayers with a heavy emphasis on god, spirituality, and immortality.

Vidyadhar Date's comments seem to be closer to some of the ideas developed in this volume.

8. Malhotra, R., *Being Different.* p. 114.

   See also Stuart Kauffman (1996), *At Home in the Universe: The Search for Self-Organization and Complexity,* to understand how spontaneous order arises in the universe; how self-organization takes place that creates new entitities. See also John Avery (2003).

9. Malhotra, op. cit. p. 114.

   Capra has also used the metaphor of Indra's Net in *Tao of Physics.* See also Herman

Harkem (2010), *Information and Self Organization: A Macroscopic Approach to Complex Systems.* Stuttgart: Springer. Harkem discusses how recognition of information is a highly cooperative process and that information is a crucial element of the very existence of life. See also John Avery, *Information Theory and Evolution*. New Jersey: World Scientific. 2003. See also Michael Talbot, *The Holographic Universe*, 1991.

Talbot writes, "Hindu Avatamsaka Sutra likened the universe to a legendary network of pearls said to hang over the palace of the god Indra and 'so arranged that if you look at one [pearl] you see all the others reflected in it.' Using this imagery, the author of Sutra explained that 'each object in the world is not merely itself, but involves every other object and in fact *is* everything else'" (Talbot, 1991:290–291). Talbot informs that in the seventh century, Fa-Tsang, the founder of the Hua-yen school of Buddhist thought, employed a remarkably similar analogy when trying to communicate the ultimate interconnectedness and interpenetration of all things. This non-local organization of the universe was explained in their unique way long before the invention of the hologram. Talbot has also noted that seventeenth century German mathematician and philosopher Leibniz were familiar with the Hua-yen school of Buddhist thought. Some have argued that this was why he proposed that the universe is constituted out of fundamental entities he called "monads", each of which contains a reflection of the whole universe (similar to nodes in Indra's Net). We should also note that Leibniz also gave the world integral calculus and it was integral calculus that enabled Dennis Gabor to invent the hologram (Ibid: 291).

The scientist Nikola Tesla (who patented 700 inventions in the US during the twentieth century) also told in one interview, "When wireless is perfectly applied the whole earth will be converted into a huge brain, which in fact it is, all things being particles of a real and rhythmic whole" (quoted from John B. Kennedy interviewing Nikola Tesla, *Collier Magazine,* January 30, 1922. Reproduced in Global Research.ca. August 25, 2018: "Who is Nikola Tesla?"). When Nikola Tesla met Swami Vivekananda he became interested in Eastern philosophy as it provided him a spiritual terminology to explain scientific phenomenon, cosmology and his dreams (he used to dream of new inventions) (video: "Missing Secrets of Nikola Tesla," by Phenomenon: The Lost Archives).

10. Today, Eastern knowledge is being used by millions of people around the world and many western academic institutions are doing more advanced research on Eastern knowledge in various fields than Indians are. The human accumulation of knowledge is no one's monopoly and we can all learn and benefit from it. Interestingly, a recent article has documented that Yoga hand *mudras* are also depicted in Orthodox Christian Art (Byzantine Art) showing the influence of Buddhist and Hindu religious practices ("Myths, Symbols and Mysteries: Rediscovering the Past" in http://www.bibhudevmisra.com/2017/11/yoga-mudras-in-ortodix-christian-art.html). This information was posted on the website of Abhinvagupta.com. See also Igunma, J. (2019), to understand how the story of Buddha came to be celebrated by Christian Europe under a different name.
11. See Review of Stanford Video Series (countercurrents.org 3/10/15). The reviewer of this series, William T. Hathaway, writes, "The surface level is our ordinary thinking awareness, which mediates our sense impressions of the macroscopic level of the universe. Beneath that surface lie subtler subconscious levels of mental activity that science is beginning to explore. Underlying it all is a transcendental field out of which thoughts arise and which mystics, artists and philosophers of all cultures have contacted and described as a reservoir of creativity and dynamism." Furthermore, he pointed out that, "theoretical and experimental evidence" shows that "the unified field of physics and the unified field of consciousness are identical—i.e. that during the meditative state, human awareness directly experiences the unified field as the foundation of the universe."

It is important to point out that when Western scholars write and experiment with Eastern ideas of consciousness, meditation and so on, they are taken more seriously than when an Indian scholar points out about Indian mystical traditions and meditation.

J. P. Das, a psychologist of Indian origin, has recently written a book on *Consciousness Quest: Where East Meets West on Mind, Meditation and Neural Correlates.* SAGE Publications: New Delhi, 2014. He writes:

Self-consciousness awareness arising out of reflection, by definition a human trait, and above it at the higher state of mental evolution is cosmic consciousness." He mentions Bucke's book (1961) on Cosmic Consciousness, who wrote the following: "Self-consciousness … a faculty upon which rests all of our life … By virtue of this faculty man is not only conscious of trees, rocks … his own limbs and body; but becomes conscious of himself as a distinct entity … Cosmic Consciousness is a third form which is as far above Self-Consciousness as is that above Simple consciousness … The prime characteristics of cosmic consciousness as its name implies, a consciousness of the cosmos, that is of the life and order of the universe … To this is added a state of moral exaltation, an indescribable feeling of elevation, and elation and joyness … With these come what may be called, a sense of immortality, a consciousness of eternal life … the consciousness that he has it already." Das pointed out that this "concept is remarkably similar to the higher level of consciousness in wisdom traditions of Vedanta and yoga" (Das, 2014:74–75).

12. See also other works on the same subject: *Journal of Happiness Studies*; Jill Lepore (2013). *The Mansion of Happiness: A History of Life and Death.* NY: Vintage Books; Christopher Peterson (2012). *Pursuing the Good Life: 100 Reflections on Positive Psychology.* Oxford University Press; Sonja Lyubomirsky (2008). *The Myths of Happiness: What Should Make You Happy; but Doesn't. What Shouldn't Make You Happy, but Does.* NY: Penguin Books; Shimon Edelman (2012). *The Happiness of Pursuit: What Neuroscience Can Teach Us About the Good Life.* NY: Basic Books; Oliver Burkeman (2012). *The Antidote: Happiness for People Who Can't Stand Positive Thinking.* Faber and Faber; Robert Skidelsky and Edward Skidelsky (2013). *How Much is Enough? Money and the Good Life.* NY: Other Press; Ashis Nandy, "The Idea of Happiness," *Economic and Political Weekly*, January 14, 2012, 47(2):45–48. Universities in the US are also promoting Happiness Studies.
13. See also David Graeber (2015). *The Utopia of Rules: On Technology, Stupidity and the Secret Joys of Bureaucracy.* NY: Melville House. We learn in this book about how "audit culture" has spread throughout all spheres of life and clerical work has been outsourced to consumers turning them into part-time, unpaid administrators for corporations.
14. There are studies exposing Google's deliberate use of algorithms to influence viewer support in favor of Hillary Clinton.

SECTION III

Applying the Alternative Perspective

CHAPTER 3

Interaction and Conjunction of International Historical Forces, 1800–1913

"The West won the world not by the superiority of its ideas or values or religion (to which few members of other civilizations were converted) but rather by its superiority in applying organized violence. Westerners often forget this fact; non-Westerns never do" (Huntington, 1998).

"Interaction exists in international life just as it does in the internal life of peoples. It is a natural and inevitable process … the ideologies of every particular age are always most closely connected—whether positively or negatively—with the ideologies of the preceding age" (Plekhenov, 1947).

"If contingency played little part in how history turned out, if the present was inevitable, then it makes little sense to challenge the status quo. However, if contingency dominates history, the future is open, and the world can be another way" (Stephen Jay Gould, quoted in York and Clark, 2011).

"Regions are also a social constructs that are created by the use that people make of certain resource that are found within a geographical 'space' " (Ågren, 1998).

INTRODUCTION

Before we discuss the emergence of the large-scale steel industry in the four chosen countries, we shall locate these societies within the larger international context of that time because the interaction and conjunction of historical forces internationally were produced through intra-societal interactions as well as through inter-societal interactions. In subsequent chapters, we shall focus on each society's specific societal context which is created by the conjunction of historical forces within each society. This organization of historical information is necessary because the history of every society/country is also the history of its interdependence with other countries. They influence one another either in reciprocal ways or with asymmetric perceptions, relationships, or by force. Through these entangled processes, societies/countries help constitute and co-produce one another. That is why the history of different societies should not be treated as separate autonomous units for comparison with labels as "core/periphery," or "developed /undeveloped." Our methodology does not deny that some societies do become powerful, controlling, and colonize other societies, compelling them to become peripheral and underdeveloped. Today this is done through the actions of the World Bank and IMF (in Europe it also includes the European Central Bank) by forcing structural adjustment programs on certain ex-colonies which leads to more poverty in those countries. World System theory has explained the historical global processes in the making of the global condition (Wallerstein, 1974; Frank, 1967). What is being suggested here is that no society should be considered "developed or underdeveloped" as it's natural and inevitable original organic condition.

For example, England did not come into being initially as a "developed" country. Moreover, it is not possible to write the history of nineteenth-century England without situating it simultaneously within the framework of nineteenth-century world history, which evolved through the repeated interaction of various societies of the world creating specific international conditions. Similarly, nineteenth-century world history cannot be written without explaining the respective roles of strengths and weaknesses, and of hegemony and subjection played by each society and by regional "actors" simultaneously. Similarly, England's industrialization was not simply an internal process because Britain could not industrialize without the availability of world markets in the fifteenth–seventeenth centuries [(1)]. In order to explain this historical process, we need to be aware of various pitfalls. For instance, we cannot simply summarize by combining national and regional history and then synthesize it because this would make the internal complex diversity within each country indiscernible. On the other hand, if we simply focus on differences that would lead us to treat each society as an autonomous system operating without any interaction with other societies. Similarly, if we focus only on "class struggle" it will make other forms of dominations—racial, caste, national, and gender—invisible. Therefore, in order to avoid all these pitfalls, the history of any society can be written by understanding the complex interactions within each society and amongst societies over a long period of time. For example, it includes, in addition to the interaction of societies with other societies, their interaction with various constantly changing systems of social labor relations, political power relations, and centers of cultures, which existed and were destroyed and recreated many times in these societies. Even though each culture is different, they are all related at the same time as they all learn, adopt and adapt many ideas, technology, and ways of life through inter-societal and intra-societal interactions.

For example, as Anievas and Nişancioğlu (2015) have pointed out, it was the Mongol Empire and Ottoman Empire that created crucial conditions—access to new trade routes, new technologies of navigation, arts of war, military technology, mathematics and other useful inventions and knowledge, links to large Eastern regions, and access to Chinese ideas and technology, awareness of the vastness of the world—which made it possible for Europe to develop the capitalist system through which it acquired global dominance. Mongol invasions and its Empire also created special conditions for England that allowed it to develop as an industrial country. However, the threat of Mongol invasion affected China differently as China completely ceased its oceanic voyages, and concentrated on the defense of its boundaries from Mongols. This withdrawal of China gave Europeans, who had become aware of the vastness of the world, an opportunity to expand in the Americas and later in East Asia.

Elaborating further, Anievas and Nişancioğlu suggest that the Mongol Empire played an important role in facilitating the shift in European class relations in the thirteenth century. The Black Death in Europe, which triggered a crisis in the European feudal mode of production, was due to Europe's interactions with Asia. The high mortality rate in Europe decreased the population and created a shortage of labor, which in turn pushed up wages and increased the need for labor saving machines and technology. The development of new types of productive forces with labor saving machines and technology changed class relations in Northwest Europe, and forced a change from feudalism to capitalism. After the collapse of the Mongol Empire, Europe easily captured maritime trade routes and networks (they did not have to pioneer them), which were developed by Mongol Empire over a long period of time as an alternative to a costly overland trade system. These maritime routes, which were connected to the Indian Ocean, proved very useful for Britain in becoming a dominant world power later on (Anievas and Nişancioğlu, 2015).

Europe also took advantage of this international trade to gain access to Eastern production and social and technological knowledge, which the Ottoman Empire had developed and established. Furthermore, when the Ottoman Empire blocked European merchants from the Mediterranean route, Europeans were forced to search for new routes, which shifted the commercial centers to Northwest Europe on the Atlantic. This Atlantic trade (based on extremely brutal exploitation) later made European dominance in the world possible. Anievas and Nişancioğlu suggest that it was the struggle between the Ottoman Empire and Habsburg Empire in 1600 that gave rise to the Reformation leading to the breakup of the Habsburg Empire, which then resulted in the dismantling of Christian centers, and accelerated the process of state building. The struggle between the Ottoman Empire and Habsburg Empire also facilitated the peculiar development of an English state, as England was isolated from Hapsburg's geopolitical pressures. Under these new circumstances, England became more "'responsive to commercial-capitalist interests' and did not squander its resources in Continental wars" (Ibid., 117).

Other scholars have also corroborated such interactions and their influences on Europe. For example, Conner (2005) has highlighted the many ways Europe benefitted from its interaction with the non-Western countries that contributed to its rise and dominance in the world. Earlier, Historian Janet Abu-Lughod also provided details about inter-societal and intra-societal interactions and exchanges during the thirteenth century that contributed to the formation of modern Europe (Abu-Lughod, 1989). While focusing on Egypt between 1760 and 1840, historian Peter Gran explored the Islamic roots of capitalism, which shows that the "Industrial Revolution was a global event" (Gran, 1979:xii). These observations illustrate that all of these societies were continuously co-producing and co-constituting one another.

Keeping in mind such complex historical processes in the making of any society, we shall locate the emergence of a large-scale steel industry in each of the four chosen societies both within its specific context, and within the larger international historical context of the 1880s. In this chapter, the focus is on international context to identify what types of historical, political, financial, technological, social, cultural, and religious developments had taken place in Europe during the nineteenth century.

CONJUNCTION OF INTERNATIONAL HISTORICAL FORCES

One of the historical forces that emerged during this period (1600–1900) was the formation of an international bourgeoisie class. However, its emergence and growth were intertwined with the process of state formation, primacy of science, and with the structural formation of an international political economy. These structural changes also triggered various social, nationalist, and labor movements demanding political rights and better living conditions. These historical processes were also intertwined with various social, cultural, technological, and ideological changes of that time and it is not possible to separate one historical process from the other. However, for the sake of clarity and comprehension, we shall elaborate on various broad historical processes and shifts, which contributed in the creation of powerful historical forces at that time, including the following: The formation of the transnational class of Freemasons; shifts in ideas about science and religion; liberalism and counter movements; changing structure of international political economy (improved transportation and communication systems; demographic shifts; science-based industries, increased bureaucracy and experts); new economic forces (colonialism and imperialism; trade and tariffs, monetary and financial systems; corporate cartels; urbanization); social reforms, and social changes, socialist challenge; the emergence of labor movements and social movements, emergence of nationalist movements and state formation, alliances and international treaties; the struggle for the new international balance of power.

1. THE FORMATION OF A TRANSNATIONAL CLASS: FREEMASONS

> Freemasonry was one of the most revolutionary phenomena of the 'rationalist' age and its rise is directly linked to the triumph of a new science culture, to the Newtonian version of Enlightenment—English science and English revolution—are central to the history of Radical Enlightenment and Freemasonry (Jacob, 1981:106).

Available literature on the Freemasons is very large. However, I have used information from selected important published works to trace the broad contours of the formation of this transnational class.

Elite groups within the transnational network formed a separate cosmopolitan brotherhood, called Freemasons (van der Pijl, 1998). In the eighteenth century, it was a most powerful and influential set of secret or semisecret societies with secret and esoteric doctrines. The secret nature of these societies did not allow a clear formulation of Freemasonry ideology. However, this much is known—Freemasons believed in the universal brotherhood of man, and their goal was to achieve moral self-perfection while creating a golden age without linking their ideas to a specific systematic program of political action (Ibid.).

Freemasonry performed a dual function of filling the vacuum created by the decline of the authority of the Church and the disintegration of feudal society. Thus, Freemasonry stood halfway between traditional religious faith and rationalism, while their Masonic lodges incorporated elements of the Church's hierarchical order and elaborate cult rituals (Walicki, 1979 cited in van der Pijl, 1998). This dual function made Freemasonry both a quasi-religious and also a secular institution at the same time. For example, as van der Pijl pointed out, Freemasonry drew people away from the official Church, and at the same time provided a rationalized religious experience, while secularizing its followers' world view. Yet, many people also went back to religion leaving behind Enlightenment ideas of rationality and secularism. The rationalistic and deistic wing of Freemasonry, which flourished in England and France, was able to assert not only the authority of reason against that of the Church, but also was able to promote tolerance and freedom of the individual. In the regions that were not economically developed, including Germany, the mystical

Freemasonry prevailed. At the same time, an extremely rationalist branch of Freemasonry called Illuminati, which was very active politically, also came into being in Germany. However, as van der Pijl pointed out, under the force of the Freemasonry movement, which was based on the anti-ecclesiastical model, religious faith was modernized with rational ideas, and in that process the individual soul received direct and immediate contact with God (van der Pijl, 1998).

The Masonic movement was international as it transcended national boundaries. They were able to create a transnational class that included craftsmen, intellectuals, artists, scientists, and moneyed people (merchants, bankers, and royalties) of different societies in present day Europe. They also played a major role in integrating the ascendant bourgeoisie in different states, thus contributing in the making of the political, cultural, and economic conditions that helped in the formation of Europe as an entity, which later became synonymous with Western (supposedly "developed," "civilized" and "superior") civilization. Antonio Gramsci observed that everywhere in Europe, the same topics, the same institutions, and the same principles were being discussed, and a unified consciousness of Europe was created through Masonry, which was the vehicle for that enthusiasm (quoted in Jacob, 1981:103). Freemasons not only created a unified consciousness of Europe, they also spread the capitalist ideology worldwide. However, the global spread of comprehensive capital relations took three centuries as it was a slow and gradual process. Freemasons were able to maintain their hegemonic control over the area of their influence through common strategies, as well as by adjusting their actions according to new challenges and resistance to their programs. This transnational class, along with the coercive power and structure of the state system, played an important role in the formation of Europe known as (recently invented) Western "civilization" (Appiah, 2016).

The influence of Freemasons can be noticed even in the twenty-first century. The descendants of Rothschild and other (Freemasons) today control the policy-making institutions such as the Council of Foreign Affairs, the Trilateral Commission, the American Federal Reserve Bank, and Bilderbergers[(2)]. Jim Marr (2000) has described in detail the various ways in which the Rothschild's have been connected with the Morgan, the Rockefeller, the Bilderbergers, the Council of Foreign Relation, the Trilateral Commission, and the Royal Institute of International Affairs, and how they have been able to influence different policies and projects globally (see also Quigley, 1981). The extreme secrecy of Bilderberg Group meetings maintained with the help of riot police is well known and documented in newspapers (see news report of 2015 of secret meeting of the Bilderberg Group and harsh police treatment of protesters and journalists). Moreover, Freemason symbols still decorate the American dollar bill. Since the time of the formation of this transnational class, it has mutated into many different forms, but its influence has never diminished. Instead, it has become more pervasive and more detrimental to our daily existence.

The following is a brief history of Freemasonry, its role in the making of a unified international bourgeoisie class and shaping of the modern West, while also spreading its networks worldwide.

Freemasons in the Seventeenth & Eighteenth Centuries

The first transnational bourgeoisie was the community of Freemasonry that arose after the Glorious Revolution. Those who joined Masonry during the last quarter of the seventeenth century were more interested in preserving and increasing the influence of moderately wealthy people in society and in the government, than they were in craftsmanship because they were keen on preserving the gains of the Civil War of 1642–51 (i.e., ensure limited power of the king) (van der Pijl, 1998). However, when higher level of nobility—bourgeoisie, priests, and nobles (including several brothers of Louis XVI)—increasingly entered the Masonic lodges, original Whig radicalism was restrained.

Various complex historical forces (including Freemasonry) that emerged in the eighteenth century helped in the transformation of the universal doctrine of natural law into citizens' rights (a circumscribed form) as a doctrine of cosmopolitan law. These lodges promoted the ideals of civil equality, religious toleration, and the liberation of human personality from all institutions (van der Pijl, 1998). At the same time, with their agonistic and paganized Christian rituals, Freemasons were able to include people from various sects, including Jews, into their brotherhood. This brotherhood, as van der Pijl pointed out, was similar in ways to a guild loyalty that provided exclusive "social insurance" in the face of increasingly competitive conditions. In this increasingly impersonal world, Freemasons created a system involving signs and gestures that helped its members to recognize other members from different classes in different locations. This new system enabled the members of the Masonic lodges to have access to credits from their counterparts abroad as well as providing them with new identities. Trying to link itself with the past, Masonic lodges traced their connection with earlier transnational links in medieval guilds as well as in the myths about Templar origins and other knightly orders (Ibid.). Thus, by establishing transnational links, Freemasonry was able to facilitate the idea of treating one's own society as a "colony [as if it was foreign] to be exploited. Many merchants, lawyers and accountants who entered the masonic lodges, were already alienated from their communities as they were involved in the long distance money economy [market relations]" (Ibid., 99). However, as van der Pijl pointed out, the industrial entrepreneurs in England, who were immigrants from Central Europe, did not need Masonry and its ideology to enable them to exploit their fellow men.

Since Freemasonry was not a closed system, it became possible for it to facilitate the formation of a transnational class while spreading its ideas and bourgeois elements around the world. Van der Pijl noted that in the absence of sufficient documentation, it is difficult to show a link between the role of Freemasonry in the building of Empire, or to explain how its doctrines of brotherhood sustained the world-wide activities of traders and empire builders, or to show how British cultural influences spread worldwide. However, the following offers a glimpse of their activities and influences over time.

By 1717, the upper classes in England had moved into the Grand Lodges followed by royalty from the house of Hanover. These lodges helped bring class compromises between the commercially minded aristocracy and ascendant bourgeoisie (van der Pijl, 1998). Many enlightened European monarchs had embraced Freemasonry, believing it would be able to modernize their society from above while preempting a revolution from below. Prussian King Fredrick the Great, Russian Empress Catherine II, and Austrian Emperor Joseph II were all tolerant towards it for the same reasons. However, after the French Revolution, an act of Parliament was passed that threatened private societies and future Lodges. Freemasons were able to get exemption from this act with the help of a joint intervention of two Grand Lodges in 1799. Later, a United Grand Lodge of England was created in 1813 (Ibid.).

Over the years, the power of the Freemasons (bourgeoisie) increased in relation to trade unions. By 1872, the number of Freemason in the British Empire reached four million. This was much larger than the 500,000 trade unionists and 400,000 members of the cooperative movement. Freemasons had also a strong membership among the police, which made them well-equipped with intelligence operations that aligned with their practices of extreme privacy and secrecy. Thus, as van der Pijl noted, the internal nervous system of the British ruling class and its middle class was highly developed (as it is in the US and Europe in the twenty-first century) even though both groups were weak in numbers in comparison to the vast number of the working people. This increase in ruling class (Freemasons) power was supported by a coercive apparatus at both the formal state level as well as at the informal level (Ibid.).

Since most British Masons were from the non-manual section of society, they tried to control the economy from a distance rather than by direct entrepreneurial involvement. They worked behind the scenes by preparing government policies, pulling levers, tempting with rewards, and applying sanctions. Later, the organization of British Commonwealth and subsequent international organizations adopted this model of control. For example, the French-born British Grand Master Desaguliers was the architect of the transnational spread of Masonry but he avoided the limelight, as did others after him (Ibid.).

From the early eighteenth century onwards, Masonry expanded abroad, both to English-speaking settled lands and to Europe. The first Lodge in North America was set up in 1733 in Boston. In New England and Virginia, Freemasonry united the free-thinking elite among the settlers leading to clashes between the more independent minded American bourgeoisie and British colonial interests. At least eight signatories to the Declaration of Independence (possibly thirty-two) belonged to the "craft." Benjamin Franklin became Provincial Grand Master of Pennsylvania in 1749. George Washington was initiated as a Freemason in 1752. However, as van der Pijl noted, people with opposing viewpoints and ideologies were also members of the Freemasons. For example, presidents of the early nineteenth century advocating a focus on individual rights and minimal government (Jefferson, Madison and Monroe) were Masons as was Alexander Hamilton, a champion of centralization. Even Andrew Jackson, who challenged state power and opposed the strong federal role, did not object to the federal government's role in territorial expansion (Ibid.). We can still observe the influence of Freemasonry today in Masonic symbols—including the triangle with the all-seeing eye—as printed on the US dollar note.

After the American secession and the French Revolution, British Freemasonry turned more towards conservatism while continued to expand its empire abroad. To achieve their goal of expansion, van der Pijl informs, the Masons began to interlock the network of public schools with their own lodges in order to use them as training grounds. In this way they were able to unite the English-speaking bourgeoisie as quasi-tribe, while providing them with both mystique and an elitism that was "a necessity in the imperial administrator's portfolio of tricks" (Ibid., 102). Locally, Masonic connections were and remained entwined with organizational networks such as the Rotary Club, Lions Clubs, and Chambers of Commerce. These networks were (and are) connected with productive capital and international business. The Rotary Club is a non-religious and non-secret fraternity that was set up in 1905 in Chicago as a luncheon club for businessmen. The role of this club was to serve as a transnational class network. With its expansion in the wider English-speaking world, it opened clubs in Dublin and London, and in 1922 it was renamed Rotary International. The Lions Club, founded in 1917, later helped set up the non-governmental organizations (NGO) charter for the UN in 1945 (van der Pijl, 1998). These Masonic clubs, van der Pijl informs, continue to provide the basic ingredients for the formation of an international class with their own channel of communications, and with other more restricted elite networks created with internationally operating capital.

Masonry spread through other countries as well. Canadian lodges were set up in the mid-eighteenth century, and by the early 1800s lodges began to appear in Australia. Under the British Raj, a Masonic web was created in India with the appearance of provincial Grand Lodges in Bengal in 1755, Bombay in 1764, and Madras in 1767. Non-white people were admitted much later (1860) when a Parsee entrepreneur, J. N. Tata (he started the first large-scale steel industry in India), and other Indians were allowed to join without crossing class lines (Ibid.).

In France, the lodges became hotbeds of revolutionary conspiracy, as they had been in America. The Templar Tribunal, which organized the storming of the Bastille, included Mirabeau, Robespierre, Danton, and Philippe Egalite. Under Napoleon, the lodges became nodal points for state-driven modernization as their influence spread across Europe along with the French Revolution. They created powerful networks within the army, police, and civil services. Several of Napoleon's brothers—the kings of Naples, Spain, Holland, and Westphalia—were Masons; one of the Marshals-Masons, Bernadotte, became King of Sweden and Grand Master of that country's Grand Lodge in 1811 (Ibid.). The French Revolution also inspired Latin American revolutions. Thus, Freemasonry provided the nodal points for transnationally connected bourgeois emancipation. Latin American lodges were set up in the early nineteenth century under French and American allegiance. Many Latin American revolutionary leaders were Masons including Miguel Hidalgo, Simon Bolivar, and Jose Marti (Ibid.). Lodges in Spain and Portugal were under English jurisdiction during the second quarter of the eighteenth century.

Initially, the French Revolution forced continental Freemasonry to go underground. In 1792, the Austrian lodges closed of their own accord to avoid being subjected to persecution, while in Russia, Tsar Paul I outlawed them. But after the Restoration of the monarchy, van der Pijl pointed out, Masons played a part in the commitment of the bourgeois state to modernization but in a passive revolutionary mode. This modernization allowed the advances of the bourgeoisie while preserving the prevailing structure of political power. In this preservation of enlightened monarchy as well as the formation of democratic institutions, Masonry was able to influence both processes (Ibid.). In France, Louis Philippe, the son of Philippe

Egalitee, was installed in 1830 to lead a bourgeois monarchy. Louis Blanc, a leader of the 1848 revolution, represented the radical egalitarian tradition with which he equated Masonry at large. Giuseppe Garibaldi, who came back a Mason from South America to lead the campaign for Italian unification in 1873, established Masonry in Italy as a political institution, however, it did not have much communication with England (Ibid.).

However, imperialist rivalry and revolution caused a split in the once unified transnational brotherhood of Freemasonry, except in the heartland. Even though relations between British and German Freemasonry remained friendly, the War of 1870 destroyed whatever intimate bonds had existed between masonic France and Prussia-Germany. In spite of these divisions, Masons had been successful in establishing transnational networks in core regions.

Freemasons at the Turn of the Century

Towards the close of the nineteenth century, Germany unified after its victory over Napoleon III, and became one of the powerful competitive states with a new mode of capital accumulation, which challenged British hegemony (van der Pijl, 1998:106). It also undermined the cosmopolitanism of Freemasonry as it rested on the dominance of British hegemony. Even though Freemasons had a stronghold in banking in London, they could not adequately deal with the huge emerging challenges at the turn of the nineteenth century. However, their broader function was "intellectual," as they were functioning as an international force operating within each nation in the form of an international political party (van der Pijl, 1998). In the words of Antonio Gramsci, "Freemasonry, Rotary, Jews, etc. can be subsumed into the social category of 'intellectuals,' whose function, the technical discoveries which provide the impetus for all activities of leadership, of devising compromises between, and ways out of, extreme solutions" (Gramsci, 1971, quoted in van der Pijl, 1998:107).

Faced with declining British hegemony and other challenges, European ruling classes began to focus increasingly on the national level, which in turn created the real possibility of the emergence of state monopoly. Since capitalist relation of production were not compatible with a full state monopoly, van der Pijl pointed out, this possibility was averted by the most powerful segment of the capitalist class of that time, the international investment bankers or *haute finance.* One of those bankers was Rothschild who was able to challenge the dominance of earlier merchant bankers, the Barings family [(3)]. Another British financier, Cecil Rhodes, who built the South African empire, took over the task of redefining the function of Freemasons in this new context.

Rhodes pioneered the formation of a refined Freemasonry and created a quasi-Masonic secret society to which he left his entire fortune (Quigley, 1981). The model for Rhodes' secret society was the Jesuits. His society was to be, in the words of the American secretary to the Rhodes Trust, "a church for the extension of the British Empire." William T. Stead claimed afterwards that "Mr. Rhodes ... aspired to be the creator of one of those vast semi-religious, quasi-political associations which, like the Society of Jesus, have played so large a part in the history of the world" (quoted in van der Pijl:109). However, Caroll Quigley wrote (1966) that Cecil Rhodes created a secret society in London in 1891 and the aim of this society was to expand the British

Empire to all habitable parts of the world.

After Cecil Rhodes' death in 1902, this secret society evolved and became transnational, as English elite merged with the American money-powers and the secret society moved to New York (Quigley, 1981; Docherty and Macgregor, 2013). They created various institutions (The Royal Institute of International Affairs in London, Council of Foreign Relations, Trilateral Commission, and United Nations) as instruments to create a "New World Order." The Milner Group, which took over the secret society after the death of Cecil Rhodes, as Quigley noted, was connected with a publication called, *International Conciliations.* It was through this publication that The Milner Group connected indirectly with a parallel group in America that was organized by the associates of J. P. Morgan and Company before World War I (Quigley, 1981:260). Furthermore, The Milner Group used its connections with Council of Foreign Relations and the Institute of Pacific Relations to reach the wider American public with their ideas.

Milner believed that the British way of life helps "unfolding all the best, the highest capabilities of mankind" (quoted in Ibid., 110; see also Docherty and Macgregor, 2013). Therefore, in order to maintain the existence of the British way of life, it was necessary to extend and integrate its Empire along with the development of social welfare. The leaders of this movement were trained at and recruited from Oxford College. Their influence extended to other universities in Britain and Canada with the creation of particular chairs. The Rhodes-Milner Group developed other networks that recruited promising English-speaking students. For example, it established the Royal Institute of International Affairs and its publications; the Carnegie foundations in the US, and key newspapers such as *The Times of London.* Van der Pijl noted that these institutions enabled the ruling class to achieve cohesion in their outlook. Thus, the Rhodes-Milner Group was able to both lead and serve the ruling class at the same time as it operated behind the scenes at crucial junctures and places. For example, it was the planning work of the Rhodes-Milner Group that shaped the Union of South Africa, the British Commonwealth, as well as the League of Nations (Quigley, 1981; quoted in van der Pijl:109; see also Docherty and Macgregor, 2013). All subsequent policy planning groups followed the model of the Rhodes-Milner Group.

Another concern of the Rhodes-Milner Group was to co-opt a privileged segment of the workers into an alliance with the ruling class. For that purpose, they tried to reinforce the racist prejudices of the white working class. One of Milner's recruits in South Africa, Lionel Curtis, outlined the nature of class compromise that underlaid corporate liberalism of that time: He wrote, "Whites were turned indolent and incompetent by the presence of large number of blacks … The tendency of Trade Union to exclude coloured labor should be fostered by all patriotic men in Australia and America" (quoted in van der Pijl, 1998:110–11).

While the European bourgeoisie was organizing policy planning behind the scenes to influence the nature and conduct of class struggle, its counterparts on the working-class side were emerging in the form of trade unions with the political agenda of socialism. In the late nineteenth century, these working-class organizations were becoming a threat to the traditional ruling class and their control over policy making. The ruling class dealt with this threat through imperialist expansion, as a famous quote from Rhodes (used by Lenin in his tract on imperialism) affirms this, "If you want to avoid civil war, you must become imperialist" (Quoted in van der Pijl:109).

2. SHIFTING IDEAS ON SCIENCE AND MYSTICISM

Along with the formation and worldwide spreading of the international bourgeoisie class, new ideological forces were also emerging in Europe (from the fifteenth century onward), which started challenging the power of the Church as well as the relationship between science and mysticism. These challenges included a new understanding of the natural world, of human body and mind [(4)]. The historical process of this shifting of ideas in Europe was complex.

Earlier, during the time of the Renaissance when old classics were rediscovered, mysticism and science were not seen as contradictory; rather, they went hand in hand, as magic, astrology and alchemy all flourished during this time. Magic also influenced European alchemists but later they renounced it and became empiricists and developed the "scientific method." Newton was a student of alchemy; astronomer Johannes Kepler was interested in astrology; and Francis Bacon did not rule out the possibility of the existence of phenomenon involving sorcery, witchcraft, and dreams (Jacob, 1981; Northcote, 2007). Renaissance intellectuals believed that the study of anomalies could help understand the "deeper disclosure" of the natural world (Northcote, 2007). Some of them were skeptical of church institutions and they decided to explore natural and supernatural forces. Such skepticism and explorations created a favorable environment for experimentation which in turn led to modern science. For example, Newton while pursuing an interest in alchemy also developed his theory of gravity and later discovered calculus. However, as Northcote noted, the Church believed that these ideas were the manifestation of Satan's influence and deviated people from the Scriptures. Therefore, the Church branded those intellectuals who were interested in "high" magic and occult as heretics. The Church received support from skeptics, who were also opposed to the existence of the paranormal (Ibid.).

From the late seventeenth century to the late eighteenth century, a new perspective on nature was emerging, which made many intellectuals skeptical of "high" magic. These intellectuals became more interested in the idea of empirically observing and describing things and reading literally (not symbolically) nature as an "open" book (Ibid.). With the foundation of modern mathematics at that time, calculus was discovered and geometry was formalized. These mathematical discoveries enhanced the sense of Europeans that "the universe operated under laws discoverable and calculable by humankind" (Lachmann, 2000:3).

It was also during this time that Descartes and Galileo rejected occult thinking and laid the foundation of modern mechanical physics and the mechanical model. Northcote informs that Descartes suggested a division between "subjective" imagination (creativity) and the "objective" reality of the physical world because he believed that imagination should not play a leading role in attempting to understand the objective world (Northcote, 2007). Other thinkers, such as Hume and Kant, rejected occult and "pseudoscientific" ideas on the grounds that such ideas were threats to the social, moral, and civic order. With the growing popularity of these new ideas of rejecting occult, the Church became concerned about saving the reality of God, as it feared that people would become atheists and would reject the reality of Satan, and in effect also the reality of God (Ibid). However, by the end of the seventeenth century, as Northcote noted, Humanist sentiments developed among certain Christians which helped in ending the witch hunts, and later in the eighteenth century, Humanism also helped in decreasing the state sanctioned death penalty.

While Humanist ideas were emerging, people also began to challenge scientific ideas as they felt an increased "alienation of human experience from a world of scientific fact" (Ibid., 42; see also Stremlin, 2004). This challenge came from the movement of Romanticism. Many other groups of people during this era—Rosicrucian, Illuminati, and Freemasons—wanted to relate scientific principles to certain occult ideas as they believed in the occult and in mystical philosophies. In 1824, this effort led to the publishing of a weekly astrological almanac (Northcote, 2007). By the mid-nineteenth century, a Spiritualist movement was becoming popular as interest in clairvoyance, telepathy, necromancy, channeling, and hypnotism increased. Intellectuals who were religiously inclined began to seek a unity between religion (Eastern religions), spiritualism, and scientific perspectives. For that purpose, they formed societies. For instance, the Theosophical Society focused on divining a knowledge of the mysteries of life, and was founded by Helena Petrovna Blavatsky (who claimed to be initiated by Buddhist masters in Asia) in New York in 1875, and it soon spread all around the world (Ibid.). Another society—The Society for Psychical Research—was founded in England in 1882–83 by those who were frustrated with both scientists and the Orthodox Church because scientists refused to embrace religious ideas as an integral aspect of science, and the Orthodox Church refused to embrace science as an integral aspect of religious knowledge (Ibid.).

Moreover, Enlightenment thought (based on the idea of rationality and science) in the nineteenth century also succeeded in separating philosophical thinking into distinct disciplines, while leaving the search for the absolute—a metaphysical concern—and reconciling of faith and reason, to theologians. However, scientific methods gained currency in other fields as well, which helped in decreasing the power of Church. For example, Germany established a nationwide system of lay education in 1882 to weaken the power of church in schools (Joll, 1973). In the middle of the nineteenth century, the ideas of political liberalism, and a belief that the analytical methods applicable to the natural sciences could also be applied to all problems, began to emerge. This belief led to the idea of precise historical scholarship based on detailed work in the archives with detachment and impartial accuracy. In Germany, efforts were made to reconcile religion and science by applying the criteria of rational scholarship to the study of the Bible and to the evidence of the gospels. These efforts, Joll pointed out, resulted in the creation of a new Protestant theology.

In spite of these opposing ideological shifts in the realm of religion and science, science received a wider acceptance. Each one of the political, social and intellectual movements, which later transformed Europe, also generated a counter-movement. For example, the imperialist movement led to a movement of radical criticism in imperialist countries questioning Europe's right to rule "backward" people (Ibid.). Many other such counter-movements also emerged at the time as discussed below.

3. LIBERALISM AND COUNTER MOVEMENTS

According to James Joll, the period from 1890 until the outbreak of World War I was one of the most interesting and creative in the history of Europe. The imperialist movement led to the radical criticism of imperialist ideology, which subsequently created revolutionary forces in Europe, which later also helped the process of decolonization. At the same time, the emergence of revolutionary forces also led to a renewed fear of revolution in Europe, which in turn resulted in new counter-revolutionary and anti-socialist ideologies (Joll, 1973). For example, to meet the challenges—dangers of socialist revolutions—of the modern industrial conditions and the emerging liberal state, there developed an effective Christian social movement to stem the rising tide of the socialists (Ibid.).

In the area of politics, liberal ideas of universal suffrage and a representative government were becoming the political norm. For example, the conservative empires of Germany and Austria-Hungary began implementing liberal ideas. In Russia, after the Revolution of 1905, a national parliament and some form of constitutionalism was established for the first time (Ibid., 113). Similarly, Italy and Spain accepted the form of parliamentary government. Britain and France were already functioning as parliamentary democracies—though each functioning differently—and became examples to emulate. However, in England, the principle of universal suffrage also contributed in the making of the Women's Social and Political Union (WSPU) in 1903 which fought for women's right to vote. In order to achieve their goal, by 1912 the WSPU resorted to direct action: bomb attacks, hunger strikes, interruption of political meetings and public demonstration on occasion. The WSPU was successful using shocking tactics to make the right of women to vote a live political issue. Joll has noted that similar movements also emerged in smaller democracies of Europe: Belgium, Norway, and Sweden (Ibid., 118).

In the intellectual sphere, a new generation of sociological thinkers, psychologists, historians, philosophers and physicists were becoming more interested in understanding the complex nature of society, and began looking into the deeper causes of social change. Some of the important names are August Comte, Herbert Spencer, Karl Marx, and Emile Durkheim. By the end of the nineteenth century, Max Weber focused on the importance of religious belief as a motive for social action. Anthropological studies challenged the notion that "all societies are bound by the law of nature to evolve in the same direction." Instead, they suggested that there are many possible alternative ways of organizing society besides the European ways (Ibid., 136–137). By the end of the nineteenth century, scholars also began to challenge the emphasis on certainty and the widespread belief that scientific progress would solve almost all problems. In addition, they challenged the notion that the methods of the natural sciences could be applied to the study of history, or of society, or of literature. Suggesting an alternative approach, these scholars began to place emphasis on the "irrational element in man and on the importance of the instinctive and subconscious emotions" (Joll, 1973:138). For example, Croce challenged positivist historians and emphasized "imaginative recreation of historical writing." Henri Bergson criticized the mechanistic view of mental processes, as he believed that we cannot ignore the role of time and memory in creating an image of the world in our minds. Thus, he focused on the importance of understanding the instinctual side of man's nature and the role of the subconscious in making his perception of the world. According to him, "There is one reality at least ... which we all seize from within, by intuition and not by simple analysis. It is our own personality in it flowing through time—our self that endures" (quoted in Joll, 1973:138).

Similarly, people also started reacting to their transformed environment in the wake of industrial and technical advances. They rejected industrialism and the presuppositions of industrial and mechanized thinking and began to seek new ways to live a simple life and regain contact with a more natural world. (It should be noted that in the twenty-first century, we are witnessing a similar reaction of people towards the policies of "neo-liberalism," globalization of trade, manufacturing and finances, technological advances, and environmental disasters.)

4. CHANGING STRUCTURE OF INTERNATIONAL POLITICAL ECONOMY

The domination of science along with the formation of an international bourgeoisie class (discussed earlier) played an important role in facilitating the formation of an integrated Europe. However, complete integration also required a structure of international political economy, centered in the West, and an interrelated Western nation-state system. This structure of international political economy was formed in the process of various historical developments in Europe: The growth, expansion and integration of international economy with population movement, and capital flow. Increased economic freedom led to the increased mobility of capital, labor and trade. Foreign trade also increased with new forms of transportation, communication, technological innovations, population growth, supply of natural resources, and growth of real income. All these historical developments were also deeply and extensively intertwined with Western imperialism, colonialism, and capitalist ideology. These developments are elaborated below.

a. Growth of World Economy via Improved Transportation & Communication

In the transportation area, most important was the introduction of railways in the nineteenth century—first in England and later in America. Subsequently, railways spread throughout Europe and to other continents around the world, including Russia. It was through railways that America and Russia could expand their territories within their continents. However, the experience of colonized countries was different, as railways required heavy capital investments as they operated with coal, and their components were made of iron and later of steel. Britain was the only one that was well positioned to provide credit to other societies, including its colonies, for building railways and making them buy British goods, while increasing the volume of its own trade. Britain achieved that position of power by accumulating a huge capital reserve through empire building, overseas commerce, and financial transactions across many decades. Railways also helped Western powers create an informal empire by making other countries dependent on them for loans, technology, and know-how. This was accomplished through contracts and other such means (Clarence, Wilburn, and Robinson, 1991). In this regard, Britain remained unchallenged in Europe and elsewhere until the rise of Germany and the US in the 1880s.

In addition to railways, the improvement in steamships contributed in the expansion of the world economy. Later, the carrying capacity of steamships increased (which increased population migration) with the introduction of steel, while the opening of the Suez and Panama canals brought down freight rates, thus expanded trade. In addition to improvements in transportation, the communication system also improved with the newly invented telegraph and telephone (Kenwood and Lougheed, 1971). This also helped the newspaper industry to become efficient in receiving news and expanding their reach to a large audience with their daily paper. Even governments used the services of the press to spread its own ideas among the people to garner support for war or other major issues. The improvements in communication increased the efficiency not only in the management of the transportation system but also in every area of production, distribution, exchange, trade, management of labor and capital, as well as in the arena of politics and socio-cultural life.

Thus, the spread of railways, steamships, and other communication technologies triggered many other changes in the world at that time. One of those major changes was a series of shifts in global demographics.

b. Global Demographic Shifts

Europe's population had grown very fast between 1800 and 1900. With the easing of state control between 1820 and 1913 over the flow of capital, labor, and trade, mass migration of European people to other continents began. The heaviest emigration was from Britain and Germany, but in 1880, it was more from Italy (Ibid.). British emigrants went to the US and to other dominions, Italians went to the US and Latin America; Spaniards and Portuguese went to Latin America, and Germans went to the US with a small number going to Argentina and Brazil. This migration was facilitated by the growth (rapid after 1850) of the steamship industry as it was able to reduce transportation time. Along with steamships, the invention of telegraphs helped in the circulation of information about opportunities abroad, and many people started taking these long journeys in the hope of improving their lives. Over time, passenger facilities improved with increased competition between these companies as well as with government regulations. However, the cost of travelling after 1850 did not change much (Ibid.).

The additional reasons for this large migration between 1815 and 1870 was the lack of land to accomodate an increased population, and the agricultural blight which resulted in the famine in Ireland from 1845–1852. Moreover, the inflow of cheap grain from the US further depressed prices, which reduced agricultural profits in Ireland, Britain and the rest of Europe. In the absence of any provision for British farmer protections, its rural population, hit by the collapse of the agricultural sector, also began migrating overseas in large numbers. After 1880, the migration flow to the US increased from eastern and southern European countries due to population growth in some regions and increased political oppression in other regions.

From 1848–1873 many Asian laborers from China and India went to the US and other areas. Chinese went to Cuba, the Philippines, Peru, California (following the Gold Rush before 1882) and to Australia in the 1850s. Under the Chinese Exclusion Act of 1882, Chinese population movement was restricted within the US. In Russia, mostly peasant settlers moved further eastward into Asia. Those who moved into Siberia were mostly prisoners and exiles. Many Russians moved southward into the steppe regions of eastern Asia and Turkistan (Kenwood and Lougheed, 1971).

However, these migrations could not have taken place if restrictions on migration were not removed in the receiving countries. After 1850, the governments of the receiving countries offered aids to migrants. Brazil provided initial help to immigrants with free passage, free land, and sometimes machinery, seeds and livestock as well as monthly cash allowances. Many philanthropic organizations, trade unions, individuals, and relatives of family members helped provide money and other needs for migrants (Ibid.). However, a vast majority of migrants received help from their families and friends for resources and transportation, and many others used their own resources.

The receiving countries benefited from this large immigrant population as it provided them with a large labor force and a market for goods, which led to increased growth of investment, income and employment. Many entrepreneurial immigrants brought the capital and knowledge to build new manufacturing industries involving textiles, furniture, chemicals, glass making and brewing, whereas artisans played a role in supplying the technical skills needed for the initial success of these new industries. Immigrants also provided the worker power required to build railways and transport facilities to erect cities, and to equip them with public utilities, sanitation operations, and other urban requirements. They also provided the factory workforce necessary for a rapid and sustained industrial growth in the receiving country. In turn, these workers became consumers of many of these products they helped in producing (Ibid.).

c. Increased Consumption

The growth of population and migration patterns also increased the demand for international goods. The rising price of land pushed many people to move to both rural and urban areas. The migration to urban areas and the development of new colonies contributed to the increased exploitation of natural resources that, in turn, required the expansion of colonies to acquire more land. During the nineteenth century, it was mostly in the Americas and Oceania that the supply of natural resources increased greatly. This increase was facilitated by the expansion of new knowledge about natural resources and their economic accessibility. The availability of cheap and adequate transportation, the knowledge of techniques that could exploit these natural resources with little capital, as well as an abundant availability of capital with which to exploit the mineral wealth, made the accessibility to these natural resources possible (Ibid.). In Africa and Asia, however, it proved difficult to exploit natural resources due to cost considerations, climate and topographical difficulties, and the resistance of local institutions.

However, with new production methods, better organization and improved transportation, productivity increased immensely, which raised the real income of people in certain countries. One can observe an income increase in the US and Canada after 1850, in Argentina after 1880, in Australia and New Zealand in the 1890s, and in Japan between 1870 and 1913 (Ibid.). This rise in income created an increased demand for capital goods, manufactured consumer goods, and services. Consumer goods like bicycles, sewing machines, typewriters and telephones were in demand, and by 1900 automobiles became available to the rich. In the US, with the standard of living increasing, people started consuming more dairy and meat products instead of cereals. There was more demand for sugar, tobacco, tea, coffee and luxuries. New opera houses were constructed for the entertainment of the rich, and for their luxury goods department stores were built in the 1870s. The first department store, Bon Marche in Paris, was built in 1853. Soon the idea of department stores was adopted in other places and chain stores started spreading around Europe. The growth of consumption was noticed in every social class including that of the peasants (though mildly), who were now using iron ploughs and oil lamps in their homes (Ibid.). However, as the living standard rose, Britain lost the market for low-grade cotton textile.

In the 1880s, when the Second Industrial Revolution was creating science-based industries, artificial refrigeration became possible, which allowed the importation of meat and dairy products from Argentina, Australia, and New Zealand. By the end of 1914, the consumption of tropical fruits also became important in the US.

d. Emergence of Science Based Industries

The Second Industrial Revolution (1880) was built on science-based industries that vastly reconstructed the capitalist economy and helped maintain the global economic pattern of development along with exploitation, and subordination of other societies. P. J. Hull writes that, it was at the point of production—in the science-based industries—that Western hegemony was manufactured (Hull, 2003:62). This reconstruction of production was accomplished by controlling the productive process through the instrumentation of measurement, which reduced every action in the production process into numbers. This required the development of a new technical language based on this measurement and a new conceptual apparatus that could be used by a new type of technician (Ibid.).

The earlier attempt to measure and quantify work began during the First Industrial Revolution with the help of engineering science so that the owners of capital could control the production process while maximizing its efficiency. This need for efficiency and control of the production process required a new way of measuring production and a new technical vocabulary. With the control of testing and monitoring, instrumentation became important and "the machine came to measure the measurer" (Ibid., 65). In order to achieve the goal of mass production quickly, it was important that a product be of uniformed output and easy to duplicate. To fulfill these requirements, the reorganization of workplace production and a science-based process of control became imperative. Fredrick Taylor (a member of Boston's aristocracy, who chose to become a machinist at a steel mill in Bethlehem, PA) developed his scientific management system, a series of techniques that he had begun working on in the 1870s, which became useful in the reorganization of the workplace. Conversion tables became a part of the process of routinizing and standardizing industrial measurement (Ibid.). Later, metallurgists dismissed earlier practices—an experienced eye and some rules of thumb—as obsolete. However, these nomenclatures remained in usage. Thus, with the use of instrumentation, measurement, and a new technical vocabulary, college-trained engineers and industrial scientists devalued the craft traditions, long experienced and involving the skilled hands and eyes of the workers, and established themselves as experts and authorities at the workplace. It was not difficult for these engineers and scientists to succeed in this new production system because the changing nature of the market required a large integrated firm with an expanded and extremely fast rate of production (Joll, 1973).

All of Europe was affected by the Second Industrial Revolution, because many businesses in most European countries were facing the competitive international economic system that required them to cut the cost of the means of production in order to maintain profits. These pressures further contributed to the adoption of intensified industrial production processes using modern methods and Taylor's system of scientific management. Taylor's was a new system of labor process that "converted the operatives into an automaton to match and keep pace with this equipment" (Ibid., 143). In Europe, Germany took the lead in these developments starting with education, by increasing its overall number of university students. By 1913, Germany had 60,000 university students while Britain had only 9,000 (Kennedy, 1988). Germany also increased the centralization of financial control over industry, which also contributed in creating massive industrial trusts and cartels in most areas of the economy. These new institutions and industries were run on the principles of scientific management, instrumentation, measurement, statistics, and technical vocabulary.

However, these changes could not be implemented and operationalized without a vast structure of bureaucracy and specialized experts.

e. Increased Bureaucracy and the Dependence on Experts

In the second half of the nineteenth century, experts were needed not only in the workplace, but in other areas, as well. The management of increasingly larger armies and navies, as well as the complicated administration of the newly built railway systems required more organization and planning. This requirement created a demand for professionals who held the following qualifications: knowledgeable about foreign countries and various foreign languages, possessing the organizational abilities to create and control a railway or an ammunition supply system, being well-acquainted with technological innovations, and possessing the ability to study and assimilate the latest tactical and strategical writing. Thus, in the late nineteenth century, the role of the expert became dominant and staff officers were required to improve their educational qualifications and training upon entering the service. Similar changes were introduced in virtually all other sectors of the government and the administration, as well as in foreign and colonial ministries, the educational department, and commercial and financial offices (Joll, 1973).

As the mass production of goods brought more prosperity, more people and politicians started demanding more efficient state organization as well (Hull, 2003). Following the lead of industry, both a new technical language and the concept of measurement at the workplace began to be applied to the growing bureaucracy and other governmental structures. The state began using technical codes and standards to regulate industries functioning more like a "secretariat of a confederation of trade association" (5). Economic and technological information was also used in the functioning of secondary industrial organization such as trusts, cartels, Japanese zaibatsu, freight car pools, power grids, patent pooling and cross-licensing. The measurement and technological language surrounding these functions became the foundation for all production, as well as for many other areas of human life. Nothing was left outside of measurement and everything was reduced into numbers based on a criteria of measurement set by technical experts.

Middle-class intellectuals started demanding that social legislation be scientifically based, and the London School of Economics was created for that purpose in 1895. The school emphasized the collection of data and documentation as critical for providing scientific credentials to any social reform (Joll, 1973). Thus, started the era of dissemination of facts and figures, as all social, economic, or any other social condition were explained away with the help of data. The legacy of this measurement and instrumentation of measurement in almost every sphere of life is well and alive in our time. For example, in the twenty-first century, most political, social, economic, and cultural decisions are made based on statistical data, which means everything has to be measured. Moreover, data collection and documentation also proved useful in controlling public opinion for political or other purposes as is also the case in our own time (collection of metadata by the government and other private corporations) in the twenty-first century.

f. Increased Urbanization and Industrial Art

With increased industrialization, more and more people started moving to urban areas. From the mid-nineteenth century onwards, iron and glass was increasingly used for building urban monuments. Important examples of this is the Crystal Palace built in London to hold the technology exhibit in 1851 and the Eiffel Tower built to showcase technology as part of the 1889 World's Fair. By the end of the nineteenth century, steel and reinforced concrete became more important, and in America steel-framed buildings were constructed from the 1890s onward. Other exciting new discoveries—motor cars, airplanes, cinema, radio—also made urban city life more glamorous with all its glitter and fast pace. In this newly mechanized glamorous urban environment, the attitude of some artists became more positive towards industrialism by the beginning of the twentieth century (Ibid.). For example, the first Impressionist exhibition took place in 1874, and by 1914, artists reacting to the emergence of photography began creating abstract work. Joll noted, post-impressionist painters like Paul Gauguin, Vincent Van Gogh, and Paul Cezanne focused on "inner formal structure and emotional meaning in the figure and landscape" (Ibid., 139). In France, the Cubist techniques developed in 1907, and thereafter by Pablo Picasso, Georges Braque, and others, who broke up space and depicted objects from "several simultaneous viewpoints in an effort to convey the dynamism of urban life" (Ibid., 140). (It should be noted that the scramble of Africa gave Picasso access to the African art world, which deeply influenced the artwork that made him world famous). However, futurist artists were more interested in showing the positive aspects of the Machine Age.

5. SOCIAL CHANGES AND SOCIAL REFORMS

With the rapid growth of urbanization and industry—which was based on complex industrial process and increased size—along with the emergence of liberal ideas, the notion of universal suffrage and representative government, the new industrial society faced acute social and health problems greater than any other time previously. At the same time, new discoveries in science and technology brought the understanding that by using rational means human beings would be able to control and remove many evils of human existence. To remove the social evils of the Industrial Revolution, Britain (first to face such problems) passed a Factory Act of 1847 to limit the length of the working day to 10 hours in the textile mills. The issue of working hours was also a major concern in the 1848 French Revolution.

Similar changes were made in other countries, as well. For example, in Prussia, laws were enacted (1830–1840) which gave the landowner the right to rule his workers with patriarchal justice. Later, this law was also extended to factory owners. In 1836, Italy prohibited child labor. In Germany, Bismarck introduced legislation (1878) which forbade the employment of child labor under 12. This law also changed the working hours for labor under the age of 16. However, all these laws were difficult to enforce (Joll, 1973).

Other improvements were made in the area of health with discoveries of new medicines and immunization. These improvements became effective due to improvement in sanitation with a new sewage system, availability of clean water, better housing and the availability of better food. However, improved transportation created a new commuter age as people moved into the suburbs. Many advances in medicines, such as anesthesia and antiseptic medicine, were made to meet the needs of growing injuries during wars, which were becoming bloodier with the use of powerful weapons. These growing wars also increased a popular demand for making war more "humane," and as a result, The International Red Cross was created in the 1860s to mitigate the sufferings of war (Ibid.).

6. EMERGENCE OF NEW ECONOMIC FORCES

The integration of Europe also reflected in the integration of the European elite as Walther Rathenau wrote in 1909, "Three hundred men all acquainted with each other control the economic destiny of the continent" (quoted in Joll, 1989:33). However, this economic destiny of the continent was not due to some inevitability, but due to the conjunction of various emerging new economic forces, as discussed below.

a. Growth of Finance Capital: Increased International Lending and Foreign Investment

An increase in international lending contributed in the formation of an international economic system by incorporating different regions of the world. After the Napoleonic Wars (1803–1815), the specialized financial institutions involved in international lending began to grow. The major players in international lending in the last decade before World War I were Britain, Germany, and the US. These players had flooded the world market with capital flow. However, the Netherlands and Switzerland also began investing significantly overseas (Kenwood and Lougheed, 1971). Sergei Witte, the Russian Foreign Minister in 1902, explained this phenomena,

> In every country which has reached a high level of industrial and commercial development and where the political horizon is calm and cloudless, a surplus of capital is experienced ... If in addition, small capitalists possess to a high degree the taste for savings—a taste which for many years has been innate in the French nations—the need for the export of capital becomes an absolute and ineluctable necessity (quoted in Joll, 1989:127).

Globally, total foreign investment rose from 4,750 million pounds by 1900 to 9,500 million pounds in 1914. The major borrowers by 1914 of these investment funds were Russia, the Balkans and Turkey, but investment also flowed to Canada, Argentina, Brazil, Mexico, India, Ceylon, China and Japan. On the continent of Africa, the Union of South Africa received the greatest portion of funds, while the remainder was invested in the African colonies belonging to Britain, France, Germany and Belgium. In the Oceania region, Australia received the largest fund amount (Kenwood and Lougheed, 1971).

Further incentive to invest came from the establishment of the gold standard and the free trade movement (1860–70). In fact, the reasons for investment in a country were also influenced by various political situations. For example, in the 1850s, Britain sympathized with the rebel states in Greece, Belgium, and several Latin American countries and invested in those regions as well as in many counter-revolutionary states in order to preserve the status quo in European politics. Sometimes the reasons for investment were influenced by religious affinities or geographical proximity. The increased investment in the US, Australia, Argentina, and Brazil by 1913 was due to their capacity to absorb capital (Ibid.).

However, after the 1890s the political priority of building military alliances for the much-anticipated forthcoming power struggle became more important. For example, France invested heavily in Russian government securities, and Britain also gave loans to Russia in the years leading up to 1914 for the same reasons (Ibid.). Thus, market capitalism was maintained through alliances and increasing interdependency among the European nation-states. Increased industrial development required more foreign resources, and that led to increased overseas investment as well as colonization of other societies. The increased industrial development also raised workers' income, which increased the demand for imported food and other consumer goods, and in turn, it also pushed up overseas investment (and expansion of imperialism and colonization) to meet those demands.

b. New Actors in the Global Trading System

Until the 1870s, three separate triangular systems of trade existed. One was comprised of the UK, Western Europe, and the Baltic countries that dominated Northern Europe's trade. Another was the slave trade triangle linking Britain, Africa, and the West Indies, and the various ports in the Americas. In the third trade triangle that became well established in 1860s, Britain covered its trade deficits with the US by obtaining surpluses from Latin America. Similarly, Britain's trade deficit with China was offset by surpluses from India (Ibid.).

After the 1870s, a new payment network system began to evolve due to the growing importance of other regions and countries in world trade, and it brought in new players. At the same time, the existing triangular systems began to merge. Although Britain remained the central player, its status and relations with others changed within the new system. After the 1880s, the US and Germany became an important separate link in the chain of international trade and payment systems. For example, between 1910 and 1914, US trade with the tropical countries of India and Brazil was fast growing and the US paid its trade deficit with these countries with export surplus from the Great Plains of Canada. During the period of 1910–1914, when other countries had put up high tariff protection for manufactured goods, Britain was able to use the Indian market to sell its manufactured goods, as well as obtain large quantities of food and raw materials from highly protected countries without having to increase its own export to these countries (Ibid.).

c. The Spread of the Gold Standard

This international global trade system was connected with the international monetary system, which changed in 1867. Two developments compelled this sudden change in the international monetary situation. One, Germany shifted to the gold standard because its commercial relations with several East European countries were affected when these countries shifted from the silver standard to inconvertible paper. Germany also had to consider the fact that its commercial relations with non-European countries were financed through Britain, which operated under the gold standard (Ibid.). Two, at the 1867 International Monetary Congress in Paris, a large number of delegates from many European counties had supported the adoption of the universal gold standard. The decision by the US Congress to adopt the gold standard was directly related to the discovery of large silver deposits in Nevada and elsewhere which increased the output and the price of silver dropped (Ibid.). By the end of the century, the gold standard was adopted everywhere and it remained dominant between 1897 and 1914. This global trading system had a direct connection with the economic imperialism of Western countries and the colonization of people of other continents in Asia, Africa, Latin America, and Middle East.

7. TARIFF PROTECTION IN EUROPE AND THE MYTH OF FREE TRADE

Trade protection in the nineteenth century was not a new phenomenon, as France used trade protection in the thirteenth century to protect its textile production from the threats posed by superior woolen textiles of Bruges and Ghent (Abu-Lughod, 1989).

In the nineteenth century, the British claim that its industrialization was founded on free trade, is not correct, as it was based on moderate protectionism. For example, British tariffs stood at a substantial 20 percent during 1846 and 1860 and remained significant at 10 percent between 1860 and 1879, and only dropped to a modest 6 percent as late as 1880–1913 (Hobson, 2004). Indeed, in 1875 (at the peak of "liberalization") average tariff rates on manufactures stood at 10 percent for Europe, and 14 percent when including the US. Moreover, during the era of "free trade" Britain had made very few treaties with European powers, and it remained indifferent to European protectionism between 1877 and 1879 (Ibid.).

In the late nineteenth century, the unification of Germany and Italy promoted nationalism and contributed to the rigidity of national borders and people's national identities (Joll, 1973:71). These nationalist feelings along with the global depression of 1873–1879, increased the demand for protection. Merchants and manufacturers became more nationalistic as they faced declining profits and intense competition and began to look for government help in the form of protective tariffs for their products (Ibid.). Similarly, different special interest factions in each country also began to pressure for tariffs. In the US, the government adopted "free trade" in the 1830s but reversed it in 1861 even though the US was not inside Europe (Ibid.). Earlier Russia had reverted to protectionism in 1868 to promote domestic industrialization. The import duty on coal, steel, machinery and chemicals was increased so much that the demand for these goods practically ceased (Ibid.). Russia increased duties in 1893 and again in 1900.

In spite of the imposition of tariffs, European leaders were also interested in keeping the increased international trade functioning smoothly, and for that purpose they made many international treaties. In 1860, the Anglo-French Treaty of Commerce opened more tariff negotiations (Ibid.). To facilitate international communication using railways, canals, telegraphs, postal arrangements, and other communication systems, many conventions were signed. Similarly, the Latin Monetary Union was created in 1865 in France to standardize the value of coinage in France, Italy, Switzerland, and Belgium to facilitate commerce among these countries. Thus, market capitalism was maintained through alliances and an increasing interdependency among nation-states.

8. FORMATION OF INTERNATIONAL CARTELS

In order to control prices, markets, supplies, and technological changes, about one hundred international cartels were formed in industries related to shipping, armaments, steel rails, electric bulbs, aluminum, calcium carbide, plate glass, tobacco, enamelware, and bottles. Since Britain was not a cartel member, the economic power of these cartels was greatly limited by the threat of British competition (Ibid.). Some foreign companies tried to break these trade barriers by investing directly in those countries. However, such direct investments were not very common before 1913 and they were not on a large scale.

9. IMPERIALISM, COLONIALISM, AND POWER STRUGGLES FOR MARKETS AND HEGEMONY

Within the European world, which was becoming more integrated by 1800, it was Britain that had acquired global dominance in naval mastery, as well as in its system of financial credit and commercial expertise. Britain remained dominant in the world arena until the 1850s, as its manufacturing production peaked due to the Industrial Revolution in the 1860s (Kennedy, 1988). The following quote by English economist William Stanley Jevons in 1865 indicates the colonial and imperial reach of Britain:

> The plains of North America and Russia are our corn field, Chicago and Odessa our granaries, Canada and Balkan are our timber forest, Australia contains our sheep farms, and in Argentina and on the Western prairies of North America are our fields of oxen, Peru send the silver, and the gold of South Africa and Australia flows to London; the Hindus and the Chinese grew tea for us, and our coffee sugar and spice plantation are in all Indies, Spain and France are our Vineyards, and the Mediterranean our fruit garden; and our cotton grounds ... occupied the southern United States, are now being extended everywhere in the warm regions of the earth (Quoted in Ibid., 194).

Between 1815 and 1880 Britain was able to maintain its dominance and its Empire as it had no rival in the international arena during this time. Britain's dominance was challenged when power and productive capacity of Germany and the US began to rise. British dominance was also challenged in the 'scramble of Africa' and in China. The expansion of European influence in Africa was very wide. By 1914 the whole of Africa was divided among European powers except for Liberia and Ethiopia. Britain held the largest territorial areas in Africa. This 'scramble for Africa' led to many conflicts and confrontations among European powers.

In China, Britain was the most influential and important trading power as Britain had forced China (through gun boat diplomacy) to open its ports to foreign traders. After Japan defeated China in 1895, the situation changed and other European countries—France, Russia, and Germany—also began to intervene in China's affairs. Kennedy noted that under the pretext of saving the integrity of the Chinese Empire from Japanese demands, these European powers, while intervening in China, imposed a sphere of influence and got concessions for trading rights, railway concessions, naval stations, mining rights and whatever direct or indirect control they could come up with.

Britain also extended its control over Burma and Malaya while imposing direct rule on India in 1858. Furthermore, in order to protect the route to its Indian colony, Britain colonized Egypt in 1882. The Dutch also extended their control over all of modern-day Indochina. Similarly, France took steps in strengthening its hold on its Indo-Chinese empire, while also taking over Laos and a small piece of China in 1893. Germany, being the late comer in the game of imperialism, could build only a limited empire in the East and southwest Africa and on the coast of China. However, it did succeed in gaining colonies in the Pacific Southwest: the Solomon, Marshall and Caroline Islands. Japan was able to avoid being colonized as it had already adopted European industrial techniques, and by 1894 it also became free from the trade "capitulations" which were imposed on it in 1858. Japan's strength was reflected in its winning successive wars with China and Russia in 1905. The US began to expand its influence abroad by colonizing the Philippine archipelago in 1898 after defeating Spain. In 1904, the US was able to block a German advance in the Western Hemisphere. Moreover, the US established the republic of Hawaii and intervened in Mexico, Costa Rica, Dominica, Colombia and Nicaragua. With the completion of the Trans-Siberian Railway, Russia was also able to establish itself as a major Pacific power (Kennedy, 1988).

The expansion of territories was also related to the question of international prestige, as French statesman Leon Gambetta remarked, "[T]o know a great nation or to become one, you must colonize" (quoted in Joll, 1973:81). In this game of imperialism, many European countries held overseas territories in the eighteenth century, although some lost them (Spain, for example lost its territories to the US and Britain in 1898). With the expansion of imperialism, the colonial governments not only colonized non-European countries, but also colonized surrounding regional areas to protect their existing strategic colonies, their boundaries, and the routes to them.

Thus, on the eve of World War I in 1914, every continent was carved out for colonization among the Western powers. However, Russia was expanding its territories within the continent through internal colonization. As historian Kennedy noted, Europe's control of the land surface of the world increased from 35 percent in 1800 to 67 percent in 1878. Britain had an empire 140 times its own size, Belgium, an empire 80 times its size, Holland, 60 times, and France, 20 times (Kennedy, 1988:143).

10. CHRISTIANITY, COMMERCE, AND COLONIZATION

The colonization of the non-Western world was also facilitated by the non-state actors who prepared the groundwork for it because "Christianity, commerce, civilization went hand and hand" (Livingstone quoted in Joll, 1973:80). For example, the Scottish merchants who founded the Imperial British East Africa Company were equally interested in both setting up trade posts and spreading Christianity. Scottish merchants along with other non-state actors—European trade, missionary activities, individual exploration, and scientific discoveries—were intricately involved with each other. This involvement was clearly explained by the president of the French Geographical Society in this 1874 address,

> Abstract science, gentlemen, does not suffice for humanity. Science is only really fruitful when it is an instrument of progress and production. It is not just in the interest of curiosity that exploration and geographical discoveries have been made. The discovery of America ... explorations of the interior of Africa ... have had besides a scientific end, a political and commercial object (quoted in Joll, 1973:80).

The exploration of unknown territories was made by certain Europeans who were inspired by an urge for scientific discovery. Their explorations opened up these unknown territories to the European traders and colonizers. Similarly, the quest of Christian missionaries to reach remote parts of the world to convert heathens and establish centers, facilitated European colonization of these regions. (It is similar to NGO efforts, since the introduction of "neoliberalism," to prepare people of poor countries to accept without agitation the negative consequences of multinational corporations' takeover of natural resources in those countries.) However, as Joll (1973) pointed out, the rivalries between Catholic and Protestant missionaries sometimes turned into a rivalry between French and British governments to protect their citizens in those regions.

Thus, the actions and choices of various merchants, Christian missionaries, and individual scientific explorers, who prepared the groundwork for colonization of remote regions, proved very beneficial for the colonizer countries not only for the access to new resources, new markets and various types of raw materials, but also to find an outlet for their educated unemployed, find inspiration in Africa for modern art, and in Turkey for music. However, these are just a few examples as this is not an exhaustive list of benefits [(6)].

11. SOCIALIST CHALLENGE

During the 1870s, when industrialization was increasing in Europe, an international socialist movement was emerging based on the idea that it was possible for people to create a totally new (utopian) society. (This idea is similar to the Judeo-Christian myth of creating a utopia with redemption of a flawed humanity.) (See Crooke, 2018). The First International, which was actually The International Working Men's Association, was formed in London in 1864. This Association helped disseminate Karl Marx's ideas, which influenced the working-class movement in Europe and abroad. The Paris Commune was formed in 1871. In addition to Marx's theories, there were other thinkers whose ideas were also spreading in Europe, and separate movements were emerging as each held a different assumption from Marx's: Pierre-Joseph Proudhon, Mikhail Bakunin, and Ferdinand Lassalle (Joll, 1973). However, the First International split in 1872 due to a quarrel between Marx (socialism) and Bakunin (anarchism).

By 1875, socialism was becoming a mass movement and workers were becoming aware of the theories of socialism. At the same time, even though the number of industrial proletariat was increasing, the number of trade unions were also increasing in Europe (Ibid.). For example, when the membership of trade unions increased in Britain it began a series of dramatic strikes: the London dock strike in 1889, a series of strikes during 1910 in the coal mines, strikes by the seaman and dock workers in 1911, and a national rail strike in 1911. Consequently, over the next twenty years, workers' bargaining power increased. In France, two strikes were held by public employees of the post office in 1909 and 1910, and railway workers went on a nationwide strike. During the period between 1900 and 1914, real wages had declined after a prolonged period of rising wages, which led to increasing labor unrest (Ibid.).

By 1900, social democracy as a movement gained recognition in European countries, except in Spain and Russia. An aggressive women's movement also developed in Britain (discussed earlier) and in the US during this time demanding political participation.

12. FORMATION OF NATION-STATE AND RISE OF NATIONALISM

Before the emergence of nationalism and nation-states between 1850 and the 1870s, Portugal, Spain, Britain, and France were the first monarchical nation-states who were free from the Holy Roman Empire. Between 1547 and 1584 the Russian Czar unified the government and created the first Russian nation-state. These newly emerging nation-states in the sixteenth and seventeenth centuries had a complex relationship with the predominant transnational power of the time, the Catholic Church. Some monarchs, like Henry VIII of England, wanted to attain absolute power, which led to a dispute over the question: Who controls the English church? This dispute ultimately broke England free from the Pope, and in the 1530s it established an independent Protestant Church.

Later, the legal foundation of the nation-state was established after the end of the Thirty Years' War, which was fought between Protestants and Catholics throughout central Europe from 1618–1648. In the treaty of Westphalia at the end of the war, the concept of a sovereign state ruler was created who would have power over all elements of both the nation and the state including religion, thus elevating state above civil society. According to this concept, final power rested with the central government, which made uniform laws and practices across the country. Consequently, between 1500 and 1700, these monarchical states became centralized and created a growing bureaucracy and a permanent mercenary army. However, to maintain an army, to conduct wars, and to meet the needs of monarchy required more revenue through increased taxes. These monarchs, being a single centralized authority, were able to quickly develop their economy, which enabled them to have, without dependence on nobility, a strong military and national armies. Pumped up with such military power, each of these nation-states wanted to expand its sphere of influence, which led to the search for new territories and colonization. In the sixteenth century it resulted in the creation of the Spanish Empire (Joll, 1973).

Earlier, France and England had built their national identities through constant conflict with each other. Linda Collins contends, "Britain was an invention forged above all by war. Time and time again, war with France brought Britons, whether they heralded from Wales, or Scotland or England, into confrontation with an obviously hostile other and encouraged them to define themselves collectively against it" (Collins, 1992:5). Thus, the necessity for consolidating diverse cultural groups within England, France, Spain, and Germany led to the rise of national identity and nationalism. Napoleon's military victories also paved the way for the emergence of nation-states in the rest of Europe. In places, the people rallied together as a nation in order to defeat Napoleon.

Inspired by notions of nationalism, Italians created a nation-state from a large number of smaller principalities. European Germans followed the same path as they organized into a loose confederation of more than 30 states after the defeat of Napoleon, and in 1871 Germany was unified following the Treaty of Versailles. Nationalism also gripped Eastern Europe, where ethnic groups were increasingly becoming aware of their own cultures and languages. This nationalism was based on ethnic identity.

The European working class also became interested in nationalism (loyalty to the state) instead of social justice movements because they liked the idea of popular sovereignty as it would enable them to play a part in determining political leadership. However, it also meant that as citizens they should be supporting and defending the sovereignty of the nation (Joll, 1973), including fighting in its wars if and when needed.

Soon these nationalist movements became a threat to the stability and security of three great empires: Russia, Austria, and Ottoman. However, monarchs, while making compromises with nationalism, used it to their advantage by promoting wars as heroic acts to save the nation while not worrying about domestic tension (Ibid.).

13. FEAR OF WAR AND NEW INTERNATIONAL BALANCE OF POWER

> The triumph of monarchical conservatism over the forces of liberalism and its compromise with nationalism enabled it to survive into the late nineteenth century, when it was confronted with a new challenge from socialism and socialist internationalism. The response of the ruling elites to their new opponents profoundly affected great-power relations in the half century between the Treaty of Frankfurt and the outbreak of the First World War (Bridge and Bullen, 1960:111).

The European state system did not change much between 1871–1914 as policy making remained in the hands of a small elite—as had been the case for the previous 200 hundred years. They followed a general policy in their inter-state relations, according to which, nations would settle adjustable interests with bargaining. However, any threat to vital interests to any one of them would be fought over. This state system managed to keep relative peace on the continent, while colonial rivalries were increasing (Ibid.).

However, the unification of the German Empire changed the balance of power in Europe, as Germany began to expand its industrial power along with strengthening it's military capabilities. Moreover, France, Austria-Hungary, and Russia had also acquired large land armies by the 1890s that had no match, except for one another. In addition to these developments, colonial rivalries began to increase after the 1880s. The main imperial rivalries were between Britain and France in Africa, and Britain and Russia in the Far East. By 1900, China had become an object in a struggle for influence among the European powers. These colonial rivalries and their ambitions to expand their area of influence fueled an apprehension of war, which led them to forge the Triple Alliance.

The Triple Alliance consisted of the following: German Austrian treaty of 1879, which Italy joined in 1882, and the Franco-Russian alliance of 1893. This Triple Alliance was renewed in 1912. In 1904, England and France made a less formal *Entente,* and in 1907 England created another similar alliance with Russia. In making these alliances, a major shift in British thinking was that Germany's increasing power was a more immediate threat to Britain's imperial position than either France or Russia. Moreover, to face these new challenges and maintain Britain's position as the strongest imperial power, Britain did not have sufficient resources as it saw the limits of its military strength during South African War (Joll, 1989). Thus, a new international balance of power emerged hoping to prevent war by stopping any power to upset the balance. However, the existence of an alliance system actually strengthened the division amongst these groups, and every European country began to frame their own policies in accordance to the divisions that they might be confronting in a possible war (Joll, 1973).

This fear of war led to increased mass production of weapons and other related products, such as steel. We shall take up the emergence of the large-scale steel production in each of the four countries in the following chapters.

SUMMATION

In this chapter we discussed the conjunction of various international historical forces that emerged and shaped international conditions, which in turn, shaped and influenced the choices and actions of people in each society who came into contact with these forces and also helped create these forces. The following topics are covered to elaborate on various broad historical processes and shifts: the formation of the transnational class of Freemasons; shifts in ideas about science and religion; Liberalism and counter-movements, Changing Structure of International political economy (improved transportation and communication systems; demographic shifts; science-based industries, increased bureaucracy and experts), New economic forces—colonialism and imperialism; trade and tariffs, monetary and financial systems—urbanization, social reforms, and social changes, socialist challenge; nationalism and social movements; alliances and international treaties; the struggle in the international balance of power.

With the conjunction of these international historical forces and the more immediate fear of a possible World War, the need to become well-equipped with weapons became urgent. This fear gave boost to the production of steel industry at that time leading to the emergence of the large-scale steel industry in the US, Russia and in colonized India. In the following four chapters, we shall focus specifically on the question of how and why the large-scale steel industry emerged in Imperial Russia, Imperial USA, and colonized India, but not in Imperial Britain, within their specific historical contexts from 1880–1914.

ENDNOTES

1. See Chapter 5 in this volume on Britain.
2. Marrs, J. (2000). *Rule By Secrecy: The Hidden History that Connects the Trilateral Commission, the Freemasons and the Great Pyramids.* New York: Harper Collins. See also van der Pijl, op. cit. We may not agree with everything Marrs has presented. However, I find the information on Freemasons, Rothschild, and all others including the Trilateral Commission convincing as we witness in our own time these connections taking place at Davos in the meetings of World Economic Forum and the role of various banks controlled by Rothschild and others.
3. These merchant bankers used to be traders, as earlier English foreign trade was in the hands of the nobility until the Glorious Revolution. The first of these merchant bankers were the Barings, who were descended of Bremen wool merchants. The Barings family started their banking business in 1762 and held many aristocratic titles. Over time, the Baring family not only became one of the most powerful in the ruling class but also the most powerful dynasties in the British Empire (van der Pijl, 1998). By the turn of the nineteenth century, Rothschild, a money changer in Frankfurt's Jewish quarters, was able to challenge Baring's dominance. Rothschild moved from his cotton trade office in Manchester to set up a bank in London in 1804. He expanded his connection with a web of European families as well as with the Masonic brotherhood. Rothschild's banking business operated in Paris, Frankfurt, Vienna, and Naples. Other banks also created a comparable transnational network: J. Henry Schroder & Company, another merchant bank, opened in 1818 and had its operations in Hamburg and New York; in 1877 the Lazards family operation opened its banks in Paris and in New York (van der Pijl, 1998).
4. It needed to be noted that it was not the first time in the history of humanity that the ideas of scientific objectivity occurred. Five centuries earlier in China elements of rational social thoughts free from religious dogma were present. In the Muslim world Ibn Khaldoun also wrote about such ideas (Amin 2012, monthlyreview.org).
5. Hull, 2003. We see it clearly today, in every sphere including academia, where only statistical data is considered scientific. This has pushed some scholars of English literature to interpret literature mathematically so that English literature would gain the credibility of science.
6. The colonial governments, who took over the governance of these newly acquired regions, needed more information about the people they were governing, which led to the creation of the science of anthropology. In addition to the introduction of a new academic discipline

for British research scholars, colonized India was also used as a training ground for the British army and to acquire cheap Indian soldiers for its army (Joll, 1973). India also provided careers for the most able graduates of Oxford and Cambridge in the Indian Civil Services. Their number must be very high because most British middle-class families had contact with the Indian Empire through either a son in the Indian administration or a cousin in the army.

Moreover, the colonization of Africa helped bring about a revolution in European painting styles initiated by Spanish artist Pablo Picasso in about 1907 (Joll, 1973). Fifteen years earlier, French artist Paul Gauguin, inspired by the South Seas, had settled in the French colony of Tahiti. The sounds of Oriental music inspired French composer Claude Debussy when those sounds were introduced at the great Paris International Exhibition of 1889. Earlier, Turkish music had influenced the works of Beethoven, Hayden, and Mozart. The Ottomans used giant war drums and cannons to frighten their enemies on the battlefield and to terrify the public in places like Vienna, Austria. Western Europeans adopted many Turkish cultural practices, including military music. Hayden wrote his "Military" symphony and Mozart wrote his piano sonata "Rondo Alla Turca" ("The Turkish March") with the influence of Turkish music (http//archives.cnx.org).

CHAPTER 4

The Emergence of the Large-Scale Steel Industry in Imperial Russia, 1880–1914

> "The temptation to describe pre-revolutionary Russia as a backward economy is powerful, but it is a temptation that should be resisted. The truth is that the tsarist economy grew rapidly between 1850 and 1917 ... a more nuanced assessment is also required in respect of the capital market ... As Lenin observed in 1899, 'the process of transformation must, by the very nature of capitalism, take place in the midst of much that is uneven and disproportionate'" (Peter Gatrell, 1986).

> "There are many ways to be 'capitalist,' many combinations of public and private ownership, various forms of government intervention in economic life, countless incarnations of the mythical entrepreneur. An invisible hand after all is not likely to look the same to all observers" (McCaffray, 1996).

INTRODUCTION

The comparative historical approach as practiced in its present form is not useful because it focuses on (supposedly) separate, autonomous social entities that are compared on the assumptions of being either "developed" or "underdeveloped." The challenge to this binary distinction is critical because historians have continued to label Imperial Russia (and other ex-colonies) as a "backward" country despite the fact that it was able to build and control a large empire (as did Britain and the US), and had a large-scale steel industry at the same time as that the US had one, although, Britain did not. Historian Madhavan Palat pointed out that Russian imperialism has been neglected in general theory, history, and fiction (of the West) due to the assumption that, "Russia was too backward to have sustained a genuine imperialism" (Palat, 1988:160). Even imperial bureaucrats and Russian intelligentsia asserted Russia's "backwardness" in order to measure the distance from their goal of becoming an industrial society. According to Palat, "The concept of her [Russia's] backwardness was as much a strategy [for Russian bureaucrats] as the fact of it might have been obviously true by the usual comparative indices of growth" (Ibid.).

This labeling of Russia as backward by both Russian bureaucrats and scholars is based on the assumption within the binary distinction of "progressive/backward" and "developed/underdeveloped," that European historical experience was a universal phenomenon, and, thus, a yardstick of progress. Evaluating other societies with this yardstick, scholars automatically categorized them as inferior or backward. Such scholars do not seem to be aware that this assumption and yardstick of progress is irrelevant to understand other societies. For example, as Alessandro Stanziani pointed out, a European model that ranks peasants, soldiers, military, landed elite, and the bureaucracy as separate hierarchical entities is not relevant in understanding Russian military strategies (Stanziani, 2014). Furthermore, it is a myth that Russian history began with Peter the Great and it is also a myth that progress was (and is) possible only by using Western techniques. These erroneous beliefs ignore the fact that the, "Western military revolution occurred long after Peter [Muscovy expansion took place before Peter] and in fact Western military revolution was influenced by the method of Russian conscription" (Ibid., 160).

Refuting the erroneous approach of Eurocentric universal historical experience, it is suggested here that Russia's "backwardness" is a misnomer as evidenced by its development of a large-scale iron industry beginning in the seventeenth century (1). The Russian state owned a large integrated iron industry in the Urals that produced a massive amount of iron, some of which was exported to England. A large-scale integrated steel industry was also built in the Donets Basin in the Ukraine during the 1880s (at the same time the US had one). By the eve of World War I, Russia had a highly developed large-scale steel industry that was on par with other "developed" societies. Scholars have consistently claimed that only those countries with a large-scale steel industry at the end of the nineteenth century could follow the path of development. Given this claim, it is perplexing that scholars do not consider Russia as developed in light of Russia having a large-scale steel industry at the end of the nineteenth century, and having also achieved the status of a major industrial power. In that regard, Peter Gatrell wrote that by 1900,

> Russia had achieved the status of a major industrial power … By the beginning of the twentieth century, Russia had joined the ranks of the world's major producers of iron and steel. Russia contributed around 6 percent of total world output and occupies fourth place after United States, Germany, and Britain … Russia possessed an integrated iron and steel industry that stood the test of comparison with best practices elsewhere in Europe (Gatrell, 1994:14).

A recent anthology addressing the issue of Russia being part of the European family suggests that Europe was not simply one homogenous "progressive" place, as it also had its machine breakers, holy wanderers, indolent landowners, communal farmers, fortune tellers, "all of whom existed until at least the twentieth century" (McCaffray and Melancon, 2005:5). The articles in this anthology suggest that both Russian thinkers and European elites were having similar thoughts as both were participating in the same dialogue. In fact, Peter Mathias, a British economic historian, wrote, "The elemental truth must be stressed that the characteristic of any country before its industrial revolution and modernization is poverty" (Mathias, 1990:4).

Based on this information it is hard to understand why scholars such as Gerschenkron (1962) and others continued promoting the idea of the "backwardness" of Imperial Russia. One reason for their conclusion might be that to understand Russia they used a yardstick based on the experiences of industrialization of European and British societies/countries. These scholars ignored the fact that the broad trajectory of most societies/countries is very similar, and that no society/country began with an original condition of being "progressive" or "backward."

Such scholars also ignore the observable reality that most societies have been interacting with other societies for centuries. Over time, this society-to-society interaction tended to become increasingly about trade, interaction of religions and intellectuals, migration, gaining territories or resources, and often leading to battles and wars. It was in this process of various interactions and through wars and colonization that each society, over time, became a complex mix of various cultures, languages, and polity. As discussed in Chapter 2, both of these social processes—inter-societal and intra-societal interactions—are created by spontaneous human creativity which expresses itself in human agency (actions). However, human actions in every society are guided by four basic needs: survival, prosperity, security, and reproduction. It is through the human agency (actions) of various actors (caste, ethnic group, gender groups, different classes), through state (or elite) control, and through power struggles (within a society and internationally), and the conjunction and combination of larger historical forces that are taking place at a particular time, both within a particular society as well as internationally (just as they do today) that a society takes on a specific political, economic, social, and cultural form.

With this understanding, the process of the making of Imperial Russia (as also of Imperial Britain, postcolonial Imperial US, and colonial India) does not look very different from other European experiences. Therefore, instead of using the arbitrary labels of developed/underdeveloped, progressive/backward, this volume, using a yardstick of parity (see Chapter 2), we not only look into universal and specific elements of Russian society, but also conjunction and combination of historical forces within a society and in the larger international arena which contributed in the making of Russian society. Furthermore, we explore the history of the emergence of the large-scale steel industry in Russia as a simultaneous historical process that was as much a specific history of Russian society as that of its intertwined relationships with larger international forces and other societies of that time.

In this chapter, based on information drawn from existing studies (only in the English language), the focus is on refuting the label of the "backwardness" of Russian society by erasing the binary distinction of developed/underdeveloped with a yardstick of parity (discussed in Chapter 2). This refutation assumes (see Chapter 2) that no society is a finished product because all societies are in a continuous process of emerging. No society begins as "developed" or "underdeveloped" (as discussed in Chapter 1, these labels were assigned in the middle of the twentieth century by individuals with a Eurocentric understanding of the world's social reality). By removing the cobwebs spun by these labels it becomes possible to see how each society emerged in similar ways historically through complex interaction processes among different social actors with various social relationships (based on class, race, gender or any other) within these societies, as well as with other societies over time. However, to substantiate our argument, the historical material about Russia's industrialization (as well as for the other three countries) is organized around the main issue of the volume: Erasing the binary distinction of developed/underdeveloped with a yardstick of parity. Therefore, the reader will only get a synoptic historical account of Russia's industrialization, and not a conventional in-depth chronological history of Russia.

The chapter is divided in two parts. In Part I (Erasing the Binary Distinction with A Yardstick of Parity), using the yardstick of parity (discussed in Chapter 2), we examine both universal and specific characteristics in the making of Russian society and its industrialization. This discussion shows that it is possible to do comparative history without categorizing societies as developed or underdeveloped. In Part II (Conjunction and Confluence of Historical Forces: Emergence of the Large-Scale Steel Industry), within this larger context of the making of Russian society with its universal and specific characteristics, and historical processes in the international arena (discussed in Chapter 3), the related issue of Russia's industrialization and the emergence of the large-scale steel industry in Russia in the late nineteenth century is explicated. This discussion elucidates that the large-scale steel industry in Russia emerged due to the conjunction of historical forces within Russia and in the international arena, as it did also in the other three chosen countries. The chapter ends with a summation.

PART I

ERASING THE BINARY DISTINCTION WITH A YARDSTICK OF PARITY

The uniqueness of each society is a universal situation. In other words, uniqueness is nothing more than the ways in which historical processes manifest in each society and creates specific conditions through the interaction of historical forces within and outside of a society. The Russian story is no different in that regard, as the trajectory of Russia's history is not much different from that of the other three societies chosen for this volume. The important point is that people in each society behaved in a similar manner—as human beings, all of them were involved in the creation of their society in the process of fulfilling their human needs. Those individuals or groups who were successful in controlling their society's resources tried to keep them under their control. Inevitably, social conflicts followed and people from other societies tried to take advantage of these conflicts and other internal weaknesses within the society. Individually, who became successful, how and why, are important questions in their own right. However, every society is created and reproduced in every historical time through its members in the process of their interaction with other members within society and its social institutions. At the same time, the actions and choices of each member of a society are not autonomous from their societal and larger historical context, which is also connected with other societies in a particular historical time. The observation of McCaffray and Melancon is pertinent in this regard as they write, "Europe is a civilization where we find 'the same things [as in Russia], but in a different way'" (McCaffray and Melancon, 2005:9). However, it should be added that being in a "different way" does not mean one is either superior (advanced) or inferior (backward).

With this understanding, it is suggested here that by using a yardstick of parity we can comprehend the making of Russian society and its industrialization on par with others and without categorizing it as either developed or underdeveloped. This is done by focusing on both universal and specific elements (also existant in the other three chosen societies) in the making of Russian society, which shaped it and its choices of actions.

UNIVERSAL ELEMENTS IN THE MAKING OF RUSSIAN SOCIETY

Russia, like any other society, was built by both the universal process of society-to-society interaction, invasions, and migration as well as by its specific history which was constructed from the interaction and choices made by its ruling elite and different groups of people across different historical times within a specific natural geographical region. Like any other society, Russia did not start as a "developed" or "underdeveloped" society. Like any other society, Russia was constructed through the choices and actions of its people over the years when its people and their ruling elite decided to expand their territory from its origin as a small Muscovy duchy. A long history of invasions and power struggles ultimately gave birth to the Moscow state.

As in other societies, the historical trajectory of Russia was influenced by its geography and the conjunction of historical forces both within and outside of Russia, which were emerging in each historical epoch. For example, the territorial growth of the Russian state was possible due to the lack of natural obstacles and it could advance all the way to the Pacific and beyond to Alaska and California. At the same time, its vastness and distance provided effective protection from outside attacks. However, in spite of having a vast empire, Russia remained landlocked and this situation led to Russian interest in the Baltic Sea, Black Sea, and multitudinous Straits (Riasanovsky, 1984). Furthermore, Asiatic nomads (Mongols) used Russia's southern steppe as a highway to penetrate into Europe, which impacted Russian history as well. Harsh climate and poor soil along with a short growing season made the subsistence of Russian farmers very difficult. In response, farmers had to rely on collective, cooperative action to prepare crops and harvest them quickly. Consequently, there was no significant development of private land ownership in Russia. Under these geographical conditions, ancillary, non-agricultural activities, and institutions became important for Russian peasants many centuries ago (Buck, 2003). Even on the eve of World War I, serf-entrepreneurs and *kustar* together were responsible for over five million individual workers (Falkus, 1972). Prior to the building of railways it was not possible for Russia to utilize the mineral resources as they were mostly located in the periphery. Moreover, rivers in Russia could not be utilized year-round due to the direction of these rivers, harsh climate, and the size of the Russian territory, which made Russia's economy a seasonal activity with slow commodity circulation. Thus, the unique problem in Russia was the overwhelming distances and sparseness (not the lack of transportation networks, towns, banks, or capital), which became a major problem for both officials and entrepreneurs to stimulate economic development (McCaffray and Melancon, 2005).

Russia was able to expand its territory connecting with natural boundaries in order to acquire vast natural resources for the creation of a prosperous Russia. However, having natural resources alone does not create prosperity in any society unless people work on them and create an internal cohesion of the relations between people and places (Ågren, 1998). Like the constituents of other societies, Russians also started socially constructing their geographical region while interacting with the vast natural resources that were available to them. The socially organized production of iron in the Urals (discussed later) is a good example of how that region in Russia was shaped. This example also reflects the specificity of iron production in Russia at that time.

Like other societies, Russia was made up of various cultures as many people of different cultures and ethnicities migrated there and many were brought in from other places by the tsar to improve Russian society. Kiev was the first Russian state; its people were Eastern Slavs. Kiev was destroyed by the Mongols in 1240 after having been savaged by earlier invaders including Scythian, Greek, Iranian, Cimmerian, Sarmatian, German, Finno-Ugrian, Bulgar, and Turk. These myriad invaders, along with

Kiev's local population, contributed to the formation of Russia's social structure. At the same time, these invasions and destruction prompted heightened concerns over military security, and to ensure greater security Russia embarked on a search for resources. In 1380, Dimitri Ivanovich, the Grand Prince of Moscow, who had defeated the Mongols, followed a policy of expansion which his successors would continue.

Russia's territorial expansion and its consolidation was not unique, a fact that can be discerned by looking into the history of the making of both Britain and the US. By the middle of the sixteenth century, Russia had entered Siberia and reached the mouth of the Yenisei River. Throughout the process of expansion the Russian state remained in a constant state of emergency, which created a siege mentality, which in turn prompted the Russian state to acquire a disproportionate amount of power (Crisp, 1976). (It should be noted that the US also expanded to its natural boundaries and created a siege mentality to justify its imperialist wars. See Chapter 6). Over time, Russia moved from security concerns to territory expansion into the east, south, and west while groping for natural frontiers and sea outlets. (At the time when Russia was emerging as a state, many persecuted Europeans, adventurers, and criminals were moving to the US where they settled by exterminating many of the native people who were already living there). Russia used diplomatic means to deal with powerful neighboring states—the Safavids of Persia, the Ottoman Empire, Mongolian Khanates, the kingdoms of Poland, Lithuania, and Sweden—so that Moscow could expand territorially without much conflict (Stanziani, 2014). Consequently, Russia became an empire and achieved great power status internationally. However, Europe treated her as an outsider because Russia adopted the Christian religion from Byzantium and not from Rome. In spite of this treatment, Russia was greatly influenced by changes that were taking place in Europe.

Russia became a strong powerful centralized state through territorial expansion and unification leading to a unified Russian identity. This was not different from English people becoming conscious of their national identity in the process of fighting long wars with France and later colonizing large number of countries around the world. Like any other society, Russia experienced many types of power struggles, but the forms and outcomes were specific to each society.

Similar to other societies, Russian society also had its own specific characteristics which shaped its history including its industrialization.

SPECIFIC CHARACTERISTICS OF RUSSIAN SOCIETY

Highlighting the specific characteristics of Russian society, McCaffray and Melancon (2005) noted that Russia was comparable to Europe as both faced similar types of challenges, but each country made a different choice in responding to those challenges due to the specific cultural and geographical context that gave a "unique cast to many of their solutions" (McCaffray and Melancon, 2005:6). Russia and Europe had different cultural traditions that colored their choices and actions. For example, Russia's culture was rooted in eastern Orthodoxy, and Europe was under the influence of Roman Catholicism or radical Calvinism. However, there was also a difference between Roman Catholicism and radical Calvinism. Russian institutions decisions in governance were influenced by specific geographical concerns; the vast territory of rugged plains. England, as a small maritime island, developed its institutions differently and made different choices. Thus, it is not surprising that people of Russia and England see life differently, as Russians had to labor long and hard to prepare for a dark and dangerous winter, while people of England lived in a comparatively more carefree and bountiful environment (Ibid.). In spite of the particularities of location, climate, history, tradition, language, and religion in Russia and in Europe and their peculiar responses to these problems, they were also similar in many ways. For example, the European people stuck to their regional, linguistic, and "national" distinctions as did the Russians. Similarly, England had its power struggles as did Russia, but they manifested differently in each country in a specific way.

The most important specific features of Russia were strong rulers and a centralized state. (Between 1500–1700 some European states were also centralized). Russian rulers became strong by eliminating the elite power struggle and by shaping Russian society, culture, labor force, industrialization, and entrepreneurship. Unlike Europe, Russia had various types of entrepreneurial groups, including serfs, who were involved in manufacturing under various types of production relationships. Unlike Europe, Russian merchants could not become an autonomous force as capitalists remained subordinate to the state. Unlike Europe and England, Russia had developed a large-scale iron industry prior to England's Industrial Revolution. In the following, these specific characteristics of Russia are elaborated with a focus on its industrialization.

1. POWER STRUGGLES

As happened in other societies, Russia also dealt with various conflicts between different interest groups within Russia, as well as power struggles between the *boyars* (the nobility) and the tsar, as was reflected in Russia's political process. Russia, like England, had no written constitution and political practices were based on customs. Therefore, the first tsar Mikhail Fyodorovich Romanov was selected at the end of the Time of Troubles in 1613 by an assembly known as the *zemskii sobor* that consisted of 500–700 members (Riasanovsky, 1984). Several hundred signatures on the final document included members of the clergy, boyars, gentry, townspeople, and individuals who represented the state peasants of northern Russia but not the serfs. The *zemskii sobor* and its relationship to Muscovite autocracy was complicated because it was essentially a sporadic gathering convened by the tsar when he wanted to discuss and decide on a particularly important issue "with all the land." Over time the *zemskii sobor* became an integral part of the supreme authority of the land rather than merely a government department or agency (Ibid.). Muscovite aristocracy interests were in conflict with this new situation because the tsar wanted to minimize the influence of aristocracy on governance and to create a strong monarchy. For that purpose, the tsar decided to appoint non-aristocratic bureaucrats to the *zemskii sobor*. Their number slowly increased from 30 to 59 to 167. Since there were no written rules to follow, the *zemskii sobo*r was allowed to assume direct authority during the absence of the tsar from Moscow, and in the case of an interruption (Ibid.).

The other power struggle was between the tsar and landed elite and nobility because these interest groups were opposed to territorial expansion. Therefore, the tsar used state authority to subordinate the Russian military, nobility, and the landed elite, and to further neutralize that opposition, the tsar created peasant soldiers who would colonize new land as well as provide for their own provisions. Thus, Moscow was able to win the loyalty of the peasants while avoiding the need for a centralized bureaucracy or a standing army that would require moving soldiers and provisions (Ibid.). Since Moscow's territorial expansion was dictated by commercial and geo-political interests of the state, merchants (unlike in England) did not play a big role. The goal of Russian rulers was to develop a Eurasian market by gradually integrating the local merchants, and political and religious elites of newly acquired territories into their Empire (Ibid.).

Furthermore, Russian rulers introduced more reforms to further secure the increased state power which eliminated many local practices. For example, the self-government of towns in Poland and Lithuania was replaced with a central authority and laws that later helped Peter the Great implement his reforms and impose serfdom in Russia. However, Siberia escaped the infliction of serfdom because it had very few gentry and endless space for fugitives (Ibid.). Siberian society was able to develop independently because it profited from European migration and from assimilation through intermarriages. Thus, Siberia came to represent a freer and more democratic social system than the one across the Urals. It also exhibited certain qualities of sturdiness and independence that are often associated with the American frontier culture. In a different context, many Russians fled to the borderlands and beyond, joining the free-living Cossacks on the steppes, when Ivan Vasilyevich IV, commonly known as Ivan the Terrible, enacted severe methods to implement necessary reforms to modernize Russia in the sixteenth century.

However, by the early seventeenth century, Russia was becoming a formidable European power with the expansion and unification of its territory despite its inability to conquer the Baltic States to the west. To maintain its strength in the power struggle within the international arena, Russia needed to increase the pace of its industrialization as well as to eliminate power struggles between different groups within Russia. It achieved both by creating a centralized bureaucratic state.

2. CENTRALIZED AND BUREAUCRATIC STATE

Russia's strong rulers and centralized state used reforms and legislation to subordinate various interest groups while increasing their own power. For example, until the seventeenth century there was no 'pure' feudal system in Russia, however, there existed an intermediate, tax paying, service class of *dvoryane* between the *boyar* landowners and the peasants. Peter the Great, who wanted to make the Russian State more powerful, combined *dvoryane* and *boyar* and made them both liable to military or civil service. Thereafter, the Russian agricultural system came increasingly under state influence, as it assigned serfs to masters, and also attached large number of serfs to the estates belonging to the Russian government (Buck, 2003). Therefore, power struggles between different interest groups in Russia did not take the same form as they did in other European countries.

Russia's strong rulers were continuously expanding Russian territory while also trying to protect its national sovereignty, and the Russian state was gradually centralized in the process. To protect national sovereignty the Russian state began mobilizing national resources to industrialize the country long before Peter the Great. However, industrialization got a great push under Peter the Great. To promote his agenda of industrialization, Peter the Great made the Russian state more powerful with a more efficient bureaucratic structure and unified market by converting *prikazy* into *kollegii* or functional ministries with centralized functions (Buck, 2003). To increase efficiency he created a centralized administrative structure based on written documentation and routine work known as the *General Regulations* (1720) to guide the working of all branches of government and bureaucracy. To further modernize his administration, Peter promoted the idea of creating a cadre of educated personnel for future administrative jobs. For that purpose, he established the Academy of Science and advocated the study of Russian law both as an academic discipline and as a tool for future administration. Later, Catherine II also vigorously promoted education, sending students abroad to study law and inviting foreign scholars to lecture on jurisprudence, thus encouraging the formation of an intellectually creative elite. Efforts were also made to base laws on Russian social reality by initiating an investigation of the Empire's history and traditions. At the same time, by ending the state monopoly of printing presses, private initiative was opened up so that both Russian and Western writings became readily available to the public.

3. STATE PROMOTION OF INDUSTRIALIZATION

The other major push for Russia's industrialization came from the wars of the state in the first quarter of the eighteenth century. In order to fulfill its military needs, the Russian state, under Peter I, set up and operated numerous enterprises that gave a boost to iron and copper mining. To acquire armaments, Peter the Great established two shipyards, an armory at Tula, and a gunpowder factory on the Okhta River between 1712 and 1719. For a century and a half, these enterprises, supplemented by the Izhevsk arsenals in the Urals, remained the main source of the Russian defense industry. The largest works were in the Urals iron industries (discussed later) and the mining enterprises in the province of Perm that employed roughly 25,000 workers. The government also procured artillery pieces from several privately-owned metallurgical factories that were scattered around the Urals (Gatrell, 1994).

In order to achieve its industrial goals, the Russian state encouraged the private sector to set up new industrial establishments. After 1720, most state enterprises were sold or leased to private entrepreneurs, and private industries received assistance through subsidies, tax exemptions, monopolies, and other concessions. Private entrepreneurs from the merchant class also joined the state enterprises. Most of all, the state became the main customer for the products of these new factories because at that time a mass market for manufactured goods did not exist in Russia (Ibid.). Thus, the Russian state provided the market, capital and labor force for the development of mining, metallurgy, armaments, and textile industries. Consequently, these industries not only came into being, but also started yielding high annual growth rates (Crisp, 1976).

In 1725, Peter I made a major attempt to promote industrialization by connecting production with the needs of the state. Therefore, he forced merchants and entrepreneurs in urban areas to join government guild organizations so that their production and activities could fulfill the state's needs and services. Similarly, peasants and townspeople were also drafted by the state to provide transport, food, and material to military establishments and service personnel. With the promotion of the Western lifestyle for Russian nobility the demand increased not only for more produce but also for more artisanal labor to build homes, maintain townhouses, and provide recreational activities. These needs were fulfilled through the labor of migrant peasants who moved to the capital and its garrison towns. The emerging industrial sector, requiring a detailed administration, increased the bureaucratic control over the process of industrialization. At the same time, private operators were given licenses for state monopolies in consumer goods. However, they were required to meet state procurement at fixed prices (Ibid.).

These reforms and the reorganization of relations of production led to the growth of Russian industries. "The last 25 years of Peter's life saw the growth of a substantial manufacturing sector which gave employment to several thousands of industrial workers" (Falkus, 1977:21). Foreign commerce grew and shifted from the White Sea to the Baltic and from the ancient port of Arkhangelsk (Archangel) to Peter's newly-constructed capital at St. Petersburg. Earlier, in the 1630s, certain foreigners had established ironworks and estate owners had set up manorial factories using the labor of their own serfs. Over time, specialization began to emerge in some regions. For example, the Tula and Moscow regions specialized in iron products, the Tver and Moscow regions in linen, Nizhny-Novgorod in leather, and the Kama and Upper Volga regions in salt. Some small-scale village handicrafts and peasant cottage industries had also started producing for a wider market (Ibid.)

i. Shaping of Culture and Social Structure

Russian rulers, in addition to promoting industrialization, also created necessary social and cultural conditions to facilitate this process. For example, Peter I, and earlier, Ivan III, began to change the culture of the Russian court and nobility by introducing the Western lifestyle—including Western dress, manners, and language as well as openness for women. These changes not only threatened existing religious traditions and the power of the Church, but they also brought about a clash between Church authority and Peter's authority. Peter the Great began to flex his authority over the Church by replacing the Muscovite clergy with more aggressive, better educated, and sophisticated clergymen from the Ukraine[(2)], while also imposing increased fines on the Church. The new, educated clergymen trained in logic, Western language, and rhetoric, helped to introduce the concept of natural law and Neo-Scholastic philosophy to Russia. (It should be noted that the challenge to Church authority was also occurring in England, France, Germany, and the Habsburg lands at that time).

Furthermore, the Russian government was aware that the unified state could not successfully operate without the cooperation of various social groups involved in the political process. There existed no such single cohesive group in Russia at that time. Therefore, the Russian state introduced reforms to reorganize class structure and also spread the network of its institutions and administration to the provincial and local level. Through these state institutions and administrations, the Russian state, while maintaining peace, law, and order, was able to affect and direct the lifestyles of the people at the local level.

Catherine II created an entity known as "the third estate" that consisted of commercial, artistic, and professional individuals (musicians, painters, architects, and teachers) who could contribute to the material and cultural progress of Russia. It was open to everyone, including the urban population, freed serfs, peasants, and even orphans. To further promote "estate consciousness" and increase local participation in the political process, she convened the Legislative Commission in 1767 (Raeff, 1983). Under its directive, every town was legally recognized as constituting a unit with an identity of its own. This recognition created a sense of group identity or "estate consciousness" among the town dwellers. The statute of 1775, *The Fundamental Law for the Administration of the Provinces of the All-Russian Empire*, allowed local nobles to elect an official who would have the power to execute the governor's directives and to enforce law and order. Subsequently, a necessary institutional framework was set up in 1785 for the estate organization of the provincial and urban elites. Catherine II allowed the urban leadership to establish and administer medical, philanthropic, and educational enterprises, as well as to supervise public health and security matters. She hoped that this structure, and the security of persons and property that it guaranteed, would mold the nobility into a dynamic, enterprising, and productive class that would contribute to the Russian Empire's material and cultural progress (Ibid.).

In the border regions, Catherine II transformed the existing agrarian elites into Russian nobles by extending to them nearly all the benefits and privileges enjoyed by other Russian nobles but without requiring them to convert to Christianity. Thus, these agrarian elites gained control over peasant labor, access to ranks in service, and the admission of their children to state educational institutions. However, the state remained in command through a large and strong bureaucratic structure and retained the initiative for industrialization until the end of the nineteenth century [3].

Catherine II, influenced by both French Enlightenment philosophy and critical attitude, realized the need for an elite social group of intelligentsia. The intelligentsia that emerged in Russia was not much influenced by the Masonic movement [4] but by Enlightenment philosophy, and they were independent of the main body of nobility and the state (Walicki, 1979). They played an important role in the making of public opinion during the nineteenth century debate on Russia's industrialization. Bureaucrats were also part of the Russian intelligentsia, and their views and biases also played an important role in Russia's industrialization.

The intelligentsia was concerned about Russia's future national identity, while having differences in opinion amongst themselves (many were opposed to government policies), they nonetheless judged Russia's condition from the perspective of more advanced societies (Ibid). Western ideas fascinated the Russian intellectuals, and many members of the gentry and other educated persons began expressing discontent with their own closed society. They were keen on reforming the system. This situation created a dilemma for Catherine II: how to maintain Russia's position as a world power while using Western know-how, but at the same time, avoiding the threat to tsardom that Western ideas would bring. The tsar responded to this explosion of Western ideas with repression, and crushed the Decembrist revolt of 1825 that was demanding a constitution. Faced with such suppression, many enlightened educated Russians migrated to France, England, and Switzerland in order to pursue their agenda for a constitution and additional reforms in Russia.

ii. Creating Labor Force for Industrialization

The most important ingredient for industrialization, a continued supply of labor force—skilled and unskilled—was difficult to get in Russia. Therefore, Russian rulers began restructuring the class system. For example, Ivan III had limited the peasant freedom of moving from one landowner to another by law in an effort to protect the landlord. At first, a peasant was bound to an estate and not to its owner. Later his bondage became personal; he was the chattel of the estate owner who, with impunity, could sell him off or move him from the field into the manor house to work as a personal servant. Thus, a peasant became, in every sense, a slave. After 1721, a law was passed that allowed merchants (those living in towns) to buy whole villages of serfs and attach them to factories. They were known as *pssessiini selliany* (possessional peasants). However, peasants owned by the state were either consigned in perpetuity, or leased out to factories. This was particularly important in the Urals iron industries (Falkus, 1972).

The restructuring of the Russian class system continued under Peter the Great as he wanted to increase revenues through taxes and acquire more recruits for factories and the army. He strengthened serfdom and increased taxation on the peasants, while drafting beggars, orphans, criminals, prisoners of war, and heretics to the factories. The bondage system of 1649 affected all classes of society. Men born into any class—peasantry, gentry, and townsmen—inherited their class status and could not cast it aside. According to this new system, sons of the gentry were mandated to take up army service and be prepared to become officers. It was decreed that townsmen must live out their lives in the localities of their birth, and that each son must succeed to his father's trade[(5)].

In addition to the restructuring of the class system, Russia, under Ivan III, also began to acquire skilled labor from Western countries. Russian rulers wanted to make Russia strong in its army, its administration, and its production. They were aware that only by improving Russian technical knowledge and skill would they achieve their goal of expanding Russian territory, as well as safeguarding Russia's sovereignty from European powers. To achieve these goals, Ivan IV attempted to establish firm contact with Tudor England so that Russia could win British naval support and obtain better access to Western scholarship, technical skills, industries, and trade. Russian rulers imported doctors, artisans, and artists from Western Europe to train and build new palaces and new churches. Italian gunsmiths were brought in to improve Russian techniques for making arms and minting coins. Western technicians were brought to build weapon factories and to teach Russians how to operate them. The first Russian weapon factory at Tula was built in 1632. In no time, Russians excelled in skills such as goldsmithery, tanning, clock making, masonry, glass manufacturing, and bell making.

By 1613, hundreds of German, Irish, Scots, Englishmen, Greeks, Swedes, and Poles had been hired to serve as officers in the Russian army. By 1645, more than one thousand foreign families lived in Moscow's German quarter, which also included many Dutch, as trade with the Netherlands had become significant. Dutch sea captains, shipwrights, and carpenters were brought to Russia to train the Russians in Western skills. Others such as the French Huguenots, who were fleeing persecution in their own country, joined the Russian services. Similarly, many Catholics who managed to escape from Cromwell and his Puritan saints had also fled to Russia. Russia benefited from the presence of these foreigners, as the Russians learned many new skills while also incorporating changes in their dress, manners, and court customs.

In 1698, Peter I also tried to resolve the skilled labor shortage by bringing in hundreds of foreign technicians and skilled artisans. He encouraged foreign entrepreneurs to set up establishments in Russia. At the same time, he sent young Russians to Europe to learn the secrets of Western industrial processes. Russia also made more active commercial contacts with the West. For example, by 1725, the mining and metallurgical industries of the Urals had made substantial progress in increasing their large export trade with England. During the second half of the eighteenth century, Russian trade continued to grow under the rule of Catherine II. With the expansion of Russian territories, more regional specialization began to evolve that fostered internal trade and territorial division of labor, which in turn doubled the Russian population between the 1740s and the 1790s. During this time, as Lyashchenko would later point out, it was possible to achieve large-scale production with merely the simple cooperation of a poorly skilled mass labor force (Lyashchenko, 1949:277). However, in 1762, merchants were no longer allowed to buy serfs. Instead, serfs paid their owners dues in money or in kind rather than providing labor service. Many serfs became industrial entrepreneurs (discussed later) and bought their freedom with large sums of money (Falkus, 1977).

However, legislative reforms also gave more power to the Russian gentry over their serfs and allowed them to punish serfs, whereas the peasantry was forbidden to make complaints against their masters. Not surprisingly, a revolt known as Pugachev's Rebellion broke out in 1773 (also at the time of the emerging Industrial Revolution in the West) and became the greatest peasant war in Russian history, posing a serious threat to the Empire. Nonetheless, Catherine the Great suppressed the rebellion successfully.

iii. Promotion of Entrepreneurship

The Russian state took many steps to develop conditions for the promotion of industries. It created, supported and privileged trading companies (especially for the development of foreign trade), improved existing roads and canals, eliminated tolls at the entrances of towns, and dropped restrictive passport requirements. The state also passed a law on bills of exchange in order to secure the circulation of credit instruments. Numerous fiscal and administrative constraints on foreign trade were also eliminated in an effort to encourage foreign entrepreneurs to increase their trade with Russia. Individual initiatives and freer entrepreneurial activities increased with the passing of new laws that ensured the security of property titles and improved effectiveness of the justice administration. In 1773, Russia removed many existing restrictions on trade and internal custom duties, complying with the demands of the nobility and traders to abolish individual and commercial monopolies. The manifesto of 1775 allowed anyone to start any type of mill and to produce in these mills any type of handiwork. Industries were further protected by high tariffs on foreign goods.

With all these reforms, laws, changes, and incentives, Russia saw increased activity in trade, commerce, and industrial production. The Russian nobility became involved in industrial production and created a monopoly on distillation. Many urban citizens as well as free and state peasants started trading freely within the Empire [6]. These policies and reforms of the Russian state also created various types of entrepreneurial groups.

4. VARIOUS TYPES OF ENTREPRENEURIAL GROUPS

Unlike Europe, Russia had various types of entrepreneurial groups that contributed in its industrialization. As discussed earlier, both Peter I and Catherine II recognized the importance of the entrepreneurial class in promoting Russia's industrialization. However, they wanted to retain state power and control over this class while also increasing Russia's competitiveness in manufacturing and increasing Russian wealth. Thus, their policies created a complex social class structure with many types of entrepreneurs involved in manufacturing for the state as well as for the market. For example, one set of entrepreneurs came from the class of peasant serfs, some of whom became very rich and successful. Their success in the field of manufacturing belies the idea that entrepreneurship was possible only in a free market with the initiatives of a merchant class.

As Reiber has pointed out, we should not assume and expect a fixed uniform pattern of behavior from all groups of people to internal changes or external pressures on a society because there can be a variety of social identities and groupings in any society. Instead we should study each group of people to understand their choices and actions in their specific historical context (Rieber, 1982: xix-xx). The following sections discuss the various entrepreneurial groups that contributed to Russia's industrialization: merchants, private industrial enterprises, serf entrepreneurs, foreign banks and investors, and private foreign entrepreneurs.

i. Merchants

The role of Russian merchants in the process of its industrialization was very different than it was in Europe. Their responses depended on how the Russian state defined and ordered the social organization because state services were the basis for determining social stratification. Thus, the choices and actions of Russian merchants were the outcome of historical processes taking place within Russia (Reiber, 1982). Reiber informs that from the mid-seventeenth century to the second half of the nineteenth century, state service defined the status of a person in Russia. In the Collection of Laws of 1649 *(Ulozhenie)* the state administration partitioned society into three closed hereditary categories—service, urban (including merchants), and peasants (Ibid.). Each group was assigned specific duties and obligations that were also hereditary. However, within each of these groups was a mix of many types of social groups with their own rankings, access to economic advantages, and legal status. The social mobility among these official ranking groups or even within each rank was virtually impossible, as Reiber pointed out.

With the social stratification tied up with service, merchants could not function as an independent force as they were caught up between bondage and opportunity. Peter did not give merchants monopoly over trade, at the same time, he tied their function with responsibility to preserve the integrity of urban communities. Merchants were responsible for protecting commercial privileges and tax paying capabilities of the towns. Under these circumstances merchants could not compete in the market place. Even though these bonds were loosened under Catherine II, merchants (and nobility) could not enjoy complete autonomy. The reason for the lack of autonomy was the growth of bureaucratic absolutism under the absolutist state which kept a tight control over the internal affairs of these groups (Ibid.). In addition, merchants were facing competition from ethnic and foreign merchants, as well as from a large number of trading peasants who were emancipated and joining guilds.

Capitalism was expanding within Russia during the second half of the nineteenth century. In the wake of this development it became necessary for the Russian government to reorganize its population into four *sosloviia* (status group): nobility, clergy, townspeople (included merchants and artisans), and rural inhabitants. The Russian government also opened up membership in the merchant guilds to anyone who paid guild tax. However, in practice, merchants were treated as a distinctive legally defined social group as *soslovie,* and Russian manufacturers remained dependent on the state for protection against the anti-protectionist wave in 1896 (Ibid.). Thus, merchants could not emerge as an independent force in Russia's development. However, the *soslovie* system came to an end with succession of rapid changes within Russia and internationally: the Revolution of 1905, the elections of the duma, the creation of national parties and lobbying organizations, the Stolypin reforms, the renewed industrial surge after 1910, and finally World War I (Ibid.).

ii. Private Industrial Enterprise

Unlike Europe, Russian capitalists came from many walks of Russian society: outcasts, outsiders, disadvantaged elements of society, serfs, religious minorities, foreigners, as well as members of the indigenous commercial class. Aside from the merchant class, it was mostly the lower classes, peasants, and urban masses that provided the major supply of industrial entrepreneurs in the early nineteenth century (Blackwell, 1968). At the same time, foreign businesses and technical skills also played an important role in the development of private industry in Russia. It was during 1820–1830 that Russia witnessed the origin of private industrial capital, the formation of an entrepreneurial class, and the development of the consumer market in the area of the new textile industry that used a hired labor force. Most Russian entrepreneurs were truly "self-made men," but many of them also benefited from their communal traditions and from connections in accessing capital for their ventures (Ibid.). The role of communal tradition was very important to the capitalist development of Russia as many early industrialists and commercial and financial capitalists came from dissenting religious sects, such as the Old Believers, the Skoptsy, and the Jews [(7)].

The Russian middle class, which was converted into the nobility during the eighteenth century, got involved in industry only after 1800 as they began to influence state policies by making contributions to the war chest and by petitioning for high tariffs. By the reign of Nicholas I, a new Westernized industrial middle class was making its appearance in Moscow, St. Petersburg, Ivanovo, and other emerging factory towns. Modern industry and commerce had created a rich and powerful social class that was replacing the traditional merchant class. For example, Moscow could boast of having 12 millionaires, St. Petersburg had as many, and Ivanovo had three (New York had 20 millionaires in 1855) (Blackwell, 1968). By the 1850s, these businessmen had become Europeanized—adopting the use of a foreign language, joining dancing clubs, and taking trips to Europe to maintain their European lifestyles.

While the state was curtailing traditional commercial monopolies and privileges, it was also giving peasants and nobles limited rights to engage in trade. In 1842, the government further dismantled the century-old wall of protection that had been built around the Russian merchant class by permitting factory owners to retail their products directly in the cities and at fairs. Soon cities became magnets for merchants who wanted to explore industrial ventures. Many enterprising ex-serfs, craftsmen, construction bosses, and others were able to establish various small manufacturing enterprises. Over time, these entrepreneurs were allowed to join the ranks of the country's three merchant guilds enabling them to legally expand their manufacturing into large-scale industrial enterprises. Many ex-serfs, who began their career pounding the road in St. Petersburg and Moscow, became wealthy, whereas other merchants remained traders (Ibid.).

The guilds were ranked. Those belonging to the first and second guilds were invested heavily in industry by the middle of nineteenth century, while the lower ranking gentry set up small factories on their estates to generate income. The Russian state relaxed the rules for the entry of nobility in the higher merchant guilds, so that their members could invest their vast wealth in production rather than on the conspicuous consumption of country houses, servants, personal ornaments, and temples. However, to generate the income necessary to keep up their Westernized lifestyles and status, much of the nobility opened factories on their estates. It was only the wealthier nobility that could build large factories and attract the government cooperation that was necessary for the survival of their enterprise. Interestingly, the nobility was not as much involved in bulk stock market purchases as were the middle class or foreigners (Blackwell, 1968).

iii. Serf Entrepreneurs

A very important specific unique feature of the Russian capitalist class was "the lord who owns not the capital but the capitalist and of the serf who is the master of hundreds of hired laborers" (Blackwell, 1968:204). Serf entrepreneurs in the north of Russia came into being through a combination of various social conditions in the late eighteenth century. Land was decreasing in productivity while the population was on the rise. The circulation of money also had increased with the expansion of commercial activities. At the same time, the newly Westernized nobility needed more cash to maintain their enhanced status. They found that they could generate more cash by permitting their serfs to work for wages in factories or to produce handicrafts and remit to the nobles a tax, the *obrok*. The nobles awarded protection and began handing over local government of the factory villages to their serf entrepreneurs. Such factories were rising in numerous villages throughout the Vladimir, Kostroma, and Moscow provinces. It was in these small villages during the early nineteenth century that some of the wealthiest and most prominent industrialist families of Tsarist

Russia founded their enterprises. Many serf entrepreneurs willingly accepted their bondage, because the privileges of the nobles to whom they were legally attached provided protection from competitors and from the state. However, with the expanding mechanized industry and its consequences many serfs bought their freedom as early as 1825. They used any available means to enhance their efforts. For instance, certain serf craftsmen tried to acquire new skills and knowledge about cotton printing by sending peasants to work at a foreign cotton mill to learn the secrets of the work process. Upon the return of the peasants, the serf craftsmen used this new knowledge to modernize and expand their enterprises (Blackwell, 1968).

The Great Fire of 1812 in the Moscow textile industry created an opportunity for many serf-craftsmen to build up their trades. Nobles started demanding higher taxes from these productive serfs. Over time, as certain serfs became rich they were able to purchase their freedom for a sizable sum. Many merchants did not want these former serfs joining the guild system and tried to influence the state to restrict membership. However, these merchants failed in their efforts because both nobility and bureaucrats were invested in the modernization of Russia and were keen on increasing the pace of industrialization. One can find in the history of the city of Ivanovo the existence of a large number of successful serf-entrepreneurs, "peasant captains of industry"[(8)].

iv. Foreign Bankers and Investors

In the modernization of Russia, the role of foreigners was not less important. By 1860, foreigners controlled the external trade of Russia but not its industry (Blackwell, 1968). However, there was a distinction among the foreign investment in trade and factories, the foreign enterprise in Russia, and the foreign investment in Russia's industrialization. The English and the Germans had controlled the large-scale European import and export trades in Russia during the early nineteenth century. Most of these were based in St. Petersburg. Some had also begun investing in Russian industries. Before 1860, most foreign enterprises were commercial. Between 1769 and 1862, the money supply came from wealthy banking houses in Amsterdam and London. England directly subsidized the Russian government during the Napoleonic period to equip and pay Russian troops. After 1815, the Russian government began receiving money from the houses of Baring and Rothschild in England. Baring marketed Russian bonds issues (1818, 1832, and 1833) in England and those funds were used to repress the Polish uprising. Baring also aided railroad construction between St. Petersburg and Moscow with five-and a-half million pounds and financed a large-scale rail network extending 1500 miles across the European part of the Russian Empire. In addition, Baring cooperated with Russian banking firms to sell Russian iron to the US (Ibid.). In 1822, Russia received six million pounds from Rothschild and his family bankers in London and Paris. However, when the Russian government sought loans from Rothschild to finance its war against the Turks, the request was turned down at the behest of the German government (Ibid.). In 1856, France took over the financing of Russian interests with the formation of La Grande Société des Chemins de Fer Russes.

Under Nicholas I, it was difficult for foreign businessmen to operate factories in Russia without being a citizen. Under Catherine II it was less of a problem. In 1807, laws were created to limit foreign merchants, which were further extended in

1824. But these laws were not strictly enforced as foreigners were still able to make large profits and the Russian government also offered them special privileges (Ibid.). By 1863, Russia largely controlled fifty-five of its largest factories with over one-and a-half-million spindles in cotton spinning. In the Russian machine industry, foreign entrepreneurs dominated until the mid-century, but, overall, it appears that foreign involvement was insignificant at that time. However, by 1914 around a one-third of Russia's total industrial investment was foreign (Ibid.)

Foreign industrialists brought different types of expertise and technical knowledge to Russia. For example, French entrepreneurs in Russia catered primarily to the Russian upper-class demand for consumer goods and luxury items that had become fashionable in France. The German industrialists in Russia brought capital, as well as new methods of banking and finance to Russian industry. In the 1840s, with the lifting of a ban on the export of machinery from England, English businessmen were able to bring machinery to Russia (Ibid.).

Many entrepreneurs and skilled workers from England also played a dominant role in the development of the Russian machine industry. One of the English-speaking machinists of the early nineteenth century at St. Petersburg was Charles Baird. He applied his skills in Russia between 1786–1843. He developed Russia's first steam machine factory in 1792, which would become one of the largest iron foundries in St Petersburg. It produced Russia's first steam engine and steam-propelled industrial machines. Aided initially by a government monopoly, Baird also expanded in other directions with his own efforts (Ibid.).

v. Private Foreign Enterprise

The Russian state had a close relationship with private foreign enterprises because the state was the major purchaser of industrial goods such as railways, shipbuilding, munitions, and metallurgy (McCay, 1970). McCay pointed out that the Old Russian regime was deeply concerned with the survival of the state sector due to political, ideological, and security reasons. Politically, government dockyards and armories were necessary to check the power of the emergent industrial elite as well as to show that the Tsarist state could not be swayed by their power. Moreover, it was necessary during war times that the Russian government had direct access to industrial production for its own defense. To achieve these goals, Russian industrialists and foreign enterprises were forced to accept a strict subordinate status within the existing political system that placed limits on their economic strength.

Foreign entrepreneurs worked within the state's broad development scheme and through contracts or direct/indirect relations. Moreover, the Russian state had put in place many constraints on foreign entrepreneurs so that they could not use their technical and financial superiority to fleece the country. One of those constraints was that the Russian state could withdraw from a foreign enterprise the permission to operate within Russia at any time (Ibid.). For example, the Russian government actually refused to ratify the creation of a steel cartel on the American model of Trust in 1908 (Ibid.).

Foreign capital also faced opposition from Russian landed nobility. During the 1890s, the attack on foreign capital came from landed nobility, who by that time were able to dominate both the upper bureaucracy and the Tsar's entourage. Together these two interest groups carried out violent press campaigns against foreign capital between 1896 and 1900. However, Sergei Witte, Russian minister of finance from 1893–1903, was able to successfully promote a campaign in favor of foreign capital and industrialization with a vigorous counter attack on landed nobility and local businesses (Ibid.). Thus, the efforts of the Russian state were to allow foreign capital to promote Russia's industrialization while keeping them under state control to maintain its own dominance.

5. INDUSTRIAL MANUFACTURING UNDER VARIOUS TYPES OF PRODUCTION RELATIONSHIPS

While promoting industrialization the Russian state also felt a competitive sense of urgency in the face of Europe's Industrial Revolution. Therefore, the Russian state made serious efforts to encourage increased productivity in all areas: agriculture, manufacturing, and mining, as well as importing knowledge of new techniques and crops. The Free Economic Society was founded in 1767 for that purpose, and the state began taking a systematic approach in the husbanding of natural resources, especially lumber. Skilled, specialized workers from different ethnic groups, such as the Germans, Georgians, Armenians, Jews, and Greeks, were moved to South (New) Russia for resettlement. In the late nineteenth century, this region became highly industrialized and would later become the center for the country's large-scale steel industry.

However, the new reforms and new rules in Russia created various types of social relationships in production as discussed below (Lyashchenko, 1949):

i. Capitalist manufacturing industries were supported by the state treasury, and run by guest merchants, large landowners, and foreigners who did not have personal capital. The main consumer for their production was the military, as well as other related needs of the state. These manufacturers acquired their labor force through an agreement with the state (under Peter the Great) to buy fully-inhabited villages under the condition that these villages remain connected with a factory. This arrangement during the eighteenth century created a constant struggle for manpower between the nobility and merchants.
ii. The state was also directly involved in manufacturing for its own needs: military, navy, army, and the construction of cities.
iii. In 1723, the state transferred certain factories to a "particular person" and individual entrepreneur, such as: a merchant, a tradesman, a foreigner, or a nobleman. This practice was known as merchant manufacturing.
iv. Yet another type of production relationship was called "possessional manufacturing" in which peasants were bound to the factory but not to the owner of the factory. They could not be sold apart from the factory, and remained under the control of the government. This arrangement denied the factory owner control over pricing, specification, and delivery of the product.
v. Manorial manufacturing was developed during the second half of the eighteenth century and gave control to the landlords. They were allowed to exploit the serfs to the extreme while running these manufactories, as they found that the sale of processed raw material was very profitable.

vi. In another arrangement for production, peasant serfs were permitted to set up industrial enterprise and use hired labor. As discussed earlier, many peasant serfs who were involved in this type of production became very rich entrepreneurs and purchased their freedom by paying large amounts of money.

vii. Along with these new types of production relationships, small-scale artisan production continued including carriage builders, book binders, watchmakers, barbers, and dress makers. In order to organize all these urban handicrafts along the lines of Western European models, Peter I created two guilds in 1721. In the first guild were big merchants, doctors, apothecaries, and goldsmiths. Petty traders, and small artisans were included in the second guild and were further divided based on specialty. All the guilds were headed by aldermen who kept records of the artisans and their reliability for good work.

viii. Finally, there was the old system of home industry known as *Kustar.*

6. RUSSIA'S UNIQUE LARGE-SCALE IRON WORKS PRIOR TO ENGLAND'S INDUSTRIAL REVOLUTION

Another important unique feature of Russia was the establishment of large-scale iron industry well before England's Industrial Revolution. It was established in the first half of the eighteenth century with the initiative of the Russian state when it needed new supplies of iron for more war materials and no foreign businessmen were interested in investing in Urals due to the harsh conditions of life and severe climate. In the mid-eighteenth century, the Russian production of iron expanded due to the enlargement of forges which increased the efficiency and pace of work (Florén, 1994). This expansion became possible with the availability of migrant peasants from the western part of Russia as they were attracted by the socially and religiously tolerant Siberia (Florén et al. in Ågren, 1998). With the expansion of iron industry, it became possible to train foremen and workers (Crisp, 1976) for employment in various industries. The main product was bar iron that was transported to the western part of Russia for refining and for exporting.

Urals furnaces and forges formed part of a large industrial complex, which also included workshops, mills, and smithies for the making of different metal wares. Thus, the Russian blast furnaces were much larger in construction than their Swedish counterparts. The centralization of the Urals large-scale iron industry became necessary in order to control the costs of production as well as to run it efficiently for increased revenue (Florén et al. in Ågren, 1998). However, improvements in efficiency did not require the traditional fuel power or advanced technology because accessible lake ore deposits were easy to process and use for making products (Ibid.).

During the latter part of the eighteenth century, when many of the state-owned works were sold to the aristocracy, the ironworks became an integral part of a feudal estate economy. From the mid-eighteenth century through the next hundred years, dramatic changes occurred in the international market for bar iron. The British market had expanded rapidly since the late seventeenth century, but British iron producers could not meet the demand. Spanish iron had played an important role in that British market, although beginning in the mid-eighteenth century, iron from Sweden became an increasingly dominant force followed by iron from the Urals. In

Britain, the iron imported from different countries and regions was used for different purposes, therefore other countries did not enter into direct mutual competition with Britain except for Russia, as Russian iron shared many of the qualities of British iron (Florén et al. in Ågren, 1998). In spite of competition with Sweden, Russians had overtaken Sweden in sales to the British iron market by the end of the century. However, the technological changes that took place during the second quarter of the nineteenth century in the Western world reflected the need for producing iron at lower cost and higher quality. Russian iron masters did not see the sense in adopting rolling mills as labor was still very cheap until the 1850s (Gatrell, 1986). Therefore, instead of competing in the international market, Russia chose to withdraw from it and turned its resources to meet home demand for a variety of iron and metal wares as Russia's internal market had grown to a considerable size by the beginning of the nineteenth century (Ågren, 1998).

The above discussion shows that Russia was way ahead of the Western Industrial Revolution, as Russia, along with Sweden, became a front runner in European development with a highly advanced large-scale iron industry (Florén et al. in Ågren, 1998). By the eighteenth century, the Russian iron industry in the Urals was already centralized and hierarchical with a clear division of labor. Whereas, at that same time in Belgium, France, and Britain, the social organization of both coal mining and charcoal-burning was based mainly on work performed by peasants and petty producers (Florén et al. in Ågren, 1998).

SUMMATION

In Part I, based on the yardstick of parity, we did not categorize Russia as developed or underdeveloped. Instead, we discussed the universal and specific elements in the making of Russian society and its industrialization. After broadly discussing the universal elements, we identified Russia's specific historical conditions as follows: elimination of power struggle and creation of centralized state, the role of the Russian state in creating conditions for the promotion of industrialization while also shaping the social structure and culture of Russian society, the role of different entrepreneurial groups in creating industries, industrial manufacturing under various types of social relationships, and the unique emergence of a large-scale iron industry in Russia during the early eighteenth century long before the Western Industrial Revolution. In Part II, again using a yardstick of parity and not categorizing Russia either developed or underdeveloped, we shall focus on the conjunction of historical forces within which the large-scale steel industry in Russia came into being as it did in other three chosen countries.

PART II

CONJUNCTION AND CONFLUENCE OF HISTORICAL FORCES IN THE EMERGENCE OF THE LARGE-SCALE STEEL INDUSTRY IN RUSSIA

As suggested in the beginning of the chapter, we are using the same yardstick to understand the industrialization and the emergence of the large-scale steel industry during 1880–1914 in Russia, as we do for the other three chosen countries. With this yardstick of parity, it has become possible to erase the binary distinction of developed/underdeveloped. Instead of categorizing Russia as either developed or underdeveloped, we focus on complex intertwined historical processes, which show that it was the conjunction and confluence of historical forces developing within Russia (inter-societal interactions), and within the international arena (intra-societal interactions), which created conditions for the emergence of the large-scale steel industry. These simultaneous historical processes were as much a specific history of each society as that of their intertwined relationships with larger international forces (discussed in Chapter 3) and other societies of that time. These statements are substantiated in the following discussion.

TERRITORIAL EXPANSION, IMPROVED TRANSPORTATION AND LIMITED INTERNAL MARKET

As pointed out in Part I, Russian rulers created a huge empire by continuously expanding Russia's territory. This expansion created an internal market for Russian goods. Russia expanded further by adding Georgia to its empire in 1801, and Caucasus in the 1790s, which provided an additional internal market for manufactured goods. During the second half of the eighteenth century, Russia was exporting half of the iron output of the Urals industry, and three-quarters of this was exported to Britain. It also exported high-quality iron (Gatrell, 1986).

It is also noted in Part I that Russia began to industrialize under Peter the Great and that the Russian state had been aggressively creating conditions to promote industrialization for a long time. The most important of these actions were improvements in communication and transportation, which expanded internal trade in Russia between 1830 and 1855. Canals were built in the Baltic provinces during the beginning of the nineteenth century. Steam navigation was rapidly improving in the 1850s on Russia's inland waterways along the Volga River. Railway construction had started in the 1830s. Consequently, the number of merchants, who belonged to guilds, more than doubled during this time (Falkus, 1972). According to Gatrell, before the reforms of 1860, private enterprise in Russia was increasingly providing for the private market and they were not dependent on the state for buying their products as was the case in the early eighteenth century. This private market was created by the desires and needs of gentry landowners who wanted to emulate the lifestyle of the Western European aristocracy.

Apart from village workshops and textile mills, and the unique large-scale iron industry in the Urals, Russia's industrialization had been slow. Moreover, most industrial products were sold at regional fairs that were not held regularly.

GLOBAL PRESSURE AND LOCAL HINDRANCES, 1850–1870

Russia's defeat in the Crimean War of 1854–56 revealed an inadequate supply of industrial material and transportation infrastructure. At the same time, nationalism was spreading all over Europe as first Italy and later Germany unified and emerged as developed industrial nations. By 1870, Russia was growing increasingly alarmed as Germany moved towards the domination of Europe, and thus possibly changing the international power structure. Russia realized that if it did not industrialize fast enough, Germany would be able to subjugate Europe after defeating Britain because the empires of Austria-Hungary and Turkey were already on decay. It became obvious to Russia that the future of Europe hinged on Russia's strength and its industrialization (Gatrell, 1994).

However, the industrialization of Russia was not an easy task due to the country's vast distances, harsh climate, and inaccessibility of mineral wealth. Moreover, the pyramid structure of Russia's stratified society, with it's huge peasant base and small elite of landed gentry, did not allow for the emergence of a prosperous middle class (McCay, 1970). In addition, there existed other disincentives for industrial development: lack of a network of private commercial banks to support industrial development and native capital, merchants were not interested in investing in industry as trade was more profitable, the Russian landed gentry was also not interested in investment in industry as it was getting regular income from interest on bonds and their estates using serf labor, and moreover, the legal process of incorporation was very difficult in Russia (Ibid.). Russia's industrialization also suffered as Nicholas I was interested in war, and in case of a clash between war and industrialization, he sacrificed industrialization (Blackwell, 1968). He did not have a consistent policy for industrialization, and consequently many projects that could have helped with Russia's industrialization were not implemented. Under Nicholas I, a conservative, traditionalist, and nationalist approach was dominant, but no one opposed the ultimate industrialization of Russia. In fact, Russia's industrialization was a subject of constant debate among the bureaucrats.

DEBATE WITHIN RUSSIA OVER INDUSTRIALIZATION

As pointed out earlier, Peter the Great and Catherine II, created a strong centralized bureaucracy to run the administration efficiently. However, this bureaucracy was divided on the issue of the pace of industrialization and this division influenced the implementation of industrial policies in the nineteenth century. The other debate at that time was whether Russia should industrialize on a large-scale or remain an agricultural nation (Prior to US industrialization, there was a debate as to whether the US should remain an agrarian economy or to industrialize. Farmers did not want to become wage laborers in the US, and they revolted against it).

The issue of dispute was the choice between free trade versus the protective tariff of 1811 (Blackwell, 1968:123–125). Free trade promoters in the Russian bureaucracy, mostly upper ranking officials during the time of Alexander I (1801–1825), were inspired by the ideas of Adam Smith. They asserted that industrialization and factory legislation corrupted the physical, moral, and spiritual health of workers, and that it would lead to workers' uprisings. According to free traders, the Russian peasant was better off economically and morally under serfdom than under the dehumanized English factory workers enslaved by a machine. They also charged that protective tariffs favored a monopoly system, stimulated corruption and smuggling, and discouraged competition. However, free traders were not unanimous in their views; Decembrists and other liberals supported the abolition of serfdom (Ibid.). Protectionists were critics of Adam Smith's theories, and they argued that by following the example of Western industrial nations, Russia could also develop sufficient capital to industrialize through tariff policies. They warned that if Russia did not industrialize, it would become economically and politically dependent upon Europe. They argued that this dependence would lead to the outflow of precious metal from Russia which would result in stagnation, inflation, and poverty.

Free trade ideas were in tune with the interests of the majority of the nobility who wished to preserve serfdom and profit from village handicraft, industries, exports of raw materials, and purchase of luxury goods. Since the time of Catherine II, many magnate industrialists, officials and families had established factories on their estates with serf labor (Ibid.). The needs of this growing Russian industrial class were represented by the protectionists. Merchant factory owners, plus an increasing number of landlords and influential magnates, along with the decision makers of economic policy, supported protectionist ideas. In the end, the protectionist policy won and it remained in place for forty years. Thus, the tariff and industrial policies of Russia reflected various trends and pressures both within the country and from outside: foreign competition, the demands of war, the influence of European economic theory, and a conflict of interests among social groups (Ibid.).

RUSSIAN STATE CREATING CONDITIONS FOR INDUSTRIAL GROWTH, 1860–1870

In spite of clashes of interests and debates over the issue of industrialization, the Russian government realized with its defeat in the Crimean War that it would not be able to improve its own strength in the international power structure without swiftly developing its industries. Therefore, the Russian government took various steps to remedy its industrial and infrastructure inadequacies, which created conditions for subsequent industrial growth. The following liberal reforms were introduced between 1860 and 1874: modernization of the banking system, abolition of institutional serfdom, creation of the organs of local self-government, modernization of the Russian army, and changing people's deep-seated prejudices against the railways (Falkus, 1972). Because of the lack of information about the history of the preparation for the reforms and their connection with the legislation of the 1860s and 1870s, it is not possible to elaborate on the crisis in the ruling elite [(9)]. However, Russia had a large number of serf-entrepreneurs (discussed earlier), therefore, in implementing its new industrial policy, the Tsarist government moved carefully, as it did not wish to sacrifice the traditional noble estate while sustaining the interest of the country's businessmen.

In 1863, to remove the disincentives for industrial growth, the state subsidized new private railways, but eventually took them over when two of its banks dominated total deposits. The Russian government also opened the purchasing of certificates to everyone, including women and foreigners, as all of them were outside of merchant estates (Buck, 2003).

Industrial development also required the regulation of working conditions. New regulations were introduced between 1882–1893: hours of work and age requirement of the workers, banning women and youths under seventeen years old from working at night in the textile industries, workers were to be paid twice a month (using a pay booklet) only in cash, with no deduction for doctor, education, or use of tools; rules for both employers and workers to give prior notice for terminating/leaving the job (McCay, 1972). In addition to these regulations, the Russian state also introduced a law in 1882 for the creation of a factory inspectorate, and published detailed rules to be followed by the employers for the terms of hiring. The following year, laws were passed to increase the quality of work and to improve working conditions within mines and factories. For example, hiring a person with an appropriate engineering degree to oversee mines or factories and building hospitals staffed with a full-time doctor or medical assistant for workers. In spite of these new laws, employers were able to ignore mining regulations with impunity for many years (Ibid.).

Other reforms were in the area of taxes and tariffs. Before the Crimean War, the government had maintained extremely protective tariff rates, enough to inhibit the importation of iron through Azov ports. By the late 1850s, the tsar's advisers pushed for lower tariffs in order to support the construction of a railroad system. Consequently, iron bound for certain machine industries entered the country more cheaply after 1859. Thus, between 1878 and 1880, more than 50 percent of the pig iron imported into the country entered duty-free. However, with the efforts of the Association of Southern Coal and Steel Producers (discussed below), the iron tariffs rose substantially during the next seven years.

The import of coal and coke also followed a similar trajectory. These new tariffs on iron and coal convinced prospective investors in 1880 that the imperial government intended to support the development of the domestic coal and steel industry along with expanding the empire's rail network. Their confidence further increased as progressive income taxes were introduced in 1890, which allowed firms to both incorporate and increase their nominal foundation capital (Gartell, 1986).

INDUSTRIAL DEVELOPMENT IN RUSSIA AFTER 1861

Through various reforms between the serf emancipation in 1861 and World War I, Russia's industrial structure was transformed, and the area and volume of agriculture increased. New centers of production emerged—the Ukraine in the 1880s, and the Caucasus between 1881 and 1890s—and with the introduction of steam power the position of handicraft workers was steadily eroded (Gatrell, 1986). From 1880s the volume of agriculture had been increasing with the expansion of the area under cultivation, and introduction of the use of machinery, fertilizer, and scientific methods. In 1885, The Peasant's Land Bank was founded and was encouraged to buy gentry land and resell to peasants. The country's population increased between 1860 and 1916, and railroad expansion increased from 1,000 miles in 1860 to 40,000 miles in 1916. The enormous Trans-Siberian line was built between 1891 and 1903. With the expansion of railroads, manufacturing and mining production in the areas of coal, oil, iron, and steel, increased rapidly in 1860s. The huge railway network also offered the prospect of further economic gains by reducing transportation costs, improving inter-regional trade, and stimulating the migration of population to areas of greater economic opportunity. After 1905, the migration of peasants to Siberia was encouraged, and by 1913 western Siberia became an important dairy region with peasant marketing cooperatives (Ibid).

While absorbing one third of the Russian iron output, and a large quantity of coal, the railway industry was also stimulating the establishment of large locomotive works. A modern iron and steel industry was established and by 1894 there were 4 major steel producers in the southern region, and in 1900 their number increased to 18. This increase does not include several firms whose plans or installations were cut short by the crisis of 1900, nor does it include certain coal companies that were planning to become metallurgical firms (McKay, 1970). In addition to steel, Russia created a modern engineering industry and a basic chemical industry. In 1900, Russia was the world's largest oil producer (Ibid.), and with the growth of urban populations, consumer goods industries also began to thrive. Russia improved its industrialization and reached fifth in rank in its rail network in comparison to other states in 1890, and by 1900, Russia jumped to second place, behind the US. By 1900, Russia had achieved the status of a major industrial power (Gatrell, 1994).

However, this industrial development was taking place under the shadow of international tension, which brought Russia closer to France and France began to invest heavily in Russia's industrial development.

TENSION IN INTERNATIONAL ARENA

In June 1881, a new Alliance of Three Emperors' League—Germany, Austria-Hungary, Russia—was founded for three years, and was renewed in 1884 for another three years. This alliance was essentially to declare that if one of the contracting powers engaged in a war with a fourth power, except Turkey, the other two were to maintain friendly neutrality (Riasanovsky, 1984). However, conflicting interests in the Balkans did not keep them together for long and in 1887 Russia and Germany concluded a secret Reinsurance Treaty to remain neutral in case the other fought a war, except if Germany went to war with France and if Russia went against Austria-Hungary. However, this treaty also did not work out as Germany had obligations to Austria-Hungary. In 1885, Anglo-Russian tension over the expansion of the Russian Empire in Central Asia was increasing as it threatened British Colonial India. Even though conflict was avoided they remained hostile as they competed for influence and control in the vast lands south of Russia, especially in Iran.

In this tense international context, France remained the only possible partner for Russia. Their alliance was consolidated between 1891–1894. In the final form, the alliance provided that if Russia were attacked by Germany, or by Austria-Hungary supported by Germany, France would employ all available forces against Germany. This treaty remained in force for the duration of the Triple Alliance of Germany, Austria-Hungary, and Italy. The treaty with France proved very useful for Russia's industrial development (discussed later). Paris alone provided a great market for Russian state loans as Berlin's financial market was closed to Russia in 1887. Moreover, Frenchmen proved remarkably eager to subscribe to these loans as well as to invest directly in the Russian economy (McCay, 1972; McCaffrey, 1996).

SEARCH FOR CAPITAL

The massive expansion and growth of the mining and metallurgy industry depended on the import of machineries and electrical equipment, as well as on foreign capital and foreign technical aid. The Russian state supported these developments by bringing a huge amount of foreign capital into the economy—by promoting a high tariff on iron and steel in 1887 and 1891, by creating currency stabilization, by giving long term orders, and providing subsidies and bonuses (Crisp, 1986).

It was Russian foreign minister Sergei V. Witte who successfully attracted foreign capital with various incentives, including exceptionally low worldwide interest rates in the 1890s (Buck, 2003). He laid down his strategy for industrial development in his famous Memorandum (Gatrell, 1986) and noted that "extensive railroad construction would stimulate the growth of the metallurgical and fuel industries, which in turn would promote lighter industries and agriculture" (McCay, 1972:57).

Witte took many steps to attract foreign capital. He undertook budget balancing and currency reform measures aimed at putting the ruble on the gold standard in 1897. Foreign investors (details in the following section) approved of these efforts. As pointed out previously, in the 1880, France was the only choice left for Russia to partner with in the prevailing tense international climate. Interestingly, French were also keen on having this partnership and to invest in Russia. Within this context it became easy for Witte to attract state loans from prominent French banking houses such as the Crédit Lyonnais, and kept up with dividend payments made in gold by maintaining a favorable balance of trade, which he ensured through a system of incentives granted to Russian exporters. He established favorable freight rates for grain producers shipping to the ports and promoted the formation of beet sugar and oil syndicates that organized the markets for these two key Russian exports. He also successfully used the power of media to create pro-Russian sentiment in French newspapers, which enabled him to tap into liquid capital from the ladies and gentlemen of western European commercial families, who were looking for new opportunities to invest their surplus capital in the industrialization of the late nineteenth century. The closer financial ties between Paris and St. Petersburg, within a shifting diplomatic climate, brought direct French investments, particularly to the coal and steel companies in South Russia (Ibid.; see also Crisp, 1976). Witte encouraged heavy industry by virtually every means at his command, including government orders, liberal credits, unceasing efforts to obtain investments from abroad, tariff regulations, and improved transportation.

Moreover, the Russian government did not create any barrier for engaging in steel production (McCaffrey, 1996), and this resulted in a large number of foreigners joining the industry. For example, Makeevak Steel was controlled by the Socéité Générale of France, and Donets Steel at Druzhkovka and Huta Bankova both formed part of the French Bonnardel group (Ibid.). The Russian state made a large amount of new capital available to the railway economy, and to ports and ships between 1893 and 1900 (Crisp, 1986). The state also made capital available to the economy through the banking system between 1892 and 1900. In addition, the state encouraged the influx of foreign capital into Russian joint stock companies by stabilizing the currency and introducing convertibility (1894–97) (Ibid).

In 1897, Russia also adopted the gold standard (Falkus, 1972:12) as other major industrial nations of the world were already on the gold standard or about to adopt it. Thus, 80 percent of new industrial investment came from foreign capital and Russia's economy grew rapidly from 1903–1905. Between 1889 and 1892, and between 1901 and 1904 the total industrial output grew by about 4.7 percent per annum in real terms, or by about 3.4 percent per capita (Gatrell, 1994:14). Thus, with heavy foreign investment a large-scale steel industry could emerge in Russia. This foreign capital came mostly from France and Belgium (discussed below), though a small amount of capital came from Britain, Germany, and Netherlands.

FOREIGN INVESTORS

Before investing in the Donets Basin steel industry in the 1880s, French investors had been involved in many branches of Russian industry. They were attracted to steel only when the new Ekaterina Railroad was opened and the government raised the level of tariff protection. French investors received help in their venture from the powerful French investment bank, the Société Générale. The bank was no stranger to Russian industry, as it was already directly involved with the Rutchankia mine through a Franco-Russian company. When in 1887 the Laveissière investment group invested in the Brianak Iron Company's new Aleksandrovsk steel mill, a rolling mill, and a mechanical factory (which would employ 4,500 workers by 1905), other foreign investors became interested in South Russian industries (McCaffray, 1996; see also Crisp, 1960). French investors also gave a boost to coal production operating in the Donbas area. By the 1890s, there was a steady French investment in Donets Basin helping to deepen the mines, construct rail links and adding machinery for lifting and pumping (McCaffray, 1996). In 1895, the Tsarist government decorated Eugene Verdic and Gabriel Channove for "the successful mechanical improvement for the Huta Bankowa factories and the construction of the Druzhkovka steel factory in the southern Russia" (Ibid., 63.).

French and Belgian investors also supported native capitalist A. K. Alchevskii as he set up the Lurievka Iron and Steel Company in 1895. Direct French investment in mining rose from 31.2 million francs in 1880 to 274.1 million francs in 1900. In metallurgy, investment rose in the same period from 70.6 million to 298 million francs. By 1899 French investment paid handsome dividends. It is not clear why the net share of invested French capital dedicated to mining and especially to metallurgy rose after 1895 even when earnings in other areas were somewhat higher (Ibid., 64).

Belgian entrepreneurs were also interested in Donets Basin, and they also played an important role in building industries in South Russia. These entrepreneurs had access to information about the technicalities of doing business in Russia through commercial sections of their own foreign affairs ministry as well as from their representative in St. Petersburg. They had kept track of various economic, social, and legal developments in Russia for more than forty years. In 1873, a report (from Belgian sources) noted that even though Russian iron was the finest in Europe, it was importing coal and iron from England and Silesia due to distances and transportation difficulties. It was explained in the report that in order to develop Donets Basin the tsarist government made it a requirement for the railroad to buy rails from

Russian firms. However, it did not yield the desired results. It was suggested in the report that Belgians could find a place in this situation in Russia. No wonder, once the Ekaterina Railroad provided a link to coal and iron ore in the mid-1880s, several Belgian metallurgical firms, which were among the most advanced in Europe, became interested in Donets Basin. By the 1890s, most of the Belgian steel companies had formed Russian branches (McCaffray, 1996).

There were a few British, German, and Dutch companies, and one founded jointly by a Russian subject and an American citizen. In addition to these, at least fourteen new coal or metallurgical firms opened in Donets Basin between 1895–1900. These were Russian firms whose capital sources remain unknown (Ibid.).

However, foreign investors could not succeed in Russia without the help of a class of native administrators who knew how to satisfy their foreign masters while maintaining their own considerable autonomy (McCaffray, 1996). These administrators were also keen supports of promoting the steel industry in Russia to enhance Russia's ranking in the international arena. These middlemen were engineer managers who were in control of the Association of Southern Coal and Steel Producers. They were the "best organized and most permanent industrial interest group in the empire" (Reiber, 1982:233).

UNIQUE ROLE OF ENGINEER MANAGERS

Most people, both native and foreigners, who came to Donets Basin during the 1880s and 1890s were newcomers and outsiders (Ibid.). Everyone in Donets including capitalists, foreigners, and engineer managers, was interested in the expansion of heavy industry and in making large profits. However, in the promotion of the large-scale Russian steel industry, the role of engineer managers was extremely important. They consisted of enterprising landlords, newly arrived entrepreneurs, and trained mining engineers and they took over the leadership of the Association of Southern Coal and Steel Producers (formed in 1874 to address the issues of railroads and state's tax and tariff policies) and embraced steel producers who were also coal producers. Few of these engineer managers were proprietors themselves, but most of them simply worked for a large firm. The Southern Association was a professional organization and less a representative of foreign capital. Engineer managers, while defending foreign interests, were more concerned with making Russia a modern, industrial nation as quickly as possible (Ibid.). They saw foreigners as short-term renters and themselves as stewards of resources from which Russia would benefit in the future. They treated foreign directors as tutors for building industry and not for instructing others about how Russia should work. They used the economic power of the enterprises controlled by foreign capital to further their own careers, as well as the future economic and political development of the region and the empire as a whole (Reiber, 1982).

They did not see any distinction between their own professional interests and helping Russia's advancement. However, they resisted any obstacle even from government with regard to the growth of Russia's coal and steel industry (McCaffray, 1996; Reiber, 1982). Thus, these engineer managers became more than employees of foreign firms, and in fact became a political force in their own right promoting Russia's industries and entrepreneurship. They assumed this role because the gap between those supporting industrialization and those opposing it was very large. Their actions made sense, as McCaffray suggests, in the context of a state that wanted to promote industry without establishing a capitalist elite and without resolving the debate between pastoralists and industrialists (McCaffray, 1996). The engineer managers were not influenced by entrepreneurism or Russian merchant traditions. McCaffray points out that their vision was neither socialism, nor laissez-fair capitalism, nor corporatism. However, they were not a homogenous group ethnically, but they had developed a regional consciousness and common goal, which was to defend the southern steel industry from political manipulations (McCaffray, 1996; see also Reiber, 1982).

The views of engineer managers were based on nineteenth and early twentieth-century Enlightenment ideas, committed to popular welfare, and they were suspicious of the "pure market." They saw the market only as a way of getting goods from the place of production to the consumer and not into a "free market." They promoted the Enlightenment ideas of education, work, progress, rational organization, and meritocracy. They believed that with industrialization Russia would become cultured and prosperous. On the issues of labor and labor costs, the engineer managers disagreed with foreign bosses, and they were confrontational with local governing and taxing authorities (McCaffray, 1996). Their confrontational stance was due to the contradiction they faced. On the one hand, they belonged to an educated social class involved in investing for profit. On the other hand, their physical connection to the work site and to the work itself, and their commitment to Russianness, made them feel closer to the needs of the workers. They were more concerned with Russia's industrialization and, ultimately, with improving the living conditions of the common folk that would raise Russia's rank among the European nations (Ibid.). Engineer managers envisioned an industrial Russia of private enterprise and private property. However, they were also aware that government support and assistance to industry in its mission of social uplift was important. Thus, the role of engineer managers was crucial in the development of the Russian steel industry as it navigated between foreign investors and Russia's advancement.

The Southern Association also proved useful to the Russian government as a way to exert pressure on foreign investors lest foreigners assume too much initiative (Ibid.). During the crisis of 1900–1913, metallurgists decided to form some kind of industrial combination. However, the timing of their notion for a metallurgical trust coincided with threats to Witte's (finance minister) policy of industrialization and public hostility towards foreign investments. In order to resolve this issue, the Association of Southern Coal and Steel Producers was given the responsibility to negotiate with both the French-Belgian capitalists and St. Petersburg on behalf of the foreign owned and Russian metallurgical enterprises (Reiber, 1982). With the help of these engineer managers a complex organization of the first and most powerful prerevolutionary syndicates, the Society for the Sale of Products of the Russian Metallurgical Industry *(Prodamet)* was created.

EMERGENCE AND DEVELOPMENT OF THE LARGE-SCALE STEEL INDUSTRY

In the late nineteenth century, the iron and steel industry was turning into a large-scale organization globally, and by the end of the nineteenth century steel had become the foundation for industrial development and strategic power. Russia was well aware of these developments and, specifically, after its defeat in Crimean War it began to improve its industries in ernest. The Russian state introduced various reforms for that purpose while also improving its transportation network with increased railroads. Since local capital was not interested in investing in industry, Russia had to look outside to get capital for industrial development. As pointed out earlier, the foreign minister Witte was successful in attracting foreign capital. The international tensions of the time had brought France and Russia closer and French capital was very keen on investing in Russian industries. All these reforms and improvements along with tariffs on the import of iron and coal convinced French and Belgian capitalists to invest in the Russian metallurgical industry. However, the Russian state was interested in industrialization without establishing a capitalist elite and without resolving the debate between pastoralists and industrialists. This particular state concern was resolved with the creation of The Association of Southern Coal and Steel Producers run by technocrats known as engineer managers, who became a political force in their own right.

In addition to these historical developments, many changes were taking place within South Russia's Donets Basin, which further prepared the ground for the emergence of the large-scale steel industry. Many unsuccessful attempts were made earlier in the Ukraine to start a metallurgical industry before the founding of the iron industry in the Ukraine in 1869 (Falkus, 1972). In 1869, John Hughes, a British iron founder, contracted with the Russian Government to establish an ironworks near Lugansk in the Donets Basin. The Russian government offered him favorable terms to buy iron rails. Impressed by his success many foreign and Russian capitalists also began to invest in this industry. However, the Donbas (Donets Basin) region in South Russia, while rich in subterranean resources including coal, was not well connected with the railroad and had a scanty supply of labor. Once this area became connected in the 1870s with four new railroads it was able to develop its coal and coke industry. At that time, the main demand for coal came only from railroads and private homeowners. However, once the iron industry and, later, the steel industry started developing they directly led to the expansion of the coal industry (Ibid.). In 1873, the possibility of further development of heavy industry in the Ukraine increased with the discovery of coal in the Lugansk area, and later in 1882 the discovery of very rich iron deposits in the Krivoi Rog region.

Coal had to be hauled on a locomotive, which needed additional coal to run (McCay, 1970). In the 1880s, the Southern Association (discussed earlier) supported the rapid development of the local steel industry for the enormous consumption of Donbas coal. However, the Southern Association was aware that the infant steel industry needed protection from foreign competition, so it requested tariffs on imported pig iron (Ibid.). The Russian state complied with the tariff request, announced a gradual increase in duties on pig iron, and, by 1886, pig iron imports dropped dramatically. These stiff tariffs were maintained by the new finance minister, Sergei Iulevich Witte, who had become the Head of the Railway Ministry in 1892 (Ibid.).

However, these tariffs brought Russia in conflict with Germany and a tariff war broke out between them. The situation was resolved in 1894 with a signed trade treaty that reduced duties on finished steel and iron products. This tariff structure benefited the southern region far more than the Urals industrialists, who strenuously objected to this agreement (Gatrell, 1986). Interestingly, the Urals industrialists began to think about improving their works when two French companies in 1896 and 1897 were founded to use Urals iron ores. One company—Société Métallurgique de l'Oural-Volga—was founded to build a steel mill at Tsaritsyn on the lower Volga in order to use the ore of the Urals and the coals of the Donets Basin. The second one—Volga Vishera—was founded to smelt the ore in the northern Urals using timber, and to construct a steel works near Kazan in Paratov. However, these companies did not become a huge success (Ibid.).

With foreign capital pouring in after 1892, the Donets Basin (south Russia) was converted from a coal producing region to a major center of heavy industry. By 1894, there were four major steel producers in the southern region of Russia. In 1895, Southern Russia surpassed the Urals in pig iron production for the first time. To sustain the new iron and steel industries and the nascent engineering industry, the tsarist government created further demand for iron and steel by investing in the rails and rolling stock. Thus, the foreign-sponsored steel industry in Donets Basin grew rapidly (Gatrell, 1986). Most of Russian rail output came from southern Russian factories where a handful of enterprises controlled the industry and the volume of orders enabled them to achieve the economies of scale in iron and steel production. By 1898, in southern Russia there were seventeen large works for the smelting of pig iron, with twenty-nine blast furnaces in operation and a further twelve under construction. Only one of these works was entirely Russian (Crisp, 1976).

Russia was also catching up technologically. In the Ukraine, innovations were introduced by foreign capitalists that increased the capacity of the blast furnace, improved the use of byproducts and modernized iron and steel rolling. The integrated steel plant used both the Bessemer and Martin methods in order to meet the requirements of the market. Most of the growth in output was contributed by the new iron and steel works located in the Ukraine where iron and steel grew nine-fold between 1890 and 1900. Foreign entrepreneurs installed new Bessemer converters and Siemens Martin's open-hearth furnaces (both were invented in England) that were capable of producing high quality steel because high quality iron ore was available in that area (Ibid.). The establishment of new rolling mills supplying steel rails, structural shapes, and steel sheets were other important additions to the steel industry. Gatrell informs that Bessemer steel production in Russia was no less sophisticated than Western methods. The capacity of the hearth in Russia doubled between 1895 and 1913 from 20 to 40/50 tons, approaching the contemporary German norm. Rolling-mills were also following Western practices. Thus, the emergence of Russia as a modern industrial power owed much to the creation of the dynamic iron and steel industry in southern Russia, which was one of the world's most technologically advanced and highly integrated industrial complexes (Gatrell, 1986). As a result, Russia possessed an integrated iron and steel industry that "stood the test of comparison with best practices elsewhere in Europe" (Ibid., 47). Gatrell pointed out that Russia's investment in rails and rolling stock between 1896 and 1900 exceeded the 25 percent of total investment, which Germany earlier claimed was the necessary percentage for its own industrialization. The situation in Russia at that time was the same as in Germany a generation ago.

The development of the steel industry made Russia self-sufficient in basic metallurgical products. In 1893 local production accounted for 90 percent of consumption; in 1898, 95 percent; in 1903, 99 percent; in 1908, 100 percent; and in 1913, 99 percent. A continuing trickle of imports was due primarily to costs of transportation to St. Petersburg and the Baltic provinces from the Donets Basin. These imports were offset by exports primarily of rails through the Black Sea to a number of countries in the Balkans, the Mediterranean, and South America (Ibid.).

The foreign response in the late 1890s was so great that steel mills operated at only 50 to 60 percent capacity from 1900–1909. This excess capacity permitted southern producers to increase their production by 50 percent between 1910–1913 with ease and with profound relief. As the industry moved toward full capacity in 1913, further expansion through new investments posed few serious problems (McCay, 1970). Rapid industrialization in South Russia created a new situation that led to the profound transformation of the Donets coal industry in a single decade. Foreign entrepreneurs as a group also felt that they could profitably operate there in other related ventures in the steel industry (Ibid.).

Earlier in the 1860s and 1870s, the machine building industry emerged and produced complex items, such as agricultural machinery, ships, and railway equipment (Gatrell, 1994). Technological improvements were made in these industries during the recession of 1900 by replacing some old steam engines with electrical and internal combustion engines that increased the output per worker by 18 percent. The increase in steel output was also due to lower cost of production which became possible with the abolition of an excise tax on iron and the decline in the input prices (Ibid.). By the beginning of the twentieth century, Russia had joined the ranks of the world's major producers of iron and steel, contributing about six percent of the total world output, and occupied fourth place after the United States, Germany, and Britain. The Russo-Japanese War (1903) brought a further increase in steel output.

DURING DEPRESSION, 1900–1914

During the depression of 1900–1904, Russian officials took a number of steps to alleviate the critical position of the iron and steel producers. The state bank extended long-term credit facilities to the *zemstvos,* enabling them to purchase agricultural equipment from Russian suppliers. The government also approved the formation of a syndicate in the iron and steel industry that was initiated by the directors of a handful of metallurgical firms, most of them operating in Southern Russia. These firms had close links with French financial institutions, notably the Société Générale and the Banqué de l'Union Parisiénne, as well as with Belgian capital (Gatrell, 1994). These combines were formed as a remedy against the losses due to over-production, as happened between 1900 and 1903 (Falkus, 1972). By 1913, twelve iron and steel works had acquired more than thirty iron ore mines through backward integration because it gave them competitive advantage in the rising market prices of iron ore, pig iron, and coal (Gatrell, 1994). Finance Minister Witte supported the syndicate as he wanted to reassure the French and other foreign investors that the Russian state would not take over French-owned assets at cut prices during the crisis.

From 1902 to 1914, the Russian state permitted and even encouraged the growth of syndicates/cartels based on the German Kombinat model, i.e. vertical integration between mines and metallurgy. The formation of cartels was useful for the Russian state because it could easily regulate and effectively control the concentrated private industries during a national emergency. For example, with the onset of World War I, State Councils were established for procurements of the products of militarily strategic industries such as defense, fuel, transport, and food. It also issued prices and orders for iron and steel.

For the metallurgical firms, the formation of the syndicate would help create a more unified sales system, which would decrease the power of merchant houses in imposing heavy credit terms on them. In July 1902, the Tsarist government approved the statutes of the new joint stock company, and the syndicate *Prodamet* came into being. Each party agreed to sell its output through *Prodamet,* and in the event of refusal to comply, the firm had to pay a financial penalty. This syndicate forced up the price of iron and steel products because competition was eliminated (Ibid.). Along with the approval of the syndicate, the Russian government took other measures to deal with the Depression. For example, it extended the law on receivership to foreign-owned corporations that allowed them to suspend debt payment indefinitely.

At the same time, as Gatrell pointed out, the Russian government kept its distance from monopoly capital and did not subordinate its own interests to big business. For example, the newly formed "Society for the Trade in Products of Russian Locomotive Factories" *(Prodparovoz)* did not become a formal joint stock company as the Russian government did not give permission. Eleven companies, trading in wagons, also reached an agreement to form a syndicate, *Prodavagon,* but they were also unsuccessful in getting more government orders (Gatrell, 1994:61). However, the Russian government did yield ground to the private sector before 1905, when they produced important new innovations: the manufacture of smokeless powder, light artillery, and new cartridges (Ibid.). At the same time, there was no surety that the Russian government would yield to the expansion of the private sector only on this basis. For a private enterprise to operate it had to convince the government that it would be offering a substantially new product. However, the enterprise was not allowed to expand in their product as they wished as the government was concerned with the welfare of the labor force in the private sector.

In 1913, the government became more open to the idea of industrial syndicates, but in practice it did not protect them from the criticism of government officials and the Russian public, who were against the iron and coal syndicates. For example, a faction within the Ministry of Transport gained temporary ascendancy and began to play a more influential role in the formulation of industrial policy (Ibid.). The first step was taken by Rukhlov, the Minister of Transport, to initiate a legal action against *Produgol* and *Prodamet* with backing from the Minister of Justice. However, this legal action was stymied by the diplomatic intervention of the French and Belgian governments, as they wanted to protect their investments in the Russian coal and iron industries (Ibid.).

After 1909, rolling mills started introducing improved technology in Russia by replacing steam power with electric power in order to increase profits. However, the largest firms used their monopoly status as part of the syndicates to reap large profits without investing anything in technical improvements. With the industrial boom of 1913, iron and steel producers were able to make handsome profits and recover at least some losses that they had sustained during the Recession (Ibid.). On the eve of World War I Russia saw its industrial output, investment, prices, and profits increase. According to Gatrell, the "First World War was a godsend for Russian heavy industry" (Gatrell, 1986: 185). However, Russia was also now confronted with a new challenge from socialism and socialist internationalism.

SUMMATION

In this chapter, the notion of the pre-revolutionary Russia's "backwardness" is refuted with evidence that Russia had a large-scale iron industry at a time when neither the United Kingdom nor the United States had a comparable large-scale iron industry. In fact, Russia was exporting iron to Britain. Moreover, Russia had its large-scale steel industry in operation at the same time the US was developing its incipient operation in the 1880s. The United Kingdom did not have a large-scale steel industry until the 1930s, and its steel was produced by family-owned, small-scale businesses. Russia became a major industrial power in 1900 and occupied fourth place in the production of iron and steel. Russia achieved this status largely with the help of state policies and various reform efforts as well as with foreign capital.

Another major point highlighted in this chapter is that it is possible to understand the making of Russia with a yardstick of parity, which will not categorize Russia as either developed or underdeveloped. This was achieved by first focusing on universal aspects in the making of Russian society that were present in other societies as well. Following this, the focus moved to the specific historical and geographical conditions within which the Russian people and their ruling class made specific choices to build and industrialize their society.

Elaborating on those specificities, and especially on Russia's industrialization, it is pointed out that state policies were guided by Russia's need to expand for commercial and security purposes. It needed a large army to conquer more land, and maintaining this army required all sorts of equipment, weapons, transportation, and many other items. To fulfill the needs of the army, industrial development became necessary. These needs of the Russian state also guided its policy of subordinating the nobility to the Russian state as the nobility was not supportive of expansion. Thus, the Russian state played an active role in the social organization of Russian society by creating various categories of social relationships for production. Consequently, no one system of social relationship for production dominated the Russian industrial sector.

Peter the Great had been very particular in industrializing Russia, and he introduced many reforms for that purpose. Later, Catherine II actively promoted the formation of a Russian intelligentsia that played an important role in the debate about industrialization. A strong, centralized bureaucracy (a common feature in all European countries) was created to help promote Russia's industrialization.

However, the defeat of Russia in the Crimean War exposed the weaknesses of Russian infrastructure and production. There was also pressure from the changing international power structure and emerging nationalism on the continent. Therefore, to strengthen Russia and its security, as it was surrounded by big empires and aggressive international forces, industrialization was imperative. In order to boost its industrialization in the middle of the nineteenth century, the Russian state introduced many reforms in tariffs, taxes, incorporation policies, promoted the building of railways, and the gold standard was introduced. The Russian government also encouraged entrepreneurs and investors from the private sector to invest in the steel industry. All these reforms and actions of the Russian government gave incentives to foreign capitalists to invest in the country, and they came in droves during the 1880s and invested in Russia's large-scale steel industry. However, they had to operate within the Russian system and the state could take away investors' rights at any moment. Thus, while promoting industrialization the Russian government did not subordinate its own authority to big business.

A unique feature in these developments was the role of the engineer managers in the Association of Southern Coal and Steel Producers. Their role was decisive in the development and growth of Russia's steel industry even though the investment in steel industry came from foreign capital. There was a large gap in Russia between those supporting industrialization and those opposing it and engineer managers were able to navigate between Russian government and foreign capital while promoting Russia's industrialization. The vision of these engineer managers was neither socialism, nor laissez-faire capitalism, nor corporatism. They were influenced by Enlightenment ideas and were dedicated to the growth of the steel industry so that Russia would become an industrial nation as quickly as possible—raising its rank among European nations.

By the beginning of the twentieth century, Russia had joined the ranks of the world's major producers of iron and steel, contributing about six percent of the total world output, and occupied fourth place after the United States, Germany, and Britain. The Russian state did not subordinate its interest to foreign capital or big business, but it did rescue the steel industry during the downturn in 1900 as well as allowed the formation of the syndicate *Prodamet*. It should be pointed out that the state's support of industry was not unique to Russia, as most of the European and US industrialization took off only with the help of state protection, including tariffs.

It is shown in this chapter how the choices and actions of the Russian state and its people (as also in other societies) did not take place in a vacuum. It was the conjunction and confluence of various historical forces both within and outside of Russian society that created the need for building a large-scale steel industry in 1880, and also to protect it during the economic depression. While examining these conjunctions of historical forces it is also demonstrated that it is possible to write comparative history with a yardstick of parity, without categorizing any society as developed or underdeveloped as the naturally given condition of any society.

ENDNOTES

1. Scholars, who believe in this binary approach, generally do not give credit to those societies which are able to achieve a higher standard of living and industrialization in a much shorter time after their independence in spite of being subjugated for a very long time, squeezed of all their resources, and plundered by imperialist forces. For example, China

is becoming the second largest economy in the world within a few decades. Similarly, Russia, after being plundered by the West in the 1990s, has regained status in the world arena within a decade. India, colonized for 200 years, plundered of its resources and facing many famines, has achieved a growth rate of 6–7 percent in the twenty-first century.

2. Summary based on Raeff, M. (1983). *The Well-Ordered Police State: Social and Institutional Change through Law in the Germanies and Russia, 1600–1800.* New Haven ; London: Yale University Press.
3. Discussion in this whole section is based on Raeff (1983).
4. Discussion based on Walicki, A. (1979), *A History of Russian Thought from the Enlightenment to Marxism.* CA: Stanford University Press.
5. Discussion in this section is based on Falkus (1972).
6. Summary based on Lyashchenko (1949). p. 301.
7. Blackwell (1968).
    a. The Moscow Old Believers came to Moscow in the tenth century and developed the textile industry. But in the 1840s, the Old Believers came under heavy scrutiny because of the suspicion that theirs was a hot bed of subversion and corruption. In 1847, the Russian government struck them hard by taking over their homes, forced them to marry, and locking down their Churches (Blackwell, 1968:225–227).
    b. Jewish entrepreneurs and bankers faced anti-Semitic bias in Russia. In 1847, a large number of Russian Jews were unskilled, unemployed, and were forced to live in ghettos. Jews were always insecure so they had to work harder to establish themselves. Since they were barred from military and civil services, they concentrated in the economic and commercial sphere. However, a group of Jews worked as peddlers, and also smuggled goods across European frontiers. Ghetto and Pale provided a common way of life, an identity, a sense of kinship, a mutual dependence. This created cooperation of Jewish businessmen and they hired Jews only. Jews assumed the economic function of the community in the western part of Russian empire. They refused to become farmers. Yet a few thousands of them worked as tailors and a small number of them ran saloons. Those few who were involved in export trade became wealthy and they played an important role in the industrialization of western provinces of the Russian Empire. With their role in industrialization and having wealth, this group of Jews emerged in 1820–30 as an economic force particularly in Ukraine and Belorussia. As a group they were able to accumulate wealth, as many of them were local dealers of the general store, inn or saloon keepers, some of them were actively trading at the Ukraine fairs, or money lending. By the mid-nineteenth century some of them became private bankers and also branched out into industrial ventures. They also fulfilled the needs of the Tsar's army including money lending to the government during the Napoleonic wars, as the army desperately needed cloth and money. The Russian government during Alexander I time also helped many pauper Jews learn useful occupations, and also helped many Polish Russian Jews to grow the woolen industry. When the railroad developed in Russia it provided more investment opportunities for Jewish bankers. In Germany, by the end of the nineteenth century a fourth of the boards of directors of electrical, mining and brewing firms were Jews. In England at the same time, half of the big bankers were Jewish, in Russia only a very few Jews were able to battle their way to the top (Blackwell, 1968:230–237).
    c. Skoptsy was another religious group that was very wealthy. It consisted of many millionaires, industrialists, and financers with an underground kingdom which was spread from Siberia to Romava. The first Skoptsy 'shop' in Moscow was set up by Luginien and from there Skoptsy spread all over main cities of Russia, but most of

them went to St. Petersburg. Many became craftsmen as jewelers and goldsmiths while others joined commerce and industry. Skoptsy flourished in Siberia as a religious community. They were able to accumulate a vast amount of capital with a stipulation that all individuals wealth was bequeathed to the community. This large capital, which grew quickly, was used for loans to merchants, for other investments, and also to help a member of the sect. However, in the late nineteenth century, the Skoptsy community faced arrests, confiscation and a series of group trials and banishments, which effectively weakened them (Blackwell, 1968:237–238).

8. For stories of serfs becoming rich see Blackwell, pp. 207–208. See also Rosovsky, H. (1954). "The Serf Entrepreneurs in Russia." *Exploration in Entrepreneurial History*, Vol. 6. pp. 207–33.
9. Larisa Georgievna Zakharova raised the question about the history of the preparation for the reforms and their connection with the bourgeois legislation of the 1860s and 1870s. She asks what was "the class essence of the governmental program for the abolition of serfdom; connection between this program and preceding legislation; between this program and liberal bourgeois ideas of the 1850s?" According to her, the activities leading to the reform reflect the "crisis of the elites—a crisis within the ruling class and in the government's policy toward the nobility" ("Autocracy and the Abolition of Serfdom in Russia, 1856–1861." *Soviet Studies in History*, Fall 1987:12–24, 13).

CHAPTER 5

The (Non)Emergence of the Large-Scale Steel Industry in Britain, 1880–1914

"If it was just the natural genius of the British people to do these things [*technological innovations*], there is an onus of proof on explaining just why that genius saw fit to wait until the mid-eighteenth century to throw aside its disguise, and why it faded in relation to that of other countries a brief century later on" (Mathias, 1990; emphasis mine).

"There was no inherent English advance position—indeed, often it was backwardness which created the favourable circumstances for capital accumulation. ... [T]he English system of law with its many feudal elements and guild-like professional structures, in term of its suitability for a capitalist system, has proven superior to the continental rational institutionalised system of law, and has crowded out the latter wherever the two could compete directly, as in Canada" (van der Pijl, 1998).

"Britain's own emergent Modernity was crucially dependent on its relation with the outside world and, in particular, on an aggressive commercialism and imperialism .... The combining of monarchical authority and 'property-power' was achieved only at the expense of regicide, two revolutions and civil war. The unification of the British nation, in the eighteenth century itself, was the work of two wars with the Scots and a savage process of attrition against the Irish. The 'stabilisation' of British society, in the phrase of J. H. Plumb, involved a brutalizing class war symbolised, perhaps by the Peterloo Massacre when more British troops were stationed on Lancashire than in the whole of the Indian Empire... [*With so much blood shed, wars, and massacres,*] Britain was starting to build a new kind of global empire and to unleash the forces of industrialisation onto the world" (Washbrook, 1997; emphasis mine).

"The historical context producing Britain's initial turn toward industrialization, then, were multi-faceted and complex. But two features about it now seem paramount. It took place in and is scarcely explicable outside a broad global context of relationships and exchanges, and it involved relations of imperialism from the first. Britain's rise to world power was as much a cause as a consequence of its industrialisation—and India was heavily imbricated in the process for a long time before industrialisation finally 'emerged'" (Washbrook, 1997).

"Great Britain was first (*in modern times*) among the world's producers of steel in 1880, by 1890 she was second and by 1900 she was third" (Temin, 1966; emphasis mine).

"We [*Great Britain*] did not have to compete but could evade. And our [*Britain's*] ability to evade helped to perpetuate the archaic and increasingly obsolete industrial and social structure of the pioneer age" (Hobsbawm, 1968; emphasis mine).

INTRODUCTION

The quotes at the beginning of this chapter highlight how Britain's industrialization and its specific internal history were constructed through brutal class wars, bloodshed, and interaction with the larger world in the form of aggressive imperialism, including the colonization of India and other countries. This information suggests that there was no inherent English advance position or "natural genius" of the British people from which it emerged as "the first industrial nation." This observation is discussed in this chapter with a yardstick of parity without categorizing England as either developed or underdeveloped. This is achieved by first looking very broadly into the universal and specific elements in the making of British society, and then by focusing on the conjunction and confluence of historical processes within Britain and internationally to understand its industrialization. Within this larger context we tried to locate the non-emergence of the large-scale steel industry in England.

The focus on large-scale steel industry is important because there is a general agreement among scholars that the large-scale steel industry was the gateway to "development" between 1880 and 1914. However, this claim seems dubious as Britain did not have a large-scale steel industry until the 1930s and is labeled as "developed" (progressive), whereas Russia (during 1880s) and India (in 1912) had established large-scale integrated steel industries, but were labeled as "undeveloped" (backward). How does one explain this double standard? Instead of raising this question, economic historian Joel Mokyr has reinforced this double standard in his book, *Enlightened Economy* (2009). He admires England's industrial revolution while labeling Asia and China as being "backward." However, when he compares England with Europe, he changes the argument. He writes, "It makes little sense to think of the rest of Europe as 'slow' or 'backward.' Each continental country had its own specific constraints and obstacles that needed to be removed or overcome before it could do what Britain did, and follow its own variation on the theme of industrialization and modernization" (Mokyr, 2009:11). Why does Mokyr find it difficult to use the same argument for India and China?

A similar double standard is noticeable in the claim that Britain was the "pioneer" in modern industrialization. This "neat-and-tidy" narrative of Britain's "Industrial Revolution" is problematic. The "Industrial Revolution" (a misnomer) was not simply a product of technological development, or the "genius" of a few people, or the leadership of the bourgeoisie, or the presence of a market economy. It was a long-drawn out process in which many actors, including the state system and international forces, played important roles along with many other evolving political, social, economic, and cultural institutions that were controlled by different interest groups at different time periods. Moreover, as pointed out by some historians, the state system was influenced by conflicts on the European continent, conflicts between different sections of the ruling classes, between the ruling classes and working class—including their trade unions, and between the ruling classes and common people. Above all, it was the daily survival strategies of different social groups in different locales and regions of Britain, and of those who migrated to Britain, that created specific internal conditions for the rise of an industrial economy, and subsequently for the steel industry.

In addition, the important fact that Britain, like any other society, did not exist in a vacuum as it was continuously interacting with other societies and learning from them. It was intertwined with the regional dynamics of early modern Europe, which was largely non-capitalist (Park, 2000:19–20). Most of all, as Mokyr pointed out, "Britain learned from inventions made in other societies. Most ideas came from Europe" (Mokyr, 2009:106). However, Europe learned various inventions, skills, and information from its contacts with the Mongol Empire and Ottoman Empire, and through them Europeans came in contact with China and other Eastern countries and their inventions in various fields (Anievas and Nişancioğlu, 2015). Daniel Defoe noted that in the early eighteenth century that, "English are justily fam'ed for improving Arts rather than inventing" [1]. In light of this information, I find it strange that scholars (see Mokyr, 2009; Mokyr, 2016) have been privileging the process of improving upon skills and inventions learned from China (or other places), as an act of "genius" inherent in those people (generally applied to English people only), and not the process of original invention made by Chinese people (or by any other group of people).

These double standards need to be replaced with a yardstick of parity that can be applied to all societies without the arbitrary labels of developed/underdeveloped, progressive/backward. The comparative historical approach, based on the Eurocentric understanding of social reality, as practiced in its present form is not useful because this approach focuses on separate autonomous social entities that are compared using a prior assumption of being either "developed" or "underdeveloped." No society begins as "developed" or "underdeveloped." These labels were assigned in the middle of the twentieth century by scholars with a Eurocentric understanding of the social reality of the world. The facts are ignored that no society is a finished product, as all are in the continuous process of emerging, and that most present-day societies have been interacting with other societies for a long time (Frank, 1998; Hobson, 2004; Sahu, 2016). Over time, this society-to-society interaction tended to become increasingly about trade, gaining territories, or resources (colonizing), and frequently led to battles and wars. It was in this process of interactions through wars and colonization that each society became a complex mix of various cultures, languages, and polity. The making of England (and also of Imperial Russia, postcolonial Imperial US, and colonial India) is no different in that regard. The often repeated argument of the "technological superiority" of Britain in its industrialization ignores the fact that it was a product of Britain's interaction with other societies over a long period of time. "British were rarely coy about utilizing foreign ideas or about reverse-engineering imported inventions. Trade created so-called *exposure affects*, inspiring imitation and innovation through the observation of what foreigners could do" (emphasis in the original, Mokyr, 2009:19; see also Parthasarathi, 2011; Raj, 2006; Washbrook, 1997).

Challenging ongoing double standards in order to understand the making of England and other societies, while using a yardstick of parity, this volume suggests that both social processes (inter-societal and intra-societal interactions) were (and are) being created by spontaneous human creativity which expresses itself through human agency (actions). It is human agency, through interactions with others, that creates society, class conflicts, intra-class conflicts, and larger historical forces within a society as well as in the international arena. Based on this understanding, we can comprehend the making of any society with a yardstick of parity, which is to look into not only the universal and specific elements of a society, but also the conjunction and combination of historical forces within a society and in the larger international arena which contribute in the making of a modern society. In this way, it will be possible to erase the constraints of binary distinction of developed/underdeveloped, which in turn will facilitate an understanding that the historical processes and the formation of British society were no different than those of any other society at that time, even though (as of every society) its historical specificities were different. Thus, by removing the cobweb spun by these labels, it would become possible to see how each society emerged in similar ways historically through complex interaction processes among different social actors with various social relationships, based on class, race, gender or any other, within these societies, as well as with other societies over time. However, to substantiate our argument, the historical material about Britain's industrialization (as well as for the other three countries) is organized around the main issue of the volume: Erasing the binary distinction of developed/underdeveloped with a yardstick of parity. Therefore, reader will get only a synoptic historical account of Britain's industrialization, and not a conventional in-depth chronological history of Britain.

In the following, based on information from selected existing published studies, in Part I (Erasing the Binary with a Yardstick of Parity), instead of categorizing England as either developed or underdeveloped, we shall treat England with the same yardstick of parity which is also used for the other three chosen societies. According to this yardstick, all societies have both universal and specific elements. Therefore, we shall focus on these elements while understanding the making of England and its industrialization. In Part II (Conjunction of Historical Forces: (Non)Emergence of Large-Scale Steel Industry), instead of assuming that England's industrialization was due to some special quality of its people, or superior technology, we show, using a yardstick of parity, how England's industrialization, as well as the non-emergence of the large-scale steel industry in Britain during 1880–1914 was due to the conjunction of historical forces developing within England and in the international arena at that time, as was also the case with the other three countries. In the end we shall examine the reasons for the continuation of the small-scale family firms in British steel industry well into the mid-twentieth century.

PART I

ERASING THE BINARY DISTINCTION WITH A YARDSTICK OF PARITY

According to the yardstick of parity, the trajectory of Britain's history is not much different from that of the other three societies examined in this volume. Aside from specific details, the larger story of invasion, constant territorial wars, trade, interaction with other societies, migration, borrowing of ideas and technology, power struggle among various groups, political conspiracies, and so on, remain the same. People in every society are concerned with four basic needs: survival, prosperity, security and reproduction. Specific details vary for each society, as does the time period of their trajectories. The important point is that people in each society behaved in similar manner—as human beings, all of them were involved in shaping their society to fulfill their human needs. The individuals or groups who were successful in controlling the resources of their society tried to keep those elements under their control. Inevitably, social conflicts followed, and often people from other societies tried to take advantage of these social conflicts and other internal weaknesses within the society. Individually, who became successful, how, and why, are important questions in their own right. However, every society is created and reproduced in every historical time through its members in the process of interaction with other members of the society and its social institutions. At the same time, the actions and choices of each member of a society are not autonomous from their societal and larger historical context, which is also connected with other societies in a particular historical time.

Based on this suggested yardstick of parity, in this chapter England is not categorized as either developed or underdeveloped. Instead we focus on universal and specific elements in the making of England, as we do for the other three societies.

UNIVERSAL ELEMENTS IN THE MAKING OF ENGLAND

The universal characteristics of British society are as follows: connections and interaction with other societies, interactions among people within society and choices made by different sections of society, power struggles, mix of many cultures, a concern with four basic human needs: survival, prosperity, security and reproduction, and the choices and actions based on geographical location, terrain, and climate.

Like other societies, the making of England was deeply connected with its interactions with other surrounding societies and later with far off ones. Therefore, it is not possible to discuss in isolation any phase of the internal historical processes in Britain (or other modern societies) without connecting it with the history of the making of Europe, and more specifically from the sixteenth century onwards with the Americas, Asia, Africa, Middle East, South Asia and Australia, and without connecting to British imperialist wars and colonialism, which led to the making of a modern world economic structure with related political and international networks and structures.

Like other European countries, Britain emerged through centuries of outside invasions by different groups; Romans, Scandinavian, Danish, and French, who in turn linked England to Christianity and Europe. From the first through thirteenth centuries, England was controlled by various foreign occupiers who colonized and exploited it. Thus, right from the beginning England was connected with other societies politically, technologically, economically, socially and culturally. The name England is derived from the Germanic tribe known as Angles, and its language was influenced by Scandinavian and other invading cultures (Ackroyd, 2012). The efforts made by different local kings of England to stabilize their societies created a specific social, economic, cultural and political structure in England. Wessex King Alfred tried to introduce a new defense system with levies, promoting urbanization, intellectual regeneration and culture among the English people. Norman King, William the Conqueror, created a hierarchical structure with the promotion of earls, barons and knights. He also conducted a huge survey of England and Wales and commissioned the "Doomsday Book" (2) in an effort to record conditions and to regulate the country. The British monarchy was able to increase its power (1137–1453) as it was constantly at war with France over a complex inheritance of possession. Noblemen supported the King's power in order to get opportunities for acquiring booty and ransom. At the same time, these conflicts helped England develop a separate national identity. Later, when England was able to expand its empire into India, it strengthened its state and national identity, as Washbrook pointed out, "[T]he unitary imperial project eased the transformation of recalcitrant Scottish and Irish gentries into Britons" (Washbrook, 1997:424).

In addition to its European wars, as in other societies, many complex (specific to England) combinations of power struggles within England also contributed in the making of England, while each power struggle also created new conditions for the later ones (Mann, 1996:17). These multiple struggles brought various transformations in England. However, these transformations did not eliminate the traditional dominant power group and did not revolutionize distributive power (Ibid., 18). We shall discuss in another section that even though power struggles are a universal phenomenon, they are also specific in their forms and outcome as people in their specific context make specific choices.

However, these multiple struggles were also influenced by European conflicts as Anievas and Nişancioğlu (2015:190) have explained while focusing on the English Revolutions of 1640–42, 1688, and 1745. These authors suggest that European conflicts provided the English a necessary, but temporary, geopolitical isolation, which enabled Britain to concentrate on its state-building practices and socio-economic development. However, this process was not a peaceful one because there was a struggle for power between Parliament and the Crown. This power struggle became more intense with the Irish Rebellion of October 1641 because then the question arose who would have control of English armed forces to suppress the rebellion. These unresolvable conflicts eventually pushed England into a Civil War in 1642 (Ibid.). According to Anievas and Nişancioğlu, the social transformation of England during and before Revolutions were thus "a result and part of an international process, involving foreign trade, changes in intra-European relations following on from the discovery of the Americas, and the rivalry of rising mercantile powers in Europe" (Ibid., 195). For example, merchant capitalists who gained with overseas colonial expansion in the Atlantics were more interested in political change against monarchy, whereas the older merchant elite, associated with the East India Company and the Levant trade, depended on Crown charters and therefore, supported the Crown during the Civil War (Ibid.). After the Glorious Revolution of 1688, which overthrew James II, the Netherland's William of Orange became the ruler of England and involved England with Dutch led wars against the French.

Thus, the geopolitics of the European continent shaped and reshaped the relationship between the English state and English society. England went through many dramatic transformations during the Anglo-Dutch wars of 1665–67 and 1672–74, and Anglo-French wars of 1689–1714. In these transformations England adopted advanced fiscal, military, and administrative practices that were developed by the Dutch, which later became very useful for England to gather resources for wars and "the establishment of a form of state conducive to the maximization of capitalist development" (Ibid., 196).

Like other societies, the United Kingdom is also made of many cultures. In the initial making of England, many invading groups of people from different regions also settled in England contributing to its culture and way of life: Anglo-Saxon, Danish, Norman, and French. England's interaction with other societies through trade, wars, colonization and slave trade contributed to the migration of people from various cultures to England, making it a multicultural society. The import of different spices, tea, sugar, and coffee from colonized countries changed the tastes and habits of the British people. More specifically, Indian fabrics and cotton cloth became highly desirable goods in England, though later their import was banned in order to promote the English textile industry.

Like other societies, England's early history was also influenced by its geographical location as well as its climate, natural resources, and terrain. However, these exogenous factors do not operate on their own in any society, but only within a given economic, social, and institutional framework of a society (Hobsbawm, 1968). For example, its natural resources proved a boon when England was able to develop appropriate skills and other resources to exploit them. It has access to sea as no part of Britain is further than seventy miles from the sea and even less from a navigable waterway, which allowed people to move bulk goods cheaply. Coal and other natural resources were located near water carriages in many regions of the island. However, these natural advantages were turned into economic assets with technological changes and an improved and extended river navigation system in the eighteenth century (Mathias, 1990).

In addition to the aforementioned universal elements in the making of England, it also had numerous specific elements (as in the case of other societies) which gave it a distinct character.

SPECIFIC CHARACTERISTICS IN THE MAKING OF MODERN ENGLAND

In the making of modern England, the choices and actions of different elite groups and common people also shaped the political economy of the emerging country, as it also happened in other societies. However, elite groups and common people in each society acted differently in their specific context. Unlike in Russia, where a strong state eliminated power struggles between different groups by subordinating them to the state, in Britain it was the power struggle between various interest groups at a micro and macro level that shaped British state, society, other social and political institutions, its national market, industrial structure and relationship with other countries in a specific way. Even the process of making Britain a dominant global power, and its colonization of large number of countries, was intertwined with these power struggles. In the following we discuss briefly these specific elements in the making of England, including its industrial structure.

1. POWER STRUGGLE AND THE CREATION OF A WEAK MONARCHY

The British Crown established its symbolic "absolute" control over the economy by issuing the "*Book of Orders*," in 1587 (Lie, 293). However, the Crown did not have the means to enforce its control and turned to London merchants for assistance during the fiscal crisis. Merchants, in turn, used this opportunity to play an important political role that created tension between Parliament and the Lord Alders against the Crown, eventually leading to the Civil War (Ibid.). However, after the Civil War and Revolution, the English monarchy's efforts to create a stable economic, political, and cultural structure was not possible without the support of local noblemen, landed gentry, merchants and other vested interest groups within England. However, these noblemen and other interest groups were constantly engaged in power struggles. These power struggles among different groups as well as with the monarchy created new conditions that shaped Britain's various political, social, economic institutions, including its national markets.

For example, George III allowed the gentry elite to consolidate their power in the localities in exchange for their support of far-reaching financial and administrative reforms and retention of executive privileges (Price, 1999). The noblemen supported the King and won property rights protected by the state, and a provision that the state could not tax anyone without permission of Parliament. Under this agreement the King became subordinated to Parliament while Parliament was controlled by an oligarchy of landowning aristocrats comprised of post-revolutionary elite (Hobsbawm, 1968:51). Thus, the British state avoided taxing lands in order to ensure domestic political stability by not alienating the landed gentry. In this context, it is not surprising that the British state had to keep shifting its priorities and allegiances across time based on the nature of the power struggles between different interest groups.

The choices made by different elite groups based on each group's own interest also contributed in making a weak monarchy while restructuring agrarian relationships. For example, it was only through its position within the manorial structure that the landed elite could exercise their rights of extraction and rights to regulate (Lachmann, 1987:144). Therefore, the gentry's struggle for the control and reordering of agrarian class relations excluded the crown elite from positions of regulations or extraction at the local level and thus curtailed crown and clerical authority over manorial land rights (Ibid., 141). They were able to attain that position by organizing its access to production within manors, which determined the structure of peasant communities at the local level. This dual elite structure remained intact in which the gentry held all positions of extraction and regulation within manors, and could also control peasants without interference from rival extractors at the local level (Ibid., 147). These feudal elite were also actors at the national level, and with their control over the local market and class relations they were able to constrain other elites including the Crown from transforming the organization of agricultural production. Defeated in the conflicts with the feudal elite, the Crown was forced to confine itself exclusively at the national level. Since it had no position within the local organizational structure of production, and it had no fiscal instrument to capture agrarian surpluses, the Crown was deprived of agrarian revenue. This situation led the Crown to search for alternative sources for revenue.

State Search for Alternative Sources for Revenue

While the landed elite was successful in creating a weak monarchy, the King began to use patronage to strengthen his political position. However, to meet the needs of wars, debts and political patronage, the King looked to alternative sources of income from free trade by promoting overseas trade to generate custom revenue and excise duties. This free trade helped keep intact landed interests at home while it also helped in connecting with the British diaspora abroad through the movement of international commercial capital. The new landed elite, which was also becoming active in national politics in Parliament, was more interested in making war or peace for profit by controlling the colonies and markets in an effort to stamp out competitors, rather than looking for prestige and honors (Hobsbawm, 1968:32). Under Elizabeth I, the British state began to organize adventures to explore new markets for the export of wool cloth by sending trade envoys to negotiate with Russians, Moguls, and Persians. Thus, Britain's foreign policy became completely subordinated to its economic ends. However, in order to protect its overseas trade, it needed to increase investment in building the country's naval supremacy. Unsurprisingly, the Royal Navy became the most important weapon in the success of British business overseas, and thus investment in the Navy was increased (Ibid., 26). By the mid-seventeenth century, England's fiscal military state had created the most fearsome military apparatus in the Western world. Thus, England emerged over the course of the eighteenth century as the most dynamic economy in Europe as well as a formidable military power (Chibber, 2013:78). In the words of one observer, "British commerce was both businesslike and warlike in 1750 as it was closely linked with the political system of Britain" (Voltair quoted in Hobsbawm, 1968:25).

2. POWER STRUGGLE BETWEEN BRITISH ELITE AND COMMON PEOPLE

In the process of constructing the state system common people also played an important role. However, after the Revolution (1688), the elite found ways to keep them out of it, as they were not interested in including the common persons in the process of making the state. Earlier, during the Civil War the landed class and their elite allies found it advantageous to support the ideals of political rights of the people to justify and legitimize their own actions in the name of public interests (Zaret, 2000 quoted in Chibber, 2013:62–63). But soon after the Civil War, the landed class became keenly interested in the restoration of order as new groups of people with radical ideas were entering a position of authority, and began challenging the old order. To restore its own order, the landed elite were willing to revive once again the monarchical rule minus the absolutist state, and the old social hierarchy. Moreover, in this new order, sovereignty would reside in the nation and not in the monarchy.

However, the landed elite could not check the expansion of political space due to the increases in election frequency and the number of electorates between 1689 and 1710. Therefore, they began to place one obstacle after another in the political process to minimize the political participation of the lower classes. The landed elite was finally successful in keeping the lower classes out of the new power structure of the nation, as well as excluding new petit-bourgeoisie from the voting process and from holding state offices in 1714 when George I succeeded Queen Anne to the British throne (Ibid.; see also Mann, 1993). In the 1760s, these diverse groups consisted of a mix of various elites at the local and national levels: the Old Regime (monarch, church, aristocracy, country gentry, and commercial merchant oligarchs), the petit bourgeoisie (small capitalists, tradesmen, manufacturers, artisan, intellectuals, lawyers, teachers and journalists), the peasant farmers (small property owners using family labor), and the capitalist class (merger of the old regime and the upper petite bourgeoisie across land, commerce and industry) (Mann, 1993:97).

Besides keeping the poor outside the political process, the elite also denied legal protection to trade unions, and continued the practice of indentured labor, while the legal system was used to impose draconian penalties, even capital punishment, for petty theft. By the 1720s, the groups such as the Levellers (Brailsford, 1961) and the Quakers went underground, although their radical ideas spread throughout France and in other places on the Continent. When the middle class began joining the Parliament in 1820, they were able to check further expansion of elite power by cleaning up the criminal laws and the fiscal system. Reforms continued after 1832 when old abuses of the state system were further attacked, and a public system of education was instituted (Porter, 1990:127–128; quoted in Chibber, 2013). In spite of these reforms, by the 1840s, a single capitalist ruling class emerged in England which was comprised of the core of the old regime and the petite bourgeoisie. By 1870, this capitalist ruling class was able to bring the Church, the landed aristocracy, the financial institutions, the industrial corporation and the nation-state under its control.

3. CONTENDING SOCIAL GROUPS AT LOCAL LEVEL AND THE FORMATION OF A NATIONAL MARKET

In addition to the re-formation of the elite group, the ruling class was able to create and control the national market. The formation of a national market involved social organization, norms, values and power struggles (including the working people's struggle), that created the structure and operation of concrete historical markets. In the sixteenth century, England was an open market. However, by the eighteenth century a national market came into being in the process of power struggles among various social groups that were pursuing their micro interests (Lie, 1993:297).

Earlier, the struggle against serfdom led to the peasant uprising in 1381, which resulted in the creation of more free market, productive and exchange activities. During this time, production of commodities and markets required simple tools and low capital. These earlier markets and productive activities could flourish because the British monarchy was devoting more energy to overseas trade to increase its own power and income, instead of investing in Britain's internal infrastructural capacity to generate revenue. In this environment, the market for local country crafts began expanding on an unprecedented level through peddlers and chapmen, who were walking all throughout the Kingdom selling their wares from door to door. During the same time, the number of provincial shops (mostly located in market towns) were rising (Ibid.).

Later, in the seventeenth century, it was the travelling merchants who stimulated industries and laid the basis for the rise of manufacturing centers. These merchants provided both credit for consumers as well as capital for producers (Ibid., 289). Their transactions were based on kinship networks. Over time, these simple commodity producers and traders transformed themselves into capitalists and merchants. They brought local production under their control through the use of the putting-out system and by creating unequal relations between weavers and clothiers. The new relations of production were now between the capitalist and the worker.

While travelling merchants were becoming capitalists, an alliance of rural capitalists and lords was also taking place that constructed another interregional organization of commodity exchange with a different social base (Ibid., 290). Polarization between the classes emerged within the market region as prices rose over the next century. Many people, who were dependent on the open market for their sustenance, became poorer, as smaller landholders began to engage in enclosure practices, consolidating and fencing in their land to promote agricultural efficiency. Even though an anti-enclosure policy existed, enforcement began to decline because the same landlords or local notables who were supposed to enforce this law comprised the social force advocating further enclosures. The local elites were interested in enclosures because they enabled the rapid expansion of commercial farming. This was also reflected in the rising rates of deforestation of parks and forests, especially during the reign of Charles I. As a result of these developments, speculations in the land market increased, and landholding became concentrated, which in turn encouraged and entrenched agrarian capitalism—enriching landlords, while creating dispossessed rural wage earners (Lie, 1993).

In the absence of any national bureaucracy, the upwardly mobile rural gentry controlled local regions and invested in commercial pursuits (Ibid.). These local commercial elites essentially joined the national elite in London, as they allied with local justice of peace. The role of the local justice of peace was to uphold the rules of the market place. However, these justices now began making decisions in favor of furthering the commercial interests of traders, as they themselves were involved in commerce. By the late seventeenth century, 60%–70% of land was owned by the gentry, 25%–33% by the yeomanry, and 5%–10% by the Church and Crown (Ibid.). This consolidation destroyed the peasantry, while increasing the number of agrarian wage laborers and rural poor. Many of these dispossessed people migrated to London.

Over time, London became the dominant export trade center, as England's trade with other countries was increasingly centralized in London. By 1700, up to one-half of the London population was employed in jobs related to shipping and the city's port. The needs of shipping and insurance also fostered the growth of the mercantile marine and the City of London itself. Furthermore, a demand for the stocks of overseas trading companies created conditions for the emergence of a stock market (McKendrick, Brewer and Plumb, 1982).

London also emerged as a major consumption and commercial center, as roughly two-thirds of the rapid urbanization of seventeenth-century English society took place there. The city became the national social center for elites as well as for their retinues, and many services emerged to cater to their demands. Culturally, England saw a shift from the earlier ideal of country gentry to the ideal of civility in city life. The arrival of Indian cottons promoted a revolution in domestic consumption patterns as did the arrival of tea, coffee, sugar and porcelain, which helped in laying the basis of the first "national" markets in Britain (Washbrook, 1997).

In the late eighteenth and early nineteenth century, a large mercantile organization was created that integrated independent shops and traveling merchants who were engaged in direct sales to consumers. John Lie informs, middlemen in London created a new set of rules to govern trade and started selling commodities by sample, rather than taking commodities to the market place. Retail became a branch of wholesale in large markets, and merchant organizations pushed for more profits in their overseas trade. In their efforts to crush travelling merchants, middlemen got help from the state through a royal grant. This royal grant allowed London-based merchants the right to hire "agents" to harass and crush local manufacturers and peddlers who threatened their monopolies. However, this encroachment of middlemen met with resistance by all those who were involved in the market, resulting in riots (Lie, 286).

In spite of riots, the middlemen were successful in maintaining their monopoly because they were able to monopolize information and resources necessary for maintaining virtual dominance over the internal flow of an important commodity—wheat. With this control, larger wholesalers were able to increasingly expand export trade profitably during the late seventeenth century, which established them as a corporate body controlling enormous parts of the economy (Ibid., 295). Thus, the wholesale system became the dominant mode of exchange and distribution in the national market of England.

4. STRUGGLE OVER THE CREATION OF A NEW FINANCIAL SYSTEM

It should be noted that in the seventeenth century many intellectuals and other public-spirited individuals were concerned with the question of how to increase the money supply. England did not have gold mines. One group of merchants that had been appointed to investigate a 1620 fiasco in the wool trade with Holland did not consider credit to be a viable alternative to metallic currency. Another group of intellectuals known as Hartlib's Circle believed that with the knowledge of alchemy, they could solve the problem of money scarcity by transforming lead into gold. But the effort proved futile (Ghosh, 2012).

Certain pre-conditions for financial revolution in England had long been present such as the existence of London's merchants and goldsmiths, their cosmopolitan connections, as well as their extensive international trade. However, financial revolution could not take place before 1688 because James II was pro-French, and his pro-Catholic policies frightened the predominantly Protestant bankers and investors, and without their support, financial revolution was not possible (Cains and Hopkins, 1993:63). This fear was removed with the "gentlemanly revolution" of 1688, as the newly installed monarch did not have financial independence and was compelled to govern through Parliament in order to secure an adequate income. The new type of monarchy also had to acknowledge the political dominance of the landed gentry's interests. In return, the new Monarch and his successors demanded finances for participation in the Continental war, and that led to the expansion of the national debt (Ibid., 64).

The Whig party gained the majority in Parliament after the Revolution of 1688 with the help of various interest groups, including the gold smiths, bankers, and creditors who had suffered severely when Charles II had earlier defaulted on the loans owed to them. Therefore, the Whigs wanted a financial system that could be backed by strong and effective fiscal and administrative machinery. Moreover, Britain needed a sound credit system for overseas expansion as it was at a disadvantage in its struggle with the Dutch, and only with improved credit would it be able to defend its overseas expansion (Cains and Hopkins, 1993). The Whig party was successful in getting a commitment from the administration that became the foundation for the smooth functioning of the public credit system, which in turn provided political and financial stability. However, for the success of a public credit system, it was necessary to win public trust and thus public opinion became an important arbiter of public credit and therefore politicized. Importantly, writers and intellectuals helped in convincing the public in this regard by producing future values of market through their power of imaginative use of social imagery of reality. This was reflected in connection with the stocks of the South Sea Company for the transnational slave economy, which in turn, created a credit bubble (Ghosh, 2012). However, this new credit system enabled England to become financially dominant in the world during the eighteenth and nineteenth centuries.

5. POWER STRUGGLES BETWEEN VARIOUS MERCHANT GROUPS, BETWEEN LANDED GENTRY AND PEASANTS AND THE FORMATION OF NEW CLASSES

By the mid-seventeenth century, British commercial and property classes were becoming restless due to the inefficiency of the economic system engendered by the Crown's promotion of patronage to increase its own political power. Their restlessness manifested in changing social, religious and economic values of British society, and in various power struggles, which led to the rearrangement of the British class structure (Mukherjee, 1974). Below is the discussion about power struggles between the following groups: Merchant Guilds and Craftsmen Guilds, Foreign Merchants, English Merchant Bourgeoisie and Merchant Adventurers, Landed Gentry, and Peasants.

i. Merchant Guilds and Craftsmen Guilds

Most towns in England had won their freedom from feudal exaction and attained a certain measure of self-government by the end of the thirteenth century (Ibid., 9). These towns tried to keep trade in the hands of their own burgesses by creating Merchant Gilds (same as 'guild' in modern usage. Charles Gross, 1890, quoted in Mukherjee, 1974). These guilds were based on the principle that only those who paid their share towards the freedom of the town had the right to share in its privileges, including all the traders. These new interest groups were based on the control of capital and credit (Ibid., 11). They strictly implemented regulations with fines and, in extreme cases, with expulsion. However, all people in the burgess had a common interest, as everyone in the town was connected with trade in some way. Over time, as the town grew in size, Craft G[u]ilds came into being which challenged the Merchant Gilds (Ibid., 12). With the rapid development and specialization of industry, Craft G[u]ilds further increased and grew in power during the reigns of the three Edwards—particularly, under Edward III. Many master craftsmen became wealthy, dealing extensively with the wares, and started employing wage labor to produce those wares. At the end of the thirteenth century, as Mukherjee pointed out, sharper class divisions emerged in these towns as the number of journeymen, who remained wage earners all their lives, increased. The dealers or merchants, who traded in different branches of production, distinguished themselves from the trading artisans by forming separate fraternities. These new class formations led to the demise of the old Merchant G[u]ild and by the fourteenth and fifteenth centuries, the Craft G[u]ilds were at the peak of their power[3].

ii. Power Struggle Among Foreign Merchants, English Merchants, Bourgeoisie and Merchant Adventurers

It should be pointed out that the term "merchant" has held different meanings in different times. For example, as discussed earlier, old guild merchants were initially very powerful in their towns, both politically and economically. However, they later lost their power to rich craftsmen (Mukherjee, 1974:18). Under this new power elite, the idea of citizenship changed as it was no longer connected to the ownership of property, residence, birth, purchase, gift or marriage. Instead, the "right to trade or exercise a craft became a preeminent privilege" (Ibid., 19). However, when merchant companies known as the Staplers and the Adventures emerged, the craftsmen lost their privileged status in the face of a growing merchant bourgeoisie[(4)]. Early on, England was able to attain peace by suppressing private wars, as well as acquiring a monopoly over the rapidly developing foreign trade in wool (Mukherjee, 1974:22). During the reign of Henry III, English merchants, who had been trading in wool, hides, tin and lead, formed an association called the Fellowship of the Staple. They were able to receive monopoly rights in the valuable wool export trade in exchange for providing loans to the Crown (Ibid., 24). They were also successful in diminishing the role of their entrenched rivals (Flemish and Italian merchants in London), as the Crown began to rely on export taxes on wool and on wool loans from English wool exporters for state revenue.

When wool prices went down, the English cloth making industry began to grow. The export trade in cloth developed and became lucrative with official encouragement. Along with this new lucrative trade emerged the Merchant Adventurers who had broken away from the Fellowship of the Staplers at the beginning of the thirteenth century. These English Merchant Adventurers made fortunes in foreign trade, and some ventured beyond European borders. For example, in 1580 Captain Francis Drake returned to England from his first world tour "with half a million pounds worth of loot, as much as the whole revenue of the Crown for a year" (Ibid., 35).

These Merchant Adventurers wanted a monopoly on the export of various manufactured goods, especially cloth, and for that purpose, as Mukherjee noted, they formed various companies: the Russia Company wanted the sole rights to trade with Muscovy, the East Africa Company and South Africa Company wanted monopolies "to kidnap or purchase and work to death without compunction the natives of Africa" (Ibid., 26), the Eastland Company wanted a monopoly over "trade through the Sound into Norway, Sweden, Poland, Lithuania, Prussia and also Pomerania from the river Oder eastward to Dantzick, Elbing, Konigsberg, to Copenhagen and Elsinore and to Finland, Gothland, Barnhom and Oeland," the Spanish Company wanted to monopolize the lucrative trade in wine, oil, and fruit with Spain and Portugal, and the Levant Company wanted a monopoly over trade with Turkey (Ibid.).

These companies were successful in securing monopoly power from a Royal charter, but, as Mukherjee noted, the members of the company were forbidden to engage in the manual occupations of retail shopkeepers or to marry outside of England (Ibid., 32). These companies were given a wide range of powers, in addition to trade, military, and political authority. In their sphere of trade, they were allowed to make by-laws, and to impose imprisonment or fines on all non-freemen trading in these foreign parts. Out of all these companies it was the East India Company that turned out to be the most powerful (Ibid., 27). Queen Elizabeth was one of the shareholders of the East India Company and its charter of monopoly was renewed to perpetuity by James I in 1805 (Ibid., 26). These companies were successful in imposing laws, fines, and imprisonment on people of foreign countries because local producers, in the absence of developed markets, were unable to influence the exchange price of their products (Ibid., 30). Moreover, the English merchants were interested only in large profits, and that was possible only by buying goods at a very low price or with no payment at all. English merchants decided to achieve this goal by controlling the buying power of foreign countries by colonizing those regions (Ibid., 35). English merchants were successful with this goal because their idea of colonization was in tune with the British people's growing desire at that time for "the spirit of conquest" and "the expansion of British power overseas."

Theological Support for Merchant Capital

These new class formations were legitimized with new theological interpretations, as Calvinism is "perhaps the first systematic body of religious teaching which can be said to recognize and applaud the economic virtues" of merchant capital (Mukherjee, 1974:4). Over time, the followers of Calvinism saw it "as a frank idealization of the life of trader, as the service of God and the training ground of the soul" (Ibid., 6). However, there existed diverse Protestant ideologies which English Puritans and German Pietists adapted to their purely theological doctrines to address issues of economics and politics. But they did it only when, and to the extent, rulers challenged their institutional freedoms (Fullbrook quoted in Lachmann, 2013:19).

Ramakrishna Mukherjee has pointed out that in England, where the Puritan moralists derived their teaching "most directly from Calvin," usury—in the sense of payment for a loan—was not considered in itself as unlawful for Christians[(5)]. Therefore, it is not surprising that in the seventeenth century English upper classes favored Calvinism. Under Elizabeth I, Calvinism developed into a vigorous Puritan movement more strongly among the trading and commercial classes. The leading businessmen, who advised Charles II's government on commercial policy, came from the ultra-Protestantism of the city and some came from London's French Huguenot church. As a rule, most iron masters of the eighteenth century belonged to the Puritan connection (Ibid., 7). However, as Tawney noted, it was the "development of sixteenth century capitalism [*which*] drove the spread of English Calvinist Puritanism" (Tawney quoted in Heller, 2011:15). Moreover, government officials and employers were attracted to Calvinism's idea of discipline as it would help them to control their subjects and employees[(6)].

However, it should be noted that every Protestant region did not industrialize (Hobsbawm, 1968; See also Mathias, 1990). In fact, Protestantism declined rapidly when commercial capitalism lost out in Poland, Spain, Italy, or Hungary. At the same time, when export agriculture expanded in those areas, Catholicism was reinstated (Wallerstein, 1976:105–106).

iii. Power Struggle between Landed Gentry and Peasants: Formation of Wage Labor

Until the middle of the eighteenth century, industry and manufacturing in Britain were rural. It was the village artisan or a small holder in his cottage who was the worker himself. This village artisan/small holder began to specialize increasingly in the manufacturing of certain products: cloth, hosiery or metal goods. Later, these craftsmen and small farmers would become wage laborers. English historian Eric Hobsbawm noted that the villages where men spent their spare time weaving, knitting and mining became industrial villages of full-time workers, whereas, other villages developed into industrial towns. Many villages became market centers where transactions took place: buying of village products, distributing raw material, and renting out looms or frames to cottage workers. Over time, some of these villages developed into towns with workshops creating a primitive manufacturing system where scattered outworkers prepared and finished materials and goods (Hobsbawm, 1968).

As the system of the rural domestic or putting-out industry began spreading widely throughout the countryside it led to an increase in cash transactions as well as greater dependence on other areas for food. In the wake of these developments, the landlord class developed an interest in the mines that were beneath their lands, and also in the manufacturing sector that was evolving in the village. With this new interest in manufacturing and mining, the local nobility and gentry started investing in canals and turnpikes in order to widen the market for local agricultural produce, and local mining and manufacturing with a cheap transportation system (Hobsbawm, 1968). Thus, the conjunction of different developments and the choices made by different classes of people, created conditions for the emergence of a wage labor force, as well as an increase in production and manufacturing in certain villages.

The creation of this wage labor market took place between 1570 and 1640 when "the portion of English peasants who were *proletarianized*—that is, who lost their land rights and were forced to work for wages or for poor relief payments, rose to 40 percent. By 1688, a majority, 56 percent of English rural laborers were proletarian" (Lachmann, 1987:16, emphasis in the original).

However, the creation of wage labor was part of the gentry's strategy for land control. Richard Lachmann noted that the gentry was positioned (discussed earlier) between two structural levels—the national and the local—and was engaged in two forms of conflict—elite and class. This dual engagement created conflict at both levels; structure of land, and labor allocation and control (Ibid.). When landlords won the battle for control over the manors, it created a pool of landless peasants (Ibid., 141). The labor market now became part of the country-level structures that prevented former tenants from making any claims to the land. The only way these former tenants and landless individuals could gain access to land was to become a wage laborer or to stay on poor relief. Landlords used these two structures to their advantage; they wanted labor to work on their estate so that the peasant class could not make claims on the land, and that in turn would keep away Crown and clergy intervention with regard to any such land claims. Thus, according to Lachmann, "[T]he market allocation of agrarian labor in England was the historical outcome of gentry strategies for land control" (Ibid.).

Overseas Slave Trade and Commercial Revolution

While English landed gentry was creating wage labor within the country, English merchants were depending on slave trade and slave labor in the colonial plantations for tropical goods and produce. With the sale of these tropical and colonial products (produced through plantation slavery) British merchants became instrumental in creating a commercial revolution while generating a substantial part of Britain's tax revenue. This intertwined relationship between merchant capital, slave trade, and the royal navy gave Britain greater sea power and control. Britain needed a continuous supply of these colonial products, which could be maintained only with an enormous mercantile marine. No wonder the abolition of the slave trade from Africa was considered a threat towards diminishing British sea power in the world (Washbrook, 1997:422).

Thus, the plantation slavery system and slave trade with Africa and the Caribbean played a major role in the financing of British commercial and industrial revolutions (Williams, 1944). This link between slave trade and Britain's industrialization is corroborated in the biographies of slave-ship captains and traders in the northwest of England (Rice and Poulter, n.d). It is also noticeable that cotton for Manchester came from slave plantations, and Manchester's population increased from 17,000 in 1760 to 180,000 in 1830.

6. WEAK INDUSTRIALISTS AND POWERFUL GENTLEMANLY CLASS

Since Britain's foreign policy was guided by its commercial interests overseas, it was dominated by domestic commercial and financial interests. However, the manufacturing sector, initially the woolen industry and later others, also increasingly began to put pressure on the state to accommodate their interest. For example, British textile producers were able to win protection against Indian textile imports, which was contrary to the interests of the East India Company. Later in 1813, the East India Company lost its monopoly in India when India was opened up for the massive import of Lancashire cotton (Hobsbawm, 1968). However, British industrialists remained less integrated in the policy making structure in spite of the Industrial Revolution. At the same time, the "gentlemanly class," which had joined the British Civil Services after 1850, detested manual labor and looked down on industrialists (Hopkins and Cains, 1987), but treated bankers with the utmost respect. With the formation of joint-stock companies, the power of the "gentlemanly class" increased in the form of family capitalism during the nineteenth century. Most of these gentlemen were on the boards of these companies. They maintained their power through social networks, marriages, heirships, and leisurely social interaction (Hopkins and Cains, 1986:518).

Faced with the strong power of the gentlemanly class, industrialists had no choice but to support their agenda to save their own class interests. Moreover, after 1850, the industrial sector was becoming less dynamic and its representatives did not have direct access to the "charmed circles" of policy formulation (Hopkins sand Cains, 1987). Thus, industrialists were less integrated into the policy-making structure, and being small firm enterprises they were unable to speak with one voice about major issues concerning their interests. Furthermore, they were not powerful enough to change the overseas alliances between London and existing export industries. Nonetheless, industrialists were aware that they would benefit from British marketing of export of all kinds of goods, therefore, they went on supporting free trade as well as the stringent monetary and fiscal policies (Ibid.). It was only after World War I, with the growth of big business, that industry gained more political power [(7)]. At that time, international finance was contracting and London's interests in domestic industrial finance started increasing.

7. INCREASE IN SERVICE SECTOR AND RESTRUCTURING OF CLASSES

The British government's dependence on London for advances in money made London more powerful, even though many of these monetary advances came from people with aristocratic, landed, or service backgrounds (Hopkins and Cains, 1987). After 1850, London and all of Southeast England developed a dynamic service sector with the highest rate of growth for employment, which created a new middle class. The members of the middle class were employed in civil services, in the armed forces, in the Church and in other professions that were based on meritocratic selection. After the 1870s, Britain's invisible export—that is, services—increased rapidly. However, the service economy became successful only after 1880s when London became the chief market of the world with an open economy and free trade creating more opportunities for the service sector. Britain became a financial power with an invisible empire, which was facilitated by an invisible trade and by developing the interior of continents with a network of railways. This invisible trade and invisible empire saved Britain when its influence in America and Europe started diminishing in 1880.

During 1880–1900, Britain increased its presence overseas with service and finance generating a greater impact than the industrial sector. The shift from industry to service incomes and employment was reflected in the changing composition of British foreign trade. With these shifts, members of the new 'upper class,' located mostly in London, were able to amass wealth and prestige equal to that held by members of the landed aristocracy. This new 'upper class' consisted of rentier money, service employments, and the remnants of landed society, which influenced the politics and culture of the late nineteenth and twentieth centuries.

It is notable that both the British government and its financial sector shared the same assumptions about international policies because their members came from the same communities. For example, the sons of the professional class, educated at public schools in South England, were given administrative and army jobs in India (Hopkins and Cains, 1987). Moreover, small numbers of banking dynasties and their associates could unite more easily to promote their interests. For instance, certain leading figures were able to influence banks via interlocking and directorship of major financial institutions. After 1880, as Hopkins and Cains explained, these financial leaders used investment trusts to influence financial decisions that spread London's influence across the globe. Thus, London became a breeding ground for the newer forms of "gentlemanly capitalism."

However, in 1914 the financial elite turned to domestic investment as big business and industry started dominating international policies.

8. IDEOLOGY OF PROSPERITY, FREEDOM, AND IMPERIALIST CONQUESTS

Earlier, Britain was deriving its state revenue from a stagnant economic base or from an expanding population or geographic region. By modernizing and reforming its fiscal apparatus Britain was able to generate revenue by increasing labor productivity, which in turn increased per capita income. Britain became a dynamic and self-expanding capitalist economy and it also acquired a major share of the overseas market with the rapid expansion of the international economy. With the help of the centralized military state, Britain became powerful by subordinating all of its foreign policy to economic ends as her war aims were always commercial and naval (Hobsbawm, 1968). With the rise of British power, it became imperative for European states to have a huge amount of resources for its political survival (Chibber, 2013:264), which led to political centralization across the European continent. Thus, Britain's emergence as a prosperous and powerful state changed the rules of the game in international relations. By 1815, Britain established itself as one of two preeminent global players along with Russia. As a global player with an expanding capitalist economy, Britain achieved prosperity at home and simultaneously expanded its imperial conquests abroad (Ibid., 265). John Locke (1691) defined this prosperity as follow:

> Riches do not consist in having more Gold and Silver, but in having more in proportion than the rest of the World, or than our Neighbours, whereby we are enabled to procure to ourselves a greater Plenty of the Conveniences of Life than comes within the reach of Neighbouring Kingdom and States (Locke, 1691, quoted in Williams, 1980:15).

Similarly, Bacon provided a justification for British imperialism abroad with these words: "The increase of any estate must be upon the foreigner, for whatsoever is somewhere gotten is somewhere lost" (Ibid., 20). This imperial outlook and strategy were not challenged by any coalition of interests or classes who had participated in the Glorious Revolution and created the republic of the Commonwealth. Even the Levellers vigorously supported an imperialist outlook (Ibid.). Though the Revolution had strengthened the rights of free Englishmen and created a strong momentum toward a more representative and responsible government, England remained "backward and underdeveloped." To address this issue of backwardness, British elites continued to expand the centrally directed imperial system, which created an intense paradox between the ideas of freedom on one hand, and order and prosperity on the other. John Locke, both a philosopher and an advisor to the Chancellor of the Exchequer under Charles II, provided a model for colonial Englishmen who sought power in the name of the "exercise of freedom" (Ibid., 22). Thus, as Williams (1980) pointed out, the interaction between economic activities and political, intellectual and social developments produced a new culture that was based on the proposition that expansion was the key to freedom, prosperity, and social peace.

English and other European empire builders later developed contradictory and complex arguments to justify their imperial activities in India, Africa, Asia and America. They could not use the argument of self-defense against the colonized societies as these areas were thousands of miles away, and none of them had attacked these European societies. Therefore, they justified their initial invasion by asserting their "superiority," and this system of ideas became the base and excuse for aggressive action (Ibid.).

However, the assertion of "superiority" became possible with the formation of a strong national identity, and that was achieved during the process of power struggles at the international level including wars with France and the colonization of India.

SUMMATION PART I

In Part I, we focused on erasing the binary of developed/underdeveloped by using a yardstick of parity to understand the making of English society and its industrialization process. Accordingly, we did not categorize England as either developed or underdeveloped. Instead, we looked into universal and specific elements in the making of England and its industrialization as we also applied to three other societies. We noted England's universal characteristics as follows: interactions with many societies, people trying to meet their four basic needs: survival, security, prosperity, reproduction; power struggles at micro and macro levels and geographical features impacting people's choices. However, England's interaction with other societies was of a specific nature i.e. wars, invasions, colonization, commerce, and slave trade. Similarly, various power struggles in England were of a specific nature within its specific historical context. We highlighted those specific elements that contributed to England's industrialization as follows: various power struggles between different groups at micro and macro levels that shaped British state (weak monarchy); society, culture, its economic, social and political institutions; its national market, industrial structure and production relationships, as well as Britain's interaction with other societies and the world at large. These power struggles were also connected with the process of making Britain a dominant global power including the colonization of a large number of countries. It is also noted that England's industrial sector was not well represented within the structure of power and policy making, even though it generated the first so-called Industrial Revolution in the world that theoretically put Britain on the path of "development" and made it a super power. Within this larger historical context, we locate in Part II the non-emergence of the large-scale steel industry in England, we use the same yardstick of parity to explain, after an overview of the history of England's industrialization, that like the other three societies chosen for this volume, the non-emergence of a large-scale steel industry in England (1880–1914) was due to intertwined historical processes of conjunction and confluence of historical forces at that time.

PART II

CONJUNCTION AND CONFLUENCE OF HISTORICAL FORCES IN THE NON-EMERGENCE OF THE LARGE-SCALE STEEL INDUSTRY IN BRITAIN

> Leadership in economic matters passed slowly from the Mediterranean to the north, and as the Italian cities declined, those of the Netherlands rose: but there was little in the way of business or industrial technique in use in northern economies that would have been unfamiliar to the Venetian merchant or a Florentine clothier of the fifteenth century (Wallerstein, 1976:108).

As suggested in the beginning of the chapter, we are using the same yardstick of parity to understand Britain's industrialization and the (non)emergence of the large-scale steel industry (1880–1914) in England, as we are doing for the other three chosen countries. Instead of categorizing England as either developed or underdeveloped, we focus on complex intertwined historical processes, which show that it was the conjunction of historical forces developing within England (inter-societal interactions) and within international arena (intra-societal interactions) which created conditions for the (non)emergence of the large-scale steel industry in England. After all, England's "Industrial Revolution" was a slow process spanning three centuries, and within these three centuries various historical developments took place within Britain and in the international arena. That is why these simultaneous complex historical processes became as much a specific history of England as that of its intertwined relationships with larger international forces (see Chapter 3) and other societies of that time. In the following we first discuss the conjunction of historical forces (within Britain and internationally) which led to the industrial development of Britain. Within this larger context we shall then locate the non-emergence of steel industry between 1880 and 1914 in Britain.

HISTORICAL DEVELOPMENTS WITHIN BRITAIN

We discussed in Part I that various power struggles between various sections of people created specific conditions within Britain, which led to the restructuring of classes, making of a national market, and a foreign policy that was completely subordinated to commercial interests. It was also noted that as commerce grew, London became the center of both commerce and finance. Even before industrialization, Britain was able to increase its revenue by modernizing and reforming its fiscal apparatus, which increased labor productivity and household income.

However, in creating economic prosperity in the country the role of the British government remained important. For example, England was able to start its wool industry only after seizing Calais from France during the conflicts over the inheritance of territorial possessions. Before the takeover of Calais, Britain, until the thirteenth and fourteenth centuries, was dependent on Europe for technological help and for exports of raw wool and cheap wool cloth to the Low Countries. Calais provided England with a connection to Flanders, a cluster of manufacturing towns. Thus, England was able to lay a foundation for its wool cloth manufacturing industry with the help of Flemish weavers who were brought into the country by Edward III. He centralized the trade in raw wool and banned the import of woolen cloth so that the local industry could develop. Thus, England became a formidable wool manufacturing nation by the time of the reign of Elizabeth I and Henry VII (Cheng, 2002). Similarly, when there arose a tussle between British industry and commerce—represented by the East India Company—the British government protected British manufacturers against Indian textile imports.

The role of British government further increased because after the English Civil War people began to expect that their government should maintain a stable society and also promote a systematic fostering of national wealth (Hobsbawm, 1968:227). Consequently, the British state started playing a more direct role in creating those conditions within which its economy could flourish. It introduced economic reforms that brought the separation of private and public funds as well as the systematic accounting for such funds, and the creation of salaried public servants. Since every part of England was within 70 miles of the sea and most regions were connected to navigable waterways, transportation and communication was cheap and easy. However, further improvements in transportation and rivers were made following Parliament's passage of the Petition of Right under Charles I, as coastal shipping had tripled between 1628–83 (Hobsbawm, 1968). The centralization of the infrastructure with an improved administrative network between major cities boosted the industrial economy. By the mid-seventeenth century, four-wheeled wagons were moving all over England. In 1750, land transportation was facilitated with the completion of a turnpike road system centered in London. The British government also supported technological innovations and the development of capital goods industries in order to raise more revenue.

Even though the pre-industrial British domestic market was not of a sufficient scale, it was steady and great in size, which not only allowed for economic growth, but also saved Britain during crisis, as it did in the 1780s, when war and the American Revolution disrupted exports. Most of all, the home market provided the broad foundation for a generalized industrial economy. As Hobsbawm wrote, "The domestic market may not have provided the spark, but it provided fuel and sufficient draught to keep it burning" (Hobsbawm, 1968:48).

The home market began to expand with increased urbanization which brought improvements to inland transportation and many technological innovations in the coal industry, as well as in the flour milling and beer brewing industries. All these improvements, in turn, enabled many small entrepreneurs and skilled traditional artisans to start their own industries, as it was economically easy to start a production establishment on a small-scale without having any specialized training in science. The only requirement for a small-scale entrepreneur was to have practical experience, ordinary literacy, familiarity with simple mechanical devises, and a knowledge of how to work with metals (Ibid., 51).

The home market also provided a major outlet for what later became capital goods, such as coal and iron. Coal grew almost entirely with the number of urban and especially metropolitan fire-places, but the iron industry did not grow as much because the demand was only in domestic pots, pans, nails, stoves, and in agriculture. Thus, the pre-industrial base of the coal industry was much sounder and its output was already being measured in millions of tons. In 1769, a hundred atmospheric engines (in coal mines) were working around Newcastle on Tyne, and fifty-seven were actually at work (Ibid., 47).

In addition to the development of a general industrial economy, England also made huge profits by monopolizing high technology industries, and by controlling the outflow of its core technologies (Chang, 2008:127). When other countries tried to recruit skilled British workers, Britain banned the migration of those workers for jobs abroad in practically all industries, including wool, steel, iron, brass, other metal and watch making industries (Ibid., 129). In 1750, when machines became more complex and more important, Britain first banned the export of tools and utensils related to the wool and silk industries, and later those of the cotton and linen industries. In 1785, the Tools Act was introduced to ban the export of many different types of machinery (Ibid., 130). But by the end of the century, with the development of science, disembodied knowledge increased and was difficult to protect (Ibid., 131), as it was easy to copy a written down idea. Thus, the concept of protecting ideas developed, and consequently the creation of patent laws, through which the flow of ideas across the continent were managed. Britain created a copyright law in 1709 and a trademark law in 1862. The idea of patent spread around the world, and eventually led to an international agreement on intellectual property rights. However, these laws and agreements did not end the use of "illegal" means to acquire technological knowledge [(8)].

All these developments in the British industrial economy, and the subsequent industrial revolution, were simultaneously connected with Britain's relationship with other countries and its foreign policy of aggressive colonization to capture overseas markets. For example, in 1813, after abolishing East India Company's monopoly over India, the British government began exporting a massive amount of Lancashire cotton to colonized India, which simultaneously stimulated the English industrial revolution, and deindustrialization of India.

HISTORICAL DEVELOPMENTS IN THE INTERNATIONAL ARENA

Britain's industrialization and its historical context is complex and multifaceted, but from the very beginning the global trade exchange was based on relations of imperialism (Washbrook, 1997). Even before its industrialization, Britain's rise to world power was deeply connected to its imperial relation with India as cotton had been imported from India in the century prior to Britain's industrialization. As Washbrook noted, this was part of the large-scale "transfer" of science and technology from the East to the West that occurred during later medieval times. For example, the British learned from India the techniques of weaving as well as the science of dyeing with 'indigo' blue. These manufacturing industries had received an earlier boost in 1721 when Robert Walpole, first Prime Minister of Britain, banned exports from colonies of those products that would compete with British products at home and abroad. The British state employed high tariffs and banned the import of superior products (such as Irish wool and Indian cotton products) from the colonies if those imports threatened British industry (Hobsbawm, 1968:45). Consequently, Britain was able to protect the British textile industry by killing the Irish wool industry and banning Indian cotton products. It also later protected the British iron and steel industries by stifling colonial America's development of its iron and steel industries by banning the construction of new rolling and slitting steel mill, refining of iron, and manufacture of finished articles from iron (Mathias, 1969:79). The British cotton industry developed and industrialized as foreign demand increased. Britain began to export to its colonies the greater part of its total output of cotton at the end of the eighteenth century. For example, until 1770 over ninety percent of British cotton exports went to colonial markets; mainly Africa. After the middle of the nineteenth century it found its staple outlet in India and the Far East.

Moreover, the massive British domestic economy was closely connected with the rapidly expanding international economy, which generated the industrial revolution. The international economy was expanding due to the simultaneous developments of a potentially expanding market in Europe for overseas products of everyday use, which were being produced in large quantities and cheaply with slave labor in colonies under an overseas economic system. This economic system was set up in a way that it served the interests and advantages of European owners (Hobsbawm, 1968).

In this expanding international economy, Britain was successful in cornering and protecting a major share of overseas international markets, which enabled it to expand and widen the flow of British commerce. Moreover, the British economy flourished under the British government's ruthless, and aggressive economic discrimination policies against all possible international rivals. Thus, British merchants were able to sell to British manufacturers; primarily tropical products produced in British colonies' slave plantations. By 1780, the characteristic imports from the tropics were consumer goods such as sugar, tea, coffee, tobacco and similar products, and from Eastern Europe it was wheat, linen, iron, hemp, and timber. Moreover, probably seven million slaves were transferred from Africa to the Americas during the eighteenth century. A large number of British industries—producing clothing, footwear, building and household furniture—continued to work in entirely traditional ways, except for the use of novel materials here and there. This pattern remained intact throughout the nineteenth century. Thus, resources from outside Europe contributed to commercial growth in various ways, which stimulated mechanization. For example, the growing demand for guns in the colonies shifted the gun-making industry from Germany to England where British workers had acquired skills in gun making in the late seventeenth century (Washbrook, 1997).

Wars also contributed in the promotion of Britain's technological innovations and industrialization as well as exports. For example, wars required huge amounts of iron to make cannons and the East India Company demanded a lot of them. With this lucrative prospect, Henry Cort, an iron producer, revolutionized iron manufacturing by using the method of puddling and rolling, to meet the Navy's needs. The demand for iron remained high due to the various wars Britain fought during the eighteenth century with France in the Spanish succession (1702–13), Austrian Succession (1739–48), the Seven Years War (1756–63), the American War of Independence (1776–83), and Revolutionary and Napoleonic Wars (1793–1815). No wonder, by the end of the Napoleonic wars, Britain's position became unassailable as the only industrial power and there was no competitor in the international arena.

After the Napoleonic Wars, other countries also began to industrialize, creating huge demands for iron. The innovations in iron production—smelting iron with coke, puddling and rolling—stimulated the coal industry, which invented the steam engine, and which, in turn, created railways. In spite of all this demand, iron and coal did not undergo its real industrial revolution until the middle decades of the nineteenth century, or about fifty years later than cotton. The production of coal and iron increased three-fold in twenty years, and essentially created the steel industry with the incoming age of the railway.

RAILWAYS AND CAPITAL GOODS INDUSTRIES

With its worldwide empire and no parallel competitor on the international arena, Britain entered a new phase of industrialization with the capital goods industry, which gave it a much firmer foundation for economic growth. However, capital goods like iron could not transform on an industrial level with regards to the domestic market because demand was mostly for agricultural items—ploughs and other implements, horse shoes, wheel rims and so on—and for domestic pots, pans, nails, and stoves. Whereas, coal had a solid foundation as the demand for it grew with increased urbanization and everyone needed fire-places. It was the coming of railway construction that provided a breakthrough to iron and coal. However, steam engines were needed in the coal fields so that inland coal fields could be linked to the coast (Hobsbawm, 1968:111). Experiments in the mines demonstrated the feasibility of a profitable railway system, and soon others from outside of the mining areas began copying this idea and further improved upon it for their own benefits.

In addition to the feasibility of a profitable railway system, there were two other reasons that investors became interested in the railways. One, as the rest of the world was industrializing, there was a rapidly increasing market for capital goods. However, these industrializing countries were not equipped to produce sufficient quantities of capital goods to meet their needs. Therefore, the possibility of exporting capital goods to these industrializing countries was an additional incentive for British investors. Domestically, there already existed a great capacity to absorb massive quantities of iron and coal in the railways and steamship.

The second reason for investment in railways had nothing to do with the growth of demand. It was not industry, but investors looking for new areas of profitable investment for their vast accumulation of capital who wanted railway construction prioritized as a major national project. They needed it because they had their fingers burnt by lending money to Britain's allies for wars and reestablishing continental governments (Hobsbawm, 1968:112). Thus, railway construction happened "by accident rather by design—an admirable solution to the crisis of the first phase of British capitalism" (Ibid., 114). The people who benefited the most were those whose profits were made not by running the railway but by planning or building them. This effort became the most expensive construction in the world. (A similar process took place in the US as the first Transcontinental railroad was created not because there was a demand for it, but to increase investment. In this venture, those who projected and planned this railroad made large sums of money) (White, 2011). Between 1830 and 1850 some six thousand miles of railways were opened in Britain, mostly as the result of two extraordinary bursts of concentrated investment followed by railway construction, the little 'railway mania' of 1835–37 and the gigantic one of 1845–57 (Hobsbawm, 1968:110). Thus, railways, besides being a transport system, became a new means of mobilizing capital accumulation of all kinds for industrial purposes. They also became a vast new source of employment as well as a huge and lasting stimulus to the capital goods industries (coal, iron, and steel) of Britain. Below, we shall focus only on the emergence and development of two capital goods industries—iron and steel.

IRON INDUSTRY

Initially the dynamic expansion of the British iron industry became possible when iron producing methods of "indirect processing" and Walloon forging techniques were transferred to Britain through migrants from France (Awty, 1981:536). These techniques were developed in France almost a century before and were introduced in England around 1500 by the first Francophone migrants (from Liège, Namur and Franchimont in the Walloon region of the Netherlands and Normandy). These techniques remained in use for two-and a-half centuries (Ibid., 530–531). Confirming this transfer of technology, Crossley and others suggest that this method could not have developed from within England as "there is nothing to indicate that indirect reduction was anticipated by native iron workers" (Crossley, 1981; Bjorkenstam, 1995; quoted in Evans and Ryden, 2005:16).

Henry VII's constant wars with Scotland and France gave a boost to the iron industry and investment in it was increased (Hobsbawm, 39). He not only created a market for iron wares through his wars, but also made serious efforts to recruit increasing numbers of skilled iron workers from France. Many French speaking men from France were hired during the time of Henry VIII at the Wealden Iron Works in Sussex primarily to develop high quality iron smelting for the making of armaments (Parthasarathi, 2011). With the availability of a sizeable secure market and a supply of skilled labor, Britain's political and commercial interests began to collaborate to invest in the iron industry. These investors were banking on the idea, as Hobsbawm pointed out, that customers at home and abroad would accept their products as common people had not developed finer tastes yet (Hobsbawm,1968:62). It was not too costly to start an industry at that time, and no technological breakthroughs or individual inventive genius was required. The more important skill required was how workers could solve a practical situation at the workplace (Ibid., 60). As related industries started emerging, the iron industry became more important to both foreign and domestic markets.

Thus, England's industrial base and iron industry expanded where new industrial techniques could be tested and skilled workers like the Huguenots could also be absorbed (Awty, 1981). However, the non-ferrous metal industry was organized similarly to that of the textile industry (Burt:269), whereas extractive and mineral processing industries remained a small production unit. The output was increased not by creating large units of production but by having a larger number of small units (Clay, 1984; cited in Burt, 1991:268). Even though the knowledge of different techniques was continuously being disseminated, changes in these industries were introduced slowly and thoughtfully as a small-scale improvement, and not as claimed, "revolutionary forces introduced by heroic inventors or visitors" (Ibid.). For example, the steam engine (used for pumping water out of mines came into being long before James Watt's refined steam engine in 1781) was a product of its creator's involvement with mining industry and it made its way to the mines very slowly. By 1769, "atmospheric engines" were being built in Newcastle upon Tyne, and 57 of them were working. Later, railways were invented by developing and employing the improved versions of the steam engine for winding gear (Hobsbawm,1968:47), which created a big market for the iron industry.

Even before the coming of the railways, the demand for iron increased due to the choices and actions of iron masters. They began to use coke and the steam engine in iron making, and the iron masters in the Midlands, South Wales, and Scotland started to tap into their coal mines (Carr and Taplin, 1962:1). The ironmasters of South Wales were among the first to build ironworks utilizing coke smelting and puddling in the 1790s (Hyde, 1977) because they could sell their rapidly growing output to other regions due to the development of the canal network, which was initiated by local landed gentry to widen the market for their agricultural products and minerals. These developments created further demand for new machinery, which required more iron works. Thus, the structural changes in the iron market affected the course of technical change. For example, to meet this growing demand, by the end of the eighteenth century the iron works industry became highly capital intensive creating integrated units of production with a large labor force. This integrated system was connected with the iron master's own ore and coal supplies, as well as with the process of smelting, refining, rolling, and slitting the iron into its finished form of bars, plates and sheets, or into finished casting ranging from domestic pots and pans to cannons and machinery. By the first decade of the nineteenth century, Carron and Walsh works of Dowlais and Cyfarthfa in Wales were employing more than 2000 workers (Ibid., 2).

The iron industry also got a boost (starting in 1830 and peaking during 1845–1847) from the development of the steamship and the industrial economy, and flourished with the inauguration of the railways. Domestic demand for iron increased not only for machines and tools, but also for bridges, pipes, building material and domestic utensils (Hobsbawm, 1968:70). The iron industry acquired an important export market after the Napoleonic Wars when other countries began to industrialize. The major stimulus for the export of capital goods came from railway construction abroad, which continued until the 1880s (Ibid., 114). Moreover, Britain was able to provide its economy abundant supplies of iron and steel by getting more raw material from new markets in China and Japan, which Britain acquired with gun boat diplomacy and war flotilla (Ibid., 115).

The national market for the iron industry further increased with lower transportation costs after the growth and expansion of the railway network in the 1830s and the rapid growth of the Scottish iron industry. These developments encouraged innovative iron masters to expand output, which in turn increased the competitive pressures on other ironmasters to innovate also. However, there were significantly different levels of productivity and costs associated with each production technique, which created vigorous price competition among ironmasters. It should be pointed out that innovations in Britain were not made by any particularly trained technicians. Rather, there was a cluster of interdependent innovations that developed over time by various untutored working technicians (Ibid., 193; see also Mokyr, 2009). Iron-making technology advanced through a process of gradual continuous change rather than through a series of sharp discrete innovations [(9)]. However, whether inventions in iron making technique were developed by sheer chance or by individual efforts, their application diffusion was determined by market forces—that is, whether it was profitable or not.

For example, as Hyde pointed out, most of these innovations were adopted during the years of rapid economic expansion between 1775 and 1815 [(10)]. But the increased demand for iron, which kept prices high, helped in producing huge profit margins from the early innovations, thus slowing the diffusion of new technology. Iron masters made higher profits by utilizing outdated methods, and not by investing in new techniques because it would require new equipment and new sites. In fact, after 1815, iron masters adopted new methods under opposite conditions when prices declined between 1815 and 1870 with the rapid production of iron. Railways generated temporary high prices, but the cycle of boom and bust and the post-Napoleonic depression imposed a long-run decline in both prices and profits. The iron masters adopted the hot-blast method between 1835 and 1845 in order to stabilize falling profits rather than seeking a windfall in an attempt to ensure survival in a competitive industry. Moreover, as Hyde pointed out, the risk of adopting new innovations were small as it did not require much capital investment because most innovations could be installed relatively easily in an existing structure on a limited basis at a low cost.

However, the long-term accumulated effect of all innovations was a radical change in both the smelting and refining sectors. The iron making techniques that British ironmasters adopted in the eighteenth and early nineteenth centuries radically altered production costs and Britain's position in world markets. Britain had achieved cost parity by the early nineteenth century and by the early 1870s was exporting nearly half of its total output, which had increased roughly 250-fold since the mid-eighteenth century. Actually, Britain survived international competition and the depression through its export of iron and steel to its colonies (India and Australia), as the British iron and steel industries relied on its overseas markets and its colonies for forty percent of its production beginning in the mid-nineteenth century (Hyde, 1977:204).

STEEL INDUSTRY

In addition to iron-making, the steel-making industry was developing during the mid-eighteenth century on a small-scale. It was localized mainly in the South Yorkshire town of Sheffield. The cutlery of Sheffield was already very popular by the Tudor times (Carr and Taplin, 1962:3). Tinplate was also made in this town. Sheffield was the main center of British steelmaking producing crucible steel and its products: local blister, shear bars and cutler's scrap. Over time, the region increased its use of high-quality imported Swedish iron in larger quantities (Ibid., 4), and Sheffield monopolized the entire British steel-making industry. However, during the post-Napoleonic depression after the war, the country's steel production dropped by 50 percent. The growth of the industry picked up again in the 1830s and 1840s when Josiah Marshall Heath found a way to produce a superior quality crucible steel that could be welded by adding manganese to common-grade Swedish and Russian iron. This new method reduced the price in the Sheffield market by 30 to 40 percent (Ibid., 11). However, the new steel represented only a small part of Britain's iron and steel production until 1875 (Ibid., 94).

Carr and Taplin noted that three connected, but distinct, steel industries existed in Sheffield by 1875 (Ibid., 131). Crucible steelmaking, linked with the production of tools and cutlery, was the oldest one. Crucible steelmaking not only flourished but enlarged in scope to include the manufacture of guns, projectiles, and large steel castings and forgings. The heavy wrought iron industry specialized in naval armor and also produced ordinary strip and boiler plates. The newest method, the Bessemer process (invented in 1856), was useful in the mass production of steel that was used for making rails and railway springs, buffers, tires, wheels and axels and other related products.

The transport revolution of railways and the steamship created the major markets for British iron, steel, and coal exports. This stimulated not only new markets but also expanded old ones (Hobsbawm, 1968). Steel was increasingly being used instead of iron during the next two decades because it had a more consistent quality and was becoming less expensive. Thus, the increase in the demand for steel was directly connected with the expansion of the coal industry, the coming of steam engines, and the widening transport system. The expansion of coal in turn was due to the expansion of railways, as it trebled the production of the coal and iron that virtually created the steel industry. The increased demand for mass-produced steel also required new innovations. The first such innovation came about in 1856 with the development of the Bessemer converter, the next in the 1860s with the open-hearth furnace, and by the late 1870s the basic-process came into being. the economy stagnated in the Great Depression of 1873–1896. However, when open-hearth steelmaking came about in the 1880s, the Bessemer steel industry found it hard to compete and by 1896, wrought iron production was declining everywhere (Ibid.).

Britain maintained its free trade policy and did not create a steel cartel or a trust or a large-scale steel industry using these new innovations. Meanwhile, the US and Germany had begun surpassing Britain in the production of steel between 1890 and 1895. With the rise of production in those two countries, Britain had lost its monopoly in the "underdeveloped" world. Subsequently, it became necessary to formally mark out regions of imperial influence against these potential competitors. Thus, Britain was able to ride the crisis by conquering unexploited areas of the world and through the partition of Africa in the 1880s.

It is noteworthy that British steel manufacturers made multiple innovations for the mass production of steel, but they did not apply many of these innovations within Britain, or they did it very slowly. Instead, it was the US and Germany that benefitted the most from British innovation in the steel industry. Why did British steel manufacturers make such choices? Why did they remain as small-scale family businesses, and not create a large-scale steel industry or cartels? These questions are explored in the following section.

REASONS FOR THE NON-EMERGENCE OF LARGE-SCALE STEEL INDUSTRY

In the late nineteenth century, iron and steel industry in the world was transformed from the earlier small-scale competitive structure to predominantly large-scale organizations. The transition to the mass production of steel became possible with the introduction of the Bessemer process, which was developed in England. Once established, mass production could not be reversed even when the importance of rail production declined. Interestingly, even though Britain had introduced three different inventions for the mass production of steel, it did not adopt them fully. One of the many reasons for this non-adoption was that Bessemer process required an iron ore that had an exceedingly low phosphorus content, which was not available in England. Only Spain and the US possessed large supplies of non-phosphoric iron ores. The other reasons for the non-adoption of large-scale organization in steel included the following: the larger historical context of the time, the structure of the British steel industry, the individual choices and actions of British steel manufacturers, the role of labor union and class struggle, the role of the judiciary in industrial relations, the social, economic and cultural constraints of the time, and the availability of colonial markets.

As discussed earlier, Britain had a highly developed iron industry. However, wrought iron producers switched to steel production when the overall rate of demand growth in wrought iron slowed down. Many large iron producers built small open-hearth furnaces to produce steel for finishing in the existing rolling mills, while others turned to re-rolling, using mostly imported semi-finished steel (Elbaum and Wilkinson, 1979). These choices and actions of British iron producers further reinforced the traditional industrial structure in Britain, which in turn reduced any incentive for introducing new techniques in the production of steel (Ibid.). One British expert explains this situation in *Indian Engineering* as follows:

> We hear much about the non-adaptability of English manufacturers, that they refuse to undertake work which is a little outside their line, which work the Americans jump at; and that John Bull's prices compared with Jonathan's are prohibitive. But this is purely the result of a great stress of work when a man has his shops full of work of the kind for which they were built, and for which his machines are specially designed; and when, as far as he can see, orders of that kind are likely to continue flowing in, it is hardly likely that he will stop, and not only alter his machines but teach his workmen new ways, in order merely to keep work in the country. And not only that, but plenty of work for all means high prices; and the manufacturer is hardly likely to take in work at a low price which will "crowd out" work he is doing for a better profit. Nay, even if his hands are not quite full, but if he sees a prospect of getting work of his own kind and price at a near date, he will hesitate to fill his shops with cheap and new work (*Indian Engineering,* April 20, 1901:253).

British industries in general remained largely comprised of highly specialized firms that were of a medium size (except for the copper industry, which was organized on a large-scale with the help of the government, but failed and collapsed), highly localized, often specialized even within their branch, and linked with each other by a complex set of individual business transactions in the market (Hobsbawm, 1968). According to Payne, this was due partly to the pride of British industrialist in being self-sufficient and their ability to utilize the methods of market control (Payne, 1967). In the context of a well-established industrial structure it was hard to make any changes. For example, when an opportunity for massive growth presented itself, British manufacturers did not make any changes in the industrial structure, instead they increased their product differentiation. They were able to exploit marginal differences in quality by increasing specialization while exaggerating differences. British manufacturers made this choice because they had already invested in the specialization of their product, which involved special mercantile relationships, a highly skilled labor force, and the evolution of particular types of managerial talent. All of these features could not be achieved easily nor were they easily reversible as they were expensive. Moreover, as Payne pointed out, the British were especially reluctant to raise new capital (that required a new procedure), which would have weakened their control over their family firms. They were able to meet product demand without borrowing from the domestic market, as they could rely on their own accumulated sources of capital (Ibid.). Thus, British manufacturers tried to insulate themselves from the pricing policies of their rivals. At the same time, with an increased degree of product differentiation, they were able to create monopolistic position for themselves, which made higher profit margins possible. These tendencies strengthened after 1850 with the spread of overseas market because there was a demand for articles made to detailed local specifications (Ibid). Thus, British firms were able to successfully resist the formation of any combination (cartels).

Before 1905, big firm combination was rare in Britain. However, even when such amalgamations were formed the terms were set in such a way that the individuality of the participant firm was largely maintained (Payne, 1967:532). It was only in the production of warships and armaments that the largest vertical combination was formed, as manufacturing of these complex products required that a many-sided firm be formed to handle various mechanisms and processes. However, even in this vertical combination, management was loosely centralized and organizational changes were also very slow to come about. Manufacturers' resistance to cartel formation was echoed in the British judiciary as it was also against any formation of pools or cartel, or any loosely knit associations from becoming more permanent organizations. This was specifically discouraged in the iron and steel industry.

Thus, in absence of a cartel in steel, the British steel industry remained trapped in the market of small-scale family firms and they were unable to benefit from the invention of the Bessemer process for mass production. This was noted by Lord Hamilton, Secretary of State for India. He wrote to the Viceroy of India:

> In America the great mass of the railway companies brought their locomotive engines from the outside trade and thus there is enormous plant laid down and in working order for the production of locomotives; which enables its owners to tender for the supply of engines in any part of the world. All the engines in America are more or less of a standard pattern, and their parts are interchangeable, and this enables these great firms, when business is slack, to employ a certain number of men in making certain parts of engines which they can utilize fully when trade becomes brisk. Here, (in Britain) an entirely different system prevails. Nearly all the great companies make their own locomotives, and each company has a pattern for locomotives, which is according to the fancy and idea of the Locomotive superintendent for the time being. The outside firms, therefore, who make locomotives, are very much less powerful, and have less capital behind them than those which exist in America, and therefore, it is clear to me that, if time being a consideration, it is to be one of the factors taken into account (that) when tenders are invited, the American engineering trade must beat ours in point of delivery [(11)].

Moreover, in absence of large cartels or trusts, no one could compel the small-scale steel industry to improve its production methods, increase its productive capacity, or control its prices. In this regard Lord Hamilton, Secretary of State for India, noted:

> There is an inevitable objection in this country (Britain) amongst manufacturers and producers of all kinds to combine. They all like working according to their own ideas and their own particular plans, and according to their own particular methods, and it is here whereas the American, who is quite as independent in his character and action as the Englishman, beats us. They have brought to a fine art the power of combinations although it looks as if the millionaires had somewhat over reached themselves in the gigantic steel trusts they have created [(12)].

The reasons for the lack of cartel formation in Britain, as pointed out by Friedman, were the following: Alternative restrictive practices were still available to British firms, British mergers did not survive long as these were a collective of several firms without much inter-firm coordination as no one firm clearly dominated the merger, British mergers were limited as British industrialists were able to turn to exports to underdeveloped countries, and British financial interests were able to invest in foreign countries and continue to make good profit (Friedman, 1977:38).

In this context, it is not surprising that despite Britain's specialization in open-hearth steel making, the scale of operation in this process also lagged behind that of the US. In 1890, the average size of furnaces in Britain was 10 tons, one-third the average size in the US, and by 1900 US furnaces were four times as productive as their British counterparts (Elbaum and Wilkinson, 1987).

The slow rate of increase in output and the continued existence of small producers further hampered the prospects of any large-scale steel industry. "Many of these producers were family firms operating on narrow margins who were unwilling to scrap obsolete capacity while it remained intermittently profitable" (*Indian Engineering*, April 20, 1901:253). Moreover, there was a shift in the composition of foreign trade as it increasingly moved away from industry to service income and employment [(13)]. Manufacturing exports grew much more slowly after 1870 than before, and Britain's share of visible world trade fell. Invisible trade, on the other hand, increased rapidly until 1914. According to Hopkins, there is no single causal relationship between the increased propensity to export capital and the loss of industrial dynamism (Hopkins). Hopkins and Cains suggest:

> While the perpetuation of the small firm in manufacturing may have been a rational response to the conditions prevailing in that sector, it was politically inefficient because atomistic units had difficulty combining, even in their own interests, and were plagued by the problem of free riders. Growing concentration in finance and distribution, on the other hand, was not only a rational response to the opportunities created by the expansion of this sector, but was also politically efficient because the relatively small number of banking dynasties and their associates could unite more easily to promote their interests (Hopkins and Cains, 1987:4–5).

Another problem was that Britain's industrialization had proceeded without any substantial utilization of banking for long-term investment purposes. "The more gradual character of the industrialization process and the more considerable accumulation of capital, first from earnings in trade and modernized agriculture, and later from industry itself, obviated the pressure for developing any special institutional devices for provision of long-term capital to industry" (Ibid.). This nature of relations between banking and industry in Britain was detrimental to the development of its steel industry.

In addition, the British steel industry did not invest in large-scale production techniques because the market for wrought iron was already unstable and was leading to wide price fluctuations (Mitchel and Deane, 1962). Moreover, British manufacturers were unable to control prices through their regional associations when the number of firms and producing regions increased. During economic recession, this inability to control prices became even more problematic, as the inter-regional dumping increased. Faced with this situation, the manufacturers became more concerned with scrambling for declining orders and also selling below full cost. They further lost their control of the market as they began to depend on intermediaries (those providing market outlets for the output of small firms and imported steel) for selling their product (Carr and Taplin, 1962:293; Burnham and Hoskins, 1942:211; Burn, 1940:278, cited in Elbaum and Wilkinson, 1979). All these factors not only reduced producer control of the market, but also hindered the formation of steel cartels in Britain.

Interestingly, Britain's "free trade" policy, which was closely linked to its service economy and small-firm industrial structure, was reinforced by the emergence of strong trade unions in the steel industry and the development of collective bargaining in wages and prices. This further hindered the formation of steel cartels in Britain.

Holt (1977) has pointed out that in Britain, the earlier industrial relations in the iron industry changed when it became involved in steel. The system of bargaining, that developed in Britain in 1889, virtually eliminated strikes and lockouts laying the foundation for industrial peace (Elbaum and Wilkinson, 1979). These peaceful industrial relations became possible because the British iron and steel industry achieved limited growth, and in the absence of any cartels steel manufacturers had no control over prices. Each manufacturer depended on the support of his workers to fix a price (linking wages and prices), which gave British workers more bargaining power. Both British employers and workers agreed with this arrangement, as workers would not face competitive wage cutting during the recession, and manufacturers would not face costly stoppages. Thus, labor unionism in Britain while surviving the industrial change from iron to steel, also broadened its base to include less-skilled workers (Pugh, 1951 quoted in Ibid.).

Moreover, unions in the British iron and steel industry did not resist the introduction of new methods (Elbaum and Wilkinson, 1979), as they expected some share in the benefits of technical improvements. For example, the unions were successful at resisting widespread rate reductions if there was a substantial increase in productivity. The unions were also successful at maintaining control over the labor process in the British steel industry, and Taylor's theory of scientific management made little or no impact in Britain (Gintz, 1954 quoted in Ibid.). Moreover, in Britain the rules and procedures for resolving local disputes made it very difficult for the employer to change tonnage rates. These rules and procedures were the result of determined fights of British trade unions in the last quarter of the nineteenth century for the right to exist on both industrial and political fronts. Through many such battles, British trade unions gained acceptance as a legitimate institution and also acquired strength. Faced with the strength of the unions, British employers did not adopt stronger anti-union policies as they themselves lacked confidence in their own resources (Elbaum and Wilkinson, 1979).

In England, the division between work and politics was not sharply drawn because the Labor party and its trade union allies tried explicitly to infuse British politics with workplace concerns. Moreover, after 1875, the English courts, while deferring to Parliament's authority, stopped connecting workers with conspiracy and began narrowing interpretations of power against the use of violence and intimidation (Hatam, 1992). However, this division of political power between Parliament and the judiciary was itself a legacy of past political struggles and negotiations at the end of the English Civil War (Chibber, 2013:148).

Moreover, as Hobsbawm noted (1968:184), there is some truth in the suggestion that the British felt they had manifested already, as now sons of grocers and cotton spinners were joining the aristocracy. When a person achieved the status of "gentleman" or aristocrat, that person ceased to strive further as he lacked the entrepreneurial urge to maintain a constant rate of technical progress for its own sake. Moreover, the small family firms, the characteristic type of enterprise, were fairly effectively insulated against excessive growth, which would have posed a risk of the loss of family control. Consequently, each generation became less enterprising and individuals felt no need to be entrepreneurs (Ibid., 183). This idea was reinforced further as the risk of loss through bankruptcy was decreasing, which freed British businessmen from "the specter of sudden impoverishment and social ostracism." Consequently, British did not feel the need to work too much (Ibid., 185).

In addition, British industry, though remaining an industrial power for a long time, lost its dynamism early on as private enterprises were difficult to modernize. This lack of dynamism did not affect these small family firms, which were able to maintain satisfactory profits with their old ways. Small family firms in Britain, and specifically in the iron and steel industries, were not concerned with either the larger economy or global competition. For example, as Hobsbawm pointed out, British iron masters were slow to adopt the Gilchrist-Thomas "basic" process for extracting phosphorus from veins of local iron ore, because they could import non-phosphoric ores easily and cheaply. Moreover, they were concerned that a great deal of capital sunk in their plants for the production of acid steel would lose its value (Ibid.). Thus, the British steel industry remained largely tied up with an obsolete technology. The railways and the coal industries were not modernized until 1947 (when they were nationalized) because any decision to modernize required a joint decision of both, and they could never agree (Ibid., 190). As mentioned earlier, there were no cartels in Britain that could pressure industries to modernize. The reasons for this resistance to modernization were that the traditional methods of making a profit were not yet exhausted and that small family-owned British firms could still make a profit in cheaper and more convenient ways (discussed above).

Moreover, the British iron and steel industry relied on the British Empire and the "underdeveloped" world, as did the cotton industry, because Britain had gained the historic advantages of being a strong commercial power, which made it the greatest source of international loan capital. Britain also had acquired immense power to protect its home market, and it used this power to sell its products around its own large Empire. For example, Argentina and India alone bought more British iron and steel exports in 1913 than did the whole of Europe. Similarly, Australia alone bought double the volume of iron and steel than the US. In addition, the steel industry—like the coal industry—tended to rely increasingly on the protection of the home market. Thus, Britain was becoming a parasite rather than a competitive economy, living off the remains of a world monopoly, the "underdeveloped" world, and its own past accumulation of wealth. Under these conditions, as Hobsbawm pointed out, the rich also became increasingly complacent (Ibid., 193).

In addition, British capitalists found the tasks of modernization and integration of British industry much more difficult than making profits through foreign investments and exports to semi-protected regions. Britain's annual investment abroad actually began to exceed its net capital formation at home around the 1870s (Hobsbawm, 1968:192). Until the middle of nineteenth century, "free trade" was the symbol of British industrial capitalism, whose world superiority was so strong as to dominate the markets without a need for artificial aid. The tariff was defended as only a temporary measure for the protection of a young and weak industry. However, with growing world competition, the tariff became the most important weapon of advanced capitalist countries. This process of protectionism started with Germany's tariff of 1879 (engineered by Bismarck), and was followed by French tariffs from 1883–1892, and US tariffs in 1883, 1890, 1897, and 1907. The question of tariffs and trade in the steel industry was tied to the rise of "trusts." Due to its unique industrial structure and so-called "gentlemanly capitalism," Britain followed more free trade procedures ("modified free trade" as discussed by Bhattacharya and others) (Bhattacharya, 1965:47) and extended its Empire to keep up profits in finance and trade. In turn, the US and Germany relied on tariffs, first to increase production and then to compete with Britain (Yeager, 1980). "This mode of protection when dealing with international markets was in contrast to that of the previous period ... This period of negotiated exchange agreements changed the previous period's private inverse-protective mode into a public mode of mutual, reciprocal protection" (Ibid., 48).

In the last quarter of the nineteenth century, the effectiveness of protection depended on the ability of a country to maintain international agreements on steel production and exports, which in turn depended on the cohesiveness of the country's national financial groups. According to Elbaum and Wilkinson (1979), Britain could not provide that cohesiveness to its own steel industry (run by small family firms), whereas the US and Germany could. Britain tried to overcome its weaknesses in world competition by increasing its reliance on its colonies for profits and trade relations. These strategies kept the British steel industry within its "old" small-scale production mode, which remained under the control of family firms. Thus, British steel industry remained vulnerable and it continued to maintain small, inefficient and technically backward plants.

EMERGENCE OF THE LARGE-SCALE STEEL INDUSTRY IN THE 1930S

It was not until the 1930s that Britain tried to create a large-scale steel industry when a steel cartel was created with the help of banks and a government mandate. This process began after World War I with the collapse of the 1921 boom when many banks began to lend money on a large scale to heavy industry, especially steel, for expansion and possible amalgamations. "The banks then used this position–debenture stock—in cooperation with the leading groups of steel owners to cartelize the steel industry so as to improve its profitability. Thus, arose the Iron and Steel Federation in 1932" (Aatonovitch, 1955:51–52).

For a short time, the British steel industry continued to expand after World War I with loans from the banks. The slump that followed the short-lived boom after the war made it urgent that the steel industry should begin it's internal reorganization and rationalization (McEachron, 1980:48). The initiative came from the Bank of England as it prepared plans for reconstruction in the steel industry and attempted to rationalize its structure. In 1916, a protectionist committee chaired by G. Scoby-Smith, was set up by Lord Balfour and Iron and Steel Trades for conducting a general investigation into the reconstruction of the steel industry. The committee was not opposed to accepting formal assistance, but it did not want the government interfering with the plants or organization of the industry (Ibid., 19). Consequently, it underestimated the necessary contribution of both the government and the Bank of England (Ibid., 47). However, these changes were short-lived and did not strengthen the internal organization of the industry.

Again, in 1932, the British steel industry was granted a large measure of tariff protection, but those steel firms which relied on the import of semi-finished production were in favor of free trade and not protection. As the slump deepened, the demand for tariff protection increased and the disastrous state of the industry convinced the government that it would have to grant a tariff. The import duties advisory committee recommended that government could use protectionism to pressure the steel industry to make necessary structural changes and increase technical efficiency. The British government enacted the formation of the British Iron and Steel Federation (BISF) and the Import Duties Advisory Committee (IDAC) to help construct agreements with international steel cartels (Ibid., 51). However, these did not produce a cohesive and industry wide plan as they relied on the initiative and veto of individual firms. The Bank of England became involved, and gradually the board brought in those members who conformed to the Federation's objectives (Ibid., 52).

While the British government and banks were devising various schemes for the future of the steel industry, the steel workers were also determining what their position would be. These contrasting positions, which were developing in the 1930s, led to the conflict over the ownership and control of the steel industry (Ibid., 59). However, the Bank of England did try to impose a comprehensive plan for the development of the steel industry and it had a measure of success in consolidating the financial and firm structure of the industry through a series of sponsored amalgamations. In the long run, the Bank initiative was unsuccessful, largely because it lacked adequate machinery for determining and implementing the collective policies of the elite class. As McEachron pointed out, the Bank's overriding perspective was financial prosperity, which limited the kinds of changes it could encourage (Ibid., 62).

The steel industry remained a problem both for capital as a whole and for the banks in three ways. First, steel was a basic industry supplying essential raw materials to the manufacturing sector upon which the health of the capitalist economy depended. Second, the level of unemployment in the industry was high. It should be noted that although the Bank of England was prompted to act due to the unemployment situation, it ignored the consequences of its action plans on unemployment. In fact, many of its proposed schemes would have further increased unemployment. Third, the un-rationalized structure of the steel industry was a serious drain on limited financial resources (McEachern, 1980). Consequently, it remained difficult for the British steel industry to modernize for a very long time.

SUMMATION PART II

By using a yardstick of parity we showed that similar to the other three societies discussed in this volume, the non-emergence of a large-scale steel industry in England was due to the conjunction and confluence of various historical forces developing within England, as well as internationally. These simultaneous complex international historical processes were the outcome of interactions between England and other societies, and thus, they became as much a specific history of England as that of its intertwined relationships with larger international forces (Chapter 3) and other societies of that time. This approach to understand England's 'Industrial Revolution' is important because it was a slow process spanning three centuries, and during these centuries various historical developments took place within Britain and in the international arena, which also formed it. In Part II, we elaborated on the interaction of these historical forces to understand England's industrialization. Within this larger context we then located the specific development of British iron and steel industries and highlighted the reasons for the continuation of the family owned, medium-scale steel industry until the mid-twentieth century. It is pointed out, in addition to other historical processes, that the British government played an important part in creating conditions for England's industrialization with its naval strength, aggressive colonization and capturing overseas markets, tariff, improved infrastructure including railways, protection of overseas commerce and trade, recruiting skilled iron workers from other countries, controlling the outflow of industrial technology, banning the migration of skilled workers, and patent laws.

However, it was the railways that boosted the capital goods industry such as coal and iron and actually created the market for steel. Nevertheless, the coming of the British railways had nothing to do with the real need for transportation because most of the country was within easy access of water transport by sea, river, or canal and that was cheaper for moving bulk goods. It was investors who really needed railway construction as a national program, as they were looking for profitable investment for their vast accumulated capital. Thus, railway construction, which created a huge market for the steel industry, happened "by accident rather by design" (Hobsbawm, 1968:114). However, the second phase of the Industrial Revolution did take off from this 'happy accident.'

It is also pointed out that even though three different methods to mass produce steel was invented in England, steel producers did not fully apply them, as Britain did not have non-phosphoric iron ore necessary for these methods. Nonetheless, British steel producers had no problem selling their products profitably because they could rely on Britain's safe colonial markets. They also did not modernize their mills as they could easily make sufficient profits from selling their specialized products. Moreover, the unions controlled the labor process in the British steel industry, as Taylor's scientific management did not make an impact in Britain, and the rules and procedures for resolving local disputes were too complicated for the employer to change tonnage rates. Therefore, British steel industry did not create any cartels and remained highly specialized family owned medium-scale industry until much later in the twentieth century.

CHAPTER SUMMARY

In this chapter, using a yardstick of parity, we try to show that the making of England was no different than that of the other three chosen countries for this volume, as it was created and constructed through the interaction of people within Britain and Britain's interaction with other societies and with larger international historical forces. Various social actors also made choices in this process of interaction that included in addition to common people, the ruling elite, landed elite, merchant elites, and the 'gentlemanly classes'. This statement is explained not by categorizing Britain as either developed or underdeveloped, but by focusing on it's universal and specific characteristics (as we did for the other societies). Furthermore, the yardstick of parity is used to explain Britain's industrialization and the non-emergence of the large-scale steel industry in Britain between 1880 and 1914. This is demonstrated by showing how the conjunction and combination of historical forces developing within Britain and in the international arena created conditions for the non-emergence of large-scale steel industry in Britain. In Part I, we traced the various historical processes that were taking place within England and internationally over time. The international historical processes show that England was part of a wider "world economy of the European maritime states," which was a network of economic relationships with a "system of economic flows—of trade, of international payments, of capital transfers of migration" (Hobsbawm, 1968:35). It is emphasized that the British government played an important role in creating conditions for the promotion of trade, commerce, and industrialization with improved infrastructure (roads, canals, railways), controlling the outflow of technology, banning the migration of skilled workers, tariffs, and a strong Royal Navy to protect overseas commerce and control colonies.

We tried to show that Britain, which was considered to be a "developed" country during the span of 1880–1914, could not develop the large-scale steel industry that was claimed to be the basis for "development" of a country during this time period. However, when a large-scale steel industry did emerge in Britain during the middle of the twentieth century, it occurred only with the initiative of the government and its banks—creating steel cartels and forcing the modernization of the British steel industry. It did not occur due to internal dynamics of free market, nor was it a product of dynamic entrepreneurship, as generally claimed. This information and other details discussed in this chapter suggest that there was no inherent advanced position with England or "natural genius" of British people from which it emerged as "the first industrial nation."

It is suggested in this chapter that it is possible to understand the making of England and its industrialization, including the making of its medium-scale steel industry, with the same yardstick of parity as is used for other societies, and not by categorizing it as developed or underdeveloped.

ENDNOTES

1. Mokyr, 2009. He quoted Daniel Defoe [1726–27], 2001, p. 162. "A General History of Discovery of and Improvement." Reprinted. In W. R. Owens and P. N. Furbank, (Eds.), *Writing on Travel, Discovery, and History by Daniel Defoe.* London: Pickering and Chatto.
2. *Doomsday Book.* Housed in The National Archives in Kew, London. This book was commissioned in December 1085 by William the Conqueror—who invaded England in 1086. It contains records of 12,418 settlements in English counties south of the Ribble and Tees Rivers. Doomsdaybook.co.uk.
3. Mukherjee, 1974. p. 13. He is quoting from Charles Gross (1890), *The Gild Merchants.* Oxford: Clarendon Press. Vol. I. p. 93.
   Mokyr, J. op. cit. p. 71. Mokyr quoting from Thomas Hodgskin, "all technical innovation emanated from working class ingenuity, and that if the laborers could only acquire such knowledge as the middle class possessed, they would no longer need the masters." Hodgskin, T. (1825). *Labour Defended Against the Claims of Capital.* 2nd ed. London: Knight and Lacey.
4. Discussion based on Mukherjee, 1974.
5. Mukherjee, 1974. pp. 4–5.
   The following is the information about how usury became acceptable to the Christians.

Usury was reinterpreted for the benefit of the merchant capital because in the middle ages lending money at interest was forbidden to the Christians. The serious shortage of the precious metal coins that were the official medium of exchange, created a need to expand the money supply with loans on credit. To meet this important need, an exception was made to the proscription against usury for the Jews, whose Scriptures forbade usury only to "brothers" (meaning other Jews). This gave them a virtual monopoly on lending [to the Christians], however, allowing them to charge excessively high rates because there were no competitors. Interest sometime went as high as 60 percent. These rates were particularly devastating to the poor. To remedy the situation Franciscan monks, defying the prohibitions of the Dominicans and Augustinians, formed charitable pawnshops called *monte pietatus* (non-speculative collections of funds). These shops lent at low or no interest on the security of valuable left with the institutions. Unfortunately, it went broke in the process and it eventually had to close. Franciscan monks then established *montes pietatus* in Italy that lent at low rates of interest. They did not seek to make a profit on their loans. But they faced bitter opposition not only from their banking competitors but from other theologians. It was not until 1515 that the *montes* were officially declared to be meritorious. After that, they spread rapidly in Italy and other European countries. They soon evolved into banks, which were public in nature and served public and charitable purposes. This public bank tradition became the modern European tradition of public, cooperative and saving banks. (www.bankofengland.co.uk/publicaitons/Documents/quarterlybulletin/2014qb14q1prereleasemoneycreaton.pdf Quoted in alternet.org/economy/revolutionary-pope-calls-rethniking-outdated-thinking-rules-world. Viewed 7/14/15).

6. Gorski, P. (2003). *Disciplinary Revolution: Calvinism and the Rise of the State in Early Modern Europe*. Chicago University Press. Quoted in Lachmann (2013). op. cit. p. 77.
7. Discussion based on Hopkins and Cains, 1987.
8. Ha Joon Chang (2008) has pointed out that in the nineteenth century, copyrights were routinely violated as people started patenting borrowed ideas from other countries [it is similar to the acts of American corporations who are trying to patent India's herbs and trees along with Ayurvedic medicines, as if these are "new inventions" of American corporations] as well as by extensive counterfeiting of trademarks. The United States, a net importer of copyright materials, only protected American authors and refused to protect foreigners' copyright agreement of 1891. Moreover, for another century (until 1988), the United States did not recognize copyright on materials that were printed outside of the US (133).

   Many other countries also grew rapidly by using protective barriers. Those countries were Germany, Sweden, France, Finland, Austria, Japan, Taiwan, and Korea. Other countries achieved similar goal through policy intervention, creating state owned enterprises, giving subsidies and supporting intensively export marketing. For example, in the eighteenth century, Prussia used these methods to promote its linen, iron and steel industries which made it an industrial leader. Similarly, Japan started steel, shipbuilding and railway industries through state ownership and targeted subsidies (Chang, 2008:55–57).
9. Hyde, 1977. p. 194.

   Chris Evan (2005) explained that the spread of new technology in the iron industry was dependent on the sponsorship of landed magnates. For example, it was Sir Henry Sydney of South Wales, who had political privilege as Lord President of the Council of the Marches, and an entrepreneur activist owning estates and iron works in Sussex, who was able to establish a blast furnace in early 1560 outside southeast England. Similarly, the English elite, who received the seized Irish land—rich in woodland—after Ireland was conquered and re-conquered first by Elizabeth I and later by Cromwell, brought in iron workers and settled them on the south and west coasts of Ireland. In other areas of England, old methods of producing iron remained intact and blast furnace technology was not introduced until the 1690s.

   In the seventeenth century, inter-regional exchanges and integration within the iron industry became possible with the rapid growth and differentiation of the market for iron wares. However, the supply of vegetable energy in Britain was limited and made the cooperation between furnace and forge operators necessary, which in turn led to the horizontal as well as vertical integration of the iron industry. This type of integration was not very efficient for handling a larger production network. To handle this new situation, landlords started leasing furnaces and forges to the new generation of iron masters who could create partnerships in variety of processing sites: furnaces, forges and slitting mills. "Very often, these partnerships were based around a small number of families whose interests, by the early eighteenth century, spanned the British Isles ... In this way, widely dispersed sites were brought together in a network of loosely articulated partnership" (Evans, 2005 in Evans and Ryden:17–18).

With this network of structure of production, it became possible to diffuse technical knowledge and soon new ideas began spreading quickly from district to district. It is important to note, as Roger Burt wrote, that innovations and their diffusion occurred spontaneously through untutored working technicians and not by a great savant or a technical genius as generally believed. Actually, it was carried over by rank and file furnace men and forge men who moved from site to site on a regular basis. These migrations of iron workers were facilitated by family connections, as skilled ironworkers and iron masters were organized on a dynastic basis. Many were descendent of Francophone migrants of the early sixteenth century. In this way, iron workers ensured that incremental improvements were quickly generalized across the British Isles. Moreover, there were no social constraints in the spread of ideas. However, sometime it was difficult to introduce a change due to the power of labor market that was also organized on a dynastic basis.

For example, the small and self-contained workforce that had characterized the British iron trade during the period of Walloon forging (1500–1750) organized on a dynastic basis, was able to control recruitment to the industry. They would admit no other man to work at the refinery but what have been 'Bred up to it from Their Cradles' (Burt, 1991). However, by the early years of nineteenth century, puddling and rolling transformed the British iron industry. Henry Cort, who was looking for super profits in supplying iron to Navy, introduced new form of industrial organization, which led to more efficient production and also eliminated dynastic control of workforce. He tried to use puddling and rolling methods to increase iron production to 200 tons a week, instead of 13 tons of bloom weekly with existing method of stamping and potting. Another of his associates, Richard Crawshay, was also interested in this method as it would de-skill work in the forge. He was specifically concerned with finding a technique for refining that could be imparted quickly to a large number of workers who had no background in the metal trades. Crawshay thought that through this method iron producers would be able to break the power of the labor market. [Note that later Taylor developed his scientific management on the same lines]. (Roger Burt: "The International diffusion of technology in the early modern period: The case of the British non-ferrous mining industry" (*Economic History Review*, 1991, 44(2):249–271).

10. Discussion based on Hyde, p. 194.
11. Hamilton Papers, Eur. Mss. C-126/3m Secretary of State to Colonial Government of India. July 18, 1901. India Office Library, London. Much of the information in this section is based on Chapter 1 in Bahl, 1995 and Chapter 8 in Bahl, 2005.
12. "Trade of the British Empire and Foreign Competition." C-8449 of 1899. p. 577. Cited in Amartya Sen. (1963), "Sociological and Economic Explanations: An Illustration from the Indian Iron and Steel Industry." *Economic Weekly*, February, pp. 183–86.
13. Hopkins and Cains, (1987) op. cit.

CHAPTER 6

The Emergence of the Large-Scale Steel Industry in Postcolonial Imperial US, 1880–1914

"Responding to the requirements of paradoxical age of Renaissance and Inquisition, the West's first modern discourses of conquest articulated a vision of all human kind united under a rule of law discoverable solely by human reason. Unfortunately for the American Indians, the West's first tentative step toward this noble vision of Law of Nations contained a mandate for Europe's subjugation of all peoples whose radical divergence from European-derived norms of right conduct signified their need for conquest and remediation...the very existence of the country [US] is a result of the looting of an entire continent and its resources [*and its original settlers*]" (Dunbar-Ortiz, 2014. Emphasis mine).

"Ironically, the founders of the republic [USA] have been hailed and lionized by left, right and center for—in effect—creating the first apartheid state" (Horne, 2014).

"Madison, one of the founding fathers, boldly argued that 'empire was essential for freedom' and Americans accepted it" (Williams, 1980).

"America has been at war 93% of the time—222 out of 239 years—since 1776" (globalresearch.ca. 1/2/17).

"The possession of money will acquire influence, influence will lead to authority, and authority will open the purses of people." Words of Robert Morris, the financier of the American Revolution (quoted in Hogeland, 2012).

"Tension between capitalism and democracy has characterized American life for two centuries ... during the first half of the nineteenth century, democracy [*only for white men*—my emphasis] took the lead, as the states abandoned property qualifications for voting and the parties responded by courting the masses of ordinary men...Andrew Jackson waged political war on the pet projects of the big capitalists of his day, smashing the Bank of the United States... But capitalism fought back during the Civil War .... Government became the sponsor of business rather than its foe, underwriting railroad construction, rising tariffs rates, creating a national currency, and allowing the likes of Morgan to troll for fortunes in the troubled waters of the war .... By the century's end the imperatives of capitalism mattered more to the daily existence of most Americans than the principles of democracy" (Brands, 2010).

INTRODUCTION

As mentioned in previous chapters, the comparative historical approach as practiced in its present form is not useful, as it focuses on separate autonomous social entities that are compared using a prior assumption of being either "developed" or "underdeveloped." It is often ignored that most present-day societies have been interacting with other societies for a long time. Over time, this society-to-society interaction tended to become increasingly about trade, gaining territories or resources, and, frequently, leading to battles and wars. It was in this process of interaction through wars and colonization that each society became a complex mix of various cultures, languages, and polity. The case of the US (and also of Imperial Russia, Imperial Britain and colonial India) is no different in that regard. The making of US society included both factors: the interaction among the invaders and indigenous population and amongst different groups, and the process of US interaction with other societies. Both of these social processes (inter-societal and intra-societal interactions) were (and are) created by spontaneous human creativity that expresses itself through human agency (actions). This human agency in the process of interaction with others creates society, class conflicts, intra-class conflicts, and the conjunction and combination of larger historical forces (see Chapter 3 for modern era), which take place at a particular time, both within the society as well as internationally. We can use this yardstick of parity to understand all societies, including the US and its industrialization instead of categorizing US as developed or underdeveloped.

By removing the cobwebs spun by these labels, it would become possible to see how each society emerged in historically similar ways through complex interaction processes amongst different social actors with various social relationships, based on class, race, gender or any other, within these societies—as well as with other societies over time. Thus, this approach will help erase the constraints of binary distinction while facilitating an understanding that the historical processes and the formation of the US society were no different than those of any other society at that time, even though, as is the case with every society, its historical specificities were different. However, to substantiate our argument, the historical material about US industrialization (as well as for the other three countries) is organized around the main issue of the volume: Erasing the binary distinction of developed/underdeveloped with a yardstick of parity. Therefore, the reader will get only a synoptic historical account of US industrialization, and not a conventional in-depth chronological history of the US.

In this chapter, based on information from selected published studies written in English only, in Part I (Erasing the Binary with a Yardstick of Parity) we shall treat the US with the same yardstick of parity and not categorize it as either developed or underdeveloped. According to this yardstick, all societies have both universal and specific elements, therefore, we shall focus on these elements to understand the making of US society and its industrialization. In Part II, (Conjunction and Confluence of Historical Forces in the Emergence of the Large-Scale Steel Industry) using the same yardstick of parity we shall show that the emergence of the large-scale steel industry in the US (as also in other three chosen societies) was due to the conjunction and combination of larger historical forces within the US as well as internationally during 1880–1914. The chapter ends with a summation.

PART I

ERASING THE BINARY DISTINCTION WITH A YARDSTICK OF PARITY

The basic trajectory of the US history is not much different from that of the other three societies examined in this volume. Aside from specific details, the larger story of invasion, constant territorial wars, territorial claims, migration, trade, borrowing of technology, political intrigues and alliances, and so on, remain the same. Specific details vary for each society, as does the time period of their trajectories. The important point is that people in each society behaved in a similar manner—as human beings, all of them were involved in shaping their society to fulfill their human needs. The individuals or groups who were successful in controlling the resources of their society tried to keep those elements under their control. Inevitably, social conflicts arose that manifested in class conflicts, compromises, and repressions, that in turn created new material conditions (modes of production, new class conflicts, power struggles, social relations and social structures—economies, political systems and culture—values, world view and so on), which then affect the choices people make in those new conditions. Thus, the cycle goes on. Individually, who became successful, how, and why, are important questions in their own right. However, every society is created and reproduced in every historical time through its members in the process of their interaction with other members of the society and its social institutions. At the same time, the actions and choices of each member of a society are not autonomous from their societal and larger historical context, which is also connected with other societies in a particular historical time.

Based on this understanding and using the yardstick of parity, we focus below on the universal and specific elements in the making of US society and its industrialization instead of categorizing US as either developed or underdeveloped.

UNIVERSAL ELEMENTS IN THE MAKING OF US SOCIETY

The universal characteristics of US society are: connections and interaction with other societies, interactions among people within society and choices made by different sections of society, power struggles, mix of many cultures, a concern with four basic human needs (survival, prosperity, security and reproduction), and people's choices and actions based on geographical conditions (climate, terrain, locale, and natural resources).

The social institutions of US society were created through the interaction of people, like any other society. Some of its specific characteristics are shared by countries like Australia and Canada: the colonization of territories following the annihilation of the original indigenous people, a country built with a large population of immigrants, adopting British social structure and using slave labor to produce wealth. However, the US, Australia, and Canada were not created in a vacuum. They came into being as a result of the needs of British imperialism and capitalism to expand overseas. Thus, the histories, social structures, values, and social institutions of these three countries (ex-colonies of Britain) were intertwined with British capitalism and imperialism.

Moreover, right from its inception, the US was tightly connected with the history of Britain. For example, the US War of Independence became necessary due to slaveholders' fears that the growing anti-abolition sentiments in Britain would support a slave uprising in the US (Horne, 2014).

> By the mid-1770s, incessant rumors calculated that the British would not merely incite the slaves to revolt, but would go so far as to arm them against their white masters. As early as 1774, the Virginian Arthur Lee read a pamphlet in London which suggested that the patriots might not go to war if their slaves were inspired to revolt against them.

> Likewise, James Madison thought a bill freeing slaves had been introduced in Parliament, although no such bill has ever been located. This type of volatile gossip spread with lightning speed. In May 1775, the South Carolina Gazette printed a letter from London in which the writer speculated that the English government had sent 78,000 guns to America to 'put into the hands of N***s' (Joyce 2016, Alternet.org, July 3; see also Hadden, 2001).

As a colony of Britain, the US was an extension of British and Northern European societies and their values. However, it also had connections with other societies, as people came from European countries to gain access to greater resources, to make profits, and to live better lives. Slaves from the African continent, of course, did not come to make a profit, as they were chained and forcibly brought to the US to work on the land and produce wealth for their owners. Chinese, Filipinos and Japanese workers arrived later, and they did not get much better treatment as employers pitted one ethnic group against the other as a control mechanism, keeping them divided (Roediger and Esch, 2012). The US also acquired other labor from the countries it colonized: Hawaii, the Philippines, Guam, and Cuba in addition to the region of Mexico taken after the Mexican-American War. The US was, and still is, connected to various other societies in Europe, Russia, Africa, Asia, South Asia, and Latin America, as waves of people have migrated to the US over the course of its history, looking for opportunities for a better life. Early in its history, under the banner of the Monroe Doctrine (1823), the US invaded Mexico and interfered (and continues to do so) in many other Latin American countries in attempts to bring them under its hegemony (Herring, 2008).

Moreover, in winning independence from Britain, the US looked for help from France and negotiated with Spain and Portugal, as well. It also needed recognition from other countries and required trade treaties with them so that it could survive and flourish (Herring, 2008). However, US interaction within the continent was mostly violent as it was initially the British who arrived with their violent colonization project, which was continued by the independent US. In fact, the US was created by colonizing Native American land while the original settlers were violently exterminated and forced out of their homes (also happened in Australia and other white colonies) through dubious treaties and means (Dunbar-Ortiz, 2014; Janson, 2016). The violence of slave trade from Africa and slave breeding within the US are some other examples. It was through a violent revolution that the US was created when it brought together separate colonies to challenge British control in the late eighteenth century. Southern slave owning and plantation states were brought under US control through the Civil War between 1861 and 1865. The US used vicious and brutal violent attacks on its labor force, which were migrants from other countries [(1)]. Similarly, Hawaii, Cuba, the Philippines, and Guam became US colonies through war.

The US not only learned the ideal of violent empire building from Britain, but also instituted this ideal into the US Constitution. As happened in Britain, the ideal of empire building in the US was, and continues to be, promoted by and for the needs of merchants, bankers, and stockbrokers (Ibid.; see also Beard, 1913). Even though many of the early American colonialists did not want the British form of strong centralized government, they did want, like the British imperialists, more land and trade to achieve the goals of prosperity and freedom at home. James Madison, one of the country's founding fathers boldly argued that "an empire was essential for freedom" (Williams 1980: 44). This ideology was clearly stated in the Federalist Paper No. XI. "American society was founded on the logic and the instrument of empire to achieve a future of liberty, freedom, opportunity, stability, and material welfare. It was stated, "Let us 'concur in erecting one great American system, superior to the control of all transatlantic force or influence, and able to dictate the terms of the connection between the old and new world'" (quoted in Ibid., 48). Based on these imperialist ideas, people in the US and their ruling classes made certain choices and took actions at every historical time. There were also those who criticized these ideas, but in the end, both promoters and objectors to imperialism accepted it in the name of freedom and prosperity. Consequently, this ideology of imperialism and related actions shaped the formation of American society and its industrialization. William Appleman Williams summarized this as follows:

> Americans viewed themselves as agents of God's will and purpose … equating Godliness with individual or collective success on earth … If other people refuse to 'open their minds to the idea of improvement' they are agents of the Devil who must be dealt with by force ... Americans came very quickly to view themselves as having discovered the ultimate solution to mankind's long search for the proper way to organize society … 'America the world's best hope'… Americans considered themselves perpetually beleaguered, an attitude that led on to the conviction that military security was initially to be found in controlling the entire continent—and ultimately prompted them to deny any distinction in between domestic and foreign policy. Americans apparently considered that no natural right of another was inalienable upon occasion—that on which it conflicted with the always inalienable rights of Americans themselves … leaving no medium between Safety and Conquest" (Williams, 1980:52 and 73–79).

It was in this same spirit that the Monroe Doctrine in 1823 clearly stated that European powers would not be allowed to re-conquer former colonies in any form, while asserting the right of the US to support Greek revolutionaries as well as to control other regions (Ibid.; see also Josephson, 1962; Hofstadter, 1955; Brands, 2010).

In addition to following imperial ideas of Britain, US also adopted British social order. The European settlers in the US were "thoroughly indoctrinated with prevailing [in Britain and Holland] ideas of social inequality ... and they certainly had never heard of classless society" (Zinn, 1970:66). Only a few people had a chance for social mobility, as the US was born amidst slavery, semi-slavery, poverty and land monopolies, class privileges, and class conflicts (Ibid., 69). European migrants saw the US as an emerging society in which they had opportunities to make wealth and carve out a space for themselves. However, those who could not be successful or who were brought as slaves or bonded labor, were compelled to accept a subordinate status. It was primarily this group that created wealth for the US and also helped in the creation of a "middle class." This "middle class" believed in the ideas of "born free" (except for slaves), because as Howard Zinn pointed out, the servitude system provided some comforts to a large number of the non-slave population. However, when those creating the wealth demanded their share of it, they were subjected to repression, as the US state always sided with the ruling class and employers, while keeping the subordinated classes in lowly status and without power (Josephson, 1962; Trachtenberg, 2007).

In this power and class struggle, different cultural and ethnic groups—migrated from various countries—were treated differently at different historical time. For example, when Irish, Germans, and Italians came they were not treated on par with British and Scottish migrants. In fact, employers used different ethnic groups against one another to control the labor force (Roediger and Esch, 2012). The fate of Chinese, Japanese, and Mexican labor workers was much worse than many European migrants. However, America became a multiethnic and multicultural society with a diverse migrant population.

These different power struggles and class conflicts seem to be a universal phenomenon. How these power struggles played out and how class conflicts were resolved or compromised remained tied to specific historical situations within a society and to a conjunction and combination of historical forces of the time, internationally and nationally.

Like other societies, the geographical location, climate, available resources and access to waterways also played an important part in shaping American society. For example, the US had the advantage of a favorable geography with vast fertile land and a great supply of natural resources. These favorable geographical locations allowed Americans to develop resource-intensive machines. For example, as Cross and Szostak pointed out, the circular saw wasted much wood but it was far faster and required far fewer workers than a reciprocating saw or a hand saw. Thus, the availability of cheap raw materials combined with a scarcity of labor and costly transportation directed US innovation toward labor saving technology that "featured the use of wood and developed transport and communications innovations such as steamboats and the telegraph" (Cross and Szostak, 1995:64). At the same time, the abundance of natural resources also discouraged Americans from introducing new technologies. For example, until 1850 many industries in the US still used waterwheels and did not switch to steam power, even though it was available.

SPECIFIC CHARACTERISTICS IN THE MAKING OF US SOCIETY AND ITS INDUSTRIALIZATION

The specific historical conditions within the US were equally important in the making of American society. For example, immediately following the American Revolution in 1776, there was a power struggle between different ideological interests to control the state structure. The specific institution of slavery (which also existed in other white colonies) contributed heavily to shaping its historical trajectory. Specific social, moral and ethical values (used by US corporations to control workers) of the US society, which were shaped by occult movements (transported from Europe), prepared people to accept poor working and living conditions. In the US, a liberal democracy was promoted in the nineteenth century which transformed democracy from being a participatory practice to a passive enjoyment of constitutional safeguards and rights (Post, 2011). The US government actively contributed in creating necessary conditions for industrialization, by promoting military, weapons, transportation and communication, banks, the legal system, geographical surveys and other relevant information. Furthermore, the US government provided incentives for merchants, promoted the formation of cartels, helped in the creation of a national market, promoted technology, education, flow of migrant workers to replenish the labor force, while controlling the labor force by crushing unions, and favoring corporations and industrialists. All these specific historical processes, along with the choices and role of the state actor within the US, set the stage for the country's future roadmap leading to its industrialization.

In the following section we elaborate on these specificities while focusing on US industrialization.

1. INSTITUTION OF SLAVERY, TERRITORIAL EXPANSION & CREATION OF WEALTH

One specific element basic for US existence and the capitalist growth that made it a first world nation, was the institution of slavery. For example, the evolution and modernization of the US after the War of Independence was driven mainly by the expansion of slavery while also protecting the interests of white slave owners' and their property through a police force specifically created to control the slave population. In a recent study, historian Edward Baptist illustrates how the South grew from a narrow coastal strip of worn-out tobacco plantations to a continental cotton empire which helped the US to become a modern, industrial, and capitalist economy. The key raw material of the Industrial Revolution was cotton, which was produced through a system of brutal slavery. The US seized control of the world market for cotton (at the time, constituting 50 percent of the country's export) and became a prosperous and powerful nation. According to Baptist, the dominant US economy today—real estate, insurance, and finance—owes its existence to slavery. For example, it was African slaves who built the physical wall that gives Wall Street its name, and in 1711, New York officials established a slave market on Wall Street to formalize slave trade (Baptist, 2016). Many prominent American banks such as J. P. Morgan and Wachovia National made fortunes from slavery and accepted slaves as "collateral." J. P. Morgan acknowledged, as documents reveal, that the company "accepted approximately 13,000 enslaved individuals as collateral on loans and took possession of approximately 1, 250 enslaved individuals" (Farrow, Lang and Frank, 2006). The holdings of Warren Buffet, one of the richest billionaires in the US, are derived from an antecedent firm in Rhode Island with a history of textile manufacturing and slavery profiteering.

New England was the home of America's cotton textile industry and without the availability of cotton from the South (produced with slave labor) the industrial revolution in New England would not have taken place (Ibid.). Anne Farrow (2006) illustrates the ways the Northern American bourgeoisie were connected to the slave system by a 'million threads': they bought molasses, which was made with slave labor, and sold rum as part of the Triangle Trade; they lent money to Southern planters, and most of the cotton that was sold to Britain was shipped through New England ports.

The American slave system also included a slave breeding industry which treated slaves as a form of capital. For the functioning of this industry a sophisticated infrastructure was created involving financiers, plantation owners, traders, haulers, marketers, lawmakers, and law enforcers. The slave breeding industry became vastly bigger in the US than the transatlantic slave trade ever was, and to protect this industry and trading business from competition, the Slave Trade Act of 1807 abolished the transport of slaves in and out of the country. Ned and Constance Sublette (2016) pointed out in their investigative book on the breeding industry that US President Jefferson was well aware of the economic potential of slaves as a form of capital. In this regard

Jefferson wrote a letter in 1819 stating, "I consider the labor of a breeding woman as no object, and that a child raised every 2 years is of more profit than the crop of the best laboring man ... I must pray you to inculcate upon the overseers that it is not their labor, but their increase which is first consideration with us" (quoted in Joyce, 2016).

Since slave breeding was a capitalist enterprise it needed continuous growth to survive, especially since cotton was emerging as the primary cash crop in the world at that time. In other words, the US needed more territory to expand its plantation economy which was possible only by exterminating or forcibly relocating and controlling the Native American population. US army General Andrew Jackson, who also owned slaves, brutally achieved this goal with the help of Federal troops. His "achievements" helped earn him the position of US President (1829–1837), and he used that position to acquire even more territory that could be used for slave plantations and slave breeding (Ibid).

2. POWER STRUGGLES IN THE MAKING OF THE US AND VICTORY OF FINANCIAL ELITE

Even though power struggle is a universal phenomenon, how it develops and what forms it takes, its outcome and influences, are very specific to each society. Ideologically, the power struggle in the US was between those (militia private, armed labors, and leaders like Cannon and Young) who wanted an egalitarian society (only for whites) and those (merchants, plantation owners, landlords, and lenders) who opposed it (Beard, 1913:70). However, those who wanted an egalitarian society lost the struggle because the US Constitution favored the elite, and the financial elite gained complete control of American policies (Ibid.).

The financial elite prevailed because some of the first nationalists, who were also among the first high financers, saw in the War of Independence new and exciting financial opportunities not only for themselves and their friends, but also for the country. When the war created US foreign debt the size of which exceeded domestic debt, merchants became not only investors and private creditors, but also public creditors for the US government. Hogeland pointed out, debt was considered as a catalyst for nationhood, therefore paying interest on the large public debt and sustaining it was considered necessary. Robert Morris, then the most financially successful merchant of Philadelphia, believed that the democratic law-making process was a hindrance to the growth of commerce. Therefore, he suggested that if Congress could obtain wartime powers to eliminate democratic law-making processes, America could become a competitive commercial power. Morris was of the opinion that to unify America, war was necessary. According to Hogeland, Morris believed "the best way to support public investment was war; the best way to support war was public investment" (Hogeland, 2012:75).

But to conduct a war, the US also needed to borrow money from domestic lenders. Thus, a new creditor class emerged in response to the necessity to pay for the country's wartime debts. The strategy, as Morris said, was that, "The possession of money will acquire influence ... Influence will lead to authority, and authority will open the purses of the people" (quoted in Ibid., 70). Morris was successful in getting the Continental Congress to issue federal bonds and make a strong investment

(Ibid., 78). Based on this strength, $2.5 million in loans was borrowed from France to pay off US war debts. As for US financiers, there was no need to buy bonds with gold or silver, as Congress agreed to accept continental paper as payment assurances. Thus, Morris became the "financier of the American Revolution," using both his own funds and public funds for personal speculation. Not surprisingly, as Hogeland noted, many land-holders did not approve of this way of making money as they considered it (making money out of paper work) to be a form of corruption (Ibid., 79).

Morris was also interested in the formation of a central bank to stabilize the finances of Congress. The bank was to be privately financed by Morris and others, including his business partner, lawyer Thomas Willing, while they served simultaneously as both subscribers and governing board. Moreover, the bank would operate as a public corporation, publicly chartered both by Pennsylvania and by Congress. The charter would make board members immune from personal lawsuits and allow them to use bank capital for investments for anything they would consider useful. Meanwhile, the bank lent money to Congress and also managed its finances. Congress appointed Morris as the superintendent of finance, and gave him free reign, which allowed him to mix public finances with his own money. Under this arrangement, Morris and his governing board evolved into executive departments of the US state, necessitating that all information about finance, foreign affairs, and war be reported to Morris (Ibid., 81). Thus, he became the richest man in the US by controlling Congress and the first national bank.

Soon Alexander Hamilton joined Morris (Ibid., 82) in further maneuvering the bank in an effort to combine and integrate high finance with the military hierarchy (Ibid., 92). William Pitt, Chancellor of the Exchequer in England, said at the inauguration of the first privately-owned central bank of the US under Alexander Hamilton: "Let the American people go into their debt funding schemes and banking systems, and from that hour their boasted independence will be a mere phantom" (quoted in Cushing, 2013:272–273).

This movement transformed US military officers into wealthy gentlemen who then became both US investors and creditors. In 1783 these officers founded the Society of the Cincinnati, a hereditary social organization. The Society unified the families of those who were later among the country's most influential men. One of its functions was to oversee and safeguard certain financial matters. The officers, now bondholders of high standing, refused to support soldiers when Pennsylvania troops rebelled over the non-payment of promissory notes. Instead, the rebellion was put down (Ibid.).

Thus, the financial elite won the power struggle by controlling the US treasury, foreign affairs, war, and domestic banking. Over time, through the formation of corporations and by tweaking the law with assistance from the Supreme Court, the financial elite were successful not only in retaining their power but also increasing it.

Challenges to Power Elite

There were revolts such as Shay's Rebellion of 1786–1787 by Massachusetts farmers who were revolting against the burden of debts, taxes, and the possible loss of their landed property under increasing market competition (Post, 2011:189). Hogeland pointed out that Herman Husband, a North Carolina assemblyman, was involved during the 1760s with the Regulator Movement in North Carolina—a populist uprising against wealthy, corrupt, colonial officials—and in the 1794 Whiskey Rebellion in Western Pennsylvania against federal taxes on distilleries. Husband had started pondering these ideas of "regulations" in the 1750s and 1760s believing that ordinary people could restrain the power of wealth. He thought that the rich should submit to a government that would actually be interested in equalizing wealth, income, and benefits. He represented the thinking of many thousands of people who had completely different ideas about finance and economics than those embraced by the Founding Fathers [(3)]. In the end, however, it was the financial elite (discussed in last section) and industrial capital that won the debate, and they continued to control US state power structures and created new policies favoring the industrial elite.

3. STRUGGLE OVER THE QUESTION OF INDUSTRIALIZATION

The specific historical context of the debt problem pushed the American elite to face the question of promoting industrialization. America did not start as an industrial society because it was basically dependent on Britain for manufactured goods. Every village in the US was part of the empire of goods as peddlers brought manufactured goods to them, thus, linking people with merchants in Boston, London, and other manufacturers in England. This expanding Atlantic economy changed the material culture of every person, including the well-off and average people (Breen, 1986). The initial making of US society was really the story of the vast number of links between people living both in America and in England.

After the War of Independence, a vast amount of goods from Britain coming to the US alarmed country leaders as it came under a huge debt that it was unable to pay. This inability to pay off its debt plunged the US into an economic depression. This debt condition and economic depression strengthened the argument of those who favored encouraging domestic manufacturing and establishing an independent and balanced economy in order to provide for the new republic. One of many interesting arguments that were put forward in favor of domestic manufacturing included the idea of divine utilitarianism: "Nature had been so 'profusely liberal' to America, it became her to use her gifts to the utmost" (Kasson, 1976 quoted in Kornblith, 1998:9). By 1787, more and more people were supporting the idea of domestic manufacturing and a few organizations were formed specifically for the promotion of manufacturing, and "the useful arts." Some of these organizations also promoted the idea that America could solve the problem of its scarcity of labor with more machinery in the workshops.

By 1791, ideas favoring domestic manufacturing culminated in Hamilton's *Report on the Subject of Manufactures* which not only promoted manufacturing but also justified the expansion of America's protectionist policy to help its infant domestic industries. Hamilton did not see nationalism and industrialization as separate processes. He was convinced that American independence and greatness could be ensured with English-style industrialization. With this conviction, he recruited English artisans and imported British textile technology (Cross and Szostak, 1995). Jefferson, who wished to keep the US as an agrarian republic, lost the argument and the US began to pursue industrialization. Southern interest groups, however, opted for solutions according to their plantation interests. After 1817, Adam Smith's technical vocabulary and new science of economics became more prevalent replacing old republican terms such as virtue, independence, and corruption (Matthew, 1991:143).

4. CHANGING SOCIAL RELATIONSHIPS & THE TRIUMPH OF INDUSTRIAL CAPITAL

In addition to an open debate over the question of industrialization, there were other specific developments taking place within the US which changed the social relationship of production and led to the industrialization of agricultural products.

The American Revolution and its immediate aftermath radically changed the relationship between Northern farmers, merchants, and speculators. The Revolutionary War temporarily disrupted the non-market reproduction as state governments were buying food, cloth, and other supplies to meet the demands of the war. Northern farmers and households fell into debt, and higher taxes after the war forced these farmers to market increasingly larger portions of both their subsistence and surplus output. This dire situation led to the rural unrest that followed in the 1780s and 1790s. Thus, as Post pointed out, the class struggle of this time effectively ended independent household production in the original areas of colonial settlement (Post, 2011:231). Northern farmers were now transformed from independent households to petty commodity producers, which increased the pace of capitalist manufacturing growth in the two decades before the Civil War (Ibid., 233). These commodity producer farmers stopped producing their implements themselves and began to purchase the most advanced tools and machinery on the market. Consequently, the North concentrated mostly on producing farm machinery, tools and supplies, which could process agricultural raw material for other agro-industries such as meat packing, leather tanning, caning, flour milling, and baking (Ibid.). Subsequently, the agro-industrial complex began to expand in the mid-nineteenth century.

The stimulation for commodity production and circulation came from merchant capital at that time because the dominant form of social production in all regions of the US during this time was non-capitalist (Ibid.). For example, as Post elaborated, the finances for the slave-based cotton cultivation and the organization of raw cotton sales to textile manufacturers in New England and Great Britain came from Northern and Southern merchants and bankers. Similarly, land speculators were purchasing land from the federal government at public auctions and then re-selling it to family farmers in the North, and to planters in the South. Before the mid-1840s, as Post pointed out, the geographical expansion of plantation slavery was important because Northern merchants were able to accumulate capital directly from the slave-created cotton which was sold to Britain. They also provided capital for land and for the building of transport infrastructures. Post writes, "The unintended consequence of the merchants' pursuit of their own non-capitalist strategy for reproduction, buying land cheap and selling it dear—created the condition for the development of industrial capitalism in the US" (Ibid., 234).

Over time, even the activities of manufacturers and commercial family farmers also became the main stimulus of commodity production and circulation while increasingly deepening the division of labor. For example, the agrarian petty production for market, which was expanding geographically, encouraged the growth in capitalist manufacturing of consumer goods. In turn, the growth of both manufacturing and cities further led to more rural specialization, innovation, and accumulation. According to Post, these new social property relations transformed the role of Northern rural merchants, as well as stimulating increased investment in railroads. For example, large, specialized grain-and-livestock merchants, located in the growing rail, river and lake cities of the Ohio Valley and the Great Plains, displaced many local merchant shop keepers, which led to the subordination of merchant to industrial capital. Post explained that following the financial crisis of 1837–1842, with the banks becoming a main source of credit for both farmers and manufactures, manufacturers became financially independent of the merchants. In the 1840s and 1850s, industrial capital became the dominant form of capital. However, it could not extend into the Southern region due to the geographical expansion of plantation slavery (Ibid., 235). This conflict between the need for expansion of industrial capital and the expansion of plantation slavery culminated in the Civil War. Another party to this conflict was the legally free producers in the North—wage earners and self-employed small producers more generally (Levine, 2012:39). However, at the end of the Civil War, it was industrial capital that triumphed [(4)].

5. SPECIFIC FEATURES OF US INDUSTRIALIZATION

Once the issue of industrialization was settled, the US government started creating other necessary conditions for the development of industrialization. In this endeavor, the country had the advantage of a very favorable geography with vast fertile land and other great supplies of natural resources. The favorable geographical location, availability of cheap raw materials combined with a scarcity of labor and costly transportation directed US innovations toward labor saving technology that "featured the use of wood and developed transport and communications innovations such as steamboats and the telegraph" (Cross and Szostak, 1995:64).

However, favorable geography in itself could not make the US an industrialized country unless it was worked upon to achieve that goal. The country had to build new institutions that would create legal, financial and other necessary social and cultural conditions which would promote and favor industrialization. It also needed information about the geological location of resources, a better transport infrastructure and a skilled workforce for its industries, as well as an ideology to make people accept their plight and status. How did the US achieve these goals within a short time span, especially when in the 1790s, there were only 3.9 million people inhabiting the US, and 18 percent of whom were slaves and two thirds of whom were subsistence farmers? In the following sections, we discuss the development of those specific historical forces that created conditions for the promotion of America's industrialization.

We begin by looking into the shaping of American values; specifically, the myth of the "self-made man." This myth was necessary in order to make workers passively accept their living and working conditions so that American industrialization would have little resistance.

i. The Myth of the "Self-Made Man"

American values and ethical behavior are deeply affected by Protestant Evangelical ideas of self-discipline and self-control, which were being renewed in the early nineteenth century. However, their ideas of social progress and individual betterment are rooted in the spiritual (occult) movements that migrated to the US from Europe at different times (Horowitz, 2009). In these spiritual movements, spiritual practices (for example, mesmerism) were combined with a self-improvement philosophy, which created a new culture of self-empowering and healing spirituality. In this new culture, science and religion were seen as allies in the march toward progress (Ibid., 63), which created a conviction that divine mysteries are within the settings of ordinary life (Ibid., 81–82).

These spiritual ideas are clearly reflected in Protestant Evangelical ideas of self-discipline and self-control, which became an important part of the American value system. These Protestant evangelical ideas helped shape both workers and the middle class. The idea of self-discipline and self-control helped in creating docile workers, which also helped in bridging the social division of labor among different types of labor, different forms of economic organization, and people of different social backgrounds as they were having different experiences in the transition to industrial work, while also involved in the expansion of industry at that time (George, 1982:55).

Protestant evangelical ideas of self-discipline and self-control also shaped a distinct middle class [(5)]. According to these ideas, any individual can be successful in life with sheer self-discipline, self-control, and determination because individual success is not predestined by God and the individual has the power to choose their path to eternal life. With this criteria of success Americans began celebrating the status of family business, proprietors, and simple partnerships (George, 1982:81), while newspapers and other publications began glorifying economic advancement and material welfare. For example, Benjamin Franklin's *Poor Richard's Almanac* encouraged self-reliance for achieving material success during the eighteenth century [(6)]. However, the cult of "self-reliance" and the "self-made man" condemned government regulations with regard to economic affairs, but it had no problem with approving strong government support for private investment and stemming the rise of labor organizations. For example, Eli Whitney's firearms manufacturing firm was an early recipient of government financial assistance, as were the private initiatives for the development of US transportation improvement, both canals and railways (George, 1982:60).

Remarkably, the cult of the "self-made man" became more pronounced precisely at a time when large monopolies were emerging and more people were losing their land, while craftsmen were being reduced to wage laborers, and the American frontier reached the Pacific Ocean. At the same time, both the US government and its courts were actively reducing opportunities for the common man to become a "self-made man" by continuously siding with industrialists and employers in conflicts between workers and employers, or between land-owner farmers and industrial needs. As Miller's and other studies show, the idea of the "self-made man" in reality is a myth, as is also the story of "rags to riches" (Ibid., 64–68). However, these myths and values proved very beneficial to employers and industrialists in controlling the labor force.

Along with the establishment of the myth of the self-made man, in the late nineteenth century, the idea of the individual citizen was created to turn American democracy into a liberal democracy making it a passive enjoyment of constitutional and procedural safeguards and rights (Post, 2011). Thus, people began to perceive themselves as individual citizens living private lives in isolation from one another believing in the myth of the self-made man. These values stabilized and established capitalist social relationships in the North as liberalism, and in the South in the form of legal racial segregation, disenfranchisement, and a reign of terror (Ibid.).

ii. Federal Government Facilitating Industrialization

An important specific feature of US industrialization was that it was not market forces that created industrial development, but the state, which granted special privileges and subsidies for transportation, canals, banks, and railroads. For example, it was not the demand of the people that railroads were built in new territories. It was after railroads were built with high cost in new territories subsidized by the government that people were given incentives to settle in those newly opened areas (White, 2011).

Railroads were not the only industry that received subsidies and privileges from Federal government, the whole project of American industrialization was facilitated by the Federal government's actions and laws privileging entrepreneurs and industrialists. The most important initial industry Federal government promoted was the weapons industry to fulfill the needs of its standing army. This army was created after the War of Independence to enforce the laws of the land, to crush the rural rebellions of 1780 and 1790, for westward expansion, and for class warfare between workers and federal troops (Trachtenberg, 2007). With the coming of the weapons industry many related industries began to rapidly develop within the US.

The Federal government was also actively facilitating American industrialization by systematically exploring unsettled regions in search of suitable routes for railroads to the Pacific with the help of the US army (Ibid.). Furthermore, in 1879, the US government established the Geographical Survey Institute, which took up scientific expeditions to explore natural resources and to provide detailed information (data and photographs) about the terrain, the mineral and timber resources, and the climate and water supply in various regions of the US for the benefits of the industries, while also gaining public support for government's policy of conquest, settlement and exploitation (Ibid., 20). With the availability of reliable information, including maps and photographs, and government incentives, railroads and telegraphs were able to open up vast spaces for further industrial and agricultural production. This in turn, attracted commercial and industrial businesses to extract raw materials—timber, oil, natural gas, iron ore and other minerals—for processing and manufacturing goods for the market.

The federal government further helped railroad companies with the Homestead Act, under which it donated more than million and a half acres of public domain in the form of "land grants to railroad companies operating west of the Mississippi" (Ibid., 22), which, in fact, turned railroad companies into private colonizers. Similarly, Congress gave land grants and right to access that land to mining and timber interests by passing various Acts between 1866 and 1873. All these Acts increased the privatization of the public domain and individual entrepreneurs were sidelined (they later became wage laborers) as large companies began buying out land and replacing small-scale mining, timber cutting, and farming with capital intensive methods (Ibid., 23). Similar changes took place in the food production and processing industries, as by 1890 they all became capital intensive and highly mechanized. These developments changed the relations of corporation to agriculture, as agriculture became integrated in a productive and marketing structure, which was connected to the international market system (Ibid.).

Following is the discussion of various steps the federal government took to facilitate the industrialization of America.

a. Integration of Federal Military, Industrial Corporations, Science and Universities

As pointed out earlier, military production was an integral part of the American system of manufacturing as it led to the production of weapons, goods, iron, railroads, etc. Thus, the mass production of weapons and other related items for the army brought war, military, science, engineering, and industry into a new relationship, which was reflected in the closer partnership between the US state, corporations, and universities (Noble, 1979:xii). For example, to develop interchangeable parts necessary for the mass production of guns, new sophisticated machine tools were adapted from clockmaker Eli Terry's special purpose machinery for mass producing timepieces (Ibid). While mass-produced guns (in factories) were used for conquering and controlling the colonies, railways and telegraphs also became an essential part of the military as they helped in the rapid deployment of armies, weapons, and supplies to the war front (Ibid., 185).

The development of new efficient weapons required scientific research, which could be conducted in universities and big laboratories with the help of engineers and scientists. Therefore, the federal government established an extensive education system with land grant colleges and engineering schools immediately after the Civil War, and, later, industrial research labs. The availability of engineers and chemists later helped Carnegie, Edison, and others affiliated with large corporations to promote and expand their enterprises (Ibid., 162). Their employment of large numbers of trained specialists gave these corporations a monopoly over professional engineers. Thus, these engineers began playing key roles in technical and industrial research funded by large corporations. In this way a few giant firms began dominating science based electrical and chemical industries through consolidation, patent monopolies, and mergers (Ibid., xx). Consequently military, railways, industries, corporations, universities, and science became integrated. Soon this process of integration became part of the global and international historical processes, as the US began to compete with European nations to become a world power.

b. Promotion of Transportation and Creation of National Market

The US became fully industrialized and developed a national market after building an infrastructural system of transportation: a system of interregional roads, the construction of canals, innovations in riverboats powered with steam, and the introduction of railroads (Cross and Szostak, 1995).

Initially there existed a national market in the US with an existing regional waterway system as many of the waterways were linked to the coastal areas—the Hudson and Mohawk Rivers in the North, the Potomac and Savannah Rivers in the South. The Ohio and Mississippi River system facilitated the early colonization of vast lands. The US also had the advantage of an "increase[d] population in a resource rich land that created market for industrial goods, capital favored by the legal and political system, a workforce that did not impede and even encouraged mechanizing in some case, and a culture that in the long run was hospitable to imitating British innovation" (Ibid., 65). These advantages multiplied with the help of the US government as it gave protection to the textile industry with the Tariff Act of 1816, and initiated and subsidized the transportation revolution, which connected major agricultural and industrial areas with turnpikes and river improvement companies.

Beginning in 1810, states started offering full subsidies for the development of canals and further expansion of roads and waterways systems (Ibid., 92). In certain states, private investors were also offered other attractive rewards: subsidies, tax exemption and government backing for privately issued bonds, special banking options, lottery franchises, and exclusive corporate charters conferring lucrative monopoly privileges. Many merchants, who suffered in the international market due to fierce competition after the War of Independence, were attracted by the offer of generous government subsidies and began investing in improvements in transportation: the construction and maintenance of roads, turnpikes, bridges, and canals, and soon thereafter, steamboats and railroads (*American Social History Project,* 2000).

The improvement of the transportation system—canals and railways—connected various geographic regions with national markets, which reduced the cost of production and the distribution of goods. By the early 1840s, the US was able to export locomotives to Europe and to design railroads overseas as it was able to make numerous technical innovations in the areas of safety, the manual signal system, use of the telegraph, electrical signals for air brakes and train dispatch systems. Its biggest developments were in bridges and tunnels, and between 1867 and 1873 the first steel bridge was built over the Mississippi River in St. Louis followed by a suspension bridge over Niagara Falls between 1852 and 1855, and the first steel suspension bridge connecting New York and Brooklyn a decade later (Cross and Szostak, 1995:98–100). The railroads also helped in increasing the role and importance of stock markets, as railroads needed vast amount of funding that no one private person could afford to provide. It also created conditions for the development of large retailing companies, Montgomery Ward in 1872 and Sears, Roebuck & Company in 1887, as they relied on railroad delivery for mail orders of goods (Cross and Szostak, 1995).

With all these developments a new national market emerged that provided incentives and opportunities that encouraged further innovations which business owners, industrialists, and investors fully utilized while making the US both an industrial society and consumer society. At the same time, these developments created new social relationships and a new culture in the US, as production moved out of households and people became dependent on the market and transportation for consumer goods, which changed their daily lives profoundly.

Cochran has rightly summed up that,

> In America up to 1820 at least, efficient communication, transportation, finance, marketing and law ... were collectively more important in reducing cost than were contemporary improvements in the fabrication of goods ... the new world they lived in was more the product of faster and cheaper finance, trade, and transportation than the result of steam engines, power saws, and other new machines. Speeding the movement of goods from maker to receiver was the chief economizer of scarce working capital (Cochran, 1981 in Kornblith, 1998:18; see also Kaul, 2013).

c. Reforming and Building New Institutions

Industrialization required new institutions and laws for both mobilizing capital and for controlling the labor force. To achieve these goals, the US followed the English models of banking and insurance institutions for its own commercial and manufacturing investments.

With a reformed legal system and help from business lawyers the US government created the groundwork of rules for banking and insurance institutions to grow economically without any hindrance from the old legal order. Thus, the country's economic growth became possible with the creation of a "well-coordinated and flexible business system" (Cross and Szostak, 1998:2).

Legal System

A new groundwork of rules protected private property, and encouraged enterprise and corporate venture. However, in practice it was the right of the party, who used resources in a dynamic and enterprising way, that was protected, and not the right of the inheritor of land. For example, beginning in the 1820s the states awarded turnpike companies the right of eminent domain, which forced landowners to sell rather than to block proposed road-projects. Similarly, the US legal system tended to favor the forces of technological change. For example, whenever any vested interests used legal avenues to halt technological change that they deem threatening to their interest, the legal system would favor the side of technological change (Ibid.). Thus, under the pressure of business lawyers, the law courts became the promoters of entrepreneurial action and contract laws became more important in commercial and property transactions, as they were enforced based on the contract agreement and not whether it was fair or not to the loser (Matthew, 1991).

Even state governments were becoming innovative in corporate law. For example, in 1811, New York retracted an earlier rule that required new corporations to obtain a special charter from the legislature, thus, greatly easing the formation of manufacturing corporations. Many states passed legislation to provide businesses relief from bankruptcy by gradually replacing imprisonment for bad debts with debt forgiveness. By the mid-nineteenth century, state governments had also introduced limited liability, which freed the investors in corporations from personal responsibility for the debts of their corporation beyond the value of their investment.

Another important legal change in the promotion of industrialization was the Patent Act of 1790 which allowed the government to encourage industrialization without giving subsidies. Individual innovation was now rewarded with a legal monopoly over the patented invention and the inventor was encouraged to license or sell his inventions. However, in reality it was hard to win patent infringement suits and inventions were quick to pass into the competitive market (Ibid.).

The US legal system was also geared towards helping employers to control the labor force, and the judiciary played an important role in this regard. For example, throughout the nineteenth century US courts repeatedly overrode many legislative initiatives that would have helped the cause of workers unions. The US judiciary was so powerful that when it foiled legislation for labor's right to collective action, the state legislatures of New York and Pennsylvania could not override them (Hattam, 1992:138).

All these new laws and new legal system encouraged more businesses to take risks, which in turn stimulated investment, as it became not only easy to incorporate but also to get the protection of contracts against state interference. In addition to these new laws, industrial development required an existence of a good monetary system and banking. However, there was a constant struggle between private bankers and the federal government for control of the money supply until 1913 when the Federal Reserve Bank was founded. The importance of who controls monetary system and banks, and its political and social implications, are well expressed in the following two quotes:

> Give me control of a Nation's money supply, and I care not who makes its laws (Attributed to Mayer Amschel Bauer Rothschild).

> It is well enough that people of the nation do not understand our banking and monetary system, for if they did, I believe there would be a revolution before tomorrow morning (Henry Ford).

Banks

However, as Nissami noted, US bankers acquired wealth through a series of poorly managed fractional reserve practices that in turn gave rise to numerous scams, hoaxes, and machinations. These scams and hoaxes dragged the US through various wars, creating poverty, helplessness, declining health and environmental disasters, while all the time transferring massive wealth from the people to the bankers (Nissami, 2016).

As late as 1896, certain political leaders objected to the power and influence of banks on governance. US Presidential candidate William Jennings Bryan said on July 8, 1896,

> We believe that the right to coin and issue money is a function of government ... It is a part of sovereignty, and can no more with safety be delegated to private individuals than we could afford to delegate to private individuals the power to make penal statues or levy taxes ... I stand with Jefferson ... that the issue of money is a function of government, and that the banks ought to go out of the governing business ... When we have restored the money to the Constitution, all other reforms will be possible, but until it is done there is no other reform that can be accomplished" [(2)].

In the early US, banks needed special permission from the government to operate because the earlier US policymakers well understood the importance of controlling the money supply, and they resisted entrusting the profit-driven private banks with the critical task of overseeing the money supply and the credit system. Jefferson wrote,

> The [private] Central Bank is an institution of the most deadly hostility existing against the principles and form of our constitution ... If the American people allow private banks to control the issuance of their currency ... the banks and corporations that will grow up around them will deprive the people of all their property until their children will wake up homeless on the continent their fathers conquered (quoted in Hussein-Zadeh, 2015).

In 1835, Andrew Jackson abolished the Bank of the US, arguing that it exerted an undue and unhealthy influence over the course of the national economy. From then until 1913, the US did not allow the formation of a private central bank, and the government did not issue any paper money until 1862. During that period of nearly three-quarters of a century, monetary policies were carried out, more or less, according to the US Constitution: Only the "Congress shall have power ... To coin money, regulate the value thereof" (Article I, Section 8, US Constitution quoted in Hussein-Zadeh, 2015). Moreover, the role of earlier financial institutions had been to serve as channels for funneling national savings to productive investments without creating big financial bubbles.

The first central/national bank was founded in 1791 with a ten-year charter. After that charter expired, a second bank was created in 1816 with a charter that ended in 1836, although it closed in 1833. Following these short-lived attempts, the US government took over the job of supervising banks. Each bank had its own currency, but the problem of fake currency was also very high (Fraser, 2005). In 1860, when a large number of banks declared bankruptcy, the demand for a uniform national currency grew. In response, the National Currency Act of 1863 was passed that led to the creation of a system of new banks and a new government agency that was headed by the comptroller of the currency. Now the nation's mainstay of its money supply became National Bank notes until the Federal Reserve Bank was created in 1913.

From then on, the US government began relying on borrowing from the Federal Reserve rather than on self-financing (free money) as it had been doing prior to the creation of this bank. With this borrowing, the US began facing a new phenomenon—the rise of national debt and banks became the main source of industrial investment.

iii. Creating Industrial Labor Force

Industrialization needed a large labor force as fuel. Most of the workforce in American textile mills before 1850, primarily in the New England and Mid-Atlantic States, consisted of urban populations and newly arrived European immigrants. Before 1850 very few goods were mass produced in the US as most of the early manufacturing took place within the households (Kornblith, 1998). Only ship building and iron working were conducted on a larger scale. When the demand for goods started rising during the early nineteenth century, merchant investors moved household manufacturing—yarn, cloth and thread production—to factories using imported European machines developed in the late eighteenth century. Their products were protected from foreign competition under the existing US import tariff of 1816 (*American Social History Project,* 2000). Along with merchants turning into industrialists, master artisans were also transforming the traditional handicraft trades into modern capitalist industries [(7)]. These factories generated the need for a large labor force.

The historical European mass migration between 1840 and 1900 provided the needed labor force. Later on, after the Spanish War, the US colonized Cuba, Guam, the Philippines, and Puerto Rico, which also provided labor for the US needs. These migrants could not develop specialization in any one trade as they were changing their jobs all the time and moving around. However, they did develop various skills which gave craftsmen confidence that they could make any machinery work. These artisans learned to make crude but effective machines through observation, practice, and apprenticeship. These all-purpose artisan immigrants were able to move "from making furniture or hoes to erecting textile machinery and ultimately to fashioning parts of steam engines; or from building houses to constructing paper mills; or from working for wages to becoming independent entrepreneurs" (Cochran, 1981 in Kornblith, 1998:18). Over time, a flexible labor supply with a relatively high competence became possible in America and workers began to innovate. However, many young white people saw the possibility of social mobility (economic rationality) in America, and they left their families early in life, took risks and pushed hard to achieve this goal (Ibid., 21). The choices of these migrants turned small market centers into bustling towns, and turned larger ports such as New York, Philadelphia, and Baltimore into teeming metropolises. Many migrants who were involved in manufacturing activities became the first US industrial workforce.

In the South, America solved the scarcity of labor problem by bringing slaves from Africa to work on their plantation. They were replenished by the slave breeding industry (discussed earlier) and through the transatlantic slave trade. After the Civil War, freed black laborers in the South became sharecroppers and developed alliances with white farmers. However, these alliances did not last long, as under the Jim Crow segregation laws such alliances were crushed. With that defeat, planters reorganized cotton production along capitalist lines with a system of centrally supervised wage labor (Post, 2011:277). From the 1890s on, planters began to mechanize Southern agriculture as they were able to organize the labor process and also to fire workers at will.

Immigrant Women Labor Force

There were only men in the first settlements in America and they had to import women to be their companions, child bearers, and sex slaves (Zinn, 2005:104). In 1619, ninety women arrived on a ship to Jamestown and they were sold to the settlers as wives. At that same time, the first black slave was brought to Virginia. Many women came from Europe as indentured servants, especially teenaged girls, but their lives were not much different from those of slaves and they were also routinely sexually abused by their masters. The only difference from slave labor was that these indentured servants came under specific terms of service, which meant that that their slavery and abuse would end one day (Ibid., 105).

Before industrialization, women on the frontier worked important jobs: shopkeepers, innkeepers, bakers, tin workers, brewers, tanners, rope makers, lumberjacks, printers, morticians, woodworkers, stay makers, publishing newspapers, managing tanneries, keeping taverns, engaging in skilled work. They also had a monopoly on midwifery (Zinn, 2005:111–112). These frontier women had to work very hard, but they also gained respect. If their husbands died, these women would run their husbands' businesses as well as running their homes. With the coming of textile mills in New England many young women took jobs in the mills and later joined in strikes to improve their living and working conditions (Dublin, 1979). These women were not passively accepting the system, and they rebelled against it and demanded equality and equal wages (Zinn:112–115).

Poor women and black women toiled in the fields and factories or as domestic servants for wages. Middle-class and upper-class white women were forbidden from working outside the home by cultural norms. However, some tried to influence the direction of public institutions (specifically, social welfare) by using their "moral" role in religious and charitable organizations. They also became health reformers (Stansell, 1982 in Kornblith, 1998). Since middle-class women were barred from higher education, they began to monopolize the profession of primary school teaching, which doubled the literacy among women between 1780 and 1840 (Zinn:117).

iv. Technology for Industrialization

A specific feature of US industrialization was that it borrowed and stole all its technology from England or other places. It did not make any sophisticated breakthrough innovations in the early nineteenth century as US manufacturers did not invest in research and development. They learned new principles from Europe and applied them to new market conditions. For example, advanced technology for the textile industry already existed when US manufacturers began the mechanization of that industry. Later, the US also borrowed and adapted from the existing locomotive and steel industry in Britain. To borrow technologies for the textile industry (as they did later in the 1830s for locomotive construction), US manufacturers regularly visited Britain. Even after US manufacturers had developed their own particular forms of innovation, they went on borrowing or copying from the Europeans.

The American upper class believed in practical innovations. American innovation was directed towards lowering cost of production and high-volume output. Benjamin Franklin said, "A discovery which … is not good for something is good for nothing." He created a practical "stove" insert for the fireplace that saved fuel and increased efficiency in heating rooms. His lightning rod reduced fires (Cross and Szostak, 1995:65). Franklin's American Philosophical Society became an important conduit for mechanical and engineering information, which further contributed to the development of innovations in the US. The US manufacturers' main concern was to achieve low-cost, high-volume output that required speed and the control of the production process. The newly arrived immigrants were useful for achieving this goal as they did not resist working on machines because they were desperate to earn a living. They worked in streamlined factories where each worker performed smaller and simplified tasks. Moreover, there was no tradition of European type guilds in America to hinder innovations. Thus, manufacturers were able to achieve three goals by introducing machines at the work place: they eliminated the old apprenticeship system; they increased productivity with a lower cost, and they disempowered those highly priced skilled workers who were attempting to slow the pace of mechanization (Ibid., 111).

After 1790, with the concentration of population in certain regions, businesses could easily connect with technically skilled workers, which led to increased industrialization. For example, Cochran writes, "[I]n a large urban area the man who wants credit can apply to a nearby bank, the shop supervisor who needs a new part can walk a few blocks down the street to get it. The innovator with a fresh inspiration can study existing practices, talk with informed friends, and consult useful books at hand" (Cochran, 1981 quoted in Kornblith, 1998:18). This concentration of workshops produced an informal all-purpose machine tool industry which was essential for autonomous economic growth as well as for successful borrowing.

In addition to learning from Europe, the US also gained from the technical knowledge that migrant workers and the many businessmen moving between two countries (Britain and the US), brought with them. For example, during the 1820s Pennsylvania coal mines benefitted from British immigrants' knowledge of black powder for blasting, steam engines for pumping water from the shafts, and rails to move heavy coal from the mine for deep coal mining. Scotsman Henry Burden brought the English technology for rolling and slitting iron to make rails and railroad spikes to Troy, New York. In 1774, Joseph Hague, an English immigrant, built two spinning jenny machines in Philadelphia replicating James Hargreaves's recent invention in England. Thomas Digges, using his art of smuggling, brought 20 English textile machine makers to the US. In 1793 Samuel Slater, a British immigrant, built water frames and carding machines from memory. Moreover, the early US chemical and pharmaceutical industries owed their origins to Swiss, English, and German immigrants (Cross and Szotsak, 1995). By the 1860s, the US mill began to resemble the English factory and not an enlightened model factory of the 1820s (Ibid., 80).

However, the availability of technology in and of itself did not bring industrialization to the US. For example, even when steam power became available, Americans did not use it until much later as they found water power cheaper and located their textile and other mills along rivers. Even though the American iron industry lost its export market after 1776, the US was not quick to adopt British iron making technology because it had access to unlimited forest resources (Cross and Szostak, 1995) and cheap imports from Britain. The situation changed in the early nineteenth century when coal fields near Pittsburgh were opened up (Ibid., 91). With the help of immigrant British workmen who were familiar with coke furnaces, with puddling and rolling, British iron making techniques were adopted and adapted. The US government supported the iron industry by imposing tariffs against foreign imports (Ibid.).

Once technological advancement and economic expansion took off in the 1840s, it did not slow down during the economic slump of 1854–55. In fact, during this time investment shifted from trade to factories, and the number of banks increased. The demand for manufactured goods started growing, and improved technology such as looms, sewing machines, reapers, lathes, and steam boilers increased productivity. Soon, general stores were replaced by specialty shops. The introduction of the railroad further changed America's landscape. By the 1850s, ten thousand miles of railroad track linked Western farmers to older railroad lines, while both the telegraph and the circulation of newspapers allowed better communication and the spreading of ideas across great distances (George, 1982:71).

Assembly Line and Mass Production

The increased demand for consumer goods required mass production, which was possible by the mechanization of the production process. An early example of a successful continuous processing was Oliver Evans's "automatic" flour mill in 1785. However, in the early nineteenth century, the form of an assembly line was stationary, where inputs were brought as needed to a stationary assembly points and workers would assemble the final products. During the 1870s and the 1880s, the earlier stationary form was replaced by a continuous assembly process in the meat packing industry. Later on, Henry Ford was able to mass produce automobiles at the turn of the nineteenth century by using the idea of a continuous assembly process and the idea of interchangeable parts (along with Taylor's scientific management) drawn from the innovations in firearms production (Ibid.). According to Ford, "mass production is the focusing upon a manufacturing project of the principles of power, accuracy, economy, system, continuity and speed ... And the normal result is a productive organization that delivers in quantities a useful commodity of standard material workmanship and design at minimum cost" (Ibid., 72). Once this system was established, it spread throughout many fields of work and production giving the employers and capitalists complete control over the workplace, which affected everyone's life in the US and beyond.

v. Increased Power of Corporations

The US Civil War had already boosted manufacturing under direct orders from the federal government as Northern factories, with 1.3 million industrial workers, were turning out weapons, ammunitions, blankets, clothing, shoes, and other wartime products, and were building shipyards fleets for Southern ports (*American Social History Project,* Vol. I, 2000:624). The federal government not only granted large contracts to Northern railroads to carry troops and supplies, but also gave loans and land grants to finance the postwar expansion of the railroads. Laws were passed to impose steep tariffs on imported manufactured goods to protect American manufacturers from competition while encouraging domestic industrial development. The Republican Party, led by iron manufacturers and coal mine owners, passed many new laws that stimulated growth and innovation in industry (Ibid.). After the Civil War, the access to Southern markets, the availability of vast natural resources, and the expansion of railroads pushed up economic growth (George, 1982:9), which further increased the power of corporations. Lincoln had warned about this increase of corporate power and feared that the Republic would be destroyed. In fact, during the last third of the nineteenth century, corporations became very powerful. However, their power and success did not come from proverbial 'rugged individualism' and heroic personal sacrifice in the pursuit of a dream. They got their power and gained advantages for themselves by using politicians and the federal government to punish rival corporations, which in turn blurred the line between corporate competition and federal regulation.

Initially, people were suspicious of corporations, as the American Revolution was against British corporations as much as it was against the British monarch and parliament (Lasn, 2012). After the Revolution, corporations were conceived as agencies of the state to meet community needs such as turnpikes, banks, railroads and canals, many of which, in essence, took the form of public utilities (Trechenberg, 2007:79).

The US Civil War was the turning point. During war time, corporations made huge profits and they were able to buy legislatures, judges, and presidents. Having lawmakers and judges in their pockets, corporations were able to guide the government to amend laws that governed them, while judges granted them small legal victories conceding rights and privileges which these corporations did not have before. An important event in 1866 that gave corporations more power involved a dispute over rail bed routes. While interpreting the law, the Supreme Court ruled that a private corporation was a "natural person" under the US Constitution, and therefore entitled to protection under the Bill of Rights (Ibid.). With this interpretation, corporations acquired all the rights, including the right to free speech, and sovereignty previously enjoyed only by the people. In other words, corporations had the same power as private citizens. However, corporations had the resources to defend and exploit their rights and freedoms more vigorously than any individual, and that gave them more freedom. From then on, the whole idea of democratic government was changed substantially and profoundly. Using these rights, railroads and mining companies were able to take over vast tracts of land with very little money. The market power of business firms also increased, as they were able to exploit technological and organizational innovations to greatly increase the size of their establishments.

After the 1870s, corporate formation was adjusted to meet the increasing demand for industrial incorporation, and thus, the legislature's control was removed transferring to the corporations themselves (Ibid.). These changes strengthened the power of corporate management in the late nineteenth century as mergers and consolidation of corporations followed. "It was the large 'modern' corporate controllable by strategically organized blocs of shares and virtually self-perpetuating boards of directors that made this concentration of power possible" (Ibid., 7). These corporations controlled banking, railroad, insurance, and power companies. In Massachusetts, where Lowell's textile industry had been described as "a miniature of the corporate industrial society of the 20th century," was also under corporate control as were the great textile mills in that city and those scattered around the state.

Corporations also benefitted from the liberal general incorporation laws in New Jersey and Delaware during the late 1890s and early 1900s. In order to generate income, these two states followed liberal laws for the creation of chartering fees and annual franchise levies. Consequently, between 1898 and 1902, about 90 corporations were chartered in New Jersey, with about fifty in 1899 alone (Ibid., 81). One-half of these corporations were manufacturing, and the remainders were public utilities and services. Businessmen liked the corporate form, as it gave their firms a personality as separate legal entities, attracting small shareholders to invest in the company, which then increased corporate capital. As the corporate system facilitated the management of large accumulations of capital, it also gave rise to a professional managerial class that was separate from the ownership of the company. Moreover, in this set up, shareholders were only liable to the extent of the capital which they had invested and not for the whole of a company's investments. Most of all, as George pointed out, corporations were largely freed from government interference because the government could only interfere by changing the legislation under which a corporation had been chartered, or through the interpretation of a corporate charter by the courts (George, 1982:78). By 1919, corporations had become more powerful as they employed more than 80 percent of the US workforce and produced most of the country's wealth.

By 1894, the US had become the world's leading industrial power, US capitalists became very wealthy and corporations became very powerful. Now they wanted to have access to foreign market and resources, as improved transport and communication system had lowered the cost and risk of foreign business. However, that was not possible without a change in federal policies. Therefore, corporations began focusing on the federal government to sway its members to promote corporate interests. In these efforts, the federal judiciary proved very helpful because most federal judges had begun their careers in corporation law, and after joining the Supreme Court, they supported their former business associates (Ibid., 38). Initially, corporations expanded their domestic market into nearby regions such as Canada and Mexico. During the country's economic depression of 1893–1897, it became imperative to sell US products abroad: sewing machines, petroleum products, electrical equipment and chemicals.

By the end of the century, as George pointed out, US companies also started to manufacture or assemble their products abroad and, in some cases, they had begun investing in the extraction of raw materials from foreign resources. By 1914, Canada had more US controlled manufacturing plants than any other country (Ibid., 105). With this direct investment, US corporations were able to acquire ownership and legal control over foreign assets adding to their portfolio investments (Ibid., 101). These ownership rights facilitated the consumption of US products abroad as well as extended US technology and management techniques to these countries (Ibid., 103). During World War I, US exports increased and industrial production rose, which helped it to recover from the severe economic recession of 1913. Thus, with expansion abroad, the already existing powerful corporations within the US, by the end of the century, "became the most powerful institutions in the American economy, and its managers the most influential group of economic decision makers" (Ibid., 107).

SUMMATION PART I

In Part I, we focused on erasing the binary of developed/underdeveloped by using a yardstick of parity to understand the making of US society and its industrialization. According to this understanding we did not categorize the US as either developed or underdeveloped. Instead, we looked into universal and specific elements in the making of US society and its industrialization as we also applied to three other societies. We noted the universal characteristics as follows: interactions with many societies, people trying to meet their four basic needs (survival, security, prosperity, reproduction), and power struggles at micro and macro levels. However, US interaction with other societies was and continues to be of specific nature i.e. immigration, invasion, colonization and slave trade. Similarly, various power struggles in the US were of specific nature within its specific historical context. We particularly highlighted those specific elements which contributed to US industrialization as follows: institution of slavery, financial elite winning the power struggle, debate over "to industrialize or not industrialize," various actions, factors and historical developments which contributed to US industrialization; a culture and myth of self-made man; business friendly legal system and banking system; creation of a labor force by turning farmers into wage laborers, promoting immigration and through slave trade and slave breeding; borrowed technology for industrialization, and corporate takeover of finance, economy, industry and politics.

In Part II, using the same yardstick of parity to understand the issue of the emergence of the large-scale steel industry in the US (1880–1914), we explain that like the other three chosen societies for this volume, the US large-scale steel industry also emerged with the intertwined historical processes of conjunction and confluence of historical forces at that time, even though specific history of each society was different.

PART II

CONJUNCTION AND CONFLUENCE OF HISTORICAL FORCES IN THE EMERGENCE OF THE LARGE-SCALE STEEL INDUSTRY

As suggested in the beginning of this chapter, we are using the same yardstick to understand the industrialization and the emergence of the large-scale steel industry (1880–1914) in the US, as we do for the other three chosen countries. With this yardstick of parity, we do not categorize the US as developed or underdeveloped, instead we focus on complex intertwined historical processes, which show that similar to other societies it was the conjunction and confluence of historical forces developing within (inter-societal interactions) the US and within international arena (intra-societal interactions) which created conditions for the emergence of the large-scale steel industry. These simultaneous historical processes were as much a specific history of the US as that of its intertwined relationship with larger international forces (see Chapter 3) and with other societies of that time.

In 1800, America had only 5 million people, however, by 1860 America was already on its way to industrial development. This development in such a short period did not happen by the actions of some genius but due to various simultaneous historical processes (within the US and internationally) coming together along with favorable geography and resources. We have already discussed in Part I how in the making of the US society and its industrialization it benefited from various historical and natural advantages. For example, increased population—due to an international migration trend—in a resource rich land (occupied and colonized) that created markets for industrial goods, capital was favored by the legal and political system, a workforce which was not against mechanization and sometimes encouraged it, and a culture which had no problem in imitating British innovation, and a government which whole heartedly supported and promoted capitalists and industrialization. For example, the US government promoted industrialization by improving the transportation and communication system by working upon the existing waterways with further construction of canals, built a system of interregional roads, innovated riverboats powered with steam, and later construction of railroads. Moreover, the US benefited from the ongoing international slave trade to run their plantation economy with slaves, and later Americans started the slave breeding industry within the US and banned the import of slaves from Africa.

In Chapter 3 we also discussed the historical forces developing internationally which directly influenced US economy and industrialization. For example, the population in Europe was moving to different locales in the early nineteenth century, as many colonial governments in different countries were offering incentives to attract the labor force. Many were choosing to migrate due to famine condition, or due to political persecution looking for a better life in the new world. A large number of these immigrants came to the US in waves and increased its population to 30 million in 1860. They provided the necessary labor force to build industries, waterways and farming, while also creating demands for farm tools and common household goods (Cross and Szotak:60). Large arable land provided higher wages and relatively cheap food and allowed households the spare wealth to buy industrial goods.

As discussed in Part I, for technological development Americans took advantage of the experience of earlier innovations undertaken in England and Europe, and learned to become skillful borrowers and adapters of another people's technology. Moreover, Americans took a practical approach towards technology. Many British immigrants helped in transferring British technology to the US. Even the US government copied from the English system of banking, insurance and corporate organizing methods for gathering money for commercial and manufacturing investment. The government also encouraged industrialization by creating a legal climate which was conducive to industrial capital and innovation, such as debt forgiveness, and limited liability. Moreover, American law tended to favor the developer (as was also the case in England) rather than the inheritor of land. All these changes in legal principles encouraged risk taking. The most important legal innovation was the Patent Law of 1790, which provided a legal monopoly over an invention (17 years) and thus, encouraged individual innovation. Aside from a favorable legal climate, the US government also helped the infant textile industry with a tariff in 1816 on imports and an embargo on British imports in 1807 (Ibid., 61). It also helped in creating a national market by linking important manufacturing centers with a network of turnpikes, canals, steamboats, and railroads. The US government also organized geological explorations of new lands, as well as promoted the railroads, which opened up these lands for industrial exploitation.

The other incentive for industrial development came from the needs of rich farmers in the North as they lacked a cheap and reliable labor force. These farmers were market oriented and had increasing access to markets as America was improving its transportation system, specifically the railways. These farmers had a strong incentive to employ labor saving machinery to maximize the quantity of land that they could cultivate. To meet this demand, agricultural tool manufacturing and food and raw material processing industries came into being (Ibid., 63). In the South the plantation economy solved this problem of scarcity of labor with forced slave labor from Africa.

American industrialization was further facilitated by a labor force which was ready to adapt to innovations and not resist mechanization of the industries. Workers did not try to sabotage mechanization because they were earning higher wages with increased mechanization. Moreover, these migrant workers were more flexible to changing industrial conditions as they were becoming jacks-of-all-trades while hopping from job to job. Thus, did not develop any personal stake in any given skill or set of tools. In fact, some workers even initiated innovation. In addition, government had also stopped enforcing the old apprenticeship system after 1810, and after 1840 newly arrived immigrant labor was put straight to work on machines.

The US government also helped promote manufacturing companies and railroads, specifically during the Civil War with direct orders to Northern factories to produce large quantities of weapons, ammunitions, blankets, clothing, shoes, and other wartime products employing 1.3 million industrial workers. These factories were also building shipyards fleets for Southern ports (*American Social History Project,* Vol. I, 2000:624). To carry troops and supplies during the Civil War, Northern railroads also got contracts from the federal government. In addition to giving contract to railroad, the government also financed the postwar expansion of the railroad with loans and land grants. The Republican Party, led by iron manufacturers and coal mine owners, passed many new laws that further stimulated growth and innovation in industry (Ibid.). For example, the federal government imposed steep tariff on imported manufactured goods to protect American manufacturers from competition while encouraging domestic industrial development. Furthermore, various Acts were passed which gave power to the federal government to create currency, to issue federal charters to banks and to create a national debt which made the government the largest single employer with a growing bureaucracy. After the Civil War, the access to Southern markets, the availability of vast natural resources, and the expansion of railroads pushed up economic growth (George, 1982:9). Urban growth further helped in creating demand for manufactured goods. By 1894, the US had become the top industrial power in the world making American capitalists and corporations wealthy and powerful. It is no wonder that within fifteen years after the war, Carnegie's first steel mill, Rockefeller's Standard Oil refinery and Bell's first telephone—all soon to become monopolies—came into being. By 1919 corporations were employing 80 percent of the US workforce.

It is within this larger context of conjunction and confluence of historical forces within the US and internationally, we locate the emergence of the large-scale steel industry in the US.

THE EMERGENCE OF THE LARGE-SCALE STEEL INDUSTRY

Since it was the iron producers who began to invest in steel making, it is imperative to understand at what point and why the iron industry began to produce steel. In 1750, England prohibited North American colonies from making steel, the refining of iron and manufacture of finished articles from iron so that these colonies would buy these products from England (Mathias, 1983:79). However, these colonies were encouraged to produce pig iron for the British iron and steel industries so that the Britain could stop importing pig iron from Sweden and Russia as they were not under British political control. Thus, until the American Revolution, the US was supplying pig and bar iron for domestic use as well as exporting to Britain. But soon after the American Revolution, the American iron industry lost its export market in Britain as well as faced competition domestically because Britain was able to produce cheap and better-quality iron with improved technology. However, in spite of the loss of market the US did not adopt the new methods developed in Britain, as the US had access to unlimited forest resources. Moreover, cheap imported iron from Britain did not create incentive for starting new iron works. The situation changed in the early nineteenth century when the US government placed a tariff on iron imports protecting the domestic iron industry from competition, and immigrant British workmen familiar with the new British technology helped in its adaptation to American resources (Cross and Szostak, 1995).

In the early 1830s American iron was still being produced by charcoal, but that changed when Americans began to use coal in the making of wrought iron, and coal using furnaces to produce cast iron in the 1840s in eastern Pennsylvania. By the 1840s, shovels, saws, scythes, stoves, pots, pans, wire, plows, reapers, harvesters, as well as axes and nails, were being produced in the factories. At the end of the decade, guns were being produced for nongovernment markets through the fabrication and assembling of interchangeable parts. During the same decade steam began to be used extensively in industrial production, and large enterprises began to spread quickly including metal working. Iron industries were modernized and the availability of large quantities of iron and coal encouraged large scale manufacturing of iron products for the first time, and soon production units moved to the larger towns which separated iron mining from iron manufacturing. Between 1842 and 1847—a time of mass migration from Europe, emerging larger towns, and the spread of railroads—the American consumption of iron had tripled. Production of various types of goods was now taking place in large factories, which gave rise to a new working class and a new management class in American industry. By the 1850s the output and technology of American factory production was very impressive (McCraw, 1988:314).

While iron production was moving into large-scale integrated establishments, steel remained until the first half of the nineteenth century an expensive refinement of wrought iron and was used in limited ways for military, knife blades, or watches or time pieces. Even though the advantage of steel was well understood, it could not be produced cheaply on a mass scale until Henry Bessemer's process in 1856 was invented in England. The Bessemer process was useful for the mass production of quality steel at a lower cost. Later, two other English innovations in steel—the open-hearth process and Sidney-Gilchrist Thomas—further helped to increase the output of steel at a lower cost. Unlike England, the US was able to effectively use the Bessemer process for producing steel on a massive scale because it had a large supply of the non-phosphoric iron ore necessary to use this process.

In addition to benefiting from British innovations in steel making, the US expansion of the railroads gave various manufacturers access to consumers everywhere, and spurred the expansion of other industries including the ones railroads needed for its own consumption: coal, iron, steel, stone, and lumber. Railroads also stimulated the communication industry through the use of the electric telegraph and transmission lines that ran along the railroad tracks. As White's study (2011) shows, government subsidies in this railroad venture played a huge role and, thus, indirectly also facilitated the mass production of steel. Along with the railroad's huge demand for steel, in the 1860s it also opened up access to Western iron ore fields (Cross and Szostak, 1995). In fact, railroads provided much of the capital investment required in all new Bessemer works so that essential supply of steel was assured. Railways also helped in increasing the importance of the stock market as railways required large investments that no one individual could provide. Andrew Carnegie, who built the most efficient steel mill, benefitted from these developments. He and other industrialists also benefited from the availability of professional engineers and scientists who were trained in universities and science laboratories established with government land grants. Thus, with the availability of a huge market, large fields of non-phosphoric iron ore and a technology to mass produce quality steel cheaply, along with the availability of a large migrant labor force, as well as educated engineers, it became possible for entrepreneurs to think of investing in large-scale steel production.

It is in this above mentioned larger historical context within the US and in the international arena, that the newly invented Bessemer steel process was introduced in the late 1860s and early 1870s (during the American Civil War) in the existing integrated iron mills. Few newly constructed works—Andrew Carnegie's Edgar Thomson Steel Works in Pittsburg and one and two other rail plants—also introduced this system (Chandler in Kornblith, 1998:143). With the new Bessemer process the average annual output of the blast furnaces rose from 5,000 to 65,000 tons and that for steel works and rolling mills from 3,000 to 23,000 tons between 1869 and 1899. During the same period, the average capital investment for a blast furnace establishment increased four and a half times, from $145,000 to $643,000, and rolling mills eight times, from $156,000 to $967,000. However, the work force grew more slowly. The expansion needed immense amount of fuel consumption which reached 8.1 million tons of coal in 1885 (Ibid., 146). In 1900, the US was producing 10 million tons of steel and in 1910, 26.1 million (Cross and Szotask, 1995:152).

ANDREW CARNEGIE'S STEEL MILL

Carnegie was not the first person in the US to invest in steel, as many iron industries had also installed Bessemer process to produce steel during the 1870s. But Carnegie's steel plant was the largest, technically most innovative and efficient early steel company in America producing tremendous profits. Andrew Carnegie, who learned his skills of administration and investment while working for railroads, had already accumulated a substantial amount of wealth with successful investments in various companies in oil wells, iron, steamer on the Great Lakes, and railroads. He also drew the idea of the administrative structure and organization for his steel mill from railways, as he had worked there as a railroad executive and remained in close relationship with railroads in order to sell Bessemer steel. Learning most of the needed skills from railways, it is not surprising that he got his general manager and other important employees for the steel mill from railroad companies. During one of his trips to England, Carnegie met steel makers and learned about the new steel making methods of mass production and saw the possibilities for steel-making in the US. In 1875 he started a steel factory in the US using the Bessemer process of steel making with the help of British engineers. Carnegie had brought these engineers from England because they were familiar with the new processes and could adapt these techniques for use in the US.

As Alfred D. Chandler pointed out, in the metal-making and metal-working industries, design of the works and plant is as equally important as the use of intense energy, and intricate costly machines for mass production. At the same time, it was important for these industries to develop systematic practices and procedures of factory management to deal with the challenges of scheduling, coordination and controlling the flow of work in an integrated steel mill. These requirements made the job of overall management more challenging because each part of the production process involved different activities. Carnegie, who had learned the complex administrative system and coordination challenges when he was working on the railroad and later running his own companies, obviously had understood these challenges and he systematically dealt with each one of these issues successfully. He decided to not only control the labor process through technological innovations, but also by controlling workers with ruthless management.

He appointed engineer Alexander Lyman Holley to design his steel mill, Edgar Thomson Steel Works, in the mid-1870s in such a way that it became the most efficient steel producer in the nation. The location for this new work was chosen carefully. It was on the Monongahela River at the junction of three railroads—the Pennsylvania, Baltimore and Ohio, and the Pittsburgh and Lake Erie, which made the fullest use of existing railroad transportation. The plant was designed to assure as continuous a flow as possible from the suppliers of the raw materials through the processes of production to the shipment of the finished goods to the customers (Cross and Szostak, 1995). At the same time, it was done in a way that unnecessary manual handling of materials was eliminated so that material moved smoothly through the various stages of the steel-making process. To that end, Holley introduced elevated trains that carried coal overhead throughout the huge mill, which eliminated the need for employing hundreds of workers to shovel coal. Carnegie's blast furnaces were the largest and most energy consuming in the world. With the profits made in this factory, he bought other mills, including the Homestead mills, and combined them in 1889 as Carnegie steel mills. He reinvested profits into new technical innovations that would improve the efficiency of the mill. In 1886 he had installed an open-hearth furnace system to produce steel which was suitable for structural beams and armor plates fetching him premium prices.

Carnegie tried to improve efficiency within the factory using systematic methods of production and management. However, this improvement could not be achieved without a guaranteed supply of necessary raw material, effective ways to market their products, and the elimination of any competition (George, 1982). Therefore, Carnegie integrated his steel industry vertically, and allying with Henry Clay Frick, he acquired sources of iron ore, coke and coal, and developed a fleet of steamships and a railroad for transporting raw material directly to his steel mills (Ibid., 31). Carnegie used his control over key oil fields to compel railroad management into cutting the rates they charged for hauling his oil, and he coerced them into giving him kickbacks on the inflated rates they charged his competitors (Ibid.). (It should be pointed out that Rockefeller followed similar tactics with railroad management for the transportation of oil.)

Chandler noted that Andrew Carnegie was the only one out of all the metal-making enterprises who had developed an effective technique of coordination and control. Carnegie had learned the skills of coordination and control in the railroads where he was working earlier as a railroad executive. He was able to transfer the administrative methods and control developed on the railroads to his manufacturing system by using them imaginatively. To implement these ideas, Carnegie appointed

William P. Shinn, a highly competent railroad executive, as his general manager, who was able to coordinate the various parts and also developed statistical data needed for coordination and control. This was accomplished with a voucher system of accounting (borrowed from railroads). According to this system, each department would list the amount and cost of materials and labor used on each order as it moved through each subunit. Shinn used this data to prepare monthly statement of cost sheets, which were then send to Carnegie. Later, Shinn also began to produce daily statements on costs of each material, repairs, and labor for each ton of rail produced. Through these everyday minute details of cost of materials and labor in every department, Carnegie and his managers—Shinn and Captain William Jones—were able to evaluate the performance of department managers, foremen, and workers while also checking the quality and mix of raw materials. They also used these statements to evaluate improvements in the product and production process, and examine the possibility of developing by-products (Chandler in Kornblith, 1998).

However, within his mechanized, technologically innovative steel mill there was no concern for worker's safety, and large numbers of workers were injured or died due to lack of safety equipment and long hours of grueling shifts. In addition, workers faced the prospect of lower wages as Carnegie was continuously trying to drive down costs of production, not only by introducing more innovative technology but also by lowering wages. However, he could not implement his plan of lowering wages without removing the hold of powerful skilled union workers from his plant. Therefore, he prepared carefully for a showdown. Henry Clay Frick, who became the director of the works at the Homestead mills, had the reputation of smashing strikes in the coal and coke industry. He immediately started the fortification of the plant. The timing was also opportune for a showdown because the railroad construction boom had come to an end, rail prices were falling, and many mills were laying off workers and shutting down plants. Therefore, when the workers union asked for a compromise on the proposed drastic tonnage reductions, Frick refused and closed down parts of the mill and discharged all its workers and served a notice that the "Homestead steel works will operate as a non-union mill" (Montgomery in Kornblith, 1998:175). Union workers fought back in the bloody Homestead Strike of 1892. But Carnegie was successful in breaking the unions by pitting union workers against non-union workers (Montgomery, 1987). Local management used Pinkerton guards to break the hold of the Amalgamated Association of Iron, Steel and Tin workers and in this skirmish many workers died. Later with the help of the Pennsylvania National Guard and strike breakers Frick was able to reopen the mill.

After this strike, Carnegie was able to effectively break the link between output and earnings, which gave management control over its wage costs (Gintz, 1954). Thus, under the supervision of Henry Frick he was able to implement an increase in the length of the working day (12-hour shifts, 7 days a week) in all of the company's plants at the same daily rate of pay. These changes also made the initiatives and prerogatives of management more important in directing and controlling machine, workers and final product. Thus, unionism in the US was weakened and workers lost their bargaining power with the development of large-scale steel production and the emergence of large firms. All these changes and control mechanisms paid off, and by 1900, Carnegie was dictating the price at which steel should be sold across the country (Ibid.).

In addition to improving efficiency and cost cutting, Carnegie was constantly re-fitting and mechanizing his steel mill with the help of engineers to deal with evolving steel markets ranging from railroads rails, to structural steel for construction, to sheets for industrial machinery, and for building automobiles. For example, when the market for steel rail began to stagnate, Carnegie tried to tap into the new markets in growing urban areas that required a specific type of steel structure for skyscrapers, bridges, and subways (Misa, 1995). Bessemer steel was not useful for those structural shapes, or even for the rails that could bear the strain of heavy locomotives and trains. Therefore, Carnegie refitted his steel mill in 1890s with the basic open-hearth process to meet the needs of this new market. Open-hearth steel was also used for making rails at the end of the century when the second generation of the railroad industry began to use heavier locomotives and trains. Carnegie also benefited from the naval arms race which intensified between 1885 and 1914, as battleships were all protected by technically identical armors. The price of armor plates in the US was fifteen times as high as rail prices and it required acid open-hearth steel. The Carnegie and Bethlehem companies were able to provide these armor plates and made large profits which consolidated their leading positions in the industry (Ibid). In 1885, the American steel industry was looking for an outlet overseas for its surplus production of steel. At the same time, a growth in the formation of Trusts was also emerging in the US. In the steel industry, it culminated into the formation of the US Steel Company in 1901 when J. P. Morgan bought Carnegie's steel industry and relieved Carnegie from its control.

In 1901, Morgan consolidated half of the US steel companies and formed the US Steel Company, the nation's first billion-dollar corporation (Elbaum and Wilkinson, 1979). The purpose of the formation of this giant corporation was to stabilize the steel industry because Carnegie was purchasing iron ore lands in order to destabilize the railroad industry—in direct conflict with J. P. Morgan, who had played a leading role in reorganizing bankrupt railroads in the 1890s. Therefore, the main reason for the US Steel merger was, as one contemporary understood, "to eliminate Mr. Carnegie from the trade" (quoted in Misa, 1995: xxii). However, the creation of large cartels and trusts enabled the US steel industry to compete in the world arena, as well as to eliminate unionism in 1909 by locking out US steel workers. These unions could not match the power of monopoly capital as it did not have the mass organization and central control necessary to challenge it.

The American steel industry kept on changing its structure and mechanization with new demands of the market. For example, metal cutting factories required entirely different steel made in hundred-pound batches inside clay or graphite crucibles and then forged into tool steel. In 1905, automobile production became the final industrial sector to alter basic patterns in the steel industry as it was the leading user of steel (Misa, 1995). It required a specific type of high-tech steel alloy which could be produced with electric furnaces because it yielded exceptionally clean steel. Moreover, they also preserved the expensive alloying elements that other steel-making processes wasted. The requirements of the automobile industry gave the steel industry its modern form. American industry on the whole was transformed with the availability of cheaper steel and specialist alloys, as American industries now were able to produce more machine tools and more complex products. With the coming of World War I, America was able to export a large number of products, which boosted its economy and it thus was able to recover from the severe economic recession of 1913.

SUMMATION PART II

By using the yardstick of parity, we showed that similar to the other three societies discussed in this volume, the large-scale steel industry in the US also emerged due to the conjunction and confluence of various historical forces developing within the US (inter-societal interactions) as well as internationally (intra-societal interactions) during the 1880s. We traced in Part I, various historical processes which were taking place within the US and internationally over time. It is emphasized that in addition to natural and historical advantages (mass immigration from Europe, technology), US government played an important role in promoting industrialization through improved infrastructure (roads, canals, railways), a legal system favorable to investors, patent laws, tariff, geological exploration and providing data for exploitation of resources, direct orders to meet the needs of the military during the Civil War, and undermining worker's unionization.

The iron industry was already developing in the US during the 1840s, and with the introduction of steam in production process, a large quantity of iron became available, which in turn encouraged the large-scale manufacturing of iron products. The consumption of iron further increased with mass immigration from Europe, increased urbanization, and expansion of railways. Thus, a mass market already existed for iron when the mass production of steel was introduced in iron mills during the Civil War. This shift to mass production of steel became possible at that time because in 1856 the new Bessemer's process invented in England became available for that purpose. Through that process, steel could be produced in large quantities inexpensively, and moreover, the US had the large reserve of non-phosphoric iron ore necessary to use in this process. Many iron mills introduced the Bessemer process to produce steel. However, we elaborated on Carnegie's steel mill because he was able to create a successful and efficient steel mill. He was successful in transferring the skills of organization, administration and management that he learned while working in the railways to the production of steel. He made his mills most efficient by constantly improving methods of production, cost of production, and controlling his workers with strict discipline and ultimately breaking their hold on the labor process by breaking unions. He was able to refit his mills according to the changing steel market and new inventions while constantly increasing profitability. By 1900 he was dictating the price of steel in the US. In 1901, J. P. Morgan created the nation's first billion-dollar corporation, US steel, combining half of the US steel mills including Carnegie's mills. US steel kept on changing its structure and mechanization with new demands of the market, which included the needs of the automobile industry.

CHAPTER SUMMATION

In this chapter we try to show that the making of the US was no different than that of the other three chosen countries as it was created and constructed through the interaction of people within the US and through larger international historical forces. People also made choices in this process of interaction that included the ruling elite, the business class, the professionals—lawyers, engineers, and others who controlled the social, religious, economic and political institutions —as well as migrant workers (men and women). However, these people made choices in a larger context that was created earlier based on choices made by previous generations to open the new world for profits. The previous generations made their choices in the European context where the rush for territorial expansion was in full force with the development of capitalism. Similar to other societies, the US has both universal characteristics as well as a specific history unique to itself. In this chapter, I have tried to explain both these traits (universal and specific) in the making of the US while also connecting them to the issue of industrialization and, ultimately, to the matter of the emergence of the large-scale steel industry during 1880–1914.

It is pointed out that the role of the Federal government was very decisive in creating conditions for industrialization and later for the large-scale steel industry. Moreover, the US state and society made a conscious choice to industrialize. Once the decision was made to industrialize, then Federal government took steps to help create those institutions to achieve this goal. It gave incentives in every area and at every stage to investors, business people and employers to promote industry and also passed laws and policies to protect the industry from unions. The migration of Europeans was encouraged, which replenished the US labor force and also enriched US knowledge of various technologies that these immigrants brought with them. The Federal government established educational institutions to help generate more knowledge and innovations. The needs of the US military created the evolution of advances in weapon technologies that were then used for private interests to make profit from them. The steel industry also benefitted from government orders for steel armors.

Right from the beginning, the US had been borrowing technology from abroad for producing various goods. The case of steel industry is not different because the US started large scale steel industry only when Bessemer process of mass production became available in England. It was first installed in many existing iron mills during the American Civil War. A few mills—Carnegie and two others—were newly constructed to mass produce steel. Carnegie was more successful in creating a well-organized, highly efficient, cost effective and profitable steel mill, which he was constantly upgrading, and refitting to meet the evolving demands of the steel market. However, in 1901 he sold it to J. P. Morgan, the financial magnate, who created the first billion-dollar large corporation of US steel by combining half of the existing steel mills including Carnegie's.

Thus, the emergence and development of the US large-scale steel industry is intertwined with the invention of Bessemer Process in England, expansion of railroads and railways, and later with urbanization and the automobile industry. It evolved along with the demands of evolving market in the US. The steel industry benefitted from tariffs and from government subsidies for expansion of railways, even though there was no real demand for railway expansion. It has also been pointed out that the large-scale steel industry was not simply a product of technological breakthroughs or the genius of one person. It was a long drawn out process in which numerous actors (including historical processes internationally) played parts creating conjunction of various historical processes, which allowed the emergence of the large-scale steel industry in the US in the 1880s, and its development up to the First World War giving it a specific form and structure.

ENDNOTES

1. Michael Yates reviewing Henry Giroux's book, *America's Addiction to Terrorism,* NY: Monthly Review Press (2016), highlighted the following:

    Nation (the US) was founded upon terrorism, namely that of slavery, whose unspeakable degradations hardly ended with formal emancipation. Jim Crow, the KKK, thousands of lynching, mass imprisonment, and an orgy of police torture and murder have tormented the lives of black men and women right up to the present day. Black men, women and children became the nation's torture template, and what has happened to them set the stage for that directed at workers who dared defy their employers, and to the peoples of the world as the US rained misery down on its many enemies, reaching to apogee but by no means its end with the atomic bombing of Hiroshima and Nagasaki .... Giroux excoriates all this terror, as well its contemporary raw, naked and ever more diabolical forms: drone strikes, waterboarding, renditions, rape, presidential kill lists, and all of these horrors documented in the US senate's recent Committee Study of the Central Intelligence Agency's Detention and Interrogation Program" (Michael D. Yates, "On Henry Giroux," in *Monthly Review,* January 2016. pp. 44–45).

    Comparing the violent history of America and its continuation in the present time, Garikai Chengu wrote recently the following in *The Guardian* newspaper:

    During the late nineteenth and early twentieth century on average two African Americans were lynched every week ... today FBI data shows that a Black person is killed by a white police officer more than twice a week ... lynching also included humiliation, torture, burning, dismemberment and castration. A public ritual that often took place in front of large crowds that sometimes numbered in the thousands and children played during the festivities ... [in one issue of 1899 *Springfield Weekly* information is available about how torture and dismemberment of black people took place. "Bones crushed to small pieces and ... selling small bones for 25 cents"] it went hand in hand the imprisonment of Blacks ... to this day American government refuses to designate the KKK as a domestic terrorist organization ... Racially motivated war on drugs ... profit system depends on imprisoning Blacks for its survival ... Capitalism was created by slavery and slavery in turn created the enduring legacy of Racial Capitalism that persists in America today" (Garikai Chengu, "How Slaves Built American Capitalism" (12/18/15) in counterpunch.org).

2. William Jennings Bryan's Cross of Gold Speech, July 8, 1896. See "American History from Revolution to Reconstruction and Beyond Documents." (http//www.let.rug.nl/usa/documents/1876–1900).
3. Hogeland interviewed by David V. Johnson in "How Big Finance Won the American Revolution." ReadersSupportedNews.org, December 2, 2012.
4. In 1862, a document known as the Hazard Circular prepared by British banking interests, was circulated among US bankers. This circular revealed the ploy of European financiers to support wage labor instead of slavery because it would allow capitalists to exploit labor by controlling the money supply while labor would be feeding itself.

    Slavery is likely to be abolished by the war power and chattel slavery destroyed. This, I and my European friends are glad of, for slavery is but the owning the labor and carries with it the care of the laborers, while the *European plan,* led by England, is that capital shall control labor by controlling wages. This can be done by controlling the money. The great debt that capitalists will see to it is made out of the war, must be used as a means to control the volume of money. To accomplish this, the bonds [government debt to the bankers] must be used as a banking basis ... It *will* not do to allow the greenbacks, as it is called, to circulate as money any length of time, as we cannot control that [(3)].

    The wish of British banking interests was fulfilled, as after the Civil War slaves were turned into wage labor. "Hazard Circular" 1862, quoted in Charles Lindburgh, *Banking and Currency and the Money Trust.* Washington, DC: National Capital Press. 1913. p. 102; Ellen Brown, quoted from Lindburgh in her article, "'Today We're All Irish': Debt Serfdom Comes to America." Global Research.ca. March 18, 2017.

5. American Social History Project: CUNY (2000) *Who Built America? Working People and the Nation's Economy, Politics, Culture and Society: From Conquest to Colonization Through 1877.* Vol. I. New York: Worth Publishers. p. 382.
6. In the early twentieth century, Andrew Carnegie (in his *Gospel of Wealth* and his autobiography) promoted similar ideas. Rockefeller and Morgan were also portrayed at that time as models of virtue in the fiction of "rags to riches," while conflicts in real life were ignored. Similarly, the media promoted an image of Edison as a hero, genius, an example of ingenuity and self-reliance, while ignoring that he was a businessman who employed a large number of engineers who helped him create new things by experimenting continuously. He collaborated with media to promote this image as he well understood the power of media to promote his products and attract financial investment (Morus, 2018).
7. Kornblith, J. G. "The Entrepreneurial Ethic." In Gary J. Kornblith (Ed.), *Problems in American Civilization: The Industrial Revolution in America.* Boston ; NY: Houghton Mifflin Co. 1998. pp. 71–79.

   Kornblith wrote about a master craftsman, Jonas Chickering, who was America's premier piano maker and how he became a capitalist by adopting the division of labor. Chickering adopted production strategies that paralleled innovative development in several other trades: the expansion of a wage-earning work force, the subdivision of the manufacturing process into highly specialized tasks, the use of new materials and new technologies, and the design of relatively standardized products appropriate for sale to a national clientele. He started as a cabinet maker and learned his trade as an apprentice at the age of seventeen to local cabinet maker. Later he went to work for piano maker John Osborn a true master of the trade. After Chickering became sole owner of the small piano manufactory, he transformed the way piano was made and his partner Mackay transformed the way in which they were sold. Later, Chickering bought the company from Mackey's son (as Mackey had died) and organized his workers of 100 into over twenty separate departments, each devoted to a different step of the manufacturing process. Workers were trained only in a small part of the production process. Kornblith wrote,

   > Consequently with the exception of his sons—at least two of whom enjoyed the benefits of a regular apprenticeship under his supervision—Chickering's employees lacked the range of knowledge to become masters in their own right and could expect to remain wage earners for the duration of their careers within the trade. For him there was no inherent contradiction between the 'modern' goal of maximizing one's profits and the 'traditional' goal of perfecting one's craft. He turned his shop into a factory and his craft into an industry and he conferred the legitimacy of the new even though he was trained under the old productive order. By infusing industrial capitalism with the authority of craft tradition, he and other artisan entrepreneurs obscured the emerging conflict of interest between capital and labor, and made innovations more palatable to workers and consumers alike. As a result, support for technological change and economic development cut across class lines, and there emerged a broad-based coalition in favor of the Industrial Revolution in America (p. 79).

CHAPTER 7

The Emergence of the Large-Scale Indian Steel Industry under British Colonial Rule, 1880–1914

> The image of 'holistic' ideology mainly [was achieved] by marginalising in India's historical culture all those elements which might conceivable correspond to some kind of 'individualism'—such as Brahmanic ethic and *bhakt*-ism ... just as it achieves its image of Modern West as 'individualistic' by overlooking Europe's own holistic ideologies—Catholicism, monarchism, Fascism. Similarly, it denies Traditional India ideologies of equality by focusing exclusively on caste at the expense of systems of kinship, temple sect and 'community,' where hierarchy was never easy to establish. Just as its inference that Modern Western society is no longer dominated by ideologies of hierarchy disposes, at a stroke, of the entire subject matters of the sociologies of gender, generation and race (Washbrook, 1997:415).

> "Between 1765 and 1938, the [Britain's] drain [of India 's wealth] amounted to 9.2 trillion pounds ($45 trillion), taking India's export surplus earnings as the measure, and compounding it as a 5 per cent rate of interest" (Patnaik, 2018).

INTRODUCTION

David Washbrook and many other scholars have challenged the essentialized images of both India and of the Western world. Sumit Sarkar, a renowned Indian Marxist historian, has also alluded to similar observations in his recent volume on India (Sarkar, 2014) by highlighting the circulatory processes in various economic and environmental interactions within colonial India [(1)].

While agreeing with these scholars, I wish to not simply challenge the binary distinction, but to erase it so that we can find an alternative perspective that does not require the binary distinction of developed/underdeveloped to understand any society. With this in mind, my specific focus in this volume is on the binary distinction of development/underdevelopment and how to erase it, because as practiced in its present form a comparative historical approach is not useful. This existing approach focuses on supposedly separate autonomous social entities that are compared using a prior assumption of being either developed or underdeveloped. The challenge to this binary distinction is critical because historians have continued to label India as a "backward" country despite the fact that pre-British India exported cotton textiles in large quantities to the world market for centuries (Parthasarathi, 2011). Moreover, throughout a long history of 5000 years, India was able to innovate and contribute in many fields of art, literature, architecture, trade, mathematics, sciences, technology, commerce, shipbuilding, culinary art, apparel, and various other fields. It is pointed out in Chapter 1 that modern science is a product of innovations, skills, and knowledge learned from India and other advanced civilizations such as China, as well as from the West. There was no one group of geniuses located in one place who created on their own, in a vacuum, all of the sciences and knowledge. As is also noted in the introductory chapter, common people had been gathering knowledge for thousands of years while hunting, fishing, and other survival activities. Today, all of us benefit from the cumulative knowledge gathered by our common human ancestors around the world for thousands of years.

In this chapter our focus is on refuting the label of India's so called backwardness and being underdeveloped, while also suggesting an alternative way of understanding India's present condition without the binary label of developed/underdeveloped. The question of India's underdevelopment has been raised in debates dealing with the question of India's de-industrialization under colonial rule by Indian nationalist leaders and economic historians (2). During the 1960s this debate was undertaken with great vigor. One group of thinkers blamed colonial rule for India's underdevelopment, whereas another group attributed it to India's static traditional society (3). It is notable that Indian nationalists' discourse in the late nineteenth century on India's de-industrialization seems strikingly similar to the arguments extended in the dependency theory (with better terminology and conceptualization) of the mid-twentieth century (Chandra, 1991). However, the literature on theories of development does not reflect the contribution made in this regard by nationalist Indian economists of the late nineteenth century.

The approaches stemming from the 1960s debate on India's de-industrialization are inadequate to help explain the exceptional historical emergence of the large-scale steel industry in India at the beginning of the twentieth century under British colonial rule. The developmentalists are interested in explaining either underdevelopment or the positive effects of imperialism. Moreover, their analysis of the phenomenon of "underdevelopment" is often severed from the specific histories of the countries in question; a lacuna that creates more problems in understanding "underdevelopment" than it resolves. Meanwhile, most Indian economists and economic historians accept the conclusion that India was de-industrialized under British colonial rule (4). However, Sumit Sarkar, an Indian Marxist historian, recently highlighted the problem of the nationalist Indian economists' idea about Naoroji's 'drain theory' and finds the idea of a "circulatory" process more useful in understanding the issue of India's industrialization (Sarkar, 2014).

In my earlier book (1995), I pointed out that contrary to the approaches based on the idea of the stage theory of transition, the issue of India's industrialization under colonial rule should be examined by looking at the conjunction of historical forces of the time with regard to how they were formed and how, in turn, they formed each other. Based on this understanding I showed how the large-scale Indian steel industry was not the outcome of different stages of economic and technological development within India, as Rostow suggests in his theory of modernization (stages of economic growth). Nor did it emerge due to inevitable historical change (so called continuous and progressive) with a shift in the productive base (also a stage theory idea) as Marx would have it (5). Instead, as discussed in Part II of this chapter, it was the conjunction of various historical forces developing within India and in the international arena at that time that created the conditions for the emergence of the large-scale Indian steel industry under colonial rule.

To carry my argument further, I suggest here that we should stop using the existing binary distinction of developed/underdeveloped to categorize any society. Instead, we need to use a yardstick of parity to understand every society by looking into the universal and specific elements in the making of each society. This suggestion (discussed in detail in Chapter 2) is based on the understanding that each society is made by its members (human agency), their actions and choices that include power struggles, class struggle (a continuously changing process) within a society, and by society to society interactions (intra-societal). In all of these social and historical processes, it is the innate characteristic of human creativity (inherited from nature's innate creativity, as human beings are one of the infinite expressions of nature's creativity) that expresses itself in human agency (actions). However, human action is guided by four basic needs: survival, prosperity, security, and reproduction. These human choices and actions in each society create a conjunction and combination of larger historical forces both within the society as well as internationally. In turn, societies and countries make choices and act within this vast, continuously changing historical context from both within a society and also internationally. Thus, it is not possible to simply look into the specific history of a society and ignore the interaction and mutual influence of larger historical processes both within a society and internationally, which are in turn the products of the actions and choices of people of each society.

This yardstick was used in earlier chapters for understanding postcolonial Imperial US, the Imperial UK, and Imperial Russian societies. In this chapter we apply the same yardstick to understand colonial India's industrialization with a special focus on the emergence of the country's large-scale steel industry (as was also done for the above mentioned countries). By doing so, it is possible to establish that all societies—including the colonized—can be understood without the binary distinction of "developed/underdeveloped" or "progressive/backward," while locating them in their specific context of conjunction of historical forces within and internationally. By removing the cobwebs spun by these labels, it becomes possible to see how each society emerged in similar ways historically through complex interaction processes among different social actors with various social relationships, based on class, race, gender or any other, within these societies—as well as with other societies over time. However, to substantiate our argument, the historical material about India's industrialization (as well as for the other three countries) is organized around the main issue of this volume: Erasing the binary distinction of developed and underdeveloped with a yardstick of parity. Therefore, readers will only get a synoptic historical account of India's industrialization, and not a conventional in-depth chronological history of India.

In Part I of this chapter, after tracing the universal and specific elements in the making of Indian society/country (as was done for other societies in this volume), I shall locate India in the context of British Imperial colonialism and within other larger historical forces which were developing at that time within India, as well as in the international arena. In Part II, within these larger contexts, I shall explain how and why the large-scale steel industry in colonial India came into being. In other words, our focus will be on the conjunction and confluence of historical forces, both internationally and from within India, that created conditions for the emergence of the large-scale steel industry in India. Our methodology will also refute the Western myth that the lack of technology, technical knowledge, or cultural constraints were major impediments in the industrialization of India.

PART I

ERASING THE BINARY DISTINCTION WITH A YARDSTICK OF PARITY

India's history spans over 5000 years, and its civilization had been developing in every area of human life while contributing a great deal of knowledge to the fields of science, literature, philosophy, mathematics, fine arts, and technology—including steel production. However, in this chapter we focus only on more recent times and find that the basic trajectory of Indian history is not much different from that of the three other societies examined in this volume. Aside from specific details, the larger story of invasion, constant territorial wars, territorial claims, migration, trade, borrowing of technology, political intrigues and alliances, power struggles, and so on, remain similar. Specific details vary for each society, as does the time period of their trajectories. The important point is that people in each society behaved in a similar manner. As human beings, all of them were involved in shaping their society to fulfill their human needs. The individuals or groups who were successful in controlling the resources of their society tried to keep those elements under their control. Inevitably, social conflicts emerged and manifested into class conflicts, compromises, and repressions, which in turn created new material conditions (modes of production, new class conflicts, power struggles, social relations and social structures—economies, political systems and culture—values, world view and so on), which then affected the choices people made in those new conditions. Thus, the cycle continues. Individually, who became successful, how, and why, are important questions in their own right. However, every society is created and reproduced in every historical time through its members in the process of their interaction with other members of the society and its social institutions. At the same time, the actions and choices of each member of a society are not autonomous from their societal and larger historical context which is also connected with other societies in a particular historical time.

Based on this understanding and using the yardstick of parity, we focus below on the universal and specific elements in the making of Indian society and its industrialization instead of categorizing India as either developed or underdeveloped.

UNIVERSAL ELEMENTS IN THE MAKING OF COLONIAL INDIA

The universal characteristics of Indian society are as follows: connections and interaction with other societies, interactions among people within society and choices made by different sections of society, power struggles, mix of many cultures, a concern with four basic human needs: survival, prosperity, security, and reproduction; and the choices and actions based on geographical conditions.

> Like people everywhere, Indian people are also doubters and believers, conformists, and non-conformists. They are defiant, compliant, selfish, magnanimous, independent, innovative, tradition bound, fearful, courageous, optimistic, pessimistic. They hope, aspire, despair, subvert, connive, abide, enforce, manipulate and choose among alternatives as they cope with their society and its values (Berreman, 1971:18).

As with Imperial Russia, Imperial Britain and the postcolonial Imperial US, we can discern the elements of both universality and specificity in the making of modern

India as well. India's long history across thousands of years evolved through many invasions along its western borders, through traders interacting with neighboring countries along coastal areas, and through the migration of people for various purposes, both from outside as well as within the subcontinent. Regarding India's earlier relations with Europe, Oscar Pujol (N.d.) noted that it "began in the sixth century BC and ended with the fall of the Roman Empire." Thus, India was constructed with a mix of diverse religions, sects, traditions, social practices, ethnicities, languages, political systems, economic and financial structures, and cultures. Recently, writing about the alternative history of early medieval India, Bhariabi Sahu suggested similar ideas. It is worthwhile to quote at length from her article as it corroborates the point being made here:

> The cultural unity of India represented in a pool of common ideas, values, symbols and motifs was not naturally inherent or inherited, but derived from the intra-and inter-regional cultural transactions which shaped the formation of the regions during the early medieval period and beyond. So it emerges that regions are part of the whole and not the whole itself ... while regions shape and are continuously reshaped by trans-regional/pan-Indian cultural strands, the sense of shared tradition engendering the experience of belonging to a felt community in a spatially distinguishable and culturally identifiable entity evolves historically ... The interaction and spread of 'imitable models,' first Buddhism and later Brahmanical ideology, with all their associated ideas and ingredients, created conditions for the spread of state societies and overarching cultural forms, while allowing space for both cultural confluence as well as diversity to thrive even in situations ... of 'antagonistic tolerance.' ... There have always been networks of cultural interactions. Linkages between South and South-east Asia continued in the post–Gupta times. The rise of early subregional/regional kingdoms provided the context and the Brahmanas, epics and the temples, trade and politics—among others—became the agencies in the evolving long term, lively interrelationship. ... The interaction between the world of Islam and regional cultures of South Asia precedes the Ghuri conquests by almost half a millennium. ... A trade charter from Kerala dated to the mid-ninth century, which is bilingual and multi-script—with Hebrew, Kufic (for Arabic) and Pahlavi scripts beside those to do with Malayalam and Sanskrit—easily points to the ongoing multilateral transactions.... the large-scale migration of frontier groups at the turn of the thirteenth century ... they carried with themselves their social networks 'and their households carried steppe and frontier traditions with them to their new homes' ... Such transregional influences were not new to the North-West and the Punjab; they had comparable experiences in the early historical times with the coming of the Bactrians, Indo-Greeks, Sakas, Pahlavas, Kushanas, and the Huns ... Studies such as these make it possible for us to recognize the permeable borders and appreciate the transcultural influences in the shaping of the regions and Indian civilization in pre-modern times ... It appears that all through there was change, but change through continuities, instead of the earlier perceived breaks or ruptures (Sahu, 2016:34–35).

Thus, according to Sahu, there was no empirical or conceptual break in transition from early medieval to medieval times, as these transitions were negotiated in the process of structural evolution in different domains, which allowed the gradual integration of state and society.

Along the same lines, we explore the universal characteristics in the making of India, and find that, like other societies, India had been interacting with other societies from its very beginning through invasions, migrations, trade, and travel. For example, from the north-west came the Greeks, Shungas, Kushans, Turks, Mongols, and Persians. They brought their religion, language, culture, and practices to India—making it a mix of many cultures and languages. The specific history of modern India was made within this universal historical process of the formation of modern societies. The unification of large parts of present-day India was enabled by both local rulers and foreign invaders-turned rulers at different points of time in Indian history. Among these early rulers were: Ashoka, Samudragupta, Alauddin Khilji, and Muhammad Tughlaq. However, these early imperial unities did not survive for long, and, consequently, did not make a major impact on the economy. Under the Moghul Emperor Akbar, the subcontinent was partially reunited during the sixteenth century. It was under Aurangzeb's rule in the seventeenth century that nearly the whole subcontinent was united.

During the time of the Moghul Empire, as Washbrook (1997) pointed out, the Indian economy underwent many changes and was linked with the world through three networks of trade and civilization. One link was connected from India's west coast to Arabia and the Levant. The second link was from India's northwest to Central Asia and Iran. The third link was from India's southeast to Southeast Asia. These links facilitated the interaction of a variety of people, ideas and goods, which contributed in creating a materially rich Indian civilization. Elaborating on this material richness of Indian civilization, Washbrook (1997) noted that from the West and Northwest India received Islam, the Persian wheel, systems of commercial and state organizations, various military technologies, and vast quantities of silver. It received copper, silk, spices, and large quantities of gold from the East. However, it was not a one-way process, as India also sent back many things in all directions, including the most important export item, cotton cloth. Europeans were not directly connected with this network of Asian trade and civilizations until the eighteenth century.

In the late eighteenth century, Britain was successful in controlling the destiny of India, and once again the complex mix of people in India—with its various religions, sects, languages, cultures and social structures—came under the control of yet another outside ruler. Under British colonial rule, India's social institutions, polity, economy, social organization, culture, languages, and way of life were substantially restructured and reshaped. However, it was not a one-way process because the British way of life and British ideologies were also influenced by their interactions with India. The colonization of India and North America paved the way for Britain's Industrial Revolution because India and the Atlantic colonies provided Britain with the raw material, mass consumption commodities, capital, and external markets, which were crucial for the industrial success of Britain. Moreover, the Indian economy played a crucial role in providing a continual balance-of-payments surplus for the Empire, and those huge surpluses helped Britain to gain 'mastery of the world finance' (Anievas, and Nişancioğlu, 2015:261–262; see also Patnaik, 2017a and 2017b). The Indian colony also provided a cheap land army that helped Britain to defeat France in various wars and also evict Napoleon from Egypt when the Indian based army joined the British navy in a joint operation (Washbrook, 1997; see also Bayly, 1988).

Like other societies, the varied physical features of the sub-continent and its natural barriers contributed in the making of its specific history. For example, foreign invaders came to India from the northwestern mountain passes and created a very mixed culture. Indian defense was weak in this region due to the Thar desert, which separated two regions into two different units. However, Himalaya in the north protected India from invaders, whereas the sea protected it from three other sides. These natural protections allowed India to evolve her own style of life and development. Moreover, the region of Utter Pradesh, Bihar, and Bengal had a tropical climate and many rivers running from Himalaya throughout the year, which made this region very prosperous. However, the natural division that separated South India from the North created two separate histories and, to a large extent, South India remained immune to the political turmoil of the North.

Like other societies, India as a modern entity was created by bringing various principalities and empires under one ruler. Even though large parts of India were unified under Mughal emperors Akbar and Aurangzeb, India as it exists today is the creation of British colonial rule. Britain was able to colonize India by getting involved in the power struggles among various regional princes after the breakup of the Mughal Empire.

Power struggles are a universal phenomena and it was no different in the case of India. However, internal power struggles soon became proxy wars between the French and British, thus intertwining local conflicts with global conflicts for territorial gains. A detailed story of these power struggles is not the focus of this volume. However, a short summary of the major power struggles will be discussed below to explain the specific form it acquired in the process of people's interactions within India, as they were simultaneously interacting with the larger international historical forces of that time. This discussion will show how modern India was a product of all these various interactions, and power struggles.

SPECIFIC ELEMENTS IN THE MAKING OF COLONIAL INDIA

To understand the specificities of power struggles, we need to also understand the specific larger historical context in which these power struggles were taking place, how the Europeans and British became involved in these local wars, and how, in the end, the British were successful at colonizing the whole of India; defeating various Indian princes and European rivals. Once Britain was able to colonize and unify different local rulers under the new entity called India under British rule, it was able to create mechanisms to stabilize and organize it in such a way that it could utilize Indian resources for its own needs and profits. However, Britain and Europeans were not dealing with a static society but a dynamic one with a thriving textile industry, amongst a number of other industries—the finished products of which were already being exported around the world.

1. INDIA'S DYNAMISM UNDER THE MUGHALS

Those believing in the idea, as promoted by British colonialists, about India being a "static, traditional and hierarchical society" and therefore, "it did not develop its economy due to its religion and caste system," do not take into account the fact that between the twelfth and eighteenth centuries, "the same constraints did not prevent India from generating an industrial system of major global importance, which pioneered the first world market in manufactured goods" (Washbrook, 1997:416).

Today, we have a vast amount of information about the existence of various industries, and technical knowledge in numerous fields as well as the existence of scientific thinking in pre-British India. Moreover, historians have brought to light much information about the prevailing applied techniques and practical skills that existed in Mughal India, which cannot be labeled any more "backward" and stagnant than the early modern West (Parthasarathi, 2011; Raj 2007). In addition, under Mughal India, the sugar industry was well developed in Bengal, Gujarat, and Punjab. Utensils, renowned for their beauty, were made with copper, brass, and bell metal. Gold mining, and copper mining, and diamond mining were developed, as was the pearl industry. Indians also built good ships and the iron industry was well developed although steel was produced in a small quantity. Indians made sword, javelins and other traditional arms of good quality. The most important famous and largest industry was cloth of different varieties of cotton, silk, and wool. Indian cotton enjoyed a worldwide reputation and this industry flourished for a long time. Carpets and shawls of good quality were also produced in India. The Mughal emperors also started many *Karkhanas* (factories) for producing woolen cloth.

Mughal India also created new possibilities to open up and develop by allowing contacts with the Europeans. For example, in the areas of agriculture, India adapted to the new crops that were brought from the Americas—tobacco, tapioca, potatoes, and above all the chilies—which made a significant change in Indian diet and in production. Similar was the case in the area of production of goods and commerce. Washbrook noted that such contacts allowed cotton weaving artisans to create various types of fabric designs for multiple markets in the world. Similarly, blacksmiths produced high qualities of sword steel. In this expansion of commerce, the need to control the movements of money and resources over longer distance became important, and thus, new accountancy and management skills were developed (Washbrook, 1997:427). India also acquired a substantial supply of gold and silver from Africa and Asia in this expansion of commerce. Moreover, India was also able to get American bullion, which Europeans took from them and exchanged for Indian textiles.

2. EUROPEAN AND BRITISH TRADING COMPANIES IN INDIA AND THEIR MILITARIZATION

The Europeans and British were successful after the 1600s in controlling Indian commerce and industry, as reflected in the economy of Bengal where substantial growth occurred between the 1660s and 1730s through European investment in trade. In the sixteenth century, the Portuguese and Dutch had started arming the Asian seas in an effort to increase their power and profits in Asian trade. The limited response by Indian states to this activity enabled Europeans to increasingly take over India's long-distance sea trade during the seventeenth century. By the early eighteenth century, English merchants held predominant control over Indian trade. Consequently, Indian products began to lose market shares, first due to the increase of tariffs in European countries to protect European industries, and second, due to the disruption to the Ottoman Empire (Washbrook, 1997).

To further expand its trade, British traders of the East India Company began to build an Indian land army (militarization of the East India Company) to defeat its major rival, France, in many wars. The creation of the Indian army was pivotal in making Britain a world super power. Thereafter, as Washbrook noted, the joint forces of the Indian land army and British naval power began to dominate most of the world between the Mediterranean and the China Sea (Ibid.; see also Bayly, 1988).

The British were able to build up one of the largest European style standing armies composed of Indians because they were able to seize the land revenue of India between 1750 and 1881. The Indian army was useful in winning over regional power struggles after the decline of Mughal Empire. In addition, this army was used to control the subcontinent itself, which enabled the British to increasingly employ its army and naval power to construct informal empires of influence and trade in the Middle East, the coast of China, and East Africa during the first two decades of the nineteenth century. Thus, the Indian army became an imperial reserve, as questions relating to the Indian military were now debated in an international context. For example, it was used against the French in Egypt in 1801, and for the seizure of the Cape of Good Hope in 1795 and 1806 (Bayly, 1988).

Once the British gained a foothold in the Asian trading world, they began selling Indian opium and raw cotton on the Chinese market. Later, these British merchants expanded their trade operations to the Philippines and Latin America, which were then part of the Spanish Empire. These new trading operations made it possible for British merchants to open trade back to Europe with new products including tea and porcelain (Ibid. and Washbrook, 1997).

In addition to expanding and controlling its trade within India and internationally, the British and Europeans also got involved in the ongoing power struggles amongst various regional principalities, as the subcontinent was fragmenting due to the decline of the Mughal Empire. This involvement enabled them to play an important part in the colonization and subsequent formation of future India.

3. FRAGMENTATION OF THE SUBCONTINENT

With the weakening of the Mughal Empire from the early eighteenth century, the subcontinent was broken up into a series of de facto regional states. There is no consensus among historians on why and how this happened. However, Washbrook (1997) believes there is enough evidence to show that the earlier loose relations among the state, labor, and capital began to change with the expansion of commercialization during the seventeenth century, which probably led to the break up. He explains the situation as follows:

The Mughal state was dependent upon merchant capital and therefore, encouraged it. Many nobles under the Mughal state not only had close relations with merchants but also traded on their own accounts. Under the Mughal state the bureaucratic structure was patrimonial, which was designed to enrich the state and its nobility, and not the commercial classes. Under this insecure condition, merchants and bankers tried to control these conditions by developing their own organizations through networks of caste and kinship. However, even in this context their control was not secure, because the relationship between merchant capital and production was also open-ended. The households that were involved in production also controlled the process of production as they possessed the skills and knowledge for it.

Their control over production was further strengthened with the structure of caste and kinship within which these households were grouped together. However, according to Washbrook, in the course of the eighteenth century, these loose relations among merchant capital, labor, the production process, and the state started becoming tighter and more compact (Ibid., 429–430), which created new dynamics.

In this new context, merchants and bankers got an opportunity to strengthen their positions when a regional state system emerged. The rulers of these principalities depended on bankers and merchants for money to protect their territory and power. Thus, profit and power became intertwined as this arrangement gave these merchants and bankers an opportunity to gain greater and more secure access to state power as well as more profit and security. While the "commercialization of royal power" brought commercial prosperity and economic growth, it also increased rack-renting, exploitation, and the oppression of peasants and producers (Ibid., 431). This arrangement did not last long as these regional rulers themselves slowly came under the direct control of European trading companies, and thus, once again, changed the collaborative business arrangement among Indian rulers, merchants, and bankers.

4. INVOLVEMENT OF EUROPEANS AND BRITISH TRADING COMPANIES IN THE REGIONAL POWER STRUGGLES

The Mughal Empire slowly disintegrated as rulers of the outlying provinces rebelled by refusing to remit revenue and refusing to submit to imperial authority and thus creating a regional state system. The rulers of these principalities became involved in a power struggle among themselves as each one of them wanted to retain his local power, control his own territory, and increase revenue collections by defeating rival powers. However, to achieve these goals they needed a permanently full treasury to hire the services of mercenaries and purchase European muskets and cannons, which they believed were superior. To acquire a full treasury, these rulers auctioned off their revenue and monopoly privileges to merchants and bankers and acquired European guns, flintlock muskets, and rapid-fire cannons (Washbrook, 1997). Moreover, some Indian rulers also 'invited' the East India Company to run their treasuries and to organize their 'new model' army. It did not take long for the British, Dutch, and French merchant colonialists to use these opportunities to achieve their own goals of trade expansion and influence in India. In the case of the British East India Company, it broadened its goal beyond the expansion of trade to include the possibility of political domination over India. The Company eventually achieved its goal of conquering India, as Washbrook noted, "more by stealth than by outright invasion while largely using India's own resources of men and money to capture it" (Ibid., 434). Only a few regional rulers such as Hyder Ali of Mysore and Ranjit Singh of Punjab were able to sustain a long-term resistance to the Company's political ambitions. British merchant colonialists used various dubious methods including trickery, weapons, and agreements to conquer most of the principalities after defeating both Dutch and French forces in India. Subsequently, the British East India Company was able to create a unified India under its rule that lasted until 1858 when the British government took over the formal governance of India.

5. COLLABORATION OF INDIAN BANKERS, FINANCIERS & INDIAN PRINCES WITH BRITISH EAST INDIA COMPANY IN REGIONAL POWER STRUGGLE

British success in India was not a one-way process; it was also facilitated by the collaboration of Indian princes, merchants, and bankers. Indian princes collaborated with British and European colonizers because they did not see them as a threat, since the British did not portray themselves as local rulers. Moreover, Indian rulers and other commercial and gentry classes were enamored by the modernity of the British and Europeans, and they wanted to gain from it to achieve their own specific goals. Furthermore, the British East India Company presented itself not as a competitor to Indian princes but as commercial and mercenary services for sale to the highest bidder (Washbrook, 1997). The Company successfully kept up a façade composed of appropriate symbols and gestures reflecting respect towards provincial rulers while disguising its real aims and position. It displayed deference to indigenous statecraft by following appropriate etiquette, and presented itself as a mere servant of the Mughals. Thus, local princes, who did not suspect British trickery and façades, happily collaborated with their own future rival in order to defeat their immediate rival at that time.

Indian bankers' collaboration with the East India Company unfolded as follows: After 1712, as discussed earlier, the number of successor states began competing and fighting with one another. These states increasingly depended on credit from particular bankers or sets of bankers to fund wars and to retain their power. However, these Indian financers soon changed their loyalty to the Company because they thought that their future would be better protected by the victors who had superior military force and organization, and not with those rulers who were about to be defeated by the British (Bagchi, 2002:xvi). For example, the House of Jagatseth conspired against Sirajud-daula and later against Mir Kasim in Bengal, while the firm of Nathji Arjuni Travadi sided with the British in western India helping them against the Marathas. Explaining these actions of Indian firms Amiya Bagchi wrote,

> The Indian Princes opposing the European marauders not only failed to match the European technology of warfare on the sea and land, they could not create a state structure that would depend on the credit of a mass of loyal subjects rather than that of a small group of financers whose loyalty would shift as they saw the fortunes of their erstwhile patrons seriously threatened, or who would actively conspire, for reasons of short sighted gain, against their patrons ... during the Anglo Maratha wars from the later eighteenth century the British repeatedly utilized the services of not only the local bankers but also those of the bankers of Banaras for raising funds and transferring subsidies from their richest prize till that date, namely, the Presidency of Bengal (Ibid., xvi–xvii).

Company rule between the 1780s and 1810 proved to be "good for business" for local bankers and other collaborators (Washbrook, 1997:436). This shifting loyalty and collaboration of Indian bankers and merchants with the East India Company needs to be understood within the historical context of the time. Since India then did not exist as a unified nation, it was not possible for anyone, including the bankers, to develop any sense of loyalty to a non-existing entity. Moreover, as Washbrook noted, these Indian bankers and elites collaborated with the British Company according to their own interests as they probably shared with the colonial elite the same ideologies of profit and power, which in turn provided "the effectiveness with which England consolidated and maintained its rule" in India (Ibid., 438).

However, British rule did not remain "good for business" for local bankers and collaborators for long. When Britain actually became the sovereign power in those kingdoms, many of these merchants and collaborators were ruined because with its domination of India, Britain had the ability to mobilize resources without soliciting the help of Indian financiers (Bagchi, 2002). Furthermore, the Company's own interest was to take and remit its profits from overseas activities to Britain, which eventually clashed with that of the Indian merchants, who initially had serviced it. Subsequently, these Indian merchants were pushed out. From 1810 onwards, most of the "collaborators" of the eighteenth century faced similar fates. Those merchants who sided with regional rulers were also ruined as these merchants did not have a large clientele and relied solely on these rulers who were later overthrown (Washbrook, 1997). For example, as Bagchi (2002) noted, the group of bankers who had earlier financed the operations of the Peshwa's treasury and operated out of Pune were virtually decimated with the onset of British rule after 1818. Moneylenders lost out completely as Peshwa territories became impoverished with de-industrialization as well as a decline in public expenditure. Summing it up Bayly wrote,

> Much of the amazing dynamism of early British penetration and conquest of the subcontinent was due to the underlying tides of petty commodity production, marketing and financial speculation within Indian society. By acting as an Indian merchant, fiscal entrepreneur and mercenary bank leader writ large, the Company was able to suborn and conquer India. Relying on the support of Indian literati and financial expertise, the British were able to push forward the processes of peasantisation and create a sporadically productive export economy" (Bayly, 1988:204).

6. DE-INDUSTRIALIZATION OF INDIA AND INDUSTRIALIZATION OF BRITAIN UNDER BRITISH COMPANY RULE

It was not only bankers and merchants that were ruined when the British East India Company took over power in India, but also all Indian agencies as these were demoted into passive and inferior roles. For example, when Europe was entering the "Age of Steam" in the second quarter of the nineteenth century, India was being reduced to a "simple" agricultural colony to meet the needs of British industries (Habib, 2002). Along with this reduced status in the larger imperial project, India was also now depicted as naturally a "static, traditional and hierarchical society," while Britain's national identity was defined as belonging to a so called "superior nation" based on "superior" values (Washbrook, 1997). This contrast of image and national identity vis-à-vis colonial India strengthened the British state and nation as it transformed, according to Washbrook, "recalcitrant Scottish and Irish gentries into Britons" (Washbrook, 1997:423). The administration of the Indian colony also required a professional bureaucracy both in Britain and in India which created job openings for many educated but unemployed young British men. These bureaucracies of "civil services" then facilitated the British elite's efforts to rule the world for the next one hundred and fifty years.

There is also ample information about how Indian industries were demolished in certain areas under British rule, and about how British turned the drought of the late nineteenth century into a series of famines in which 30 million people died (Davis,

2001). India's textile manufacturing later declined under British Company rule. In fact, England's industrialization and commercial revolution was deeply connected within the Indian textile industry and other British colonial territories worldwide (Habib, 2002). For example, Britain's industrialization, which was initially the mechanization of cotton textile manufacturing, was "part of a much longer 'global' history of the fabric itself" (Washbrook, 1997:417). This history of fabric is also the history of interaction between different societies over time that brought the technology, science, and mechanism of textile and fabric manufacturing to England. For example, England, before industrialization, not only learned about cotton from India but also how to design, weave and dye it with 'indigo' blue. The Indian locale names attached to many fabric types in England are proof of it—Calicoes (from Calicut), Gingams (from Gingee), Chintzes (Telugu term in Andhra coast), and Muslin (Muslim Dhaka) (Ibid.). As Washbrook (1997) noted, this "transfer" of technology and science from the East to the West had been taking place at a larger scale since medieval times. England's commercial revolution in the late seventeenth and early eighteenth centuries was connected with the importation of tropical and colonial crops: Indian cotton, tea, coffee, sugar, and porcelain. These imported goods and crops revolutionized the pattern of domestic consumption, as well as created for the first time the basis for a national market in England. This increased trade required a growth of mercantile marine, shipping, and insurance, which in turn made the City of London the center of the world [(6)].

7. REVOLTS AND CONFLICTS UNDER BRITISH COMPANY RULE

As Britain was pursuing its aim of developing a capitalist economy, it needed more new resources, which it obtained through its world empire—including India. However, the policies followed in India to extract more resources for Britain created such conditions that many armed revolts against British Company rule continued in all parts of India throughout the early nineteenth century and climaxed in 1857. The British Company was successful in suppressing these revolts/conflicts because it could always rely on the support of some part of the local population ranging from the raja and zamindar to the poor and even from people who were very low in hierarchy (Bayly, 1988:172).

These nineteenth-century resistance movements targeted both the more privileged groups of Indians as well as the British. These revolts (1800–1860) can be categorized broadly as follows: Revolts by zamindars and other superior landlords against the demands of higher revenue; Conflicts between landlords and groups of tenants or under-tenants on the violation of the obligations or the transformation of customary dues into landlord rights; Conflicts due to tension between wandering or tribal people and settled peasant farmers over the control of forests, grazing grounds or communally used resources; Revolts in the towns and cities due to various reasons including market control and taxation; Bloody conflict between caste or religious groups or among artisan communities. These widespread conflicts of different types took an exaggerated form when the Mutiny of 1857 broke out (Bayly, 1988:170–171).

Political organization and agitation created another form of tension under the Company's rule. In fact, as Bayly pointed out, modern nationalism has its roots in the early nineteenth century. For example, during the taxation riots which occurred between 1809–1818 in cities, there was a widespread awareness of the theory that Indian wealth was being "drained" by the British Company. In 1806, there was a combined effort by Indian traders and scribal people with the un-official European community in Madras to petition for the retention of a Welsh judge who had lost favor with the Madras government. Similarly, much of the cultural activities of Calcutta in the 1820s and 30s was an implied critique of colonial rule (Ibid., 196). However, these political agitations of early nineteenth century did not have an all-India organization which could combine and channel these agitations and activities against the British rule itself. This had to wait until 1885 when the Indian National Congress was founded.

8. COMPLETE SUBORDINATION OF INDIA & CONSOLIDATION OF BRITISH COLONIAL RULE

After the Mutiny of 1857, India was brought directly under the governance of British government from London, and thus under imperial subordination. The destruction of Delhi and the show trial of the last Mughal finally released the British from their theoretical submission to the authority of the House of Timur (Ibid.). Under the Act for the Better Government of India in 1858, a Secretary of State for India was appointed who would be assisted by a Council with fifteen members. Under the Indian Council Act of 1861, the number of members in the Viceroy of India's Council and also the Council at Bombay and Madras was increased. These additional members were to be drawn from a selection of non-official Europeans and Indians so that public opinion and expression were accommodated as a safety valve. Thus, British parliament began to intervene more frequently in Indian affairs as they became part of British political debates (Bayly, 1988).

To further consolidate the Crown's rule, Delhi Darbar was organized in 1877 where British Queen Victoria was proclaimed Queen-Empress. During Darbar there was also a ranking and honoring of local princes and people based on the combination of concepts about royalty and loyalty as followed by Mughals, and feudal lords, as well as the concept of race practiced by Anglo-Normans (Ibid.). Even the Indian National Congress in its first meeting in 1885 to criticize the shortcomings of British rule, had to proclaim that "loyalty is part of our constitution" (Ibid.).

In addition, the British government created a small group of local partners to consolidate its rule in India. For example, recruits for the collector's office and for district courts came from Hindu intelligentsia. Talukdar's sons in the north were enrolled in agricultural colleges to learn about crop varieties and agricultural improvements. Peasant farmers in the west became rich with the cotton boom. Conservative Muslims were coopted to imperial rule (Sir Sayyid Ahmed's, *An account of the Loyal Mohammedens of India,* 1860, quoted in Bayly, 1988). The British government changed its policies towards the native states and tried to influence their decision by relying on their British residents for 'modernizing' diwans of important native states. These English educated rajas and diwans proved more effective in promoting British interests in their respective states (Bayly, 1988) than the earlier British policy of direct intervention.

British government in India also made major changes in the Indian army after the Mutiny. As Punjabi recruits remained loyal during the Mutiny of 1857 their number was increased along with the numbers of Gurkhas from Nepal. Moreover, the British carefully fostered division among them by dividing them based on their sense of caste or tribe; Punjabi Muslims, Dogras, and Jats were kept in separate units. The British government followed a policy that the number of Indian sepoys would never outnumber European troops in the subcontinent by more than two to one. At the same time Europeans were placed in charge of artillery in well-fortified and segregated army cantonments (Ibid.).

9. INDIAN ECONOMY UNDER BRITISH COLONIAL RULE, 1860–1880

Soon after Britain took over the direct rule of India, the export of British manufacture textiles to India picked up sharply. For example, by 1860, one-third of the demand for moderate to finer cloth from Bengal and Bihar was met by British imports. At the same time, the expansion of railway lines allowed for increased exports of raw material from India to other countries. Between the 1860s and 1880 communication networks rapidly expanded and railway lines reached 4,300 miles in 1880.

Developments in the international arena also affected the Indian economy. For example, with the opening of the Suez Canal in 1869 the grain supply increased, and the American Civil War led to an increased demand for Indian cotton. The demand for jute from Bengal also grew due to the rapid growth in the volume of world shipping after 1860. Indian opium exports to China continued, as it accounted for more than ten percent of the income of the Indian government. Another important export from India at that time was indentured laborers to Ceylon, Malaysia, the Caribbean, and southern Africa to replace earlier slave populations. At the same time, plantation crops of coffee and tea were now firmly established in India.

Indian merchants' inland retailing system for Lancashire goods in eastern and southern India was now linked to seaports by railway lines. Thus, international development and the expansion of railway lines made it much easier to sell India's agricultural products on the world market and this enriched some Indian farmers and merchant entrepreneurs. These developments made the landowning, commercial, and urban elites more stable and they continued to acquiesce to the distant rule of foreigners for the time being (Bayly, 1988). However, the growth of India's economy in the years from 1860 to 1890 did not make much difference to rural poverty. Explaining the reasons for continued poverty in India, an Indian Marxist economist Utsa Patnaik (2017a and 2017b) wrote that Britain had set up a complicated mechanism to transfer India's export earnings to London for Britain's use, thus enabling it to gain international purchasing power and also to re-export capital for the industrialization of new European settlements. None of the Indian export earnings were invested in India as Indian exporters were paid from the budget (taxes paid by these exporters and others) of the colonial Indian government.

Interestingly, in spite of complete subordination of the Indian economy to colonial rule, a small group of Marwari traders who had migrated to Calcutta and merchants in Bombay were able to keep a hold on some parts of their regional economies. The first generation of India's industrialists emerged from these groups. Rural industries such as sugar-making and rice-husking, which were equally significant for modern India's economy, survived and consolidated themselves. Even in the service industry, which developed quite rapidly in the early nineteenth century, people connected with literacy and law mostly relied on indigenous traditions of learning while also creatively responding to Western methods of organization (Bayly, 1988). Educated Indian experts emerged from these groups during the first colonial age, and they played an important role in the making of modern India.

SUMMATION PART I

So far, we have discussed that it is possible to understand the making of colonial India without categorizing it as either developed or underdeveloped. Instead, we can use a yardstick of parity to look into the universal and specific elements in the making of colonial India as we did with the three other chosen societies. India, like any other society, is a product of interactions with various societies that included invasions, migrations, trade and traveling. These interactions made India a mix of many cultures, ethnicities, languages, and religions. Like any other society, power struggles had been a constant feature in the making of India. However, power struggles take specific form and have specific outcomes in every society. It is noted that before the coming of the British, India was a dynamic society with many industries including the most important—a large textile industry, which was exported worldwide. With the arrival of European and British traders, things started changing in India as the Mughal Empire was already on decline. These foreigners took advantage of the power struggles among the local principalities and over time they were able to take control of this regional state system. However, bankers, merchants, and local princes facilitated this task by collaborating with European and British merchants. Once the British were able to colonize India, they also began to de-industrialize India while simultaneously boosting Britain's industrialization. There were many revolts and conflicts against the British Company's policies, which eventually culminated as a major revolt—the Indian Mutiny, or Sepoy Mutiny of 1857. After suppressing this revolt the British government established direct rule over the Indian colony and increased exports of raw material from India. Despite all of these assaults on Indian society and economy, some Indian traders and merchants in Bombay and Calcutta were able to keep control of some parts of their regional economy. It is from this group of merchants and traders that future Indian industrialists emerged.

In this larger context of the interaction of constantly changing historical forces within India and in the international arena, we locate in Part II the emergence of the large-scale steel industry in India.

PART II

CONJUNCTION AND CONFLUENCE OF HISTORICAL FORCES IN THE EMERGENCE OF THE LARGE-SCALE STEEL INDUSTRY IN INDIA

As suggested in the beginning of this chapter, we are using the same yardstick to understand the industrialization and emergence of the large-scale steel industry (1880–1914) in India, as we do for the three other chosen countries. With this yardstick of parity it has become possible to erase the conceptual binary distinction of developed/underdeveloped. Instead of categorizing India as either developed or underdeveloped, we focus on complex intertwined historical processes, which show that it was the conjunction and confluence of historical forces developing within colonial India (inter-societal interactions) and within the international arena (intra-societal interactions) that created conditions for the emergence of a large-scale steel industry. These simultaneous historical processes were as much a specific history of India as that of its intertwined relationship with larger international forces (see Chapter 3) and with other societies of that time.

Long before the large-scale steel industry came into being under colonial rule, India was well known for its high-quality steel. For example, Indian Wootz steel was the first known steel in the world for centuries. It was much in demand for its strength and known as Damascus steel in Persia until the nineteenth century. Hobson points out that "even by the end of the eighteenth century the British production remained inferior to that of the Damascus variety ... And even as late as 1842 Indian iron and steel was not only as good, if not superior to the British production but was much cheaper than that produced in Sheffield" (Hobson, 2004:211). Western producers were in awe of the high quality of Indian and Persian steel (Ibid., 212). More recently, Indian historian, Parthasarathi, has noted that both East India Company officials and European experts had tremendous praise for the quality of the metal as well as for the knowledge and skill of Indian workers (Parthasarathi, 2011:235). Parthasarathi informs that the wide acclaim in Europe for Indian steel and the description of the iron and steel produced in India have been noted in many publications: *Philosophical Transactions of the Royal Society of London*, the *Journal of the Royal Asiatic Society*, the *Proceedings of the Royal Society of London*, the *Quarterly Journal of Science, Literature, and the Arts* as well as in numerous traveler's accounts (Ibid.).

BRITISH ENTREPRENEUR'S FAILED EFFORTS TO CREATE STEEL INDUSTRY IN INDIA

In 1740, Benjamin Huntsman made the first attempt to replicate the process of making steel in Sheffield, and those attempts continued for the next eighty years (Hobson 2004). However, in spite of these efforts, in 1873, the peak year, India had ten times the number of blast furnaces found in Britain (Ibid., 212). Allured by information about the high quality of Indian steel acclaimed in British journals and across Europe, many British steel producers attempted to build large-scale steel works in India. For example, Michael Faraday conducted experiments on Wootz Indian steel. Several Europeans made proposals for the building of a large-scale iron works in Bengal. As Parthasarathi noted, in 1812 the Bagpore Iron Foundry was established there but it failed quickly. It had been established under the leadership of iron man, Andrew Duncan from Carion, Scotland, who had fifteen years of experience in Russia setting up iron works. The reason for these early failures in the establishment of the large-scale iron industry was that as long as British iron was in demand, the prospect of Indian iron making was bleak. Consequently, the Calcutta government concluded that "not much advantage will [would] be derived from an iron foundry in this country" (quoted in Parthasarathi, 2011:235).

However, a similar effort for a large-scale steel industry in South India was more successful, at least for a few decades. In 1825, J. M. Heath sent a proposal to the Madras Council for developing an iron smelting works in its presidency. In his proposal Heath requested an exclusive privilege to produce iron by European methods for the duration of the East India Company's charter. In 1829, he again requested protection from competition for a reasonable period on the basis that such protection had also been given in England and in Russia. Heath wrote that in England "such protection was given in the reign of King James, I think, to the persons who first attempted to make iron with pit coal," and in Russia, "such protection was afforded to the first persons who established iron works" (quoted in Ibid., 236). In the end, Heath obtained the privileges and protections on the condition that the iron he produced should not compete against British iron, whether in India or Britain. Instead, he would export his iron to Europe and pose a challenge to Sweden's high quality iron. With these assurances and agreement, Heath erected his iron works in the town of Porto Novo, on the coast of Tamil country, 125 miles south of Madras. He found that the iron ore in this area was "inexhaustible" and of the highest quality, as declared by British experts (Ibid.). Porto Novo iron ore was extremely cheap, as well, and by 1839 it replaced Swedish iron imports to the Royal Arsenal of Woolwich in London (Ibid., 237). However, even with Heath's great success with Indian workers, and while he was able to transfer and adapt British technology and knowhow into the Indian context, as Parthasarathi pointed out there still remained the problem of the realization of capital due to a long gestation period. It also needed working capital to develop market for its iron in Britain, which further lengthened the time for the realization of any investment. Moreover, the following economic conditions contributed to his problems: the great economic depression following the US panic of 1837, and the bleak commercial conditions in Madras due to the great depression in South India since the mid-1820s (Ibid., 238). Besides, Porto Novo could not sell goods locally, as by the 1830s, British pig iron was flowing into India in large quantities. Even though the British iron was of inferior quality, it was cheaper than Proto Novo iron because British iron was free from import duty. Under these constraints, Parthasarathi noted, the Porto Novo iron works closed in the 1860s after a few decades of operation.

REASONS FOR THE SUCCESS OF AN INDIAN CAPITALIST IN STEEL MAKING

As discussed above, the efforts of British investors to build a large-scale iron industry in India did not succeed. The obvious question is: how could an Indian capitalist be successful in building a large-scale steel industry in India under colonial rule? As mentioned earlier, we shall seek the answer in an examination of the conjunction of various historical processes in both the global and the colonial/local context.

Based on this understanding, I explained that the large-scale steel industry in India under colonial rule emerged neither due to any "benevolent" policies of British colonial rule nor as a natural culmination of Indian economic development. Instead, it was the conjunction of historical forces within India and in the international arena that created conditions within which the British colonial government permitted Jamshetji Nasserwanji Tata known as J. N. Tata, to invest in a large-scale steel industry in 1899. This conclusion is reached by examining the following questions: What prompted the Colonial Government of India (hereafter CGI) to begin responding favorably to the idea of a large-scale Indian steel industry? Was it the continuation of old policies of the CGI or was it an historical anomaly? Was the CGI interested in India's industrialization? If so, what then were the new compulsions that brought a change in attitude among CGI members to favor steel, but not the growth of related industries? How did the overseers of steel interests in Britain react? How could CGI, while proclaiming a policy of free trade, justify the protection of steel? Why only in 1899, and not earlier, did the CGI change its attitude toward the iron and steel industry in India? Given the pressure since 1883 from the nationalist leadership and national economists' for this change, why did the CGI respond favorably only after 1899? Different explanations have been given ranging from, "the imperial vision of Lord Curzon" (Ray, 1992:46–47, see also Headrick, 1988) to "the entrepreneurial vision of Tata" (8). Bhagwati explains Tata Steel as "a happy historical accident and the work of a visionary entrepreneur" (Bhagwati and Desai, 1970:28).

None of these statements allow us to explore why an "historical accident" occurs at a particular time and not at any other time, or why the entrepreneur J. N. Tata was successful with his "vision" in 1907 rather than earlier in 1883 when he first made a proposal to the CGI. Why did earlier experiments by Europeans in the same field fail, while Tata, an Indian capitalist, succeeded under colonial rule? Why did the CGI change its attitude toward the Tata in 1899? Morris D. Morris writes, "Given that they [Tata] did go to London we do not yet really know why they [Tata] were unable to get solid financial support for their project [steel]" (Morris, 1987:140). These questions direct us to explore a different set of factors to find our answer.

I. Changing Policies and Role of the CGI

It is important to understand the CGI's policies related to the development of the large-scale Indian steel industry for three reasons. One, CGI was the biggest purchaser of iron and steel for military purposes and railways. Two, CGI had to change mining regulations and improve transport arrangements for the success and profitability of the iron and steel industry. Three, the long gestation period of a large iron and steel industry needed CGI's support. The failure of earlier attempts at large-scale steel production in India, in want of CGI's help, very well demonstrates CGI's crucial role in any future successful venture in this area (7).

The shifts in CGI policy first occurred in the 1850s, at a time when the export of British iron and steel to India was expanding phenomenally due to the growth of Indian railways. As discussed earlier, Heath's attempt in the 1830s to begin the manufacture of bar iron in India for export to England, competing on highly favorable terms with Swedish iron (Fraser, 1919:5), did not last long due to a lack of the CGI's support for competing with British iron imports. Only in the last quarter of the nineteenth century did the CGI changed its attitude toward replacing imports of British iron and steel through domestic production in India itself. This change in CGI's attitude was due to major changes that were taking place both in the pattern of iron and steel imports, and in the political situation within and outside India. In 1880, Britain had a virtual monopoly over the export of iron and steel to India. However, as shown in Table 1, by the time Lord Curzon came to serve as Governor General in

1899, Belgium had become a serious competitor, and had superseded Britain in steel exports to India.

TABLE 1: IMPORTS OF STEEL IN INDIA - IN TONS - COUNTRY STEEL

	1885–86	1895–96
UK	98, 000	274,000
Belgium	8,000	280,000

Source: S. B. Saul: *Studies in British Overseas Trade, 1870–1914.* 1960, p. 199, Liverpool.

As seen in the table, Belgian exports jumped from 8,000 tons from 1885–1886 to 280,000 tons from 1895–1896, whereas, British exports increased from 98,000–274,000 tons during the same period. These changes in export figures were cause for great concern to the colonial government, prior to the arrival of Lord Curzon, as was reflected in the CGI's reply to the Chamberlain Enquiry of 1895:

> It is well known to the India office that Belgian iron and steel are of inferior quality. In Lord Cross's Financial Dispatch No. 3, dated, 8 January 1891, it was enjoined on us that for public purposes only English metal should be purchased in consequences of the inferiority of Continental iron and steel. These metals are, however, regarded as sufficiently good by the Indian consumer and, the goods being cheap, the displacement of English by Belgium iron and steel in recent years has been very marked (9).

The personality of Lord Curzon, his creativity and his role were important within this new context and not merely factors for change in their own right.

II. Global and Local Context

Between J. N. Tata's 1883 proposal and his 1900 proposal to develop a steel industry, the economic situation had changed fundamentally both at home and internationally. The following questions come to mind, Why was Britain losing its monopoly in steel, despite its pioneering position and its development of far-flung imperial markets? What made Britain a declining hegemonic power by the end of the nineteenth century?

The need to raise the question of British hegemony, as pointed out by McMichael, is that market relations and the movement of capital and labor go beyond geopolitical boundaries (10). States both constitute and are in turn constituted by the social relations of production and circulation that may be particular to a national economy but simultaneously define its world historical context (McMichael, 1984:242). Based on this understanding, social and economic changes cannot be understood by looking exclusively at the processes that are internal to the state. We must analyze these processes in the global context as well to determine how the socioeconomic and political dynamics of a state are created by the intersections of domestic and international forces.

Britain could unify world trading to its advantage in the third quarter of the nineteenth century due to the political and military organization of the markets and not due to its supreme economic strength (11). Britain's efforts to strengthen its markets were forced by the circumstances which were the outcome of conflicts of interest at home and in the world arena, such as: the evolution of the mass production of steel, the development of railways and communication, the formation of various cartels that control prices, dwindling revenues for the CGI, a crisis of debt balance, the pressures of class formation in India, and the emergence of the Indian nationalist movement. It is within this larger context that we seek an explanation for the changed policies of the CGI towards India's steel industry. First, we shall look at the industrial structure of two main contenders: Imperial Britain and the postcolonial Imperial US. It is to the declining British hegemonic power in the world that we shall then relate the industrial and political situation in India and, in that context, define the formative process of the large-scale Indian steel industry.

i. Changing Global and Local Socio-Economic Forces in Imperial Britain and in Postcolonial Imperial US

In the late nineteenth century, an important global change occurred in the transformation of the world's iron and steel industry into a large-scale organization. This transformation was most visible in the US, but not in Britain, as British steel producers found it difficult to move out of the earlier model due to various economic, technical, and structural constraints (12). In addition, the important decisive factor in their position in the global market was deeply connected with ongoing internal class struggles in both the US and Britain. However, due to various reasons discussed below, Britain was unable to gain competitive power in the world steel market, which in turn shaped Britain's policies towards the industrialization of its colonies.

As pointed out in Chapter 5, the Western world was able to move towards a large-scale steel industry due to the high demand for steel with the coming of railways, which they were able to meet with the installation of the newly invented Bessemer process. Even though the importance of rail production had declined, Elbaum and Wilkinson noted, large-scale production processes could not be reversed. However, the US was able to benefit during this slack period, but not Britain as its steel industry was run by family-owned, small-scale producers (see Chapter 5). This was noted by the Secretary of State for India, Lord Hamilton. He wrote to the Viceroy of India:

> In America the great mass of the railway companies bring their locomotive engines from the outside trade and thus there is enormous plant laid down and in working order for the production of locomotives; which enables its owners to tender for the supply of engines in any part of the world. All the engines in America are more or less of a standard pattern, and their parts are interchangeable, and this enables these great firms, when business is slack, to employ a certain number of men in making certain parts of engines which they can utilize fully when trade becomes brisk. Here, (in Britain) an entirely different system prevails. Nearly all the great companies make their own locomotives, and each company has a pattern for locomotives, which is according to the fancy and idea of the Locomotive superintendent for the time being. The outside firms, therefore, who make locomotives, are very much less powerful, and have less capital behind them than those which exist in America, and therefore, it is clear to me that, if time being a consideration, it is to be one of the factors taken into account (that) when tenders are invited, the American engineering trade must beat ours in point of delivery (13).

Despite Britain's specialization in open-hearth steel making, it was not able to increase the scale of operation in comparison to the US. For example, in 1890, Britain's furnaces were 10 tons in average size, which was one-third of those in the US. Moreover, by 1900 the US furnaces were producing four times more than British furnaces [14]. It seems even the growth of open-hearth production in no way slowed down the process of industrial concentration in the US.

The reasons for Britain's industrial "backwardness" in steel were many and intertwined. Even though Britain had a highly developed iron industry, Elbaum and Wilkinson pointed out, its overall rate of demand growth was slow, and that forced many wrought iron producers to switch to steel production. For example, even the large producers built small open-hearth furnaces to produce steel for finishing in the existing rolling mills. Others turned to re-rolling, using mostly imported semi-finished steel. Thus, the differentiation of products further reinforced the traditional industrial structure in Britain, which in turn reduced the incentive for introducing new techniques in the production of steel (Elbaum and Wilkinson, 1979). A British expert wrote in *Indian Engineering*:

> We hear much about the non-adaptability of English manufacturers, that they refuse to undertake work which is a little outside their line, which work the Americans jump at; and that John Bull's prices compared with Jonathan's are prohibitive. But this is purely the result of a great stress of work when a man has his shops full of work of the kind for which they were built, and for which his machines are specially designed; and when, as far as he can see, orders of that kind are likely to continue flowing in, it is hardly likely that he will stop, and not only alter his machines but teach his workmen new ways, in order merely to keep work in the country. And not only that, but plenty of work for all means high prices; and the manufacturer is hardly likely to take in work at a low price which will "crowd out" work he is doing for a better profit. Nay, even if his hands are not quite full, but if he sees a prospect of getting work of his own kind and price at a near date, he will hesitate to fill his shops with cheap and new work [15].

Thus, the continued existence of traditional small-scale producers leading to a slow rate of increase in production diminished any possible prospect for Britain's large-scale steel industry. Moreover, "many of these producers were family firms operating on narrow margins who were unwilling to scrap obsolete capacity while it remained intermittently profitable" (Elbaum and Wilkinson, 1979:29). The slow increase in production reflected in the changing composition of Britain's foreign trade [16]. For example, after 1870, manufacturing exports grew much more slowly than before, and Britain's share of world visible trade fell. Invisible trade, on the other hand, increased rapidly until 1914. However, as Hopkins and Cains pointed out, there was no single causal relationship between the increased propensity to export capital and the loss of industrial dynamism. They suggest:

> [W]hile the perpetuation of the small firm in manufacturing may have been a rational response to the conditions prevailing in that sector, it was politically inefficient because atomistic units had difficulty combining, even in their own interests, and were plagued by the problem of free-riders. Growing concentration in finance and distribution, on the other hand, was not only a rational response to the opportunities created by the expansion of this sector, but was also politically efficient because the relatively small number of banking dynasties and their associates could unite more easily to promote their interests (Ibid., 5, fn, 26).

The other reason for the lack of dynamism in the British industry was that manufacturers did not depend on banks for long term investment purposes. The industrial development in Britain was a gradual process as was capital accumulation. This condition eliminated the pressure for investing or looking for any institutional device to provide for a long-term capital for industry. In fact, as Gerschenkron (1962) informs, initial British capital accumulation did not come from industry but came from trade and modernized agriculture. Thus, it is no surprise that when the British steel industry came along it followed the same path as previous industries had taken.

In addition, British steel industry did not invest in large-scale production techniques because the market for wrought iron was already unstable and was leading to wide price fluctuations (Mitchel and Deane, 1962). Moreover, British manufacturers were unable to control prices through their regional associations when the number of firms and producing regions increased (17). During economic recession, the inability to control prices became even more problematic, as inter-regional dumping increased. Faced with this situation, manufacturers became more concerned with scrambling for declining orders and also selling below full cost. They further lost control of the market as they began to depend on intermediaries (those providing market outlets for the output of small firms and imported steel) for selling their product (Carr and Taplin, 1962:293; Burham and Hoskins, 1942:211; Burn, 1940:278, cited in Elbaum and Wilkinson, 1979). All of these factors not only reduced producers' control of the market, but also hindered the formation of steel cartels in Britain.

As Elbaum and Wilkinson noted, Britain's small-firm industrial structure was further reinforced by the emergence of strong trade unions in steel, and by the development of collective bargaining for wages and prices. It is interesting to note that the history of the emergence of industrial relations in the iron industry was paralleled in the US and Britain in their earlier days. However, when they switched to steel, as Elbaum and Wilkinson (1979) noted, their development diverged. These early similarities can be attributed to their use of similar basic technology, having similar form of labor organizations, wage payment systems, and product market structure (Elbaum and Wilkinson, 1979). For example, after the formation of trade unions in both countries, an intense period of industrial conflict followed, which then led to the establishment of the procedures for collective bargaining. However, the system of bargaining that emerged in the US and in Britain had a different outcome. For example, as Elbaum and Wilkinson noted, in Britain it virtually eliminated strikes and lockouts, and laid the foundation for industrial peace. The reasons for the emergence of peaceful industrial relations in Britain were: the limited growth of the British iron and steel industries and in absence of cartels manufacturers had no control over prices. Whereas in the US, there were inter-union conflicts (18) due to craft exclusiveness of the unions, which helped in breaking strikes and forced unions to abandon central control and switch to local bargaining.

In both countries, collective bargaining was impacted by the general wage level which was regulated by the market price of iron. The US was able to cut the cost of production due to the presence of strong US steel cartels as they competed in the world market. In the US, where contracts were periodically renegotiated, management was more powerful and labeled the unions demand for a share in the benefits of technological change "a tax on progress" (Brody, 1960). US workers could not challenge wage rates because of the fixed-term nature of the union contracts and their rates were mandated during the annual revision of scales at the union's conventions.

Thus, in the US powerful management was able to control wage costs by effectively breaking the link between output and earnings.

Workers unions in the British steel industry did not resist the introduction of new methods, but they did expect some share of the benefits from technical improvements (Elbaum and Wilkinson, 1979). Since the British steel industry did not form any cartels, it was not possible for small steel firms to cut costs. However, they joined hands with skilled workers and made agreements to link wages and prices by regulating competitive wage cutting during recessions and also ending costly stoppages. At the same time, the rules and procedures for resolving local disputes made it very difficult for the employers to change tonnage rates. Under this arrangement British unions were able to broaden their base by including less skilled workers (Pugh, 1951 cited in Elbaum and Wilkinson, 1979). They also succeeded in maintaining control over the labor process as scientific management made little or no impact in Britain (Gintz, 1954 cited in Elbaum and Wilkinson, 1979). However, the strength of union organization damaged the chances of British steel firms (small scale family firms) to successfully compete in the world market.

In the US, unionism was eliminated from the corporate domain when the U.S. Steel Corporation, which included about half of US steel firms, locked out workers in 1909. This lockout was the culmination of a process that first began in 1893 with a drastic reduction in wage rates and was repeated during the depression years of the late 1890s and again in 1909. The weakening of the craft basis of unionism in the US became possible because the development of large-scale steel production created large corporate firms and cartels. Trade unions could not match the power of monopoly capital as it did not have the mass organization and central control necessary to challenge it. Thus, "the large firms could, by securing more effective control of its labor costs, use its massive productive resources to capture larger and larger shares of the market and consequently the benefits of collusion with rival producers and trade unions declined rapidly" (Elbaum and Wilkinson, 1979:301).

Another major threat to British steel markets (domestic production and exports), was the rapidly growing and low cost of German steel products. Moreover, German producers organized all large integrated steel works into Kartells, and were protected by tariffs, further intensified competition with British steel products (Burn, 1940, cited in Elbaum and Wilkinson). Germans were able to successfully compete in the world market as their integrated works helped them to increase their hold on the home market. With a safe and profitable home base, it became possible for Germans to compete successfully in export market. Similarly, in the US, increasingly fewer hands began to control production and prices, which initiated a period of intense competition among the leading firms. These firms were able to compete due to the availability of new improved production methods, growth of productive capacity, and the monopolization of raw material supplies (Elbaum and Wilkinson, 1979). However, with the formation of the U.S. Steel Corporation in 1901, which brought together rival firms, this phase of competition came to an end (Burns, 1936).

But the same process could not prevail in Britain. Lord Hamilton, the Secretary of State for India, noted:

> There is an inevitable objection in this country (Britain) amongst manufacturers and producers of all kinds to combine. They all like working according to their own ideas and

> their own particular plans, and according to their own particular methods, and it is here whereas the American, who is quite as independent in his character and action as the Englishman, beats us. They have brought to a fine art the power of combinations although it looks as if the millionaires had somewhat over reached themselves in the gigantic steel trusts they have created [(19)].

The reasons for the lack of cartel formation in Britain, as pointed out by Friedman, were that alternative restrictive practices were still available to British firms. British mergers did not survive long as these were collective of several firms without much inter-firm coordination as no one firm clearly dominated the merger. British mergers were limited as British industrialists were able to turn to exports to underdeveloped countries and British financial interests were able to invest in foreign countries and continue to make good profit (Friedman, 1977:38).

During the last quarter of the nineteenth century, British capitalists found modernization and the integration of British industry a much more difficult task than making profits through foreign investment and exportation to semi-protected regions. Until the middle of that century, free trade was the symbol of British industrial capitalism, whose world superiority was so strong as to dominate the markets without need of an artificial aid. However, amid growing world competition, the tariff became the most important weapon of capitalist countries. This process of protectionism had begun with Bismarck's Tariff of 1879, and was followed by a series of French tariffs in 1883–1892, and US tariffs in 1883, 1890, 1897, and 1907. The tariff was defended as only a temporary measure for the protection of a young and weak industry, at the same time the question of tariffs and trade in the steel industry was tied to the rise of "trusts." Due to its different industrial structure and its so-called "gentlemanly capitalism," Britain followed more "free trade" procedures (in fact "modified free trade" as discussed by Bhattacharya and others) (Bhattacharya, 1965), and extended its Empire to keep up profits in finance and trade. In their turn, the US and Germany relied on tariffs, first to increase production and then to compete with Britain. These tariffs were unilateral, nationalist, and home-market oriented.

In the last quarter of nineteenth century, the effectiveness of protection depended on the ability of a country to maintain international agreements on steel production and exports, which in turn depended on the cohesiveness of the country's financial national groups. As Elbaum and Wilkinson pointed out, Britain could not provide that cohesiveness to its steel industry, whereas the US and Germany could. Britain tried to overcome its weaknesses in world competition by increasing its reliance on its colonies for profits and trade relations. Thus, the declining competitive power of Britain in the world market and the class struggle within Britain from 1870–1900 (as well as the role of various emerging socio-economic and political forces within India) had a direct impact on the policies of the CGI, which in turn, contributed to the shaping of the future of India's steel industry and the country's overall industrialization.

ii. Social and Economic Forces Developing within Colonial India

The changes taking place during the late nineteenth century in the British economic, social, and political scenes were clearly influencing the changes in the CGI's policy towards the Indian steel industry. A look at the lengthy and complicated procedure of making tariff policies in India [20] shows that the CGI was far from being an autonomous, powerful body making independent decisions. The CGI had foreseen the necessity for change in its industrial policy 20 years before India's Secretary of State in London agreed to it. However, the CGI could not change its policy on its own, and Britain had no interest in converting India into another industrial giant when Britain herself was losing out to other world industrial giants. Within India, British officials generally accepted the view of the classical school of political economy thought—that international trade would be the vehicle for the transmission of economic "development" throughout the world [21]. Therefore, such development was viewed as the result of international specialization which could be maximized by pursuing a policy of "free trade" (Yeager, 1980). However, by 1870–1875, the CGI found that it could not keep up with the revenue demands of Britain if it continued to uphold "free trade," as the CGI was then facing its own set of problems and crises in the Indian front as discussed below.

a. Railroad Building and CGI's Crises in Balance of Trade

The CGI was developing railways in India using imported rails from Britain. Following a series of famines in India, the CGI faced problems starting in 1860 related to the balance of trade that were exacerbated by the loss of revenue from declining opium and silver prices [22]. The CGI realized that it could no longer afford to invest in building railroads and would have to invite private capital in for that purpose. Consequently, the CGI's purchasing policies became less hostile toward private enterprise [23].

The idea of promoting private entrepreneurs to fund railways was first proposed in 1879. However, since the state did not guarantee any protection, the proposal failed to bring many private investors into the field [24]. In 1881, a new proposal was advanced for building railway lines. It offered guarantees of limited amounts and duration only for those items for which there was no enterprise obtainable. However, Lord Hartington, then nominal Secretary of State objected to this proposal on the grounds that "the guarantees and not the profitableness of the project would be the attraction to private entrepreneurs, and that when it failed, the state might find itself morally bound to relieve the shareholders of unproductive undertakings in which they had embarked at its solicitation" [25]. This objection was made despite the fact that the Secretary of State, Lord Hartington, was in complete agreement with the CGI about the promotion of local industries. He wrote:

> Fully sharing the views of your Government as to the importance of development to the utmost of local industries and manufacturing, and of rendering India as independent as possible of home supplies, I caused an enquiry to be addressed to the War office on the subject of your present letter. It will now rest with your Government to adopt such measures as you may deem most conducive to stimulate the growth and development of local manufacturers essential to the needs of the state in its several departments, and you may rely on my hearty co-operation in any steps which your government may take with the object of dispensing with supplies from home [26].

In 1883 Lord Ripon, then the Governor General of India, again wrote to the Secretary of State:

> Our standard of value is unstable, and that the price of silver, on which its variations

> mainly depend, shows a downward tendency. The second is that the opium revenue is precarious and shows a tendency to diminish. Under these circumstances the Government should, in our opinion, exercise caution in incurring any fresh liabilities. Great as the importance we attach to the speedy development of the railing system, we are not prepared to recommend for the attainment of this object the adoption of any measures which are likely to lead to an increase of taxation. We should regard increased taxation as a greater evil than relatively slow progress in railway construction.

With these problems in mind he observed that:

> The railways have cost the tax payers of India about pound 25,000,000. They are now beginning to yield a profit. There is very fair reason to suppose that the profits will be considerable. Looking to the facts connected with Opium and Exchange, we think it not impossible that the practical necessities of the financial situation may oblige us to treat these profits as substitutes for taxation in the immediate future ... the most we can do is to recognize the course which is economically the most sound, and to endeavour gradually to conform to it [(27)].

According to Ripon, the sound course was to allow "as far as possible, to exclude the action of the State altogether from the field of enterprise, and that, as a general rule the Government should only undertake the construction of railways which, for their unprofitable character in a commercial sense or other causes, cannot be made by the private enterprises" [(28)]. This course of action, according to Ripon, would stop state expenditure on railways altogether and allow private development, thereby reducing government debt. Interestingly, an article in the July 1880 issue of The Englishman's Journal highlighted this strategy in a broader context:

> Now that the Afghan War is drawing to an end it may be expected that the material progress of India will again engage the attention of the Indian Government ... As a means of famine prevention, the development of industrial enterprises, is to be ranked with, if it should not take precedence of, irrigation works and railways; and among such enterprises none, perhaps, holds out fairer prospects than that which has contributed so largely to British prosperity—iron manufacturing [(29)].

After 1880, the production of rails in Britain declined and the country steadily began losing its monopoly on the world market. However, it was still gaining momentum in the triangular trade with India, involving continental Europe, the US and the rest of the world (Saul, 1960; Cecco, 1974; Latham, 1978). To maintain its rate of profit in this trade while losing its worldwide monopoly status on the market, Britain required the perpetuation of free trade. That is why Britain was reluctant to grant India tariff protection for the development of its industry. This reluctance to change the "free trade" policy was clearly reflected in Britain's attitude towards the iron and steel industry in India.

b. First Proposal for a Large-Scale Steel Industry in India, 1882

When Lord Ripon proposed in 1882 to introduce iron and steel production in India as a way to acquire cheaper material for railways and other construction works by using private capital and providing governmental protection, the issue was widely discussed in the British press [(30)] and in Parliament [(31)]. Ripon's analysis explained with remarkable clarity the need to create new avenues of employment, reduce British Home charges, and lower the cost of railway construction. Moreover, there was a large, growing demand for iron for railways, water works, buildings, and bridges. Ripon wrote:

> The government of India have, for some time past, had under special consideration the importance of developing the iron industry in India. The advantages which such development would afford both to the State and the public, by cheapening the cost of railway construction and maintenance, and of works for improving the water supply; by substituting metal for more perishable materials in buildings; by reducing the home charges and their concomitant loss by exchange; by creating for the population non-agricultural employment; and by increasing the means for profitable investment of capital—are too well known to require lengthened exposition. It may be accepted as proved that India possesses the means of supplying all her wants in respect of cast iron, wrought iron and steel, and that such supply could be produced remuneratively on a strictly commercial basis [(32)].

Nevertheless, it was to take twenty more years before the manufacture of iron in India would become a reality. Secretary of State, Huntington, in a dispatch dated November 16, 1882, refused to sanction Ripon's proposal. He maintained that Indian manufacturers of iron "must be supported by their own strength and not relieved by artificial means from the natural competition of other countries" [(33)]. He said to the House of Commons during its debate about the matter that, "I have informed the Government of India that an engagement on their part to take fixed quantities of iron and steel at fixed prices annually for a term of years is, in my opinion, open to serious objection" [(34)].

It seemed that the Secretary of State agreed in principle to the idea of allowing the development of private capital, but only on the basis of free competition rather than with protection for any infant industries. The reason for the British government's attitude was well understood by T. C. Hope, a commissioner in the Public Works department of the Viceroy's Council in India. He wrote to Lord Ripon, "Our two main proposals now before the Secretary of State on Railway policy and on Iron Works in India are apparently not in a fair way for acceptance" [(35)]. He further added:

> But the real issue is between the development of Indian industry and the relief of the Indian exchequer, on the one hand, the interest of English iron masters, and of another class to whom the transmission of Stores to India is a source of profit, on the other. All that we are asking is to be allowed to contract for Indian iron, as we do for Indian beer, boots and on fair and unprotective terms, in order to effect economy and efficiency in railway administration. There is, however, another aspect of both these questions, namely, their relation to public opinion. The postponement of railway development, the refusal to allow Indian wheat, for instance in fair chance against American, must produce a growing discontent and agitation in the English mercantile world. Again, the objections to allowing a fair chance to the Indian iron industry have already got wind in India and have been noticed in two or three native newspapers. There can be no doubt that a definite refusal would establish a grievance on the part of the natives the converse of that regarding the cotton duties, which would be effectively worked, because better founded. On the other hand, the announcement of a definite and intelligible policy of Railway expansion, and the starting of iron and steel manufacture, would be a measure most popular with all classes, and certain to bring credit to the government [(36)].

c. Demise of the First Proposal for a Large-Scale Steel Industry in India

The British government did not treat the case for promoting iron and steel development in India as an ordinary one, such as contracting for boots or beer. It was concerned with the more important issue of British competitiveness in iron and steel around the world. Although Commissioner Hope understood the debate, he insisted that:

> We cannot afford to wait while rival schools are discussing abstract principles. Nor is there, in reality, any necessity at all for deciding which of the schools is right, we want all the aid which both theories of railway construction are capable of affording ... Unaided private enterprise would be very nice, but is not to be had. The aid we, therefore, offer is the very least under which enterprise can be attracted at all [(37)].

The efforts of Ripon's government brought about a minor change; that is, from 1883 onwards, the objective of the various revisions to the Government Stores rules was to encourage the purchase of articles from bona fide local manufacturers. The main controversy that surrounded the Store purchasing policy of the CGI involved the question of what constituted a bona fide Indian manufacturer. The India Office insisted that articles wholly manufactured in Europe and only assembled in India were not bona fide Indian manufacturers. It further added that all Stores supplies not of bona fide Indian manufacture should be purchased through the Store's department of the India Office. Engineering firms, largely British-owned, then had to obtain their inputs from Europe due to the absence of a steel industry in India. Efforts to purchase locally-made manufactures under this changed policy mainly benefited woolens, paper, and leather manufactures (Sen, 1964:98; Sen, 1966:11).

Thus, the CGI's purchasing policy was formulated with the intent of reducing purchasing in London and saving on the "Home Charges," with the intention of fostering the development of a private industrial sector. To reduce purchasing in London, the CGI established a broad range of public-sector industries. It owned and operated engineering workshops that supplied the Public Works Department, the railways, the factories which supplied the Indian army, and numerous printing presses. It engaged in the operation of coal mines in the Central Provinces and Central India, and from 1882 to 1889, it ran the Barakar Iron Works as a state enterprise. Railway workshops were primarily concerned with the repairs and construction of rolling stock, but after the 1890s they produced some of their own inputs (Sen, 1964).

In 1901 the Jamalpur Workshops of the East Indian Railway began the production of steel on a small-scale. At this time the CGI did not attempt to promote specific economic activities by granting protection from import competition. Eventually, however, the CGI concluded that under certain conditions, tariff protection might be an appropriate means of directing economic development. Rider argues that between 1894 and 1914, the CGI attempted only to ensure that its revenue tariff did not generate a hardship to Indian industries (Rider, 1971:11). In fact, the Indian tariff policy between 1894 and 1914 can be characterized as modified free trade (Ibid.). The CGI did not impose protective tariffs, and it treated goods from all sources equally, however, it did impose a general duty on all imports to generate revenue. By 1859, when the preference for British goods in the Indian market was abolished, British domination of the Indian import trade was secure. Britain continued to hold over half of that trade, even though its share had been diminishing slowly (Ibid.).

In the middle of the nineteenth century, the CGI's free trade policy consolidated the traditional colonial pattern of Indian trade (Saul, 1960). While Britain's exports to its traditional markets in Europe, the US, and South America were crippled by tariff protection, colonial India's exports—mostly raw materials—did not face the same high tariff barriers. They continued to flow to world markets in excess of India's imports. Colonial India's payments to Britain, then, allowed Britain to continue purchasing from foreign countries quantities of food, raw materials, and manufactured products in excess of what Britain exported to them in the form of goods and services. Britain's free access to the Indian market combined with the worldwide demand for Indian agricultural exports facilitated the continued expansion of world trade between 1870 and 1914. This arrangement allowed Britain to play a central role in that expansion. Secretary of State Lord Hamilton wrote to the Viceroy of India Lord Curzon:

> It seems clearer that the issues raised by Chamberlain (in Britain) divide themselves into two groups, first, the question of retaliation as a means of protection to our colonies or as an instrument for negotiation with foreign countries—it seems to me that retaliation is a practical policy, but it has further advantage of being exceedingly popular—so far as I have been able to investigate the figures, it seems to me that, in any scheme that can be put forward, the colonies would gain very greatly at our expense; and, believing as I do that the foundation of our industrial edifice is the constant and large supply of cheap food and raw material, any tax upon either, sufficiently high to add to the cost of production, would be detrimental in every way to our commercial and industrial interest [(38)].

This letter explains, in part, why British tariff reformers found India difficult to incorporate into their empire-wide trading system. The export earnings of colonial India obtained in non-empire markets were more valuable to Britain than the increase in Indo-British trade anticipated from some scheme of imperial preference would have been. Certainly, there was little interest in allowing colonial India the same protection for its industries as was enjoyed by the self-governing colonies because as Rider noted, British goods did not face high tariffs in India. As long as the nature of the world economy was not disturbed, it was in Britain's interest that colonial India continued its tariff policy of modified 'free trade' (Rider, 1971).

In 1883, the reply of Ripon's government to the Secretary of State was revealing in its understanding of both the Indian situation and the British attitude to it. Ripon's dispatch on January 23rd read as follows:

> It is, we presume, certain that the establishment of the iron and steel industry would be viewed with disfavor by the persons interested in the manufacture of these articles in England in this connection. It is by no means improbable that even the most legitimate efforts to develop and encourage local industry will be represented by those interested in the matter as though such efforts involved the adoption of a protective policy on the part of the Government of India [(39)].

In spite of this appeal, Ripon did not succeed in his effort to grant assistance to private iron and steel concerns by purchasing guarantees. Since it was opposed both by British import concerns in India as well the India Office in London, the idea was subsequently dropped by Ripon's successor (Sen, 1964).

d. Second Proposal for Large-Scale Steel Industry in India, 1890s

The issue of establishing a steel industry in India was raised again because of two factors: increased US production and its Free Trade campaign of the mid 1890s, and the importance of rail production as a declining market for Bessemer steel beginning in 1890. The US, in its constant search for lower production costs for steel, had begun experimenting with Taylorism which gave management control over workers. This production system proved very useful, and the US was able to vastly increase its steel production. The growth in production of US steel at a lower cost intensified world competition.

The growth of US steel production gave the impetus to British politicians, such as Joseph Chamberlain, to advocate for protectionist policies. A plan was proposed in Britain that centered on developing an Imperial customs union with self-governing colonies: Australia, New Zealand, South Africa and Canada (Mehrotra, 1961). India, though Britain's best customer within the Empire, was ignored by tariff reformers for several reasons. India was not a self-governing colony and did not have the fiscal autonomy, which meant that India did not have the same liberty to erect tariffs against British goods that the self-governing colonies had. In addition, India was a major source of export earnings for the Empire, and Britain had a substantial trade surplus with India (Ibid.). Therefore, increasing Indo-British trade at the possible expense of India's export trade made no sense, as the summary report of government Administration points out:

> She (India) is exposed to a peculiar risk which differentiates her case from that of any other member of the Empire. India is a debtor country owing pounds 16 million per annum in a currency other than that in which her revenues are collected. Her financial stability is absolutely dependent on the maintenance of a sufficient excess of exports over imports. A series of tariff wars with powerful countries would undoubtedly be fraught with grave injury to the export trade in the certain cost of the struggle and the severe penalties of defeat would be too heavy a price to pay [(40)].

This statement was substantiated as follows:

> Three fourths of India's total imports came from the British Empire, and of the remaining fourth a substantial part consists of articles which the British Empire either does not produce at all or is not in a favourable position to supply. Thus without the assistance of discriminating tariff the British manufacturers have already obtained the bulk of the inward trade, and in the case of some of the more important articles, such as cotton goods, they seem adequately secured in the possession of the market-for a long time to come. In the case of exports the conditions are completely reversed. 3/8th of the total exports are taken by Great Britain and her possessions, a great part being raw materials, the taxation of which is not understood to be contemplated. In the production and supply of tea and wheat, which are two of the most important food-stuffs, India would still compete with other British possessions even if foreign countries were effectively excluded. She already supplies 2/3 of the England's rice demand, and for coffee she has a profitable market abroad. Thus, while the British manufacturer might profit to a small extent by India's adoption of a system of preferential duties, India herself has little if anything to gain. On the other hand, she has far more to risk, partly in the possible prejudice to her fiscal independence and injury to her customs revenue, but mainly from the retaliatory action of foreign countries [(41)].

The solution to this situation was predicted in an editorial in *Indian Engineering:*

> It may be that the true solution of any real difficulty that may be distracting manufacturers of pig iron will come not from either advocates of cornering regulation or from disciples of the school of increasing the output of raw material in order to take the wind out of the sails of the importers of finished products, but from the rival schools of political economy which are at present engaged in discussing the relative advantages of Free

> Trade and Protection—not overlooking, while so engaged, the possible middle course of an Imperial Preference, which shall be neither Protection nor Free Trade, but give the British Empire, that is Great and Greater Britain, some safeguards against the inevitable underselling of domestic products which result from the unfettered dumping of foreign produce on British and Colonial marts (42).

This solution of preferential treatment rather than the enactment of a tariff was taken up by British politicians. At Chamberlain's urging, the Colonial Conference of 1902 and 1907 passed resolutions approving the principle of Imperial preference (Burt, 1956:582).

Along with the problems of competition with the US, Britain also faced a competitive threat from Germany. This precarious situation of the British steel industry, along with its reluctance to and limitations in changing the British industrial structure in steel, directly resulted into the renewed efforts of the CGI to attract private capital for investment in the Indian iron and steel industry. In a resolution of the CGI of 25 June, 1891, it was declared:

> With the view of encouraging local industries and the development of technical education, His Excellency the Governor General in Council has now resolved to modify as a tentative measure, the existing orders prohibiting the local purchase of manufactured articles of iron and steel made up from imported materials. In so doing, the Governor General in Council desires it to be clearly understood that this relaxation of existing rules is sanctioned solely in the hope of thereby effecting economy in the public administration both by actual saving in the cost of articles purchased locally and by avoiding the delays that are sometimes inevitable when the articles have to be procured by indent in England. It is not intended to sanction thereby a procedure in any degree of a protective nature. It is also intended that relaxation of the rules regarding local manufacture shall be limited to the less important supplies, e.g. bridges and roofs of small span required for the Buildings and Roads and Irrigation Branches of PWD and, for Municipalities and District Boards. In the case of Railways under construction, the whole of the necessary supplies, as far as can be foreseen, will continue as heretofore, to be procured by indent of the Secretary of State (43).

However, this resolution contributed very little to the process of Indian industrial development except for allowing restricted competition to a specified number of firms in India. The resolution did not promote technical education or encourage local industries, because the firms that would compete had been long established with British capital and had all the necessary equipment to meet the demands of the State. Even these firms would get no more than some less-important tenders. This partial, half-hearted 'encouragement' was further dampened with the comments that "it was not intended to be a protection to the industry." It was observed in *Indian Engineering*:

> Every indent (purchase request) that is sent by the Indian Government to the India Office in London is so much taken away from the possibilities of the development of the industry in India; and in these days of a steadily falling exchange, it is an aggravation, by no means insignificant, of the exchange difficulty. One has only to look at the large aggregate of the orders for ironwork sent to the India Office to realise that this interdict on a legitimate Indian Industry plays a very important part in sending down the value of the Rupee, besides handicapping the industry itself, and yet we are told that this half-hearted removal of a small portion of the interdict must not encourage Indian manufacturers into the belief that Government intends to protect the Indian Iron Industry (44).

Clearly, the resolution of June 25, 1891 did not change much about the industrial scene of India. Barakar Iron Works, owned by British capital and worked as a state enterprise between 1882 and 1889, was refused any special consideration. In a letter written in reply to Barakar's request for preferential treatment the CGI's agent stated, "I am to add that modification of these orders is under consideration, and that in the event of their modifications your company would necessarily have to compete on the usual terms with other local suppliers" (45).

Not surprisingly, within two years, Barakar Iron Works ran into trouble and asked the CGI for financial help. The CGI refused to consider its application (46). In 1889, the Secretary of State gave over the property of Barakar Iron Works to the Bengal Iron and Steel Company (hereafter BISCO) which was incorporated in England (Sen, 1964:31). It received government orders for iron. By this time Britain's production of rails and steel had declined due to lack of demand at home and increased competition abroad. In 1894, BISCO requested the CGI for loans, as it could not make profits, which was refused. The crisis of BISCO led to the initiation of a discussion about official policy for the Indian iron and steel industry. In May 1896, Jeremiah Head, (an engineer appointed by the government) (47), reviewed the history of the unsuccessful attempts of iron manufacturing at Proto Novo, referring to the difficulty of "obtaining a continuous and sufficient supply of fuel." S. N. Sen mentions that George Watt, in a report dated, September 11, 1896, pleaded for the adoption of a policy that would "place the local industry on a permanent footing" because according to him, there was a future possibility of continental iron and steel reaching India, which could be cheaper than the same from the United Kingdom (Sen, 1964:52–53).

However, J. E. O'Connor, the Director General of Statistics, posed new problems in connection with the production of iron and steel in India. He stated that the Indian iron industry should limit itself to the production of pig iron and cast iron. The demand was great for "wrought iron, merchant iron, and steel, in all their various forms from bars and plates to rails" (48). However, he noted, "such operations cannot be undertaken except by persons possessed of very large capital." Reviving Ripon's ideas, O'Connor proposed that the company should undertake the production of wrought iron and steel and that the government should buy from them for a number of years "a certain quantity of their products" (49).

e. Increased Threat of Competition from Foreign Steel

The CGI did modify its policy in 1896 and offered BISCO a contract (Sen, 1964). It appears that with the increasing British realization that it was losing to US competition, one way of checking the competition was to bring down the cost of production by utilizing inexpensive iron ore and cheap labor from India. As was reported in *Indian Engineering*:

> The chairman of the Madras Railway has lately been giving voice to the general feeling of regret that must be felt by all his countrymen at seeing so much work taken out of the hands of English manufacturers by the Americans; while there seems a prospect that the latter will, in the near future, get even a larger share of any orders that may be going. Colonel Gardiner further proposes as a remedy that English manufacturers should set up establishments in this country, to work up the indigenous raw materials, in the hope

> that the cheap labour to be obtained here will enable us to bring our prices down to the American limit (50).

For the article's British author, the case for Indian steel rested exclusively on the need for British manufacturers to compete with US steel. As he wrote further:

> The only result of opening works here (India) would be to lighten the over pressure on English shops when work is plenty, and therefore dear, by relieving them of a part of that done for India; while at the same time the capital expended would be English, as also would the pockets into which the profits would flow. This is one of the businesses in which native owners could not even hope to compete with Englishmen (51).

Again, he explains,

> If, then, there is work which must be sent elsewhere than to England, which we contend to be the case, there is no doubt that it will benefit England most to keep it in one of her own dependencies. The benefits to India itself would not be few ... the establishment of large factories would tend to create an inland traffic and fill the wagons which now return empty (52).

According to the author of the article,

> The one advantage we have is cheap adaptable labor, and it is this which should be made most of. It will also give an impetus to the iron founding trade at home, whose outturn, now that so many countries produce their own, must be largely limited by the home consumption (53).

Another author wrote for *The Englishman's Journal* that:

> We know of no ores in the world which are fully equal to those of Central India in purity, in richness, and quantity over a given area ... Now 'Spiegeleisen' and acier sauvage (necessary for making ductible iron for wire) can only be obtained from the *purest* iron ores, and of these there are inexhaustible mines in Central India. ... if it would be possible to make finished iron or steel direct from ore, the pure ores would greatly increase in value and become eventually a most important article of export from India ... the production of iron in India per maund will get a profit of Rs 5 to 6 ... of all the half products of iron, every ounce required by England, America and other countries, should be supplied by India owing to its excellent and cheap iron ores, fuel and low wages ... Here we have then a most valuable raw material for export which would not interfere with England's commercial policy as regards India, which has hitherto consisted in the principle of taking India's raw produce and returning it to her in the shape of manufactured goods (54).

f. Making Way for a Large-Scale Steel Industry in India, 1899

Shortly after these developments on the world economic scene, the CGI began thinking seriously about clearing the way for a large-scale iron and steel industry in India, and two definitive steps were taken in this direction. In 1899 the mining rules were revised. These rules had been the biggest hindrances to the development of an iron industry in India (55). In the same year, Major R. H. Mahon, the Deputy Director General of Ordinance who had been appointed to investigate the matter, published the details in "A Report upon the Manufacture of Iron and Steel in India" and addressed the coking qualities of Indian-coal (56). Soon after, the CGI appointed several persons to explore the new areas for iron ore in the Kumaon Hills and the Chanda district so that the information could be made available to prospective manufacturers. On the basis of these investigations, the government published various monographs in 1905 on iron and steel manufacturing in Punjab, Shillong, Bengal and the Central Provinces [57]. It seems the CGI was planning for two or three iron and steel industries in India and assumed that they would be owned by British capital. To attract that British capital, the Secretary of State wrote to Lord Curzon:

> A prompt reply is essential if private enterprise is to be promoted and big men encouraged to embark in Indian enterprises. They cannot afford to keep any large proportion of their capital lying idle, and if they do not receive replies within a reasonable period, the money they had proposed to devote, or were ready to devote, to one purpose, has in the meantime, been applied to another from which it cannot be withdrawn [58].

Sir Arthur Godley, the Permanent Under-Secretary of State for India, wrote, "It is most important for us to get this matter right if we are to have the gold standard (as we hope) and to attract British capital" [59]. By then, the rupee had also stabilized [60]. It was expressed by Lord Curzon's government that "without a surplus of exports over imports all purely financial measures for supporting exchange must ultimately prove ineffectual" [61].

In 1900, the first measure to facilitate the investment in and production of steel in India was taken and the Indian Companies Act was passed. The object of this Act was to encourage the investment of British capital in Indian enterprise, constituted on a rupee basis. The Act, which followed English legislation, enabled an Indian company to open a register in Britain for membership. This placed the company in a better position to obtain a quotation on the London Stock Exchange [62]. Thus, between 1895 and 1900, the CGI felt compelled, in the long-term interest of British capital, to address questions of production, matters relating to finances, and particularly, the question of the exchange value of the rupee. It also began to take an increasingly oppositional stance in relation to the anti-protectionist stance adopted in London [63]. It was this opposition of the colonial state as much as anything else, which, between 1893 and 1899, brought the reform of the exchange question. However, this oppositional stance did not change the "free trade" and anti-protectionist policies of the British government. Secretary of State Hamilton wrote to Lord Curzon, the Viceroy of India, on January 13, 1901:

> We are not only a great manufacturing nation, but England, in addition, is an enormous exchange mart, and free trade in this respect specially benefits us. And, as regards the rest of the Empire, I do not think it would be possible to draw them together in closer relations if protectionist principles are to regulate our fiscal policy by which the manufacturing interests of different localities are placed in antagonism one to another ... I do not think it would be possible to contemplate in India any assistance to any industry which took the form of levying protective duties for its benefits, however small or slight the protection or assistance might be. On the other hand, I do think that, by instruction, by special bounties, and by pecuniary assistance, we can help agriculture [64].

Agriculture was still an important export item for Britain and its promotion was supported, but the promotion of the industrial sector was not acceptable to the Secretary of State.

g. Pressure from the Emerging Indian Nationalist Movement

The CGI, while trying to resolve its exchange problems, was not immune to the emergence of nationalist leaders at this time. These leaders, who exposed CGI's industrial policy as one opposed to Indian interests, also contributed to the shift of government policies. The situation in India was complicated by the decay of the country's traditional cottage industries under British colonial rule. The economic strategy pursued by the British did not generate sufficient employment for an expanding educated middle class, and that failure had political implications (Chandra, 1966:737–738; Desai, 1948:296). The CGI was well aware of this. As it noted,

> The attitude of the Indian public towards the important question [Industrialisation of India] is unanimous, and cannot be left out of account. Manufacturers, politicians and the literate public have for long been pressing their demands for a definite and accepted policy of state-aid to Indian industries and the demand is one which evokes the sympathy of all classes of India whose position or intelligence leads them to take any degree of interest in such matters ... As far back as 1906, the opponents of the partition of Bengal found a rallying cry that united all sections to see India a manufacturing country as well as more exporter of raw materials, and expressed the duty which lay on every patriotic Indian to help to the consummation of this end, whether as a consumer or as an investor ... Public sentiments, have again and again expressed itself in the form of resolutions and questions in the Imperial and British Councils, of resolutions in the Indian National Congress and at public meetings, and of articles in the press. In Bombay particularly, where Indian commercial opinion is relatively more highly educated and has been stimulated to greater keenness by foreign competition, the movement in this direction of enlisting Government sympathy in an active propaganda of industrial expansion has been most marked for some years past [(65)].

The CGI was equally conscious of the nature of the national movement emerging in India, as it was pointed out in its correspondence with the Secretary of State in London,

> This movement which has acquired considerable political significance in India generally has followed two particular lines of expression. In the first place, there is the constant assertion that the British Government in India have with malice intent or, if not with malice, by their attitude of indifference, allowed indigenous industries to be overwhelmed by foreign and especially by British competition. The second charge is that the British system of education has confined the energies of educated young men to literary pursuits and the learned professions, and has created among them a demand for employment limited to Government service, the law and medicine. It is to the overcrowding of these avenues of employment that much discontent and unrest are attributable. These contentions emphasise one aspect of the need for an industrial policy which will enable technical education in India to produce its best results, which will lighten the pressure on purely literary course, and reduce the excessive demand for employment in the services of calling to which these courses lead up [(66)].

The nationalist critique of British policy and economic demands was largely formulated before 1905. Until World War I, moderates [(67)] dominated the Indian National Congress. As Chandra has noted, they generally viewed the British connection favorably, welcoming the introduction of Western education, the establishment of the rule of law, economic and political unification, and the centralized administration. In their view, British administration was essential to the process of 'modernization,' a process that had only begun. Moderates did not deny that the British occupation had brought certain material benefits. Nevertheless, they believed that mistaken policies of the British bureaucracy had contributed to India's "underdevelopment" (Chandra, 1960:2–7; Naoroji, 1886:22). In 1886, the nationalists sought to nationalize economic policy hoping that it would help India's economic development.

Much of the controversy over economic policy centered on the "poverty of India" matter, which was crucial to the nationalist critique of economic policy (Dutt, 1901; Naoroji, 1901). While refuting the argument of overpopulation as a cause for India's poverty, Naoroji wrote, "To talk of overpopulation at present is just as reasonable as to cut off a man's hands, and then to taunt him that he was not able to maintain himself or move his hands" (Naoroji, 1901:217). Economic progress was an essential part of the moderates' vision of India's future. They argued that the absence of an adequate measure of economic development had led to the growing incidence of famine in India and its increasing poverty. They also deplored the export of primary resources out of India as an economic loss to India (Iyer, 1903; Rai, 1917; Dutt, 1904; Ranade, 1899). Of India's exported resources G. S. Iyer wrote:

> Treasure was carried away by British adventurers and it created a class of capitalists with large accumulations of Indian money. This money stimulated the credit of this class, imparted mobility to their energy and enterprise. By the beginning of the 19th century, the foundation of British prosperity had been well laid on the spoilation of India and Ireland (Iyer, 1903:243).

The CGI had understood the importance of appeasing these moderates long before the formation of the Indian National Congress. In 1883, T. C. Hope, had written to Ripon with a suggestion:

> Objections to allowing a fair chance to the Indian Iron industry have already got wind, and have been noticed in two or three native newspapers. There can be no doubt that a definite refusal would establish a grievance on the part of the natives the converse of that regarding the cotton duties, which would be effectively worked, because better founded. On the other hand, the announcement of a definite and intelligible policy of Railway expansion and the starting of the iron and steel manufacture would be a measure most popular with all classes and certain to bring credit to the government [(68)].

This was fully supported by Evelyn Baring, the finance member of the Viceroy's Council, who wrote,

> The issue is an important one on its own merits, and moreover, there is something in the political argument, that if any action from Home stops the establishment of the iron industry, the public in India are sure, whether rightly or wrongly, to regard that action as dictated by a feeling of hostility to Indians, and sympathy to English commercial interest [(69)].

Therefore, CGI was not surprised at the formulations of the drain theory by nationalist leaders who criticized the colonial regime. Dadabhai Naoroji and R. C. Dutt, both responsible for the "drain theory" in connection with India's poverty, argued that the extent to which the annual volume of interest payments and profits remitted to England exceeded the inflow of new capital represented a drain of wealth out of India. India's foreign trade at that time was dominated by Europeans, and hence India received fewer benefits from that trade (Naoroji, 1901; Chaudhuri, 1968, Sen, 1966). Surendranath Banerjee said at the Congress presidential address, "It had been the settled policy of England in India ever since her rise in political power to convert India into a land of raw produce for the benefits of the manufacturers and operatives of England" [(70)]. The British commercial community had been able to exert its influence over economic policy to the detriment of the overall interests of India.

These leaders placed a high priority on industrial "development" as a way to end India's poverty. They maintained that first the East India Company, and then the CGI had discouraged Indian industries, and had encouraged the production and export of primary products to Britain. They argued that the character of India's foreign trade had been shaped by British commercial and exchange policies. For example, colonial India's comparative advantage in agricultural exports was not the result of "natural endowments but rather the work of British policy in England and India." M. G. Ranade, G. V. Joshi, G. Subramaniam, S. Iyer and G. K. Gokhale all believed that a policy of forced industrialization would alleviate India's poverty [(71)]. But they were skeptical of the benefits to India of foreign capital and enterprise and believed that efforts by the government to encourage capital migration had led to currency and exchange policies detrimental to Indian interests. They believed that private Indian capital would become the instrument for the development of the industrial sector. Justice Ranade wrote:

> This is the practical work which Providence has set down for us to learn under the best of teachers ... We have to improve our Raw Materials, or Import them when our Soil is unsuited to their production. We have to organise Labour and Capital by co-operation and import freely foreign skill and machinery, till we learn our lessons properly and need no help. We have rusticated too long; we have now to turn our apt hand to new work, and bend our muscles to sturdier and honester labour. This is the Civic Virtue we have to learn, and according as we learn it or spurn it we shall win or lose in the contest. I feel sure it will soon become the creed of the whole Nation, and ensure the permanent triumph of the modern spirit in the ancient land (quoted in Chandra, 1966:66).

While arguing in this manner, the nationalist leaders in fact supported the idea of the Western model of industrial development—i.e., development within the private sector. They believed that laissez-faire, the absence of economic regulation, was essential to that development. However, they also insisted that the government purchase its stores in India, support technical and industrial education, provide technical assistance, make available cheap capital, and reduce expenditure and taxation. Ranade believed that infant industries should receive government protection. Lord Minto, then Secretary of State, and Sir Denzil Ibbeston, the Director of Board of Revenue, admitted the justice of the nationalist charges of discrimination against Bombay textiles: "'The excise duty on cotton' was 'quite inexcusable' of course, it exists simply in the interests of Manchester goods—'no self-governing country would stand such things for five minutes'" [(72)]. By 1910, the nationalists were nearly unanimous in their demand for protecting infant industries.

Creativity of Indian Capitalist Class, J. N. Tata and the Indian Nationalists

Ascension of Emerging Indian Capitalist Class

The actions and decisions of the Indian nationalist leaders and Indian capitalist class are more visible examples of human creativity (human agency) in finding solutions under subservient circumstances.

i. Revival of Indian Tradition of Industrial Mela & Swadeshi-Movement

To fight against the discrimination policy of the colonial government, the nationalist leaders began to revive the tradition of the industrial *mela* (fair) in order to awaken the Indian entrepreneurial spirit for the Swadeshi movement. Thus, as Sumit Sarkar pointed out, Swadeshi may be defined as the sentiment closely associated with many phases of Indian nationalism. For example, P. N. Bose, a prominent geologist and son-in law of the renowned economist R. C. Dutt, wrote a pamphlet in 1886 pleading for the formation of the following: a proper science curriculum in the university syllabus, a separate Science and Technical institute, and a Society for the Development of Indian Industries and technical education (Sarkar, 1973:111). Bose believed that the essential prerequisite for starting what he termed "the science industries" was technical education, and by 1891, under his leadership an Indian Industrial Association was set up in the meeting of the Indian National Congress at Bengal Provincial Conference. From 1893, this Association began to revive the Hindu *mela t*radition of holding a periodic exhibition of Swadeshi products. In 1901 the Indian National Congress made industrial *mela* a regular feature of its annual session (Ibid., 115).

Soon the Indian National Congress became a forum for the discussion of popular themes on industrial devastation, economic drain and the need for Swadeshi and boycott. Indian historian Sumit Sarkar writes that such topics were not only discussed in formal treatises and newspapers but also found their way in songs, plays, jatras (Bengali folk theatre), and, most importantly, in vernacular pamphlets (Ibid., 98). For Moderate economists industrial revival was just one item in a comprehensive program of economic and political reform. But others who were swept into the euphoria generated in the country considered Swadeshi and boycott as "a sort of panacea for all the ills of India" (Ibid, 98). This wave of Swadeshi movement was successful in making a point that "classical development theory was not an adequate basis for a development strategy in the Indian context" (73). This point was well reflected in what Lord Minto wrote to Morley on March 10, 1910:

> I have long thought that the great battle of future Indian policy will be fought over tariffs. The natural desire to foster Indian industries must be in opposition to any favourtism of imports from home. All the more so as the demand for employment in India is becoming daily more pressing, and of greater political importance, and as far as I can see, the development of Indian Industries is the only practical way of meeting it to any great extent. Also my belief is that the Imperial Council when it feels itself firm on its legs will be inclined to assert itself, especially on matters of taxation and more especially as to taxation suspected of favouring home interests (74).

A report on the existing *Art and Industries of Bengal* in 1890 admitted that all Bengali handicrafts were declining except for woodwork, brassware, matwork and pottery (75). G. N. Gupta's publication, *A Survey of the Industries and Resources of Eastern Bengal and Assam for 1907–08*, spoke of a five percent decrease in the number of weavers and their dependents in Bengal between 1891 and 1901 (quoted in Sarkar, 1973:93). Swadeshi meant that consumers should buy indigenous goods, even if they were more expensive than, or inferior in quality to, their imported substitute, and that it was the patriotic duty of those with capital to pioneer such industries even though profits initially might be minimal or nonexistent. With the forceful arguments of the nationalist leaders and deteriorating economic and political conditions in India, a Swadeshi movement emerged in 1906. These conditions influenced Swadeshi thinking profoundly, as its propaganda advocated both the boycott of foreign goods and passive resistance. This propaganda had two aspects: promotion of indigenous industries and the employment-creating potential of industrialization. These ideas were based on a widespread feeling in Bengal that a "faulty system of education combined with lack of industrial development had led to the services and the professions becoming seriously overcrowded" (Ibid., 99). This feeling was expressed in the organization of technical education and industrial research under the Swadeshi movement. Sarkar pointed out that there were five strands in it: (a) the promotion of Swadeshi sale through exhibitions, (b) shops and cost price hawking by volunteers; (c) the fostering and revival of the traditional indigenous crafts, (d) the starting of new industries based on modern techniques, and (e) the floating of Swadeshi banks, insurance companies, and inland shipping concerns (Ibid., 110–111).

ii. Entrepreneurship of J. N. Tata

Another important development which was taking place even before the Swadeshi Movement on the eastern coast of India was the emergence of Parsi entrepreneurs on the western coast. One of these Parsi entrepreneurs was J.N.Tata who was able to form a company for steel production which then created the first large-scale steel industry (Tata Iron and Steel Company) in India with exclusive indigenous capital. J.N. Tata was the son of Nusserwanji Tata and they belonged to the community of Parsi merchants in Bombay. Parsi merchants, who migrated from Persia to Gujarat, were ousted in large number from Surat in the 1750s by the Gujaratis (Sen, 1975:2). In Surat, they, along with other Indian merchants, had been useful to foreign merchants as interpreters, brokers, and contractors. When Parsis migrated to Bombay with the encouragement of the British Company government in Bombay, they continued to collaborate with foreign firms. British mercantile firms in Bombay frequently relied on the Parsis for finance and generally turned to Indian brokers and traders for the supply of cotton, opium, piece goods, cardamoms, cloves, indigo, coffee (Ibid., 1; see also Desai, 1992; Oonk, n.d.). Parsis had been loyal to the British for a long time as they partly financed the military defense of the Bombay, and remained loyal to the British during the Mutiny of 1857, while financing the British military apparatus. Moreover, they recognized the need to learn the English language and adopt British customs so that they could improve their socio-economic status in Western India by making close connections with the British Company government in Bombay [(76)].

Parsis worked with British companies to learn about international trade, and thus became wealthy. For example, Jamsetjee Jejeebhoy, a Parsi businessman, founded Jamsetjee Jejeebhoy Co. in 1818 and became very rich. By 1830 he was the largest consigner of opium to the British company Jardine Matheson and Co. This opium trade was very lucrative and when China tried to ban it, Britain colonized China in 1839. Jejeebhoy was knighted by Queen Victoria in 1842, and in 1856 he was made baronet. As we noted in Chapter 3, J. N. Tata was also allowed to join (1860) the provincial Bombay branch of the Grand Lodge of Masons.

Similar to Jejeebhoy, Nasserwanji Tata was also trading cotton and opium to Japan and China and bringing back tea, silk goods, camphor, cinnamon, copper, brass and gold to India. J. N. Tata joined his father's business in 1858 and became wealthy between 1862 and 1867 by shipping large amounts of cotton to Liverpool during the US Civil War, and later by providing supplies to the British Indian army during the 1867 invasion of Abyssinia. J. N. Tata used his share of the fortune to extend his trade to Shanghai and Yokohama, and he opened branches in Paris, London and New York supplying Indian cotton, Persian Gulf pearls, and opium. He also started investing in real estate, and built several cotton mills and the Taj Mahal Hotel in Bombay. Thus, with his shrewd investments in textile and other foreign ventures J. N. Tata was able to accumulate significant capital. In 1883, he submitted to CGI a proposal plan for a large-scale Indian steel industry, hydroelectric syndicate, and an institute of science. In 1887, he established Tata Sons Private Limited (later renamed Tata Sons and Company in 1917) which was linked to only profits and not sales or production. Later, between 1916 and 1939, Tata Sons grew to be a giant interlocking managing agency with interests in finance, real estate, trading, and industrial ventures.

J. N. Tata had cultivated a public image both as a loyal colonial subject of Britain and as a nationalist by donating funds to the Indian National Congress Party's annual session. However, his efforts bore fruit only when CGI agreed to support his venture in an Indian steel industry in 1899. The decision by the CGI, showing a change in its attitude towards industrial policy in India, was partly influenced by rising imports from Belgium and Germany, along with reasons discussed above. The challenge was patently evident according to Thomas Holland, then Director of the Geological Survey of India, who noted the following:

> Government imports came mostly from England, while 'about half the private imports of iron and steel came from Germany and Belgium'. The imports of British iron and steel into India formed an unimportant fraction of the total production at home. Yet there were iron makers I know at home who would willingly see the industry strangled in India for the sake of the small fraction of their total profits (77).

Holland warned that unless a steel industry was developed in India, "it will soon become as much a market for German as for British goods." In another letter he noted, "the British merchants were interested in simple trade and reluctant to invest capital in industries" (78).

Thus, the conjunction of the historical forces discussed above, both inside and outside India, created favorable circumstances for the emergence of the first large-scale Indian steel industry. The CGI, which as early as 1883 had contemplated a change in its attitude towards Indian industrialization, at least in principle, began making concessions in 1899 in the form of new mining rules and subsequently gave encouragement to private British capital to invest in India. The CGI, which was very keen to have a large-scale steel operation in India for the development of railways so that it could improve its balance of payments, allowed the Indian capitalist, J. N. Tata, to initiate a technical education institute as well as a steel industry.

BIRTH OF TATA IRON AND STEEL COMPANY

By 1899, the CGI was ready to revise the mining rules in an effort to encourage private enterprise in iron and other mining industries (79). Without sacrificing Britain's free trade policy, and assuming that British capital would dominate India's industrialization, the Secretary of State Hamilton suggested the following to the CGI in 1900:

> One thing you cannot do is to protect by tariff any existing or infant industry in India, but short of that, much could be done by encouragement, by assistance ... it is the practice of the war office and Admirality when they wish, for national purposes, to increase the supply of any particular article to give specially remunerative contracts to firms ... I have so strong a belief in the coming prosperity of India, that I want to associate increased investment of British capital there with a simultaneous action on the part of the Government in developing industry enterprise [(80)].

Earlier support encouraged change in 1897, as the Secretary of State Hamilton wrote to the officials working on Salem ore in South India, "if it is expedient to promise concessions on conditions that iron-works are started and successfully worked at Madras, I shall be ready to consider favourably any proposal you make on the subject" [(81)]. In an effort to import British capital, the Secretary of State and the CGI had suggested relaxing the rules for that purpose. Lord Curzon wrote that since "Cassel is much more inclined to bring his money to India, we shall not be inclined in dealing with him to sit too strongly upon rules or conditions which might hamper him in an enterprise (steel industry)" [(82)].

In 1901, BISCO was also encouraged to promote steel, and Curzon wrote to the Secretary of State Hamilton about it on September of that year [(83)]. The CGI was not keen on starting any pioneer industry for iron but was ready to accept if one such industry would start.

> We fully realize however, the great advantages that will result from the successful establishment of iron and steel works in India and desire to offer all encouragement in our power to the promoters of such enterprises. We shall not only be willing but anxious to place as many orders as possible for iron and steel sections which can be manufactured in this country, provided that quality is not below the standard of our requirement [(84)].

This statement was repeated by the CGI in 1903 to the East India Iron and Steel Syndicate [(85)] and to the governors of Madras, Bombay, the United Provinces, Punjab and Burma [(86)]. In spite of CGI's encouragement, however, no company was able to successfully manufacture steel in India at that time. BISCO made a failed attempt but was shut down in 1907. The cause of failure was recorded by the Stores Committee appointed by the CGI. The record shows that the lack of orders and an inability to attain full capacity had increased the cost of production of steel manufacturing beyond profitability [(87)]. The CGI seriously encouraged the best British firms to open branches in India so that the standard of Indian manufacturing might be raised [(88)]. But British firms did not care about developing the Indian engineering industry, and the firms that existed in India preferred, as the Indian Industrial Commission noted, "a safe profit from trade, or from such established industries as jute and cotton manufacture, to a doubtful return from such ventures as metallurgical and chemical manufacturing" [(89)]. The possibility of a British firm to invest in the steel industry in India also evaporated because The East India Iron and Steel Syndicate, which was formed in London in 1901 for the purpose of starting a steel industry in India, lost favor with the CGI due to its shady dealings in Britain, while another British capitalist, Cassel, lost interest in investing in the Indian steel industry [(90)].

With the development of railways, ports and docks, trade and commerce expanded, which meant the foreign mercantile firms had before them the prospects of making great profits. The prospect of "a safe profit from trade" cooled their interest in developing heavy industry which entailed large capital investment. It was under these circumstances that the CGI and the Secretary of State Hamilton asked J. N. Tata to invest in the manufacture of iron and steel in India.

A letter written to B. J. Padshah, special director of Tata Sons Ltd. (managing agency firm) on September 14, 1906 by V. B. Godrej (from Paris) gives us an idea of the reasons for the lack of British interest in Indian steel as well as about the general mood in Europe regarding such a risky investment:

> Baron Pfeffel said that during the recent state of money market it was useless trying to find capital either in England or in France. The English with their big speculative losses in the U.S., their heavy purchases of American securities at very favourable prices after the San Francisco disaster, their colonial loans etc, would not think of putting their money in the new enterprise especially when old and tried industries were offering as more favourable and safer investment. As regards the French investors, he is of opinion that as long as the Russian question is not settled, every financiar would be unwilling to give even a hearing. France has already lost over 5 million of francs in their Russian loans, so just at present they are not in a humor to entertain proposals for investment in out of the way places like India, however tempting the proposals may be. Till the end of the present year, in his opinion, there is positively nothing to do [(91)].

Under this climate of lack of interest among the European capitalists that the idea of Tata Iron and Steel Company was conceived by J. N. Tata [(92)]. As noted earlier, Tata was enthusiastic about the modern industry and wanted to invest in heavy industries and technical education. Lord Curzon agreed to build a railway line 45 miles long from the iron mines to a proposed iron works location, and to procure a reduction in railway freight charges on materials required for construction, for iron ore and coal, and on finished products for shipment to Calcutta. The CGI also promised to buy a large quantity of steel rails—20,000 tons—of prescribed quality every year from Tata instead of purchasing abroad, provided the prices were identical [(93)]. In 1906 the CGI promised to purchase as much pig iron as possible from the proposed works if the quality and price of the product were suitable [(94)]. Further encouragement ensued in 1909 with the sanction of the CGI, the Bengal Nagpur Railway entered into an agreement with the Tata Company to the effect that materials for the initial construction of the steel works would be carried by the Railway "from any station on the railway to Kalimati at the reduced rate of 1/15th pie [*smallest currency unit in India until 1947. It is 1/192 of a rupee*] per mile" [(95)]. The Bengal Nagpur Railway also constructed a broad-gauge railway from Kalimati to the ore mines at Gurumaishini and the line was opened in 1911 [(96)]. Stimulated by such assistance and an assured market, the Tata Sons & Co. (J. N. Tata died in 1904 and his sons took over the managing company) placed the scheme (Tata Iron and Steel Company—TISCO) on the market in 1907. Tata also tried to benefit from the growing eagerness in 1906 of the Indian bourgeoisie to invest in Swadeshi enterprises and got all the capital from Indian market (Fraser, 1919: 51; Johnson, 1966:243).

The CGI support for Tata Steel was crucial. But it did not come as an exceptional gesture. It was, in fact a continuation of the CGI policies toward the Indian iron and steel industry that had emerged in 1890. Indeed, the CGI felt as early as 1883 that private industries, especially iron, should be promoted in India in order to save the foreign exchange and at the same time expand the railways. Secretary of State Hamilton became aware of the policy at the time his appointment began in 1895, when the specific conjunction of different historical forces within the world economic situation—including Britain's reluctance to improve its steel industry structure—and within India came into being. These circumstances did not leave many alternatives for London, and Hamilton had to support the idea of giving encouragement to the private enterprises in India. He wrote that such persons should be employed who "will encourage private, as well as public, enterprises, and who will try and create conditions which will automatically promote industrial enterprise" (97).

Since 1899, J. N. Tata had also been trying to get the support of the CGI for a Tata family endowment to create a technical institute in India (98). In spite of the keen interest of Lord Curzon in the formation of this institute, the institution could not be approved. Sir William Ramsay of London University, appointed by the CGI to examine the merits of Tata's project, suggested that Tata's offer be withdrawn as the effort could not be fulfilled without outside aid—e. g., CGI's support. Instead, Ramsay suggested, Tata should devote his capital to the development of the iron and steel industry (99). With the development of steel, the CGI could reap the benefits without risking a penny, whereas, with the formation of a technical institute, the CGI might be instrumental in adding "new members of the discontented educated class" (100). As noted by the Secretary of State in his letter to Curzon,

> Ramsey told me that he expressed to him (Tata) very strongly the opinion that, unless he can get pound 13,000 a year, it is useless attempting to initiate a university, and this advise, coupled with the letter from Ritchie, will, I expect, have such an effect upon Tata that he will withdraw his scheme, and devote a certain (endowment to the manufacturing of iron and steel) (101).

This time, the CGI was careful to ensure that Tata was not put off by any unwitting action of the government and refused to give any more favors to BISCO. The gesture of promoting Tata Steel was also seen as important way to enhance the CGI's image in political circles in India.

It appears from the confidential files of the Department of Commerce and Industry that TISCO revised its original design for the works, modifying the capital requirements. The company unofficially inquired from the Secretary of the Geological Survey Office in India whether "the Government would be willing to take about 50 lakhs of Rupees worth of 5% debentures in TISCO, in case they failed to raise the money in the open market" (102). The Company made this request as it feared that in consequence of "the discount on the ordinary shares in the Bombay money market the London financiers are liable to demand terms that would counterbalance the saving due to raising part of the capital as debentures instead of in ordinary and preference shares" (103).

But the request was turned down by the Secretary of Commerce and Industry, B. Robertson, who explained that "the Government has already made certain concessions with a view to helping the company" (104). He noted in the file that,

> When these were being discussed the question was raised by Sir F. Upcott of government guaranteeing the project. The suggestion was dismissed by Sir John Hewett. He wished to see them entirely carried out by private effort assisted by such concessions as government feel able to give the scheme. This attitude should be strictly maintained ... it is a

> different matter altogether for the Government to give concession to the Company to enable it get on its own legs and the other thing to join in its undertakings. The Government could not escape criticism if it allowed its encouragement of the enterprise to take the shape of practically going into the business itself [(105)].

The TISCO management showed its willingness to give a representative of the government a seat on the Board "in order that the Government may be fully acquainted with what is going on, and be able to control to a certain extent any apparent extravagance" [(106)]. But the government refused to spend any more money on this project except for those concessions that had earlier been given to BISCO and now the same were promised to TISCO in the form of purchasing orders, the building of railway lines from the iron ore mines to the works and cheaper railway freights.

This refusal did not hamper the Tata Company's plans. Concessions granted were important savings in the initial stages of construction. Moreover, the promise from the CGI, which was the main customer for steel in India, to buy 20,000 tons of TISCO steel every year created considerable optimism about starting the steel industry. Steel work was established by TISCO at Jamshedpur, which was located in a very suitable area. Holland made the case for assistance to TISCO by the CGI as follows:

> So far as I can judge there should not be the slightest risk regarding the money required for debenture. The project possesses very unusual advantages as regards the cost of the ore required and extended prospecting operations have shown beyond questions that they have enormous supplies in sight of a quality far superior to the average material utilized in Europe and America. The total costs of the assemblage of raw material should be very much less than … in areas of Europe and America [(107)].

TISCO was formed to create blast furnaces, open-hearth, steel furnaces, rolling mills, pig iron, steel, rails, bars, plates etc. Tata Sons & Co. was appointed the agent of TISCO. This management system helped Tatas to establish "dynastic" (generational control by one family) domination over the companies managed by them (Sen, 1964:144). Sir Dorabji Tata, son of J. N. Tata, was appointed the Chairman of the Tata Sons & Co. The first steel was produced in Jamshedpur in 1912. The TISCO prospectus gives us an idea of how the company hoped to profitably run the steel works under a colonial economy.

> The import of iron and steel in India of the classes intended to be produced by the company has increased during the past 12 years to 409,000 tons annually. Import is amounting to 615,000 tons in 1905–1906 and is therefore largely in excess of the capacity of the plant which it is now proposed to erect for an output of 120, 00 tons of pig iron and the conversion of 85,000 tons thereof into 72,000 tons of finished steel. There is thus every probability of a ready market on the spot for the whole production ... this will realise a gross profit of over 24 lakhs a year (Fraser, 1919:60).

The demand for agricultural products called for the industrial processing of manufacturing finished goods, e.g. sugar and oil, while the demand for modern machinery remained insignificant. *The Indian Industrial Commission* pointed out in 1918:

> Though India's greatest industry is agriculture the demand for agricultural machinery is limited to the products of a few small local manufacturer, supplemented by import value at about 2 1/2 lakhs of rupees ... The direction of Indian industrial development has been thus pre-determined by the existence of a large export trade in raw material and by the ease with which most classes of manufactured articles could be imported from abroad [(108)].

Thus, on the basis of import figures for five years in the first decade of the twentieth century, it is clear that from the beginning, the large-scale iron and steel manufacturer in India was to cater to a demand situation that made it imperative to produce mostly finished products for the railways and public work departments. In addition, there was a demand for semi-finished products by certain engineering industrial plants manufacturing structures, and also possibly for existing Ordinance factories in the country. From the entrepreneur's point of view, concerning profit maximization, an unlimited potential for industrial growth, or growth as such in the country, was not essential since there were alternative products to produce and sell. Therefore, even when the demand for steel was expanding, the TISCO chose a particular set of steel goods for production because under the colonial economy only such a sharing of the market was possible. In the table below one can deduce which product mix was chosen by TISCO across time.

TABLE 2: TISCO Production of Different Articles 1913–1945

YEAR	ARTICLES
1913–1945	Rails, Fish plates, Structures
1916–1918	Shells
1916–1918	Ferro manganese
1924–1945	Tin plates, sleepers, blooms, billets, black sheets, galvanized sheets
1927–1945	Other steel
1932–1945	Corrugated sheets, beams, bars, channels, angles, tees, sleepers bars
1937–1939	Wires, wire nails
1938	Hoops
1942–1945	Wheels, tires

Sources: Table is constructed from following sources: *TISCO annual reports. Metallurgical Department Inspectorate. Munitions Board Handbook. Monthly Statistics of Production of Selected Industries in India 1932. CISI Department. Indian Tariff Board Report 1926.*

The table clearly points at the constraints of choice because at the time of its inception, TISCO had only CGI as a customer. That is why TISCO began by producing rails, fish plates and structurals. During World War I it produced shells and ferromanganese to help the CGI in its war efforts. Later when TISCO created subsidiaries, it added other products. Another way of putting it is to say that neither the size of capital nor the level of technology at TISCO permitted a different type of production preference under a colonial economy. But that was the manifestation of the situation and not its cause. As entrepreneur, the Tata Company was not free (due to the constraints of the demand situation created in the colonial economy) to accomplish what entrepreneurs in a free capitalist country could have accomplished in an identical position.

The London Secretary of the East India Iron and Steel Syndicate—which was also trying to launch a steel industry in India at the same time as the Tata Company—pointed out in his letter of 10 October 1902 to the Secretary to the CGI Department of Revenue and Agriculture:

> The market which India at present affords for the steel industry is a comparatively limited one, and one which would be met by one or two works on modern lines ... American

> Steel Manufacturers have now fully mastered the fact that for economical production, there must be a large output, with its necessary market equal to absorbing the same, and it will be a pity if their experience is not taken advantage of in initiating large iron and steel works for India. The dispatch of the CGI seems to foreshadow the establishment of three or four industries of the kind, and in the opinion of my Directors, even if the capital could be produced, the plan would result in a large increase in the cost of production and very uncertain results to the shareholders, with such a limited market as India at present afford [(109)].

This analysis of the Indian market makes it clear that only one, or, at most, two large-scale steel firms could be initiated successfully. As the correspondence between Lord Curzon and Lord Hamilton shows, only the Tata operation received full cooperation because Sir Ernest Cassell, a British capitalist who was earlier interested in investing in Indian steel, bowed out. The syndicate, called EIISS lost favor, because of political scandal in London and Parliament, and BISCO, which had tried to produce steel in 1906, had closed down almost immediately as it found the cost of production too high. Thus, the field was left open for Tata, who had petitioned since 1883 to start a steel industry. The CGI, which was already very keen on starting iron and steel production in India, was glad to help Tata in this venture when it found the British ventures had come to naught and, moreover, that British firms were asking too many favors and applying pressure from home. In any case, special favors to TISCO were not required because BISCO earlier was given such favors, and the government files show that the CGI was ready to give all concessions short of getting into the business itself. Such support was politically useful in undercutting the nationalist agitators and winning the loyalty of the most important capitalist to their side (Saklatvala and Khosla, 1980:58–59). It would also lead to the production of steel in India where the CGI itself could control the product, prices, and market without risking British money. Moreover, the production of steel in India would assure the supply of steel and ammunition in preparation for the coming world war.

SUMMATION, PART II

The development of the first large-scale steel industry in India was neither the only source of dynamism within the economy nor a natural culmination of India's economic development. Rather, its emergence demonstrates that contrary to the simplistic approach of dependency theory, the path of industrial development was constructed through the interaction of various historical, social, political and economic forces inside and outside India. No single cause led to the circumstances allowing the Indian steel industry to emerge. It was rather the outcome of changing conflicts of interest involving state and capital in Britain, India, and the world arena. The emergence of the mass production of steel in the world market and the development of railways and communication led to the formation of cartels dividing up world markets. This in turn created new circumstances for the decline of British hegemony and rise of US hegemony that also influenced the CGI's priorities and policies concerning India's industrialization. Therefore, the country's industrialization did not follow a predetermined line or proceed toward a single, ultimate destination as propounded by the stage theory of modernization or of Marxism. The entrepreneurial legacy of J. N. Tata could take form only from 1907, and not in 1883. In spite of being a very aggressive entrepreneur, Tata could not implement his steel project plan until the conditions were favorable in the world steel market and in Britain and India. By 1899, Britain was losing competitive advantage in the world market. At the same time, it was not able to restructure its domestic steel industry. The CGI was concerned about railway expansion, the lack of revenue sources, the falling rate of the rupee, and exchange rates. Swadeshi sentiments, which had been developing in India during the last two decades of the nineteenth century, added to the CGI's worries. The CGI felt a real political threat and tried not to alienate its supporters, particularly Indian moderates and big capitalists. On the other hand, the development of Swadeshi made it possible for Tata to generate Indian capital to finance a national steel industry when British financiers refused to cooperate.

Thus, the conjunction of global, colonial, local, individual actions, social, political, economic, and historical forces created conditions (in all of which human creativity was the primary force) in which the CGI could not prevent the Indian capitalist J. N. Tata, from investing in steel. More so, because all earlier efforts of the CGI to acquire British capital to invest in the steel industry in India had failed. In the case of Tata, the CGI had another advantage: it was not risking any money or waiting during a long gestation period without making a profit. The risk was exclusively shouldered by Indian capital. This enabled the CGI to obtain a cheap supply of steel with quality control and without either risking money or losing control of the Indian market to foreign competitors.

J. N. Tata, who had accumulated capital through the cotton industry, the opium trade, and pearls trade, was an ambitious industrialist. He was also admitted into the Mason's Lodge, thus became part of the international bourgeoisie class. The home market for steel was provided largely by the CGI because the government was the main purchaser of the steel product. Therefore, once Tata had the assurance that the CGI would buy all the company's products, he could begin to think of starting to produce steel. From the entrepreneur's point of view of profit maximization, an unlimited potential for industrial growth, or growth as such, was not essential since he had alternative products to produce and sell. From the home marketing point of view, colonial conditions largely determined the scale of growth for the industry as well as its character. The entire set of government policies, pricing, tariffs, wages, exports, imports, and purchases modified this situation from time to time. These policies also came to be determined to a great extent by the fundamental character of the home market. This process of interaction, the changes in CGI's policies due to the changing nature of the home market, which in turn was affected by changes in the world economic situation, the decline of British hegemony, the looming threat of world war, the impact of class struggle and the industrial structure within Britain, the pressures of the Indian nationalist movement—together with the level of technology and product mix is what shaped the emergence, growth, and development of the Indian steel industry. In this schema of complicated interaction among historical forces, it is hard to agree with those who believe in the existence of an independent capitalist class in India that used the simple tactics of pressure-compromise-pressure (PCP) for their gains.

SUMMARY

In this chapter, I have asserted the primacy of various complicated historical forces, including human creativity as individual entrepreneurship, as in the nationalist movements and as in the working class struggles within the colonial Indian context, while relating them to the class struggles and imperial policies in Britain and in the US within the process of the formation of a global economy at that time. This approach also treats all societies on equal terms (and not as primitive or civilized; developed or underdeveloped) in the sense that each society, colonial and colonized, was created and recreated in the process of its social formation from within as much as by its interaction with other societies and with world economic and social forces. These world economic and social forces were also formed by all these interacting societies, as much as they helped in the formation of all societies. This analysis shows that no society is superior or inferior in its formation process as each is a product of human creativity and human interaction. Inequalities between societies are created when one society is unable to solve its internal problems generated by class struggles, and tries to resolve them by controlling other societies, as is the case of Britain colonizing so many countries, including India. But the social formation process within a society remains the same everywhere: that is, the daily social reproduction of society through people's interaction to fulfill their "humaneness."

Based on these assumptions I have demonstrated that the conjunction of historical forces globally and within Britain, within the US and within India, together, created the conditions for the emergence of the large-scale steel industry in India in 1907. Thus, by giving primacy to human creativity and the conjunction of historical forces while using the yardstick of parity, it became possible to eliminate the binary distinction of developed/underdeveloped, and also allow us to move away from the stage theory of Rostow's economic growth, and stage theory of Marx's idea about shifts in the mode of production, both of which actually privileges Europe's uniqueness.

ENDNOTES

1. Sarkar wrote, "The property principle under colonialism, … could be enacted only 'through coalitions cutting across elements in the heterogeneous state and a differentiated society'… environmental studies join the critique of the homogenized binaries deployed by some analysis of colonial discourse … *Modern Forests* emphasizes in particular the need to not 'conflate policy intent with practical outcome,' and seeks to 'question the simple divide often instituted between universal Western modernity and its indigenous Other' " (p. 102).

   Writing about the relationship between Forest Laws and shifting cultivation, Sarkar wrote, "'Development' and 'underdevelopment' thus fed each other, not just globally, but also with regard to relationship within the colonized country" (p. 127). Again he wrote, "Relations between traditional and modern, indigenous and European business life in late colonial India were marked by both interconnections and varying degrees of mutually beneficial adjustments, as well as by a basic and growing subordination of the traditional indigenous. The latter produced conflicts, but did not rule out collaboration. In fact, it seems appropriate to think in terms of not two but three levels, for below the world of bazaar—of traditional merchants, bankers (shroffs) and commission agents (arhatiyas) operating through hundis—there lay a subsistence economy of poorer peasants and artisans where monetization was low or negligible and among whom loans and payments were often still made in kind" (p. 191–192). Sumit Sarkar, 2014; *Modern Times: India 1880–1950s*. Ranikhet: Permanent Black.

2. The debate on India's deindustrialization in the turn of nineteenth century was mainly carried on by the following economic historians: R. C. Dutt. *Economic History of India*, London. 1901; D. Naoroji, *Poverty and UnBritish Rule in India,* London. G. A. Nateson And Co. 1901; G. Subramaniam Iyer, *Some Aspects of British Rule in India,* Madras 1903.
3. Morris. D. Morris, "Towards a Re-interpretation of Nineteenth Century Indian Economic History," *Journal of Economic History,* 23(4), 1963. All the essays in the famous 're-interpretation' debate refer, directly or indirectly, to the issue, cf. Morris. D. Morris et al., *Indian Economy in the Nineteenth Century*. Delhi, 1969.
4. Joan Robinson, T. Balogh, Paul Baran, A. G. Frank and Keith Griffin have used the 'Indian example' (accepting the case for de-industrialization) to illustrate the effects of imperialism. There is a long list of those who have written on India's de-industrialization, for example: Daniel Thorner, "De-industrialisation in India, 1881–1931," in Daniel and Alice Thorner, *Land and Labour in India* (Bombay, 1965, pp. 70–81); M. Desai, "Demand for Cotton Textiles in Nineteenth Century India," *Indian Economic and Social History Review,* 10(4), 1971; J. Krishnamurthy, "Changes in the Composition of the Working Force in Manufacturing 1905–1951: A Theoretical and Empirical Analysis," in *Indian Economic and Social History Review,* IV (I) 1967; "De-Industrialisation Revisited," *Economic and Political Weekly,* 2(26) June 1976, and *The Cambridge Economic History of India*, vol. 2, ch. VI; R. Chattopadhyay," De-Industrialisation in India Reconsidered," *Economic and Political Weekly* 10, March 12, 1975; A. K. Bagchi, "De-industrialisation in Gangetic Bihar, 1809–1910," in B. De (Ed.), *Essays in Honour of Professor S. C. Sarkar.* New Delhi, 1976, pp. 499–522; "De-Industrialisation in India in the Nineteenth Century: Some Theoretical Implications," *Journal of Development Studies,* 12(2) 1976; M. Vicziany, "The Deindustrialization of India in the Nineteenth Century: A Methodological Critique of Amiya Kumar Bagchi," and A. K. Bagchi "A Reply," both in the *Indian Economic and Social History Review,* XVI(2) 1979; A . Orr, "De-industrialisation in India—A Note." *Journal of Development Studies,* 16(1) 1980; and M. J. Twomey, "Employment in Nineteenth Century Indian Textiles." *Exploration in Economic History,* 20(1) 1983; W. J. Macpherson, "Economic Development in India under the British Crown, 1858–1947." In A. J. Youngson (Ed.), *Economic Development in the Long Run.* London. 1972. pp. 138–43; N. Charlesworth, *British Rule and the Indian Economy, 1800–1914.* London. 1982. ch. 3; P. Robb, "British Rule and Indian 'Improvement'," *Economic History Review,* 34(4) 1981; and F. Perlin, "Proto-Industrialization and Pre-Colonial South Asia," *Past and Present,* No. 98, 1983, esp. pp. 34–53; Rajat Kant Ray (Ed.), *Entrepreneurship and Industry in India, 1800–1947.* Delhi: OUP, 1992.
5. Harry D. Harootunian writes while critiquing Marx's historiography that it has never moved beyond the concept of transition and addressed its consequences for a relationship between past and present. He further explains, "Marxist historiography has been driven by distinct stages whose movement reflects shifts in the productive base ... Implanted in this theory is a logic of inevitable historical change (continuist and progressive) and the dependence of superstructural forms on the productive base which is external to the social topography it directs. The consequence of this interpretative strategy has been to forfeit both the autonomy (or semi-autonomy) of the political present ... and the historical experiences of the world outside Euro-America" (p. 97). (Harry D. Harootunian "Historical Materialism's Task in an 'Age of Globalization'." *Radical Historical Review,* 2000, p. 95–98.).
6. Washbrook, 1997:419. Washbrook wrote that Indian society had been using a form of writing for two thousand years, and Indians had learned from the Portuguese the theoretical knowledge of printing in the sixteenth century. However, Indians did not use print technology until the nineteenth century, as there was no need for it. The techniques and skills to make textiles, manufacturing, weaving and dyeing, were all kept secret as they were embodied in the Indian artisans. Thus, it was difficult to make technical knowledge

publicly available. This situation changed when merchant capital became dominant in India and had a control over production while consolidating a new form of class structure that the embodied knowledge and skills of Indian artisans could become accessible to the public through publications (Ibid., 421).

7. M. G. Ranade, *Development of Iron Industry in India*, 1892 National Archives of India (NAI). Before the emergence of Tata Steel in 1907, the first serious attempt to manufacture iron and steel in India on a large scale was made by Mr. Heath in 1830. The Madras Presidency was supportive of Mr. Heath's project and helped it financially. It never succeeded in producing steel due to problems of bad management and lack of reliable fuel. Therefore, it closed down in 1874. In 1875 an iron work was established in Barkar, which in 1889 passed into the hands of the newly formed Bengal Iron and Steel Co. (hereafter BISCO). During the nineteenth century it did not manufacture any steel and confined itself to iron making on a relatively small scale.

   See also Lovat Fraser, *Iron and Steel in India*, Bombay. 1919. p. 6. Fraser noted that BISCO did not receive any assistance from the CGI up until 1900.
8. D. R. Headrick, *The Tentacles of Progress.* Oxford University Press. 1988. p. 283. Headrick writes "Government hesitation to develop an iron industry was a result of the split system of authority between the viceroy on the one hand and the India office on the other" (p. 290).
9. "Trade of the British Empire and Foreign Competition," C 8449 of 1899, p. 577. Quoted in Amartya Sen "Sociological and Economic Explanations; An Illustration from the Indian Iron and Steel" *Economic Weekly,* Feb 1963. pp. 183–186.
10. McMichael, P. (1984), *Settlers and the Agrarian Question: Foundation of Capitalism in Colonial Australia.* Cambridge. London. p. 242. McMichael writes, "Besides being actors in the world market, the role of the states is also to mobilize finances, centralise capital, secure forms of labour organisation, provide labour, commodity and capital markets and much more along with being part of world market" (p. 25). In this role, McMichael further points out, "States certainly secure these economic exchanges, but they remain part of the broader historical setting that results from the international character of capital and its market" p. 26.
11. The discussion is based on McMichael (1984) op. cit. pp. xiii-xiv. He summarizes this process as follows:

    > The international dimensions of the agrarian question concern not only the trading position of a particular or producing region in the world market, but also more fundamentally, the way such international relations are expressed within the particular state through the balance of class and political forces. Of course, these balances alter as the world capitalist economy develops, so that it is fair to say that there is some correspondence between the structural position of a state within the world economy and the way in which the agrarian question is both posed and resolved (if at all). British hegemony imparted a unique structural dynamic to the nineteenth century world economy, and that the political and economic consequences of British hegemony shaped Australian colonial development in a particular way.

12. Elbaum, B and Wilkinson, F. (1979). "Industrial Relation and Uneven Development: A Comparative Study of the American and British Steel Industry." *Cambridge Journal of Economics*, 3. I have borrowed heavily from them to get information on the industrial relations of British and the United States steel industry during the late nineteenth century.
13. Hamilton Papers, F. No. Eur. Mss. C-126/3 Secretary of State to the CGI, July 18, 1901 India Office Library (IOL).
14. "The traditional open hearth furnace was tapped at the bottom. The Talbot furnaces were designed to tilt so that finished steel could be poured from the tap of the 'bath'. At each casting only a proportion of the steel was removed from the bath and the molten pig iron was charged into a furnace containing a quantity of finished steel. This accelerated the conversion process and allowed open hearth furnace to check" Quoted in Elbaum and Wilkinson. op. cit.

15. *Indian Engineering.* April 20, 1901. p. 253.
16. Hopkins, A. G. and Cains, P. J. (1987). "Gentlemanly Capitalism and British Overseas Expansion: New Imperialism 1850–1945" *Economic History Review,* 2nd ser, XL 7. pp 2–3.

    Hopkins writes: "The gentlemanly capitalist of the service sector proved to be the more successful and enduring element in the complex interplay between 'money managers' and manufacturers'. Furthermore, services and finance had a greater impact than industry on Britain's presence overseas between the 1850s and 1945 … It was an amalgam of rentier money, service employments and the remnants of landed society which came together to form the new upper class after 1850 … The gulf between this gentlemanly 'consumers' England' and the 'producers' England' of the provinces, was deep, and reflected a dualism in the Victorian economy which divided southern trade and finance, the landed classes, the public schools, ancient universities and conservative politics from northern industry and a society separate from these establishment institutions" (p. 36).
17. *Royal Commission on Labour (1892).* Minutes of Evidence, taken before a Group A. London. HMSO. Quoted in Elbaum and Wilkinson, 1979. op. cit.
18. Elbaum and Wilkinson write, "The Amalgamated and Ironworkers bargaining strength lay in the skills of their members and their control of the contract system: their weakness lay in craft exclusiveness and the divisive nature of the contractor/underhand relationship. In the US, where the underhands failed to break down the craft barriers within the Amalgamated, these weaknesses proved fatal when combined with the revolution in technology and industrial organisation accompanying the transition to steel" (1979:293).
19. Hamilton Papers, Mss. C-126/3, July 18, 1901. IOL.
20. Rider has explained the whole process as follows. "The formulation of tariff policy originated in the Finance and Commerce Department of India which then circulated them to other departments, to the Governors, perhaps back to Finance and Commerce for revision, and finally to the Indian Governor General in Council. If agreed to by Governor General in Council, the proposals were submitted for approval to the Secretary of State for India in London, a member of the British Cabinet. The India Office Secretariat, over which the Secretary of State presided, would comment on the proposals and occasionally members of the Council of India might be asked by the Secretary of State for written opinions (This council was composed of 15 members, 9 of whom had lived in India within the last 5 years. The latter members were generally either retired civil servants or businessmen returning from India). The Secretary of State, after considering these comments, would give his approval or order revision and communicate that decision to the CGI. The Secretary of State's decision was partially determined by the reaction of the British cabinet. Various economic interests in Britain and in the colonies generally exerted influence on the formulation of tariff policy in India through the Secretary of State for India in London. Indian Viceroys (or Governor General) were generally not important politicians and hence had little personal influence over the British cabinet. They rarely decided the fate of Indian government proposals in London. Thus in general changes in the CGI attitude followed changes in the attitudes of the British Government toward India" (T. D. Rider, "The Tariff Policy of Government of India and its Development Stratagy 1884–1924." Unpublished Ph. D. University of Minnesota. 1971).
21. Cains and Hopkins mention that "In 'backward' areas, the Palmerstonian assumption that trade and finance flow would automatically westernise indigeneous societies, proved illusionary" in *Economic History Review,* vol XL. No 1. Feb 1987. P. J. Cains and A. G. Hopkins, "Gentlemanly Capitalism and British Expansion Overseas, New Imperialism: 1850–1945."
22. *Lord Ripon's correspondence with Persons in India*, Vol. I, 1883, No. 276. British Museum Library. London.

    B. N. Ganguli has noted, "Indian export of opium declined from 91,798 chests in 1882–83 to 75,384 chests in 1892–93 … After the closure of the mint to silver in 1893, in spite of the fall of exchange, the decline of exports to China was mainly due to the operation of competition for countries whose currencies had depreciated equally or to a greater extent" ("Dadabhai Naoroji and the Mechanism of 'External Drain' " (*Indian Economic and Social History Review,* 2(2). April 1965).

23. Letter from Baring (Finance member of Viceroy's Council) to Ripon (Viceroy of India), 14 May 1881, "No more hostility of PWD to Private enterprise. PWD on the other extreme too favourable to companies. There is a change between the general monetary condition of the present and the past. We should not say publicly anything—we should say, "This is the project, we give you all information—you give us an offer, PWD should be out of the discussion. The Rothschilds should tell us what railway and canals they want, what it will cost—how much they can buy. Then we shall take up purely finance side then a scheme put up before Government as a Corporate body." (*Correspondence with persons in India*, No. 278, Vol. I, 1881, BP 7/6 British Museum).
24. Proceedings of the Department of Finance and Commerce Branch-Account and Finance, P-2096. 1883, No. 29. Letter from (Colonial) Government of India to Secretary of State, 23 Jan. IOL.
25. Department of Finance and Comm. P-2096, November 16, 1882 (Stores). Letter of Secretary of State to Government of India-Proposal to transfer the BISCO to a Private co.
26. Department of Finance and Comm. P-2096, November 16, 1882 (Stores). Letter of Secretary of State to Government of India Proposal to transfer the BISCO to a Private co.
27. Department of Finance and Comm. P-2096, January 23, 1883, No. 29.
28. Ibid.
29. "Iron Making in India," *Englishman*, July 14, 16, 17, 1880. Reproduced in *Indian Forester*. v, VI, pp. 203–208.
30. Baring to Ripon, April 24, 1883, No 236. *Correspondence with Persons in India*, British Museum.
    The Economist wrote on November 18, 1882, "higher prices are to be paid for native than for imported products simply because they are native, this difference in price is neither more nor less than a state subsidy to the home products." Again, in December 2, 1882 it was mentioned, "But the utmost care is necessary to prevent their commendable zeal for the extension of Indian manufactures developing into a policy of protection to native industries, which could not fail to be injurious both to India and this country" CD-Coal and Iron, Feb, 1883-B. Cited in Sen, "*Industrial Policy.*" op. cit.
31. Parliament Debates, 1882, Oct–Nov, vol. 274, p. 542. British Museum Library.
32. Proceedings of Commerce Department (CD), Branch-Coal and Iron. September, 1882-B. Quoted in Sunil Sen. p. 47. op. cit.
33. CD-Coal and Iron, February 1883-B. Quoted in Sen. op. cit.
34. Parliament Debates, 1882, Oct–Nov. vol. 274. British Museum Library. P 1542. Trade and Commerce (Iron Work). Also Proceedings Department of CD-Coal and Iron, Feb. 1883-B. P-2096, Government of India letter to Secretary of State, Jan. 23, 1883, Proceedings of Finance and Commerce, No. 28. 1883.
35. T. C. Hope, (Public Works Department, member of Viceroy's Council) to Ripon, 22 April, 1883, *Marquis of Ripon Correspondence with Persons in India, 1883*. Vol. I, No. 236.
36. T. C. Hope, (Public Works Department, member of Viceroy's Council) to Ripon, 22 April, 1883, *Marquis of Ripon Correspondence with Persons in India, 1883*. Vol. I, No. 236.
37. T. C. Hope, (Public Works Department, member of Viceroy's Council) to Ripon, April 22, 1883, *Marquis of Ripon Correspondence with Persons in India, 1883*. Vol. I, No. 236.
38. Eur Mss. C-126/5, June 19, 1903, Lord Hamilton to Lord Curzon. Hamilton Papers IOL.
39. CD-Coal and Iron, February 1883. Quoted in Sen, *Industrial Policy*. op. cit. p. 49.
40. Eur. MSS. F-111/515, 1906, Summary of the Administration of Curzon of Kedleston, Finance and Commerce, Pt. I and II. IOL.
41. Eur. MSS. F-111/515, 1906, Summary of the Administration of Curzon of Kedleston, Finance and Commerce, Pt. I and II. IOL.
42. *Indian Engineering*, December 3, 1910, "Hints of the Pig Iron Market to Political Economists." p. 312.
43. P-3955, Proceedings of the Department of Finance and Commerce (Stores) Industry and Stores, June 25, 1891. GOI letter. IOL.
44. *Indian Engineering*, Nov. 5, 1892, "Iron Industry in India." p. 389, Calcutta.
45. P-3913, Proceedings of Public Works Department, 9 Feb 1891, Letter from CGI to BISCO.

46. P-5218, Proceedings of PWD, Coal and Iron, letter from Viceroy to the Secretary of State, 23 June, 1896. IOL.
47. CD, Coal and Iron, Jan 1897-B. Quoted and discussed in Sunil Sen pp. 52–53. op. cit.
48. CD, Coal and Iron, Jan 1897-B. Quoted and discussed in Sunil Sen pp. 52–53. op. cit.
49. CD-Coal and Iron, March 1897-B. Telegram from Government of India to BISCO. 15 September 1896. CD-Coal and Iron. Jan 1897(B) quoted in Sen. p. 53.
50. *Indian Engineering*, April 20, 1901, pg. 253–4, JNDL, "Production of Iron and Steel and the manufacturing in India."
51. *Indian Engineering*, April 20, 1901, pg. 253–4, JNDL, "Production of Iron and Steel and the manufacturing in India."
52. *Indian Engineering*, April 20, 1901, pg. 253–4, JNDL, "Production of Iron and Steel and the manufacturing in India."
53. *Indian Engineering*, April 20, 1901, pg. 253–4, JNDL, "Production of Iron and Steel and the manufacturing in India."
54. *Englishman*, 1880, "Iron making in India." Also reproduced in *Indian Forester*, 1880: 203–08.
55. Resolution of the Government of India, May 20, 1899, CD Coal and Iron, June 1899-B. Quoted in Sunil Sen. p. 54.
56. Proceedings of the Department of Commerce, Coal and Iron. Oct. 1899-B.
57. Begbia, L. F. (1908). *A Monograph on Iron and Steel Industry in C.P.* Nagpur: The Secretariat Press.
58. Eur. Mss. F-111/158, 1899, No. 15. Hamilton to Curzon, April 21. Curzon Correspondence. IOL
59. Eur. Mss. F-111/158, 1899, No. 15. Hamilton to Curzon, April 21. Curzon Correspondence. IOL
60. Eur. Mss. F-111/515, 1906, Finance and Commerce, Summary of the Administration of Curzon. Pt. I and II. IOL.
61. Eur. Mss. F-111/515, 1906, Finance and Commerce, Summary of the Administration of Curzon. Pt. I and II. IOL.
62. Eur. Mss. F-111/515, 1906, Finance and Commerce, Summary of the Administration of Curzon. Pt. I and II. IOL
63. McGuire, J. (1988). "The World Economy, The Colonial State and the Establishment of the Indian National Congress." In M. Shepperdson, and E. Simmons, (Eds.), *The Indian National Congress and the Political Economy of India-1885–1985. Aveby.* England. USA. Albert Hirschman, 1958, *The Strategy of Economic Development.* New Haven, also Rider pp. 68–69. Vol I; *Report of the Indian Currency Committee,* 1893, (Herschell Committee) in reports of currency committee, Calcutta. 1931. The Herschell Committee warned that the gold value of silver was likely to fall even further and additional taxation would be necessary if the Colonial Government of India were not to have large budget deficit in the next few years.
64. Eur Mss. C-126/3, 1901, Letter from Hamilton to Curzon, January 13. Hamilton Papers.
65. L/E/3-219/1915, Department of Commerce and Industry (Industry), 26 Nov, 1915, Letter from GOI to Secretary of State, Austin Chamberlin "Future Industrial Policy of Government of India" IOL.
66. L/E/3-219/1915, Department of Commerce and Industry (Industry), 26 Nov, 1915, Letter from GOI to Secretary of State. IOL.
67. Moderate term is used in the sense as used by Stanley Wolpert, in *Tilak and Gokhale, Revolution and Reform in the Making of Modern India* Berkeley 1962, and, Daniel Argov, *Moderates and Extremist in the Indian Nationalist Movement, 1883–1920 with special reference to Surendernath Banerjee and Lajpat Rai.* Bombay, 1967.
68. Correspondence of Ripon. Vol I. 1883. No. 236. BM.
69. Correspondence of Ripon. Vol I. 1883. No. 236. BM.
70. S. *Banerjee Speeches and Writings.* Calcutta: G. A. Nateson and Co. (N.d.). p. 693.
71. For the nationalist version of India's industrial history see also the views of the late justice M.G. Ranade, *The Dawn,* VI, Feb–March, 1903, for the views of G.V. Joshi "Mining,

Metallurgy, Minerals and Metal Work." Full text in *Industrial Conference Benaras,* 1905, pp. 77–95. At the very time that Indian nationalists were describing the decay of the handloom industry in India, the Bombay mill industry worried about the growing competition of the handloom industry and Tata was forming a steel company.

72. Minto to Ibbeston, Dec. 7, 1907. Replying to a letter from November 21, 1907 in which by no means Indophile bureaucrats had suggested a private appeal to Morley for a reexamination of the excise issue. Minto felt that "political considerations such as the Manchester vote would rule out any such measure." Minto Papers, Correspondence with Persons in India, M 981. Quoted in Sumit Sarkar, *The Swadeshi Movement in Bengal, 1903–1908*. p. 93.
73. *Report of the Indian Fiscal Commission, 1921–22*, Rahimtoola Commission. BPP, 1922, II Confidential. 1764, pp. 309, 334, 335.
74. Morley Papers, D 573/23. From Minto to Morley. March 10, 1910.
75. Collins, R.W. *Report on the Existing Arts and Industries of Bengal 1890*, quoted in J. G. Cunning in *Review of the Industrial Position and Prospects in Bengal 1908*, p. 5. Quoted in Sumit Sarkar, op. cit. p. 93.
76. Gijsbert Oonk informs that Gerald Aungier, Governor of East India Company in West India, understood that Bombay's prosperity will need the support of various actors: British businessmen, indigenous traders, moneylenders and artisans. Having that in mind, he and his followers persuaded local Indian businessmen (especially Parsis) and invited them to settle in Bombay by making it profitable to them in many ways. British Governor favored Parsis because they remained loyal to British during the 1857 Mutiny, and they also financed the military defense of the Bombay fort. This fact was also mentioned in Dosabhoy Framjee's book (1858) from which Oonk quotes, "Throughout the Rebellion [1857] in the East, the Parsees have maintained an unshaken loyalty to the British whom they are proud to call their fellow subjects, and while preserving their own independence of religion and customs, their chief desire is that British rule in India should be consolidated upon a basis of strict justice and mutual interest" (Dosabhoy Framjee: *The Parsees: The History, Manners, Custom and Religion*. London. 1858. p. x).

    Oonk informs that Parsis became translators, traders, money lenders, bankers and artisans but most of them were self-employed. Parsi traders acted as intermediaries for British traders in the Indian market. Many Parsi business families sent their sons to work in British trading firms. Parsis traded raw cotton for export to Manchester factories and opium to China. While dealing with international business Parsis also learned about the Industrial revolution and mechanization in Lancashire as can be shown with the example of famous J.N. Tata. He was known for his detailed knowledge of the cotton industry in Manchester; its management, finance and production potential (G.N. Natesan (Ed.), *Famous Parsis*. Madras, 1930. pp. 217–221). With profits from their international trade and knowledge gained while working for British trading firms, and with experience acquired in international trade, Parsis were able to invest in cotton mills in Bombay. In the period between 1878 and 1915, the Parsis owned between 41 and 30 percent of the mills in the city (Oonk, G. n.d.).

    A. V. Desai (1992) has also provided a detailed account of the relationship between the Parsi community and British colonial government.
77. T. H. Holland, Director, Geological Survey of India, February 12, 1905, Curzon Papers, Vol. 499. Holland noted that mineral development has been almost "pure robbery of the natural resources," in the form of export of manganese ores to Germany and America. Later, Holland became the Chairman of Indian Industrial Commission in 1916. Quoted in Sunil Sen, *House of Tata*, pp. 43–44.
78. Curzon Papers. Vol. 499. Quoted in Sen, *House of Tata*. p. 43.
79. Hamilton Papers. Eur. Mss. F. No. C-126/1, 1899.
80. Hamilton Papers. Eur. Mss. F-111/159, 1900.
81. Proceedings of the Department of Geology and Minerals, P-5895. Sept. 7, 1900. ILO.
82. Hamilton Papers. F. No. F-111-161, Feb. 6, 1902, Lord Curzon to Lord Hamilton.
83. Proceedings of Public Works Department, Sept. 5, 1901. F. No. P-6594. India Office Library.
84. Proceedings of the Public Works Department. 1901. F. No. P-6594. India Office Library.

85. Proceedings of the department of Revenue and Agriculture. Branch-Geology and Minerals. May. 1903. P-6594 ILO.
86. Proceedings of the Department of Geology and Minerals. Branch-Commerce and Industry. F. No. P-7135. June 14. Letter from Secretary to CGI and to Secretary to the Government of Madras, Bombay, UP, Punjab and Burma. ILO.
87. Proceedings of the Department of Geology and Minerals. Branch-Commerce and Industry, July 1906. F. No. P-7398, ILO.
88. Proceedings of the Department of Revenue and Agriculture. Branch-Geology and Minerals. F. No. P-6594, 1903 and D 510/10, Vol. XXII, March 13, 1902. ILO.
89. Despatch of Secretary of State, August 18, CD-Stores 1913, Proceeding vols. ILO.
90. *Report of the Indian Industrial Commission, 1916–1918*. p. 5.
91. TISCO papers. Bombay. C-6- V. B. Godrej (from Paris) to Padshah, September 14, 1906.
92. J. L. Keenan (1943). *A Steel Man in India*. NY: Duell, Stoan and Pearce. Keenan has noted that the name Tata originally meant 'hot headed.' J.N. Tata's biography can be traced from F. Harris, *Jamsetji Nusserwanji Tata: A Chronicle of His Life,* London ; Bombay: Blackie and Sons Ltd. (2nd ed.). 1958; and Lovat Fraser, *Iron and Steel in India,* Bombay: The Times Press. 1919.
93. Information on this point is from Proceedings of Department of Commerce, Branch-Stores, September 1912.
94. Letter of Harvey, Secretary to the CGI, Public Works Department, July 16, 1906. CD-Stores, June F. No. 48-B. ILO.
95. Proceedings of the Department of Commerce and Industry, Branch-Industry, October, 1910, F. No. 29. National Archives of India (NAI).
96. Annual Report TISCO, June 1911. Proceedings of the department of Commerce and Industry. Branch-Industry. Nov. 1911, F. No. 28. National Archives of India (NAI).
97. Hamilton Papers. Eur. Mss. F. No. C-125/1, 1895.
98. Hamilton Papers 1899. F. No. C/125/1. IOL. Letter from Hamilton to Curzon. 2 June and 30 June, 1899.
99. Hamilton Papers, F. No. C-126/1. May 2, 1901. IOL.
100. Hamilton Papers, F. No. C-126/1. May 9, 1901.
101. Hamilton Papers, F. No. C-126/3. June 13, 1901.
102. Proceedings, Department of Commerce and Industry. Branch Industry. 1909. Confidential. NAI.
103. Proceedings, Department of Commerce and Industry. Branch Industry. 1909. Confidential. NAI.
104. Proceedings, Department of Commerce and Industry. Branch Industry. 1909. Confidential. NAI.
105. Proceedings, Department of Commerce and Industry. Branch Industry. July 3, 1909. NAI.
106. Proceedings, Department of Commerce and Industry. Branch Industry. July 3, 1909. NAI.
107. Proceedings, Department of Commerce and Industry. Branch Industry. July 3, 1909. NAI.
108. *Indian Industrial Commission Report, 1916–18*. p. 49.
109. P-6362. Department of Revenue and Agriculture, October 10, 1902. Letter from H. A. Grimsdick, Secretary to the EIISS Co. to the Secretary of Government of India. ILO.

SUMMARY AND OBSERVATIONS

> "Each social group sought to preserve its privileges and powers and interest they already enjoyed. Non-elite tried always to improve their conditions. None of them were trying to change consciously social relations or create new ones. But their actions and choices created new conditions and unintended consequences" (Lachmann, 2000).

> "Marxist historiography has been driven by distinct stages whose movement reflects shifts in the productive base. Implanted in this theory is a logic of inevitable historical change (continuist and progressive) and the dependence of superstructural forms on the productive base which is external to the social topography it directs. The consequence of this interpretative strategy has been to forfeit both the autonomy (or semi-autonomy) of the political present … and the historical experience of the world outside Euro-America" (Harootunian, 2001).

Marxist historiography has never moved beyond the concept of "transition," and, as Harry Harootunian has pointed out, it did not include the historical experience of the world outside of Euro-America. However, when the world outside of Euro-America was included in the theory of modernization, it was categorized as third world and was located within the binary distinction of developed/underdeveloped, while the Soviet Union was considered Second World (less than Euro-America, as it categorized itself as First World). The Soviet Union does not exist anymore, therefore the term second or third world has no purchase. However, countries are still being categorized with the binary distinction of developed or underdeveloped by all policy makers and scholars everywhere including those who claim to be challenging imperialism and colonialism.

This book is about challenging this binary distinction of developed/underdeveloped to categorize any country, and also proposing to erase this binary with a yardstick of parity. It is suggested that different societies/countries should not be framed within this Eurocentric binary distinction because it does not allow for any possibility to find an alternative to the vicious "catch up game" and cycle of growth, in which poor ex-colonies are trapped, and they are also now contributing, along with Western countries, in the destruction of the planet. I believe that it is possible to write comparative history without categorizing countries and societies as either developed or underdeveloped because no country or society was begun with the initial condition of being developed or underdeveloped, and it is not an inevitable natural fate for any society (unless artificially created with economic sanctions, assassinations of leaders, wars, and force of military, coup d'état, as is playing out right now in Venezuela, and other non-Western countries).

This historical veracity seems to be pointing towards an alternative yardstick of parity for doing comparative history. However, this realization also makes clear that a yardstick of parity for a comparative history is possible only by erasing the existing binary distinction of developed/underdeveloped, as well as by rejecting the ideas of stage theory that includes "transition to socialism." I also became aware that to build this yardstick of parity I would need different concepts, a different metaphor, and a different narrative because all existing comparative studies are generally framed in the same existing binary distinction mode. Therefore, to find different concepts and metaphor for this yardstick of parity, I did not limit myself within any one particular discipline. Instead, I tried to learn from various sources of knowledge and areas of studies including social sciences, history, religious studies, science (including the ideas of physicists and neurosciences), and technology [(1)].

However, the idea of treating all societies with a yardstick of parity does not mean we ignore the differences among them, or that we ignore the unequal relationships between societies and within each society. Scholars have been explaining the unequal relationship among countries for a long time, but the problem remains that they maintain Eurocentric binary distinctions. For example, scholars have explained, based on Western narrative, that the emergence of capitalism in the West was responsible for its "industrial development." Even though scholars go far back in history, they do not break away from these Western binary distinctions. Moreover, many scholars in the so called "underdeveloped" countries (as in India) also reinforce this binary by trying to establish that India was already on the path of capitalist development which was thwarted by British colonization. Such efforts, though useful in many ways, keep the Western narrative incorporating the binary distinction of "developed/underdeveloped" alive while privileging the supremacy of "capitalist development."

Recently, Banerjee et al. deliberated upon similar concerns in connection with two leading alternative ideas of modernity: nativism and an indiscriminate acceptance of Enlightenment ideology [(2)]. They correctly argue that the nativist approach is problematic as it promotes the tendencies of reviving dead practices and nostalgia. Moreover, this approach ignores the fact that 'indigenous' thought is constantly being recreated by indigenous people in the process of their interaction with others and larger historical forces. Those who indiscriminately accept the Enlightenment ideology are actually reproducing dominant power relations and problematic categories of thought. However, the endless critique of Enlightenment rationality has not helped either, as it has led to a blind alley creating a sense of despair. Offering an alternative to these approaches, Banerjee et al. have suggested to think across traditions (without instrumentalizing, cannibalizing, or exoticizing them), and the possibility of multiple readings of certain social practices in order to build conceptual frameworks by critically engaging with everyday life. This, according to them, should include the "contemporizing" of multiple strands of thought. Thus, according to them the question of theory can also become a question of contemporizing traditions that might appear arcane or foreign today, but can bring new insights to our times [(3)].

It seems to me that Banerjee et al. have made an important move towards breaking out of the impasse we have reached in our understanding of current global/local and social reality. While agreeing with their ideas, I believe that to find an alternative perspective we also need to use all available human knowledge created by our collective human ancestors. In addition, we need to understand our present social reality as the product of a combination of contingencies and conjunctions of small and large events that came into being through human creativity, human actions and human drives that occurred within a specific ecological environment in which these humans found themselves at a particular moment in history. Of course, people envisage their everyday lives based on past experiences, traditions and mythologies prevailing in their societies. This common phenomenon can be observed everywhere, however, the Western narrative keeps treating certain societies (always poor and ex-colonies) as inferior, and others (always Western) as superior. In this Western narrative England's uniqueness made it a first industrialized country. This narrative ignores the fact that China's industrial revolution spans a period of 1500 years and it was able to produce large quantity of steel by the end of eleventh century as comparable to what combined Europe would produce in late 1700. Moreover, from the second century BCE, the Chinese had developed methods for making steel from cast iron, which over time eventually reached Europe through traders, merchants, slaves, and other travelers.

We need to challenge the Western narrative of the uniqueness of England with an alternative perspective because, "Everything in the world is ultimately unique" [(4)]. The only way we can find out "what is specific to one culture, society or situation and what is common to types or categories of social organization or is common to recurrent processes and historical circumstances," is by comparing common aspects, elements, principles, and relationships in societies [(5)]. This approach does not deny the uniqueness of any culture, any institution, any object or any event. In other words, the uniqueness is nothing more than the way historical processes manifest in each country during the process of interaction of historical forces both within and outside the country, in a web of interaction that resembles Indra's Net. No one disagrees that every country has distinct physical and geographical conditions that contribute to the specificity of its history while its people make choices about moving in a certain direction. In that sense, India is no more unique than Russia, Britain or the US. As Berreman has pointed out, Indian people have always been as human as any other people in the world with similar human needs in day-to-day life.

> Like people everywhere, Indian people are also doubters, and believers, conformists and non-conformists. They are defiant, compliant, selfish, magnanimous, independent, innovative, tradition bound, fearful, courageous, optimistic, pessimistic. They hope, aspire, despair, subvert, connive, abide, enforce, manipulate and choose among alternatives as they cope with their society and its values [(6)].

This observation is as relevant in the twenty first century as it was when Berreman wrote them in the twentieth century. In the age of the internet, cell phones and other forms of electronic communication, Indian people are behaving in a similar manner (and as addicted to it) as in any other country including the US and Britain. According to Berreman, "unique is scientifically incomprehensible," because in any scientific study it is imperative to identify and compare common phenomena in the universe of unique elements. He states that such a study "does not require that all phenomenon be in all respects identical because that requirement would deny the possibility of a science of society" [(7)]. There cannot be distinctly Indian, or British or Russian properties in chemistry or biology.

While agreeing with Berreman, I used a yardstick of parity to compare four chosen societies without categorizing any one of them either developed or underdeveloped. According to this approach we need to understand every society by looking into its universal traits as well as specific traits. Universal traits include human creativity, the four cardinal values of all societies—survival, security, prosperity and progress—social interaction, the building of social institutions, and culture, the process of creating of each society with human interaction, invasions, power struggles and class struggles. The specific traits are the products of various (universal) factors that include interactions, actions and choices of the people within each society that they make based on how they perceive their reality and possibilities (including geography) at a particular historical time, while interacting with the historical forces of the time. Therefore, no society is superior or inferior in its formation process, as all are products of human creativity and human interaction and thus human constructs. Humans can and do change their societies in many respects as societies are always in the process of becoming; none of them is a final product. Beyond that we are all connected to the larger cosmos, as human beings are part of nature and nature itself is within human beings (human body, its organs and billions, trillions of cells, and bacteria exist and thrive in human body), and a human survives only through its interaction with nature for food and other resources. In fact, humans themselves, having an innate capacity for creativity, which they inherited from nature, are one of infinite expressions of nature's creativity.

Therefore, the concept of "human creativity" seemed very appropriate as a yardstick of parity to erase the binary distinction to evaluate any society. It is different than understanding human beings only in their bodily capacity called labor. Similarly, the metaphor of Indra's Net (see Chapter 2) seems useful in understanding each society as both unique and interconnected at the same time, thus, co-constituting and co-producing each other. Moreover, the social formation process within a society remains the same everywhere—the daily social reproduction of society through people's interaction to fulfill their "humaneness." However, none of people's actions and choices exists in a vacuum, as international historical forces—those created in the process of interaction among societies—also create conditions that are impinging on each society. Thus, the specific historical trajectory of any society is the product of a conjunction of various historical forces developing and interacting within each country, as well as internationally. In turn, these historical forces were and are being created by the choices people make in each society at a given historical time, and thus the cycle goes on. There is no end to this process except when if the planet would cease to exist, along with humanity. With this understanding one can explain that inequalities among societies are created when one society cannot solve its internal problems created by class struggles and other micro/macro conflicts, and when that society tries to solve its problems by controlling other societies for resources and labor. These unequal relationships are products of violence and force, and not due to any "innate greatness" of any one society or people.

Based on these alternative ideas including the concepts of human creativity, human interactions (elaborated in Chapters 1 and 2) and a yardstick of parity, I have attempted a comparative study of four countries (Imperial Russia, Imperial Britain, postcolonial Imperial US and colonial India) while focusing on the issue of the emergence of the large-scale steel industry between 1880 and 1914 in these countries. I have chosen two countries considered to be "developed" and two considered being "underdeveloped" for this comparison. And I have chosen to focus on the matter of a large-scale steel industry because of a general claim that this industry propelled certain countries into becoming "developed" nations. Thus, using the yardstick of parity I have not categorized any one of these four countries as developed or underdeveloped. Instead I considered them, like in Indra's Net, as both unique and part of a larger web of interconnectedness co-constituting and co-producing one another. Based on this understanding I traced both universal and specific elements in each one of these four societies to comprehend the making of each one of them and their industrialization. After understanding the similarities and differences in the making of these four societies and their industrialization, I challenged the claim that the emergence of a large-scale steel industry between 1880 and 1914 propelled certain countries into becoming "developed" nations.

The challenge is based on available, obvious information that directs us to a different conclusion. For example, postcolonial Imperial US, colonial India, and Imperial Russia each had a large-scale steel industry prior to 1914, while Imperial Britain did not. However, Britain and the US are considered developed and Imperial Russia and colonial India are not. The question is, How could Britain be considered developed without a large-scale steel industry if that phenomenon was considered to be the gateway to development? Moreover, industrialization is not an autonomous force determined by neutral technology shaping society inevitably in a single direction. There was no standard experience of industrialization worldwide, there is no inevitability that agriculture must be replaced by industry, nor any inevitability that capitalism must move towards socialism. Industrialization did not evolve the same way everywhere, and it does not have to. Furthermore, industrialization in these countries did not happen by some natural force as an inevitability, or due to internal dynamics, but by deliberate efforts and actions (including wars, invasions and colonization) of political and economic leaders, and other actors within these countries. Based on these observations, I have proposed in this volume that we should use the same yardstick of parity to understand the combination of conjunctions and confluence of larger and smaller historical forces (products of human actions, interaction and choices) within each society and within the international sphere, which created conditions for the emergence of a large-scale steel industry in three countries between 1880 and 1914. However, the conjunction of historical forces developing within Britain and internationally affected Britain differently due to its vast empire and lack of global competition, which kept the British steel industry as a medium-scale family business until almost the middle of the twentieth century.

In addition to refuting the Western narrative and the related claim of uniqueness of the West, we can observe other common elements in the making of these four countries and their industrialization. For example, all four countries were formed through a similar process involving foreign invasion, power struggles, class wars, bloodshed, expansion of territories, and, in the case of Imperial Britain, going abroad and colonizing India and other countries. There was no inherently advanced English position from which it emerged as "the first industrial nation." In all cases, the story of the large-scale steel industry is connected with the development of railroads and railways. The US steel industry benefited from federal government subsidies which helped expand railroads even though there was no real demand for the expansion of railways. Similarly, in Britain, there was no need for railways as the country had a good system of transportation via waterways, and all of its regions were within 70 miles of a river. However, it was the needs of investors to invest in the railways which created the railway system in England as it did in the US. The Russian government invested in railroads to improve its industrialization for war needs. In colonial India, the colonial government invested in railroads to transport resources and troops in an effort to control different parts of the country and to export raw material to England. Later, to assure the constant supply of steel and ammunition in preparation for the coming World War, the colonial government promised Tata Company to build railway links between its iron mines, coal mines, and steel factory.

Another common element is the crucial role of the state (including Britain) in creating conditions with specific policies favorable to industrialization, and in its support of the steel industry with tariff protection and subsidies for national railroads (indirectly in the case of Britain). In turn, the choices made by the governments of each state were guided by the conditions created in the international arena, where two of these countries, Imperial Russia, and Imperial Britain—along with France and Germany, were big players. Even though Britain did not have a large-scale steel industry until the 1930s, it was the initiative of the British government and the country's banks that created the steel cartels which forced the modernization of the British steel industry during that decade. The reason for the British steel producer's resistance to modernization was that the traditional methods of making a profit were not yet exhausted, and small British firms could still profit using cheaper and more convenient methods while relying on the British Empire for safe markets. For example, by 1913, Argentina and India alone bought more British iron and steel exports than did the whole of Europe. Australia bought twice as much iron and steel than the US did. Thus, Imperial Britain became a parasite rather than a competitive economy, as it was living off the remains of a world monopoly, the "underdeveloped" world, and its past accumulation of wealth. In addition, the steel industry, like the coal industry, tended to rely increasingly on the state protection of its home market.

The other common factor among societies is that people make choices to guide and build their society in one direction or another. For example, in the US there were long debates and struggles over the issue of whether "to industrialize or not." In Imperial Russia, there were debates among different sections of the bureaucracy as to whether Russia should engage in free trade or follow protectionist policies. In colonial India the nationalist leaders had been debating continuously on the question of India's poverty and believed that India's poverty could be removed only with industrialization. With this understanding they started a *Swadeshi* movement to promote industrialization under colonial rule. Thus, choices had been made (and are being made continuously) by people who have invested in specific industries, by people who have chosen to migrate as laborer, by those who promoted industry and business through their profession such as lawyers, and engineers as well as by nationalist leaders, and by those controlling social, religious, economic and political institutions. However, all of these people have made choices within a larger context of development of historical forces within their society and internationally, which were earlier created from choices made by previous generation. For example, previous generations in the US had made their choices in the European context, where the rush for territorial expansion was in full swing under the force of capitalist development during the eighteenth century.

In addition to making choices, people of all societies learn and borrow from other societies all the time, and no innovation is created by one isolated individual.

For example, the English learned about indirect iron processing from skilled French migrant workers who came from Normandy in the late fifteenth century. France had developed this method roughly "a century before it was used in England." It has been observed that this method could not have developed from within England, as "There is nothing to indicate that indirect reduction was anticipated by native iron workers." The Walloon forging technique was introduced in England circa 1500 by the first Francophone migrants (from Liege, Namu and Franchimont in the Walloon area of the Netherlands) and the same technique was kept in use for two-and-a-half centuries. However, the real market for iron-wares at that time was created by Henry VII's constant wars with Scotland. France also needed iron for its wars against England. Under the rule of Henry VII, efforts were made to recruit more skilled iron workers and by around 1560, many foreigners, all speaking the French language, had been hired by Weald iron works industry in southeast England. Going further back in history, one can see that the French had learned iron and steel making from information circulated by the traders and merchants who traveled to France from China, where sophisticated methods of steel making had been developed since the second century BCE. The eventual patenting in 1856 of the Bessemer steel process in the West, in fact, was anticipated in 1853 by William Kelly, who had brought four Chinese steel experts to Kentucky in 1845, from whom Kelly learned the principles of steel production that had been used in China for more than two thousand years.

Even though the British developed the Bessemer process, as well as the open-hearth system to mass produce steel, the other innovations necessary to invent the Bessemer process were not made by any specially trained technicians. Instead, a cluster of interdependent innovations were developed over time by various untutored working technicians. Similarly, iron making technology advanced through a process of gradual continuous changes rather than through a series of sharp discrete innovations. Over time, the production period became progressively shorter with each successive innovation. While inventions in iron-making techniques were developed by sheer chance or by various individual efforts, their application diffusion was determined by market forces—whether or not it was profitable. Most of industry's innovations were adopted during the rapid economic expansion period of 1775–1815. The increased demand then for iron, which kept prices high and helped generate huge profit margins for the early innovators, may have slowed the diffusion of new technology. Thus, English iron masters made high profits by utilizing outdated methods and not by investing in new techniques. The demand for iron at the time resulted in high prices and accelerated the diffusion of coke smelting and puddling. Without large profits, the investment would not have been possible as the industry's operations demanded new equipment and new sites. However, after 1815, the English iron-masters had to adopt new methods under opposite conditions. Prices declined between 1815 and 1870 with the rapid production of iron. Railways yielded temporarily high prices, but the cycle of boom-and-bust and economic depression imposed long-run decline in both prices and profits. The hot-blast method was adopted in 1835–1845 when prices were declining. Then the reason for innovation was to maintain falling profits, rather than getting a windfall, and to survive in a competitive industry. The nature of innovation changed also, because the risk associated with these innovations was small, and not much capital investment was required. Most of these innovations could be easily installed in an existing structure on a limited basis at small cost. However, when Britain invented the Bessemer process it was not extensively adopted due to the lack of non-phosphoric iron ore necessary for this process; whereas, the US and Germany adopted it and became competitors in the world market of steel.

Thus, the emergence of the large-scale steel industry was not simply due to technological breakthroughs or the genius of any one person in the Western world. It was a long, drawn-out process in which various actors played parts that included borrowing from other societies and cultures. This point has been raised by many other scholars but somehow the idea that technology is an independent force remains deeply embedded in people's minds. Moreover, the idea that a society had to have prerequisites for industrialization does not hold. For example, the claim that industrialization requires the existence of entrepreneurs and free wage labor did not apply in the case of Russia, where a large number of serfs were successful entrepreneurs. In Russia, the role of technocrats such as engineer managers was critical in the promotion and success of the large-scale steel industry. Those technocrats were managing steel and coal companies for foreign bosses, but their decisions were guided by their deep concern for improving Russian culture and its material well-being. Their views were based on nineteenth and early twentieth-century Enlightenment ideas, committed to popular welfare, and suspicious of the "pure market." They saw the market only as a way of getting goods from the site of production to the consumer, and not as a "free market." Moreover, they were not influenced by either entrepreneurism or Russian merchant traditions because, in Russia, the gap between those supporting industrialization and those opposing it was so large, these technocrats took over the task of promoting Russia's industries and entrepreneurship. Their actions made sense in the context of a state that wanted to promote industry without establishing a capitalist elite and without resolving the debate between pastoralists and industrialization. The Western narrative of industrialization does not take these specificities into account.

In light of all the arguments above and within previous chapters it can be suggested that the distinct historical trajectory of each society was not due to any of them being superior (developed) or inferior (underdeveloped), but rather to how people interacted within their own society, with their geographical surroundings, and how they interacted with larger historical forces within their society and in the world arena at a particular historical time. All societies are co-produced and co-constituted as all borrow from other societies. For example, the US (earlier under British colonial rule the US was banned from producing iron and steel) borrowed steel making technology from Britain (as mentioned above, Britain learned from French people, who in turn, learned indirectly from Chinese innovations) and produced cheaper steel and special steel alloys that transformed the US industry, as it became possible to produce more durable machines, tools, and more complex products than was previously possible. The US had vast resources of iron and coal, and a large market that was conducive to the mass production, that other countries lacked. In the case of colonized India, where high quality steelmaking was known and developed since antiquity, Tata Company learned from the US modern methods of organization and management to create and run a large-scale steel industry. However, the British policies towards colonized India limited Tata Company's choices of products as well as further development and industrialization of India. Therefore, we cannot understand any society in isolation and label it as "superior" or "inferior" based on any existing criteria of Western concepts about binary distinctions.

Even the anomalous case of the large-scale steel industry in colonial India cannot be explained simply by glorifying the role of Tata's entrepreneurship or the so-called "generosity" of the colonial government. It can be explained, similar to other societies, by examining the conjunction and confluence of various historical forces developing at that time within India and throughout the larger international arena. Thus, this apparent anomaly was created by the same universal processes involved in the making of any society. No single cause led to the circumstances allowing the Indian steel industry to emerge. It was the outcome of changing conflicts of interest involving state and capital in Britain, within India and in the world arena. The emergence of the mass production of steel in the world market and the development of railways and communication, led to the formation of cartels dividing up world markets. This in turn created new circumstances for the decline of British hegemony and rise of the US hegemony that also influenced the CGI's priorities and policies concerning India's industrialization. Therefore, the country's industrialization did not follow a predetermined line or proceed toward a single, ultimate destination as propounded by the stage theory of modernization or of Marxism. The entrepreneurial legacy of J. N. Tata could take form only from 1907, and not in 1883. In spite of being a very aggressive entrepreneur, Tata could not implement his steel project plan until the conditions were favorable in the world steel market and in Britain and India. By 1899, Britain was losing competitive advantage in the world market. At the same time, it was not able to restructure its domestic steel industry. The Colonial Government of India (CGI) was concerned about railway expansion, the lack of revenue sources, the falling rate of the rupee, and exchange rates. *Swadeshi* sentiments, which had been developing in India during the last two decades of the nineteenth century, added to the CGI's worries. The CGI felt a real political threat and tried not to alienate its supporters, particularly Indian moderates and big capitalists. On the other hand, the development of *Swadeshi* made it possible for Tata to generate Indian capital to finance a national steel industry when British financiers refused to cooperate. This process of interaction, the changes in CGI's policies due to the changing nature of the home market, which in turn was affected by changes in the world economic situation, the decline of British hegemony, the impact of class struggle and the industrial structure within Britain, the pressures of the Indian nationalist movement—together with the level of technology and product mix is what shaped the growth and development of Indian steel industry during colonial rule.

To conclude, the questions raised and methodology used for this comparative study has removed the need for continuously proving the capitalist/modernist credentials of a so-called "underdeveloped" society. In other words, we do not have to worry about proving why Asia or any other region of the world did not industrialize first. By eliminating the need to answer this question, we can stop being complicit in the promotion of the Western binary distinction—which is racist—and the Western myths of "lacking" and "not yet." This method of organizing (as suggested in this volume) historical information for comparative study is necessary because the history of every society is also the history of interdependence and interconnection. Societies mutually influence one another through reciprocal or asymmetric perceptions and relationships. Through these entangled processes, societies constitute one another and "co-produce" one another because each society, while interacting with other societies, also interact with systems of various forms of social labor, forms of political power relations, and various centers of cultures. However, these centers of cultures have been destroyed and re-created over time, and in spite of each being different, they remain related at the same time. This is why the history of different societies must be understood as interconnected and intertwined (as in Indra's Net) instead of considered as separate units for comparison. However, our methodology does not deny that some societies become powerful by controlling and colonizing other societies with the use of trickery, dubious agreements, invasion, wars, force, and violence, compelling them to become peripheral and to be labeled as "underdeveloped."

Nevertheless, the goal of this book is to treat all societies with the same yardstick so that it will be possible to avoid using the binary label of "core/periphery" or "developed /undeveloped" or consider any society as unique existing in a vacuum. We tried to achieve this goal by giving primacy to human creativity while looking for universal and specific elements in each society chosen for this volume, and also by focusing on the conjunction of historical forces within each society and internationally during 1880–1914. With this approach it became possible to move away from Rostow's stage theory of economic growth and stage theory of Marx's idea about shifts in the mode of production both of which actually privileges Europe's uniqueness.

In recent years, the concepts of growth and globalization are increasingly losing their legitimacy in the Western world, and elites at Davos (World Economic Forum) are fearfully witnessing the rise of populism worldwide that challenges their economic model of perpetual growth and perpetual wars leading to extreme inequalities. The hegemony of the super power US is obviously declining and its binary approach is not working anymore in classifying different societies in the wake of the rise of China and other rising economies in the non-Western world. We should use this opening of a space to find and implement alternative ideas and change the direction of history towards parity and a better future for everyone and the planet. Even though China is challenging US hegemony, it is also (as are other rising economies in the non-Western world) following the same Western model of development and perpetual growth (Kin Chi, 2018). Without rejecting the Western model of development and perpetual growth, which links growth to progress and prosperity, these growing economies and the Western economies will remain incapable of producing alternative ideas. Alternatives will emerge from the creativity of those human beings who would like to make an alternative history and not promote "growth and development." Hopefully, such alternative ideas will emerge if we try hard enough to use our creativity consciously while benefiting from the vast human knowledge available to us that was created by our common human ancestors. Of course, there are no inevitabilities or guarantees, but we must keep trying—as this is an existential issue. It is more urgent now because the pulsed microwave technology to remotely control and manipulate human creativity and consciousness has already manifested (Babacek, 2019).

ENDNOTES

1. Interestingly, after I wrote the concluding remarks, I found some echo of them in S. C. Rajan's response to Banerjee et al. (2016) ideas as he wrote: "Allowing for pluralism, eclecticism, 'making do' with the material we find, and sharing them widely in conversation might actually give us productive results. At least, we can all claim as our common legacy a vast stock of conversational knowledge since antiquity. If nothing else, it sets up a form of democratic practice, which can at least give us the reassurance of having tried" (Rajan, S. C. 2017, "Practicing Theory in the Anthropocene: A Postcolonial Quest for Reliable Knowledge." *Economic and Political Weekly*, 52(14):72–74).
2. Banerjee, Prathama, Aditya Nigam and Rakesh Pandey (2016). "The Work of Theory: Thinking across Traditions." *Economic and Political Weekly*, 51(37):45–50.
3. Rajan, op. cit.
4. Berreman, D. G. (1971), "The Brahmanical View of Caste." *Contribution to Indian Sociology*. Harold A. Gould, (Ed.), Dec 5. 16–23. Delhi.
5. Ibid.
6. Ibid.
7. Ibid.

Bibliography
About the Author
Abstract

Bibliography

Aaronovitch, S. (1955). *Monopoly: A Study of British Monopoly Capitalism*. London: Lawrence and Wishart.

Abou-El-Haj, R. A. (2005). *Formation of the Modern State: The Ottoman Empire, Sixteenth to Eighteenth Centuries.* (2nd ed.). Syracuse, NY: Syracuse University Press.

Abu-Lughod, J. L. (1989). *Before European Hegemony: The World System A.D. 1250–1350.* New York: Oxford University Press.

Abu-Lughod, J. L. (2004). "Continuing American Provincialism and the Rest of the World." In Wallerstein, I. (Ed.), *The Modern World System in the Longue Duree*. Boulder, Colorado: Paradigm Publishers.

Ackroyd, P. (2012). *Foundation: The History of England from Its Earliest Beginnings to the Tudor.* New York: St. Martin's Press.

Adluri, V. and Bagchee, J. (2014). *The Nay Science: A History of German Indology*. New York: Oxford University Press.

Afshordi, N., Mann, R. B. and Pourhasan, R. (2014). "The Black Hole at the Beginning of Time." *Scientific American*, August: 38–43.

Agnihotri, R. K. (2016). "Gender Agenda," *Economic and Political Weekly,* 51(37). September 10. (Postscript).

Ågren, M. (Ed.). (1998). *Iron Making Societies Early Industrial Development in Sweden and Russia 1600–1900.* New York ; Oxford: Berghahn Books.

Aharonian, A. and Rangel, A. V. (2018). "The Atlas Network's Insidious Impact on the Ground." September 8. (https://mronline.org/2018/09/08/the-atlas-networks-insidious-impact-on-the-ground).

Aharonian, A. and Rangel, A. V. (2018). "Atlas Network, the right-wing libertarians." Sept. 8. (mronline.org/2018/09/07/atlas-network-the-right-wing-libertarians).

Akuno, K. and Nangwaya, A. (Eds.). (2017). *Jackson Rising: The Struggle for Economic Democracy and Black Self-Determination in Jackson, Mississippi.* Jackson, MS: Daraja Press.

Albert, M. (2016). "Marx This, Marx That, So What?" teleSUR, May 9.

Alexandra, R. (2016). "Chomsky: America is on the Decline: Guess Who's to Blame?" July 15. (https://www.alternet.org/2016/07/chomsky-america-decline-guess-whos-blame).

American Social History Project: CUNY (2000). *Who Built America? Working People and the Nation's Economy, Politics, Culture and Society From Conquest to Colonization Through 1877.* Vol. I. New York: Worth Publishers.

Amin, S. (1990). *Delinking: Towards a Polycentric World*. London: Zed Books.

Amin, S. (1998). *Specters of Capitalism: A Critique of Current Intellectual Fashions.* New York: Monthly Review Press.

Amin, S. (2009). *Eurocentrism: Modernity, Religion and Democracy: A Critique of Eurocentrism and Culturalism.* (2nd ed.). New York: Monthly Review Press.

Amin, S. (2012). "The Center Will Not Hold: The Rise and Decline of Liberalism." *Monthly Review*, January, 63(8).

Anderson, E. N. (2018). Book review, *Journal of World-Systems Research,* Winter/Spring, 24(1):266–271.

Angier, N. (2012). "Insights from the Youngest Minds." *The New York Times,* Profiles in Science. May 1. Interview with S. Elizabeth. (nytimes.com/2012/05/01/science/insights-in-human-knowledge-from-the-minds-of-babes.html).

Angus, I. (2018). "Five Revolutions: How Bacteria Created the Biosphere and Caused the First Climate Change." April 23. (https://countercurrents.org/2018/04/five-revolutions-how-bacteria-created-the-biosphere-and-caused-the-first-climate-crisis).

Anievas, A. and Nişancioğlu, K. (2015). *How the West Came to Rule: The Geopolitical Origins of Capitalism*. London: Pluto Press.

Antony, P. (2015). "Development: The Amazing Emptiness of Magic Words." November 29. (https://www.countercurrents.org/antony291115.htm).

Appiah, A. K. (2016). "Culture: Mistaken Identities." The Reith Lectures BBC. (bbc.co.uk/programmes/b081lkkj).

Archer, M. S. (1985). "Evolving Focus on Human Agency in Contemporary Social Theory." In P. Sztompka (Ed.), *Agency and Structure: Reorienting Social Theory.* (1994). Yverdon, Switzerland ; Langhorne, PA: Gordon & Breach

Archer, M. S. (1988). *Culture and Agency.* Cambridge, UK: Cambridge University Press.

Archer, M. S. (2000). *Being Human: The Problem of Agency.* Cambridge, UK: Cambridge University Press.

Argov, D. (1967). *Moderates and Extremists in the Indian Nationalist Movement, 1883–1920, with special reference to Surendranath Banerjee and Lajpat Rai.* Bombay, India: Asia Publishing House.

Ashton, K. (2015). *How to Fly a Horse: The Secret History of Creation, Invention, and Discovery.* New York: Anchor Books.

Aston, T. H. and Philpin, C. H. E. (Eds.). (2005). *The Brenner Debate: Agrarian Class Structure and Economic Development in Pre-Industrial Europe.* Delhi: Cambridge University Press and Foundation Books.

Avery, J. (2003). *Information Theory and Evolution.* River Edge, New Jersey: World Scientific Publishing Co.

Awty, B. G. (1981). "The Continental Origin of Wealden Iron Works, 1451–1544." *Economic History Review,* n.s. 34/4:524–539.

Azikiwe, A. (2016). "African American and Women Studies Majors Eliminated at Western Illinois University." June 21. (https://www.globalresearch.ca/african-american-and-women-studies-majors-eliminated-at-western-illinois-university/5532060).

Babacek, M. (2013). "Psychotronic and Electromagnet Weapons: Remote Control of Human Nervous System." January 31. (https://www.globalresearch.ca/psychotronic-and-electromagnetic-weapons-remote-control-of-the-human-nervous-system/5319111).

Babacek, M. (2019). "Remote Control of the Brain and Human Nervous System." January 23. (https://www.globalresearch.ca/remote-control-of-the-brain-and-human-nervous-system/5666202).

Babar, A. V. (2018). "When Karl Marx Fails: Discourse on Class and Caste Politics in India." July 22. (https://countercurrents.org/2018/07/when-karl-marx-fails-discourse-on-class-and-caste-politics-in-india).

Bagchi, A. K. (Ed.). (2002). *Money and Credit in Indian History from Early Medieval Times.* New Delhi: Tulika Books.

Bagchi, A. K. (2012). "Class Struggles, Ideologies, Economic Transformation and Colonialism." *Economic and Political Weekly,* 47(15):33–44.

Bagchi, A. K. (2013). "Perilous Passage: Mankind and the Global Ascendency of Capital." Lehman, MD: Rowman and Littlefield.

Bah, V. and Anumo, F. (2017). "Lesson Learned: Revolution Doesn't Come From NGOs." August 4. (https://www.alternet.org/2017/08/four-lessons-african-feminist-organizing)

Bahl, V. (1995). *The Making of the Indian Working Class: A Case Study of Tata Iron and Steel Co. 1880–1946.* New Delhi ; Thousand Oaks, CA: SAGE Publications.

Bahl, V. (1997a). "Relevance (or Irrelevance) of Subaltern Studies." *Economic and Political Weekly,* 32(23):1333–1344.

Bahl, V. (1997b). "Cultural Imperialism and Women's Movement: Thinking Globally." *Gender and History,* 9(1):1–14.

Bahl, V. (2005a). *What Went Wrong With "History from Below": Reinstating Human Agency as Human Creativity.* Kolkata, India: K. P. Bagchi and Company.

Bahl, V. (2005b). "Shifting Boundaries of 'Nativity' and 'Modernity' in the South Asian Women's Clothes." *Dialectical Anthropology,* 29(1):85–121.

Bahl, V. (2005c). "Terminology, History and Debate: 'Caste' Formation or 'Class' Formation." *Journal of Historical Sociology,* 17(2/3):265–318.

Bahl, V. (2007). "Shifting Boundaries of 'Nativity' and 'Modernity' in the South Asian Women's Clothes." T. Omoniyi and S. Gupta (Eds.), 2007.

Baldwin, J. (1998). "The Devil Finds Work." *Collected Works.* (Originally published 1976).

Banerjee, A. and Duflo, E. (2011). *Poor Economics: A Radical Rethinking of the Way to Fight Global Poverty.* New York: Public Affairs.

Banerjee, A. and Chandrasekhar, C. P. (Eds.). (2018). *Dispossession, Deprivation and Development.* New York: Columbia University Press. First published in Delhi: Tulika Press.

Bannerjee, P., Nigam, A., and Pandey, R. (2016). "The Work of Theory: Thinking Across Traditions." *Economic and Political Weekly,* 51(37):42–50.

Bannerjee, S. (2015). "The Yogi as a Pugilist: Psychotherapy-cum Martial Exercise in the Indian Armed Forces." *Economic and Political Weekly*, 1(33):10–13.

Bannerjee, S. (N.d.). *Speeches and Writings.* Calcutta (now Kolkata), India: G. A. Nateson and Co.

Baptist, E. (2016). *The Half Has Never Been Told: Slavery and the Making of American Capitalism.* New York: Basic Books.

Bard, A. and Söderqvist, J. (2012). *The Autocrats: The Futurica Trilogy*. Stockholm, Sweden: Stockholm Text.

Barkin, D. (2003). "Mexico: Towards a New Understanding." *Economic and Political Weekly*, 38(1):29–31.

Barsocchini, R. (2016). "Father of Western Economics Took 'Most of His Best Ideas' from Sharia Law." May 24. washingtonblog.com. (https://washingtonsblog.com/2016/05/father-western-economics-took-best-ideas-sharia-law.html).

Basu, P. and Biswas, N. (2017). "Revisiting Development Paradigm: Context Bhangar Movement." June 14. (https://www.countercurrents.org/wp-content/uploads/2017/06/bhangar-paper.pdf).

Bayly, C. A. (1988). *Indian Society and the Making of the British Empire.* Cambridge, UK: Cambridge University Press.

Beard, A. C. (1913). *An Economic Interpretation of the Constitution of the US*. Mineola, NY: Dover Publications.

Berkun, S. (2007). *The Myths of Innovation*. Sebastopol, California: O'Reilly Media, Inc.

Bernal, M. (1987). *Black Athena: The Afroasiatic Roots of Classical Civilization.* New Brunswick, NJ: Rutgers University Press.

Berreman, G. D. (1971). "The Brahmanical View of Caste." *Contribution to Indian Sociology,* Delhi, Harold A. Gould, (Ed.), December 5, pp. 16–23.

Betageri, A. (2015). "Is Hindu Science Possible?" March 14. (https://www.countercurrents.org/betageri140315.htm).

Bhagwati, J. N. and Desai, P. (1970). *India's Planning for Industrialization: Industrialization and Politics Since 1951.* London: Oxford University Press.

Bhatia, V. (2017). "Karnataka's Black Magic Law Targets Caste and Gender Discrimination, not Hindu Religious Practices." November 28. (https://scroll.in/article/858566/karnatakas-black-magic-law-targets-caste-and-gender-discrimination-not-hindu-religious-practices).

Bhattacharya, S. (1965). "Laissez faire in India," *Indian Economic and Social History Review,* 11(1):1–22.

Bhattacharya, S. (Ed.). *Towards a New History of Work.* New Delhi: Tulika Books.

Bisnoff, J. (2019). "Fake Politics: How Corporate and Government Groups Create and Maintain a Monopoly on Truth." New York: Skyhorse Publishing.

Black, B. Hyman, G. and Smith, G. M. (Eds.). (2014). *Confronting Secularism in Europe and India: Legitimacy and Disenchantment in Contemporary Times.* London: Bloomsbury Academic.

Blackwell, W. L. (1968). *The Beginnings of Russian Industrialization, 1800–1860.* Princeton, NJ: Princeton University Press.

Blanchard, I. (2005). "The Nineteenth-Century Russian and 'Western' Ferrous Metallurgy: Complementary or Competitive Technologies?" In Chris Evans and Göran Rydén (Eds.), *The Industrial Revolution in Iron: The Impact of British Coal Technology in Nineteenth-Century Europe.* 2005. Burlington, VT ; London: Ashgate Publishing.

Blaut, M. (1993). *The Colonizer's Model of the World: Geographical Diffusionism and Eurocentric History.* London ; New York: The Guilford Press.

Björkenstam, N. (1995). "The Blast Furnace in Europe During Medieval Times: Part of a

New System of Producing Wrought Iron," in G. Magnusson (Ed.), *The Importance of Iron Making: Technical Innovation and Social Change*. Vol. I. Stockholm, Sweden: Jernkontoret.

Bollier, D. (2016). "Beyond Development: The Commons as New/Old Paradigm of Human Flourishing." June 30. (https://www.resilience.org/stories/2016-06-27/beyond-development-the-commons-as-a-new-old-paradigm-of-human-flourishing)

Bourdieu, P. and Wacquant, L. J. D. (1992). *An Invitation to Reflexive Sociology*. Chicago, IL: Chicago University Press.

Bourdieu, P. (1991). *Language and Symbolic Power*. Cambridge, MA: Harvard University Press.

Braddick, M. J. (2000). *State Formation in Early Modern England*. Quoted in Chibber (2013). Cambridge, UK: Cambridge University Press.

Brailsford, H. N. (Edited and prepared for publication by C. Hill) (1961). *Levellers and the English Revolution*. London: The Cresset Press.

Brands, H. W. (2010). *American Colossus: The Triumph of Capitalism, 1865–1900*. New York: Doubleday.

Breen, T. H. (1986). "An Empire of Goods: The Anglicization of Colonial America, 1690–1776." *The Journal of British Studies*, 25(4):487–499.

Brennan, C. L. (2015). The *Fall of Arab Spring: From Revolution to Destruction*. San Diego, CA: Progress Press.

Brennan, T. (2006). *Wars of Position: The Cultural Politics of Left and Right*. New York: Columbia University Press.

Brennan, T. (2014). "Subaltern Stakes." *New Left Review*, 89:67–87.

Brenner, R. (1977). "The Origins of Capitalist Development: A Critique of Neo-Smithian Marxism." *New Left Review*, 104:25–92.

Bridge, F. R. and Bullen, R. (1960). *The Great Powers and the European States System, 1815–1914*. Essex, UK: Longman.

Brody, D. (1960). *Steel Workers in America: The Non-Union Era*. Cambridge, UK: Cambridge University Press.

Brown, B. (2017). *Humanity: The World Before Religion, War & Inequality*. MIT: Barry Brown.

Brown, E. (2017). "Today We're All Irish: Debt Serfdom Comes to America." March 18. (https://www.globalresearch.ca/today-we-re-all-irish-debt-serfdom-comes-to-america/8349).

Brunn, S. D. (Ed.). (2015). *The Changing World Religion Map: Sacred Places, Identities, Practices and Politics*. New York: Springer Science + Business Media.

Buck, T. (2003). "Modern Russian Corporate Governance: Convergent Forces or Product of Russia's History?" *Journal of World Business*. 38(4):299–313.

Buckley, W. (1967). *Sociology and Modern Systems Theory*. Englewood Cliffs, NJ: Prentice Hall.

Burnham, T. H. and Hoskins, G. O. (1943). *Iron and Steel in Britain, 1870–1930*. London: Allen and Unwin.

Burkeman, O. (2012). *The Antidote: Happiness for People Who Can't Stand Positive Thinking*. New York: Farrar, Straus, and Giroux.

Burns, A. R. (1936). *The Decline of Competition*. New York: McGraw-Hill.

Burn, D. L. (1940). *Story of the British Steel Industry*. Cambridge, UK: Cambridge University Press.

Burt, R. (1991). "The International Diffusion of Technology in the Early Modern Period: The Case of the British Non-Ferrous Mining Industry." *Economic History Review*, 44(2):249–271.

Bystydzienski, J. and Schacht, S. P. (Eds.). (2001). *Forging Radical Alliances Across Difference: Coalition Politics for the New Millennium*. Lanham, MD: Rowman & Littlefield.

Cains, P. J. and Hopkins, A. G. (1993). *British Imperialism: Innovation and Expansion, 1688–1919*. London: Longman.

Campbell, J. (1988). *Historical Atlas of World Mythology*. Vol. I. *The Way of the Animal Powers*, Part 2: *Mythology of the Primitive Hunters and Gatherers*. New York: Harpers Collins.

Capra, F. (1984). *Tao of Physics: An Exploration of the Parallels between Modern Physics and Eastern Mysticism*. Boston: Shambhala Publications.

Capra, F. (1996). *The Web of Life: A New Scientific Understanding of Living Systems*. New York: Random House.

Carr, E. H. (1969). "Some Reflections on Soviet Industrialization." C. H. Feinstein (Ed.), *Socialism, Capitalism, and Economic Growth: Essays Presented to Maurice Dobb*. Cambridge,

UK: Cambridge University Press.

Carr, J. C. and Taplin, W. (1962). *The Economic History of Steel Making, 1867–1939.* Cambridge, MA: Harvard University Press.

Castells, M. et al. (Eds.). (2017). *Another Economy is Possible: Culture and Economy in a Time of Crisis.* Cambridge, UK ; Malden, MA: Polity Press.

Chakrabarti, S. and Patnaik, U. (Eds.). (2017). *Agrarian and Other Histories: Essays for Binay Bhushan Chaudhuri.* New Delhi: Tulika Books.

Chakrabarty, D. (1993). "Marx after Marxism: A Subaltern Historian's Perspective." *Economic and Political Weekly,* 28(2):1094–1096.

Chakrabarty, D. (2007). *Provincializing Europe: Postcolonial Thought and Historical Difference.* (2nd ed.). Originally published in 2000. Princeton, NJ: Princeton University Press.

Chakrabarty, D. (2008). "Reply to Carola Dietze: In Defense of Provincializing Europe." *History and Theory,* 47(1):85–96.

Chakraborty, A. (2017). "Twilight of the Buddha: Tantra As it Had Risen Against Brahminism." December 7. (https://countercurrents.org/2017/12/twilight-of-the-buddha-tantra-as-it-had-risen-against-brahminism).

Chakraborty, A. (2018a). "Vastu, Ecology, Stories and Folk-Expressions: A Story of the Great Loot." February 10. (https://countercurrents.org/2018/02/vastu-ecology-stories-folk-expressions-story-great-loot).

Chakraborty, A. (2018b). "Charvaka-Jamming Against Brahminism Since Eons Before the Brahmins Happened." April 13. (countercurrents.org/2018/04/charvaka-jamming-against-brahminism-eons-before-the-brahmins-happened).

Chakraborty, A. (2018c). "Lenin and the Myths—a 'Tajik' tale." July 18. (countercurrents.org/2018/07/lenin-and-the-myths-a-tajik-tale).

Chandavarker, R. (1985). "Industrialization in India Before 1947: Conventional Approaches and Alternative Perspectives." *Modern Asian Studies,* 19(3):623–668.

Chandhoke, N. (2018). "Why I am A Hindu Review: The Power of Politics as Religion." *The Hindu,* Feb 17. (https://www.thehindu.com/books/books-reviews/why-i-am-a-hindu-review-the-power-of-politics-as-religion/article22783777.ece).

Chandler, A. D. (1977). *The Visible Hand: The Managerial Revolution in American Business.* Cambridge, MA: Harvard University Press.

Chandler, A. D. (1998). "The Coming of Mass Production and Modern Management." In Kornblith (Ed.), *Problems in American Civilization: The Industrial Revolution in America.* Boston: Houghton Mifflin Company.

Chandra, B. (1966). *The Rise and Growth of Economic Nationalism in India: Economic Politics of Indian National Leadership.* 1880–1905. New Delhi, India: People's Publishing House.

Chandra, B. (1991). "Colonial India: British versus Indian Views of Development." *Fernand Braudel Center Review,* Winter, 14(1):81–167.

Chang, H. J. (2002). *Kicking Away the Ladder: Development Strategy in Historical Perspective.* London ; New York: Anthem Press.

Chang, H. J. (2008). *Bad Samaritans: The Myth of Free Trade and the Secret History of Capitalism.* New York: Bloomsbury Press.

Chatterjee, P. (2012). "After Subaltern Studies." *Economic and Political Weekly,* 47(35):44–49.

Chaturvedi, V. (Ed.). (2000). *Mapping Subaltern Studies and the Postcolonial.* London: Verso.

Chaudhuri, K. N. (1968). "India's International Economy in the Nineteenth Century: An Historical Survey." *Modern Asian Studies,* 2(1):31–50.

Chaudhuri, K. N. (1990a). "The Historical Roots of Capitalism in the Indian Ocean: A Comparative Study of South Asia, the Middle East, and China during the Pre-Modern Period." In Sugata Bose (Ed.), *South Asia and World Capitalism.* Delhi: Oxford University Press.

Chaudhuri, K. N. (1990b). *Asia Before Europe: Economy and Civilisation of the Indian Ocean from the Rise of Islam to 1750.* Cambridge, UK: Cambridge University Press.

Cheney-Lippold, J. (2017). "We are Data: Algorithmic and the Making of Our Digital Selves." New York: NYU Press.

Chengu, G. (2015a). "How Slaves Built American Capitalism." December 18. (https://www.counterpunch.org/2015/12/18/how-slaves-built-american-capitalism).

Chengu, G. (2015b). "Before Columbus: How Africans Brought Civilization to America." December 30. (globalresearch.ca/before-columbus-how-africans-brought-civilization-to-america/5407584).

Chengu, G. (2016). "How African Slavery Civilized Britain." March 22. (globalresearch.ca/before-columbus-how-africans-brought-civilization-to-america/5407584).

Chengu, G. (2017). "History: How Africa-Muslims 'Civilized Spain'." April 8. (https://www.globalresearch.ca/history-how-african-muslims-civilized-spain/5583981).

Chibber, V. (2013). *Postcolonial Theory and the Specter of Capital.* London: Verso.

Chomsky, N. (1994). *World Orders: Old and New.* New York: Columbia University Press.

Chossudovsky, M. (1997). *The Globalisation of Poverty: Impacts of IMF and World Bank Reforms.* London: Zed Books.

Chossudovsky, M. (2018). "Social Activism Funded by Global Capitalism, Serve the Neoliberal World Order." March 28. (https://www.globalresearch.ca/social-activism-funded-by-global-capitalism-serves-the-neoliberal-world-order-the-2018-world-social-forum-wsf-in-salvador-brazil/5633926).

Christian, D. (2005). *Maps of Time: An Introduction to Big History.* Berkeley, CA: University of California Press.

Clay, C. G. A. (1984). *Economic Expansion and Social Change: England 1500–1700: Volume 2, Industry, Trade and Government.* Cambridge, UK: Cambridge University Press.

Cleere, H. and Crossley, D. (1995). *The Iron Industry of the Weald.* Cardiff, UK: Merton Priory Press.

Cochran, T. C. (1981). "An Innovative Business System." In Kornblith, G. J. (Ed.). (1998) *Problems in American Civilization: The Industrial Revolution in America.* Boston: Houghton Mifflin Co.

Collins, L. (1992). *Britons: Forging the Nation, 1707–1837.* New Haven, CT: Yale University Press.

Collins, R. (1998). *The Sociology of Philosophies: A Global Theory of Intellectual Change.* Cambridge, MA: Harvard University Press.

Collins, R. (2004). *Interaction Ritual Chains.* Princeton, NJ: Princeton University Press.

Connelly, E. (2019). "Medieval Medical Books Could Hold the Recipe for New Antibiotics." January 10. (https://www.alternet.org/2019/01/medieval-medical-books-could-hold-the-recipe-for-new-antibiotics).

Conner, C. D. (2005). *A People's History of Science: Miners, Midwives, and "Low Mechanicks."* New York: Nation Books.

Cook, H. J. (2007). *Matters of Exchange: Commerce, Medicine, and Science in the Dutch Golden Age.* New Haven, CT: Yale University Press.

Cooper, F. (2005). *Colonialism in Question: Theory, Knowledge, History.* Los Angeles: University of California Press.

Corbridge, S. (1993). "Marxism, Modernities and Moralities: Development Praxis and the Claims of Distant Strangers." *Society and Space,* 11(4):449–472.

Corbridge, S. (1998). " 'Beneath the Pavement Only Soil': The Poverty of Post-Development." *Journal of Development Studies,* 34(6):138–48.

Cowen, M. P. and Shenton, R. W. (1996). *Doctrines of Development.* London: Routledge.

Crawford, N. (2018). *Report: Human Cost of the Post 9/11 Wars: Lethality and the Need for Transparency.* November 9. (https://watson.brown.edu/costsofwar/files/cow/imce/papers/2018/Human%20Costs%2C%20Nov%208%202018%20CoW.pdf).

Crisp, O. (1960). "French Investment in Russian Joint Stock Companies, 1894–1914." *Business History,* 2(2):75–90.

Crisp, O. (1976). *Studies in the Russian Economy Before 1914.* New York: Barnes and Noble.

Crist. M. and Roquarth, R. (2018). "The Crisis of American Forensics." *The Nation,* February 26, pp. 12–25.

Cronon, W. (1998). "Railroads and the Reorganization of Nature and Time." In Kornblith, G. J. (Ed.), *Problems in American Civilization: The Industrial Revolution in America.* Boston: Houghton Mifflin Co.

Crooke, A. (2018). "The Metaphysics to our Present Global Anguish." August 21. (https://

www.globalresearch.ca/the-metaphysics-to-our-present-global-anguish/5651328).

Cross, G. and Szostak, R. (1995). *Technology and American Society: A History*. Englewood Cliffs, NJ: Prentice-Hall.

Crossley, D. W. (1981). "Medieval Iron Smelting." In D. W. Crossley (Ed.), *Medieval Industry*. York, UK: Council for British Archeology.

Cubitt, T. S., Pérez-García, D., and Wolf, M. (2018). "The Un(solv)able Problem." *Scientific American*, 319(4):29–37.

Dalit Camera (2016), "Inquiring Into the Role of CPI(M) in the Annihilation of Caste." September 21. (https://countercurrents.org/2016/09/inquiring-into-the-role-of-cpim-in-the-annihilation-of-caste).

Damon, A. and Niemuth, N. (2017). "New Google Algorithm Restricts Access to Left-Wing, Progressive Web Sites." July 27. (wsws.org/en/articles/2017/07/27/goog-j27.html).

Dangl, B. (2016). "It Took 40 Years and Millions of Lives Destroyed for Elites to Admit That Neoliberalism Has Failed." June 2. (https://www.alternet.org/2016/06/imf-admits-neoliberalism-failure).

Daniel, T. C. (2013). *Real Money Versus Banks of Issue Promises to Pay: the Most Important Factor in Civilization and Least Understood*. London: Forgotten Books.

Darder, A. (2012). "Neoliberalism in the Academic Borderland: An On-going Struggle for Equality and Human Rights." *Educational Studies: A Journal of the American Education Studies Association*. 48(5):412–426.

Dardozzi, J. (2010). "The Indiscreet Banality of the Bourgeoisie: The Church of LEED, Passive House, and the Dangers of Going Green." *Monthly Review*, December, 62(7).

da Silva Rosa, A. C. (2107). "The Metaphysical Dimensions of Reality: How to Achieve Peace, Civility and Social Well-Being." November 9. (https://www.globalresearch.ca/the-metaphysical-dimensions-of-reality-how-to-achieve-peace-civility-and-social-well-being/5617221).

Das, J. P. (2014). *Consciousness Quest: Where East Meets the West: On Mind, Meditation, and Neural Correlates*. New Delhi: SAGE Publications.

Date, V. (2015a). "Capitalism and Sports: Sports for a Few." *Economic and Political Weekly*, 43(47):22–24.

Date, V. (2015b). "Yoga, Politicians and Corporates." June 19. (https://www.countercurrents.org/date190615.htm).

Davies, W. (2015). *The Happiness Industry: How the Government and Big Business Sold Us Well-Being*. London: Verso.

Davis, C. B., Wilburn, K. E., and Robinson, R. E. (Eds.), *Railway Imperialism*. New York: Greenwood Press.

Davis, M. (2001). *Late Victorian Holocausts: El Niño Famines and the Making of the Third World*. London: Verso.

de Carteau, M. (1984). *The Practice of Everyday Life*. Berkeley: University of California Press.

de Cecco, M. (1975). *Money and Empire: The International Gold Standard, 1870–1914*. Lanham, MD: Rowman and Littlefield.

deHaven-Smith, L. (2014). *Conspiracy Theory in America (Discovering America)*. Austin, TX: University of Texas Press.

de Oliveira, F. A. (2017). "A Radical Invitation for Latin America: the Legacy of Andre Gunder Frank's 'Development of Underdevelopment'." *Monthly Review*, May, 69(1):50–59

de Paor-Evans, A. (2018). "Its Time We Stop Using the Term 'World Music' for All That Doesn't Come From the West." July 26. (https://scroll.in/article/887791/its-time-we-stop-using-the-term-world-music-for-all-that-doesnt-come-from-the-west).

De Roover, J. (2006). "Courting Con in the West." *Economic and Political Weekly*, 41(18):1764–1765.

Desai, A. (2002). *We are the Poors: Community Struggles in Post-Apartheid Africa*. New York: Monthly Review Press.

Desai, A. R. (1976). *Social Background of Indian Nationalism*. Bombay: Popular Prakashan.

Desai, A. V. (1992). The Origins of Parsi Enterprise." In R. K. Ray (Ed.), *Enterpeneurship and Industry in India, 1800–1947*. Delhi: Oxford University Press.

Deshpande, A. (2011). "Eurocentric versus Indigenous," *Economic and Political Weekly*, 46(30), July 23.
Deslandes, A. (2017). "The Zapatistas Are Building the World We Ask For." July, 46(30):87–88. (http://www.europazapatista.org/index.php?post_id=9279).
Deslippe, P. (2018). "Forgotten Histories: Yoga's Popularity in the US Long Predates Hippies and Bead-wearing Hipsters." May 21. (https://scroll.in/magazine/878928/yogas-popularity-in-the-united-states-long-predates-hippies-and-mala-bead-wearing-hipsters).
Dharwadker, V. (Ed.). (1999). *Collected Essay of A. K. Ramanujan*. New Delhi ; New York: Oxford University Press.
d'Huy, J. (2016). "The Evolution of Myths." *Scientific American*, December, 315(6):62–69.
du Guy, P. (1991). "Enterprise Culture and the Ideology of Excellence." *New Formations*, 13:45–61.
Dietz, C. (2008). "Toward a History of Equal Terms: A Discussion of 'Provincializing Europe'." *History and Theory*, 47(1):69–84.
Dirlik, A., Bahl, V., and Gran, P. (2000). *History After the Three Worlds: Post Eurocentric Historiographies*. Baltimore, MD: Rowman and Littlefield.
Dirlik, A. (2013). "Thinking Modernity Historically: Is 'Alternative Modernity' the Answer?" *Asian Review of World Histories*. 1.1 January, 5–44.
Docherty, G. and Macgregor, J. (2013). *Hidden History: The Secret Origins of the First World War*. Edinburgh ; London: Edinburgh Mainstream Publishing.
Dresser, S. (2018). "Freud versus Jung: a bitter feud over the meaning of sex." November 14. (https://aeon.co/ideas/freud-versus-jung-a-bitter-feud-over-the-meaning-of-sex).
Dublin, T. (1979). *Women at Work: The Transformation of Work and Community in Lowell, Massachusetts, 1826–1860*. New York: Columbia University Press.
Dunbar-Ortiz, R. (2014). *An Indigenous People's History of the US*. Boston: Beacon Press.
Dutt, R. C. (1901). *Economic History of India Under Early British Rule*. London: K. Paul, Trench, Trübner & Co.
Dutt, R. C. (1904). *India in the Victorian Age: An Economic History of the People*. London: K. Paul, Trench, Trübner & Co.
Eagleton, T. (2009). *Reason, Faith and Revolution: Reflections on the God Debate*. New Haven, CT: Yale University Press.
Edelman, M. and Haugerud, A. (2005). "Introduction: The Anthropology of Development and Globalization." In Edelman, M. and Haugerud, A. (Eds.), *The Anthropology of Development and Globalization*. Oxford: Oxford University Press.
Edelman, S. (2012). *The Happiness of Pursuit: What Neuroscience Can Teach Us About the Good Life*. New York: Basic Books.
Eichengreen, B. (1997). *Globalizing Capital: A History of the International Monetary System*. Princeton, NJ: Princeton University Press.
Elbaum, B. and Wilkinson, F. (1979). "Industrial Relations and Uneven Development: A Comparative Study of the American and British Steel Industry." *Cambridge Journal of Economics*, 3(3):275–303.
Ellerman, D. (2005). *Helping People Help Themselves: From the World Bank to an Alternative Philosophy of Development Assistance*. Ann Arbor, MI: University of Michigan Press.
Engdahl, W. F. (2017). "An Interview with William Engdahl: US Empire, CIA, NGOs." July 17. Interview by Dr. Ludwig Watzal. (https://countercurrents.org/2017/07/the-us-empire-the-cia-and-the-ngos).
Engels, F. (N.d.). "Dialectics of Nature." (www.marxists.org/archive/marx/works/1883/don/ch09.htm).
Escobar, A. (1995). *Encountering Development: The Making and Unmaking of the Third World*. Princeton, NJ: Princeton University Press.
Esteva, G. (2016). "The Oaxaca Commune and the Zapatistas: Hope from the Margins." August 30. (https://countercurrents.org/2016/08/the-oxaca-commune-and-the-zapitastas-hope-from-the-margins).
Evans, C. (2005). "The Industrial Revolution in Iron in the British Isles." In C. Evans and G. Rydén (Eds.), *The Industrial Revolution in Iron: The Impact of British Coal Technology in*

Nineteenth-Century Europe. London: Ashgate Publishing.

Evans, C. and Rydén, G. (Eds.). (2005). *The Industrial Revolution in Iron: The Impact of British Coal Technology in Nineteenth-Century Europe*. London: Ashgate Publishing.

Evans, J. (2019). "There's a New War on Gender Studies." January 10. (https://www.alternet.org/2019/01/theres-a-new-war-on-gender-studies).

Falkus, M. E. (1972). *The Industrialization of Russia, 1700–1914*. London: MacMillan.

Fattow, A. and Lang, J. and Frank, J. (2006), *Complicity: How the North Promoted, Prolonged, and Profited from Slavery*. New York: Ballantine Books.

Ferguson, J. (1990). *The Anti-Politics Machine: 'Development', Depoliticization, and Bureaucratic Power in Lesotho*. Cambridge, UK: Cambridge University Press.

Fernandez, R. M. (2018). "I Know Why Black Women are Wary of Reproductive Activism." February 9. (https://www.yesmagazine.org/peace-justice/i-know-why-black-women-are-wary-of-reproductive-activism-20180209).

Fernyhough, C. (2017). "Talking to Ourselves." *Scientific American*, 317(2):74–79.

Florén, A. (1994). "Social Organization of Work and Labor Conflicts in Proto-Industrial Iron Production in Sweden, Belgium and Russia." *International Review of Social History*. 39(S2):83–113.

Florén, A. (1998). "Iron-making Societies: The Development of the Iron Industry in Sweden and Russia, 1600–1900," in Ågren (Ed.), *Iron-making Societies: Early Industrial Development in Sweden and Russia, 1600–1900*. Providence, RI: Berghahn Books.

Florén, A. and Rydén, G. (1998). "The Social Organization of Work at Mines, Furnaces, and Forges," in Ågren (Ed.), *Iron-making Societies: Early Industrial Development in Sweden and Russia, 1600–1900*. Providence, RI: Berghahn Books.

Foer, F. (2017). *World Without Mind: The Existential Threat of Big Tech*. New York: Penguin Press.

Foer, J. (2011). *Moonwalking With Einstein: The Art and Science of Remembering Everything*. New York: Penguin Books.

Fox, R. G. (1990). "Gandhi's Socialism and Hindu Nationalism." In Sugata Bose (Ed.), *South Asia and World Capitalism*. New Delhi: Oxford University Press.

Frank, A. G. (1967). *Capitalism and Underdevelopment in Latin America: Historical Studies of Chile and Brazil*. New York: Monthly Review Press.

Frank, A. G. (1998a). *ReORIENT: Global Economy in the Asian Age*. Berkeley: California University Press.

Frank, A. G. (1998b). "Speaking Truth to Power about the Scientific Emperor's Clothes." *Economic and Political Weekly*, October 17–24, 33(42/43):2715–2724.

Fraser, L. (1919). *Iron and Steel in India: A Chapter From the Life of Jamshedji N. Tata*. Bombay: Times Press.

Fraser, S. (2005). *Every Man a Speculator: A History of Wall Street in American Life*. New York: Harper Perennial.

Friedman, A. L. (1977). *Industry and Labour: Class Struggle at Work and Monopoly Capitalism*. London: Macmillan Press Ltd.

Ganguli, B. N. (1965). "Dadabhai Naoroji and the Mechanism of External Drain." *Indian Economic and Social History Review*, 1(2):85–102.

Gatrell, P. (1986). *The Tsarist Economy, 1850–1917*. New York: St. Martin's Press.

Gatrell, P. (1994). *Government, Industry and Rearmament in Russia 1900–1914: The Last Argument of Tsarism*. Cambridge, UK: Cambridge University Press.

Gatade, S. (2016). "Dalit Uprising and After: Why Hindutva Would Not Be the Same Again." August 25. (https://countercurrents.org/2016/08/dalit-uprising-and-after-why-hindutva-would-not-be-the-same-again).

Gauntlett, D. (2011). *Making is Connecting: The Social Meaning of Creativity, from DIY to Knitting to YouTube and Web 2.0*. Cambridge, UK: Polity Press.

George, P. (1982). *The Emergence of Industrial America: Strategic Factors in American Economic Growth Since 1870*. Albany, NY: SUNY Press.

Ghosh, D. N. (2012). "Credit, Intellectuals and the English Financial Revolution." *Economic and Political Weekly*, October 27, 47(43):31–33.

Giddens, A. (1985). *The Constitution of Society.* Cambridge, UK: Polity Press.

Gidwani, V. and Sivaramakrishnan, K. (2003). "Circular Migration and the Spaces of Cultural Assertion." *Annals of the American Association of Geographers,* 93(1):186–213.

Gintz, H. (1954). "Effects of technological change on labour in selected sections of the iron and steel industries of Great Britain, the United States and Germany, 1901–1939." Ph.D. Diss. : University of London.

Giri, A. K. (2015). "Social Theory and Asian Dialogue: Cultivating Planetary Conversations." In Rodrigue et al. (Eds.). *Our Place in the Universe: An Introduction to Big History (From Big Bang to Galactic Civilizations: A Big History Anthology).* Delhi: Primus Books

Giroux, H. (2016). *America's Addiction to Terrorism.* New York: Monthly Review Press.

Gleig, A. and Williamson, L. (Eds.). (2013). *Homegrown Gurus: From Hinduism in America to American Hinduism.* Albany, NY: SUNY Press.

Gleiser, M. (2014). *The Island of Knowledge: The Limits of Science and the Search for Meaning.* New York: Basic Books.

"Godel's Incompleteness Theorem: The #1 Mathematical Discovery of the 20th Century." Viewed August 30, 2016. (www.perrymarshall.com/articles/religion/godels-incompleteness-theorem).

Godrej, D. (2014). "NGOs: Do They Help?" *New Internationalist,* December, No. 478:12–15.

Goldberg, P. (2010). *American Veda: From Emerson and the Beatles to Yoga and Meditation—How Indian Spirituality Changed the West.* New York: Harmony Books.

Goldsmith, W. R. (1961). "The Economic Growth of Tsarist Russia 1860–1913." *Economic Development and Cultural Change,* 9(3):441–475.

Goleman, D. (2003). "Finding Happiness: Cajole Your Brain to Lean to the Left." *The New York Times.* February 4. (https://www.nytimes.com/2003/02/04/health/behavior-finding-happiness-cajole-your-brain-to-lean-to-the-left.html).

Golingu, E. (2014). "Coloured Revolutions: A New Form of Regime Change—Made in USA." March 5. (https://www.globalresearch.ca/colored-revolutions-a-new-form-of-regime-change-made-in-the-usa/2706).

Goodman, D. (2015). "A Fight for Life." *Yes Magazine,* Spring, No. 73:28–33.

Goodman, P. (2010). *Drawing the Line Once Again: Paul Goodman's Anarchist Writings.* Oakland, CA: PM Press.

Goody, J. (1996). *The East in the West.* Cambridge, UK: Cambridge University Press.

Gorski, P. S. (2003). *The Disciplinary Revolution: Calvinism and the Rise of the State in Early Modern Europe.* Chicago: Chicago University Press.

Gorski, P. S. (2013). "What is Critical Realism? And Why Should You Care?" *Contemporary Sociology,* 42(5):658–670.

Goswami, A. (2003). "A Quantum Explanation of Sheldrake's Morphic Resonance." (http://www.stealthskater.com/Documents/Consciousness_32.pdf).

Graeber, D. (2015). *The Utopia of Rules: On Technology, Stupidity and Secret Joys of Bureaucracy.* New York: Melville House.

Graeber, G. and Wengrow, D. (2018). "How to Change the Course of Human History." March 2. (https://www.eurozine.com/change-course-human-history).

Gramsci, A. (1971). *Selections from the Prison Notebooks.* Translated and edited by Q. Hoare and G. N. Smith. New York: International Publishers.

Gran, P. (1979). *Islamic Roots of Capitalism: Egypt, 1760–1840.* Austin: University of Texas Press.

Grant, J. (1996). "Rethinking the Ottoman 'Decline' : Military Technology Diffusion in the Ottoman Empire, Fifteenth–Eighteenth Centuries." Paper at the World History Association meeting in Pomona June 21–22. Quoted in Frank (1998b).

Grove, R. (1991). "The Transfer of Botanical Knowledge between Europe and Asia, 1498–1800." *Journal of the Japan-Netherlands Institute,* 3:160–176. In Parthasarathi (2011).

Grant, R. (2012). "A Desolate Place for a Defiant People." *Smithsonian Magazine.* September 1.

Greschenkron, A. (1962). *Economic Backwardness in Historical Perspective: A Book of Essays.* Cambridge, MA: Harvard University Press.

Gudavarthy, A. (2016). "Brahmanism, Liberalism and the Postcolonial Theory." *Economic and Political Weekly,* 51(24):15–17.

Gürcan, E. C. (2015). "The Nonprofit-Corporate Complex: An Integral Component and Driving Force of Imperialism in the Phase of Monopoly-Finance Capitalism." *Monthly Review,* April. pp. 37–53.

Guru, G. (1995). "Dalit Women Talk Differently." *Economic and Political Weekly,* October 14. 30(41-42):2548–50.

Guru, G. (2016). "Shifting Categories in the Discourse on Caste and Class." *Economic and Political Weekly,* 51(47):21–25.

Gurukkal, R. (2018). "Death of Democracy: An Inevitable Possibility under Capitalism." *Economic and Political Weekly,* 53(34):104–111.

Gutiérrez y Muhs, G., Niemann, Y. F., González, C. G. and Harris, A. P. (Eds.). (2012). *Presumed Incompetent: The Intersections of Race and Class for Women in Academia.* Logan, UT: Utah State University Press.

Habib. I. (2002). "Colonization of Indian Economy." In *Essays in Indian History: Towards a Marxist Perception,* South Asian Studies. London: Anthem Press.

Hadden, S. E. (2001). *Slave Patrols: Law and Violence in Virginia and the Carolinas.* Harvard Historical Studies. Quoted in Frank Joyce, "Are You Ready for Some Hard Truths about the Birth of our Nation? Brace Yourself." July 3, 2016. (https://www.alternet.org/2016/07/o-say-can-yo u-see).

Halder, S. (2017). "Terminators." April 5. *Amor Mundi* weekly newsletter from The Hannah Arendt Center for Politics and Humanities at Bard College, N.Y.

Haley, J. (2016). "Welcoming the Digital Residents." *New Internationalist,* September, 495:40–41.

Hall, G. (2016). *The Uberfication of the University.* Minneapolis, MN: University of Minnesota Press.

Hamill, J. (2016). "Spy Nation: US Navy 'discussed plans to fit human with microchips and track their every move'." *The Sun.* June 16. (https://www.thesun.co.uk/tech/1292761/us-navy-considers-plans-to-fit-humans-with-microchips-and-track-their-every-move).

Hancock, G. (1998). *Fingerprints of the Gods.* London, UK: William Heinemann Ltd.

Hancock, G. (2015), *The Magicians of the Gods: Forgotten Wisdom of Earth's Lost Civilization.* New York: St. Martin's Press.

Hancock, G. (2019). "America Before: The Key to Earth's Lost Civilizations." London: Hodder & Staughton Ltd.

Hansen, T. (2018). "The March for Science is Being Transformed by Indigenous Knowledge." April 20. (https://www.alternet.org/2018/04/march-science-being-transformed-indigenous-knowledge). Reproduced from *Yes Magazine.*

Harari, Y. N. (2014). *Sapiens: A Brief History of Humankind.* London: Harvill Secker.

Harari, Y. N. (2017). *Homo Deus: A Brief History of Tomorrow.* New York: Harper.

Haraway, D. (1988). "Situated Knowledges: The Science Question in Feminism and the Privileging of Partial Perspective." *Feminist Studies,* 14(3):575–599.

Häring, N. (2017a), "A Well Kept Open Secret: Washington is Behind India's Brutal Demonetization Project." January 1. (https://www.globalresearch.ca/a-well-kept-open-secret-washington-is-behind-indias-brutal-demonetization-project/5566247).

Häring, N. (2017b). "How India Became Bill Gates' Guinea Pig: Conspiracy As Recounted by the Main Actors." July 27. (https://countercurrents.org/2017/07/how-india-became-bill-gates-guinea-pig-a-conspiracy-as-recounted-by-the-main-actors).

Harley, B. and Woodward, D. (Eds.). (1992). *The History of Cartography.* Book One. *Cartography in the Traditional Islamic and South Asian Societies.* Volume II. Chicago, IL: Chicago University Press.

Harootunian, H. D. (2001). "Historical Materialism's Task in an 'Age of Globalization'." *Radical History Review,* Winter, 79:95–98.

Harris, F. R. (1958). *Jamsetji Nusserwanji Tata: A Chronicle of His Life.* (2nd ed.). London; Bombay: Blackie and Sons Ltd.

Harris, R. (2017). *Rigor Mortis: How Sloppy Science Creates Worthless Cures, Crushes Hope, and Wastes Billions.* New York: Basic Books.

Harriss, J. (1998). "Development Studies and the Development of India: An Awkward Case?" *Oxford Development Studies,* 26(3):287–309.

Harriss, J. (2001). "Public Action and the Dialectics of Decentralisation: Against the Myth of Social Capital as 'the Missing Link in Development'." *Social Scientist*, Nov–Dec. 29(11/12):25–40.

Harvey, D. (1989). *The Urban Experience*. Baltimore, MD: John Hopkins University Press.

Hattam, V. C. (1992). "Institutions and Political Change: Working Class Formation in England and the United States, 1820–1895." *Politics and Society*, 20(2):133–166.

Hathaway, W. T. (2015). "Hacking Consciousness: Stanford University Video Series." Review.March 10. (https://www.countercurrents.org/hathaway100315.htm).

Haynes, J. (2008). *Development Studies*. Cambridge, UK ; Malden, MA: Polity Press.

Headrick, D. R. (1988). *The Tentacles of Progress: Technology Transfer in the Age of Imperialism, 1850–1940*. New York: Oxford University Press.

Hegde, B. M. (2017). "Science Needs to be Set Free for the Good of Mankind." April 10. (https://countercurrents.org/2017/04/science-needs-to-be-set-free-for-the-good-of-mankind).

Hegde, Z. (2018). "Is the US Government Developing Real-Life Super-soldiers, Wonder-Dog in New Research Program?" August 19. (globalresearch.ca/is-the-us-government-developing-real-life-supersoldier-wonder-dog-in-new-research-program/5651122).

Helleiner, E. (2015). "India and the Neglected Development Dimensions of Bretton Woods." *Economic and Political Weekly*, July 18, 50(29):31–39.

Heller, H. (2011). *The Birth of Capitalism: A Twenty-First Century Perspective*. London: Pluto Press.

Heredia, R. C. (2016). "Interrogating the Academy: Renegotiating the Terms of Discourse." *Economic and Political Weekly*, August 20, 51(34):18–21.

Herring, G. C. (2008). *From Colony to Superpower: U.S. Foreign Relations since 1776*. New York: Oxford University Press.

Hickelby, J. and Hickel, J. (2018). "How Britain Stole $45 Trillion From India and Lied About It." December 14. (http://www.informationclearinghouse.info/50774.htm).

Hirschman, A. O. (1958). *The Strategy of Economic Development*. New Haven, CT: Yale University Press.

Hobbs, M. (2014). "Stop Trying to Save the World: Big Ideas Are Destroying International Development." *The New Republic*. November 17. (https://newrepublic.com/article/120178/problem-international-development-and-plan-fix-it).

Hobsbawm, E. J. (1968). *Industry and Empire: An Economic History of Britain Since 1750*. Middlesex, NY. Penguin Books.

Hobson, J. M. (2004), *The Eastern Origins of Western Civilisation*. Cambridge, UK: Cambridge University Press.

Hodgskin, T. (1825). *Labour Defended Against the Claims of Capital*. (2nd ed.). London: Knight and Lacey.

Hofstadter, R. (1955). *The Age of Reform*. New York: Vintage Books.

Hogeland, W. (2012). *Founding Finance: How Debt, Speculation, Foreclosures, Protests, and Crackdowns Made Us a Nation*. Austin: Texas University Press.

Holloway, K. (2015a). "Mindfulness: Capitalism's New Favorite Tool for Maintaining the Status Quo." June 11. https://www.alternet.org/2015/07/mindfulness-capitalisms-new-favorite-tool-maintaining-status-quo).

Holloway, K. (2015b). "Why We're Sick and Tired of Wellness." August 11. (https://www.alternet.org/2015/08/why-were-sick-and-tired-wellness).

Holt, J. (1977). "Trade Unionism in the British and the US Steel Industries 1880–1914: A Comparative Study." *Labor History*, 18(1):4–35.

Hookes, D. (2015). "The Evolution of Information Systems: From the Big Bang to the Era of Globalisation."In Rodrigue et al. (Eds.), *From Big Bang to Galactic Civilizations: A Big History Anthology*. Delhi: Primus Books.

Hopkins, A. G. and Cain, P. J. (1986). "Gentlemanly Capitalism and British Expansion Overseas I. The Old Colonial System, 1688–1850." *The Economic History Review*, 2nd series, 39(4):501–525.

Hopkins, A. G. and Cain, P. J. (1987). "Gentlemanly Capitalism and British Expansion II: New Imperialism, 1850–1945." *The Economic History Review*, 2nd series, 40(1):1–26.

Horne, G. (2014). *The Counter Revolution of 1776: Slave Resistance and the Origins of the United States of America*. New York: New York University Press.

Horowitz, E. (2017). "This Company Wants to Measure Your Kid's Brainwaves." November 30. (https://www.alternet.org/2017/11/company-wants-measure-your-kids-brainwaves).

Horowitz, M. (2009). *Occult America: The Secret History of How Mysticism Shaped Our Nation.* New York: Bantam Books.

Hossein-Zadeh, I. (2015). "Who Owens the Federal Reserve Bank and Why is it Shrouded in Myths and Mysteries." December 18. (https://www.counterpunch.org/2015/12/18/who-owns-the-federal-reserve-bank-and-why-is-it-shrouded-in-myths-and-mysteries).

Hubbard, R. (N.d.). "The Mismeasure of the Gene." (www.councilforresponsiblegenetics.org/pageDocuments/0YA8FI5N1U.pdf).

Hull, J. P. (2003). "Working With Figures: Industrial Measurement as Hegemonic Discourse." *Left History*, Fall, 9(1):62–78.

Hunt, T. (2018). "This is the Everyday Mechanical Mechanism that Could Define Consciousness." November 17. (alternet.org/2018/11/everyday-mechanical-mechanism-could-define-consciousness).

Huntington, S. P. (1998). *The Clash of Civilizations and the Remaking of World Order.* London: Touchstone.

Hyde, C. K. (1977). *Technological Change and the British Iron Industry, 1700–1870.* NJ: Princeton University Press.

Ian, A. (2010). *The New Orientalists: Postmodern Representations of Islam from Foucault to Baudrillard.* London: L. B. Tauris & Co.

Ienca, M. (2017). "The Right to Cognitive Liberty." *Scientific American,* August, 317(2):10.

Igunma, J. (2019). "Christian Europe Once Celebrated the Story of Buddha Without Even Knowing It." July 4. (https://scroll.in/article/929297/christian-europe-once-celebrated-the-story-of-buddha-without-even-knowing-it).

Italie, L. (2018). "Fashion Art Installation Questions What it Means to be You." September 5. (https://www.apnews.com/9e54ba075f914684ace1a6ac811e1a3f).

Iyer, G. S. (1903). *Some Economic Aspects of British Rule in India.* Madras (now Chennai): Swadesamitran Press.

Iyer, M. S. (2011). "Decolonizing of Knowledge System," *Economic and Political Weekly.* July 23, 46(30):17–20.

Jackson, T. (2009). *Prosperity without Growth: Economics for a Finite Planet.* London: Earthscan.

Jacob, M. (1981), *The Radical Enlightenment: Pantheists, Freemasons and Republicans.* London: George Allen & Unwin.

Jain, A. R. (2015). *Selling Yoga: From Counterculture to Pop Culture.* New York: Oxford University Press.

James, P. J. (2017). "Note to the Debate on People's Development Paradigm." June 21. (https://countercurrents.org/2017/06/note-to-the-debate-on-peoples-development-paradigm).

Jangam, C. (2015). "Politics of Identity and the Project of Writing History in Postcolonial India: A Dalit Critique." *Economic and Political Weekly,* 50(40):63–70.

Jangam, C. (2016). "What is at Stake in Rewriting California School Textbooks." *Economic and Political Weekly,* 51(29):18–21.

Janson, J. (2016). "Celebrate 260 Years of Profitable Genocide—African Slaves, Native Americans, Mexicans, Filipinos, etc." July 4. (countercurrents.org/2016/07/celebrate-260-years-profitable-genocide-african-slaves-native-americans-mexicans-filipinos-etc).

Jayawardhna, J. (2015). "Our Cosmic Selves." *The New York Times.* Sunday Review. April 3. (https://www.nytimes.com/2015/04/05/opinion/sunday/our-cosmic-selves.html?ref=todayspaper).

John, M. E. (2017). "The Woman Question: Reflections on Feminism and Marxism." *Economic and Political Weekly,* December 16, 52(50):71–79.

Johnson, A. (2016). "Fairness and Accuracy in Reporting." (FAIR) Readers Supported News. July 25.

Johnson, S. (2010). *Where Good Ideas Come From: The Natural History of Innovation.* New York: Riverhead Books.

Johnson, W. A. (1966). *The Steel Industry of India.* Cambridge, MA: Harvard University Press.

Joll, J. (1990). *Europe Since 1870: An International History.* (4th ed.). (First published in

1973). London: Penguin Books.
Joll, J. (1989). *The Origins of the First World War.* (1984 reprint 1989.). London: Longman.
Josephson, M. (1962). *The Robber Barons: The Great American Capitalists 1861–1901.* London: Eyre & Spottiswoode.
Joyce, F. (2016). "Exposing America's Hidden Past As a Center for the Slave-Breeding Industry." September 12. (alternet.org/2016/09/finally-our-true-history-being-revealed).
Juluri, V. (2016). "California Textbooks Issue: A Response." *Economic and Political Weekly,* August 13, 51(31):86–89.
Kaiwar, V. (2015). *The Postcolonial Orient: The Politics of Difference and the Project of Provincialising Europe.* Chicago: Haymarket Books.
Kapoor, I. (2008). *The Postcolonial Politics of Development.* London: Routledge.
Kasbekar, S. R. (2017). "Congress Must Come Back," (Letter to Editor). *Economic and Political Weekly,* June 17, 52(24):4–5.
Kasson, F. J. (1976). "Republican Values as Dynamic Factor." In (Ed.). Gary J. Kornblith (1998), *Problem in American Civilization: The Industrial Revolution in America.* Boston: Houghton Mifflin Co.
Kauffman, S. (1996). *At Home in the Universe: The Search for the Laws of Self-Organization and Complexity.* Oxford, UK: Oxford University Press.
Kaul, V. (2013). *Easy Money: Evolution of Money from Robinson Crusoe to the First World War.* New Delhi: SAGE Publications.
Keenan, J. L. (1943). *A Steel Man in India.* New York: Duell, Sloan and Pearce.
Kenwood, A. G. and Lougheed, A. L. (1971). *The Growth of the International Economy, 1820–1990: An Introductory Text.* London: Routledge.
Kennedy, P. M. (1988). *The War Plan of the Great Powers, 1880–1914.* Boston: Unwin Hyman.
Kheel, M. (1989). "From Healing Herbs to Deadly Drugs: Western Medicine's War Against the Natural World." In Judith Plant (Ed.), *Healing the Wounds: The Promise of Ecofeminism.* Philadelphia, PA: New Society Publishers.
Kiely, R. (1994). "Development Theory and Industrialisation: Beyond the Impasse." *Journal of Contemporary Asia.* 24(2):133–160.
Kiely, R. (1999). "The Last Refuge of the Noble Savage? A Critical Assessment of Post-Development Theory." *European Journal of Development Research,* 11(1):30–55.
Kimmelman, M. (2014). "Refugee Camp for Syrians in Jordan Evolves as a Do-it-Yourself City." *New York Times.* July 4. (nytimes.com/2014/07/05/world/middleeast/zaatari-refugee-camp-in-jordan-evolves-as-a-do-it-yourself-city.html).
Kin Chi, L. (2018). "A Subaltern Perspective on China's Ecological Crisis." *Monthly Review,* October, 70(5):45–57.
King, R. (2015). "Is there a Limit to the System?" In Rodrigue et al. (Eds.), *Our Place in the Universe: An Introduction to Big History (From Big Bang to Galactic Civilizations: a Big History Anthology).* Vol I. Delhi: Primus Books.
Kitsantonis, N. (2017). "Anarchists Fill Services Void Left by Faltering Greek Governance." *The New York Times.* May 22. (https://www.nytimes.com/2017/05/22/world/europe/greece-athens-anarchy-austerity.html).
Klein, N. (2003). "No Peace Without a Fight." *The Nation.* March 13. (https://www.thenation.com/article/no-peace-without-fight/).
Klein, N. (2015). "This Changes Everything." Film. (https://thischangeseverything.org/the-documentary).
Knapton, S. (2017). "Europe Was the Birthplace of Mankind, Not Africa, Scientists Find." *The Telegraph.* May 22. (https://www.telegraph.co.uk/science/2017/05/22/europe-birthplace-mankind-not-africa-scientists-find).
Knight, F. (1932). "The Newer Economics and the Control of Economic Activity." *Journal of Political Economy,* 40(4):433–376.
Koch, C. (2016). "Does Complexity = Consciousness?" *Shambala Sun: Lion's Roar.* July. pp. 15–16.
Koepping, K. P. (1983). *Adopf Bastian and the Psychic Unity of Mankind: The Foundation of Anthropology in Nineteenth Century Germany.* St. Lucia: University of Queensland Press.

Kofas, J. (2017). "Artificial Intelligence: Socioeconomic, Political and Ethical Dimensions." April, 25. (globalresearch.ca/artificial-intelligence-socioeconomic-political-and-ethical-dimensions).

Kole, W. J. (2016). "How do You Teach Human Interaction to a Robot? Lots of TV." June 23. (https://www.southcoasttoday.com/news/20160623/how-do-you-teach-human-interaction-to-robot-lots-of-tv).

Kornblith, G. J. (Ed.). (1998). *Problem in American Civilization: The Industrial Revolution in America*. Boston: Houghton Mifflin Co.

Kornblith, G. J. (1998). "The Entrepreneurial Ethics." In Kornblith (Ed.), *Problems in American Civilization: The Industrial Revolution in America*. Boston: Houghton Mifflin Co.

Korybko, A. (2018). "Security and Counter-Intelligence: Pakistan's New Regulations Regarding International NGOs." December 27. (https://www.globalresearch.ca/security-and-counter-intelligence-pakistans-new-regulations-regarding-international-ngos/5663914).

Kumar, A. and Dar, F. A. (2015). "Marginality and Historiography: The Case of Kashmir's History." *Economic and Political Weekly*, 50(39):37–44.

Kumar, A. P. (2016). "Supreme Court's Schizophrenic Approach to Land Acquisition." *Economic and Political Weekly*, 51(38): 10–11.

Kumar, P. J. D. (2016). "Intellectual Analysis of Religion." Letter to Editor. *Economic and Political Weekly*, 51(33).

Kundu, S. (2018). "From Kanaiyah Kumar to Jignesh Mewani ..." February 13. (https://countercurrents.org/2018/02/kanaiyah-kumar-jignesh-mewani).

Kuppuram, G. and Kumudamani, K. (1990). *History of Science and Technology in India*. 12 Volumes. Delhi: Sundeep Prakashan.

Kymlicka, W. (2012). "Neoliberal Multiculturalism?" (https://www.researchgate.net/profile/Will_Kymlicka/publication/286836153_Neoliberal_multiculturalism/links/59f2993b458515bfd081d9cb/Neoliberal-multiculturalism.pdf)

Lachmann, R. (1987). *From Manor to Market: Structural Change in England, 1536–1649*. Madison, WI: University of Wisconsin Press.

Lachmann, R. (2000). *Capitalists In Spite of Themselves: Elite Conflict and Economic Transitions in Early Modern Europe*. New York: Oxford University Press.

Lachmann, R. (2013). *What is Historical Sociology*? Cambridge, UK: Polity Press.

Lal, V. and Nandy, A. (2005). *The Future of Knowledge and Culture: A Dictionary for the 21st Century*. New Delhi: Penguin Viking.

Lal, V. and Rajan, R. (eds). (2016). *India and the Unthinkable: Backwaters Collective on Metaphysics and Politics*. New Delhi: Oxford University Press.

Landes, D. S. (1969). *The Unbound Prometheus: Technological Change and Industrial Development in Western Europe from 1750 to the Present*. Cambridge, UK: Cambridge University Press.

Landes, D. S. (1998). *The Wealth and Poverty of Nations: Why Some are So Rich and Some So Poor*. New York: W. W. Norton & Company.

Landes, D. S. and Mokyer, J. (2010). *The Invention of Enterprise: Entrepreneurship from Ancient Mesopotamia to Modern Time*. Princeton, NJ: Princeton University Press.

Lasn, K. (2012). "The Unofficial History of America." (https://www.filmsforaction.org/news/the-unofficial-history-of-america).

Latham, A. J. H. (1978). *The International Economy and the Underdeveloped World, 1865–1914*. London: Croom Helm.

Lee, R. (2004a), "The 'Culture Wars' and the 'Science Wars'." In R. E. Lee and I. Wallerstein (Eds.), *Overcoming the Two Cultures: Science Versus the Humanities in the Modern World-System*. Boulder, CO: Paradigm Publishers.

Lee, R. (2004b), "Complexity Studies." In R. E. Lee and I. Wallerstein (Eds.), *Overcoming the Two Cultures: Science Versus the Humanities in the Modern World-System*. Boulder, CO: Paradigm Publishers.

Lehmann, C. (2018). "Camilla Paglia: It's Time for a new Map of Gender World." *Quillette*, November 10. (https://quillette.com/2018/11/10/camille-paglia-its-time-for-a-new-map-of-the-gender-world).

Lehmann, D. (1997). "An Opportunity Lost: Escobar's Deconstruction of Development."

The Journal of Development Studies, 33(4):568–578.

Lenin, V. I. (1975). *Collected Works*. Moscow: Progress Publishers.

Lenton, T. (2016). *Earth System Science: A Very Short Introduction*. Oxford, UK: Oxford University Press.

Lepore, J. (2013). *The Mansion of Happiness: A History of Life and Death*. New York: Vintage Books.

Levine, B. (2012). "Roots of US Capitalism." Book Review. *Against the Current,* January–February, 156:35–39.

Levites, A. (2017). "Can the 'Spiritual Left' Make the Change They Wish to See." April 9. (http://religiondispatches.org/can-the-spiritual-left-make-the-change-they-wish-to-see).

Lie, J. (1993). "Visualizing the Invisible Hand: The Social Origins of 'Market Society' in England, 1550–1750." *Politics and Society,* 21(3):275–305.

Lieten, G. K. (2002). "Faltering Development and the Post-modernist Discourse." *Social Scientist*, 30(7/8):67–83.

Lowenberg, J. S. and Davis, F. (1994). "Beyond Medicalisation-Demedicalisation: The Case of Holistic Health." *Sociology of Health and Illness*, 16(5):579–599.

Ludden, D. (Ed.). (2003). *Reading Subaltern Studies: Perspectives on History, Society and Culture in South Asia.* Delhi: Oxford University Press.

Lukacs, M. (2015). "Noam Chomsky Slams Canada's Shale Gas Energy Plan." *Guardian*. November 1.

Lummis, C. D. (2005). "Marxism." In Lal, V. and Nandy, A. (2005) *The Future of Knowledge and Culture: A Dictionary for the 21st Century*, pp. 175–179. New Delhi: Viking Penguin.

Lyashchenko, P. I. (1949). *History of the National Economy of Russia to 1917 Revolution*. New York: The Macmillan Company.

Lyubomirsky. S. (2008). *The Myth of Happiness: What Should Make You Happy, but Doesn't, What Shouldn't Make You Happy, but Does*. New York: Penguin Books.

Maclean, B. (2017). "No Pink Wooly Caps for Me." February 9. (https://www.counterpunch.org/2017/02/09/90368).

Maddison, A. (2007). *The World Economy, Vol. I: A Millennial Perspective ; Vol II: Historical Statistics*. OECD, Indian Edition.

Maheshvarananda, D. (2004), *After Capitalism: Prout's Vision for a New World*. Washington D.C. : Proutist Universal Publications.

Mahurkar, U. and Parihar, R. (1999). "Miracle of Water." *India Today,* June 7, pp. 42–45.

Malhotra, R. (2011). *Being Different: An Indian Challenge to Western Universalism*. New Delhi: HarperCollins Publishers India ; The India Today Group.

Malhotra, R. (2014). *Indra's Net: Defending Hinduism's Philosophical Unity*. New Delhi: HarperCollins Publishers India.

Mandavilli, A. (2016). "India's Government is Becoming Increasingly Anti-Science." *Scientific American,* Feb. 3. (blogs.scientificamerican.com/guest-blog/india-s-government-is-becoming-increasingly-antiscience).

Mann, C. C. (2005). *1491: New Revelations of the Americas before Columbus*. New York: Vintage Books.

Mann, M. (1993). *The Source of Social Power: The Rise of Classes and Nation States, 1760–1914*. Volume II. Cambridge, UK: Cambridge University Press.

Marean, C. (2015). "The Most Invasive Species of All." *Scientific American,* 313(2):33–39.

Marrs, J. (2001). *Rule by Secrecy: The Hidden History that Connects the Trilateral Commission, Freemasons, and the Great Pyramids*. New York: HarperCollins.

Marx, K. (1959). *Economic and Philosophical Manuscripts of 1844*. M. Milligan (Trans.). Moscow: Progressive Publishers.

Marx, K. (1974). *Early Writings*. R. Livingstone and G. Benton (Trans.). London: Penguin Books.

Mathias, P. (1990). *The First Industrial Nation: The Economic History of Britain, 1700–1914*. (2nd ed.). London ; New York: Routledge.

Matthews, J. V. (1991). *Toward a New Society: American Thought and Culture, 1800–1830*. Boston: Twayne Publishers.

Matthews, D. (2019). "Capitalism and Mental Health." *Monthly Review*, January. 70(8):49–62.

McCaffrey, S.P. (1996). *The Politics of Industrialization in Tsarist Russia: The Association of Southern Coal and Steel Producers, 1874–1914.* DeKalb, IL: Northern Illinois University Press.

McCaffray, S. P. and Melancon, M. (Eds.). (2005). *Russia in the European Context 1789–1914: A Member of the Family.* New York: Palgrave MacMillan.

McCraw, T. K. (Ed.). (1988). *The Essential Alfred Chandler: Essays Toward a Historical Theory of Big Business.* Boston, MA: Harvard Business School Press.

McEachern, D. (1980). *The Class Against Itself: Power and the Nationalization of British Steel Industry.* Cambridge, UK: Cambridge University Press.

McGuire, J. (1988). "The World Economy, The Colonial State and the Establishment of the Indian National Congress." In Shepperdson, M. and Simmons, E. (Eds.), *The Indian National Congress and the Political Economy of India, 1885–1985.* England: Avebury.

McKay, J. P. (1970). *Pioneers for Profit: Foreign Entrepreneurship and Russian Industrialization, 1885–1913.* Chicago, IL: University of Chicago Press.

McKendrick, N., Brewer, J. and Plumb, J. H. (1982). *The Birth of the Consumer Society: The Commercialization of Eighteenth-Century England.* Bloomington, IN: Indiana University Press.

McMichael, P. (1984). *Settlers and the Agrarian Question: Foundation of Capitalism in Colonial Australia.* Cambridge, UK: Cambridge University Press.

Meek, D. (2018). "Cracks in the Wall of Capitalism: The Zapatistas and the Struggle to Decolonize Science." March 17. (https://countercurrents.org/2018/03/cracks-in-the-wall-of-capitalism-the-zapatistas-and-the-struggle-to-decolonize-science).

Mehta, U. S. (1999). *Liberalism and Empire: A Study in Nineteenth-Century British Liberal Thought.* Chicago, IL: Chicago University Press.

Menand, L. (2016). "Karl Marx, Yesterday and Today." *New Yorker.* October 10. (https://www.newyorker.com/magazine/2016/10/10/karl-marx-yesterday-and-today).

Menocal, M. R. (2002). "A Golden Reign of Tolerance." *The New York Times.* March 28. (https://www.nytimes.com/2002/03/28/opinion/a-golden-reign-of-tolerance.html).

Merton, R. K. (1976). "The Unanticipated Consequences of Purposive Social Action." In *American Sociological Review,* 1(6), 894–904.

Mills, C. W. (1958). "Psychology and Social Science." *Monthly Review* (October). Reprint December 2009, 61(7):47–52.

Mintz, S. W. (1988). "The Power of Sweetness and the Sweetness of Power." 8th Duijker Lecture. Quoted in Wallerstein, 1989. Deventer, Netherlands: Van Loghum Slaterus.

Mirkovic, A. (2015). "The Real End of History." In B. Rodrigue et al. (Eds.), *From Big Bang to Galactic Civilizations: A Big History Anthology, Volume 1, Our Place in the Universe: An Introduction to Big History.* Delhi: Primus Books.

Misa, T. J. (1995). *A Nation of Steel: the Making of Modern America, 1865–1925.* Baltimore, MD: John Hopkins University Press.

Mishra, V. N. and Argullol, R. (2008). *From the Ganges to the Mediterranean: A Dialogue Between the Cultures of India and Europe.* Gurgaon, India: Shubhi Publications.

Mitchell, B. R. and Deane, P. (1962). *Abstract of British Historical Statistics.* Cambridge, UK: Cambridge University Press.

Mokyr, J. (1976). *Industrialization in the Low Countries, 1795–1850.* New Haven, CT: Yale University Press.

Mokyr, J. (1990). *The Lever of Riches: Technological Creativity and Economic Progress.* New York: Oxford University Press.

Mokyr, J. (1990). *Twenty-Five Centuries of Technological Change: An Historical Survey.* London: Routledge.

Mokyr, J. (2005). "The Intellectual Origins of Modern Economic Growth." *The Journal of Economic History,* 65:285–351.

Mokyr, J. (2009). *The Enlightened Economy: An Economic History of Britain 1700–1850.* New Haven, CT: Yale University Press.

Mokyr, J. (2016). *A Culture of Growth: The Origins of the Modern Economy.* Princeton, NJ: Princeton University Press.

Momo, S. (Ed.). (2013). "Mesoeconomy and the Clean Code." Editorial in *SPANDA Journal, Nonprofit & Anarchy: An Emerging Affair,* IV, v-xii.

Mongardini, C. (1990). "The Decadence of Modernity: The Delusions of Progress and the Search for Historical Consciousness." In J. Alexander and P. Sztompka (Eds.), *Rethinking Progress: Movements, Forces, and Ideas at the End of the 20th Century*. Boston: Unwin Hyman.

Montgomery, D. (1987). *The Fall of the House of Labor: The Workplace, the State, and American Labor Activism, 1865–1925*. Cambridge, UK: Cambridge University Press.

Montgomery, D. (1998). "The Struggle for Control of Production." In G. Kornblith (Ed.), *Problems in American Civilization: The Industrial Revolution in America*. Boston, MA: Houghton Mifflin Co.

Moore, J. W. (2015). *Capitalism in the Web of Life*. London: Verso.

Moore, R. (2018). "Cult Violence and More: We Need to Stop using the Word 'Brainwashed' to Understand People's Actions." July 21. (https://scroll.in/article/887176/cult-violence-and-more-we-need-to-stop-using-the-word-brainwashed-to-understand-peoples-actions).

Morris, M. D. (1963). "Towards a Re-interpretation of Nineteenth-Century Indian Economic History." *Journal of Economic History*, 23(4):606–618.

Morris, M. D. et al., (Eds.). (1969). *Indian Economy in the Nineteenth Century*. Delhi: Indian Economic and Social History Association.

Morris, M. D. (1987). "Indian Industry and Business in the Age of Laissez Faire." In D. Tripathi (Ed.), *State and Business in India: A Historical Perspective*. Delhi: Manohar.

Morus, I. (2018). "Why Thomas Edison's Legacy is Being Questioned—and Why That's a Lesson for America." July 14. (https://scroll.in/article/886304/why-thomas-edisons-legacy-is-being-questioned-and-why-thats-a-lesson-for-america).

Mourad, S. (2018). "Modern View of Crusades as a Clash Between Islam and Christianity Ignores Stories of Co-Existence." July 17. (https://scroll.in/article/886455/modern-view-of-crusades-as-a-clash-between-islam-and-christianity-ignores-stories-of-co-existence).

Moyn, S. (2015). "New Old Things." *The Nation*, February 9, 27–32.

Mukharji, P. B. (2016). *Doctoring Traditions: Ayurveda, Small Technologies, and Braided Science.* Chicago ; London: The University of Chicago Press.

Mukherjee, A. (2008). "The Return of the Colonial in Indian Economic History: The Last Phase of Colonialism in India. *Social Scientist,* 36(3/4):3–44.

Mukherjee, A. (2010). "Empire: How Colonial India Made Modern Britain." *Economic and Political Weekly,* December 11, 45(50):73–82.

Mukherjee, R. (1974). *The Rise and Fall of the East India Company: A Sociological Appraisal.* New York: Monthly Review Press.

Mukherjee, R. (1991). *Society, Culture, Development*. Delhi: SAGE Publications.

Mukherjee, R. (2009). *Why Unitary Social Science*? Tyne, UK: Cambridge Scholars Publishing.

Mukherji, N. (2015). "Education for the Species." *Economic and Political Weekly,* (51)32:30–35.

Mullen, J. (2016). "September 11, 2001: 9/11, The Day the Laws of Physics were Suspended. We Were Told 'People Hating our Freedoms, Attacked the Centers of American Power'." September 13. (https://www.globalresearch.ca/september-11-2001-911-the-day-the-laws-of-physics-were-suspended-we-were-told-people-hating-our-freedoms-attacked-the-centers-of-american-power/5545511).

Mumford, L. (1967). *The Myth of Machine: Technics and Human Development,* Vol. 1. New York: Harcourt Brace Jovanovich.

Mumford, L. (1970). *The Myth of the Machine: The Pentagon of Power*, Vol. II. San Diego, CA: Harvest Books.

Nanda, M. (1997). "Against Social De(con)struction of Science: Cautionary Tales from the Third World." *Monthly Review* (March): 1–20.

Nanda, M. (2005). "Intellectual Treason." January 7. (https://newhumanist.org.uk/articles/827/intellectual-treason).

Nanda, M. (2006). "How Modern Are we? Cultural Contradictions of India's Modernity." *Economic & Political Weekly*, 41(6):491–96.

Nanda, M. (2008). "God Delusion at Work: My Indian Travel Diary." *Economic & Political Weekly,* 43(42):15–19.

Nandy, A. (1990). "The Politics of Secularism and the Recovery of Religious Tolerance." In Veena Das (Ed.), *Mirrors of Violence: Communities, Riots and Survivors in South Asia.*

Delhi: OUP.

Nandy, A. (2012). "The Idea of Happiness." *Economic & Political Weekly*. 47(2):45–48.

Naoroji, D. (1901). *Poverty and UnBritish Rule in India*. London: G. A. Nateson and Co.

Nasr, S. H. (1976), *Islamic Science: An Illustrated Study*. London: World of Islam Festival Publishing Co.

Navin, T. (2016). "Una March: Challenging the Caste Barriers." August 17. countercurrents.org/2016/08/una-march-challenging-the-caste-barriers).

Nederveen, P. J. (2010). *Development Theory*. (2nd ed.). (Published in association with Theory, Culture & Society). Los Angeles: SAGE Publications.

Needham, J. (1954–2004). *Science and Civilisation in China,* (Seven Volumes). Cambridge, UK: Cambridge University Press.

Neergard, L. (2016). "Not Just Scribbles: How Tots Start Learning Text is Symbolic." January 6. (https://www.pbs.org/newshour/health/not-just-scribbles-how-tots-start-learning-text-is-symbolic).

Newberg, A. B., D'Aquili, E. G. and Rause, V. (2001). *Why God Won't Go Away: Brain Science and the Biology of Belief.* New York: Ballantine Books.

"News from Kolkata." (2016). *Times of India,* February 25.

Nicholas, G. (2018). "After Thousands of Years, Western Science is Slowly Catching up to Indigenous Knowledge." Feb. 26. (www.yesmagazine.org/people-power/after-thousands-of-years-western-science-is-slowly-catching-up-to-indigenous-knowledge-20180226).

Nigam, A. (2007). "Genealogies of Globalisation: Unpacking the 'Universal' History of Capital." *Economic and Political Weekly,* 42(12):1047–1053.

Nigam, A. (2009). "Democracy, State and Capital: The 'Unthought' of 20th Century Marxism." *Economic and Political Weekly,* 44(51):35–39.

Nigam, A. (2011). *Desire Named Development.* Delhi: Penguin Books.

Nissami, M. (2016). "The Russian Phoenix: Hope or Illusion?" (InformationClearingHouse.info/article44167.htm). February 9.

Nitesh, R. (2015). "International Yoga Day: Yoga Must Reach to Gandhi's 'Last Person'." June 20. (https://www.countercurrents.org/nitesh200615.htm).

Noble, D. F. (1979). *America by Design: Science, Technology, and The Rise of Corporate Capitalism.* Oxford, UK: Oxford University Press.

Noonan, J. (2012). "Black Children Less Likely to Get Pain Meds in ER." April 30. (https://abcnews.go.com/Health/Wellness/black-children-pain-meds-er/story?id=16231146).

Norgaard, R. (2015). "The Church of Economism and Its Discontents." December 30. (https://www.countercurrents.org/norgaard301215.htm).

Norsigian, J. (2011). *Our Bodies, Ourselves.* The Boston Women's Health Book Collective. Touchstone.

Northcote , J. (2007). *The Paranormal and the Politics of Truth: A Sociological Account*. Exeter, UK ; Charlottesville, VA : Imprint Academic.

Nour, A. (2018). "Fighting for Survival: Whither Modern Civilization?" July 18. (https://countercurrents.org/2018/07/fighting-for-survival-whither-modern-civilization).

Novak, M. (2012). "Why We Help: The Evolution of Cooperation." *Scientific American,* 307(1):34–39.

Oak, A. (2019). "Reason Does Not Make Us Ethical ... We Must Believe in Miracles, Too." Interview with Manash Firaq Bhattacharjee. June 30. (https://thewire.in/books/rightwing-nationalism-india-manash-firaq-bhattacharjee).

Olga, C. (1960). "French Investment in Russian Joint Stock Companies, 1894–1914." *Business History,* 2(1–2):75–90.

Omoniyi, T. and Gupta, S. (Eds.). (2007). *The Culture of Economic Migration: International Perspectives*. Aldershot, UK: Ashgate.

Oonk, G. (N.d.). "Industrialisation in India, 1850–1947: Three Variations in the Emergence of Indigenous Industrialists." Viewed on 12/27/14. (www.researchgate.net/publication/242148417_Industrialisation_in_India_1850-1947_Three_Variations_in_the_Emergence_of_Indigenous_Industrialists).

Oweiss, I. M. (N.d.). "Ibn Khaldun: The Father of Economics." (http://faculty.georgetown.

edu/imo3/ibn.htm).

Owen, T. C. (1981). *Capitalism and Politics in Russia: A Social History of the Moscow Merchants, 1855–1905.* Cambridge, UK. Cambridge University Press.

Owens, W. R. and Furbank, P. N. (Eds.). (2001). *Writing on Travel, Discovery and History by Daniel Defoe*. London: Pickering and Chatto.

Padmanabhan, S. (2006). "Debate on Indian History: Revisiting Textbooks in California." *Economic and Political Weekly*, 41(18):1761–1763.

Palat, M. K. (1988). "Tsarist Russian Imperialism." *Studies in History,* 4(1/2):157–297. Jawaharlal Nehru University. Centre for Historical Studies, SAGE Publications.

Pandey, A. (2015). "A Deeper Look at Vedic History Suggest A Tribal Melting Pot That May Surprise the Hindu Nationalist." March 26. (https://www.countercurrents.org/pandey260315.htm).

Pandey, S. (2018). "Why Does RSS-BJP Not Like These Hindu Monks?" July 23. (https://countercurrents.org/2018/07/why-does-rss-bjp-not-like-these-hindu-monks).

Panne, V. V. (2017). "Detroit's Underground Economy: Where Capitalism Fails, Alternatives Take Roots." July 6. (https://www.alternet.org/2017/07/detroit-alternative-economy).

Parliamentary Debates from the Year 1803 to the Present Time. Vol. 25 [March 11–May 10, 1913] Debates in the House of Lords / Marquis Wellesley's motion for the production of certain papers on East India affairs, April 9, 1813.

Parramor, L. S. (2016). "The Zentrepreneur: Ayn Rand in Lotus Position?" August 30. (https://www.alternet.org/2016/08/beware-zen-entrepreneur-they-may-be-hyped-hustlers-picking-pockets-hapless-consumers-purpose).

Parry, M. (2018). "In Defense of 'Conspiracy Theories': From 'Fake News' to the Art World." December 2. (www.globalresearch.ca/in-defense-of-conspiracy-theories-from-fake-news-to-the-art-world/5661632).

Parthasarathi, P. (2011). *Why Europe Grew Rich and Asia Did Not: Global Economic Divergence, 1600–1850.* Cambridge, UK: Cambridge University Press.

Patel, S. (2006). "Beyond Binaries: A Case of Self-reflexive Sociologies." *Current Sociology,* 54(3):381–395.

Patel, S. (2016). "The Challenge of Doing Sociology Today." *Economic and Political Weekly,* 51(46):33–40.

Patnaik, P. (2011). *Re-Envisioning Socialism*. New Delhi: Tulika

Patnaik, P. (2018). "Capitalism's Discourse on "Development." (Originally published in *People's Democracy,* July 20, 2018). August 2. (https://mronline.org/2018/08/02/capitalisms-discourse-on-development).

Patnaik, U. (2017a). "Drain of Wealth in British India." Discussion Forum. April 8. New Delhi. Jawaharlal Nehru University. Center for Informal Sector and Labour Studies. This article is also published in Banerjee and Chandrashekar, (Eds.). (2018), *Dispossession, Deprivation, and Development: Essays for Utsa Patnaik.* New York: Columbia University Press.

Patnaik, U. (2017b). "Revisiting the 'Drain', or Transfer from India to Britain in the Context of Global Diffusion of Capitalism." In S. Chakrabarti and U. Patnaik (Eds.), *Agrarian and Other Histories: Essays for Binay Bhushan Chaudhuri.* New Delhi: Tulika Books.

Patten, T. (2018). "What it Really Means to be 'Woke': Radical Activism is Spiritual as Well as Political." March 12. (https://www.alternet.org/2018/03/now-time-woke-radical-evolutionary-activism-spiritual-political).

Payne, P. L. (1967), "The Emergence of the Large-Scale Company in Great Britain, 1870–1914." *The Economic History Review,* 20(3):519–542.

Pearson, T. (2019). "Everything the Western Mainstream Media Outlets Get Wrong When Covering Poor Countries." January 9. (https://www.globalresearch.ca/everything-western-mainstream-media-outlets-get-wrong-covering-poor-countries/5665056).

Penny, L. (2016). "Life-Hacks of the Poor and Aimless." July 8. (https://thebaffler.com/war-of-nerves/laurie-penny-self-care).

Perkins, J. (2004), *Confessions of an Economic Hit Man*. New York: A Plume Book.

Peterson, C. (2012). *Pursuing the Good Life: 1000 Reflections on Positive Psychology*. Oxford, UK: Oxford University Press.

Petras, J. (2017). "Independence and Self-Determination: Weapons for Empire Building or National Liberation ?" October 20. (https://www.globalresearch.ca/independence-and-self-determination-weapons-for-empire-building-or-national-liberation/5614218).

Pieri, M. (2008). "Mind-Body Dualism/Unity in Medicine." April 10. (https://serendipstudio.org/exchange/molly-pieri/mind-body-dualismunity-medicine).

Pierscioneck, T. (2018). "How Identity Politics Makes the Left Lose its Collective Identity." August 9. (https://www.globalresearch.ca/how-identity-politics-makes-the-left-lose-its-collective-identity/5650112).

Pilger, J. (2016). "Silencing America As It Prepares for War." July 9. (informationclearinghouse.info/article45196.htm).

Plekhanov, G. V. (1947). The *Development of the Monist View of History*. London: Lawrence and Wishart.

Plant, S. J. (2009). "International Development and Belief in Progress." *Journal of International Development*. 21(6):844–55.

Pollin, R. (2018). "De-Growth vs A Green New Deal." *New Left Review*, Issue 112. July/August. (newleftreview.org/issues/II112/articles/robert-pollin-de-growth-vs-a-green-new-deal).

Polya, G. (2018). "Legacy of Colonialism: Britain Robbed India of $45 Trillion and Thence 1.8 Billion Indians Died from Deprivation." December 18. (https://www.globalresearch.ca/legacy-of-colonialism-britain-robbed-india-of-45-trillion-and-thence-1-8-billion-indians-died-from-deprivation/5663351).

Porter, R. (1990). *English Society in the Eighteenth Century*. London: Penguin Books.

Posner, L. (2018). "Corporations Do Damage to Poor Women with their Global Philanthropy." March 31. (https://www.alternet.org/2018/03/corporations-do-damage-poor-women-their-global-philanthropy/).

Post, C. (2011). *The American Road to Capitalism: Studies in Class Structure, Economic Development and Political Conflict, 1627–1877*. Leiden, Netherlands: Brill.

Prak, M. (2000). *Early Modern Capitalism*: *Economic Change in Europe, 1400–1800*. London: Routledge.

Prashad, V. (2001). *Untouchable Freedom: A Social History of a Dalit Community*. New Delhi: Oxford University Press.

Price, R. (1999). *British Society 1680–1880: Dynamism, Containment and Change*. Cambridge, UK: Cambridge University Press.

Prigogine, I. (1980). *From Being to Becoming: Time and Complexity in the Physical Sciences*. San Francisco: W. H. Freeman & Co.

Prigogine, I. and Stengers, I. (1984). *Order out of Chaos: Man's New Dialogue with Nature*. Toronto: Bantam Books.

Prigogine, I. and Stengers, I. (1979). *La Nouvelle Alliance*. Paris Gallimard. Quoted in Immanuel Wallerstein: *Geopolitics and Geoculture: Essays on the Changing World-System*, Cambridge, UK: Cambridge University Press, 1997.

Pomerantsev, P. (2016). "Why We're Post-Fact." *Granta*, July 20. (https://granta.com/why-we're-post-fact).

Pugh, A. (1951). *Men of Steel*. London: Iron and Steel Trades Confederation.

Pujol, O. (N.d.). *Six Images of India*. New Delhi. India International Center. Occasional Publication 7. Posted at svabhinava.org, November 3, 2018. (http://www.svabhinava.org/HinduCivilization/OscarPujol/India6Images-frame.php).

Purser, R. and Edwin, N. G. (2015). "Corporate Mindfulness is B.S." September 28. (https://www.alternet.org/2015/09/corporate-mindfulness-bs).

Quack, J. (2012). *Disenchanting India: Organized Rationalism and Criticism of Religion In India*. New York: Oxford University Press.

Quigley, C. (1966). *Tragedy and Hope: A History of the World in Our Time*. New York: MacMillan.

Quigley, C. (1981). *The Anglo-American Establishment*. New York: Books in Focus.

Quinn, D. (1995). *Ishmael*. New York: Bantam Books.

Raeff, M. (1983). *The Well-Ordered Police State: Social and Institutional Change Through Law in the Germanies and Russia 1600–1800*. New Haven, CT: Yale University Press.

Rahman, A. (Ed.). (1999). *History of Indian Science: Technology and Culture A.D. 1000–*

1800. Delhi: Oxford University Press.

Rahenema, M. (1997). *The Post-Development Reader*. London: Zed Books.

Rahenema, M. (2005a). "Development." In V. Lal and A. Nandy (Eds.), *The Future of Knowledge and Culture: A Dictionary for the 21st Century*. New Delhi: Viking, Penguin.

Rahenema, M. (2005b). "Poverty." In V. Lal and A. Nandy (Eds.), *The Future of Knowledge and Culture: A Dictionary for the 21st Century*. New Delhi: Viking, Penguin.

Rai, L. L. (1917). *England's Debt to India: A Historical Narrative of Britain's Fiscal Policy in India*. New York: B. W. Huebsch.

Raj, K. (2007). *Relocating Modern Science: Circulation and the Construction of Scientific Knowledge in South Asia and Europe, 1650–1900*. New York: Palgrave.

Rajan, S. C. (2017). "Practicing Theory in The Anthropocene: A Postcolonial Quest for Reliable Knowledge." *Economic and Political Weekly*, 52(14):72–74.

Rambachan, A. (2015). *A Hindu Theology of Liberation: Not-Two is Not One*. Albany, NY: SUNY Press.

Ranade, M. G. (1899). *Essays in Indian Economics*. Bombay: G. A. Natesan & Co.

Ranganathan, S. (2014). "The Rationalist Movement Against Quack Healing." *Economic and Political Weekly*, 49(1):13–15.

Rapley, J. (2017a). *Twilight of the Money Gods: Economics as a Religion and How it All Went Wrong*. New York: Simon & Schuster.

Rapley, J. (2017b). "How Economics Became a Religion." July 11. (https://www.theguardian.com/news/2017/jul/11/how-economics-became-a-religion).

Ray, R. K. (Ed.). (1992). *Entrepreneurship and Industry in India, 1880–1947*. Delhi: Oxford University Press.

Reitz, S. (2008). "Hold the Prosecco, and Pass the Edamame: Dictionary's New Entries Debut." July 7. (http://archive.boston.com/news/local/articles/2008/07/07/hold_the_prosecco_and_pass_the_edamame).

Renier, T. (2018). "The Prevailing Relevance of Dependency Theories in Caribbean Development." January 15. (globalresearch.ca/the-prevailing-relevance-of-the-dependency-theory-in-the-caribbean-development/5625911).

Riasanovsky, N. V. (1984). *The History of Russia*. (4th ed.). New York: Oxford University Press.

Ridley, M. (2010), *The Rational Optimist: How Prosperity Evolves*. New York: Harper Collins.

Rieber, J. A. (1982). *Merchants and Entrepreneurs in Imperial Russia*. Chapel Hill, NC: The University of North Carolina Press.

Rice, A. and Poulter, E. (N.d). "Fuelling the Industrial Revolution." Revealing Histories, Remembering Slavery; A partnership project from eight museums in Greater Manchester (http://revealinghistories.org.uk/how-did-money-from-slavery-help-develop-greater-manchester/articles/fuelling-the-industrial-revolution.html).

Rider, T. D. (1971). "The Tariff Policy of Government of India and its Development Strategy 1884–1924." PhD diss. : University of Minnesota.

Rikodi, C. (2015). "Development, Religion and Modernity." In E. Tomalin (Ed.), *The Routledge Handbook of Religions and Global Development*. London: Routledge.

Rist, G. (1997). *The History of Development: From Western Origins to Global Faith*. (P. Camiller, Trans.). London: Zed Books.

Roberts, P. C. (2013). "What Became of the Left." August 19. (informationclearinghouse.info/article45314.htm).

Roberts, P. C. (2019). "Kennedy and King Family Members and Advisors Call for Congress to Reopen Assassination Probes." January 21. (https://www.globalresearch.ca/kennedy-and-king-family-members-and-advisors-call-for-congress-to-reopen-assassination-probes/5666030).

Rodney, W. (1983). *How Europe Underdeveloped Africa*, London: Tanzanian Publishing House.

Rodrigue, B., Grinin, L. and Korotayev, A. (Eds.). (2015). *Our Place in the Universe: An Introduction to Big History (From Big Bang to Galactic Civilizations: a Big History Anthology): Vol. I*. Delhi: Primus Books.

Roediger, D. R. and Esch, E. D. (2012). *The Production of Difference: Race and the Management of Labor in U.S. History*. Oxford, UK: Oxford University Press.

Rogers, C. R. (1954). "Towards a Theory of Creativity." *ETC, A Review of General Semantics*, 11:249–260.

Rosenfeld, J. M. and Tardieu, B. (2000). *Artisans of Democracy: How Ordinary People, Families in Extreme Poverty and Social Institutions Become Allies to Overcome Social Exclusion*. Lanham, MD: University Press of America.

Rosovsky, H. (1954). "The Serf Entrepreneur in Russia." *Exploration in Entrepreneurial History*, 6:207–233.

Rostow, W. W. (1960). *The Stages of Economic Growth: A Non-Communist Manifesto*. Cambridge, UK: Cambridge University Press.

Rowe, J. 2018. "What History Books Left out about Depression Era Co-Ops." September 16. (https://readersupportednews.org/news-section2/318-66/52313-what-history-books-left-out-about-depression-era-co-ops).

Roy, A. (2014). *Capitalism: A Ghost Story*. Chicago: Haymarket Books.

Roy, A. (2017). *The Doctor and the Saint: Caste, Race, and Annihilation of Caste, the Debate Between B. R. Ambedkar and M. K. Gandhi*. Chicago: Haymarket Books.

Roy, T. (2006). *The Economic History of India, 1857–1947*. New Delhi: Oxford University Press.

Roy, T. (2012). *The East India Company: The World's Most Powerful Corporation*. London: Penguin

Royal, R. (1998). "Who Put the West in Western Civilization?" *The Intercollegiate Review*, Spring, pp. 3–17.

Russell, B. A. W. and Russell, D. (1923). *The Prospects for Industrial Civilization*. NY: Century Co.

Russell, R. (2014). "Rethinking Economics: From the UK, A Global Student Movement Takes Shape." Jan. 22. (www.occupy.com/article/rethinking-economics-uk-global-student-movement-takes-shape?utm_source=Website+%27Join+Us%27&utm_campaign=177fd08b55-RSS_EMAIL_#sthash.iYGfROuz.dpbs).

Sachs, W. (1992). *The Development Dictionary: A Guide to Knowledge as Power*. London: Zed Books.

Safina, C. (2016). *Beyond Words: What Animals Think and Feel*. London: Picador.

Sahlins, M. (2008). *The Western Illusion of Human Nature*. Chicago: Prickly Paradigm Press.

Sahu, B. P. (2016). "Writing Alternative Histories." *Economic and Political Weekly*. 51(18):30–36.

Saini, A. (2019). *Superior: The Return of Race Science*. New York: Harper Collins.

Saklatvala, B. S. and Khosla, K. (1980). *Jamsetji Tata, Builders of Modern India*. Series. (2nd ed.). New Delhi: Government of India Publication.

Salazar, M. (2017). "Mind Control: Stranger than Fiction." *The Nation*, November, pp. 10.

Saler, M. (2014). "Science as Salvation." Review. *The Nation*, September 15, pp. 42–45.

Saliba, G. (1996). "Arab Influence on the Renaissance." Paper at the 5th Annual Conference of the World Historical Association, Pomona, CA, June 21.

Saner, E. (2018). "Employer are Monitoring Computers, Toilet Breaks—Even Emotions. Is Your Boss Watching You?" May 16. (www.theguardian.com/world/2018/may/14/is-your-boss-secretly-or-not-so-secretly-watching-you).

Sanyal, B. (1994). "Ideas and Institutions: Why the Alternative Development Paradigm Withered Away." *Regional Development Dialogue*, 15(1):23–35.

Sanyal, K. (2014). *Rethinking Capitalist Development: Primitive Accumulation, Governmentality and Post-Colonial Capitalism*. Delhi: Routledge.

Sardar, Z. (2005a). "Islam." In Vinay Lal and Ashis Nandy (Eds.), *The Future of Knowledge and Culture: A Dictionary for the 21st Century*. New Delhi: Viking, Penguin.

Sardar, Z. (2005b). "Postmodernism." In Vinay Lal and Ashis Nandy (Eds.), *The Future of Knowledge and Culture: A Dictionary for the 21st Century*. New Delhi: Viking, Penguin.

Sardar, Z. (2007). "Beyond Development: An Islamic Perspective." *The European Journal of Development Research*, 8(2):36–55.

Sarkar, S. (1973). *The Swadeshi Movement in Bengal, 1903–1908*. New Delhi: People's Publishing House.

Sarkar, S. (2014). *Modern Times: India 1880–1950: Environment, Economy, and Culture*. Ranikhet: Permanent Black.

Sarkar, U. (2017). "Carnegie Endowment in India: Promoting US Leadership with Indian

Corporate Wealth." August 31. (https://thewire.in/business/carnegie-india-think-tank-role).

Sau, R. (2006). "How Modern Are We? Why Be Modern? Be Rational." *Eonomic and Political Weekly.* (Discussion), 41(16):1589–1591.

Saul, S. B. (1960). *Studies in British Overseas Trade, 1870–1914*. Liverpool, UK: Liverpool University Press.

Savva, A. (2017). "Cambridge University Students Launch Campaign to 'Decolonise' Courses to Include more Ethnic Minority Writers." October 25. (www.cambridge-news.co.uk/news/cambridge-news/cambridge-university-students-launch-campaign-13808830).

Sayers, S. (2003). "Creative Activity and Alienation in Hegel and Marx." *Historical Materialism,* 11(1):107–128.

Scheler, M. (1970). *The Nature of Sympathy*. Hamden, CT: Archon Books.

Schmelzer, M. (2016). "Undoing the Ideology of Growth." July 13. (https://countercurrents.org/2016/07/undoing-the-ideology-of-growth).

Schor, J. B. (2011). *True Wealth: How and Why Millions of Americans Are Creating a Time-Rich, Ecologically Light, Small-Scale, High-Satisfaction Economy*. London: Penguin Books.

Schulson, M. (2016). "Should NASA have given 1.1 million to a Theology Institute?" July 10. (https://www.alternet.org/2016/07/should-nasa-have-given-11-million-theology-institute).

Schumpeter, J. (2013). "The Mindfulness Business: Western Capitalism is Looking for Inspiration in Eastern Mysticism." *The Economist,* Nov. 16. (www.economist.com/business/2013/11/16/the-mindfulness-business).

Scott, A. (1998). "Homoeopathy as a Feminist Form of Medicine." *Sociology of Health and Illness.* 20(2):191–214.

Scott, J. C. (2013). *Two Cheers for Anarchism: Six Easy Pieces on Autonomy, Dignity, and Meaningful Work and Play*. Princeton, NJ: Princeton University Press.

Scroll Staff, (2018). "University of Ghana Removes Mahatma Gandhi Statue at the Centre of Anti-Racism Protests." December 13. (https://scroll.in/latest/905531/university-of-ghana-removes-mahatma-gandhi-statue-at-the-centre-of-anti-racism-protests).

Seabrook, J. (2012). "Deindustrializing Humanity." *The New Internationalist,* April, NI 451:54–55.

Sen, A. (1963). "Sociological and Economic Explanations: An Illustration from the Indian Iron and Steel Industry." *Economic Weekly,* February, Annual Number, pp. 183–186.

Sen, J. (2015). "Commodification of 'Giving Back' in a Neo-liberal World." *Economic and Political Weekly,* 50(42):22–25.

Sen, S. (1964). *Studies in Industrial Policy and Development of India, 1858–1914*. Calcutta: Progressive Publishers.

Sen, S. (1966). *Studies in Economic Policy and Development of India, 1848–1926*. Calcutta: Progressive Publishers.

Sen, S. (1975). *House of Tata, 1839–1939.* Calcutta: South Asia Books.

Sengupta, A. (2018). "Microbes are striking back." August 7. (https://mronline.org/2018/08/06/microbes-are-striking-back).

Shaban, A. (2017). "Geographical Epistemology and the Question of Space." *Economic and Political Weekly,* 52(48):85–89.

Shah, E. (2011). " 'Science' in the Risk Politics of Bt. Brinjal." *Economic and Political Weekly,* 46(31):31–38.

Shantz, J. (2014). "Seeds Beneath the Snow: The Sociological Anarchy of Paul Goodman, Colin Ward and James C. Scott." *Contemporary Sociology,* 43(4):468–473.

Shapin, S. (1996). *The Scientific Revolution*. Chicago: Chicago University Press.

Sheldrake, R. (2012). *The Science Delusion: Freeing the Spirit of Enquiry*. London: Coronet.

Shenk, T. (2014). "What was Socialism?" *The Nation,* May 5, pp. 27–37.

Shepperdson, M. and Simmons, C. (Eds.). (1988). *The Indian National Congress and the Political Economy of India 1885–1985*. England: Avebury.

Sherman, J. (2018). "Science Still Can't Explain This Biological Mystery, But Scientists Like to Pretend Otherwise." March 18. (alternet.org/2018/03/science-still-cant-explain-biological-mystery).

Sherner, M. (2015). "Scientia Humanitatist." *Scientific American*. June.

Shiva, V. and Jalees, K. (2009). *Farmers Suicides in India*. Research Foundation for Science,

Technology and Ecology. New Delhi, pp. 27–36.
Shukla, B. D. (1960). *A History of the Indian Liberal Party*. Allahabad: The Indian Press.
Singh, P. (2016). "IMF's Autocritique of Neo-Liberalism?" *Economic and Political Weekly*, 51(32):17–18.
Singh, V. (2015). "Yoga Made Must be Paramilitary Forces, Government Seeks Action Taken Reports." *The Indian Express*. June 29. (https://indianexpress.com/article/india/india-others/yoga-made-must-for-paramilitary-forces-government-seeks-action-taken-reports).
Sivin, N. (1982). "Why the Scientific Revolution Did Not Take Place in China—Or Didn't It?" In E. Mendelson (Ed.), *Transformation and Tradition in the Sciences*. Cambridge, UK: Cambridge University Press.
Sjöberg, M. and Tomilov, A. (1998). "Iron-Making in Peasant Communities." In M. Ågren, (Ed.), *Iron making Societies Early Industrial Development in Sweden and Russia, 1600–1900*. Oxford ; Providence, RI: Berghahn Books.
Skidelsky, R. and Skidelsky, E. (2013). *How Much is Enough? Money and the Good Life*. New York: Other Press.
Smith, A. (1776). *An Inquiry into the Nature and Causes of the Wealth of Nations*. London: Methuen & Co.
Smith, J. E. H. (2019). *Irrationality: A History of the Dark Side of Reason*. Princeton, NJ: Princeton University Press.
Smith, W. C. (1991[1962]). *The Meaning and End of Religion*. Minneapolis: Fortress Press.
Solnit, R. (2016). "The Ideology of Isolation." *Harper's Magazine*, July. pp. 4–8.
Stansell, C. (1982). "The Geography of Vice." In Kornblith (Ed.), *Problem in American Civilization: The Industrial Revolution in America*. Boston: Houghton Mifflin Co. 1998.
Stanziani, A. (2014). "Beyond Asiatic Despotism: Soldiers, Mercenaries and Peasants in Eurasia." In S. Bhattacharya (Ed.), *Towards a New History of Work*. New Delhi: Tulika Books.
Stark, R. and Finke, R. (2000). *Acts of Faith: Explaining the Human Side of Religion*. Berkeley, CA: University of California Press.
Stauber, J. and Rampton, S. (2001). *Trust Us. We're Experts! : How Industry Manipulates Science and Gambles With Your Future*. New York: Tarcher/Putnam.
Stirner, M. (2005). *The Ego and His Own: The Case of the Individual Against Authority*. New York: Dover Publications.
Stix, G. (2014). "The IT Factor." *Scientific American*, September, 311(3):74–79.
Storm, J. J. (2017). *The Myth of Disenchantment, Magic, Modernity, and the Birth of the Human Sciences*. University of Chicago Press.
Street, P. (2015). "Beyond False Dichotomies." *Z Magazine*, March 27, pp. 16–22.
Stremlin, B. (2004). "Constructing Authority: The Rise of Science in the Modern World." In R. E. Lee and I. Wallerstein, *Overcoming the Two Cultures: Science versus the Humanities in the Modern World-System*. Boulder, CO: Paradigm Publishers.
Subaltern Studies Series. Vol. 1–8. Oxford, UK: Oxford University Press.
Sublette, Ned and Constance (2016). *The American Slave Coast: A History of the Slave Breeding Industry*. Chicago: Lawrence Hill Books.
Suwandi, I., Jonna, R. J. and Foster, J. B. (2019). "Global Commodity Chains and the New Imperialism." *Monthly Review*, 70(10):1–24.
Sylvester, C. (1999). "Development Studies and Postcolonial Studies: Disparate Tales of the 'Third World'." *Third World Quarterly*, 20(4):703–721.
Syrmopoulos, J. (2016). "Fifteen Years Later, Physics Journal Concludes All Three WTC Towers Collapsed on 9/11 Due to Controlled Demolition." September 13. (https://www.globalresearch.ca/fifteen-years-later-physics-journal-concludes-all-three-wtc-towers-collapsed-on-911-due-to-controlled-demolition/5545488).
Sztompka, P. (Ed.). (1994). *Agency and Structure: Reorienting Social Theory*. Yverdon, Switzerland; Langhorne, PA: Gordon and Breach.
Talbot, M. (1991). *The Holographic Universe*. New York: Harper Perennial.
Talbot, M. (2006). "The Holographic Universe: Does Objective Reality Exist?" (http://www.rense.com/general69/holoff.htm).
Targ, R. (2012). *The Reality of ESP: A Physicist's Proof of Psychic Abilities*. Wheaton, IL: Quest Books.

Tattersall, I. (2001). "How We Came to be Human." *Scientific American,* 285(6):56–63.

Taylor, K. Y. (2016). *From #BlackLivesMatter to Black Liberation.* Chicago: Haymarket Books.

Taylor, W. C. (2006). "Here's an Idea: Let Everyone Have Ideas." *The New York Times,* March 26. (nytimes.com/2006/03/26/business/yourmoney/26mgmt.html).

teleSUR, May 26 (2016). "China Just Made a Karl Marx Hip Hop Tune to 'Educate' Its Youth." (https://www.telesurenglish.net/news/China-Just-Made-a-Karl-Marx-Hip-Hop-Tune-to-Educate-Its-Youth-20160526-0034.html).

Temin, P. (1964). *Iron and Steel in Nineteenth Century America.* Cambridge, MA: M.I.T. Press.

Temple, R. (1999). *Genius of China.* London: Prion Books.

Tezcan, B. (2010). *The Second Ottoman Empire: Political and Social Transformation in the Early Modern World.* Cambridge, UK: Cambridge University Press.

Thadeusz, F. (2010). "No Copyright Law: The Real Reason for Germany's Industrial Expansion?" *Spiegel,* August 18. (www.spiegel.de/international/zeitgeist/no-copyright-law-the-real-reason-for-germany-s-industrial-expansion-a-710976.html).

Thapar, R. (1966). *A History of India.* Volume One. London: Penguin Books.

Tharoor, S. (2016). *Inglorious Empire: What the British Did to India.* Scribe. London: Hurst & Co.

Thomas, J. (2016). "US 'Cultural Colonisation' in Asia Pacific." (New Eastern Outlook) August 30. (https://www.globalresearch.ca/us-cultural-colonisation-in-asia-pacific/5543302).

Tick, E. (2004). "Edward Tick, PhD: On Asklepios, dream healing, and talking with the dead." Interview by Bonnie Horrigan. *Alternative Therapies in Health & Medicine.* Jan./Feb. 10(1):69–71.

Times of India, September 1, 2016a.

Times of India, February 25, 2016b.

Todhunter, C. (2016). "Pro-GMO Spin Masquerading As Science Courtesy of 'Shameful White Men of Privilege'." July 1. (https://countercurrents.org/2016/07/pro-gmo-spin-masquerading-as-science-courtesy-of-shameful-white-men-of-privilege).

Todhunter, C. (2017a). "India, From the Destablization of Agriculture to Demonetization, 'Made in America'." January 6. (https://www.globalresearch.ca/india-from-the-destabilization-of-agriculture-to-demonetization-made-in-america/5566615).

Todhunter, C. (2017b). "Indian Independence: Forged in Washington?" July 30. (https://www.globalresearch.ca/indian-independence-forged-in-washington/5601615).

Tomalin, E. (Ed.). (2007). *The Routledge Handbook of Religions and Global Development.* London: Routledge.

Tombs, R. (2015). *The English and Their History.* New York: Alfred A. Knopf.

Trachtenberg, A. (2007). *The Incorporation of America: Culture and Society in the Gilded Age.* New York: Hill and Wang.

Tripathi, D. (1987) (Ed.). *State and Business in India: A Historical Perspective.* Delhi: Manohar.

Trojanow, I. and Hoskote, R. (2012). *Confluences: Forgotten Histories from East and West.* New Delhi: Yoda Press.

Vanbergen, G. (2017). "The Truth War is Being Lost to a Global Censorship Apparatus Called Google." August 8. (https://www.globalresearch.ca/the-truth-war-is-being-lost-to-a-global-censorship-apparatus-called-google/5602578).

van der Linden, M. (2008). *Workers of the World: Essays Toward a Global Labor History.* Leiden, Netherlands: Brill.

van der Pijl, K. (1998). *Transnational Classes and International Relations.* London: Routledge.

van Zanden, L. J. (2008). "The Road to the Industrial Revolution: Hypotheses and Conjectures about Medieval Origins of the 'European Miracle'." *Journal of Global History,* November, 3(3):337–359.

Varma, R. (2001). "People's Science Movements and Science War?" *Economic and Political Weekly,* 36(32):4796–4802.

Veciana, S. (2016). "Degrowth and the Global Ecovillage Network." September 15. (https://countercurrents.org/2016/09/degrowth-and-the-global-ecovillage-network).

Victor, P. (2008). *Managing without Growth: Slower by Design, not Disaster.* Cheltenham, UK: Edward Elgar Publishing.

Vilar, P. (1969). *A History of Gold and Money, 1450–1920.* London ; Atlantic-Highlands, NJ:

Humanities Press.
Visuvalingam, S. (2017). Email reply to C. Rajendran. 5 December, 2017. Abhinavagupta@yahoo.com; Hindu-Budhist@yahoogroups.com
Vombatkere, S. G. (2016). "The Dalits Rally." August 17. (https://countercurrents.org/2016/08/the-dalits-rally).
Von Laue, T. H. (1963). *Sergei Witte and the Industrialization of Russia*. New York ; London: Columbia University Press.
Vrasti, W. (2013). *Volunteer Tourism: Giving Back in Neoliberal Times*. London: Routedge.
Wagner, D. B. (1993). *Iron and Steel in Ancient China*. Leiden, Netherlands: E. J. Brill.
Waite, A. E. (1994). *A New Encyclopaedia of Freemasonry*. 2 volumes. New York: Wings Books.
Waldrop, M. M. (1992). *Complexity: The Emerging Science at the Edge of Order and Chaos*. New York. A Touchstone Book. Simon and Schuster.
Walicki, A. (1979). *A History of Russian Thought: From the Enlightenment to Marxism*. Stanford, CA: California University Press.
Wallerstein. I. (1974a). *The Modern World System: Capitalist Agriculture and the Origins of the European in the Sixteenth-Century*. London: Academic Press.
Wallerstein, I. (1974b). "The Rise and Future Demise of the World Capitalist System: Concepts for Comparative Analysis." *Comparative Studies In Society and History*, 16:387–415.
Wallerstein, I. (1976). *The Modern World-System: Capitalist Agriculture and the Origins of the European World-Economy in the Sixteenth Century*. (Text ed.). London: Academic Press.
Wallerstein, I. (1989). "Culture as the Ideological battleground of the Modern World-System." *Hitotsubashi Journal of Social Studies*, August, No. 21:5–22.
Wallerstein, I. (1991). *Geopolitics and Geoculture: Essays on the Changing World-System*. Cambridge, UK: Cambridge University Press.
Wallerstein, I. (1994). "The Agonies of Liberalism: What Hope Progress?" *New Left Review. 1/204. March–April.*
Wallerstein, I. (1996). "History in Search of Science." *Review*, Winter, 19(1):11–22.
Wallerstein, I. (1997). "Social Sciences and the Quest for a Just Society." *American Journal of Sociology*, 102(5):1241–1257.
Wallerstein, I. (1999). *As We Know It of the World, The End: Social Science for the Twenty First Century*. Minneapolis, MN: University of Minnesota Press.
Wallerstein, I. (2000). *The Essential Wallerstein*. New York: The New Press.
Wallerstein, I. (2003). *The Decline of American Power: The US in a Chaotic World*. New York: The New Press.
Wallerstein, I. (2011). *The Modern World-System: Centrist Liberalism Triumphant, 1789–1914*. Volume IV. Berkeley, CA: University of California Press.
Ward, C. (2011). *Autonomy, Solidarity, Possibility: The Colin Ward Reader*. D. F. White and C. Wilbert (Eds.). Troy, MI: Oakland Press.
Washbrook, D. (1988). "Progress and Problems: South Asian Economic and Social History, 1720–1860." *Modern Asian Studies*, 22(1):57–96.
Washbrook, D. (1997). "From Comparative Sociology to Global History: Britain and India in the Pre-History of Modernity: *Journal of the Economic and Social History of the Orient*, 40(4):410–443.
Weinstein, E. (2018). *Recipes for Good Luck: The Superstitions, Rituals, and Practices of Extraordinary People*. San Francisco: Chronicle Books.
Weinstein, M. M. (1999). "Rewriting the Book of Capitalism: How Capitalist Innovation Steals Competition's Thunder." *New York Times*. June 5. (nytimes.com/1999/06/05/arts/rewriting-book-capitalism-now-cooperative-innovation-steals-competition-s.html).
Welch, M., Feldman, B. A., and Morningstar, C. (2018). "The Non-Profit Industrial Complex and the "Parallel Left." May 12. (https://www.globalresearch.ca/the-non-profit-industrial-complex-and-the-parallel-left-a-conversation-with-cory-morningstar-and-bob-feldman/5640021).
White, R. (2011). *Railroaded: The Transcontinentals and the Making of Modern America*. New York: W. W. Norton.
Willford, J. N. (2002). "When Humans Became Human." *The New York Times*, February 26. (https://www.nytimes.com/2002/02/26/science/when-humans-became-human.html).

Williams, E. (1944). *Capitalism and Slavery.* Chapel Hill, NC: University of North Carolina Press.

Williams, J. J. (2014). "The 'Contemporary' Moment: How Postmodernism became Passé." *The Chronicle of Higher Education,* December 8.

Williams, W. A. (1980). *Empire As a Way of Life.* New York: Oxford University Press.

Willmont, H. (1993). "Strength is Ignorance, Slavery is Freedom: Managing Culture in Modern Organizations." *Journal of Management Studies,* 30(4):515–552.

Wilson, E. O. (1998). *Consilience: The Unity of Knowledge.* New York: Vintage Books.

Wolpert, S. (1962). *Tilak and Gokhale: Revolution and Reform in the Making of Modern India.* Berkeley, CA: University Press.

Woodhead, L. (2001). "Introduction: Modern Contexts of Religion." In Woodhead et al.

Woodhead, L., Kawanami, H. and Partridge, C. (Eds.). (2001). *Religions in the Modern World: Traditions and Transformations.* (2nd ed.). London: Routledge.

Wright, R. (1992). "Science, God and Man." *Time,* December 28. pp. 38–44.

Wunder, H. (1985). "Peasant Organization and Class Conflict in Eastern and Western Germany." In T.H. Aston and C.H.E. Philpin (Eds.), *Brenner Debate: Agrarian Class Structure and Economic Development in Pre-Industrial Europe.* Cambridge: Past & Present Publishers.

Yates, M. D. (2016). "On Henry Giroux: On Henry Giroux: Foreword to *America's Addiction to Terrorism.*" *Monthly Review,* January, 67(8):44–50.

York, R. and Clark, B. (2011). "Stephen Jay Gould's Critique of Progress." *Monthly Review,* February, 62(9):19–36.

Young, R. (1990). "The Mind-Body Problem." In R. C. Olby et al., (Eds.), *Companion to the History of Modern Science.* pp. 702–11. London: Routledge.

Zahn, M. (2016). "Mindfulness Has Gone Corporate: Why has America Appropriated Buddhism for Capitalist Ends?" July 18. (https://www.alternet.org/2016/07/mindfullness-buddhism-capitalist-ends)

Zaitchik, A. (2017). "The God Capsule: Can Psychedelics Prove a Biological Basis for Spirituality?" November 8. (https://www.alternet.org/2017/11/lsd-god-capsule).

Zaman, A. (2008). "Islamic Economics: A Survey of the Literature." June 1. University of Birmingham: Religions and Development Research Programme, Working Paper No. 22. (Available at SSRN: https://ssrn.com/abstract=1282786 or http://dx.doi.org/10.2139/ssrn.1282786van)

Zaret, D. (2000). *Origins of Democratic Culture: Printing, Petitions, and the Public Sphere in Early-Modern England.* Princeton, NJ: Princeton University Press.

Zinn, H. (1970). *The Politics of History.* Boston: Beacon Press.

Zinn, H. (2005). *A People's History of the United States, 1492–Present.* New York: Harper Perennial.

About the Author

Vinay Bahl, presently a non-affiliated research scholar, taught historical sociology in the United States for many years. She received her Ph.D. degree in Sociology from Binghamton University, New York and M. Phil degree in Modern Indian History from Jawaharlal Nehru University, New Delhi, India. She was an invited guest scholar of the College de France, Paris, for one academic year. She was also an Associate Fellow at the International Institute for Asian Studies in Amsterdam.

She has published three books:

What Went Wrong With "History From Below": Reinstating Human Agency as Human Creativity;

History After the Three Worlds: Post-Eurocentric Historiographies (co-edited);

The Making of the Indian Working Class: The Case Study of the Tata Iron and Steel Co. 1880–1946.

She has also published numerous articles in various scholarly journals and book chapters on subjects ranging from industrialization, working class, caste system, south Asian women's apparel, global women, social movements, historiography, culture, and Dhrupad form of Indian classical music.

Abstract

Marxist historiography has never moved beyond the concept of "transition" and it did not include the historical experience of the world outside of EuroAmerica. However, under the influence of the theory of modernization, the world outside of EuroAmerica (categorized as third world) was located within the binary distinction of developed/underdeveloped, while the Soviet Union was considered Second World (less than EuroAmerica as it categorized itself as First World). The Soviet Union does not exist anymore and therefore, the term second or third world has no purchase. However, countries are still being categorized with the binary distinction of developed/underdeveloped by all policy makers and scholars everywhere including those who claim to be challenging imperialism and colonialism.

This book challenges this binary distinction to categorize any country while proposing to erase this binary with a yardstick of parity. The erasure of this binary distinction is important as it would eliminate the need to continuously prove the capitalist or modernist credentials of a so-called underdeveloped society, as well as eliminate the need to prove why Asia (China) or any other region of the world did not industrialize first. By removing the need to answer this question, we can stop being complicit in the promotion of Western binaries and Western myths about the baseless, irrelevant and humiliating "lacking" and "not yet" labelling of other countries. Thus, no society would have to re-prove its capabilities and creativity to fit into the Western "development" mold or play the vicious "catch up game." This erasure will also create a space wherein it would be possible to imagine the alternative theoretical framework that is sorely needed to break out of this so called development model, in which the world is mired with a sense of fatalism and hopelessness. Hence, the erasing of the existing binary distinction of developed/underdeveloped became the focus and title for this volume.

The author believes that it is possible to write comparative history without categorizing countries/societies as either developed or underdeveloped because no country or society was begun with the initial condition of being "developed" or "underdeveloped," and it is not an inevitable fate for any society. No society is superior or inferior in its formation process, as all are products of human creativity and human interactions, all societies are always in the process of becoming, and none of them is a final product. At the same time, all societies are co-produced and co-constituted as all borrow from other societies. However, this co-production of societies can sometimes be based on unequal relationships when one country/society forcefully controls and colonizes another country/society for the benefit of the colonizing country. Notwithstanding this unequal and exploitative relationship between the colonizing and colonized country/society, all societies have universal and specific characteristics and they all can be compared with the same yardstick of parity. With a sample of comparative historical study of four chosen countries, two (Imperial Britain and Post-colonial Imperial US) considered "developed" and two (Imperial Russia and Colonial India) considered "underdeveloped," it is shown in this book how the yardstick of parity can be applied without categorizing societies with the binary distinction of developed or underdeveloped. This comparative historical study specifically focuses on the emergence of the large-scale steel industry between 1880 and 1914 because during this period it was considered to be the basis for the development of powerful economies. Our study repudiates the claim that it is the cultural backwardness of certain societies which made them "underdeveloped," or that it was some inherent superior capabilities of certain societies which made their country "developed." Refuting the stage theory (Rostow and Marx) it is explained that it was the conjunction of historical forces that created conditions and power structures within each society and in the international arena for the emergence (or non-emergence, as in the case of England) of the large-scale steel industry in four countries.

Hopefully, by erasing the Western binary distinction of developed/underdeveloped in comparative history and in other related academic fields, a new space can be created for scholars and societies to imagine and develop alternative perspectives, which would defend neither imperialism nor neoliberalism, nor fundamentalism of all sorts, nor indigenisim. This is important, as it is an existential issue.